CATECHISM
OF THE
CATHOLIC
CHURCH

AN IMAGE BOOK
DOUBLEDAY
NEW YORK   LONDON   TORONTO
SYDNEY   AUCKLAND

AN IMAGE BOOK
PUBLISHED BY DOUBLEDAY
a division of Bantam Doubleday Dell Publishing Group, Inc.
1540 Broadway, New York, New York 10036

IMAGE, DOUBLEDAY, and the portrayal of a deer drinking from a stream are trademarks of Doubleday, a division of Bantam Doubleday Dell Publishing Group, Inc.

First Image Books edition published April 1995.

Imprimi Potest
+ Joseph Cardinal Ratzinger
Interdicasterial Commission for the *Catechism of the Catholic Church*

ISBN 0-385-47967-0
ISBN 0-385-47985-0 (gift edition)

Printed in the United States of America

CONTENTS

APOSTOLIC CONSTITUTION
FIDEI DEPOSITUM ON THE PUBLICATION
  OF THE *CATECHISM OF THE
  CATHOLIC CHURCH*   1
PROLOGUE   9
I.   The Life of Man—To Know and Love
      God   9
II.   Handing on the Faith: Catechesis   10
III.   The Aim and Intended Readership of
      This Catechism   11
IV.   Structure of This Catechism   12
V.   Practical Directions for Using This
      Catechism   13
VI.   Necessary Adaptations   14

PART ONE: THE PROFESSION OF FAITH   17
SECTION ONE: "I BELIEVE"—"WE BELIEVE"   17
CHAPTER ONE: MAN'S CAPACITY FOR GOD   17
I.   The Desire for God   17
II.   Ways of Coming to Know God   19
III.   The Knowledge of God according to
      the Church   20
IV.   How Can We Speak about God?   21
      IN BRIEF   22
CHAPTER TWO: GOD COMES TO MEET MAN   23
ARTICLE 1: THE REVELATION OF GOD   23
I.   God Reveals His "Plan of Loving
      Goodness"   23
II.   The Stages of Revelation   24
III.   Christ Jesus—"Mediator and Fullness of
      All Revelation"   27
      IN BRIEF   28
ARTICLE 2: THE TRANSMISSION OF DIVINE
  REVELATION   29
I.   The Apostolic Tradition   29
II.   The Relationship between Tradition and
      Sacred Scripture   31
III.   The Interpretation of the Heritage of
      Faith   32
      IN BRIEF   35

ARTICLE 3: SACRED SCRIPTURE   35
I.   Christ—The Unique Word of Sacred
        Scripture   35
II.   Inspiration and Truth of Sacred
        Scripture   36
III.   The Holy Spirit, Interpreter of Scripture   37
IV.   The Canon of Scripture   40
V.   Sacred Scripture in the Life of the
        Church   43
        IN BRIEF   43
CHAPTER THREE: MAN'S RESPONSE TO GOD   44
ARTICLE 1: I BELIEVE   45
I.   The Obedience of Faith   45
II.   "I Know Whom I Have Believed"   46
III.   The Characteristics of Faith   47
ARTICLE 2: WE BELIEVE   51
I.   "Lord, Look upon the Faith of Your
        Church"   52
II.   The Language of Faith   53
III.   Only One Faith   53
        IN BRIEF   54
        THE CREDO   56
SECTION TWO: THE PROFESSION OF THE CHRISTIAN
    FAITH: THE CREEDS   58
CHAPTER ONE: I BELIEVE IN GOD THE FATHER   61
ARTICLE 1: "I BELIEVE IN GOD THE FATHER
    ALMIGHTY, CREATOR OF HEAVEN AND
    EARTH"   61
Paragraph 1. I Believe in God   61
I.   "I Believe in One God"   61
II.   God Reveals His Name   62
III.   God, "He Who *Is*," Is Truth and Love   66
IV.   The Implications of Faith in One God   67
        IN BRIEF   68
Paragraph 2. The Father   69
I.   "In the Name of the Father and of the
        Son and of the Holy Spirit"   69
II.   The Revelation of God as Trinity   71
III.   The Holy Trinity in the Teaching of
        the Faith   74

IV.   The Divine Works and the Trinitarian
       Missions   76
       IN BRIEF   78
Paragraph 3. The Almighty   79
       IN BRIEF   81
Paragraph 4. The Creator   82
I.   Catechesis on Creation   82
II.   Creation—Work of the Holy Trinity   85
III. "The World Was Created for the Glory
       of God"   86
IV.   The Mystery of Creation   87
V.   God Carries Out His Plan: Divine
       Providence   89
       IN BRIEF   94
Paragraph 5. Heaven and Earth   95
I.   The Angels   95
II.   The Visible World   98
       IN BRIEF   101
Paragraph 6. Man   101
I.   "In the Image of God"   101
II.   "Body and Soul but Truly One"   103
III. "Male and Female He Created Them"   105
IV.   Man in Paradise   106
       IN BRIEF   107
Paragraph 7. The Fall   108
I.   Where Sin Abounded, Grace Abounded
       All the More   109
II.   The Fall of the Angels   110
III. Original Sin   111
IV.   "You Did Not Abandon Him to the
       Power of Death"   116
       IN BRIEF   117
CHAPTER TWO: I BELIEVE IN JESUS CHRIST, THE
   ONLY SON OF GOD   118
ARTICLE 2: "AND IN JESUS CHRIST, HIS
   ONLY SON, OUR LORD"   120
I.   Jesus   120
II.   Christ   122
III. The Only Son of God   124
IV.   Lord   125
       IN BRIEF   127

ARTICLE 3: "HE WAS CONCEIVED BY THE
POWER OF THE HOLY SPIRIT, AND WAS
BORN OF THE VIRGIN MARY"   127
Paragraph 1. The Son of God Became Man   127
I.   Why Did the Word Become Flesh?   127
II.   The Incarnation   129
III.   True God and True Man   130
IV.   How Is the Son of God Man?   132
        IN BRIEF   135
Paragraph 2. "Conceived by the Power of the
Holy Spirit and Born of the Virgin Mary"   136
I.   Conceived by the Power of the Holy
        Spirit . . .   136
II.   . . . Born of the Virgin Mary   136
        IN BRIEF   142
Paragraph 3. The Mysteries of Christ's Life   143
I.   Christ's Whole Life Is Mystery   143
II.   The Mysteries of Jesus' Infancy and
        Hidden Life   146
III.   The Mysteries of Jesus' Public Life   150
        IN BRIEF   159
ARTICLE 4: "JESUS CHRIST SUFFERED
UNDER PONTIUS PILATE, WAS
CRUCIFIED, DIED, AND WAS BURIED"   161
Paragraph 1. Jesus and Israel   161
I.   Jesus and the Law   162
II.   Jesus and the Temple   164
III.   Jesus and Israel's Faith in the One God
        and Savior   166
        IN BRIEF   167
Paragraph 2. Jesus Died Crucified   168
I.   The Trial of Jesus   168
II.   Christ's Redemptive Death in God's Plan
        of Salvation   170
III.   Christ Offered Himself to His Father for
        Our Sins   172
        IN BRIEF   176
Paragraph 3. Jesus Christ Was Buried   177
        IN BRIEF   179
ARTICLE 5: "HE DESCENDED INTO HELL.
ON THE THIRD DAY HE ROSE AGAIN"   179

Paragraph 1. Christ Descended into Hell   180
      IN BRIEF   181
Paragraph 2. On the Third Day He Rose from
   the Dead   182
I.   The Historical and Transcendent Event   182
II.   The Resurrection—A Work of the Holy
      Trinity   186
III.   The Meaning and Saving Significance of
      the Resurrection   186
      IN BRIEF   188
ARTICLE 6: "HE ASCENDED INTO HEAVEN
   AND IS SEATED AT THE RIGHT HAND
   OF THE FATHER"   189
      IN BRIEF   191
ARTICLE 7: "FROM THENCE HE WILL
   COME AGAIN TO JUDGE THE LIVING
   AND THE DEAD"   191
I.   He Will Come Again in Glory   191
II.   To Judge the Living and the Dead   194
      IN BRIEF   195
CHAPTER THREE: I BELIEVE IN THE HOLY SPIRIT   196
ARTICLE 8: "I BELIEVE IN THE HOLY
   SPIRIT"   197
I.   The Joint Mission of the Son and the
      Spirit   198
II.   The Name, Titles, and Symbols of the
      Holy Spirit   199
III.   God's Spirit and Word in the Time of the
      Promises   203
IV.   The Spirit of Christ in the Fullness of
      Time   207
V.   The Spirit and the Church in the Last
      Days   210
      IN BRIEF   213
ARTICLE 9: "I BELIEVE IN THE HOLY
   CATHOLIC CHURCH"   214
Paragraph 1. The Church in God's Plan   215
I.   Names and Images of the Church   215
II.   The Church's Origin, Foundation, and
      Mission   217

III.   The Mystery of the Church   221
        IN BRIEF   223
Paragraph 2. The Church—People of God,
  Body of Christ, Temple of the Holy Spirit   224
I.   The Church—People of God   224
II.   The Church—Body of Christ   226
III.   The Church Is the Temple of the Holy
        Spirit   230
        IN BRIEF   231
Paragraph 3. The Church Is One, Holy,
  Catholic, and Apostolic   232
I.   The Church Is One   233
II.   The Church Is Holy   237
III.   The Church Is Catholic   239
IV.   The Church Is Apostolic   247
        IN BRIEF   250
Paragraph 4. Christ's Faithful—Hierarchy,
  Laity, Consecrated Life   251
I.   The Hierarchical Constitution of the
        Church   252
II.   The Lay Faithful   258
III.   The Consecrated Life   262
        IN BRIEF   267
Paragraph 5. The Communion of Saints   268
I.   Communion in Spiritual Goods   269
II.   The Communion of the Church of
        Heaven and Earth   270
        IN BRIEF   272
Paragraph 6. Mary—Mother of Christ, Mother
  of the Church   273
I.   Mary's Motherhood with Regard to the
        Church   273
II.   Devotion to the Blessed Virgin   275
III.   Mary—Eschatological Icon of the
        Church   275
        IN BRIEF   276
ARTICLE 10: "I BELIEVE IN THE
  FORGIVENESS OF SINS"   276
I.   One Baptism for the Forgiveness of Sins   277
II.   The Power of the Keys   278
        IN BRIEF   279

ARTICLE 11: "I BELIEVE IN THE
RESURRECTION OF THE BODY"   279
I.   Christ's Resurrection and Ours   280
II.   Dying in Christ Jesus   284
   IN BRIEF   287
ARTICLE 12: "I BELIEVE IN LIFE
EVERLASTING"   287
I.   The Particular Judgment   288
II.   Heaven   289
III.   The Final Purification, or Purgatory   291
IV.   Hell   292
V.   The Last Judgment   293
VI.   The Hope of the New Heaven and the
New Earth   295
   IN BRIEF   297
   "Amen"   298

PART TWO: THE CELEBRATION OF THE
CHRISTIAN MYSTERY   301
SECTION ONE: THE SACRAMENTAL ECONOMY   304
CHAPTER ONE: THE PASCHAL MYSTERY IN THE
AGE OF THE CHURCH   305
ARTICLE 1: THE LITURGY—WORK OF THE
HOLY TRINITY   305
I.   The Father—Source and Goal of the
Liturgy   305
II.   Christ's Work in the Liturgy   307
III.   The Holy Spirit and the Church in the
Liturgy   309
   IN BRIEF   314
ARTICLE 2: THE PASCHAL MYSTERY IN
THE CHURCH'S SACRAMENTS   315
I.   The Sacraments of Christ   315
II.   The Sacraments of the Church   316
III.   The Sacraments of Faith   317
IV.   The Sacraments of Salvation   319
V.   The Sacraments of Eternal Life   320
   IN BRIEF   320
CHAPTER TWO: THE SACRAMENTAL CELEBRATION
OF THE PASCHAL MYSTERY   321
ARTICLE 1: CELEBRATING THE CHURCH'S
LITURGY   321

I.	Who Celebrates?	321
II.	How Is the Liturgy Celebrated?	324
III.	When Is the Liturgy Celebrated?	329
IV.	Where Is the Liturgy Celebrated?	334
	IN BRIEF	336

ARTICLE 2: LITURGICAL DIVERSITY AND THE UNITY OF THE MYSTERY — 338
IN BRIEF — 340

SECTION TWO: THE SEVEN SACRAMENTS OF THE CHURCH — 341

CHAPTER ONE: THE SACRAMENTS OF CHRISTIAN INITIATION — 341

ARTICLE 1: THE SACRAMENT OF BAPTISM — 342

I.	What Is This Sacrament Called?	342
II.	Baptism in the Economy of Salvation	343
III.	How Is the Sacrament of Baptism Celebrated?	346
IV.	Who Can Receive Baptism?	349
V.	Who Can Baptize?	352
VI.	The Necessity of Baptism	352
VII.	The Grace of Baptism	353
	IN BRIEF	356

ARTICLE 2: THE SACRAMENT OF CONFIRMATION — 358

I.	Confirmation in the Economy of Salvation	358
II.	The Signs and the Rite of Confirmation	360
III.	The Effects of Confirmation	363
IV.	Who Can Receive This Sacrament?	364
V.	The Minister of Confirmation	366
	IN BRIEF	366

ARTICLE 3: THE SACRAMENT OF THE EUCHARIST — 368

I.	The Eucharist—Source and Summit of Ecclesial Life	368
II.	What Is This Sacrament Called?	369
III.	The Eucharist in the Economy of Salvation	371
IV.	The Liturgical Celebration of the Eucharist	374

V.   The Sacramental Sacrifice: Thanksgiving,
          Memorial, Presence   378
VI.   The Paschal Banquet   386
VII.   The Eucharist—"Pledge of the Glory to
          Come"   392
          IN BRIEF   393
CHAPTER TWO: THE SACRAMENTS OF HEALING   396
ARTICLE 4: THE SACRAMENT OF PENANCE
  AND RECONCILIATION   396
I.   What Is This Sacrament Called?   396
II.   Why a Sacrament of Reconciliation after
          Baptism?   397
III.   The Conversion of the Baptized   398
IV.   Interior Penance   399
V.   The Many Forms of Penance in
          Christian Life   400
VI.   The Sacrament of Penance and
          Reconciliation   401
VII.   The Acts of the Penitent   404
VIII.   The Minister of This Sacrament   408
IX.   The Effects of This Sacrament   409
X.   Indulgences   411
XI.   The Celebration of the Sacrament of
          Penance   413
          IN BRIEF   415
ARTICLE 5: THE ANOINTING OF THE SICK   417
I.   Its Foundations in the Economy of
          Salvation   417
II.   Who Receives and Who Administers
          This Sacrament?   421
III.   How Is This Sacrament Celebrated?   422
IV.   The Effects of the Celebration of This
          Sacrament   423
V.   Viaticum, the Last Sacrament of the
          Christian   424
          IN BRIEF   424
CHAPTER THREE: THE SACRAMENTS AT THE
  SERVICE OF COMMUNION   426
ARTICLE 6: THE SACRAMENT OF HOLY
  ORDERS   427
I.   Why Is This Sacrament Called "Orders"?   427

II.   The Sacrament of Holy Orders in the
       Economy of Salvation   428
III.   The Three Degrees of the Sacrament of
       Holy Orders   433
IV.   The Celebration of This Sacrament   438
V.   Who Can Confer This Sacrament?   439
VI.   Who Can Receive This Sacrament?   439
VII.   The Effects of the Sacrament of Holy
       Orders   441
       IN BRIEF   444

Article 7: THE SACRAMENT OF
   MATRIMONY   446
I.   Marriage in God's Plan   446
II.   The Celebration of Marriage   452
III.   Matrimonial Consent   453
IV.   The Effects of the Sacrament of
       Matrimony   456
V.   The Goods and Requirements of
       Conjugal Love   458
VI.   The Domestic Church   461
       IN BRIEF   462

Chapter Four: Other Liturgical
   Celebrations   464
Article 1: SACRAMENTALS   464
   IN BRIEF   467
Article 2: CHRISTIAN FUNERALS   467
I.   The Christian's Last Passover   468
II.   The Celebration of Funerals   468

PART THREE: LIFE IN CHRIST   471
Section One: Man's Vocation: Life in the
   Spirit   474
Chapter One: The Dignity of the Human
   Person   474
Article 1: MAN: THE IMAGE OF GOD   474
   IN BRIEF   476
Article 2: OUR VOCATION TO BEATITUDE   477
I.   The Beatitudes   477
II.   The Desire for Happiness   478
III.   Christian Beatitude   478
       IN BRIEF   480

ARTICLE 3: MAN'S FREEDOM 481
I.   Freedom and Responsibility 481
II. Human Freedom in the Economy of
     Salvation 482
     IN BRIEF 484
ARTICLE 4: THE MORALITY OF HUMAN
ACTS 485
I.   The Sources of Morality 485
II. Good Acts and Evil Acts 486
     IN BRIEF 487
ARTICLE 5: THE MORALITY OF THE
PASSIONS 487
I.   Passions 487
II. Passions and Moral Life 488
     IN BRIEF 489
ARTICLE 6: MORAL CONSCIENCE 490
I.   The Judgment of Conscience 490
II. The Formation of Conscience 492
III. To Choose in Accord with Conscience 492
IV. Erroneous Judgment 493
     IN BRIEF 494
ARTICLE 7: THE VIRTUES 495
I.   The Human Virtues 495
II. The Theological Virtues 498
III. The Gifts and Fruits of the Holy Spirit 502
     IN BRIEF 503
ARTICLE 8: SIN 504
I.   Mercy and Sin 504
II. The Definition of Sin 505
III. The Different Kinds of Sins 506
IV. The Gravity of Sin: Mortal and Venial Sin 506
V.   The Proliferation of Sin 509
     IN BRIEF 510
CHAPTER TWO: THE HUMAN COMMUNITY 511
ARTICLE 1: THE PERSON AND SOCIETY 511
I.   The Communal Character of the Human
     Vocation 511
II. Conversion and Society 513
     IN BRIEF 514
ARTICLE 2: PARTICIPATION IN SOCIAL LIFE 515
I.   Authority 515

II.	The Common Good	517
III.	Responsibility and Participation	519
	IN BRIEF	520
ARTICLE 3: SOCIAL JUSTICE		521
I.	Respect for the Human Person	521
II.	Equality and Differences among Men	522
III.	Human Solidarity	524
	IN BRIEF	525
CHAPTER THREE: GOD'S SALVATION: LAW AND GRACE		526
ARTICLE 1: THE MORAL LAW		526
I.	The Natural Moral Law	527
II.	The Old Law	529
III.	The New Law or the Law of the Gospel	531
	IN BRIEF	534
ARTICLE 2: GRACE AND JUSTIFICATION		535
I.	Justification	535
II.	Grace	538
III.	Merit	541
IV.	Christian Holiness	542
	IN BRIEF	544
ARTICLE 3: THE CHURCH, MOTHER AND TEACHER		545
I.	Moral Life and the Magisterium of the Church	546
II.	The Precepts of the Church	548
III.	Moral Life and Missionary Witness	549
	IN BRIEF	550
	The Ten Commandments	551
SECTION TWO: THE TEN COMMANDMENTS		553
	IN BRIEF	559
CHAPTER ONE: "YOU SHALL LOVE THE LORD YOUR GOD WITH ALL YOUR HEART, AND WITH ALL YOUR SOUL, AND WITH ALL YOUR MIND"		560
ARTICLE 1: THE FIRST COMMANDMENT		561
I.	"You Shall Worship the Lord Your God and Him Only Shall You Serve"	561
II.	"Him Only Shall You Serve"	564
III.	"You Shall Have No Other Gods before Me"	568

IV.   "You Shall Not Make for Yourself a
       Graven Image . . ."   573
       IN BRIEF   574
ARTICLE 2: THE SECOND COMMANDMENT   575
I.   The Name of the Lord Is Holy   575
II.   Taking the Name of the Lord in Vain   577
III.   The Christian Name   578
       IN BRIEF   579
ARTICLE 3: THE THIRD COMMANDMENT   580
I.   The Sabbath Day   580
II.   The Lord's Day   581
       IN BRIEF   586
CHAPTER TWO: "YOU SHALL LOVE YOUR
NEIGHBOR AS YOURSELF"   587
ARTICLE 4: THE FOURTH
COMMANDMENT   587
I.   The Family in God's Plan   589
II.   The Family and Society   590
III.   The Duties of Family Members   592
IV.   The Family and the Kingdom   596
V.   The Authorities in Civil Society   597
       IN BRIEF   601
ARTICLE 5: THE FIFTH COMMANDMENT   602
I.   Respect for Human Life   602
II.   Respect for the Dignity of Persons   609
III.   Safeguarding Peace   613
       IN BRIEF   617
ARTICLE 6: THE SIXTH COMMANDMENT   619
I.   "Male and Female He Created
       Them . . ."   619
II.   The Vocation to Chastity   620
III.   The Love of Husband and Wife   626
IV.   Offenses against the Dignity of Marriage   632
       IN BRIEF   635
ARTICLE 7: THE SEVENTH
COMMANDMENT   636
I.   The Universal Destination and the
       Private Ownership of Goods   636
II.   Respect for Persons and Their Goods   637
III.   The Social Doctrine of the Church   640
IV.   Economic Activity and Social Justice   642

V.	Justice and Solidarity among Nations	645
VI.	Love for the Poor	646
	IN BRIEF	649

ARTICLE 8: THE EIGHTH COMMANDMENT   651

I.	Living in the Truth	651
II.	To Bear Witness to the Truth	653
III.	Offenses against Truth	654
IV.	Respect for the Truth	657
V.	The Use of the Social Communications Media	658
VI.	Truth, Beauty, and Sacred Art	659
	IN BRIEF	661

ARTICLE 9: THE NINTH COMMANDMENT   662

I.	Purification of the Heart	663
II.	The Battle for Purity	664
	IN BRIEF	666

ARTICLE 10: THE TENTH COMMANDMENT   667

I.	The Disorder of Covetous Desires	667
II.	The Desires of the Spirit	669
III.	Poverty of Heart	670
IV.	"I Want to See God"	671
	IN BRIEF	672

PART FOUR: CHRISTIAN PRAYER   673

SECTION ONE: PRAYER IN THE CHRISTIAN LIFE   673

WHAT IS PRAYER?   673

CHAPTER ONE: THE REVELATION OF PRAYER   675

THE UNIVERSAL CALL TO PRAYER   675

ARTICLE 1: IN THE OLD TESTAMENT   676

IN BRIEF   683

ARTICLE 2: IN THE FULLNESS OF TIME   684

IN BRIEF   691

ARTICLE 3: IN THE AGE OF THE CHURCH   692

I.	Blessing and Adoration	693
II.	Prayer of Petition	693
III.	Prayer of Intercession	695
IV.	Prayer of Thanksgiving	696
V.	Prayer of Praise	696
	IN BRIEF	697

CHAPTER TWO: THE TRADITION OF PRAYER   698

ARTICLE 1: AT THE WELLSPRINGS OF PRAYER   699

IN BRIEF 701
ARTICLE 2: THE WAY OF PRAYER 701
    IN BRIEF 707
ARTICLE 3: GUIDES FOR PRAYER 707
    IN BRIEF 710
CHAPTER THREE: THE LIFE OF PRAYER 711
ARTICLE 1: EXPRESSIONS OF PRAYER 712
I.   Vocal Prayer 712
II.   Meditation 713
III.   Contemplative Prayer 714
    IN BRIEF 716
ARTICLE 2: THE BATTLE OF PRAYER 717
I.   Objections to Prayer 717
II.   Humble Vigilance of Heart 719
III.   Filial Trust 720
IV.   Persevering in Love 722
ARTICLE 3: THE PRAYER OF THE HOUR OF
    JESUS 723
    IN BRIEF 725
SECTION TWO: THE LORD'S PRAYER: "OUR
    FATHER!" 726
ARTICLE 1: "THE SUMMARY OF THE
    WHOLE GOSPEL" 727
I.   At the Center of the Scriptures 727
II.   "The Lord's Prayer" 728
III.   The Prayer of the Church 728
    IN BRIEF 730
ARTICLE 2: "OUR FATHER WHO ART IN
    HEAVEN" 731
I.   "We Dare to Say" 731
II.   "Father!" 731
III.   "Our" Father 734
IV.   "Who Art in Heaven" 736
    IN BRIEF 737
ARTICLE 3: THE SEVEN PETITIONS 738
I.   "Hallowed Be Thy Name" 739
II.   "Thy Kingdom Come" 742
III.   "Thy Will Be Done on Earth as It Is in
    Heaven" 743
IV.   "Give Us This Day Our Daily Bread" 745

V.   "And Forgive Us Our Trespasses, as We
         Forgive Those Who Trespass against
         Us"   748
VI.   "And Lead Us Not into Temptation"   751
VII.   "But Deliver Us from Evil"   752
ARTICLE 4: THE FINAL DOXOLOGY   754
         IN BRIEF   755
SUBJECT INDEX   757
ABBREVIATIONS   823

APOSTOLIC CONSTITUTION
FIDEI DEPOSITUM

ON THE PUBLICATION OF THE CATECHISM OF THE CATHOLIC CHURCH

PREPARED FOLLOWING THE SECOND VATICAN ECUMENICAL COUNCIL

JOHN PAUL, BISHOP
SERVANT OF THE SERVANTS OF GOD
FOR EVERLASTING MEMORY

To my Venerable Brothers the Cardinals, Patriarchs, Archbishops, Bishops, Priests, Deacons, and to all the People of God.

GUARDING THE DEPOSIT OF FAITH IS THE MISSION WHICH THE LORD ENTRUSTED TO HIS CHURCH, and which she fulfills in every age. The Second Vatican Ecumenical Council, which was opened 30 years ago by my predecessor Pope John XXIII, of happy memory, had as its intention and purpose to highlight the Church's apostolic and pastoral mission and by making the truth of the Gospel shine forth to lead all people to seek and receive Christ's love which surpasses all knowledge (cf. *Eph* 3:19).

The principal task entrusted to the Council by Pope John XXIII was to guard and present better the precious deposit of Christian doctrine in order to make it more accessible to the Christian faithful and to all people of good will. For this reason the Council was not first of all to condemn the errors of the time, but above all to strive calmly to show the strength and beauty of the doctrine of the faith. "Illumined by the light of this

Council," the Pope said, "the Church . . . will become greater in spiritual riches and gaining the strength of new energies therefrom, she will look to the future without fear. . . . Our duty is to dedicate ourselves with an earnest will and without fear to that work which our era demands of us, thus pursuing the path which the Church has followed for 20 centuries."[1]

With the help of God, the Council Fathers in four years of work were able to produce a considerable number of doctrinal statements and pastoral norms which were presented to the whole Church. There the Pastors and Christian faithful find directives for that "renewal of thought, action, practices, and moral virtue, of joy and hope, which was the very purpose of the Council."[2]

After its conclusion, the Council did not cease to inspire the Church's life. In 1985 I was able to assert, "For me, then—who had the special grace of participating in it and actively collaborating in its development—Vatican II has always been, and especially during these years of my Pontificate, the constant reference point of my every pastoral action, in the conscious commitment to implement its directives concretely and faithfully at the level of each Church and the whole Church."[3]

In this spirit, on January 25, 1985, I convoked an extraordinary assembly of the Synod of Bishops for the 20th anniversary of the close of the Council. The purpose of this assembly was to celebrate the graces and spiritual fruits of Vatican II, to study its teaching in greater depth in order that all the Christian faithful might better adhere to it and to promote knowledge and application of it.

On that occasion the Synod Fathers stated: "Very many have expressed the desire that a catechism or compendium of all catholic doctrine regarding both faith and morals be composed, that it might be, as it

---

1 John XXIII, Discourse at the Opening of the Second Vatican Ecumenical Council, October 11, 1962: AAS 54 (1962) pp. 788–91. 2 Paul VI, Discourse at the Closing of the Second Vatican Ecumenical Council, December 7, 1965: AAS 58 (1966) pp. 7–8. 3 John Paul II, Discourse of January 25, 1985: *L'Osservatore Romano,* January 27, 1985.

were, a point of reference for the catechisms or compendiums that are prepared in various regions. The presentation of doctrine must be biblical and liturgical. It must be sound doctrine suited to the present life of Christians."[4] After the Synod ended, I made this desire my own, considering it as "fully responding to a real need of the universal Church and of the particular Churches."[5]

For this reason we thank the Lord wholeheartedly on this day when we can offer the entire Church this "reference text" entitled the *Catechism of the Catholic Church* for a catechesis renewed at the living sources of the faith!

Following the renewal of the Liturgy and the new codification of the canon law of the Latin Church and that of the Oriental Catholic Churches, this catechism will make a very important contribution to that work of renewing the whole life of the Church, as desired and begun by the Second Vatican Council.

1. The Process and Spirit of Drafting the Text

The *Catechism of the Catholic Church* is the result of very extensive collaboration; it was prepared over six years of intense work done in a spirit of complete openness and fervent zeal.

In 1986, I entrusted a commission of twelve Cardinals and Bishops, chaired by Cardinal Joseph Ratzinger, with the task of preparing a draft of the catechism requested by the Synod Fathers. An editorial committee of seven diocesan Bishops, experts in theology and catechesis, assisted the commission in its work.

The commission, charged with giving directives and with overseeing the course of the work, attentively followed all the stages in editing the nine subsequent drafts. The editorial committee, for its part, assumed responsibility for writing the text, making the emendations requested by the commission and examining the

---

4 *Final Report* of the Extraordinary Synod of Bishops, December 7, 1985, *Enchiridion Vaticanum,* vol. 9, II, B, a, n. 4: p. 1758, n. 1797. 5 John Paul II, Discourse at the Closing of the Extraordinary Synod of Bishops, December 7, 1985, n. 6: AAS 78 (1986) p. 435.

observations of numerous theologians, exegetes and catechists, and, above all, of the Bishops of the whole world, in order to produce a better text. In the committee various opinions were compared with great profit, and thus a richer text has resulted whose unity and coherence are assured.

The project was the object of extensive consultation among all Catholic Bishops, their Episcopal Conferences or Synods, and of theological and catechetical institutes. As a whole, it received a broadly favorable acceptance on the part of the Episcopate. It can be said that this *Catechism* is the result of the collaboration of the whole Episcopate of the Catholic Church, who generously accepted my invitation to share responsibility for an enterprise which directly concerns the life of the Church. This response elicits in me a deep feeling of joy, because the harmony of so many voices truly expresses what could be called the "symphony" of the faith. The achievement of this *Catechism* thus reflects the collegial nature of the Episcopate; it testifies to the Church's catholicity.

2.   Arrangement of the Material

A catechism should faithfully and systematically present the teaching of Sacred Scripture, the living Tradition in the Church and the authentic Magisterium, as well as the spiritual heritage of the Fathers, Doctors, and saints of the Church, to allow for a better knowledge of the Christian mystery and for enlivening the faith of the People of God. It should take into account the doctrinal statements which down the centuries the Holy Spirit has intimated to his Church. It should also help to illumine with the light of faith the new situations and problems which had not yet emerged in the past.

This catechism will thus contain both the new and the old (cf. *Mt* 13:52), because the faith is always the same yet the source of ever new light.

To respond to this twofold demand, the *Catechism of the Catholic Church* on the one hand repeats the "old," traditional order already followed by the Catechism of St. Pius V, arranging the material in four parts: the *Creed,* the *Sacred Liturgy,* with pride of place given to the sacraments, the *Christian way of life,* explained beginning with the Ten Commandments, and finally, *Christian prayer.* At the same time, however, the contents are often presented in a "new" way in order to respond to the questions of our age.

The four parts are related one to another: the Christian mystery is the object of faith (first part); it is celebrated and communicated in liturgical actions (second part); it is present to enlighten and sustain the children of God in their actions (third part); it is the basis for our prayer, the privileged expression of which is the *Our Father,* and it represents the object of our supplication, our praise and our intercession (fourth part).

The Liturgy itself is prayer; the confession of faith finds its proper place in the celebration of worship. Grace, the fruit of the sacraments, is the irreplaceable condition for Christian living, just as participation in the Church's Liturgy requires faith. If faith is not expressed in works, it is dead (cf. *Jas* 2:14–16) and cannot bear fruit unto eternal life.

In reading the *Catechism of the Catholic Church* we can perceive the wonderful unity of the mystery of God, his saving will, as well as the central place of Jesus Christ, the only-begotten Son of God, sent by the Father, made man in the womb of the Blessed Virgin Mary by the power of the Holy Spirit, to be our Savior. Having died and risen, Christ is always present in his Church, especially in the sacraments; he is the source of our faith, the model of Christian conduct, and the Teacher of our prayer.

3.   The Doctrinal Value of the Text

The *Catechism of the Catholic Church,* which I approved June 25th last and the publication of which I today order by virtue of my Apostolic Authority, is a statement of the Church's faith and of catholic doctrine, attested to or illumined by Sacred Scripture, the Apostolic Tradition, and the Church's Magisterium. I declare it to be a sure norm for teaching the faith and thus a valid and legitimate instrument for ecclesial communion. May it serve the renewal to which the Holy Spirit ceaselessly calls the Church of God, the Body of Christ, on her pilgrimage to the undiminished light of the Kingdom!

The approval and publication of the *Catechism of the Catholic Church* represent a service which the Successor of Peter wishes to offer to the Holy Catholic Church, to all the particular Churches in peace and communion with the Apostolic See: the service, that is, of supporting and confirming the faith of all the Lord Jesus' disciples (cf. *Lk* 22:32), as well as of strengthening the bonds of unity in the same apostolic faith.

Therefore, I ask all the Church's Pastors and the Christian faithful to receive this catechism in a spirit of communion and to use it assiduously in fulfilling their mission of proclaiming the faith and calling people to the Gospel life. This catechism is given to them that it may be a sure and authentic reference text for teaching catholic doctrine and particularly for preparing local catechisms. It is also offered to all the faithful who wish to deepen their knowledge of the unfathomable riches of salvation (cf. *Eph* 3:8). It is meant to support ecumenical efforts that are moved by the holy desire for the unity of all Christians, showing carefully the content and wondrous harmony of the catholic faith. The *Catechism of the Catholic Church,* lastly, is offered to every individual who asks us to give an account of the hope that is in us (cf. *1 Pet* 3:15) and who wants to know what the Catholic Church believes.

This catechism is not intended to replace the local catechisms duly approved by the ecclesiastical authorities, the diocesan Bishops and the Episcopal Conferences, especially if they have been approved by the Apostolic See. It is meant to encourage and assist in the writing of new local catechisms, which take into account various situations and cultures, while carefully preserving the unity of faith and fidelity to catholic doctrine.

At the conclusion of this document presenting the *Catechism of the Catholic Church,* I beseech the Blessed Virgin Mary, Mother of the Incarnate Word and

Mother of the Church, to support with her powerful intercession the catechetical work of the entire Church on every level, at this time when she is called to a new effort of evangelization. May the light of the true faith free humanity from the ignorance and slavery of sin in order to lead it to the only freedom worthy of the name (cf. *Jn* 8:32): that of life in Jesus Christ under the guidance of the Holy Spirit, here below and in the Kingdom of heaven, in the fullness of the blessed vision of God face to face (cf. *1 Cor* 13:12; *2 Cor* 5:6–8)!

Given October 11, 1992, the thirtieth anniversary of the opening of the Second Vatican Ecumenical Council, in the fourteenth year of my Pontificate.

Joannes Paulus II

PROLOGUE

"FATHER, ... this is eternal life, that they may know you, the only true God, and Jesus Christ whom you have sent.[1] God our Savior desires all men to be saved and to come to the knowledge of the truth."[2] "There is no other name under heaven given among men by which we must be saved"[3] than the name of JESUS.

I. THE LIFE OF MAN—TO KNOW AND LOVE GOD

1 God, infinitely perfect and blessed in himself, in a plan of sheer goodness freely created man to make him share in his own blessed life. For this reason, at every time and in every place, God draws close to man. He calls man to seek him, to know him, to love him with all his strength. He calls together all men, scattered and divided by sin, into the unity of his family, the Church. To accomplish this, when the fullness of time had come, God sent his Son as Redeemer and Savior. In his Son and through him, he invites men to become, in the Holy Spirit, his adopted children and thus heirs of his blessed life.

2 So that this call should resound throughout the world, Christ sent forth the apostles he had chosen, commissioning them to proclaim the gospel: "Go therefore and make disciples of all nations, baptizing them in the name of the Father and of the Son and of the Holy Spirit, teaching them to observe all that I have commanded you; and lo, I am with you always, to the close of the age."[4] Strengthened by this mission, the apostles "went forth and preached everywhere, while the Lord worked with them and confirmed the message by the signs that attended it."[5]

3 Those who with God's help have welcomed Christ's call and freely responded to it are urged on by love of Christ to proclaim the Good News everywhere in the world. This treasure, received from the apostles,

---

1 *Jn* 17:3. 2 *1 Tim* 2:3–4. 3 *Acts* 4:12. 4 *Mt* 28:18–20. 5 *Mk* 16:20.

has been faithfully guarded by their successors. All Christ's faithful are called to hand it on from generation to generation, by professing the faith, by living it in fraternal sharing, and by celebrating it in liturgy and prayer.[6]

II.   HANDING ON THE FAITH: CATECHESIS

4   Quite early on, the name *catechesis* was given to the totality of the Church's efforts to make disciples, to help men believe that Jesus is the Son of God so that believing they might have life in his name, and to educate and instruct them in this life, thus building up the body of Christ.[7]

5   "Catechesis is an *education in the faith* of children, young people, and adults which includes especially the teaching of Christian doctrine imparted, generally speaking, in an organic and systematic way, with a view to initiating the hearers into the fullness of Christian life."[8]

6   While not being formally identified with them, catechesis is built on a certain number of elements of the Church's pastoral mission which have a catechetical aspect, that prepare for catechesis, or spring from it. They are: the initial proclamation of the Gospel or missionary preaching to arouse faith; examination of the reasons for belief; experience of Christian living; celebration of the sacraments; integration into the ecclesial community; and apostolic and missionary witness.[9]

7   "Catechesis is intimately bound up with the whole of the Church's life. Not only her geographical extension and numerical increase, but even more her inner growth and correspondence with God's plan depend essentially on catechesis."[10]

8   Periods of renewal in the Church are also intense moments of catechesis. In the great era of the Fathers of the Church, saintly bishops devoted an important part of their ministry to catechesis. St. Cyril of Jerusalem and St. John

---

6 Cf. *Acts* 2:42.   7 Cf. John Paul II, apostolic exhortation, *Catechesi tradendae* 1; 2.   8 *CT* 18.   9 *CT* 18.   10 *CT* 13.

Chrysostom, St. Ambrose and St. Augustine, and many other Fathers wrote catechetical works that remain models for us.[11]

9   "The ministry of catechesis draws ever fresh energy from the councils. The Council of Trent is a noteworthy example of this. It gave catechesis priority in its constitutions and decrees. It lies at the origin of the *Roman Catechism,* which is also known by the name of that council and which is a work of the first rank as a summary of Christian teaching. . . ."[12] The Council of Trent initiated a remarkable organization of the Church's catechesis. Thanks to the work of holy bishops and theologians such as St. Peter Canisius, St. Charles Borromeo, St. Turibius of Mongrovejo, or St. Robert Bellarmine, it occasioned the publication of numerous catechisms.

10   It is therefore no surprise that catechesis in the Church has again attracted attention in the wake of the Second Vatican Council, which Pope Paul VI considered the great catechism of modern times. The General Catechetical Directory (1971), the sessions of the Synod of Bishops devoted to evangelization (1974) and catechesis (1977), the apostolic exhortations *Evangelii nuntiandi* (1975) and *Catechesi tradendae* (1979) attest to this. The Extraordinary Synod of Bishops in 1985 asked "that a catechism or compendium of all Catholic doctrine regarding both faith and morals be composed."[13] The Holy Father, Pope John Paul II, made the Synod's wish his own, acknowledging that "this desire wholly corresponds to a real need of the universal Church and of the particular Churches."[14] He set in motion everything needed to carry out the Synod Fathers' wish.

III. THE AIM AND INTENDED READERSHIP OF THIS CATECHISM

11   This catechism aims at presenting an organic synthesis of the essential and fundamental contents of Catholic doctrine, as regards both faith and morals, in the light of the Second Vatican Council and the whole of the Church's Tradition. Its principal sources are the Sacred Scriptures, the Fathers of the Church, the liturgy, and the Church's Magisterium. It is intended to serve

---

11 Cf. *CT* 12.   12 *CT* 13.   13 Extraordinary Synod of Bishops 1985, *Final Report,* II B a, 4.   14 John Paul II, Discourse at the Closing of the Extraordinary Synod of Bishops, December 7, 1985: AAS 78 (1986).

"as a point of reference for the catechisms or compendia that are composed in the various countries."[15]

12   This work is intended primarily for those responsible for catechesis: first of all the bishops, as teachers of the faith and pastors of the Church. It is offered to them as an instrument in fulfilling their responsibility of teaching the People of God. Through the bishops, it is addressed to redactors of catechisms, to priests, and to catechists. It will also be useful reading for all other Christian faithful.

IV.   STRUCTURE OF THIS CATECHISM

13   The plan of this catechism is inspired by the great tradition of catechisms which build catechesis on four pillars: the baptismal profession of faith (the *Creed),* the sacraments of faith, the life of faith (the *Commandments),* and the prayer of the believer (the *Lord's Prayer).*

Part One: *The profession of faith*

14   Those who belong to Christ through faith and Baptism must confess their baptismal faith before men.[16] First therefore the Catechism expounds revelation, by which God addresses and gives himself to man, and the faith by which man responds to God *(Section One).* The profession of faith summarizes the gifts that God gives man: as the Author of all that is good; as Redeemer; and as Sanctifier. It develops these in the three chapters on our baptismal faith in the one God: the almighty *Father,* the Creator; his *Son* Jesus Christ, our Lord and Savior; and the *Holy Spirit,* the Sanctifier, in the Holy Church *(Section Two).*

Part Two: *The sacraments of faith*

15   The second part of the Catechism explains how God's salvation, accomplished once for all through Christ Jesus and the Holy Spirit, is made present in

---

15 Extraordinary Synod of Bishops 1985, *Final Report* II B a, 4.   16 Cf. *Mt* 10:32; *Rom* 10:9.

the sacred actions of the Church's liturgy *(Section One)*, especially in the seven sacraments *(Section Two)*.

Part Three: *The life of faith*

16 The third part of the Catechism deals with the final end of man created in the image of God: beatitude, and the ways of reaching it—through right conduct freely chosen, with the help of God's law and grace *(Section One)*, and through conduct that fulfills the twofold commandment of charity, specified in God's Ten Commandments *(Section Two)*.

Part Four: *Prayer in the life of faith*

17 The last part of the Catechism deals with the meaning and importance of prayer in the life of believers *(Section One)*. It concludes with a brief commentary on the seven petitions of the Lord's Prayer *(Section Two)*, for indeed we find in these the sum of all the good things which we must hope for and which our heavenly Father wants to grant us.

V. PRACTICAL DIRECTIONS FOR USING THIS CATECHISM

18 This catechism is conceived as *an organic presentation* of the Catholic faith in its entirety. It should be seen therefore as a unified whole. Numerous cross-references in the margin of the text (italicized numbers referring to other paragraphs that deal with the same theme), as well as the analytical index at the end of the volume, allow the reader to view each theme in its relationship with the entirety of the faith.

19 The texts of Sacred Scripture are often not quoted word for word but are merely indicated by a reference (cf.). For a deeper understanding of such passages, the reader should refer to the Scriptural texts themselves. Such Biblical references are a valuable working-tool in catechesis.

20 The use of small print in certain passages indicates observations of an historical or apologetic nature, or supplementary doctrinal explanations.

21   The **quotations,** also in small print, from patristic, liturgical, magisterial or hagiographical sources, are intended to enrich the doctrinal presentations. These texts have often been chosen with a view to direct catechetical use.

22   At the end of each thematic unit, a series of brief texts sum up the essentials of that unit's teaching in condensed formulae. These **IN BRIEF** summaries may suggest to local catechists brief summary formulae that could be memorized.

VI.   NECESSARY ADAPTATIONS

23   The Catechism emphasizes the exposition of doctrine. It seeks to help deepen understanding of faith. In this way it is oriented toward the maturing of that faith, its putting down roots in personal life and its shining forth in personal conduct.[17]

24   By design, this Catechism does not set out to provide the adaptation of doctrinal presentations and catechetical methods required by the differences of culture, age, spiritual maturity, and social and ecclesial condition among all those to whom it is addressed. Such indispensable adaptations are the responsibility of particular catechisms and, even more, of those who instruct the faithful:

> Whoever teaches must become "all things to all men" *(1 Cor 9:22)*, to win everyone to Christ. . . . Above all, teachers must not imagine that a single kind of soul has been entrusted to them, and that consequently it is lawful to teach and form equally all the faithful in true piety with one and the same method! Let them realize that some are in Christ as newborn babes, others as adolescents, and still others as adults in full command of their powers. . . . Those who are called to the ministry of preaching must suit their words to the maturity and understanding of their hearers, as they hand on the teaching of the mysteries of faith and the rules of moral conduct.[18]

---

17 Cf. CT 20–22, 25.   18 *Roman Catechism,* Preface, 11; cf. *1 Cor* 9:22; *1 Pet* 2:2.

Above All—Charity

25   To conclude this Prologue, it is fitting to recall this pastoral principle stated by the *Roman Catechism:*

> The whole concern of doctrine and its teaching must be directed to the love that never ends. Whether something is proposed for belief, for hope or for action, the love of our Lord must always be made accessible, so that anyone can see that all the works of perfect Christian virtue spring from love and have no other objective than to arrive at love.[19]

---

19 *Roman Catechism,* Preface, 10; cf. *1 Cor* 13:8.

PART ONE
THE PROFESSION OF FAITH

SECTION ONE
"I BELIEVE"—"WE BELIEVE"

26 We begin our profession of faith by saying: "I believe" or "We believe." Before expounding the Church's faith, as confessed in the Creed, celebrated in the liturgy, and lived in observance of God's commandments and in prayer, we must first ask what "to believe" means. Faith is man's response to God, who reveals himself and gives himself to man, at the same time bringing man a superabundant light as he searches for the ultimate meaning of his life. Thus we shall consider first that search *(Chapter One)*, then the divine Revelation by which God comes to meet man *(Chapter Two)*, and finally the response of faith *(Chapter Three)*.

CHAPTER ONE
MAN'S CAPACITY FOR GOD

I. THE DESIRE FOR GOD

27 The desire for God is written in the human heart, because man is created by God and for God; and God never ceases to draw man to himself. Only in God will he find the truth and happiness he never stops searching for:

355, 170
1718

> The dignity of man rests above all on the fact that he is called to communion with God. This invitation to converse with God is addressed to man as soon as he comes into being. For if man exists, it is because God has created him through love, and through love continues to hold him in existence. He cannot live fully according to truth unless he freely acknowledges that love and entrusts himself to his creator.[1]

28 In many ways, throughout history down to the

---

1 Vatican Council II, *GS* 19 § 1.

843,2566   present day, men have given expression to their quest
2095-2109   for God in their religious beliefs and behavior: in their
prayers, sacrifices, rituals, meditations, and so forth.
These forms of religious expression, despite the ambi-
guities they often bring with them, are so universal that
one may well call man a *religious being:*

> From one ancestor [God] made all nations to in-
> habit the whole earth, and he allotted the times
> of their existence and the boundaries of the places
> where they would live, so that they would search
> for God and perhaps grope for him and find him—
> though indeed he is not far from each one of us.
> For "in him we live and move and have our be-
> ing."[2]

2123-2128   **29**   But this "intimate and vital bond of man to
God" (*GS* 19,1) can be forgotten, overlooked, or even
explicitly rejected by man.[3] Such attitudes can have different causes: revolt against evil in the world; religious
ignorance or indifference; the cares and riches of this
world; the scandal of bad example on the part of be-
398   lievers; currents of thought hostile to religion; finally,
that attitude of sinful man which makes him hide from
God out of fear and flee his call.[4]

30   "Let the hearts of those who seek the LORD re-
2567, 845   joice."[5] Although man can forget God or reject him, He
never ceases to call every man to seek him, so as to find
life and happiness. But this search for God demands of
368   man every effort of intellect, a sound will, "an upright
heart," as well as the witness of others who teach him
to seek God.

> You are great, O Lord, and greatly to be praised:
> great is your power and your wisdom is without
> measure. And man, so small a part of your cre-
> ation, wants to praise you: this man, though
> clothed with mortality and bearing the evidence of
> sin and the proof that you withstand the proud.
> Despite everything, man, though but a small a part
> of your creation, wants to praise you. You yourself
> encourage him to delight in your praise, for you

---

2 *Acts* 17:26–28.   3 *GS* 19 § 1.   4 Cf. *GS* 19–21; *Mt* 13:22; *Gen* 3:8–10; *Jon*
1:3.   5 *Ps* 105:3.

have made us for yourself, and our heart is restless until it rests in you.[6]

II.   WAYS OF COMING TO KNOW GOD

31   Created in God's image and called to know and love him, the person who seeks God discovers certain ways of coming to know him. These are also called proofs for the existence of God, not in the sense of proofs in the natural sciences, but rather in the sense of "converging and convincing arguments," which allow us to attain certainty about the truth.

These "ways" of approaching God from creation have a twofold point of departure: the physical world and the human person.

32   The *world:* starting from movement, becoming, contingency, and the world's order and beauty, one can   54, 337
come to a knowledge of God as the origin and the end of the universe.

> As St. Paul says of the Gentiles: For what can be known about God is plain to them, because God has shown it to them. Ever since the creation of the world his invisible nature, namely, his eternal power and deity, has been clearly perceived in the things that have been made.[7]

> And St. Augustine issues this challenge: Question the beauty of the earth, question the beauty of the sea, question the beauty of the air distending and diffusing itself, question the beauty of the sky . . . question all these realities. All respond: "See, we are beautiful." Their beauty is a profession *[confessio]*. These beauties are subject to change. Who made them if not the Beautiful One *[Pulcher]* who is not subject to change?[8]

33   The *human person:* With his openness to truth and beauty, his sense of moral goodness, his freedom   1730, 2500
and the voice of his conscience, with his longings for the   1776
infinite and for happiness, man questions himself about God's existence. In all this he discerns signs of his spiri-   1703

---

6 St. Augustine, *Conf.* 1, 1, 1: PL 32, 659–661.   7 *Rom* 1:19–20; cf. *Acts* 14:15, 17; 17:27–28; *Wis* 13:1–9.   8 St. Augustine, *Sermo* 241, 2: PL 38, 1134.

366 tual soul. The soul, the "seed of eternity we bear in our-selves, irreducible to the merely material,"⁹ can have its origin only in God.

34   The world, and man, attest that they contain within themselves neither their first principle nor their final end, but rather that they participate in Being itself, which alone is without origin or end. Thus, in different ways, man can come to know that there exists a reality which is the first cause and final end of all things, a re-

199 ality "that everyone calls 'God.' "¹⁰

35   Man's faculties make him capable of coming to a knowledge of the existence of a personal God. But for man to be able to enter into real intimacy with him,

50 God willed both to reveal himself to man and to give him the grace of being able to welcome this revelation in faith. The proofs of God's existence, however, can

159 predispose one to faith and help one to see that faith is not opposed to reason.

III. THE KNOWLEDGE OF GOD ACCORDING TO THE CHURCH

36   "Our holy mother, the Church, holds and teaches that God, the first principle and last end of all things, can be known with certainty from the created world by the natural light of human reason."¹¹ Without this capacity, man would not be able to welcome God's

355 revelation. Man has this capacity because he is created "in the image of God."¹²

37   In the historical conditions in which he finds himself, however, man experiences many difficulties in

1960 coming to know God by the light of reason alone:

> Though human reason is, strictly speaking, truly capable by its own natural power and light of at-taining to a true and certain knowledge of the one personal God, who watches over and controls the world by his providence, and of the natural law written in our hearts by the Creator; yet there are

---

9 *GS* 18 § 1; cf. 14 § 2.   10 St. Thomas Aquinas, *STh* 1, 2, 3.   11 Vatican Council I, *Dei Filius* 2: DS 3004; cf. 3026; Vatican Council II, *Dei Verbum* 6.
12 Cf. *Gen* 1:27.

many obstacles which prevent reason from the effective and fruitful use of this inborn faculty. For the truths that concern the relations between God and man wholly transcend the visible order of things, and, if they are translated into human action and influence it, they call for self-surrender and abnegation. The human mind, in its turn, is hampered in the attaining of such truths, not only by the impact of the senses and the imagination, but also by disordered appetites which are the consequences of original sin. So it happens that men in such matters easily persuade themselves that what they would not like to be true is false or at least doubtful.[13]

38   This is why man stands in need of being enlightened by God's revelation, not only about those things that exceed his understanding, but also "about those religious and moral truths which of themselves are not beyond the grasp of human reason, so that even in the present condition of the human race, they can be known by all men with ease, with firm certainty and with no admixture of error."[14]   *2036*

IV.   How Can We Speak about God?

39   In defending the ability of human reason to know God, the Church is expressing her confidence in the possibility of speaking about him to all men and with all men, and therefore of dialogue with other religions, with philosophy and science, as well as with unbelievers and atheists.   *851*

40   Since our knowledge of God is limited, our language about him is equally so. We can name God only by taking creatures as our starting point, and in accordance with our limited human ways of knowing and thinking.

41   All creatures bear a certain resemblance to God, most especially man, created in the image and likeness of God. The manifold perfections of creatures—their truth, their goodness, their beauty—all reflect the infi-   *213*

---

13 Pius XII, *Humani Generis,* 561: DS 3875.   **14** Pius XII, *Humani Generis,* 561: DS 3876; cf. *Dei Filius* 2: DS 3005; *DV* 6; St. Thomas Aquinas, *STh* I, 1, 1.

299   nite perfection of God. Consequently we can name God by taking his creatures' perfections as our starting point, "for from the greatness and beauty of created things comes a corresponding perception of their Creator."[15]

42   God transcends all creatures. We must therefore
212, 300   continually purify our language of everything in it that is limited, imagebound or imperfect, if we are not to
370   confuse our image of God—"the inexpressible, the incomprehensible, the invisible, the ungraspable"—with our human representations.[16] Our human words always fall short of the mystery of God.

43   Admittedly, in speaking about God like this, our language is using human modes of expression; nevertheless it really does attain to God himself, though unable to express him in his infinite simplicity. Likewise, we must recall that "between Creator and creature no similitude can be expressed without implying an even greater dissimilitude";[17] and that "concerning God, we
206   cannot grasp what he is, but only what he is not, and how other beings stand in relation to him."[18]

IN BRIEF

44   Man is by nature and vocation a religious being. Coming from God, going toward God, man lives a fully human life only if he freely lives by his bond with God.

45   Man is made to live in communion with God in whom he finds happiness: "When I am completely united to you, there will be no more sorrow or trials; entirely full of you, my life will be complete" (St. Augustine, *Conf.* 10, 28, 39: PL 32, 795).

46   When he listens to the message of creation and to the voice of conscience, man can arrive at certainty about the existence of God, the cause and the end of everything.

---

15 *Wis* 13:5.   **16** *Liturgy of St. John Chrysostom,* Anaphora.   **17** Lateran Council IV: DS 806.   **18** St. Thomas Aquinas, *SCG* I, 30.

47   The Church teaches that the one true God, our Creator and Lord, can be known with certainty from his works, by the natural light of human reason (cf. Vatican Council I, can. 2, § 1: DS 3026).

48   We really can name God, starting from the manifold perfections of his creatures, which are likenesses of the infinitely perfect God, even if our limited language cannot exhaust the mystery.

49   "Without the Creator, the creature vanishes" (*GS* 36). This is the reason why believers know that the love of Christ urges them to bring the light of the living God to those who do not know him or who reject him.

CHAPTER TWO
GOD COMES TO MEET MAN

50   By natural reason man can know God with certainty, on the basis of his works. But there is another order of knowledge, which man cannot possibly arrive at by his own powers: the order of divine Revelation.[1]   36 Through an utterly free decision, God has revealed himself and given himself to man. This he does by revealing the mystery, his plan of loving goodness, formed from all eternity in Christ, for the benefit of all men. God has fully revealed this plan by sending us his beloved Son,   1066 our Lord Jesus Christ, and the Holy Spirit.

ARTICLE 1
THE REVELATION OF GOD

I.   GOD REVEALS HIS "PLAN OF LOVING GOODNESS"

51   "It pleased God, in his goodness and wisdom, to reveal himself and to make known the mystery of his   2823 will. His will was that men should have access to the Father, through Christ, the Word made flesh, in the

---

1 Cf. *Dei Filius*: DS 3015.

1996 Holy Spirit, and thus become sharers in the divine nature."[2]

52   God, who "dwells in unapproachable light," wants to communicate his own divine life to the men he freely created, in order to adopt them as his sons in his only-begotten Son.[3] By revealing himself God wishes to make them capable of responding to him, and of knowing him, and of loving him far beyond their own natural capacity.

53   The divine plan of Revelation is realized simultaneously "by deeds and words which are intrinsically bound up with each other"[4] and shed light on each other. It involves a specific divine pedagogy: God com-
1953, 1950 municates himself to man gradually. He prepares him to welcome by stages the supernatural Revelation that is to culminate in the person and mission of the incarnate Word, Jesus Christ.

> St. Irenaeus of Lyons repeatedly speaks of this divine pedagogy using the image of God and man becoming accustomed to one another: The Word of God dwelt in man and became the Son of man in order to accustom man to perceive God and to accustom God to dwell in man, according to the Father's pleasure.[5]

II.   THE STAGES OF REVELATION

In the beginning God makes himself known

54   "God, who creates and conserves all things by
32 his Word, provides men with constant evidence of himself in created realities. And furthermore, wishing to open up the way to heavenly salvation, he manifested himself to our first parents from the very beginning."[6] He invited them to intimate communion with
374 himself and clothed them with resplendent grace and justice.

---

2 *DV* 2; cf. *Eph* 1:9; 2:18; *2 Pet* 1:4.   3 *1 Tim* 6:16; cf. *Eph* 1:4–5.   4 *DV* 2.
5 St. Irenaeus, *Adv. haeres.* 3, 20, 2: PG 7/1, 944; cf. 3, 17, 1; 4, 12, 4; 4, 21, 3.
6 *DV* 3; cf. *Jn* 1:3; *Rom* 1:19–20.

55   This revelation was not broken off by our first parents' sin. "After the fall, [God] buoyed them up with the hope of salvation, by promising redemption; and he has never ceased to show his solicitude for the human race. For he wishes to give eternal life to all those who seek salvation by patience in well-doing."[7]   *397, 410*

> Even when he disobeyed you and lost your friendship
> you did not abandon him to the power of death. . . .
> Again and again you offered a covenant to man.[8]   *761*

The Covenant with Noah

56   After the unity of the human race was shattered by sin God at once sought to save humanity part by part. The covenant with Noah after the flood gives expression to the principle of the divine economy toward the "nations," in other words, toward men grouped "in their lands, each with [its] own language, by their families, in their nations."[9]   *401
1219*

57   This state of division into many nations, each entrusted by divine providence to the guardianship of angels, is at once cosmic, social, and religious. It is intended to limit the pride of fallen humanity,[10] united only in its perverse ambition to forge its own unity as at Babel.[11] But, because of sin, both polytheism and the idolatry of the nation and of its rulers constantly threaten this provisional economy with the perversion of paganism.[12]

58   The covenant with Noah remains in force during the times of the Gentiles, until the universal proclamation of the Gospel.[13] The Bible venerates several great figures among the Gentiles: Abel the just, the king-priest Melchizedek—a figure of Christ—and the upright "Noah, Daniel, and Job."[14] Scripture thus expresses the heights of sanctity that can be reached by those who live   *674*

---

7 *DV* 3; cf. *Gen* 3:15; *Rom* 2:6–7.   8 *Roman Missal,* Eucharistic Prayer IV, 118. 9 *Gen* 10:5; cf. 9:9–10, 16; 10:20–31.   10 Cf. *Acts* 17:26–27; *Deut* 4: 19; *Deut* (LXX) 32:8.   11 Cf. *Wis* 10:5; *Gen* 11:4–6.   12 Cf. *Rom* 1:18–25.   13 Cf. *Gen* 9:16; *Lk* 21:24; *DV* 3.   14 Cf. *Gen* 14:18; *Heb* 7:3; *Ezek* 14:14.

2569 according to the covenant of Noah, waiting for Christ to "gather into one the children of God who are scattered abroad."[15]

God chooses Abraham

59   In order to gather together scattered humanity
145, 2570 God calls Abram from his country, his kindred, and his father's house,[16] and makes him Abraham, that is, "the father of a multitude of nations." "In you all the nations of the earth shall be blessed."[17]

60   The people descended from Abraham would be the trustees of the promise made to the patriarchs, the
760 chosen people, called to prepare for that day when God
762, 781 would gather all his children into the unity of the Church.[18] They would be the root onto which the Gentiles would be grafted, once they came to believe.[19]

61   The patriarchs, prophets, and certain other Old Testament figures have been and always will be honored as saints in all the Church's liturgical traditions.

God forms his people Israel

62   After the patriarchs, God formed Israel as his
2060, 2574 people by freeing them from slavery in Egypt. He established with them the covenant of Mount Sinai and, through Moses, gave them his law so that they would recognize him and serve him as the one living and true God, the provident Father and just judge, and so that
1961 they would look for the promised Savior.[20]

204, 2801 **63**   Israel is the priestly people of God, "called by
839 the name of the LORD," and "the first to hear the word of God,"[21] the people of "elder brethren" in the faith of Abraham.

64   Through the prophets, God forms his people in the hope of salvation, in the expectation of a new and everlasting Covenant intended for all, to be written on

---

15 *Jn* 11:52.   16 *Gen* 12:1.   17 *Gen* 17:5; 12:3 (LXX); cf. *Gal* 3:8.   18 Cf.
Rom 11:28; *Jn* 11:52; 10:16.   19 Cf. *Rom* 11:17–18, 24.   20 Cf. *DV* 3.
21 *Deut* 28:10; *Roman Missal,* Good Friday, General Intercession VI; see also *Ex* 19:6.

their hearts.[22] The prophets proclaim a radical redemp- 711, 1965
tion of the People of God, purification from all their infidelities, a salvation which will include all the nations.[23]
Above all, the poor and humble of the Lord will bear
this hope. Such holy women as Sarah, Rebecca, Rachel,
Miriam, Deborah, Hannah, Judith, and Esther kept 489
alive the hope of Israel's salvation. The purest figure
among them is Mary.[24]

III. CHRIST JESUS—"MEDIATOR AND FULLNESS OF ALL REVELATION"[25]

God has said everything in his Word

65   "In many and various ways God spoke of old to
our fathers by the prophets, but in these last days he has
spoken to us by a Son."[26] Christ, the Son of God made 102
man, is the Father's one, perfect, and unsurpassable
Word. In him he has said everything; there will be no
other word than this one. St. John of the Cross, among
others, commented strikingly on *Hebrews* 1:1–2:

> In giving us his Son, his only Word (for he possesses
> no other), he spoke everything to us at once in
> this sole Word—and he has no more to say . . . be-
> cause what he spoke before to the prophets in
> parts, he has now spoken all at once by giving us
> the All Who is His Son. Any person questioning 516
> God or desiring some vision or revelation would be
> guilty not only of foolish behavior but also of of-
> fending him, by not fixing his eyes entirely upon
> Christ and by living with the desire for some other
> novelty.[27]   2717

There will be no further Revelation

66   "The Christian economy, therefore, since it is the
new and definitive Covenant, will never pass away; and
no new public revelation is to be expected before the
glorious manifestation of our Lord Jesus Christ."[28] Yet

---

22 Cf. *Isa* 2:2–4; *Jer* 31:31–34; *Heb* 10:16.   23 Cf. *Ezek* 36; *Isa* 49:5–6; 53:11.
24 Cf. *Zeph* 2:3; *Lk* 1:38.   25 *DV* 2.   26 *Heb* 1:1–2.   27 St. John of the Cross,
The Ascent of Mount Carmel, 2, 22, 3–5, in *The Collected Works*, tr. K.
Kavanaugh, OCD, and O. Rodriguez, OCD (Washington DC: Institute of
Carmelite Studies, 1979), 179–180; *LH*, OR Advent, wk 2, Mon.   28 *DV* 4; cf. *1
Tim* 6:14; *Titus* 2:13.

even if Revelation is already complete, it has not been made completely explicit; it remains for Christian faith
94 gradually to grasp its full significance over the course of the centuries.

67 Throughout the ages, there have been so-called "private" revelations, some of which have been recognized by the authority of the Church. They do not belong, how-
84 ever, to the deposit of faith. It is not their role to improve or complete Christ's definitive Revelation, but to help live more fully by it in a certain period of history. Guided by the magisterium of the Church, the *sensus fidelium* knows how to discern and welcome in these revelations whatever constitutes an authentic call of Christ or his saints to the
93 Church.

Christian faith cannot accept "revelations" that claim to surpass or correct the Revelation of which Christ is the fulfillment, as is the case in certain non-Christian religions and also in certain recent sects which base themselves on such "revelations."

IN BRIEF

68 By love, God has revealed himself and given himself to man. He has thus provided the definitive, superabundant answer to the questions that man asks himself about the meaning and purpose of his life.

69 God has revealed himself to man by gradually communicating his own mystery in deeds and in words.

70 Beyond the witness to himself that God gives in created things, he manifested himself to our first parents, spoke to them and, after the fall, promised them salvation (cf. *Gen* 3:15) and offered them his covenant.

71 God made an everlasting covenant with Noah and with all living beings (cf. *Gen* 9:16). It will remain in force as long as the world lasts.

72 God chose Abraham and made a covenant with him and his descendants. By the covenant God formed his people and revealed his law to them through Moses. Through the prophets, he prepared them to accept the salvation destined for all humanity.

73   God has revealed himself fully by sending his own Son, in whom he has established his covenant for ever. The Son is his Father's definitive Word; so there will be no further Revelation after him.

ARTICLE 2
THE TRANSMISSION OF DIVINE REVELATION

74   God "desires all men to be saved and to come to the knowledge of the truth":[29] that is, of Christ Jesus.[30] Christ must be proclaimed to all nations and individuals, so that this revelation may reach to the ends of the earth: *851*

> God graciously arranged that the things he had once revealed for the salvation of all peoples should remain in their entirety, throughout the ages, and be transmitted to all generations.[31]

I.   THE APOSTOLIC TRADITION
75   "Christ the Lord, in whom the entire Revelation of the most high God is summed up, commanded the apostles to preach the Gospel, which had been promised beforehand by the prophets, and which he fulfilled in his own person and promulgated with his own lips. In preaching the Gospel, they were to communicate the gifts of God to all men. This Gospel was to be the source of all saving truth and moral discipline."[32]   *171*

In the apostolic preaching . . .
76   In keeping with the Lord's command, the Gospel was handed on in two ways:

---

29 *1 Tim* 2:4.   **30** Cf. *Jn* 14:6.   **31** *DV* 7; cf. *2 Cor* 1:20; 3:16–4:6.   **32** *DV* 7; cf. *Mt* 28:19–20; *Mk* 16:15.

—*orally* "by the apostles who handed on, by the spoken word of their preaching, by the example they gave, by the institutions they established, what they themselves had received—whether from the lips of Christ, from his way of life and his works, or whether they had learned it at the prompting of the Holy Spirit";[33]

—*in writing* "by those apostles and other men associated with the apostles who, under the inspiration of the same Holy Spirit, committed the message of salvation to writing."[34]

. . . continued in apostolic succession

77   "In order that the full and living Gospel might always be preserved in the Church the apostles left bishops as their successors. They gave them 'their own position of teaching authority.' "[35] Indeed, "the apostolic preaching, which is expressed in a special way in the inspired books, was to be preserved in a continuous line of succession until the end of time."[36]

861

78   This living transmission, accomplished in the Holy Spirit, is called Tradition, since it is distinct from Sacred Scripture, though closely connected to it. Through Tradition, "the Church, in her doctrine, life, and worship perpetuates and transmits to every generation all that she herself is, all that she believes."[37] "The sayings of the holy Fathers are a witness to the life-giving presence of this Tradition, showing how its riches are poured out in the practice and life of the Church, in her belief and her prayer."[38]

174
1124, 2651

79   The Father's self-communication made through his Word in the Holy Spirit, remains present and active in the Church: "God, who spoke in the past, continues to converse with the Spouse of his beloved Son. And the Holy Spirit, through whom the living voice of the Gospel rings out in the Church—and through her in the world—leads believers to the full truth, and

---

33 *DV* 7.   34 *DV* 7.   35 *DV* 7 § 2; St. Irenaeus, *Adv. haeres.* 3, 3, 1: PG 7, 848; Harvey, 2, 9.   36 *DV* 8 § 1.   37 *DV* 8 § 1.   38 *DV* 8 § 3.

makes the Word of Christ dwell in them in all its richness."[39]

II. THE RELATIONSHIP BETWEEN TRADITION AND SACRED SCRIPTURE

One common source . . .

80 "Sacred Tradition and Sacred Scripture, then,
are bound closely together and communicate one with
the other. For both of them, flowing out from the same
divine well-spring, come together in some fashion to
form one thing and move towards the same goal."[40]
Each of them makes present and fruitful in the Church
the mystery of Christ, who promised to remain with his
own "always, to the close of the age."[41]

. . . two distinct modes of transmission

81 "*Sacred Scripture* is the speech of God as it is put
down in writing under the breath of the Holy Spirit."[42]

"And [Holy] *Tradition* transmits in its entirety 113
the Word of God which has been entrusted to the apostles by Christ the Lord and the Holy Spirit. It transmits
it to the successors of the apostles so that, enlightened
by the Spirit of truth, they may faithfully preserve, expound, and spread it abroad by their preaching."[43]

82 As a result the Church, to whom the transmission and interpretation of Revelation is entrusted, "does
not derive her certainty about all revealed truths from
the holy Scriptures alone. Both Scripture and Tradition
must be accepted and honored with equal sentiments of
devotion and reverence."[44]

Apostolic Tradition and ecclesial traditions

83 The Tradition here in question comes from the
apostles and hands on what they received from Jesus'
teaching and example and what they learned from the Holy
Spirit. The first generation of Christians did not yet have a
written New Testament, and the New Testament itself
demonstrates the process of living Tradition.

39 *DV* 8 § 3; cf. *Col* 3:16.   40 *DV* 9.   41 *Mt* 28:20.   42 *DV* 9.   43 *DV* 9.
44 *DV* 9.

1202, 2041   Tradition is to be distinguished from the various
2684   theological, disciplinary, liturgical, or devotional traditions, born in the local churches over time. These are the
particular forms, adapted to different places and times, in
which the great Tradition is expressed. In the light of Tradition, these traditions can be retained, modified or even
abandoned under the guidance of the Church's magisterium.

III.   THE INTERPRETATION OF THE HERITAGE OF FAITH

The heritage of faith entrusted to the whole of the Church

84   The apostles entrusted the "Sacred deposit" of
the faith (the *depositum fidei*),[45] contained in Sacred
Scripture and Tradition, to the whole of the Church.

857, 871   "By adhering to [this heritage] the entire holy people,
united to its pastors, remains always faithful to the

2033   teaching of the apostles, to the brotherhood, to the
breaking of bread and the prayers. So, in maintaining,
practicing, and professing the faith that has been
handed on, there should be a remarkable harmony between the bishops and the faithful."[46]

The Magisterium of the Church

85   "The task of giving an authentic interpretation
of the Word of God, whether in its written form or in
the form of Tradition, has been entrusted to the living,

888-892   teaching office of the Church alone. Its authority in this
2032-2040 matter is exercised in the name of Jesus Christ."[47] This
means that the task of interpretation has been entrusted
to the bishops in communion with the successor of Peter, the Bishop of Rome.

86   "Yet this Magisterium is not superior to the
Word of God, but is its servant. It teaches only what has
been handed on to it. At the divine command and with

---

45 *DV* 10 § 1; cf. *1 Tim* 6:20; *2 Tim* 1:12–14 (Vulg.).   46 *DV* 10 § 1; cf. *Acts* 2:42 (Gk.); Pius XII, apostolic constitution, *Munificentissimus Deus*, November 1, 1950: AAS 42 (1950), 756, taken along with the words of St. Cyprian, *Epist.* 66, 8: CSEL 3, 2, 733: "The Church is the people united to its Priests, the flock adhering to its Shepherd."   47 *DV* 10 § 2.

the help of the Holy Spirit, it listens to this devotedly, guards it with dedication, and expounds it faithfully. All that it proposes for belief as being divinely revealed is drawn from this single deposit of faith."[48] *688*

87   Mindful of Christ's words to his apostles: "He who hears you, hears me,"[49] the faithful receive with docility the teachings and directives that their pastors give them in different forms. *1548 2037*

The dogmas of the faith
88   The Church's Magisterium exercises the authority it holds from Christ to the fullest extent when it defines dogmas, that is, when it proposes truths contained in divine Revelation or having a necessary connection with them, in a form obliging the Christian people to an irrevocable adherence of faith.

89   There is an organic connection between our spiritual life and the dogmas. Dogmas are lights along the path of faith; they illuminate it and make it secure. Conversely, if our life is upright, our intellect and heart will be open to welcome the light shed by the dogmas of faith.[50] *2625*

90   The mutual connections between dogmas, and their coherence, can be found in the whole of the Revelation of the mystery of Christ.[51] "In Catholic doctrine there exists an order or 'hierarchy' of truths, since they vary in their relation to the foundation of the Christian faith."[52] *114, 158 234*

The supernatural sense of faith
91   All the faithful share in understanding and handing on revealed truth. They have received the anointing of the Holy Spirit, who instructs them[53] and guides them into all truth.[54] *737*

92   "The whole body of the faithful . . . cannot err in matters of belief. This characteristic is shown in the

---

48 *DV* 10 § 2.   49 *Lk* 10:16; cf. *LG* 20.   50 Cf. *Jn* 8:31–32.   51 Cf. Vatican Council I: DS 3016: *nexus mysteriorum*; *LG* 25.   52 *UR* 11.   53 Cf. *1 Jn* 2:20, 27.   54 Cf. *Jn* 16:13.

785 supernatural appreciation of faith *(sensus fidei)* on the part of the whole people, when, 'from the bishops to the last of the faithful,' they manifest a universal consent in matters of faith and morals."[55]

93   "By this appreciation of the faith, aroused and sustained by the Spirit of truth, the People of God, guided by the sacred teaching authority *(Magisterium)*,
889 . . . receives . . . the faith, once for all delivered to the saints. . . . The People unfailingly adheres to this faith, penetrates it more deeply with right judgment, and applies it more fully in daily life."[56]

Growth in understanding the faith

94   Thanks to the assistance of the Holy Spirit, the understanding of both the realities and the words of the
66 heritage of faith is able to grow in the life of the Church:

2651 —"through the contemplation and study of believers who ponder these things in their hearts";[57] it is in particular "theological research [which] deepens knowledge of revealed truth."[58]

2038, 2518 —"from the intimate sense of spiritual realities which [believers] experience,"[59] the sacred Scriptures "grow with the one who reads them."[60]

—"from the preaching of those who have received, along with their right of succession in the episcopate, the sure charism of truth."[61]

95   "It is clear therefore that, in the supremely wise arrangement of God, sacred Tradition, Sacred Scripture, and the Magisterium of the Church are so connected and associated that one of them cannot stand without the others. Working together, each in its own way, under the action of the one Holy Spirit, they all contribute effectively to the salvation of souls."[62]

---

55 *LG* 12; cf. St. Augustine, *De praed. sanct.* 14, 27: PL 44, 980.   56 *LG* 12; cf. Jude 3.   57 *DV* 8 § 2; cf. *Lk* 2:19, 51.   58 *GS* 62 § 7; cf. *GS* 44 § 2; *DV* 23, 24; *UR* 4.   59 *DV* 8 § 2.   60 St. Gregory the Great, *Hom. in Ez.* 1, 7, 8: PL 76, 843 D.   61 *DV* 8 § 2.   62 *DV* 10 § 3.

IN BRIEF

96 What Christ entrusted to the apostles, they in turn handed on by their preaching and writing, under the inspiration of the Holy Spirit, to all generations, until Christ returns in glory.

97 "Sacred Tradition and Sacred Scripture make up a single sacred deposit of the Word of God" (*DV* 10), in which, as in a mirror, the pilgrim Church contemplates God, the source of all her riches.

98 "The Church, in her doctrine, life, and worship, perpetuates and transmits to every generation all that she herself is, all that she believes" (*DV* 8 §1).

99 Thanks to its supernatural sense of faith, the People of God as a whole never ceases to welcome, to penetrate more deeply, and to live more fully from the gift of divine Revelation.

100 The task of interpreting the Word of God authentically has been entrusted solely to the Magisterium of the Church, that is, to the Pope and to the bishops in communion with him.

ARTICLE 3
SACRED SCRIPTURE

I. CHRIST—THE UNIQUE WORD OF SACRED SCRIPTURE

101 In order to reveal himself to men, in the condescension of his goodness God speaks to them in human words: "Indeed the words of God, expressed in the words of men, are in every way like human language, just as the Word of the eternal Father, when he took on himself the flesh of human weakness, became like men."[63]

102 Through all the words of Sacred Scripture, God

---

[63] *DV* 13.

65, 2763 speaks only one single Word, his one Utterance in whom he expresses himself completely:[64]

426-429
> You recall that one and the same Word of God extends throughout Scripture, that it is one and the same Utterance that resounds in the mouths of all the sacred writers, since he who was in the beginning God with God has no need of separate syllables; for he is not subject to time.[65]

103 For this reason, the Church has always venerated the Scriptures as she venerates the Lord's Body. She

1100, 1184 never ceases to present to the faithful the bread of life,
1378 taken from the one table of God's Word and Christ's Body.[66]

104 In Sacred Scripture, the Church constantly finds her nourishment and her strength, for she welcomes it not as a human word, "but as what it really is, the word of God."[67] "In the sacred books, the Father who is in heaven comes lovingly to meet his children, and talks with them."[68]

II.   INSPIRATION AND TRUTH OF SACRED SCRIPTURE

105 *God is the author of Sacred Scripture.* "The divinely revealed realities, which are contained and presented in the text of Sacred Scripture, have been written down under the inspiration of the Holy Spirit."[69]

"For Holy Mother Church, relying on the faith of the apostolic age, accepts as sacred and canonical the books of the Old and the New Testaments, whole and entire, with all their parts, on the grounds that, written under the inspiration of the Holy Spirit, they have God as their author and have been handed on as such to the Church herself."[70]

106 God inspired the human authors of the sacred books. "To compose the sacred books, God chose certain men who, all the while he employed them in this task, made full use of their own faculties and powers so

---

64 Cf. *Heb* 1:1–3.   65 St. Augustine, *En. in Ps.* 103, 4, 1: PL 37, 1378; cf. *Ps* 104; *Jn* 1:1.   66 Cf. *DV* 21.   67 *1 Thess* 2:13; cf. *DV* 24.   68 *DV* 21.   69 *DV* 11.   70 *DV* 11; cf. *Jn* 20:31; *2 Tim* 3:16; *2 Pet* 1:19–21; 3:15–16.

that, though he acted in them and by them, it was as true authors that they consigned to writing whatever he wanted written, and no more."[71]

107   The inspired books teach the truth. "Since therefore all that the inspired authors or sacred writers affirm should be regarded as affirmed by the Holy Spirit, we must acknowledge that the books of Scripture firmly, faithfully, and without error teach that truth which God, for the sake of our salvation, wished to see confided to the Sacred Scriptures."[72]   702

108   Still, the Christian faith is not a "religion of the book." Christianity is the religion of the "Word" of God, "not a written and mute word, but incarnate and living."[73] If the Scriptures are not to remain a dead letter, Christ, the eternal Word of the living God, must, through the Holy Spirit, "open [our] minds to understand the Scriptures."[74]

III.   THE HOLY SPIRIT, INTERPRETER OF SCRIPTURE

109   In Sacred Scripture, God speaks to man in a human way. To interpret Scripture correctly, the reader must be attentive to what the human authors truly wanted to affirm and to what God wanted to reveal to us by their words.[75]

110   In order to discover *the sacred authors' intention,* the reader must take into account the conditions of their time and culture, the literary genres in use at that time, and the modes of feeling, speaking, and narrating then current. "For the fact is that truth is differently presented and expressed in the various types of historical writing, in prophetical and poetical texts, and in other forms of literary expression."[76]

111   But since Sacred Scripture is inspired, there is another and no less important principle of correct interpretation, without which Scripture would remain a dead letter. "Sacred Scripture must be read and inter-

---

71 *DV* 11.   72 *DV* 11.   73 St. Bernard, *S. missus est hom.* 4, 11: PL 183, 86.
74 Cf. *Lk* 24:45.   75 Cf. *DV* 12 § 1.   76 *DV* 12 § 2.

preted in the light of the same Spirit by whom it was written."[77]

The Second Vatican Council indicates three criteria for interpreting Scripture in accordance with the Spirit who inspired it.[78]

112   1. *Be especially attentive "to the content and unity of the whole Scripture."* Different as the books which comprise it may be, Scripture is a unity by reason 128 of the unity of God's plan, of which Christ Jesus is the 368 center and heart, open since his Passover.[79]

> The phrase "heart of Christ" can refer to Sacred Scripture, which makes known his heart, closed before the Passion, as the Scripture was obscure. But the Scripture has been opened since the Passion; since those who from then on have understood it, consider and discern in what way the prophecies must be interpreted.[80]

113   2. *Read the Scripture within "the living Tradition of the whole Church."* According to a saying of the 81 Fathers, Sacred Scripture is written principally in the Church's heart rather than in documents and records, for the Church carries in her Tradition the living memorial of God's Word, and it is the Holy Spirit who gives her the spiritual interpretation of the Scripture ("according to the spiritual meaning which the Spirit grants to the Church"[81]).

90 **114**   3. *Be attentive to the analogy of faith.*[82] By "analogy of faith" we mean the coherence of the truths of faith among themselves and within the whole plan of Revelation.

The senses of Scripture
115   According to an ancient tradition, one can distinguish between two *senses* of Scripture: the literal and the spiritual, the latter being subdivided into the allegorical, moral, and anagogical senses. The profound concordance

---

77 DV 12 § 3.   78 Cf. DV 12 § 4.   79 Cf. Lk 24:25–27, 44–46.   80 St. Thomas Aquinas, *Expos. in Ps* 21, 11; cf. *Ps* 22:15.   81 Origen, *Hom. in Lev.* 5, 5: PG 12, 454D.   82 Cf. *Rom* 12:6.

of the four senses guarantees all its richness to the living reading of Scripture in the Church.

116   The *literal sense* is the meaning conveyed by the words of Scripture and discovered by exegesis, following the rules of sound interpretation: "All other senses of Sacred Scripture are based on the literal."[83]   *110*

117   The *spiritual sense.* Thanks to the unity of God's plan, not only the text of Scripture but also the realities and *1101* events about which it speaks can be signs.

    1. The *allegorical sense.* We can acquire a more profound understanding of events by recognizing their significance in Christ; thus the crossing of the Red Sea is a sign or type of Christ's victory and also of Christian Baptism.[84]

    2. The *moral sense.* The events reported in Scripture ought to lead us to act justly. As St. Paul says, they were written "for our instruction."[85]

    3. The *anagogical sense* (Greek: *anagoge,* "leading"). We can view realities and events in terms of their eternal significance, leading us toward our true homeland: thus the Church on earth is a sign of the heavenly Jerusalem.[86]

118   A medieval couplet summarizes the significance of the four senses:

> The Letter speaks of deeds; Allegory to faith;
> The Moral how to act; Anagogy our destiny.[87]

119   "It is the task of exegetes to work, according to these rules, toward a better understanding and explanation of the meaning of Sacred Scripture in order that *94* their research may help the Church to form a firmer judgment. For, of course, all that has been said about the manner of interpreting Scripture is ultimately subject to the judgment of the Church which exercises the divinely conferred commission and ministry of watching over and interpreting the Word of God."[88]

> But I would not believe in the Gospel, had not the *113* authority of the Catholic Church already moved me.[89]

---

83 St. Thomas Aquinas, *Sth* I, 1, 10, *ad* 1.   84 Cf. *1 Cor* 10:2.   85 *1 Cor* 10:11; cf. *Heb* 3–4:11.   86 Cf. *Rev* 21:1–22:5.   87 Lettera gesta docet, quid credas allegoria, moralis quid agas, quo tendas anagogia.   88 *DV* 12 § 3.   89 St. Augustine, *Contra epistolam Manichaei,* 5, 6: PL 42, 176.

IV.   THE CANON OF SCRIPTURE

120   It was by the apostolic Tradition that the Church
1117   discerned which writings are to be included in the list of
the sacred books.[90] This complete list is called the canon
of Scripture. It includes 46 books for the Old Testament
(45 if we count Jeremiah and Lamentations as one) and
27 for the New.[91]

The Old Testament: Genesis, Exodus, Leviticus,
Numbers, Deuteronomy, Joshua, Judges, Ruth, 1 *and* 2
Samuel, 1 *and* 2 Kings, 1 *and* 2 Chronicles, Ezra and Ne-
hemiah, Tobit, Judith, Esther, 1 *and* 2 Maccabees, Job,
Psalms, Proverbs, Ecclesiastes, *the* Song of Songs, Wisdom,
Sirach (Ecclesiasticus), Isaiah, Jeremiah, Lamentations,
Baruch, Ezekiel, Daniel, Hosea, Joel, Amos, Obadiah,
Jonah, Micah, Nahum, Habakkuk, Zephaniah, Haggai,
Zechariah and Malachi.

The New Testament: the Gospels according to
Matthew, Mark, Luke *and* John, the Acts of the Apostles,
the Letters of St. Paul to the Romans, 1 *and* 2 Corinthians,
Galatians, Ephesians, Philippians, Colossians, 1 *and* 2
Thessalonians, 1 *and* 2 Timothy, Titus, Philemon, *the*
Letter to the Hebrews, *the* Letters of James, 1 *and* 2 Peter,
1, 2, *and* 3 John, *and* Jude, *and* Revelation (the Apoca-
lypse).

The Old Testament

121   The Old Testament is an indispensable part of
1093   Sacred Scripture. Its books are divinely inspired and retain a permanent value,[92] for the Old Covenant has
never been revoked.

122   Indeed, "the economy of the Old Testament was
deliberately so oriented that it should prepare for and
702, 763   declare in prophecy the coming of Christ, redeemer of
all men."[93] "Even though they contain matters imperfect
and provisional,"[94] the books of the Old Testament bear
708   witness to the whole divine pedagogy of God's saving
love: these writings "are a storehouse of sublime teaching on God and of sound wisdom on human life, as well
as a wonderful treasury of prayers; in them, too, the
2568   mystery of our salvation is present in a hidden way."[95]

---

90 Cf. *DV* 8 § 3.   91 Cf. DS 179; 1334–1336; 1501–1504.   92 Cf. *DV* 14.
93 *DV* 15.   94 *DV* 15.   95 *DV* 15.

123   Christians venerate the Old Testament as true Word of God. The Church has always vigorously opposed the idea of rejecting the Old Testament under the pretext that the New has rendered it void (Marcionism).

The New Testament

124   "The Word of God, which is the power of God for salvation to everyone who has faith, is set forth and displays its power in a most wonderful way in the writings of the New Testament"[96] which hand on the ultimate truth of God's Revelation. Their central object is Jesus Christ, God's incarnate Son: his acts, teachings, Passion and glorification, and his Church's beginnings under the Spirit's guidance.[97]

125   The *Gospels* are the heart of all the Scriptures "because they are our principal source for the life and   *515* teaching of the Incarnate Word, our Savior."[98]

126   We can distinguish three stages in the formation of the Gospels:

1. *The life and teaching of Jesus.* The Church holds firmly that the four Gospels, "whose historicity she unhesitatingly affirms, faithfully hand on what Jesus, the Son of God, while he lived among men, really did and taught for their eternal salvation, until the day when he was taken up."[99]

2. *The oral tradition.* "For, after the ascension of   *76* the Lord, the apostles handed on to their hearers what he had said and done, but with that fuller understanding which they, instructed by the glorious events of Christ and enlightened by the Spirit of truth, now enjoyed."[100]

3. *The written Gospels.* "The sacred authors, in   *76* writing the four Gospels, selected certain of the many elements which had been handed on, either orally or already in written form; others they synthesized or explained with an eye to the situation of the churches, while sustaining the form of preaching, but always in such a fashion that they have told us the honest truth about Jesus."[101]

127   The fourfold Gospel holds a unique place in the   *1154* Church, as is evident both in the veneration which the

---

96 *DV* 17; cf. *Rom* 1:16.   97 Cf. *DV* 20.   98 *DV* 18.   99 *DV* 19; cf. *Acts* 1:1–2.   100 *DV* 19.   101 *DV* 19.

liturgy accords it and in the surpassing attraction it has exercised on the saints at all times:

> There is no doctrine which could be better, more precious and more splendid than the text of the Gospel. Behold and retain what our Lord and Master, Christ, has taught by his words and accomplished by his deeds.[102]

2705

> But above all it's the Gospels that occupy my mind when I'm at prayer; my poor soul has so many needs, and yet this is the one thing needful. I'm always finding fresh lights there, hidden and enthralling meanings.[103]

The unity of the Old and New Testaments

128   The Church, as early as apostolic times,[104] and then constantly in her Tradition, has illuminated the unity of the divine plan in the two Testaments through
1094 typology, which discerns in God's works of the Old
489 Covenant prefigurations of what he accomplished in the fullness of time in the person of his incarnate Son.

129   Christians therefore read the Old Testament in the light of Christ crucified and risen. Such typological
681 reading discloses the inexhaustible content of the Old Testament; but it must not make us forget that the Old Testament retains its own intrinsic value as Revelation reaffirmed by our Lord himself.[105] Besides, the New Tes-
2055 tament has to be read in the light of the Old. Early Christian catechesis made constant use of the Old Testament.[106] As an old saying put it, the New Testament
1968 lies hidden in the Old and the Old Testament is unveiled in the New.[107]

130   Typology indicates the dynamic movement toward the fulfillment of the divine plan when "God [will] be everything to everyone."[108] Nor do the calling of the patriarchs and the exodus from Egypt, for example, lose their own value in God's plan, from the mere fact that they were intermediate stages.

---

102 St. Caesaria the Younger to St. Richildis and St. Radegunde, *SCh* 345, 480.
103 St. Thérèse of Lisieux, *ms. autob.* A 83v.   104 Cf. *1 Cor* 10:6, 11; *Heb* 10:1;
1 Pet 3:21.   105 Cf. *Mk* 12:29–31.   106 Cf. *1 Cor* 5:6–8; 10:1–11.   107 Cf. St.
Augustine, *Quaest. in Hept.* 2, 73: PL 34, 623; cf. *DV* 16.   108 *1 Cor* 15:28.

V.   Sacred Scripture in the Life of the Church

131   "And such is the force and power of the Word of God that it can serve the Church as her support and vigor and the children of the Church as strength for their faith, food for the soul, and a pure and lasting font of spiritual life."[109] Hence "access to Sacred Scripture ought to be open wide to the Christian faithful."[110]

132   "Therefore, the 'study of the sacred page' should be the very soul of sacred theology. The ministry of the Word, too—pastoral preaching, catechetics, and all *94* forms of Christian instruction, among which the liturgical homily should hold pride of place—is healthily nourished and thrives in holiness through the Word of Scripture."[111]

133   The Church "forcefully and specifically exhorts all the Christian faithful . . . to learn 'the surpassing *2653* knowledge of Jesus Christ,' by frequent reading of the divine Scriptures. 'Ignorance of the Scriptures is igno- *1792* rance of Christ.' "[112]

IN BRIEF

134   "All Sacred Scripture is but one book, and that one book is Christ, because all divine Scripture speaks of Christ, and all divine Scripture is fulfilled in Christ" (Hugh of St. Victor, *De arca Noe* 2, 8: PL 176, 642).

135   "The Sacred Scriptures contain the Word of God and, because they are inspired they are truly the Word of God" (*DV* 24).

136   God is the author of Sacred Scripture because he inspired its human authors; he acts in them and by means of them. He thus gives assurance that their writings teach without error his saving truth (cf. *DV* 11).

---

109 *DV* 21.   110 *DV* 22.   111 *DV* 24.   112 *DV* 25; cf. *Phil* 3:8 and St. Jerome, *Commentariorum in Isaiam libri xviii* prol.: PL 24, 17b.

137   Interpretation of the inspired Scripture must be attentive above all to what God wants to reveal through the sacred authors for our salvation. What comes from the Spirit is not fully "understood except by the Spirit's action" (cf. Origen, *Hom. in Ex.* 4, 5: PG 12, 320).

138   The Church accepts and venerates as inspired the 46 books of the Old Testament and the 27 books of the New.

139   The four Gospels occupy a central place because Christ Jesus is their center.

140   The unity of the two Testaments proceeds from the unity of God's plan and his Revelation. The Old Testament prepares for the New and the New Testament fulfills the Old; the two shed light on each other; both are true Word of God.

141   "The Church has always venerated the divine Scriptures as she venerated the Body of the Lord" (*DV* 21): both nourish and govern the whole Christian life. "Your word is a lamp to my feet and a light to my path" (*Ps* 119:105; cf. *Isa* 50:4).

CHAPTER THREE
MAN'S RESPONSE TO GOD

142   *By his Revelation,* "the invisible God, from the fullness of his love, addresses men as his friends, and moves among them, in order to invite and receive them into his own company."[1] The adequate response to this
1102 invitation is faith.

143   *By faith,* man completely submits his intellect and his will to God.[2] With his whole being man gives his assent to God the revealer. Sacred Scripture calls this human response to God, the author of revelation, "the
2087 obedience of faith."[3]

---

1 *DV* 2; cf. *Col* 1:15; *1 Tim* 1:17; *Ex* 33:11; *Jn* 15:14–15; *Bar* 3:38 (Vulg.).
2 Cf. *DV* 5.   3 Cf. *Rom* 1:5; 16:26.

ARTICLE 1
I BELIEVE

I. THE OBEDIENCE OF FAITH

144 To obey (from the Latin *ob-audire,* to "hear or listen to") in faith is to submit freely to the word that has been heard, because its truth is guaranteed by God, who is Truth itself. Abraham is the model of such obedience offered us by Sacred Scripture. The Virgin Mary is its most perfect embodiment.

Abraham—"father of all who believe"

145 The *Letter to the Hebrews,* in its great eulogy of the faith of Israel's ancestors, lays special emphasis on Abraham's faith: "By faith, Abraham obeyed when he was called to go out to a place which he was to receive as an inheritance; and he went out, not knowing where he was to go."[4] By faith, he lived as a stranger and pilgrim in the promised land.[5] By faith, Sarah was given to conceive the son of the promise. And by faith Abraham offered his only son in sacrifice.[6] · 59, 2570 · 489

146 Abraham thus fulfills the definition of faith in *Hebrews* 11:1: "Faith is the assurance of things hoped for, the conviction of things not seen":[7] "Abraham believed God, and it was reckoned to him as righteousness."[8] Because he was "strong in his faith," Abraham became the "father of all who believe."[9] · 1819

147 The Old Testament is rich in witnesses to this faith. The *Letter to the Hebrews* proclaims its eulogy of the exemplary faith of the ancestors who "received divine approval."[10] Yet "God had foreseen something better for us": the grace of believing in his Son Jesus, "the pioneer and perfecter of our faith."[11] · 839

---

4 *Heb* 11:8; cf. *Gen* 12:1–4.   5 Cf. *Gen* 23:4.   6 Cf. *Heb* 11:17.   7 *Heb* 11:1.
8 *Rom* 4:3; cf. *Gen* 15:6.   9 *Rom* 4:11, 18; 4:20; cf. *Gen* 15:5.   10 *Heb* 11:2, 39.   11 *Heb* 11:40; 12:2.

Mary—"Blessed is she who believed"

148   The Virgin Mary most perfectly embodies the
obedience of faith. By faith Mary welcomes the tidings
and promise brought by the angel Gabriel, believing
that "with God nothing will be impossible" and so giving her assent: "Behold I am the handmaid of the Lord;
let it be [done] to me according to your word."[12] Elizabeth greeted her: "Blessed is she who believed that there
would be a fulfillment of what was spoken to her from
the Lord."[13] It is for this faith that all generations have
called Mary blessed.[14]

149   Throughout her life and until her last ordeal[15]
when Jesus her son died on the cross, Mary's faith never
wavered. She never ceased to believe in the fulfillment
of God's word. And so the Church venerates in Mary
the purest realization of faith.

II.   "I KNOW WHOM I HAVE BELIEVED"[16]

To believe in God alone

150   Faith is first of all a personal adherence of man
to God. At the same time, and inseparably, it is a *free
assent to the whole truth that God has revealed.* As
personal adherence to God and assent to his truth,
Christian faith differs from our faith in any human person. It is right and just to entrust oneself wholly to God
and to believe absolutely what he says. It would be futile and false to place such faith in a creature.[17]

To believe in Jesus Christ, the Son of God

151   For a Christian, believing in God cannot be separated from believing in the One he sent, his "beloved
Son," in whom the Father is "well pleased"; God tells
us to listen to him.[18] The Lord himself said to his disciples: "Believe in God, believe also in me."[19] We can believe in Jesus Christ because he is himself God, the Word
made flesh: "No one has ever seen God; the only Son,

---

12 *Lk* 1:37–38; cf. *Gen* 18:14.   13 *Lk* 1:45.   14 Cf. *Lk* 1:48.   15 Cf. *Lk* 2:35.
16 *2 Tim* 1:12.   17 Cf. *Jer* 17:5–6; *Ps* 40:5; 146:3–4.   18 *Mk* 1:11; cf. 9:7.
19 *Jn* 14:1.

Margin references:
494, 2617 (¶148)
506 (¶148)
969 (¶149)
507, 829 (¶149)
222 (¶150)

who is in the bosom of the Father, he has made him known."[20] Because he "has seen the Father," Jesus Christ is the only one who knows him and can reveal him.[21] *424*

To believe in the Holy Spirit

152 One cannot believe in Jesus Christ without sharing in his Spirit. It is the Holy Spirit who reveals to men who Jesus is. For "no one can say 'Jesus is Lord,' except by the Holy Spirit,"[22] who "searches everything, even the depths of God. . . . No one comprehends the thoughts of God, except the Spirit of God."[23] Only God knows God completely: we believe *in* the Holy Spirit because he is God. *243, 683*

The Church never ceases to proclaim her faith in one only God: Father, Son, and Holy Spirit. *232*

III.   THE CHARACTERISTICS OF FAITH

Faith is a grace

153 When St. Peter confessed that Jesus is the Christ, the Son of the living God, Jesus declared to him that this revelation did not come "from flesh and blood," but from "my Father who is in heaven."[24] *Faith is a gift of God, a supernatural virtue infused by him.* "Before this faith can be exercised, man must have the grace of God to move and assist him; he must have the interior helps of the Holy Spirit, who moves the heart and converts it to God, who opens the eyes of the mind and 'makes it easy for all to accept and believe the truth.' "[25] *552* *1814* *1996* *2606*

Faith is a human act

154 Believing is possible only by grace and the interior helps of the Holy Spirit. But it is no less true that believing is an authentically human act. Trusting in God and cleaving to the truths he has revealed are contrary neither to human freedom nor to human reason. Even in human relations it is not contrary to our dignity to *1749*

---

20 *Jn* 1:18.   21 *Jn* 6:46; cf. *Mt* 11:27.   22 1 *Cor* 12:3.   23 1 *Cor* 2:10–11.
24 *Mt* 16:17; cf. *Gal* 1:15; *Mt* 11:25.   25 *DV* 5; cf. *DS* 377; 3010.

believe what other persons tell us about themselves and their intentions or to trust their promises (for example, when a man and a woman marry) to share a communion of life with one another. If this is so, still less is it contrary to our dignity to "yield by faith the full submission of . . . intellect and will to God who reveals,"[26] and to share in an interior communion with him.

155   In faith, the human intellect and will cooperate with divine grace: "Believing is an act of the intellect assenting to the divine truth by command of the will moved by God through grace."[27]

Faith and understanding

156   What moves us to believe is not the fact that revealed truths appear as true and intelligible in the light of our natural reason: we believe "because of the authority of God himself who reveals them, who can neither deceive nor be deceived."[28] So "that the submission of our faith might nevertheless be in accordance with reason, God willed that external proofs of his Revelation should be joined to the internal helps of the Holy Spirit."[29] Thus the miracles of Christ and the saints, prophecies, the Church's growth and holiness, and her fruitfulness and stability "are the most certain signs of divine Revelation, adapted to the intelligence of all"; they are "motives of credibility" *(motiva credibilitatis),* which show that the assent of faith is "by no means a blind impulse of the mind."[30]

157   Faith is *certain.* It is more certain than all human knowledge because it is founded on the very word of God who cannot lie. To be sure, revealed truths can seem obscure to human reason and experience, but "the certainty that the divine light gives is greater than that which the light of natural reason gives."[31] "Ten thousand difficulties do not make one doubt."[32]

---

26 *Dei Filius* 3: DS 3008.   27 St. Thomas Aquinas, *STh* II-II, 2, 9; cf. *Dei Filius* 3: DS 3010.   28 *Dei Filius* 3: DS 3008.   29 *Dei Filius* 3: DS 3009.   30 *Dei Filius* 3: DS 3008–10; cf. *Mk* 16:20; *Heb* 2:4.   31 St. Thomas Aquinas, *STh* II-II, 171, 5, obj. 3.   32 John Henry Cardinal Newman, *Apologia pro vita sua* (London: Longman, 1878), 239.

158   "Faith *seeks understanding*":[33] it is intrinsic to faith that a believer desires to know better the One in whom he has put his faith and to understand better 2705 what He has revealed; a more penetrating knowledge will in turn call forth a greater faith, increasingly set afire by love. The grace of faith opens "the eyes of your 1827 hearts"[34] to a lively understanding of the contents of Revelation: that is, of the totality of God's plan and the mysteries of faith, of their connection with each other and with Christ, the center of the revealed mystery. 90 "The same Holy Spirit constantly perfects faith by his gifts, so that Revelation may be more and more profoundly understood."[35] In the words of St. Augustine, "I 2518 believe, in order to understand; and I understand, the better to believe."[36]

159   *Faith and science:* "Though faith is above reason, there can never be any real discrepancy between faith and reason. Since the same God who reveals mysteries and infuses faith has bestowed the light of reason on the human mind, God cannot deny him- 283 self, nor can truth ever contradict truth."[37] "Consequently, methodical research in all branches of knowledge, provided it is carried out in a truly scientific manner and does not override moral laws, can never conflict with the faith, because the things of 2293 the world and the things of faith derive from the same God. The humble and persevering investigator of the secrets of nature is being led, as it were, by the hand of God in spite of himself, for it is God, the conserver of all things, who made them what they are."[38]

The freedom of faith

160   To be human, "man's response to God by faith must be free, and . . . therefore nobody is to be forced to embrace the faith against his will. The act of faith is 1738, 2106 of its very nature a free act."[39] "God calls men to serve

---

33 St. Anselm, *Prosl. prooem.*: PL 153, 225A.   **34** *Eph* 1:18.   **35** *DV* 5.   **36** St. Augustine, *Sermo* 43, 7, 9: PL 38, 257–258.   **37** *Dei Filius* 4: DS 3017.   **38** *GS* 36 § 1.   **39** *DH* 10; cf. CIC, can. 748 § 2.

him in spirit and in truth. Consequently they are bound to him in conscience, but not coerced. . . . This fact received its fullest manifestation in Christ Jesus."[40] Indeed, Christ invited people to faith and conversion, but never coerced them. "For he bore witness to the truth but refused to use force to impose it on those who spoke against it. His kingdom . . . grows by the love with 616 which Christ, lifted up on the cross, draws men to himself."[41]

The necessity of faith

161   Believing in Jesus Christ and in the One who sent him for our salvation is necessary for obtaining 432, 1257 that salvation.[42] "Since 'without faith it is impossible to please [God]' and to attain to the fellowship of his sons, therefore without faith no one has ever attained justification, nor will anyone obtain eternal life 'but he who 846 endures to the end.' "[43]

Perseverance in faith

162   Faith is an entirely free gift that God makes to man. We can lose this priceless gift, as St. Paul indicated 2089 to St. Timothy: "Wage the good warfare, holding faith and a good conscience. By rejecting conscience, certain persons have made shipwreck of their faith."[44] To live, grow, and persevere in the faith until the end we must nourish it with the word of God; we must beg the Lord 1037, 2016 to increase our faith;[45] it must be "working through 2573, 2849 charity," abounding in hope, and rooted in the faith of the Church.[46]

Faith—the beginning of eternal life

163   Faith makes us taste in advance the light of the beatific vision, the goal of our journey here below. Then 1088 we shall see God "face to face," "as he is."[47] So faith is already the beginning of eternal life:

---

40 DH 11.   41 DH 11; cf. Jn 18:37; 12:32.   42 Cf. Mk 16:16; Jn 3:36; 6:40 et al.   43 Dei Filius 3: DS 3012; cf. Mt 10:22; 24:13 and Heb 11:6; Council of Trent: DS 1532.   44 1 Tim 1:18–19.   45 Cf. Mk 9:24; Lk 17:5; 22:32.   46 Gal 5:6; Rom 15:13; cf. Jas 2:14–26.   47 1 Cor 13:12; 1 Jn 3:2.

> When we contemplate the blessings of faith even now, as if gazing at a reflection in a mirror, it is as if we already possessed the wonderful things which our faith assures us we shall one day enjoy.[48]

164 Now, however, "we walk by faith, not by sight";[49] we perceive God as "in a mirror, dimly" and only "in part."[50] Even though enlightened by him in whom it believes, faith is often lived in darkness and can be put to the test. The world we live in often seems very far from the one promised us by faith. Our experiences of evil and suffering, injustice, and death, seem to contradict the Good News; they can shake our faith and become a temptation against it.

2846

309

1502, 1006

165 It is then we must turn to the *witnesses of faith:* to Abraham, who "in hope . . . believed against hope";[51] to the Virgin Mary, who, in "her pilgrimage of faith," walked into the "night of faith"[52] in sharing the darkness of her son's suffering and death; and to so many others: "Therefore, since we are surrounded by so great a cloud of witnesses, let us also lay aside every weight, and sin which clings so closely, and let us run with perseverance the race that is set before us, looking to Jesus the pioneer and perfecter of our faith."[53]

2719

ARTICLE 2
WE BELIEVE

166 Faith is a personal act—the free response of the human person to the initiative of God who reveals himself. But faith is not an isolated act. No one can believe alone, just as no one can live alone. You have not given yourself faith as you have not given yourself life. The believer has received faith from others and should hand it on to others. Our love for Jesus and for our neighbor

875

---

48 St. Basil, *De Spiritu Sancto,* 15, 36: PG 32, 132; cf. St. Thomas Aquinas, *STh* II-II, 4, 1. 49 *2 Cor* 5:7. 50 *1 Cor* 13:12. 51 *Rom* 4:18. 52 *LG* 58; John Paul II, *RMat* 18. 53 *Heb* 12:1–2.

impels us to speak to others about our faith. Each believer is thus a link in the great chain of believers. I
cannot believe without being carried by the faith of
others, and by my faith I help support others in the
faith.

167 "I believe" *(Apostles' Creed)* is the faith of the
1124 Church professed personally by each believer, principally during Baptism. "We believe" *(Niceno-Constantinopolitan Creed)* is the faith of the Church confessed
by the bishops assembled in council or more generally
by the liturgical assembly of believers. "I believe" is
also the Church, our mother, responding to God by
faith as she teaches us to say both "I believe" and "We
2040 believe."

I.   "LORD, LOOK UPON THE FAITH OF YOUR CHURCH"

168 It is the Church that believes first, and so bears,
nourishes, and sustains my faith. Everywhere, it is
the Church that first confesses the Lord: "Throughout
the world the holy Church acclaims you," as we sing in
the hymn *"Te Deum";* with her and in her, we are
won over and brought to confess: "I believe," "We believe." It is through the Church that we receive faith
and new life in Christ by Baptism. In the *Rituale Ro-
manum,* the minister of Baptism asks the catechumen:
"What do you ask of God's Church?" And the answer
1253 is: "Faith." "What does faith offer you?" "Eternal
life."[54]

169 Salvation comes from God alone; but because
we receive the life of faith through the Church, she is
our mother: "We believe the Church as the mother of
our new birth, and not *in* the Church as if she were the
750 author of our salvation."[55] Because she is our mother,
2030 she is also our teacher in the faith.

---

54 *Roman Ritual,* Rite of baptism of adults.   55 Faustus of Riez, *De Spiritu
Sancto* 1, 2: PL 62, 11.

II.   THE LANGUAGE OF FAITH

170   We do not believe in formulas, but in those realities they express, which faith allows us to touch. "The believer's act [of faith] does not terminate in the propositions, but in the realities [which they express]."[56] All the same, we do approach these realities with the help of formulations of the faith which permit us *186* to express the faith and to hand it on, to celebrate it in community, to assimilate and live on it more and more.

171   The Church, "the pillar and bulwark of the *78, 857,* truth," faithfully guards "the faith which was once for *84, 185* all delivered to the saints." She guards the memory of Christ's words; it is she who from generation to generation hands on the apostles' confession of faith.[57] As a mother who teaches her children to speak and so to understand and communicate, the Church our Mother teaches us the language of faith in order to introduce us to the understanding and the life of faith.

III.   ONLY ONE FAITH

172   Through the centuries, in so many languages, cultures, peoples, and nations, the Church has constantly confessed this one faith, received from the one Lord, transmitted by one Baptism, and grounded in the conviction that all people have only one God and Fa- *813* ther.[58] St. Irenaeus of Lyons, a witness of this faith, declared:

173   "Indeed, the Church, though scattered throughout the whole world, even to the ends of the earth, having received the faith from the apostles and their disciples . . . guards [this preaching and faith] with care, as dwelling in but a single house, and similarly believes *830* as if having but one soul and a single heart, and preaches, teaches, and hands on this faith with a unanimous voice, as if possessing only one mouth."[59]

---

56 St. Thomas Aquinas, *STh* II-II, 1, 2, *ad* 2.   57 1 *Tim* 3:15; *Jude* 3.   58 Cf. *Eph* 4:4–6.   59 St. Irenaeus, *Adv. haeres.* 1, 10, 1–2: PG 7/1, 549–552.

174   "For though languages differ throughout the world, the content of the Tradition is one and the same. The Churches established in Germany have no other
78 faith or Tradition, nor do those of the Iberians, nor those of the Celts, nor those of the East, of Egypt, of Libya, nor those established at the center of the world. . . ."[60] The Church's message "is true and solid, in which one and the same way of salvation appears throughout the whole world."[61]

175   "We guard with care the faith that we have received from the Church, for without ceasing, under the action of God's Spirit, this deposit of great price, as if in an excellent vessel, is constantly being renewed and causes the very vessel that contains it to be renewed."[62]

IN BRIEF

176   Faith is a personal adherence of the whole man to God who reveals himself. It involves an assent of the intellect and will to the self-revelation God has made through his deeds and words.

177   "To believe" has thus a twofold reference: to the person and to the truth: to the truth, by trust in the person who bears witness to it.

178   We must believe in no one but God: the Father, the Son, and the Holy Spirit.

179   Faith is a supernatural gift from God. In order to believe, man needs the interior helps of the Holy Spirit.

180   "Believing" is a human act, conscious and free, corresponding to the dignity of the human person.

181   "Believing" is an ecclesial act. The Church's faith precedes, engenders, supports, and nour-

---

60 St. Irenaeus, *Adv. haeres.* 1, 10, 1–2: PG 7/1, 552–553.   61 St. Irenaeus, *Adv. haeres.* 5, 20, 1: PG 7/2, 1177.   62 St. Irenaeus, *Adv. haeres.* 3, 24, 1: PG 7/1, 966.

ishes our faith. The Church is the mother of all believers. "No one can have God as Father who does not have the Church as Mother" (St. Cyprian, *De unit.* 6: PL 4, 519).

182 We believe all "that which is contained in the word of God, written or handed down, and which the Church proposes for belief as divinely revealed" (Paul VI, *CPG*, § 20).

183 Faith is necessary for salvation. The Lord himself affirms: "He who believes and is baptized will be saved; but he who does not believe will be condemned" (*Mk* 16:16).

184 "Faith is a foretaste of the knowledge that will make us blessed in the life to come" (St. Thomas Aquinas, *Comp. theol.* 1, 2).

THE CREDO

The Apostles' Creed	The Nicene Creed
I believe in God, the Father almighty, creator of heaven and earth.	We believe in one God, the Father, the Almighty, maker of heaven and earth, of all that is, seen and unseen.
I believe in Jesus Christ, his only Son, our Lord.	We believe in one Lord, Jesus Christ, the only Son of God eternally begotten of the Father, God from God, Light from Light, true God from true God, begotten, not made, one in Being with the Father. Through him all things were made. For us men and for our salvation he came down from heaven:
He was conceived by the power of the Holy Spirit and born of the Virgin Mary.	by the power of the Holy Spirit he was born of the Virgin Mary, and became man.
He suffered under Pontius Pilate, was crucified, died, and was buried. He descended into hell.	For our sake he was crucified under Pontius Pilate; he suffered, died, and was buried.
On the third day he rose again.	On the third day he rose again in fulfillment of the Scriptures;
He ascended into heaven and is seated at the right hand of the Father. He will come again to judge the living and the dead.	he ascended into heaven and is seated at the right hand of the Father. He will come again in glory to judge the living and the dead, and his

kingdom will have no end.

I believe in the Holy Spirit, the holy catholic Church, the communion of saints, the forgiveness of sins, the resurrection of the body, and the life everlasting. Amen.

We believe in the Holy Spirit, the Lord, the giver of life, who proceeds from the Father and the Son.
With the Father and the Son he is worshiped and glorified.
He has spoken through the Prophets.
We believe in one holy catholic and apostolic Church.
We acknowledge one baptism for the forgiveness of sins.
We look for the resurrection of the dead, and the life of the world to come. Amen.

Section Two
The Profession of the Christian Faith
The Creeds

185   Whoever says "I believe" says "I pledge myself
171, 949   to what *we* believe." Communion in faith needs a common language of faith, normative for all and uniting all
in the same confession of faith.

186   From the beginning, the apostolic Church expressed and handed on her faith in brief formulae for
all.[1] But already early on, the Church also wanted to
gather the essential elements of its faith into organic and
articulated summaries, intended especially for candidates for Baptism:

> This synthesis of faith was not made to accord with
> human opinions, but rather what was of the great-
> est importance was gathered from all the Scrip-
> tures, to present the one teaching of the faith in its
> entirety. And just as the mustard seed contains a
> great number of branches in a tiny grain, so too this
> summary of faith encompassed in a few words the
> whole knowledge of the true religion contained in
> the Old and New Testaments.[2]

187   Such syntheses are called "professions of faith"
since they summarize the faith that Christians profess.
They are called "creeds" on account of what is usually
their first word in Latin: *credo* ("I believe"). They are
also called "symbols of faith."

188   The Greek work *symbolon* meant half of a broken
object, for example, a seal presented as a token of recognition. The broken parts were placed together to verify the
bearer's identity. The symbol of faith, then, is a sign of
recognition and communion between believers. *Symbolon*
also means a gathering, collection, or summary. A symbol
of faith is a summary of the principal truths of the faith and
therefore serves as the first and fundamental point of reference for catechesis.

---

1 Cf. *Rom* 19:0; *1 Cor* 15:3–5, etc.   2 St. Cyril of Jerusalem, *Catech. illum.* 5,
12: PG 33, 521–524.

189   The first "profession of faith" is made during Baptism. The symbol of faith is first and foremost the *baptismal* creed. Since Baptism is given "in the name of the Father and of the Son and of the Holy Spirit,"[3] the truths of faith professed during Baptism are articulated in terms of their reference to the three persons of the Holy Trinity.

1237, 232

190   And so the Creed is divided into three parts: "the first part speaks of the first divine Person and the wonderful work of creation; the next speaks of the second divine Person and the mystery of his redemption of men; the final part speaks of the third divine Person, the origin and source of our sanctification."[4] These are "the three chapters of our [baptismal] seal."[5]

191   "These three parts are distinct although connected with one another. According to a comparison often used by the Fathers, we call them *articles*. Indeed, just as in our bodily members there are certain articulations which distinguish and separate them, so too in this profession of faith, the name *articles* has justly and rightly been given to the truths we must believe particularly and distinctly."[6] In accordance with an ancient tradition, already attested to by St. Ambrose, it is also customary to reckon the articles of the Creed as *twelve,* thus symbolizing the fullness of the apostolic faith by the number of the apostles.[7]

192   Through the centuries many professions or symbols of faith have been articulated in response to the needs of the different eras: the creeds of the different apostolic and ancient Churches,[8] e.g., the *Quicumque,* also called the Athanasian Creed;[9] the professions of faith of certain Councils, such as Toledo, Lateran, Lyons, Trent;[10] or the symbols of certain popes, e.g., the *Fides Damasi*[11] or the *Credo of the People of God* of Paul VI.[12]

---

3 Mt 28:19.   4 *Roman Catechism,* I, 1, 3.   5 St. Irenaeus, *Dem. ap.* 100: SCh 62, 170.   6 *Roman Catechism,* I, 1, 4.   7 Cf. St. Ambrose, *Expl. symb.* 8.   8 Cf. DS 1–64.   9 Cf. DS 75–76.   10 Cf. DS 525–541; 800–802; 851–861; 1862–1870.   11 Cf. DS 71–72.   12 Paul VI, *CPG* (1968).

193   None of the creeds from the difference stages in the Church's life can be considered superseded or irrelevant. They help us today to attain and deepen the faith of all times by means of the different summaries made of it.

Among all the creeds, two occupy a special place in the Church's life:

194   *The Apostles' Creed* is so called because it is rightly considered to be a faithful summary of the apostles' faith. It is the ancient baptismal symbol of the Church of Rome. Its great authority arises from this fact: it is "the Creed of the Roman Church, the See of Peter, the first of the apostles, to which he brought the common faith."[13]

195   *The Niceno-Constantinopolitan* or *Nicene Creed* draws its great authority from the fact that it stems from the first two ecumenical Councils (in 325 and 381). It remains common to all the great Churches of both East and West to this day.

242, 245
465

196   Our presentation of the faith will follow the Apostles' Creed, which constitutes, as it were, "the oldest Roman catechism." The presentation will be completed however by constant references to the Nicene Creed which is often more explicit and more detailed.

197   As on the day of our Baptism, when our whole life was entrusted to the "standard of teaching,"[14] let us embrace the Creed of our life-giving faith. To say the Credo with faith is to enter into communion with God, Father, Son, and Holy Spirit, and also with the whole Church which transmits the faith to us and in whose midst we believe:

1064

1274
> This Creed is the spiritual seal, our hearts's meditation and an ever-present guardian; it is, unquestionably, the treasure of our soul.[15]

---

13 St. Ambrose, *Expl. symb.* 7: PL 17, 1196.   14 *Rom* 6:17.   15 St. Ambrose, *Expl. symb.* 1: PL 17, 1193.

CHAPTER ONE

I BELIEVE IN GOD THE FATHER

198   Our profession of faith begins with *God*, for God is the First and the Last,[1] the beginning and the end of everything. The Credo begins with God the *Father*, for the Father is the first divine person of the Most Holy Trinity; our Creed begins with the creation of heaven and earth, for creation is the beginning and the foundation of all God's works.

ARTICLE 1
"I BELIEVE IN GOD THE FATHER ALMIGHTY, CREATOR OF HEAVEN AND EARTH"

Paragraph 1. I Believe in God

199   "I believe in God": this first affirmation of the Apostles' Creed is also the most fundamental. The whole Creed speaks of God, and when it also speaks of man and of the world it does so in relation to God. The other articles of the Creed all depend on the first, just as the remaining Commandments make the first explicit. The other articles help us to know God better as he revealed himself progressively to men. "The faithful first profess their belief in God."[2]   *2083*

I.   "I BELIEVE IN ONE GOD"

200   These are the words with which the Niceno-Constantinopolitan Creed begins. The confession of God's oneness, which has its roots in the divine revelation of the Old Covenant, is inseparable from the profession of God's existence and is equally fundamental. God is unique; there is only one God: "The Christian faith confesses that God is one in nature, substance, and essence."[3]   *2085*

201   To Israel, his chosen, God revealed himself as the

---

1 Cf. Isa 44:6. 2 *Roman Catechism*, I, 2, 2. 3 *Roman Catechism*, I, 2, 2.

2083 only One: "Hear, O Israel: The LORD our God is one
LORD; and you shall love the LORD your God with all
your heart, and with all your soul, and with all your
might."[4] Through the prophets, God calls Israel and
all nations to turn to him, the one and only God:
"Turn to me and be saved, all the ends of the earth! For
I am God, and there is no other. ... To me every
knee shall bow, every tongue shall swear. 'Only in the
LORD, it shall be said of me, are righteousness and
strength.' "[5]

202   Jesus himself affirms that God is "the one Lord"
whom you must love "with all your heart, and with all
your soul, and with all your mind, and with all your
strength."[6] At the same time Jesus gives us to under-
446 stand that he himself is "the Lord."[7] To confess that Jesus is Lord is distinctive of Christian faith. This is not
contrary to belief in the One God. Nor does believing in
152 the Holy Spirit as "Lord and giver of life" introduce any
division into the One God:

42   We firmly believe and confess without reservation
           that there is only one true God, eternal, infinite
           (immensus) and unchangeable, incomprehen-
           sible, almighty, and ineffable, the Father and the
           Son and the Holy Spirit; three persons indeed,
           but one essence, substance or nature entirely sim-
           ple.[8]

II.   GOD REVEALS HIS NAME

203   God revealed himself to his people Israel by
making his name known to them. A name expresses a
person's essence and identity and the meaning of this
2143 person's life. God has a name; he is not an anonymous
force. To disclose one's name is to make oneself known
to others; in a way it is to hand oneself over by becoming accessible, capable of being known more intimately
and addressed personally.

204   God revealed himself progressively and under
different names to his people, but the revelation that

---

4 *Deut* 6:4–5.   5 *Isa* 45:22–24; cf. *Phil* 2:10–11.   6 *Mk* 12:29–30.   7 Cf. *Mk*
12:35–37.   8 Lateran Council IV: DS 800.

proved to be the fundamental one for both the Old and the New Covenants was the revelation of the divine name to Moses in the theophany of the burning bush, *63* on the threshold of the Exodus and of the covenant on Sinai.

The living God

205 God calls Moses from the midst of a bush that burns without being consumed: "I am the God of your father, the God of Abraham, the God of Isaac, and the God of Jacob."[9] God is the God of the fathers, the One *2575* who had called and guided the patriarchs in their wanderings. He is the faithful and compassionate God who remembers them and his promises; he comes to free their descendants from slavery. He is the God who, from beyond space and time, can do this and wills to do it, the God who will put his almighty power to work for *268* this plan.

"I Am who I Am"

> Moses said to God, "If I come to the people of Israel and say to them, 'The God of your fathers has sent me to you', and they ask me, 'What is his name?' what shall I say to them?" God said to Moses, "I AM WHO I AM." And he said, "Say this to the people of Israel, 'I Am has sent me to you'... this is my name for ever, and thus I am to be remembered throughout all generations."[10]

206 In revealing his mysterious name, YHWH ("I AM HE WHO IS," "I AM WHO AM" or "I AM WHO I AM"), God says who he is and by what name he is to be called. This divine name is mysterious just as God is mystery. It is at once a name revealed and something like the refusal of a name, and hence it better expresses God as what he is—infinitely above everything that we can understand or say: he is the "hidden God," his name is ineffable, and he is the God who makes himself close to men.[11]
43

---

9 *Ex* 3:6.   10 *Ex* 3:13–15.   11 Cf. *Isa* 45:15; *Judg* 13:18.

207   By revealing his name God at the same time reveals his faithfulness which is from everlasting to everlasting, valid for the past ("I am the God of your fathers"), as for the future ("I will be with you").[12] God, who reveals his name as "I AM," reveals himself as the God who is always there, present to his people in order to save them.

724 **208**   Faced with God's fascinating and mysterious presence, man discovers his own insignificance. Before the burning bush, Moses takes off his sandals and veils his face in the presence of God's holiness.[13] Before the glory of the thrice-holy God, Isaiah cries out: "Woe is me! I am lost; for I am a man of unclean lips."[14] Before the divine signs wrought by Jesus, Peter exclaims: "De-
448 part from me, for I am a sinful man, O Lord."[15] But because God is holy, he can forgive the man who realizes that he is a sinner before him: "I will not execute my fierce anger . . . for I am God and not man, the Holy
388 One in your midst."[16] The apostle John says likewise: "We shall . . . reassure our hearts before him whenever our hearts condemn us; for God is greater than our hearts, and he knows everything."[17]

209   Out of respect for the holiness of God, the people of Israel do not pronounce his name. In the reading of Sacred Scripture, the revealed name (Yhwh) is replaced by the divine title "LORD" (in Hebrew *Adonai,* in Greek *Kyrios*). It is under this title that the divinity of Jesus will be ac-
446 claimed: "Jesus is LORD."

"A God merciful and gracious"

210   After Israel's sin, when the people had turned away from God to worship the golden calf, God hears Moses' prayer of intercession and agrees to walk in the
2116, 2577 midst of an unfaithful people, thus demonstrating his love.[18] When Moses asks to see his glory, God responds "I will make all my goodness pass before you, and will proclaim before you my name 'the LORD' [YHWH]."[19] Then the LORD passes before Moses and proclaims,

---

12 *Ex* 3:6, 12.   13 Cf. *Ex* 3:5–6.   14 *Isa* 6:5.   15 *Lk* 5:8.   16 *Hos* 11:9.
17 *1 Jn* 3:19–20.   18 Cf. *Ex* 32; 33:12–17.   19 *Ex* 33:18–19.

"YHWH, YHWH, a God merciful and gracious, slow to anger, and abounding in steadfast love and faithfulness"; Moses then confesses that the LORD is a forgiving God.[20]

211 The divine name, "I Am" or "He Is," expresses God's faithfulness: despite the faithlessness of men's sin and the punishment it deserves, he keeps "steadfast love for thousands."[21] By going so far as to give up his own Son for us, God reveals that he is "rich in mercy."[22] By giving his life to free us from sin, Jesus reveals that he himself bears the divine name: "When you have lifted up the Son of man, then you will realize that 'I Am.' "[23]

604

God alone IS

212 Over the centuries, Israel's faith was able to manifest and deepen realization of the riches contained in the revelation of the divine name. God is unique; there are no other gods besides him.[24] He transcends the world and history. He made heaven and earth: "They will perish, but you endure; they will all wear out like a garment . . . but you are the same, and your years have no end."[25] In God "there is no variation or shadow due to change."[26] God is "He who Is," from everlasting to everlasting, and as such remains ever faithful to himself and to his promises.

42

469, 2086

213 The revelation of the ineffable name "I Am who Am" contains then the truth that God alone IS. The Greek Septuagint translation of the Hebrew Scriptures, and following it the Church's Tradition, understood the divine name in this sense: God is the fullness of Being and of every perfection, without origin and without end. All creatures receive all that they are and have from him; but he alone *is* his very being, and he is of himself everything that he is.

41

---

20 *Ex* 34:5–6; cf. 34:9. 21 *Ex* 34:7. 22 *Eph* 2:4. 23 *Jn* 8:28 (Gk.). 24 Cf. *Isa* 44:6. 25 *Ps* 102:26–27. 26 *Jas* 1:17.

III.   GOD, "HE WHO IS" IS TRUTH AND LOVE

214   God, "He who is," revealed himself to Israel as the one "abounding in steadfast love and faithfulness."[27] These two terms express summarily the riches

1062 of the divine name. In all his works God displays not only his kindness, goodness, grace, and steadfast love, but also his trustworthiness, constancy, faithfulness, and truth. "I give thanks to your name for your steadfast love and your faithfulness."[28] He is the Truth, for "God is light and in him there is no darkness"; "God is love," as the apostle John teaches.[29]

God is truth

215   "The sum of your word is truth; and every one of your righteous ordinances endures forever."[30] "And

2465 now, O LORD God, you are God, and your words are
1063, 156 true;"[31] this is why God's promises always come true.[32] God is Truth itself, whose words cannot deceive. This is why one can abandon oneself in full trust to the truth and faithfulness of his word in all things. The beginning of sin and of man's fall was due to a lie of the tempter who induced doubt of God's word, kindness, and faith-

397 fulness.

216   God's truth is his wisdom, which commands the
295 whole created order and governs the world.[33] God, who alone made heaven and earth, can alone impart true
32 knowledge of every created thing in relation to himself.[34]

217   God is also truthful when he reveals himself—the teaching that comes from God is "true instruction."[35] When he sends his Son into the world it will be "to bear witness to the truth":[36] "We know that the Son
851 of God has come and has given us understanding, to
2466 know him who is true."[37]

---

27 *Ex* 34:6.   28 *Ps* 138:2; cf. *Ps* 85:11.   29 *1 Jn* 1:5; 4:8.   30 *Ps* 119:160.   31 *2 Sam* 7:28.   32 Cf. *Deut* 7:9.   33 Cf. *Wis* 13:1–9.   34 Cf. *Ps* 115:15; *Wis* 7:17–21.   35 *Mal* 2:6.   36 *Jn* 18:37.   37 *1 Jn* 5:20; cf. *Jn* 17:3.

God is love

218 In the course of its history, Israel was able to discover that God had only one reason to reveal himself to them, a single motive for choosing them from among all peoples as his special possession: his sheer gratuitous love.[38] And thanks to the prophets Israel understood *295* that it was again out of love that God never stopped saving them and pardoning their unfaithfulness and sins.[39]

219 God's love for Israel is compared to a father's *239* love for his son. His love for his people is stronger than *796, 458* a mother's for her children. God loves his people more than a bridegroom his beloved; his love will be victorious over even the worst infidelities and will extend to his most precious gift: "God so loved the world that he gave his only Son."[40]

220 God's love is "everlasting":[41] "For the mountains may depart and the hills be removed, but my steadfast love shall not depart from you."[42] Through Jeremiah, God declares to his people, "I have loved you with an everlasting love; therefore I have continued my faithfulness to you."[43]

221 But St. John goes even further when he affirms that "God is love":[44] God's very being is love. By sending *733* his only Son and the Spirit of Love in the fullness of *851* time, God has revealed his innermost secret:[45] God him- *257* self is an eternal exchange of love, Father, Son, and Holy Spirit, and he has destined us to share in that exchange.

IV. THE IMPLICATIONS OF FAITH IN ONE GOD

222 Believing in God, the only One, and loving him with all our being has enormous consequences for our whole life.

223 *It means coming to know God's greatness and* *400*

---

38 Cf. *Deut* 4:37; 7:8; 10:15.   39 Cf. *Isa* 43:1–7; *Hos* 2.   40 *Jn* 3:16; cf. *Hos* 11:1; *Isa* 49:14–15; 62:4–5; *Ezek* 16; *Hos* 11.   41 *Isa* 54:8.   42 *Isa* 54:10; cf. 54:8.   43 *Jer* 31:3.   44 *1 Jn* 4:8, 16.   45 Cf. *1 Cor* 2:7–16; *Eph* 3:9–12.

majesty: "Behold, God is great, and we know him not."[46] Therefore, we must "serve God first."[47]

2637 **224** *It means living in thanksgiving:* if God is the only One, everything we are and have comes from him: "What have you that you did not receive?"[48] "What shall I render to the Lord for all his bounty to me?"[49]

356, 360 **225** *It means knowing the unity and true dignity of* 1700, *all men:* Everyone is made in the image and likeness of 1934 God.[50]

339, 2402 **226** *It means making good use of created things:* 2415 faith in God, the only One, leads us to use everything that is not God only insofar as it brings us closer to him, and to detach ourselves from it insofar as it turns us away from him:

> My Lord and my God, take from me everything that distances me from you.
> My Lord and my God, give me everything that brings me closer to you.
> My Lord and my God, detach me from myself to give my all to you.[51]

313, 2090 **227** *It means trusting God in every circumstance,* even in adversity. A prayer of St. Teresa of Jesus wonderfully expresses this trust:

> Let nothing trouble you / Let nothing frighten you
> Everything passes / God never changes
> Patience / Obtains all
2830 > Whoever has God / Wants for nothing
1723 > God alone is enough.[52]

IN BRIEF

228 "Hear, O Israel, the LORD our God is one LORD . . ." (*Deut* 6:4; *Mk* 12:29). "The supreme being must be unique, without equal. . . . If God

---

46 *Job* 36:26.   47 St. Joan of Arc.   48 1 *Cor* 4:7.   49 *Ps* 116:12.   50 *Gen* 1:26.
51 St. Nicholas of Flüe; cf. *Mt* 5:29–30; 16:24–26.   52 St. Teresa of Jesus, *Poesías* 30, in *The Collected Works of St. Teresa of Avila*, vol. III, tr. by K. Kavanaugh, OCD, and O. Rodriguez, OCD (Washington DC: Institute of Carmelite Studies, 1985), 386 no. 9, tr. by John Wall.

is not one, he is not God" (Tertullian, *Adv. Marc.,* 1, 3, 5: PL 2, 274).

229   Faith in God leads us to turn to him alone as our first origin and our ultimate goal, and neither to prefer anything to him nor to substitute anything for him.

230   Even when he reveals himself, God remains a mystery beyond words: "If you understood him, it would not be God" (St. Augustine, *Sermo* 52, 6, 16: PL 38:360 and *Sermo* 117, 3, 5: PL 38, 663).

231   The God of our faith has revealed himself as He who is; and he has made himself known as "abounding in steadfast love and faithfulness" (*Ex* 34:6). God's very being is Truth and Love.

Paragraph 2. The Father

I.   "IN THE NAME OF THE FATHER AND OF THE SON AND OF THE HOLY SPIRIT"

232   Christians are baptized "in the name of the Father and of the Son and of the Holy Spirit."[53] Before receiving the sacrament, they respond to a three-part question when asked to confess the Father, the Son, and the Spirit: "I do." "The faith of all Christians rests on the Trinity."[54]

189, 1223

233   Christians are baptized in the *name* of the Father and of the Son and of the Holy Spirit: not in their *names,*[55] for there is only one God, the almighty Father, his only Son, and the Holy Spirit: the Most Holy Trinity.

234   The mystery of the Most Holy Trinity is the central mystery of Christian faith and life. It is the mystery of God in himself. It is therefore the source of all the other mysteries of faith, the light that enlightens them.

2157

---

53 *Mt* 28:19.   54 St. Caesarius of Arles, *Sermo* 9, *Exp. symb.:* CCL 103, 47.
55 Cf. Profession of faith of Pope Vigilius I (552): DS 415.

It is the most fundamental and essential teaching in the "hierarchy of the truths of faith."[56] The whole history
90 of salvation is identical with the history of the way
1449 and the means by which the one true God, Father, Son, and Holy Spirit, reveals himself to men "and reconciles and unites with himself those who turn away from sin."[57]

235   This paragraph expounds briefly (I) how the mystery of the Blessed Trinity was revealed, (II) how the Church has articulated the doctrine of the faith regarding this mystery, and (III) how, by the divine missions of the Son and the Holy Spirit, God the Father fulfills the "plan of his loving goodness" of creation, redemption, and sanctification.

236   The Fathers of the Church distinguish between the-
1066 ology (*theologia*) and economy (*oikonomia*). "Theology" refers to the mystery of God's inmost life within the Blessed Trinity and "economy" to all the works by which God reveals himself and communicates his life. Through the
259 *oikonomia* the *theologia* is revealed to us; but conversely, the *theologia* illuminates the whole *oikonomia*. God's works reveal who he is in himself; the mystery of his inmost being enlightens our understanding of all his works. So it is, analogously, among human persons. A person discloses himself in his actions, and the better we know a person, the better we understand his actions.

50 **237**   The Trinity is a mystery of faith in the strict sense, one of the "mysteries that are hidden in God, which can never be known unless they are revealed by God."[58] To be sure, God has left traces of his Trinitarian being in his work of creation and in his Revelation throughout the Old Testament. But his inmost Being as Holy Trinity is a mystery that is inaccessible to reason alone or even to Israel's faith before the Incarnation of God's Son and the sending of the Holy Spirit.

---

56 GCD 43.   57 GCD 47.   58 *Dei Filius* 4: DS 3015.

II.   THE REVELATION OF GOD AS TRINITY

The Father revealed by the Son

238   Many religions invoke God as "Father." The deity is often considered the "father of gods and of men." In Israel, God is called "Father" inasmuch as he is Creator of the world.[59] Even more, God is Father because of the covenant and the gift of the law to Israel, "his firstborn son."[60] God is also called the Father of the king of Israel. Most especially he is "the Father of the poor," of the orphaned and the widowed, who are under his loving protection.[61]

2443

239   By calling God "Father," the language of faith indicates two main things: that God is the first origin of everything and transcendent authority; and that he is at the same time goodness and loving care for all his children. God's parental tenderness can also be expressed by the image of motherhood,[62] which emphasizes God's immanence, the intimacy between Creator and creature. The language of faith thus draws on the human experience of parents, who are in a way the first representatives of God for man. But this experience also tells us that human parents are fallible and can disfigure the face of fatherhood and motherhood. We ought therefore to recall that God transcends the human distinction between the sexes. He is neither man nor woman: he is God. He also transcends human fatherhood and motherhood, although he is their origin and standard:[63] no one is father as God is Father.

370, 2779

240   Jesus revealed that God is Father in an unheard of sense: he is Father not only in being Creator; he is eternally Father by his relationship to his only Son who, reciprocally, is Son only in relation to his Father: "No one knows the Son except the Father, and no one knows the Father except the Son and anyone to whom the Son chooses to reveal him."[64]

2780
441-445

241   For this reason the apostles confess Jesus to be the Word: "In the beginning was the Word, and the Word was with God, and the Word was God"; as "the

---

59 Cf. *Deut* 32:6; *Mal* 2:10.   60 *Ex* 4:22.   61 Cf. *2 Sam* 7:14; *Ps* 68:6.   62 Cf. *Isa* 66:13; *Ps* 131:2.   63 Cf. *Ps* 27:10; *Eph* 3:14; *Isa* 49:15.   64 *Mt* 11:27.

image of the invisible God"; as the "radiance of the glory of God and the very stamp of his nature."[65]

242   Following this apostolic tradition, the Church confessed at the first ecumenical council at Nicaea (325) that the Son is "consubstantial" with the Father, that is, 465 one only God with him.[66] The second ecumenical council, held at Constantinople in 381, kept this expression in its formulation of the Nicene Creed and confessed "the only-begotten Son of God, eternally begotten of the Father, light from light, true God from true God, begotten not made, consubstantial with the Father."[67]

The Father and the Son revealed by the Spirit

243   Before his Passover, Jesus announced the sending 683 of "another Paraclete" (Advocate), the Holy Spirit. At work since creation, having previously "spoken through 2780 the prophets," the Spirit will now be with and in the dis- 687 ciples, to teach them and guide them "into all the truth."[68] The Holy Spirit is thus revealed as another divine person with Jesus and the Father.

244   The eternal origin of the Holy Spirit is revealed in his mission in time. The Spirit is sent to the apostles and to the Church both by the Father in the name of the Son, and by the Son in person, once he had returned to the Father.[69] The sending of the person of the Spirit after Jesus' glorification[70] reveals in its fullness the mys- 732 tery of the Holy Trinity.

152 **245**   The apostolic faith concerning the Spirit was confessed by the second ecumenical council at Constantinople (381): "We believe in the Holy Spirit, the Lord and giver of life, who proceeds from the Father."[71] By this confession, the Church recognizes the Father as "the source and origin of the whole divinity."[72] But the eternal origin of the Spirit is not unconnected with the

---

65 *Jn* 1:1; *Col* 1:15; *Heb* 1:3.   66 The English phrases "of one being" and "one in being" translate the Greek word *homoousios,* which was rendered in Latin by *consubstantialis.*   67 Niceno-Constantinopolitan Creed; cf. DS 150.   68 Cf. *Gen* 1:2; Nicene Creed (DS 150); *Jn* 14:17, 26; 16:13.   69 Cf. *Jn* 14:26; 15:26; 16:14. 70 Cf. *Jn* 7:39.   71 Nicene Creed; cf. DS 150.   72 Council of Toledo VI (638): DS 490.

Son's origin: "The Holy Spirit, the third person of the Trinity, is God, one and equal with the Father and the Son, of the same substance and also of the same nature. ... Yet he is not called the Spirit of the Father alone, ... but the Spirit of both the Father and the Son."[73] The Creed of the Church from the Council of Constantinople confesses: "With the Father and the Son, he is worshipped and glorified."[74]

685

246 The Latin tradition of the Creed confesses that the Spirit "proceeds from the Father *and the Son (filioque)*." The Council of Florence in 1438 explains: "The Holy Spirit is eternally from Father and Son; He has his nature and subsistence at once *(simul)* from the Father and the Son. He proceeds eternally from both as from one principle and through one spiration. ... And, since the Father has through generation given to the only-begotten Son everything that belongs to the Father, except being Father, the Son has also eternally from the Father, from whom he is eternally born, that the Holy Spirit proceeds from the Son."[75]

247 The affirmation of the *filioque* does not appear in the Creed confessed in 381 at Constantinople. But Pope St. Leo I, following an ancient Latin and Alexandrian tradition, had already confessed it dogmatically in 447,[76] even before Rome, in 451 at the Council of Chalcedon, came to recognize and receive the Symbol of 381. The use of this formula in the Creed was gradually admitted into the Latin liturgy (between the eighth and eleventh centuries). The introduction of the *filioque* into the Niceno-Constantinopolitan Creed by the Latin liturgy constitutes moreover, even today, a point of disagreement with the Orthodox Churches.

248 At the outset the Eastern tradition expresses the Father's character as first origin of the Spirit. By confessing the Spirit as he "who proceeds from the Father," it affirms that he *comes from* the Father *through* the Son.[77] The Western tradition expresses first the consubstantial communion between Father and Son, by saying that the Spirit proceeds from the Father and the Son *(filioque)*. It says this, "legiti-

---

73 Council of Toledo XI (675): DS 527.   74 Nicene Creed; cf. DS 150.
75 Council of Florence (1439): DS 1300–1301.   76 Cf. Leo I, *Quam laudabiliter* (447): DS 284.   77 *Jn* 15:26; cf. *AG* 2.

mately and with good reason,"[78] for the eternal order of the divine persons in their consubstantial communion implies that the Father, as "the principle without principle,"[79] is the first origin of the Spirit, but also that as Father of the only Son, he is, with the Son, the single principle from which the Holy Spirit proceeds.[80] This legitimate complementarity, provided it does not become rigid, does not affect the identity of faith in the reality of the same mystery confessed.

III. THE HOLY TRINITY IN THE TEACHING
OF THE FAITH

The formation of the Trinitarian dogma

249   From the beginning, the revealed truth of the Holy Trinity has been at the very root of the Church's
683 living faith, principally by means of Baptism. It finds its
189 expression in the rule of baptismal faith, formulated in the preaching, catechesis, and prayer of the Church. Such formulations are already found in the apostolic writings, such as this salutation taken up in the Eucharistic liturgy: "The grace of the Lord Jesus Christ and the love of God and the fellowship of the Holy Spirit be with you all."[81]

250   During the first centuries the Church sought to clarify its Trinitarian faith, both to deepen its own understanding of the faith and to defend it against the er-
94 rors that were deforming it. This clarification was the work of the early councils, aided by the theological work of the Church Fathers and sustained by the Christian people's sense of the faith.

251   In order to articulate the dogma of the Trinity, the Church had to develop its own terminology with the help of certain notions of philosophical origin: "substance," "person" or "hypostasis," "relation," and so on. In doing this, she did not submit the faith to human wisdom, but gave a new and unprecedented meaning to these terms, which from then on would be used to signify an ineffable mystery, "infinitely beyond all that we can humanly under-
170 stand."[82]

---

78 Council of Florence (1439): DS 1302.   79 Council of Florence (1442): DS 1331.   80 Cf. Council of Lyons II (1274): DS 850.   81 *2 Cor* 13:13; cf. *1 Cor* 12:4–6; *Eph* 4:4–6.   82 Paul VI, *CPG* § 2.

252   The Church uses (I) the term "substance" (rendered also at times by "essence" or "nature") to designate the divine being in its unity, (II) the term "person" or "hypostasis" to designate the Father, Son, and Holy Spirit in the real distinction among them, and (III) the term "relation" to designate the fact that their distinction lies in the relationship of each to the others.

The dogma of the Holy Trinity

253   *The Trinity is One.* We do not confess three Gods, but one God in three persons, the "consubstantial Trinity."[83] The divine persons do not share the one divinity among themselves but each of them is God whole and entire: "The Father is that which the Son is, the Son that which the Father is, the Father and the Son that which the Holy Spirit is, i.e., by nature one God."[84] In the words of the Fourth Lateran Council (1215): "Each of the persons is that supreme reality, viz., the divine substance, essence or nature."[85]

2789

590

254   *The divine persons are really distinct from one another.* "God is one but not solitary."[86] "Father," "Son," "Holy Spirit" are not simply names designating modalities of the divine being, for they are really distinct from one another: "He is not the Father who is the Son, nor is the Son he who is the Father, nor is the Holy Spirit he who is the Father or the Son."[87] They are distinct from one another in their relations of origin: "It is the Father who generates, the Son who is begotten, and the Holy Spirit who proceeds."[88] The divine Unity is Triune.

468, 689

255   *The divine persons are relative to one another.* Because it does not divide the divine unity, the real distinction of the persons from one another resides solely in the relationships which relate them to one another: "In the relational names of the persons the Father is related to the Son, the Son to the Father, and the Holy

---

83 Council of Constantinople II (553): DS 421.   84 Council of Toledo XI (675): DS 530:26.   85 Lateran Council IV (1215): DS 804.   86 *Fides Damasi:* DS 71. 87 Council of Toledo XI (675): DS 530:25.   88 Lateran Council IV (1215): DS 804.

240 Spirit to both. While they are called three persons in view of their relations, we believe in one nature or substance."[89] Indeed "everything (in them) is one where there is no opposition of relationship."[90] "Because of that unity the Father is wholly in the Son and wholly in the Holy Spirit; the Son is wholly in the Father and wholly in the Holy Spirit; the Holy Spirit is wholly in the Father and wholly in the Son."[91]

256   St. Gregory of Nazianzus, also called "the Theologian," entrusts this summary of Trinitarian faith to the catechumens of Constantinople:

236, 684
84

> Above all guard for me this great deposit of faith for which I live and fight, which I want to take with me as a companion, and which makes me bear all evils and despise all pleasures: I mean the profession of faith in the Father and the Son and the Holy Spirit. I entrust it to you today. By it I am soon going to plunge you into water and raise you up from it. I give it to you as the companion and patron of your whole life. I give you but one divinity and power, existing one in three, and containing the three in a distinct way. Divinity without disparity of substance or nature, without superior degree that raises up or inferior degree that casts down . . . the infinite co-naturality of three infinites. Each person considered in himself is entirely God . . . the three considered together. . . . I have not even begun to think of unity when the Trinity bathes me in its splendor. I have not even begun to think of the Trinity when unity grasps me. . . .[92]

IV.   THE DIVINE WORKS AND THE TRINITARIAN MISSIONS

257   "O blessed light, O Trinity and first Unity!"[93] God is eternal blessedness, undying life, unfading light.
221 God is love: Father, Son, and Holy Spirit. God freely
758 wills to communicate the glory of his blessed life. Such is the "plan of his loving kindness," conceived by the Father before the foundation of the world, in his

---

89 Council of Toledo XI (675): DS 528.   90 Council of Florence (1442): DS 1330.   91 Council of Florence (1442): DS 1331.   92 St. Gregory of Nazianzus, *Oratio* 40, 41: PG 36, 417.   93 *LH*, Hymn for Evening Prayer.

beloved Son: "He destined us in love to be his sons" and "to be conformed to the image of his Son," through "the spirit of sonship."[94] This plan is a "grace [which] was given to us in Christ Jesus before the ages began," stemming immediately from Trinitarian love.[95] It unfolds in the work of creation, the whole history of salvation after the fall, and the missions of the Son and the Spirit, which are continued in the mission of the Church.[96]

    292

    850

258   The whole divine economy is the common work of the three divine persons. For as the Trinity has only one and the same nature, so too does it have only one and the same operation: "The Father, the Son, and the Holy Spirit are not three principles of creation but one principle."[97] However each divine person performs the common work according to his unique personal property. Thus the Church confesses, following the New Testament, "one God and Father *from whom* all things are, and one Lord Jesus Christ, *through whom* all things are, and one Holy Spirit *in whom* all things are."[98] It is above all the divine missions of the Son's Incarnation and the gift of the Holy Spirit that show forth the properties of the divine persons.

    686

259   Being a work at once common and personal, the whole divine economy makes known both what is proper to the divine persons and their one divine nature. Hence the whole Christian life is a communion with each of the divine persons, without in any way separating them. Everyone who glorifies the Father does so through the Son in the Holy Spirit; everyone who follows Christ does so because the Father draws him and the Spirit moves him.[99]

    236

260   The ultimate end of the whole divine economy is the entry of God's creatures into the perfect unity of the Blessed Trinity.[100] But even now we are called to be a

    1050, 1721

---

94 *Eph* 1:4–5, 9; *Rom* 8:15, 29.   95 *2 Tim* 1:9–10.   96 Cf. *AG* 2–9.
97 Council of Florence (1442): DS 1331; cf. Council of Constantinople II (553): DS 421.   98 Council of Constantinople II: DS 421.   99 Cf. *Jn* 6:44; *Rom* 8:14.
100 Cf. *Jn* 17:21–23.

1997   dwelling for the Most Holy Trinity: "If a man loves me," says the Lord, "he will keep my word, and my Father will love him, and we will come to him, and make our home with him":[101]

2565   O my God, Trinity whom I adore, help me forget myself entirely so to establish myself in you, unmovable and peaceful as if my soul were already in eternity. May nothing be able to trouble my peace or make me leave you, O my unchanging God, but may each minute bring me more deeply into your mystery! Grant my soul peace. Make it your heaven, your beloved dwelling and the place of your rest. May I never abandon you there, but may I be there, whole and entire, completely vigilant in my faith, entirely adoring, and wholly given over to your creative action.[102]

IN BRIEF

261   The mystery of the Most Holy Trinity is the central mystery of the Christian faith and of Christian life. God alone can make it known to us by revealing himself as Father, Son, and Holy Spirit.

262   The Incarnation of God's Son reveals that God is the eternal Father and that the Son is consubstantial with the Father, which means that, in the Father and with the Father, the Son is one and the same God.

263   The mission of the Holy Spirit, sent by the Father in the name of the Son (*Jn* 14:26) and by the Son "from the Father" (*Jn* 15:26), reveals that, with them, the Spirit is one and the same God. "With the Father and the Son he is worshipped and glorified" (Nicene Creed).

264   "The Holy Spirit proceeds from the Father as the first principle and, by the eternal gift of this to the Son, from the communion of both the Father and the Son" (St. Augustine, *De Trin.* 15, 26, 47: PL 42:1095).

---

101 *Jn* 14:23.   102 Prayer of Blessed Elizabeth of the Trinity.

265 By the grace of Baptism "in the name of the Father and of the Son and of the Holy Spirit," we are called to share in the life of the Blessed Trinity, here on earth in the obscurity of faith, and after death in eternal light (Cf. Paul VI, *CPG* § 9).

266 "Now this is the Catholic faith: We worship one God in the Trinity and the Trinity in unity, without either confusing the persons or dividing the substance; for the person of the Father is one, the Son's is another, the Holy Spirit's another; but the Godhead of the Father, Son, and Holy Spirit is one, their glory equal, their majesty coeternal" (Athanasian Creed; DS 75; ND 16).

267 Inseparable in what they are, the divine persons are also inseparable in what they do. But within the single divine operation each shows forth what is proper to him in the Trinity, especially in the divine missions of the Son's Incarnation and the gift of the Holy Spirit.

Paragraph 3. The Almighty

268 Of all the divine attributes, only God's omnipotence is named in the Creed: to confess this power has great bearing on our lives. We believe that his might is *universal,* for God who created everything also rules everything and can do everything. God's power is *loving,* for he is our Father, and *mysterious,* for only faith can discern it when it "is made perfect in weakness."[103]

"He does whatever he pleases"[104]

269 The Holy Scriptures repeatedly confess the *universal* power of God. He is called the "Mighty One of Jacob," the "LORD of hosts," the "strong and mighty" one. If God is almighty "in heaven and on earth," it is because he made them.[105] Nothing is impossible with

222

---

103 Cf. *Gen* 1:1; *Jn* 1:3; *Mt* 6:9; 2 *Cor* 12:9; cf. 1 *Cor* 1:18.   104 *Ps* 115:3.
105 *Gen* 49:24; *Isa* 1:24 etc.; *Ps* 24:8–10; 135:6.

God, who disposes his works according to his will.[106] He
is the Lord of the universe, whose order he established
and which remains wholly subject to him and at his dis-
303   posal. He is master of history, governing hearts and
events in keeping with his will: "It is always in your
power to show great strength, and who can withstand
the strength of your arm?"[107]

"You are merciful to all, for you can do all things"[108]

270   God is the *Father* Almighty, whose fatherhood
and power shed light on one another: God reveals his
fatherly omnipotence by the way he takes care of our
2777   needs; by the filial adoption that he gives us ("I will be
a father to you, and you shall be my sons and daugh-
ters, says the Lord Almighty."):[109] finally by his infinite
mercy, for he displays his power at its height by freely
1441   forgiving sins.

271   God's almighty power is in no way arbitrary: "In
God, power, essence, will, intellect, wisdom, and justice
are all identical. Nothing therefore can be in God's
power which could not be in his just will or his wise intellect."[110]

The mystery of God's apparent powerlessness

272   Faith in God the Father Almighty can be put to
the test by the experience of evil and suffering. God can
sometimes seem to be absent and incapable of stopping
309   evil. But in the most mysterious way God the Father has
412   revealed his almighty power in the voluntary humiliation and Resurrection of his Son, by which he conquered evil. Christ crucified is thus "the power of God
609   and the wisdom of God. For the foolishness of God is
648   wiser than men, and the weakness of God is stronger
than men."[111] It is in Christ's Resurrection and exaltation that the Father has shown forth "the immeasurable
greatness of his power in us who believe."[112]

---

106 Cf. *Jer* 27:5; 32:17; *Lk* 1:37.   107 *Wis* 11:21; cf. *Esth* 4:17b; *Prov* 21:1; *Tob*
13:2.   108 *Wis* 11:23.   109 *2 Cor* 6:18; cf. *Mt* 6:32.   110 St. Thomas Aquinas,
STh I, 25, 5, *ad* 1.   111 *1 Cor* 1:24–25.   112 *Eph* 1:19–22.

273   Only faith can embrace the mysterious ways of God's almighty power. This faith glories in its weaknesses in order to draw to itself Christ's power.[113] The Virgin Mary is the supreme model of this faith, for she believed that "nothing will be impossible with God," and was able to magnify the Lord: "For he who is mighty has done great things for me, and holy is his name."[114]

148

274   "Nothing is more apt to confirm our faith and hope than holding it fixed in our minds that nothing is impossible with God. Once our reason has grasped the idea of God's almighty power, it will easily and without any hesitation admit everything that [the Creed] will afterwards propose for us to believe—even if they be great and marvellous things, far above the ordinary laws of nature."[115]

1814, 1817

IN BRIEF

275   With Job, the just man, we confess: "I know that you can do all things, and that no purpose of yours can be thwarted" (*Job* 42:2).

276   Faithful to the witness of Scripture, the Church often addresses its prayer to the "almighty and eternal God" ("omnipotens sempiterne Deus . . ."), believing firmly that "nothing will be impossible with God" (*Gen* 18:14; *Lk* 1:37; *Mt* 19:26).

277   God shows forth his almighty power by converting us from our sins and restoring us to his friendship by grace. "God, you show your almighty power above all in your mercy and forgiveness . . ." (*Roman Missal*, 26th Sunday, Opening Prayer).

278   If we do not believe that God's love is almighty, how can we believe that the Father could create us, the Son redeem us, and the Holy Spirit sanctify us?

---

113 Cf. 2 *Cor* 12:9; *Phil* 4:13.   114 *Lk* 1:37, 49.   115 *Roman Catechism*, I, 2, 13.

Paragraph 4. The Creator

279 "In the beginning God created the heavens and the earth."[116] Holy Scripture begins with these solemn words. The profession of faith takes them up when it confesses that God the Father almighty is "Creator of heaven and earth" *(Apostles' Creed)*, "of all that is, seen and unseen" *(Nicene Creed)*. We shall speak first of the Creator, then of creation, and finally of the fall into sin from which Jesus Christ, the Son of God, came to raise us up again.

280 Creation is the foundation of "all God's saving plans," the "beginning of the history of salvation"[117] that culminates in Christ. Conversely, the mystery of Christ casts conclusive light on the mystery of creation and reveals the end for which "in the beginning God created the heavens and the earth": from the beginning, God envisaged the glory of the new creation in Christ.[118]

281 And so the readings of the Easter Vigil, the celebration of the new creation in Christ, begin with the creation account; likewise in the Byzantine liturgy, the account of creation always constitutes the first reading at the vigils of the great feasts of the Lord. According to ancient witnesses the instruction of catechumens for Baptism followed the same itinerary.[119]

I. CATECHESIS ON CREATION

282 Catechesis on creation is of major importance. It concerns the very foundations of human and Christian life: for it makes explicit the response of the Christian faith to the basic question that men of all times have asked themselves:[120] "Where do we come from?" "Where are we going?" "What is our origin?" "What is our end?" "Where does everything that exists come from and where is it going?" The two questions, the first about the origin and the second about the end, are inseparable. They are decisive for the meaning and orientation of our life and actions.

---

116 *Gen* 1:1.   117 GCD 51.   118 *Gen* 1:1; cf. *Rom* 8:18–23.   119 Cf. Egeria, *Peregrinatio ad loca sancta*, 46: PLS I, 1047; St. Augustine, *De catechizandis rudibus* 3, 5: PL 40, 256.   120 Cf. *NA* 2.

283   The question about the origins of the world and of
man has been the object of many scientific studies which
have splendidly enriched our knowledge of the age and   159
dimensions of the cosmos, the development of life-forms
and the appearance of man. These discoveries invite us
to even greater admiration for the greatness of the Creator, prompting us to give him thanks for all his works   341
and for the understanding and wisdom he gives to scholars
and researchers. With Solomon they can say: "It is
he who gave me unerring knowledge of what exists, to
know the structure of the world and the activity of the
elements . . . for wisdom, the fashioner of all things, taught
me."[121]

284   The great interest accorded to these studies is
strongly stimulated by a question of another order, which
goes beyond the proper domain of the natural sciences. It
is not only a question of knowing when and how the universe arose physically, or when man appeared, but rather of
discovering the meaning of such an origin: is the universe
governed by chance, blind fate, anonymous necessity, or
by a transcendent, intelligent and good Being called
"God"? And if the world does come from God's wisdom and goodness, why is there evil? Where does it come
from? Who is responsible for it? Is there any liberation
from it?

285   Since the beginning the Christian faith has been
challenged by responses to the question of origins that differ from its own. Ancient religions and cultures produced
many myths concerning origins. Some philosophers have
said that everything is God, that the world is God, or that
the development of the world is the development of God
(Pantheism). Others have said that the world is a necessary   295
emanation arising from God and returning to him. Still
others have affirmed the existence of two eternal principles,
Good and Evil, Light and Darkness, locked in permanent
conflict (Dualism, Manichaeism). According to some of
these conceptions, the world (at least the physical world) is
evil, the product of a fall, and is thus to be rejected or left
behind (Gnosticism). Some admit that the world was made
by God, but as by a watchmaker who, once he has made a
watch, abandons it to itself (Deism). Finally, others reject
any transcendent origin for the world, but see it as merely
the interplay of matter that has always existed (Materialism). All these attempts bear witness to the permanence

---

121 *Wis* 7:17–22.

28 and universality of the question of origins. This inquiry is distinctively human.

32 **286**   Human intelligence is surely already capable of finding a response to the question of origins. The existence of God the Creator can be known with certainty through his works, by the light of human reason,[122] even if this knowledge is often obscured and disfigured by error. This is why faith comes to confirm and enlighten 37 reason in the correct understanding of this truth: "By faith we understand that the world was created by the word of God, so that what is seen was made out of things which do not appear."[123]

287   The truth about creation is so important for all of human life that God in his tenderness wanted to reveal to his People everything that is salutary to know on 107 the subject. Beyond the natural knowledge that every man can have of the Creator,[124] God progressively revealed to Israel the mystery of creation. He who chose the patriarchs, who brought Israel out of Egypt, and who by choosing Israel created and formed it, this same God reveals himself as the One to whom belong all the peoples of the earth, and the whole earth itself; he is the One who alone "made heaven and earth."[125]

288   Thus the revelation of creation is inseparable from the revelation and forging of the covenant of the 280, 2569 one God with his People. Creation is revealed as the first step toward this covenant, the first and universal witness to God's all-powerful love.[126] And so, the truth of creation is also expressed with growing vigor in the message of the prophets, the prayer of the psalms and the liturgy, and in the wisdom sayings of the Chosen People.[127]

289   Among all the Scriptural texts about creation, the first three chapters of Genesis occupy a unique 390 place. From a literary standpoint these texts may have had diverse sources. The inspired authors have placed

---

122 Cf. Vatican Council I, can. 2 § 1: DS 3026.   123 *Heb* 11:3.   124 Cf. *Acts* 17:24–29; *Rom* 1:19–20.   125 Cf. *Isa* 43:1; *Ps* 115:15; 124:8; 134:3.   126 Cf. *Gen* 15:5; *Jer* 33:19–26.   127 Cf. *Isa* 44:24; *Ps* 104; *Prov* 8:22–31.

them at the beginning of Scripture to express in their solemn language the truths of creation—its origin and its end in God, its order and goodness, the vocation of man, and finally the drama of sin and the hope of salvation. Read in the light of Christ, within the unity of Sacred Scripture and in the living Tradition of the Church, these texts remain the principal source for catechesis on the mysteries of the "beginning": creation, fall, and promise of salvation.

111

II. CREATION—WORK OF THE HOLY TRINITY

290 "In the beginning God created the heavens and the earth":[128] three things are affirmed in these first words of Scripture: the eternal God gave a beginning to all that exists outside of himself; he alone is Creator (the verb "create"—Hebrew *bara*—always has God for its subject). The totality of what exists (expressed by the formula "the heavens and the earth") depends on the One who gives it being.

326

291 "In the beginning was the Word . . . and the Word was God . . . all things were made through him, and without him was not anything made that was made."[129] The New Testament reveals that God created everything by the eternal Word, his beloved Son. In him "all things were created, in heaven and on earth . . . all things were created through him and for him. He is before all things, and in him all things hold together."[130] The Church's faith likewise confesses the creative action of the Holy Spirit, the "giver of life," "the Creator Spirit" *("Veni, Creator Spiritus"),* the "source of every good."[131]

241

331

703

292 The Old Testament suggests and the New Covenant reveals the creative action of the Son and the Spirit,[132] inseparably one with that of the Father. This creative cooperation is clearly affirmed in the Church's rule of faith: "There exists but one God . . . he is the Fa-

---

128 *Gen* 1:1.   129 *Jn* 1:1–3.   130 *Col* 1:16–17.   131 Cf. Nicene Creed; DS 150; Hymn *"Veni, Creator Spiritus"*; Byzantine Troparion of Pentecost vespers, *"O heavenly King, Consoler."*   132 Cf. *Ps* 33:6; 104:30; *Gen* 1:2–3.

ther, God, the Creator, the author, the giver of order. He made all things *by himself,* that is, by his Word and by his Wisdom," "by the Son and the Spirit" who, so to 699 speak, are "his hands."[133] Creation is the common work 257 of the Holy Trinity.

III.   "THE WORLD WAS CREATED FOR THE GLORY OF GOD"

293   Scripture and Tradition never cease to teach and 337, 344 celebrate this fundamental truth: "The world was made 1361 for the glory of God."[134] St. Bonaventure explains that God created all things "not to increase his glory, but to show it forth and to communicate it,"[135] for God has no other reason for creating than his love and goodness: "Creatures came into existence when the key of love opened his hand."[136] The First Vatican Council explains:

759   This one, true God, of his own goodness and "almighty power," not for increasing his own beatitude, nor for attaining his perfection, but in order to manifest this perfection through the benefits which he bestows on creatures, with absolute freedom of counsel "and from the beginning of time, made out of nothing both orders of creatures, the spiritual and the corporeal. . . ."[137]

294   The glory of God consists in the realization of this manifestation and communication of his goodness, for which the world was created. God made us "to be 2809 his sons through Jesus Christ, according to the purpose of his will, *to the praise of his glorious grace,*"[138] for "the glory of God is man fully alive; moreover man's life 1722 is the vision of God: if God's revelation through creation has already obtained life for all the beings that dwell on earth, how much more will the Word's manifestation of the Father obtain life for those who see God."[139] The ultimate purpose of creation is that God 1992 "who is the creator of all things may at last become 'all

---

133 St. Irenaeus, *Adv. haeres* 2, 30, 9; 4, 20, 1: PG 7/1, 822, 1032.   134 *Dei Filius,* can. § 5: DS 3025.   135 St. Bonaventure, *In II Sent.* I, 2, 2, 1.   136 St. Thomas Aquinas, *Sent.* 2, Prol.   137 *Dei Filius,* 1: DS 3002; cf. Lateran Council IV (1215): DS 800.   138 *Eph* 1:5–6.   139 St. Irenaeus, *Adv. haeres* 4, 20, 7: PG 7/1, 1037.

in all,' thus simultaneously assuring his own glory and our beatitude."[140]

IV.   THE MYSTERY OF CREATION

God creates by wisdom and love

295   We believe that God created the world according to his wisdom.[141] It is not the product of any necessity whatever, nor of blind fate or chance. We believe that it proceeds from God's free will; he wanted to make his creatures share in his being, wisdom, and goodness: "For you created all things, and by your will they existed and were created."[142] Therefore the Psalmist exclaims: "O LORD, how manifold are your works! In wisdom you have made them all"; and "The LORD is good to all, and his compassion is over all that he has made."[143]

216, 1951

God creates "out of nothing"

296   We believe that God needs no pre-existent thing or any help in order to create, nor is creation any sort of necessary emanation from the divine substance.[144] God creates freely "out of nothing":[145]

285

> If God had drawn the world from pre-existent matter, what would be so extraordinary in that? A human artisan makes from a given material whatever he wants, while God shows his power by starting from nothing to make all he wants.[146]

297   Scripture bears witness to faith in creation "out of nothing" as a truth full of promise and hope. Thus the mother of seven sons encourages them for martyrdom:

338

> I do not know how you came into being in my womb. It was not I who gave you life and breath, nor I who set in order the elements within each of you. Therefore the Creator of the world, who shaped the beginning of man and devised the origin

---

140 *AG* 2; cf. *1 Cor* 15:28.   141 Cf. *Wis* 9:9.   142 *Rev* 4:11.   143 *Ps* 104:24; 145:9.   144 Cf. *Dei Filius*, can. 2–4: DS 3022–3024.   145 Lateran Council IV (1215): DS 800; cf. DS 3025.   146 St. Theophilus of Antioch, *Ad Autolycum* II, 4: PG 6, 1052.

of all things, will in his mercy give life and breath
back to you again, since you now forget yourselves
for the sake of his laws. . . . Look at the heaven and
the earth and see everything that is in them, and
recognize that God did not make them out of things
that existed. Thus also mankind comes into being.[147]

298   Since God could create everything out of nothing, he can also, through the Holy Spirit, give spiritual
1375 life to sinners by creating a pure heart in them[148] and
bodily life to the dead through the Resurrection. God
"gives life to the dead and calls into existence the things
992 that do not exist."[149] And since God was able to make
light shine in darkness by his Word, he can also give the
light of faith to those who do not yet know him.[150]

God creates an ordered and good world

339 **299**   Because God creates through wisdom, his creation is ordered: "You have arranged all things by measure and number and weight."[151] The universe, created
in and by the eternal Word, the "image of the invisible
God," is destined for and addressed to man, himself created in the "image of God" and called to a personal relationship with God.[152] Our human understanding,
41, 1147 which shares in the light of the divine intellect, can understand what God tells us by means of his creation,
though not without great effort and only in a spirit of
humility and respect before the Creator and his work.[153]
Because creation comes forth from God's goodness, it
shares in that goodness—"And God saw that it was
good . . . very good"[154]—for God willed creation as a
gift addressed to man, an inheritance destined for and
entrusted to him. On many occasions the Church has
358 had to defend the goodness of creation, including that
2415 of the physical world.[155]

---

147 2 *Macc* 7:22–23, 28.   148 Cf. *Ps* 51:12.   149 *Rom* 4:17.   150 Cf. *Gen* 1:3;
2 *Cor* 4:6.   151 *Wis* 11:20.   152 *Col* 1:15; *Gen* 1:26.   153 Cf. *Ps* 19:2–5; *Job*
42:3.   154 *Gen* 1:4, 10, 12, 18, 21, 31.   155 Cf. DS 286; 455–463; 800; 1333;
3002.

God transcends creation and is present to it

300   God is infinitely greater than all his works: "You have set your glory above the heavens."[156] Indeed, God's "greatness is unsearchable."[157] But because he is the free and sovereign Creator, the first cause of all that exists, God is present to his creatures' inmost being: "In him we live and move and have our being."[158] In the words of St. Augustine, God is "higher than my highest and more inward than my innermost self."[159]

42

223

God upholds and sustains creation

301   With creation, God does not abandon his creatures to themselves. He not only gives them being and existence, but also, and at every moment, upholds and sustains them in being, enables them to act and brings them to their final end. Recognizing this utter dependence with respect to the Creator is a source of wisdom and freedom, of joy and confidence:

1951

396

> For you love all things that exist, and detest none of the things that you have made; for you would not have made anything if you had hated it. How would anything have endured, if you had not willed it? Or how would anything not called forth by you have been preserved? You spare all things, for they are yours, O Lord, you who love the living.[160]

V.   GOD CARRIES OUT HIS PLAN: DIVINE PROVIDENCE

302   Creation has its own goodness and proper perfection, but it did not spring forth complete from the hands of the Creator. The universe was created "in a state of journeying" *(in statu viae)* toward an ultimate perfection yet to be attained, to which God has destined it. We call "divine providence" the dispositions by which God guides his creation toward this perfection:

> By his providence God protects and governs all things which he has made, "reaching mightily from one end of the earth to the other, and ordering all

---

156 *Ps* 8:2; cf. *Sir* 43:28.   157 *Ps* 145:3.   158 *Acts* 17:28.   159 St. Augustine, *Conf.* 3, 6, 11: PL 32, 688.   160 *Wis* 11:24–26.

things well." For "all are open and laid bare to his eyes," even those things which are yet to come into existence through the free action of creatures.[161]

303   The witness of Scripture is unanimous that the solicitude of divine providence is *concrete* and *immediate;* God cares for all, from the least things to the great events of the world and its history. The sacred books powerfully affirm God's absolute sovereignty over the course of events: "Our God is in the heavens; he does whatever he pleases."[162] And so it is with Christ, "who opens and no one shall shut, who shuts and no one opens."[163] As the book of Proverbs states: "Many are the plans in the mind of a man, but it is the purpose of the Lord that will be established."[164]

269

304   And so we see the Holy Spirit, the principal author of Sacred Scripture, often attributing actions to God without mentioning any secondary causes. This is not a "primitive mode of speech," but a profound way of recalling God's primacy and absolute Lordship over history and the world,[165] and so of educating his people to trust in him. The prayer of the Psalms is the great school of this trust.[166]

2568

305   Jesus asks for childlike abandonment to the providence of our heavenly Father who takes care of his children's smallest needs: "Therefore do not be anxious, saying, 'What shall we eat?' or 'What shall we drink?'. . . . Your heavenly Father knows that you need them all. But seek first his kingdom and his righteousness, and all these things shall be yours as well."[167]

2115

Providence and secondary causes

306   God is the sovereign master of his plan. But to carry it out he also makes use of his creatures' cooperation. This use is not a sign of weakness, but rather a token of almighty God's greatness and goodness. For God grants his creatures not only their existence, but also the dignity of acting on their own, of being causes and prin-

1884

---

161 Vatican Council I, *Dei Filius* 1: DS 3003; cf. *Wis* 8:1; *Heb* 4:13.   162 *Ps* 115:3.   163 *Rev* 3:7.   164 *Prov* 19:21.   165 Cf. *Isa* 10:5–15; 45:5–7; *Deut* 32:39; *Sir* 11:14.   166 Cf. *Ps* 22; 32; 35; 103; 138; *et al.*   167 *Mt* 6:31–33; cf. 10:29–31.

ciples for each other, and thus of cooperating in the ac- 1951
complishment of his plan.

307   To human beings God even gives the power of
freely sharing in his providence by entrusting them with
the responsibility of "subduing" the earth and having 106, 373
dominion over it.[168] God thus enables men to be intelli- 1954
gent and free causes in order to complete the work of
creation, to perfect its harmony for their own good and 2427
that of their neighbors. Though often unconscious collaborators with God's will, they can also enter deliberately into the divine plan by their actions, their prayers,
and their sufferings.[169] They then fully become "God's 2738
fellow workers" and co-workers for his kingdom.[170] 618, 1505

308   The truth that God is at work in all the actions
of his creatures is inseparable from faith in God the Creator. God is the first cause who operates in and through
secondary causes: "For God is at work in you, both to
will and to work for his good pleasure."[171] Far from diminishing the creature's dignity, this truth enhances it.
Drawn from nothingness by God's power, wisdom, and
goodness, it can do nothing if it is cut off from its ori- 970
gin, for "without a Creator the creature vanishes."[172]
Still less can a creature attain its ultimate end without
the help of God's grace.[173]

Providence and the scandal of evil
309   If God the Father almighty, the Creator of the
ordered and good world, cares for all his creatures, why
does evil exist? To this question, as pressing as it is un-
avoidable and as painful as it is mysterious, no quick 164, 385
answer will suffice. Only Christian faith as a whole con- 2805
stitutes the answer to this question: the goodness of creation, the drama of sin, and the patient love of God who
comes to meet man by his covenants, the redemptive Incarnation of his Son, his gift of the Spirit, his gathering
of the Church, the power of the sacraments, and his call
to a blessed life to which free creatures are invited to

---

168 Cf. *Gen* 1:26–28.   169 Cf. *Col* 1:24.   170 *1 Cor* 3:9; *1 Thess* 3:2; *Col* 4:11.
171 *Phil* 2:13; cf. *1 Cor* 12:6.   172 *GS* 36 § 3.   173 Cf. *Mt* 19:26; *Jn* 15:5;
14:13.

consent in advance, but from which, by a terrible mystery, they can also turn away in advance. *There is not a single aspect of the Christian message that is not in part an answer to the question of evil.*

310   But why did God not create a world so perfect that no evil could exist in it? With infinite power God
412   could always create something better.[174] But with infinite
1042-1050   wisdom and goodness God freely willed to create a world "in a state of journeying" toward its ultimate perfection. In God's plan this process of becoming involves the appearance of certain beings and the disap-
342   pearance of others, the existence of the more perfect alongside the less perfect, both constructive and destructive forces of nature. With physical good there exists also *physical evil* as long as creation has not reached perfection.[175]

311   Angels and men, as intelligent and free creatures, have to journey toward their ultimate destinies by their
396   free choice and preferential love. They can therefore go
1849   astray. Indeed, they have sinned. Thus has *moral evil,* incommensurably more harmful than physical evil, entered the world. God is in no way, directly or indirectly, the cause of moral evil.[176] He permits it, however, because he respects the freedom of his creatures and, mysteriously, knows how to derive good from it:

> For almighty God . . . , because he is supremely good, would never allow any evil whatsoever to exist in his works if he were not so all-powerful and good as to cause good to emerge from evil itself.[177]

312   In time we can discover that God in his almighty providence can bring a good from the consequences of an evil, even a moral evil, caused by his creatures: "It was not you," said Joseph to his brothers, "who sent me here, but God. . . . You meant evil against me; but God meant it for good, to bring it about that many people

---

174 Cf. St. Thomas Aquinas, *STh* I, 25, 6.   175 Cf. St. Thomas Aquinas, *SCG* III, 71.   176 Cf. St. Augustine, *De libero arbitrio* 1, 1, 2: PL 32, 1223; St. Thomas Aquinas, *STh* I–II, 79, 1.   177 St. Augustine, *Enchiridion* 3, 11: PL 40, 236.

should be kept alive."[178] From the greatest moral evil *598–600*
ever committed—the rejection and murder of God's
only Son, caused by the sins of all men—God, by
his grace that "abounded all the more,"[179] brought
the greatest of goods: the glorification of Christ and
our redemption. But for all that, evil never becomes a
good.   *1994*

313   "We know that in everything God works for
good for those who love him."[180] The constant witness *227*
of the saints confirms this truth:

> St. Catherine of Siena said to "those who are scan-
> dalized and rebel against what happens to them":
> "Everything comes from love, all is ordained for the
> salvation of man, God does nothing without this
> goal in mind."[181]

> St. Thomas More, shortly before his martyrdom,
> consoled his daughter: "Nothing can come but that
> that God wills. And I make me very sure that what-
> soever that be, seem it never so bad in sight, it shall
> indeed be the best."[182]

> Dame Julian of Norwich: "Here I was taught by the
> grace of God that I should steadfastly keep me in
> the faith . . . and that at the same time I should take
> my stand on and earnestly believe in what our Lord
> shewed in this time—that 'all manner [of] thing
> shall be well.' "[183]

314   We firmly believe that God is master of the
world and of its history. But the ways of his providence
are often unknown to us. Only at the end, when our
partial knowledge ceases, when we see God "face to
face,"[184] will we fully know the ways by which—even *1040*
through the dramas of evil and sin—God has guided his *2550*
creation to that definitive sabbath rest[185] for which he
created heaven and earth.

---

178 *Gen* 45:8; 50:20; cf. *Tob* 2:12–18 (Vulg.).   179 Cf. *Rom* 5:20.   180 *Rom*
8:28.   181 St. Catherine of Siena, *Dialogue on Providence*, ch. IV, 138.   182 *The
Correspondence of Sir Thomas More*, ed. Elizabeth F. Rogers (Princeton:
Princeton University Press, 1947), letter 206, lines 661–663.   183 Julian of
Norwich, *The Revelations of Divine Love*, tr. James Walshe, SJ (London: 1961),
ch. 32, 99–100.   184 *1 Cor* 13:12.   185 Cf. *Gen* 2:2.

IN BRIEF

315   In the creation of the world and of man, God gave the first and universal witness to his almighty love and his wisdom, the first proclamation of the "plan of his loving goodness," which finds its goal in the new creation in Christ.

316   Though the work of creation is attributed to the Father in particular, it is equally a truth of faith that the Father, Son, and Holy Spirit together are the one, indivisible principle of creation.

317   God alone created the universe freely, directly, and without any help.

318   No creature has the infinite power necessary to "create" in the proper sense of the word, that is, to produce and give being to that which had in no way possessed it (to call into existence "out of nothing") (cf. DS 3624).

319   God created the world to show forth and communicate his glory. That his creatures should share in his truth, goodness, and beauty—this is the glory for which God created them.

320   God created the universe and keeps it in existence by his Word, the Son "upholding the universe by his word of power" (*Heb* 1:3) and by his Creator Spirit, the giver of life.

321   Divine providence consists of the dispositions by which God guides all his creatures with wisdom and love to their ultimate end.

322   Christ invites us to filial trust in the providence of our heavenly Father (cf. *Mt* 6:26–34), and St. Peter the apostle repeats: "Cast all your anxieties on him, for he cares about you" (*1 Pet* 5:7; cf. *Ps* 55:23).

323   Divine providence works also through the actions of creatures. To human beings God grants the ability to cooperate freely with his plans.

324   The fact that God permits physical and even
moral evil is a mystery that God illuminates by
his Son Jesus Christ who died and rose to vanquish evil. Faith gives us the certainty that God
would not permit an evil if he did not cause a
good to come from that very evil, by ways that
we shall fully know only in eternal life.

Paragraph 5. Heaven and Earth

325   The Apostles' Creed professes that God is "Creator of heaven and earth." The Nicene Creed makes it
explicit that this profession includes "all that is, seen
and unseen."

326   The Scriptural expression "heaven and earth"
means all that exists, creation in its entirety. It also indicates the bond, deep within creation, that both unites   290
heaven and earth and distinguishes the one from the
other: "the earth" is the world of men, while "heaven"
or "the heavens" can designate both the firmament and
God's own "place"—"our Father in heaven" and con-   1023, 2794
sequently the "heaven" too which is eschatological
glory. Finally, "heaven" refers to the saints and the
"place" of the spiritual creatures, the angels, who surround God.[186]

327   The profession of faith of the Fourth Lateran
Council (1215) affirms that God "from the beginning of
time made at once *(simul)* out of nothing both orders of
creatures, the spiritual and the corporeal, that is, the an-   296
gelic and the earthly, and then *(deinde)* the human creature, who as it were shares in both orders, being composed of spirit and body."[187]

I.   THE ANGELS

The existence of angels—a truth of faith

328   The existence of the spiritual, non-corporeal beings that Sacred Scripture usually calls "angels" is a

---

186 *Ps* 115:16; 19:2; *Mt* 5:16.   187 Lateran Council IV (1215): DS 800; cf. DS
3002 and Paul VI, *CPG* § 8.

truth of faith. The witness of Scripture is as clear as the
150 unanimity of Tradition.

Who are they?

329   St. Augustine says: " 'Angel' is the name of their
office, not of their nature. If you seek the name of their
nature, it is 'spirit'; if you seek the name of their office,
it is 'angel': from what they are, 'spirit,' from what they
do, 'angel.' "[188] With their whole beings the angels are
servants and messengers of God. Because they "always
behold the face of my Father who is in heaven" they are
the "mighty ones who do his word, hearkening to the
voice of his word."[189]

330   As purely *spiritual* creatures angels have intelligence and will: they are personal and immortal creatures, surpassing in perfection all visible creatures, as
the splendor of their glory bears witness.[190]

Christ "with all his angels"

291 **331**   Christ is the center of the angelic world. They
are *his* angels: "When the Son of man comes in his
glory, and all the angels with him. . . ."[191] They belong
to him because they were created *through* and *for* him:
"for in him all things were created in heaven and on
earth, visible and invisible, whether thrones or domin-
ions or principalities or authorities—all things were created through him and for him."[192] They belong to him
still more because he has made them messengers of his
saving plan: "Are they not all ministering spirits sent
forth to serve, for the sake of those who are to obtain
salvation?"[193]

332   Angels have been present since creation and
throughout the history of salvation, announcing this
salvation from afar or near and serving the accomplishment of the divine plan: they closed the earthly paradise; protected Lot; saved Hagar and her child; stayed
Abraham's hand; communicated the law by their min-

---

188 St. Augustine, *En. in Ps.* 103, 1, 15: PL 37, 1348.   189 *Mt* 18:10; *Ps* 103:20.
190 Cf. Pius XII, *Humani Generis*: DS 3891; *Lk* 20:36; *Dan* 10:9–12.   191 *Mt*
25:31.   192 *Col* 1:16.   193 *Heb* 1:14.

istry; led the People of God; announced births and callings; and assisted the prophets, just to cite a few examples.[194] Finally, the angel Gabriel announced the birth of the Precursor and that of Jesus himself.[195]

333 From the Incarnation to the Ascension, the life of the Word incarnate is surrounded by the adoration and service of angels. When God "brings the firstborn into the world, he says: 'Let all God's angels worship him.' "[196] Their song of praise at the birth of Christ 559 has not ceased resounding in the Church's praise: "Glory to God in the highest!"[197] They protect Jesus in his infancy, serve him in the desert, strengthen him in his agony in the garden, when he could have been saved by them from the hands of his enemies as Israel had been.[198] Again, it is the angels who "evangelize" by proclaiming the Good News of Christ's Incarnation and Resurrection.[199] They will be present at Christ's return, which they will announce, to serve at his judgment.[200]

The angels in the life of the Church

334 In the meantime, the whole life of the Church 1939 benefits from the mysterious and powerful help of angels.[201]

335 In her liturgy, the Church joins with the angels to adore the thrice-holy God. She invokes their assistance (in the Roman Canon's *Supplices te rogamus . . .* ["Almighty God, we pray that your angel . . ."]; in the 1138 funeral liturgy's *In Paradisum deducant te angeli . . .* ["May the angels lead you into Paradise . . ."]). Moreover, in the "Cherubic Hymn" of the Byzantine Liturgy, she celebrates the memory of certain angels more particularly (St. Michael, St. Gabriel, St. Raphael, and the guardian angels).

---

194 Cf. *Job* 38:7 (where angels are called "sons of God"); *Gen* 3:24; 19; 21:17; 22:11; *Acts* 7:53; *Ex* 23:20–23; *Judg* 13; 6:11–24; *Isa* 6:6; 1 *Kings* 19:5. 195 Cf. *Lk* 1:11, 26. 196 *Heb* 1:6. 197 *Lk* 2:14. 198 Cf. *Mt* 1:20; 2:13, 19; 4:11; 26:53; *Mk* 1:13; *Lk* 22:43; 2 *Macc* 10:29–30; 11:8. 199 Cf. *Lk* 2:8–14; *Mk* 16:5–7. 200 Cf. *Acts* 1:10–11; *Mt* 13:41; 24:31; *Lk* 12:8–9. 201 Cf. *Acts* 5:18–20; 8:26–29; 10:3–8; 12:6–11; 27:23–25.

336   From infancy to death human life is surrounded by their watchful care and intercession.[202] "Beside each believer stands an angel as protector and shepherd leading him to life."[203] Already here on earth the Christian life shares by faith in the blessed company of angels and men united in God.

II.   THE VISIBLE WORLD

337   God himself created the visible world in all its richness, diversity, and order. Scripture presents the work of the Creator symbolically as a succession of six days of divine "work," concluded by the "rest" of the seventh day.[204] On the subject of creation, the sacred text teaches the truths revealed by God for our salvation,[205] permitting us to "recognize the inner nature, the value, and the ordering of the whole of creation to the praise of God."[206]

338   *Nothing exists that does not owe its existence to God the Creator.* The world began when God's word drew it out of nothingness; all existent beings, all of nature, and all human history are rooted in this primordial event, the very genesis by which the world was constituted and time begun.[207]

339   *Each creature possesses its own particular goodness and perfection.* For each one of the works of the "six days" it is said: "And God saw that it was good." "By the very nature of creation, material being is endowed with its own stability, truth, and excellence, its own order and laws."[208] Each of the various creatures, willed in its own being, reflects in its own way a ray of God's infinite wisdom and goodness. Man must therefore respect the particular goodness of every creature, to avoid any disordered use of things which would be in contempt of the Creator and would bring disastrous consequences for human beings and their environment.

---

202 Cf. *Mt* 18:10; *Lk* 16:22; *Ps* 34:7; 91:10–13; *Job* 33:23–24; *Zech* 1:12; *Tob* 12:12.   203 St. Basil, *Adv. Eunomium* III, 1: PG 29, 656B.   204 *Gen* 1:1–2:4. 205 Cf. *DV* 11.   206 *LG* 36 § 2.   207 Cf. St. Augustine, *De Genesi adv. Man.* **1**, **2**, **4**: PL 34, 175.   208 *GS* 36 § 1.

340 God wills the *interdependence of creatures*. The sun and the moon, the cedar and the little flower, the eagle and the sparrow: the spectacle of their countless diversities and inequalities tells us that no creature is self-sufficient. Creatures exist only in dependence on each other, to complete each other, in the service of each other. *1937*

341 The *beauty of the universe*: The order and harmony of the created world results from the diversity of beings and from the relationships which exist among them. Man discovers them progressively as the laws of nature. They call forth the admiration of scholars. The beauty of creation reflects the infinite beauty of the Creator and ought to inspire the respect and submission of man's intellect and will. *283 2500*

342 The *hierarchy of creatures* is expressed by the order of the "six days," from the less perfect to the more perfect. God loves all his creatures[209] and takes care of each one, even the sparrow. Nevertheless, Jesus said: "You are of more value than many sparrows," or again: "Of how much more value is a man than a sheep!"[210] *310*

343 *Man is the summit* of the Creator's work, as the inspired account expresses by clearly distinguishing the creation of man from that of the other creatures.[211] *355*

344 There is a *solidarity among all creatures* arising from the fact that all have the same Creator and are all ordered to his glory: *293, 1939 2416*

> May you be praised, O Lord, in all your creatures, especially brother sun, by whom you give us light for the day; he is beautiful, radiating great splendor, and offering us a symbol of you, the Most High. . . . *1218*
>
> May you be praised, my Lord, for sister water, who is very useful and humble, precious and chaste. . . .

---

209 Cf. *Ps* 145:9.   210 *Lk* 12:6–7; *Mt* 12:12.   211 Cf. *Gen* 1:26.

May you be praised, my Lord, for sister earth, our mother, who bears and feeds us, and produces the variety of fruits and dappled flowers and grasses. . . .

Praise and bless my Lord, give thanks and serve him in all humility.[212]

345   *The sabbath—the end of the work of the six days.* The sacred text says that "on the seventh day God finished his work which he had done," that the "heavens and the earth were finished," and that God "rested" on this day and sanctified and blessed it.[213] These inspired words are rich in profitable instruction:

2168

346   In creation God laid a foundation and established laws that remain firm, on which the believer can rely with confidence, for they are the sign and pledge of the unshakeable faithfulness of God's covenant.[214] For his part man must remain faithful to this foundation and respect the laws which the Creator has written into it.

2169

347   Creation was fashioned with a view to the sabbath and therefore for the worship and adoration of God. Worship is inscribed in the order of creation.[215] As the rule of St. Benedict says, nothing should take precedence over "the work of God," that is, solemn worship.[216] This indicates the right order of human concerns.

1145-1152

348   The sabbath is at the heart of Israel's law. To keep the commandments is to correspond to the wisdom and the will of God as expressed in his work of creation.

2172

349   The *eighth day*. But for us a new day has dawned: the day of Christ's Resurrection. The seventh day completes the first creation. The eighth day begins the new creation. Thus, the work of creation culminates in the greater work of redemption. The first creation finds its meaning and its summit in the new creation in Christ, the splendor of which surpasses that of the first creation.[217]

2174

1046

---

212 St. Francis of Assisi, *Canticle of the Creatures.*   213 *Gen* 2:1–3.   214 Cf. *Heb* 4:3–4; *Jer* 31:35–37; 33:19–26.   215 Cf. *Gen* 1:14.   216 St. Benedict, *Regula* 43, 3: PL 66, 675–676.   217 Cf. *Roman Missal,* Easter Vigil 24, prayer after the first reading.

IN BRIEF

350   Angels are spiritual creatures who glorify God without ceasing and who serve his saving plans for other creatures: "The angels work together for the benefit of us all" (St. Thomas Aquinas, *STh* I, 114, 3, *ad* 3).

351   The angels surround Christ their Lord. They serve him especially in the accomplishment of his saving mission to men.

352   The Church venerates the angels who help her on her earthly pilgrimage and protect every human being.

353   God willed the diversity of his creatures and their own particular goodness, their interdependence, and their order. He destined all material creatures for the good of the human race. Man, and through him all creation, is destined for the glory of God.

354   Respect for laws inscribed in creation and the relations which derive from the nature of things is a principle of wisdom and a foundation for morality.

Paragraph 6. Man

355   "God created man in his own image, in the image of God he created him, male and female he created them."[218] Man occupies a unique place in creation: (I) he is "in the image of God"; (II) in his own nature he unites the spiritual and material worlds; (III) he is created "male and female"; (IV) God established him in his friendship.   *1700, 343*

I.   "IN THE IMAGE OF GOD"

356   Of all visible creatures only man is "able to know and love his creator."[219] He is "the only creature on earth that God has willed for its own sake,"[220] and

---

218 *Gen* 1:27.   219 *GS* 12 § 3.   220 *GS* 24 § 3.

1703, 2258   he alone is called to share, by knowledge and love, in
            God's own life. It was for this end that he was created,
    225   and this is the fundamental reason for his dignity:

    295   What made you establish man in so great a dignity?
                Certainly the incalculable love by which you have
                looked on your creature in yourself! You are taken
                with love for her; for by love indeed you created
                her, by love you have given her a being capable of
                tasting your eternal Good.[221]

        357   Being in the image of God the human individual
            possesses the dignity of a person, who is not just some-
    1935   thing, but someone. He is capable of self-knowledge, of
    1877   self-possession and of freely giving himself and entering
            into communion with other persons. And he is called by
            grace to a covenant with his Creator, to offer him a re-
            sponse of faith and love that no other creature can give
            in his stead.

        358   God created everything for man,[222] but man in
    299, 901 turn was created to serve and love God and to offer all
            creation back to him:

                What is it that is about to be created, that enjoys
                such honor? It is man—that great and wonderful
                living creature, more precious in the eyes of God
                than all other creatures! For him the heavens and
                the earth, the sea and all the rest of creation exist.
                God attached so much importance to his salvation
                that he did not spare his own Son for the sake of
                man. Nor does he ever cease to work, trying every
                possible means, until he has raised man up to him-
                self and made him sit at his right hand.[223]

    1701 **359**   "In reality it is only in the mystery of the Word
            made flesh that the mystery of man truly becomes
            clear."[224]

    388, 411   St. Paul tells us that the human race takes its origin
                from two men: Adam and Christ. . . . The first
                man, Adam, he says, became a living soul, the last
                Adam a life-giving spirit. The first Adam was made

---

221 St. Catherine of Siena, *Dialogue* 4, 13 "On Divine Providence": *LH,* Sunday,
week 19, OR.   222 Cf. *GS* 12 § 1; 24 § 3; 39 § 1.   223 St. John Chrysostom, *In
Gen. Sermo* II, 1: PG 54, 587D–588A.   224 *GS* 22 § 1.

by the last Adam, from whom he also received his soul, to give him life. . . . The second Adam stamped his image on the first Adam when he created him. That is why he took on himself the role and the name of the first Adam, in order that he might not lose what he had made in his own image. The first Adam, the last Adam: the first had a beginning, the last knows no end. The last Adam is indeed the first; as he himself says: "I am the first and the last."[225]

360 Because of its common origin *the human race forms a unity,* for "from one ancestor [God] made all nations to inhabit the whole earth":[226]

225, 404, 775, 831 842

O wondrous vision, which makes us contemplate the human race in the unity of its origin in God . . . in the unity of its nature, composed equally in all men of a material body and a spiritual soul; in the unity of its immediate end and its mission in the world; in the unity of its dwelling, the earth, whose benefits all men, by right of nature, may use to sustain and develop life; in the unity of its supernatural end: God himself, to whom all ought to tend; in the unity of the means for attaining this end; . . . in the unity of the redemption wrought by Christ for all.[227]

361 "This law of human solidarity and charity,"[228] without excluding the rich variety of persons, cultures, and peoples, assures us that all men are truly brethren.

1939

II. "BODY AND SOUL BUT TRULY ONE"

362 The human person, created in the image of God, is a being at once corporeal and spiritual. The biblical account expresses this reality in symbolic language when it affirms that "then the LORD God formed man of dust from the ground, and breathed into his nostrils the breath of life; and man became a living being."[229] Man, whole and entire, is therefore *willed* by God.

1146, 2332

363 In Sacred Scripture the term "soul" often refers

1703

---

225 St. Peter Chrysologus, *Sermo* 117; PL 52, 520–521. 226 *Acts* 17:26; cf. *Tob* 8:6. 227 Pius XII, encyclical, *Summi Pontificatus* 3; cf. *NA* 1. 228 Pius XII, *Summi Pontificatus* 3. 229 *Gen* 2:7.

to human *life* or the entire human *person*.²³⁰ But "soul" also refers to the innermost aspect of man, that which is of greatest value in him,²³¹ that by which he is most especially in God's image: "soul" signifies the *spiritual principle* in man.

364   The human body shares in the dignity of "the image of God": it is a human body precisely because it
1004   is animated by a spiritual soul, and it is the whole human person that is intended to become, in the body of Christ, a temple of the Spirit.²³²

2289   Man, though made of body and soul, is a unity. Through his very bodily condition he sums up in himself the elements of the material world. Through him they are thus brought to their highest perfection and can raise their voice in praise freely given to the Creator. For this reason man may not despise his bodily life. Rather he is obliged to regard his body as good and to hold it in honor since God has created it and will raise it up on the last day.²³³

365   The unity of soul and body is so profound that one has to consider the soul to be the "form" of the body:²³⁴ i.e., it is because of its spiritual soul that the body made of matter becomes a living, human body; spirit and matter, in man, are not two natures united, but rather their union forms a single nature.

366   The Church teaches that every spiritual soul is
1005   created immediately by God—it is not "produced" by
997   the parents—and also that it is immortal: it does not perish when it separates from the body at death, and it will be reunited with the body at the final Resurrection.²³⁵

367   Sometimes the soul is distinguished from the spirit: St. Paul for instance prays that God may sanctify
2083   his people "wholly," with "spirit and soul and body" kept sound and blameless at the Lord's coming.²³⁶ The

---

230 Cf. Mt 16:25–26; *Jn* 15:13; *Acts* 2:41.   231 Cf. *Mt* 10:28; 26:38; *Jn* 12:27; 2 *Macc* 6:30.   232 Cf. *1 Cor* 6:19–20; 15:44–45.   233 *GS* 14 § 1; cf. *Dan* 3:57–80.   234 Cf. Council of Vienne (1312): DS 902.   235 Cf. Pius XII, *Humani Generis:* DS 3896; Paul VI, *CPG* § 8; Lateran Council V (1513): DS 1440. 236 *1 Thess* 5:23.

Church teaches that this distinction does not introduce a duality into the soul.[237] "Spirit" signifies that from creation man is ordered to a supernatural end and that his soul can gratuitously be raised beyond all it deserves to communion with God.[238]

368 The spiritual tradition of the Church also emphasizes the *heart,* in the biblical sense of the depths of one's being, where the person decides for or against God.[239]

478, 582, 1431, 1764 2517, 2562 2843

III. "MALE AND FEMALE HE CREATED THEM" *2331-2336*

Equality and difference willed by God
369 Man and woman have been *created,* which is to say, *willed* by God: on the one hand, in perfect equality as human persons; on the other, in their respective beings as man and woman. "Being man" or "being woman" is a reality which is good and willed by God: man and woman possess an inalienable dignity which comes to them immediately from God their Creator.[240] Man and woman are both with one and the same dignity "in the image of God." In their "being-man" and "being-woman," they reflect the Creator's wisdom and goodness.

370 In no way is God in man's image. He is neither man nor woman. God is pure spirit in which there is no place for the difference between the sexes. But the respective "perfections" of man and woman reflect something of the *42, 239* infinite perfection of God: those of a mother and those of a father and husband.[241]

"Each for the other"—"A unity in two"
371 God created man and woman *together* and willed each *for* the other. The Word of God gives us to understand this through various features of the sacred text. "It is not good that the man should be alone. I will *1605*

237 Cf. Council of Constantinople IV (870): DS 657. **238** Cf. Vatican Council I, *Dei Filius:* DS 3005; GS 22 § 5; *Humani generis:* DS 3891. **239** Cf. *Jer* 31:33; *Deut* 6:5; 29:3; *Isa* 29:13; *Ezek* 36:26; *Mt* 6:21; *Lk* 8:15; *Rom* 5:5. **240** Cf. *Gen* 2:7, 22. **241** Cf. *Isa* 49:14–15; 66:13; *Ps* 131:2–3; *Hos* 11:1–4; *Jer* 3:4–19.

make him a helper fit for him."[242] None of the animals can be man's partner.[243] The woman God "fashions" from the man's rib and brings to him elicits on the man's part a cry of wonder, an exclamation of love and communion: "This at last is bone of my bones and flesh of my flesh."[244] Man discovers woman as another "I," sharing the same humanity.

372   Man and woman were made "for each other"— not that God left them half-made and incomplete: he created them to be a communion of persons, in which each can be "helpmate" to the other, for they are equal as persons ("bone of my bones . . .") and complementary as masculine and feminine. In marriage God unites them in such a way that, by forming "one flesh,"[245] they can transmit human life: "Be fruitful and multiply, and fill the earth."[246] By transmitting human life to their descendants, man and woman as spouses and parents cooperate in a unique way in the Creator's work.[247]

1652, 2366

373   In God's plan man and woman have the vocation of "subduing" the earth[248] as stewards of God. This sovereignty is not to be an arbitrary and destructive domination. God calls man and woman, made in the image of the Creator "who loves everything that exists,"[249] to share in his providence toward other creatures; hence their responsibility for the world God has entrusted to them.

307
2415

IV.   MAN IN PARADISE

374   The first man was not only created good, but was also established in friendship with his Creator and in harmony with himself and with the creation around him, in a state that would be surpassed only by the glory of the new creation in Christ.

54

375   The Church, interpreting the symbolism of biblical language in an authentic way, in the light of the New Testament and Tradition, teaches that our first parents,

---

242 *Gen* 2:18.   243 *Gen* 2:19–20.   244 *Gen* 2:23.   245 *Gen* 2:24.   246 *Gen* 1:28.   247 Cf. *GS* 50 § 1.   248 *Gen* 1:28.   249 *Wis* 11:24.

Adam and Eve, were constituted in an original "state of holiness and justice."[250] This grace of original holiness *1997* was "to share in . . . divine life."[251]

376 By the radiance of this grace all dimensions of man's life were confirmed. As long as he remained in the divine intimacy, man would not have to suffer or die.[252] The inner harmony of the human person, the harmony *1008, 1502* between man and woman,[253] and finally the harmony between the first couple and all creation, comprised the state called "original justice."

377 The "mastery" over the world that God offered *2514* man from the beginning was realized above all within man himself: *mastery of self.* The first man was unimpaired and ordered in his whole being because he was free from the triple concupiscence[254] that subjugates him to the pleasures of the senses, covetousness for earthly goods, and self-assertion, contrary to the dictates of reason.

378 The sign of man's familiarity with God is that *2415* God places him in the garden.[255] There he lives "to till it *2427* and keep it." Work is not yet a burden,[256] but rather the collaboration of man and woman with God in perfecting the visible creation.

379 This entire harmony of original justice, foreseen for man in God's plan, will be lost by the sin of our first parents.

IN BRIEF

380 "Father, . . . you formed man in your own likeness and set him over the whole world to serve you, his creator, and to rule over all creatures" (*Roman Missal,* EP IV 118).

381 Man is predestined to reproduce the image of God's Son made man, the "image of the invisible God" (*Col* 1:15), so that Christ shall be the first-

---

250 Cf. Council of Trent (1546): DS 1511. 251 Cf. *LG* 2. 252 Cf. *Gen* 2:17; 3:16, 19. 253 Cf. *Gen* 2:25. 254 Cf. *1 Jn* 2:16. 255 Cf. *Gen* 2:8. 256 *Gen* 2:15; cf. 3:17–19.

born of a multitude of brothers and sisters (cf. *Eph* 1:3–6; *Rom* 8:29).

382   "Man, though made of body and soul, is a unity" (*GS* 14 § 1). The doctrine of the faith affirms that the spiritual and immortal soul is created immediately by God.

383   "God did not create man a solitary being. From the beginning, 'male and female he created them' (*Gen* 1:27). This partnership of man and woman constitutes the first form of communion between persons" (*GS* 12 § 4).

384   Revelation makes known to us the state of original holiness and justice of man and woman before sin: from their friendship with God flowed the happiness of their existence in paradise.

Paragraph 7. The Fall

385   God is infinitely good and all his works are good. Yet no one can escape the experience of suffering or the evils in nature which seem to be linked to the limitations proper to creatures: and above all to the question of moral evil. Where does evil come from? "I sought whence evil comes and there was no solution," said St. Augustine,[257] and his own painful quest would only be resolved by his conversion to the living God. For "the mystery of lawlessness" is clarified only in the light of the "mystery of our religion."[258] The revelation of divine love in Christ manifested at the same time the extent of evil and the superabundance of grace.[259] We must therefore approach the question of the origin of evil by fixing the eyes of our faith on him who alone is its conqueror.[260]

309

457
1848
539

---

257 St. Augustine, *Conf.* 7, 7, 11: PL 32, 739.   258 *2 Thess* 2:7; *1 Tim* 3:16.
259 Cf. *Rom* 5:20.   260 Cf. *Lk* 11:21–22; *Jn* 16:11; *1 Jn* 3:8.

I.   WHERE SIN ABOUNDED, GRACE ABOUNDED
ALL THE MORE

The reality of sin

386   Sin is present in human history; any attempt to ignore it or to give this dark reality other names would be futile. To try to understand what sin is, one must first recognize *the profound relation of man to God,* for only in this relationship is the evil of sin unmasked in its true identity as humanity's rejection of God and opposition to him, even as it continues to weigh heavy on human life and history.   1847

387   Only the light of divine Revelation clarifies the reality of sin and particularly of the sin committed at mankind's origins. Without the knowledge Revelation gives of God we cannot recognize sin clearly and are tempted to explain it as merely a developmental flaw, a psychological weakness, a mistake, or the necessary consequence of an inadequate social structure, etc. Only in the knowledge of God's plan for man can we grasp that sin is an abuse of the freedom that God gives to created persons so that they are capable of loving him and loving one another.   1848 1739

Original Sin—an essential truth of the faith

388   With the progress of Revelation, the reality of sin is also illuminated. Although to some extent the People of God in the Old Testament had tried to understand the pathos of the human condition in the light of the history of the fall narrated in Genesis, they could not grasp this story's ultimate meaning, which is revealed only in the light of the death and Resurrection of Jesus Christ.[261] We must know Christ as the source of grace in order to know Adam as the source of sin. The Spirit-Paraclete, sent by the risen Christ, came to "convict the world concerning sin,"[262] by revealing him who is its Redeemer.   431 208 359 729

389   The doctrine of original sin is, so to speak, the

---

261 Cf. *Rom* 5:12–21.   262 *Jn* 16:8.

"reverse side" of the Good News that Jesus is the Sav-
422 ior of all men, that all need salvation, and that salvation
is offered to all through Christ. The Church, which has
the mind of Christ,[263] knows very well that we cannot
tamper with the revelation of original sin without un-
dermining the mystery of Christ.

How to read the account of the Fall

390   The account of the fall in *Genesis* 3 uses figura-
tive language, but affirms a primeval event, a deed that
289 took place *at the beginning of the history of man.*[264]
Revelation gives us the certainty of faith that the whole
of human history is marked by the original fault freely
committed by our first parents.[265]

II.   THE FALL OF THE ANGELS

391   Behind the disobedient choice of our first parents lurks a seductive voice, opposed to God, which
2538 makes them fall into death out of envy.[266] Scripture and
the Church's Tradition see in this being a fallen angel,
called "Satan" or the "devil."[267] The Church teaches
that Satan was at first a good angel, made by God: "The
devil and the other demons were indeed created naturally good by God, but they became evil by their own
doing."[268]

392   Scripture speaks of a sin of these angels.[269] This
"fall" consists in the free choice of these created spirits,
who radically and irrevocably *rejected* God and his
1850 reign. We find a reflection of that rebellion in the
tempter's words to our first parents: "You will be like
God."[270] The devil "has sinned from the beginning"; he
2482 is "a liar and the father of lies."[271]

393   It is the *irrevocable* character of their choice, and
1033-1037 not a defect in the infinite divine mercy, that makes the
1022 angels' sin unforgivable. "There is no repentance for the

---

263 Cf. *1 Cor* 2:16.   264 Cf. *GS* 13 § 1.   265 Cf. Council of Trent: DS 1513;
Pius XII: DS 3897; Paul VI: AAS 58 (1966), 654.   266 Cf. *Gen* 3:1–5; *Wis* 2:24.
267 Cf. *Jn* 8:44; *Rev* 12:9.   268 Lateran Council IV (1215): DS 800.   269 Cf. *2
Pet* 2:4.   270 *Gen* 3:5.   271 *1 Jn* 3:8; *Jn* 8:44.

angels after their fall, just as there is no repentance for men after death."[272]

394 Scripture witnesses to the disastrous influence of the one Jesus calls "a murderer from the beginning," who would even try to divert Jesus from the mission received from his Father.[273] "The reason the Son of God appeared was to destroy the works of the devil."[274] In its consequences the gravest of these works was the mendacious seduction that led man to disobey God.

538-540
550
2846-2849

395 The power of Satan is, nonetheless, not infinite. He is only a creature, powerful from the fact that he is pure spirit, but still a creature. He cannot prevent the building up of God's reign. Although Satan may act in the world out of hatred for God and his kingdom in Christ Jesus, and although his action may cause grave injuries—of a spiritual nature and, indirectly, even of a physical nature—to each man and to society, the action is permitted by divine providence which with strength and gentleness guides human and cosmic history. It is a great mystery that providence should permit diabolical activity, but "we know that in everything God works for good with those who love him."[275]

309

1673
412

2850-2854

III. ORIGINAL SIN

Freedom put to the test

396 God created man in his image and established him in his friendship. A spiritual creature, man can live this friendship only in free submission to God. The prohibition against eating "of the tree of the knowledge of good and evil" spells this out: "for in the day that you eat of it, you shall die."[276] The "tree of the knowledge of good and evil"[277] symbolically evokes the insurmountable limits that man, being a creature, must freely recognize and respect with trust. Man is dependent on his

1730
311

---

272 St. John Damascene, *De Fide orth.* 2, 4: PG 94, 877. 273 *Jn* 8:44; cf. *Mt* 4:1–11. 274 *1 Jn* 3:8. 275 *Rom* 8:28. 276 *Gen* 2:17. 277 *Gen* 2:17.

Creator and subject to the laws of creation and to the
301 moral norms that govern the use of freedom.

Man's first sin

1707, 2541 **397**   Man, tempted by the devil, let his trust in his
1850, 215 Creator die in his heart and, abusing his freedom, dis-
obeyed God's command. This is what man's first sin
consisted of.[278] All subsequent sin would be disobedience toward God and lack of trust in his goodness.

398   In that sin man *preferred* himself to God and by
that very act scorned him. He chose himself over and
2084 against God, against the requirements of his creaturely
status and therefore against his own good. Created in a
state of holiness, man was destined to be fully "di-
2113 vinized" by God in glory. Seduced by the devil, he
wanted to "be like God," but "without God, before
God, and not in accordance with God."[279]

399   Scripture portrays the tragic consequences of
this first disobedience. Adam and Eve immediately lose
the grace of original holiness.[280] They become afraid of
the God of whom they have conceived a distorted image—that of a God jealous of his prerogatives.[281]

1607 **400**   The harmony in which they had found them-
2514 selves, thanks to original justice, is now destroyed: the
602, 1008 control of the soul's spiritual faculties over the body is
shattered; the union of man and woman becomes sub-
ject to tensions, their relations henceforth marked by
lust and domination.[282] Harmony with creation is broken: visible creation has become alien and hostile to
man.[283] Because of man, creation is now subject "to its
bondage to decay."[284] Finally, the consequence explicitly
foretold for this disobedience will come true: man will
"return to the ground,"[285] for out of it he was taken.
Death makes its entrance into human history.[286]

401   After that first sin, the world is virtually inun-

---

278 Cf. *Gen* 3:1–11; *Rom* 5:19.   279 St. Maximus the Confessor, *Ambigua:* PG
91, 1156C; cf. *Gen* 3:5.   280 Cf. *Rom* 3:23.   281 Cf. *Gen* 3:5–10.   282 Cf.
Gen 3:7–16.   283 Cf. *Gen* 3:17, 19.   284 *Rom* 8:21.   285 *Gen* 3:19; cf. 2:17.
286 Cf. *Rom* 5:12.

dated by sin. There is Cain's murder of his brother Abel and the universal corruption which follows in the wake of sin. Likewise, sin frequently manifests itself in the history of Israel, especially as infidelity to the God of the Covenant and as transgression of the Law of Moses. And even after Christ's atonement, sin raises its head in countless ways among Christians.[287] Scripture and the Church's Tradition continually recall the presence and *universality of sin in man's history:*

> What Revelation makes known to us is confirmed by our own experience. For when man looks into his own heart he finds that he is drawn toward what is wrong and sunk in many evils which cannot come from his good creator. Often refusing to acknowledge God as his source, man has also upset the relationship which should link him to his last end; and at the same time he has broken the right order that should reign within himself as well as between himself and other men and all creatures.[288]

The consequences of Adam's sin for humanity

402 All men are implicated in Adam's sin, as St. Paul affirms: "By one man's disobedience many [that is, all men] were made sinners": "sin came into the world through one man and death through sin, and so death spread to all men because all men sinned. . . ."[289] The Apostle contrasts the universality of sin and death with the universality of salvation in Christ. "Then as one man's trespass led to condemnation for all men, so one man's act of righteousness leads to acquittal and life for all men."[290]

403 Following St. Paul, the Church has always taught that the overwhelming misery which oppresses men and their inclination toward evil and death cannot be understood apart from their connection with Adam's sin and the fact that he has transmitted to us a sin with which we are all born afflicted, a sin which is the "death of the soul."[291] Because of this certainty of faith, the

*Margin references: 1865, 2259, 1739, 430, 605, 2606*

---

287 Cf. *Gen* 4:3–15; 6:5, 12; *Rom* 1:18–32; *1 Cor* 1–6; *Rev* 2–3. 288 *GS* 13 § 1. 289 *Rom* 5:12, 19. 290 *Rom* 5:18. 291 Cf. Council of Trent: *DS* 1512.

1250 Church baptizes for the remission of sins even tiny infants who have not committed personal sin.[292]

404   How did the sin of Adam become the sin of all his descendants? The whole human race is in Adam "as one body of one man."[293] By this "unity of the human race" all men are implicated in Adam's sin, as all are im-
360 plicated in Christ's justice. Still, the transmission of original sin is a mystery that we cannot fully under-
50 stand. But we do know by Revelation that Adam had received original holiness and justice not for himself alone, but for all human nature. By yielding to the tempter, Adam and Eve committed a *personal sin,* but this sin affected *the human nature* that they would then transmit *in a fallen state.*[294] It is a sin which will be transmitted by propagation to all mankind, that is, by the transmission of a human nature deprived of original holiness and justice. And that is why original sin is called "sin" only in an analogical sense: it is a sin "contracted" and not "committed"—a state and not an act.

405   Although it is proper to each individual,[295] original sin does not have the character of a personal fault in any of Adam's descendants. It is a deprivation of original holiness and justice, but human nature has not been totally corrupted: it is wounded in the natural powers proper to it; subject to ignorance, suffering, and the dominion of death; and inclined to sin—an inclination to
2515 evil that is called "concupiscence." Baptism, by impart-
1264 ing the life of Christ's grace, erases original sin and turns a man back toward God, but the consequences for nature, weakened and inclined to evil, persist in man and summon him to spiritual battle.

406   The Church's teaching on the transmission of original sin was articulated more precisely in the fifth century, especially under the impulse of St. Augustine's reflections against Pelagianism, and in the sixteenth century, in opposition to the Protestant Reformation. Pelagius held that man could, by the natural power of free will and without

---

292 Cf. Council of Trent: DS 1514.   293 St. Thomas Aquinas, *De Malo* 4, 1.
294 Cf. Council of Trent: DS 1511–1512.   295 Cf. Council of Trent: DS 1513.

the necessary help of God's grace, lead a morally good life; he thus reduced the influence of Adam's fault to bad example. The first Protestant reformers, on the contrary, taught that original sin has radically perverted man and destroyed his freedom; they identified the sin inherited by each man with the tendency to evil (concupiscentia), which would be insurmountable. The Church pronounced on the meaning of the data of Revelation on original sin especially at the second Council of Orange (529)[296] and at the Council of Trent (1546).[297]

A hard battle . . .

407   The doctrine of original sin, closely connected with that of redemption by Christ, provides lucid discernment of man's situation and activity in the world. By our first parents' sin, the devil has acquired a certain domination over man, even though man remains free. Original sin entails "captivity under the power of him who thenceforth had the power of death, that is, the devil."[298] Ignorance of the fact that man has a wounded nature inclined to evil gives rise to serious errors in the areas of education, politics, social action,[299] and morals.

2015, 2852

1888

408   The consequences of original sin and of all men's personal sins put the world as a whole in the sinful condition aptly described in St. John's expression, "the sin of the world."[300] This expression can also refer to the negative influence exerted on people by communal situations and social structures that are the fruit of men's sins.[301]

1865

409   This dramatic situation of "the whole world [which] is in the power of the evil one"[302] makes man's life a battle:

2516

> The whole of man's history has been the story of dour combat with the powers of evil, stretching, so our Lord tells us, from the very dawn of history until the last day. Finding himself in the midst of the battlefield man has to struggle to do what is right, and it is at great cost to himself, and aided by God's

---

296 DS 371–372.   297 Cf. DS 1510–1516.   298 Council of Trent (1546): DS 1511; cf. *Heb* 2:14.   299 Cf. John Paul II, *CA* 25.   300 *Jn* 1:29.   301 Cf. John Paul II, *RP* 16.   302 *1 Jn* 5:19; cf. *1 Pet* 5:8.

grace, that he succeeds in achieving his own inner integrity.[303]

IV. "YOU DID NOT ABANDON HIM TO THE POWER OF DEATH"

55, 705
1609, 2568

410   After his fall, man was not abandoned by God. On the contrary, God calls him and in a mysterious way heralds the coming victory over evil and his restoration from his fall.[304] This passage in Genesis is called the *Protoevangelium* ("first gospel"): the first announcement of the Messiah and Redeemer, of a battle between the serpent and the Woman, and of the final victory of a descendant of hers.

675

359, 615

411   The Christian tradition sees in this passage an announcement of the "New Adam" who, because he "became obedient unto death, even death on a cross," makes amends superabundantly for the disobedience of Adam.[305] Furthermore many Fathers and Doctors of the Church have seen the woman announced in the *Protoevangelium* as Mary, the mother of Christ, the "new Eve." Mary benefited first of all and uniquely from Christ's victory over sin: she was preserved from all stain of original sin and by a special grace of God committed no sin of any kind during her whole earthly life.[306]

491

412   But *why did God not prevent the first man from sinning?* St. Leo the Great responds, "Christ's inexpressible grace gave us blessings better than those the demon's envy had taken away."[307] And St. Thomas Aquinas wrote, "There is nothing to prevent human nature's being raised up to something greater, even after sin; God permits evil in order to draw forth some greater good. Thus St. Paul says, 'Where sin increased, grace abounded all the more'; and the Exultet sings, 'O happy fault, . . . which gained for us so great a Redeemer!' "[308]

310, 395

272

1994

---

303 GS 37 § 2.   304 Cf. *Gen* 3:9, 15.   305 Cf. *1 Cor* 15:21–22, 45; *Phil* 2:8; *Rom* 5:19–20.   306 Cf. Pius IX, *Ineffabilis Deus*: DS 2803; Council of Trent: DS 1573.   307 St. Leo the Great, *Sermo* 73, 4: PL 54, 396.   308 St. Thomas Aquinas, *STh* III, 1, 3, *ad* 3; cf. *Rom* 5:20.

IN BRIEF

413 "God did not make death, and he does not delight in the death of the living. . . . It was through the devil's envy that death entered the world" (*Wis* 1:13; 2:24).

414 Satan or the devil and the other demons are fallen angels who have freely refused to serve God and his plan. Their choice against God is definitive. They try to associate man in their revolt against God.

415 "Although set by God in a state of rectitude, man, enticed by the evil one, abused his freedom at the very start of history. He lifted himself up against God and sought to attain his goal apart from him" (*GS* 13 § 1).

416 By his sin Adam, as the first man, lost the original holiness and justice he had received from God, not only for himself but for all human beings.

417 Adam and Eve transmitted to their descendants human nature wounded by their own first sin and hence deprived of original holiness and justice; this deprivation is called "original sin."

418 As a result of original sin, human nature is weakened in its powers; subject to ignorance, suffering, and the domination of death; and inclined to sin. (This inclination is called "concupiscence.")

419 "We therefore hold, with the Council of Trent, that original sin is transmitted with human nature, 'by propagation, not by imitation' and that it is . . . 'proper to each' " (Paul VI, *CPG* § 16).

420 The victory that Christ won over sin has given us greater blessings than those which sin had taken from us: "where sin increased, grace abounded all the more" (*Rom* 5:20).

421   Christians believe that "the world has been established and kept in being by the Creator's love; has fallen into slavery to sin but has been set free by Christ, crucified and risen to break the power of the evil one . . ." (*GS* 2 § 2).

CHAPTER TWO
I BELIEVE IN JESUS CHRIST, THE ONLY SON OF GOD

The Good News: God has sent his Son

422   "But when the time had fully come, God sent forth his Son, born of a woman, born under the law, to redeem those who were under the law, so that we might receive adoption as sons."[1] This is "the gospel of Jesus Christ, the Son of God":[2] God has visited his people. He has fulfilled the promise he made to Abraham and his descendants. He acted far beyond all expectation—he has sent his own "beloved Son."[3]

389

2763

423   We believe and confess that Jesus of Nazareth, born a Jew of a daughter of Israel at Bethlehem at the time of King Herod the Great and the emperor Caesar Augustus, a carpenter by trade, who died crucified in Jerusalem under the procurator Pontius Pilate during the reign of the emperor Tiberius, is the eternal Son of God made man. He "came from God,"[4] "descended from heaven,"[5] and "came in the flesh."[6] For "the Word became flesh and dwelt among us, full of grace and truth; we have beheld his glory, glory as of the only Son from the Father. . . . And from his fullness have we all received, grace upon grace."[7]

424   Moved by the grace of the Holy Spirit and drawn by the Father, we believe in Jesus and confess: "You are the Christ, the Son of the living God."[8] On the

---

1 *Gal* 4:4–5. 2 *Mk* 1:1. 3 *Mk* 1:11; cf. *Lk* 1:55, 68. 4 *Jn* 13:3. 5 *Jn* 3:13; 6:33. 6 1 *Jn* 4:2. 7 *Jn* 1:14, 16. 8 *Mt* 16:16.

rock of this faith confessed by St. Peter, Christ built his   683, 552
Church.[9]

"To preach . . . the unsearchable riches of Christ"[10]

425   The transmission of the Christian faith consists
primarily in proclaiming Jesus Christ in order to lead
others to faith in him. From the beginning, the first disciples burned with the desire to proclaim Christ: "We
cannot but speak of what we have seen and heard."[11]
And they invite people of every era to enter into the joy   850, 858
of their communion with Christ:

> That which was from the beginning, which we have
> heard, which we have seen with our eyes, which we
> have looked upon and touched with our hands,
> concerning the word of life—the life was made
> manifest, and we saw it, and testify to it, and pro-
> claim to you the eternal life which was with the Fa-
> ther and was made manifest to us—that which we
> have seen and heard we proclaim also to you, so
> that you may have fellowship with us; and our fel-
> lowship is with the Father and with his Son Jesus
> Christ. And we are writing this that our joy may be
> complete.[12]

At the heart of catechesis: Christ

426   "At the heart of catechesis we find, in essence, a
Person, the Person of Jesus of Nazareth, the only Son
from the Father . . . who suffered and died for us and
who now, after rising, is living with us forever."[13] To   1698
catechize is "to reveal in the Person of Christ the whole
of God's eternal design reaching fulfillment in that Person. It is to seek to understand the meaning of Christ's
actions and words and of the signs worked by him."[14]   513
Catechesis aims at putting "people . . . in communion
. . . with Jesus Christ: only he can lead us to the love of
the Father in the Spirit and make us share in the life of
the Holy Trinity."[15]   260

---

9 Cf. *Mt* 16:18; St. Leo the Great, *Sermo* 4, 3: PL 54, 150–152; 51, 1: PL 54,
308–309; 62, 2: PL 54, 350–351; 83, 3: PL 54, 431–432.   10 *Eph* 3:8.   11 *Acts*
4:20.   12 *1 Jn* 1:1–4.   13 *CT* 5.   14 *CT* 5.   15 *CT* 5.

427   In catechesis "Christ, the Incarnate Word and Son of God, ... is taught—everything else is taught with reference to him—and it is Christ alone who teaches—anyone else teaches to the extent that he is Christ's spokesman, enabling Christ to teach with his lips. ... Every catechist should be able to apply to himself the mysterious words of Jesus: 'My teaching is not mine, but his who sent me.' "[16]

428   Whoever is called "to teach Christ" must first seek "the surpassing worth of knowing Christ Jesus"; he must suffer "the loss of all things ..." in order to "gain Christ and be found in him," and "to know him and the power of his resurrection, and [to] share his sufferings, becoming like him in his death, that if possible [he] may attain the resurrection from the dead."[17]

429   From this loving knowledge of Christ springs the desire to proclaim him, to "evangelize," and to lead others to the "yes" of faith in Jesus Christ. But at the same time the need to know this faith better makes itself felt. To this end, following the order of the Creed, Jesus' principal titles—"Christ," "Son of God," and "Lord" *(article 2)*—will be presented. The Creed next confesses the chief mysteries of his life—those of his Incarnation *(article 3)*, Paschal mystery *(articles 4 and 5)*, and glorification *(articles 6 and 7)*.

ARTICLE 2
"AND IN JESUS CHRIST, HIS ONLY SON, OUR LORD"

I.   JESUS
430   Jesus means in Hebrew: "God saves." At the annunciation, the angel Gabriel gave him the name Jesus as his proper name, which expresses both his identity and his mission.[18] Since God alone can forgive sins, it is God who, in Jesus his eternal Son made man, "will save

---

16 CT 6; cf. *Jn* 7:16.   17 *Phil* 3:8–11.   18 Cf. *Lk* 1:31.

his people from their sins."[19] In Jesus, God recapitulates 402
all of his history of salvation on behalf of men.

431 In the history of salvation God was not content
to deliver Israel "out of the house of bondage"[20] by
bringing them out of Egypt. He also saves them from
their sin. Because sin is always an offense against God,
only he can forgive it.[21] For this reason Israel, becoming 1441, 1850
more and more aware of the universality of sin, will no
longer be able to seek salvation except by invoking the 388
name of the Redeemer God.[22]

432 The name "Jesus" signifies that the very name of
God is present in the person of his Son, made man for
the universal and definitive redemption from sins. It is 589, 2666
the divine name that alone brings salvation, and hence- 389
forth all can invoke his name, for Jesus united himself
to all men through his Incarnation,[23] so that "there is no 161
other name under heaven given among men by which
we must be saved."[24]

433 The name of the Savior God was invoked only
once in the year by the high priest in atonement for
the sins of Israel, after he had sprinkled the mercy seat
in the Holy of Holies with the sacrificial blood. The
mercy seat was the place of God's presence.[25] When 615
St. Paul speaks of Jesus whom "God put forward as an
expiation by his blood," he means that in Christ's
humanity "God was in Christ reconciling the world
to himself."[26]

434 Jesus' Resurrection glorifies the name of the Savior God, for from that time on it is the name of Jesus
that fully manifests the supreme power of the "name
which is above every name."[27] The evil spirits fear his 2812
name; in his name his disciples perform miracles, for the
Father grants all they ask in this name.[28] 2614

435 The name of Jesus is at the heart of Christian

19 Mt 1:21; cf. 2:7. 20 Deut 5:6. 21 Cf. Ps 51:4, 12. 22 Cf. Ps 79:9. 23 Cf.
Jn 3:18; Acts 2:21; 5:41; 3 Jn 7; Rom 10:6–13. 24 Acts 4:12; cf. 9:14; Jas 2:7.
25 Cf. Ex 25:22; Lev 16:2, 15–16; Num 7:89; Sir 50:20; Heb 9:5, 7. 26 Rom
3:25; 2 Cor 5:19. 27 Phil 2:9–10; cf. Jn 12:28. 28 Cf. Acts 16:16–18;
19:13–16; Mk 16:17; Jn 15:16.

prayer. All liturgical prayers conclude with the words
2667-2668 "through our Lord Jesus Christ." The *Hail Mary*
reaches its high point in the words "blessed is the fruit
2676 of thy womb, Jesus." The Eastern prayer of the heart,
the *Jesus Prayer,* says: "Lord Jesus Christ, Son of God,
have mercy on me, a sinner." Many Christians, such as
St. Joan of Arc, have died with the one word "Jesus" on
their lips.

II.   CHRIST

436   The word "Christ" comes from the Greek translation of the Hebrew *Messiah,* which means
"anointed." It became the name proper to Jesus only
690, 695 because he accomplished perfectly the divine mission
that "Christ" signifies. In effect, in Israel those consecrated to God for a mission that he gave were anointed
in his name. This was the case for kings, for priests and,
in rare instances, for prophets.[29] This had to be the case
all the more so for the Messiah whom God would send
to inaugurate his kingdom definitively.[30] It was necessary that the Messiah be anointed by the Spirit of the
711-716 Lord at once as king and priest, and also as prophet.[31]
Jesus fulfilled the messianic hope of Israel in his three-
783 fold office of priest, prophet, and king.

437   To the shepherds, the angel announced the birth
of Jesus as the Messiah promised to Israel: "To you is
525, 486 born this day in the city of David a Savior, who is Christ
the Lord."[32] From the beginning he was "the one whom
the Father consecrated and sent into the world," conceived as "holy" in Mary's virginal womb.[33] God called
Joseph to "take Mary as your wife, for that which is
conceived in her is of the Holy Spirit," so that Jesus,
"who is called Christ," should be born of Joseph's
spouse into the messianic lineage of David.[34]

438   Jesus' messianic consecration reveals his divine
mission, "for the name 'Christ' implies 'he who

---

29 Cf. *Ex* 29:7; *Lev* 8:12; *1 Sam* 9:16; 10:1; 16:1, 12–13; *1 Kings* 1:39; 19:16.
30 Cf. *Ps* 2:2; *Acts* 4:26–27.   31 Cf. *Isa* 11:2; 61:1; *Zech* 4:14; 6:13: *Lk* 4:16–21.
32 *Lk* 2:11.   33 *Jn* 10:36: cf. *Lk* 1:35.   34 *Mt* 1:20; cf. *Mt* 1:16; *Rom* 1:1; 2
Tim 2:8; *Rev* 22:16.

anointed,' 'he who was anointed' and 'the very anoint- 727
ing with which he was anointed.' The one who anointed
is the Father, the one who was anointed is the Son, and
he was anointed with the Spirit who is the anointing."[35]
His eternal messianic consecration was revealed during
the time of his earthly life at the moment of his baptism 535
by John, when "God anointed Jesus of Nazareth with
the Holy Spirit and with power," "that he might be revealed to Israel"[36] as its Messiah. His works and words
will manifest him as "the Holy One of God."[37]

439   Many Jews and even certain Gentiles who
shared their hope recognized in Jesus the fundamental
attributes of the messianic "Son of David," promised by 528-529
God to Israel.[38] Jesus accepted his rightful title of Mes- 547
siah, though with some reserve because it was understood by some of his contemporaries in too human a
sense, as essentially political.[39]

440   Jesus accepted Peter's profession of faith, which
acknowledged him to be the Messiah, by announcing
the imminent Passion of the Son of Man.[40] He unveiled 552
the authentic content of his messianic kingship both in
the transcendent identity of the Son of Man "who came
down from heaven," and in his redemptive mission as
the suffering Servant: "The Son of Man came not to be
served but to serve, and to give his life as a ransom for
many."[41] Hence the true meaning of his kingship is re- 550
vealed only when he is raised high on the cross.[42] Only
after his Resurrection will Peter be able to proclaim Je- 445
sus' messianic kingship to the People of God: "Let all
the house of Israel therefore know assuredly that God
has made him both Lord and Christ, this Jesus whom
you crucified."[43]

---

35 St. Irenaeus, *Adv. haeres.*, 3, 18, 3: PG 7/1, 934.   36 *Acts* 10:38; *Jn* 1:31.   37
Mk 1:24; *Jn* 6:69; *Acts* 3:14.   38 Cf. *Mt* 2:2; 9:27; 12:23; 15:22; 20:30; 21:9, 15.
39 Cf. *Jn* 4:25–26; 6:15; 11:27; *Mt* 22:41–46; *Lk* 24:21.   40 Cf. *Mt* 16:16–23.
41 *Jn* 3:13; *Mt* 20:28; cf. *Jn* 6:62; *Dan* 7:13; *Isa* 53:10–12.   42 Cf. *Jn* 19:19–22;
Lk 23:39–43.   43 *Acts* 2:36.

III.   THE ONLY SON OF GOD

441   In the Old Testament, *"son of God"* is a title given to the angels, the Chosen People, the children of Israel, and their kings.[44] It signifies an adoptive sonship that establishes a relationship of particular intimacy between God and his creature. When the promised Messiah-King is called "son of God," it does not necessarily imply that he was more than human, according to the literal meaning of these texts. Those who called Jesus "son of God," as the Messiah of Israel, perhaps meant nothing more than this.[45]

442   Such is not the case for Simon Peter when he confesses Jesus as "the Christ, the Son of the living God," for Jesus responds solemnly: "Flesh and blood has not *revealed* this to you, but *my Father* who is in heaven."[46] Similarly Paul will write, regarding his conversion on the road to Damascus, "When he who had set me apart before I was born, and had called me through his grace, was pleased to reveal his Son to me, in order that I might preach him among the Gentiles. . . ."[47] "And in the synagogues immediately [Paul] proclaimed Jesus, saying, 'He is the Son of God.' "[48] From the beginning this acknowledgment of Christ's divine sonship will be the center of the apostolic faith, first professed by Peter as the Church's foundation.[49]

443   Peter could recognize the transcendent character of the Messiah's divine sonship because Jesus had clearly allowed it to be so understood. To his accusers' question before the Sanhedrin, "Are you the Son of God, then?" Jesus answered, "You say that I am."[50] Well before this, Jesus referred to himself as "the Son" who knows the Father, as distinct from the "servants" God had earlier sent to his people; he is superior even to the angels.[51] He distinguished his sonship from that of his disciples by never saying "our Father," except to

---

44 Cf. *Deut* 14:1; (LXX) 32:8; *Job* 1:6; *Ex* 4:22; *Hos* 2:1; 11:1; *Jer* 3:19; *Sir* 36:11; *Wis* 18:13; *2 Sam* 7:14; *Ps* 82:6.   45 Cf. *1 Chr* 17:13; *Ps* 2:7; *Mt* 27:54; *Lk* 23:47.   46 *Mt* 16:16–17.   47 *Gal* 1:15–16.   48 *Acts* 9:20.   49 Cf. *1 Thess* 1:10; *Jn* 20:31; *Mt* 16:18.   50 *Lk* 22:70; cf. *Mt* 26:64; *Mk* 14:61–62.   51 Cf. *Mt* 11:27; 21:34–38; 24:36.

command them: "You, then, pray like this: 'Our Father,' " and he emphasized this distinction, saying "my Father and your Father."[52]

2786

444   The Gospels report that at two solemn moments, the Baptism and the Transfiguration of Christ, the voice of the Father designates Jesus his "beloved Son."[53] Jesus calls himself the "only Son of God," and by this title affirms his eternal preexistence.[54] He asks for faith in "the name of the only Son of God."[55] In the centurion's exclamation before the crucified Christ, "Truly this man was the Son of God,"[56] that Christian confession is already heard. Only in the Paschal mystery can the believer give the title "Son of God" its full meaning.

536, 544

445   After his Resurrection, Jesus' divine sonship becomes manifest in the power of his glorified humanity. He was "designated Son of God in power according to the Spirit of holiness by his Resurrection from the dead."[57] The apostles can confess: "We have beheld his glory, glory as of the only Son from the Father, full of grace and truth."[58]

653

IV.   LORD

446   In the Greek translation of the Old Testament, the ineffable Hebrew name YHWH, by which God revealed himself to Moses,[59] is rendered as *Kyrios,* "Lord." From then on, *"Lord"* becomes the more usual name by which to indicate the divinity of Israel's God. The New Testament uses this full sense of the title "Lord" both for the Father and—what is new—for Jesus, who is thereby recognized as God Himself.[60]

209

447   Jesus ascribes this title to himself in a veiled way when he disputes with the Pharisees about the meaning of *Psalm* 110, but also in an explicit way when he addresses his apostles.[61] Throughout his public life, he

---

52 *Mt* 5:48; 6:8–9; 7:21; *Lk* 11:13; *Jn* 20:17.   53 Cf. *Mt* 3:17; cf. *Mt* 17:5.
54 *Jn* 3:16; cf. 10:36.   55 *Jn* 3:18.   56 *Mk* 15:39.   57 *Rom* 1:3; cf. *Acts* 13:33.
58 *Jn* 1:14.   59 Cf. *Ex* 3:14.   60 Cf. *1 Cor* 2:8.   61 Cf. *Mt* 22:41–46; cf. *Acts* 2:34–36; *Heb* 1:13; *Jn* 13:13.

548   demonstrated his divine sovereignty by works of power over nature, illnesses, demons, death, and sin.

448   Very often in the Gospels people address Jesus as "Lord." This title testifies to the respect and trust of those who approach him for help and healing.[62] At the prompting of the Holy Spirit, "Lord" expresses the 208, 683 recognition of the divine mystery of Jesus.[63] In the encounter with the risen Jesus, this title becomes adoration: "My Lord and my God!" It thus takes on a connotation of love and affection that remains proper to 641 the Christian tradition: "It is the Lord!"[64]

449   By attributing to Jesus the divine title "Lord," the first confessions of the Church's faith affirm from the beginning that the power, honor, and glory due to God the Father are due also to Jesus, because "he was 461 in the form of God,"[65] and the Father manifested the 653 sovereignty of Jesus by raising him from the dead and exalting him into his glory.[66]

450   From the beginning of Christian history, the assertion of Christ's lordship over the world and over history has implicitly recognized that man should not sub- 668-672 mit his personal freedom in an absolute manner to any earthly power, but only to God the Father and the Lord 2242 Jesus Christ: Caesar is not "the Lord."[67] "The Church . . . believes that the key, the center, and the purpose of the whole of man's history is to be found in its Lord and Master."[68]

451   Christian prayer is characterized by the title 2664-2665 "Lord," whether in the invitation to prayer ("The Lord 2817 be with you."), its conclusion ("through Christ our Lord"), or the exclamation full of trust and hope: *Maran atha* ("Our Lord, come!"), or *Marana tha* ("Come, Lord!")—"Amen. Come, Lord Jesus!"[69]

---

62 Cf. *Mt* 8:2; 14:30; 15:22; *et al.*   63 Cf. *Lk* 1:43; 2:11.   64 *Jn* 20:28; *Jn* 21:7.
65 Cf. *Acts* 2:34–36; *Rom* 9:5; *Titus* 2:13; *Rev* 5:13; *Phil* 2:6.   66 Cf. *Rom* 10:9;
1 Cor 12:3; *Phil* 2:9–11.   67 Cf. *Rev* 11:15; *Mk* 12:17; *Acts* 5:29.   68 *GS* 10 §
3; cf. 45 § 2.   69 *1 Cor* 16:22; *Rev* 22:20.

IN BRIEF

452   The name Jesus means "God saves." The child
born of the Virgin Mary is called Jesus, "for he
will save his people from their sins" (*Mt* 1:21):
"there is no other name under heaven given
among men by which we must be saved" (*Acts*
4:12).

453   The title "Christ" means "Anointed One" (Messiah). Jesus is the Christ, for "God anointed Jesus of Nazareth with the Holy Spirit and with
power" (*Acts* 10:38). He was the one "who is to
come" (*Lk* 7:19), the object of "the hope of Israel" (*Acts* 28:20).

454   The title "Son of God" signifies the unique and
eternal relationship of Jesus Christ to God his
Father: he is the only Son of the Father (cf. *Jn*
1:14, 18; 3:16, 18); he is God himself (cf. *Jn*
1:1). To be a Christian, one must believe that
Jesus Christ is the Son of God (cf. *Acts* 8:37; *1
Jn* 2:23).

455   The title "Lord" indicates divine sovereignty. To
confess or invoke Jesus as Lord is to believe in
his divinity. "No one can say 'Jesus is Lord' except by the Holy Spirit" (*1 Cor* 12:3).

ARTICLE 3
"HE WAS CONCEIVED BY THE POWER OF THE HOLY SPIRIT, AND WAS BORN OF THE VIRGIN MARY"

Paragraph 1. The Son of God Became Man

I.   WHY DID THE WORD BECOME FLESH?
456   With the Nicene Creed, we answer by confessing: "For us men and for our salvation he came down
from heaven; by the power of the Holy Spirit, he be-

came incarnate of the Virgin Mary, and was made man."

457 The Word became flesh for us *in order to save us by reconciling us with God,* who "loved us and sent his Son to be the expiation for our sins": "the Father has
607 sent his Son as the Savior of the world," and "he was revealed to take away sins":[70]

385
> Sick, our nature demanded to be healed; fallen, to be raised up; dead, to rise again. We had lost the possession of the good; it was necessary for it to be given back to us. Closed in the darkness, it was necessary to bring us the light; captives, we awaited a Savior; prisoners, help; slaves, a liberator. Are these things minor or insignificant? Did they not move God to descend to human nature and visit it, since humanity was in so miserable and unhappy a state?[71]

458 The Word became flesh *so that thus we might know God's love:* "In this the love of God was made
219 manifest among us, that God sent his only Son into the world, so that we might live through him."[72] "For God so loved the world that he gave his only Son, that whoever believes in him should not perish but have eternal life."[73]

459 The Word became flesh *to be our model of holi-*
520 *ness:* "Take my yoke upon you, and learn from me." "I am the way, and the truth, and the life; no one comes to
823, 2012 the Father, but by me."[74] On the mountain of the Transfiguration, the Father commands: "Listen to him!"[75] Je-
1717, 1965 sus is the model for the Beatitudes and the norm of the new law: "Love one another as I have loved you."[76] This love implies an effective offering of oneself, after his example.[77]

460 The Word became flesh to make us *"partakers of the divine nature":*[78] "For this is why the Word became
1265, 1391 man, and the Son of God became the Son of man: so that man, by entering into communion with the Word

---

70 1 *Jn* 4:10; 4:14; 3:5.   71 St. Gregory of Nyssa, *Orat. catech.* 15: PG 45, 48B.
72 1 *Jn* 4:9.   73 *Jn* 3:16.   74 *Mt* 11:29; *Jn* 14:6.   75 *Mk* 9:7; cf. *Deut* 6:4–5.
76 *Jn* 15:12.   77 Cf. *Mk* 8:34.   78 2 *Pet* 1:4.

and thus receiving divine sonship, might become a son of God."[79] "For the Son of God became man so that we might become God."[80] "The only-begotten Son of God, wanting to make us sharers in his divinity, assumed our nature, so that he, made man, might make men gods."[81] *1988*

II.   THE INCARNATION

461   Taking up St. John's expression, "The Word became flesh,"[82] the Church calls "Incarnation" the fact that the Son of God assumed a human nature in order to accomplish our salvation in it. In a hymn cited by St. Paul, the Church sings the mystery of the Incarnation: *653, 661* *449*

> Have this mind among yourselves, which is yours in Christ Jesus, who, though he was in the form of God, did not count equality with God a thing to be grasped, but emptied himself, taking the form of a servant, being born in the likeness of men. And being found in human form he humbled himself and became obedient unto death, even death on a cross.[83]

462   The *Letter to the Hebrews* refers to the same mystery:

> Consequently, when Christ came into the world, he said, "Sacrifices and offerings you have not desired, but a body have you prepared for me; in burnt offerings and sin offerings you have taken no pleasure. Then I said, 'Lo, I have come to do your will, O God.' "[84]

463   Belief in the true Incarnation of the Son of God is the distinctive sign of Christian faith: "By this you know the Spirit of God: every spirit which confesses that Jesus Christ has come in the flesh is of God."[85] Such is the joyous conviction of the Church from her beginning whenever she sings "the mystery of our religion": "He was manifested in the flesh."[86] *90*

79 St. Irenaeus, *Adv. haeres.* 3, 19, 1: PG 7/1, 939.   80 St. Athanasius, *De inc.*, 54, 3: PG 25, 192B.   81 St. Thomas Aquinas, *Opusc.* 57: 1–4.   82 *Jn* 1:14. 83 *Phil* 2:5–8; cf. *LH*, Saturday, Canticle at Evening Prayer.   84 *Heb* 10:5–7, citing *Ps* 40:6–8 ([7–9] LXX).   85 *1 Jn* 4:2.   86 *1 Tim* 3:16.

III.   TRUE GOD AND TRUE MAN

464   The unique and altogether singular event of the Incarnation of the Son of God does not mean that Jesus Christ is part God and part man, nor does it imply that he is the result of a confused mixture of the divine and the human. He became truly man while remaining truly God. Jesus Christ is true God and true man. During the first centuries, the Church had to defend and clarify this truth of faith against the heresies that falsified it.

465   The first heresies denied not so much Christ's divinity as his true humanity (Gnostic Docetism). From apostolic times the Christian faith has insisted on the true incarnation of God's Son "come in the flesh."[87] But already in the third century, the Church in a council at Antioch had to affirm against Paul of Samosata that Jesus Christ is Son of God by nature and not by adoption. The first ecumenical council of Nicaea in 325 confessed in its Creed that the Son of God is "begotten, not made, of the same substance *(homoousios)* as the Father," and condemned Arius, who had affirmed that the Son of God "came to be from things that were not" and that he was "from another substance" than that of the Father.[88]

466   The Nestorian heresy regarded Christ as a human person joined to the divine person of God's Son. Opposing this heresy, St. Cyril of Alexandria and the third ecumenical council at Ephesus in 431 confessed "that the Word, uniting to himself in his person the flesh animated by a rational soul, became man."[89] Christ's humanity has no other subject than the divine person of the Son of God, who assumed it and made it his own, from his conception. For this reason the Council of Ephesus proclaimed in 431 that Mary truly became the Mother of God by the human conception of the Son of God in her womb: "Mother of God, not that the nature of the Word or his divinity received the beginning of its existence from the holy Virgin, but that, since the holy

---

87 Cf. *1 Jn* 4:2–3; *2 Jn* 7.   88 Council of Nicaea I (325): DS 130, 126.
89 Council of Ephesus (431): DS 250.

body, animated by a rational soul, which the Word of God united to himself according to the hypostasis, was born from her, the Word is said to be born according to the flesh."[90]

467 The Monophysites affirmed that the human nature had ceased to exist as such in Christ when the divine person of God's Son assumed it. Faced with this heresy, the fourth ecumenical council, at Chalcedon in 451, confessed:

> Following the holy Fathers, we unanimously teach and confess one and the same Son, our Lord Jesus Christ: the same perfect in divinity and perfect in humanity, the same truly God and truly man, composed of rational soul and body; consubstantial with the Father as to his divinity and consubstantial with us as to his humanity; "like us in all things but sin." He was begotten from the Father before all ages as to his divinity and in these last days, for us and for our salvation, was born as to his humanity of the virgin Mary, the Mother of God.[91]

> We confess that one and the same Christ, Lord, and only-begotten Son, is to be acknowledged in two natures without confusion, change, division, or separation. The distinction between the natures was never abolished by their union, but rather the character proper to each of the two natures was preserved as they came together in one person *(prosopon)* and one hypostasis.[92]

468 After the Council of Chalcedon, some made of Christ's human nature a kind of personal subject. Against them, the fifth ecumenical council at Constantinople in 553 confessed that "there is but one *hypostasis* [or person], which is our Lord Jesus Christ, one of the Trinity."[93] Thus everything in Christ's human nature is to be attributed to his divine person as its proper subject, not only his miracles but also his sufferings and even his death: "He who was crucified in the flesh, our

254

616

---

90 Council of Ephesus: DS 251.   91 Council of Chalcedon (451): DS 301; cf. *Heb* 4:15.   92 Council of Chalcedon: DS 302.   93 Council of Constantinople II (553): DS 424.

Lord Jesus Christ, is true God, Lord of glory, and *one of the Holy Trinity.*"[94]

469   The Church thus confesses that Jesus is inseparably true God and true man. He is truly the Son of God
who, without ceasing to be God and Lord, became a
man and our brother:

> "What he was, he remained and what he was not,
> he assumed," sings the Roman Liturgy.[95] And the
> liturgy of St. John Chrysostom proclaims and sings:
> "O only-begotten Son and Word of God, immortal
> being, you who deigned for our salvation to be-
> come incarnate of the holy Mother of God and
> ever-virgin Mary, you who without change became
> man and were crucified, O Christ our God, you
> who by your death have crushed death, you who
> are one of the Holy Trinity, glorified with the Fa-
> ther and the Holy Spirit, save us!"[96]

IV.   How Is the Son of God Man?

470   Because "human nature was assumed, not ab-
sorbed,"[97] in the mysterious union of the Incarnation,
the Church was led over the course of centuries to confess the full reality of Christ's human soul, with its operations of intellect and will, and of his human body. In
parallel fashion, she had to recall on each occasion that
Christ's human nature belongs, as his own, to the divine
person of the Son of God, who assumed it. Everything
that Christ is and does in this nature derives from "one
of the Trinity." The Son of God therefore communicates
to his humanity his own personal mode of existence in
the Trinity. In his soul as in his body, Christ thus expresses humanly the divine ways of the Trinity:[98]

> The Son of God . . . worked with human hands; he
> thought with a human mind. He acted with a hu-
> man will, and with a human heart he loved. Born of
> the Virgin Mary, he has truly been made one of us,
> like to us in all things except sin.[99]

---

94 Council of Constantinople II (553): DS 432; cf. DS 424; Council of Ephesus,
DS 255.   95 *LH,* January 1, Antiphon for Morning Prayer; cf. St. Leo the Great,
Sermo in nat. Dom. 1, 2; PL 54, 191–192.   96 Liturgy of St. John Chrysostom,
Troparion "*O monogenes.*"   97 *GS* 22 § 2.   98 Cf. *Jn* 14:9–10.   99 *GS* 22 § 2.

Christ's soul and his human knowledge

471   Apollinarius of Laodicaea asserted that in Christ the divine Word had replaced the soul or spirit. Against this error the Church confessed that the eternal Son also assumed a rational, human soul.[100]   *363*

472   This human soul that the Son of God assumed is endowed with a true human knowledge. As such, this knowledge could not in itself be unlimited: it was exercised in the historical conditions of his existence in space and time. This is why the Son of God could, when he became man, "increase in wisdom and in stature, and in favor with God and man,"[101] and would even have to inquire for himself about what one in the human condition can learn only from experience.[102] This corresponded to the reality of his voluntary emptying of himself, taking "the form of a slave."[103]

473   But at the same time, this truly human knowledge of God's Son expressed the divine life of his person.[104] "The human nature of God's Son, *not by itself but by its union with the Word,* knew and showed forth in itself everything that pertains to God."[105] Such is first of all the case with the intimate and immediate knowledge that the Son of God made man has of his Father.[106]   *240* The Son in his human knowledge also showed the divine penetration he had into the secret thoughts of human hearts.[107]

474   By its union to the divine wisdom in the person of the Word incarnate, Christ enjoyed in his human knowledge the fullness of understanding of the eternal plans he had come to reveal.[108] What he admitted to not knowing in this area, he elsewhere declared himself not sent to reveal.[109]

---

100 Cf. Damasus I: DS 149.   101 *Lk* 2:52.   102 Cf. *Mk* 6:38; 8:27; *Jn* 11:34; etc.   103 *Phil* 2:7.   104 Cf. St. Gregory the Great, *"Sicut aqua" ad Eulogium, Epist. Lib.* 10, 39: PL 77, 1097 A ff.; DS 475.   105 St. Maximus the Confessor, *Qu. et dub.* 66: PG 90, 840A.   106 Cf. *Mk* 14:36; *Mt* 11:27; *Jn* 1:18; 8:55; etc. 107 Cf. *Mk* 2:8; *Jn* 2:25; 6:61; etc.   108 Cf. *Mk* 8:31; 9:31; 10:33–34; 14:18–20, 26–30.   109 Cf. *Mk* 13:32; *Acts* 1:7.

Christ's human will

475   Similarly, at the sixth ecumenical council, Constantinople III in 681, the Church confessed that Christ possesses two wills and two natural operations, divine and human. They are not opposed to each other, but cooperate in such a way that the Word made flesh willed humanly in obedience to his Father all that he had decided divinely with the Father and the Holy Spirit for our salvation.[110] Christ's human will "does not resist or oppose but rather submits to his divine and almighty will."[111]

2008
2824

Christ's true body

476   Since the Word became flesh in assuming a true humanity, Christ's body was finite.[112] Therefore the human face of Jesus can be portrayed; at the seventh ecumenical council (Nicaea II in 787) the Church recognized its representation in holy images to be legitimate.[113]

1159-1162
2129-2132

477   At the same time the Church has always acknowledged that in the body of Jesus "we see our God made visible and so are caught up in love of the God we cannot see."[114] The individual characteristics of Christ's body express the divine person of God's Son. He has made the features of his human body his own, to the point that they can be venerated when portrayed in a holy image, for the believer "who venerates the icon is venerating in it the person of the one depicted."[115]

The heart of the Incarnate Word

478   Jesus knew and loved us each and all during his life, his agony, and his Passion and gave himself up for each one of us: "The Son of God . . . loved me and gave himself for me."[116] He has loved us all with a human

487

---

110 Cf. Council of Constantinople III (681): DS 556–559.   111 Council of Constantinople III: DS 556.   112 Cf. Council of the Lateran (649): DS 504.   113 Cf. *Gal* 3:1; cf. Council of Nicaea II (787): DS 600–603.   114 *Roman Missal*, Preface of Christmas I.   115 Council of Nicaea II: DS 601.   116 *Gal* 2:20.

heart. For this reason, the Sacred Heart of Jesus, pierced by our sins and for our salvation,[117] "is quite rightly considered the chief sign and symbol of that ... love with which the divine Redeemer continually loves the eternal Father and all human beings" without exception.[118]

368
2669
766

IN BRIEF

479 At the time appointed by God, the only Son of the Father, the eternal Word, that is, the Word and substantial Image of the Father, became incarnate; without losing his divine nature he has assumed human nature.

480 Jesus Christ is true God and true man, in the unity of his divine person; for this reason he is the one and only mediator between God and men.

481 Jesus Christ possesses two natures, one divine and the other human, not confused, but united in the one person of God's Son.

482 Christ, being true God and true man, has a human intellect and will, perfectly attuned and subject to his divine intellect and divine will, which he has in common with the Father and the Holy Spirit.

483 The Incarnation is therefore the mystery of the wonderful union of the divine and human natures in the one person of the Word.

---

117 Cf. *Jn* 19:34. 118 Pius XII, encyclical, *Haurietis aquas* (1956): DS 3924; cf. DS 3812.

Paragraph 2. "Conceived by the Power of the Holy Spirit and Born of the Virgin Mary"

I. CONCEIVED BY THE POWER OF THE HOLY SPIRIT . . .

484   The Annunciation to Mary inaugurates "the fullness of time,"[119] the time of the fulfillment of God's promises and preparations. Mary was invited to conceive him in whom the "whole fullness of deity" would dwell "bodily."[120] The divine response to her question, "How can this be, since I know not man?" was given by the power of the Spirit: "The Holy Spirit will come upon you."[121]

461

721

485   The mission of the Holy Spirit is always conjoined and ordered to that of the Son.[122] The Holy Spirit, "the Lord, the giver of Life," is sent to sanctify the womb of the Virgin Mary and divinely fecundate it, causing her to conceive the eternal Son of the Father in a humanity drawn from her own.

689, 723

486   The Father's only Son, conceived as man in the womb of the Virgin Mary, is "Christ," that is to say, anointed by the Holy Spirit, from the beginning of his human existence, though the manifestation of this fact takes place only progressively: to the shepherds, to the magi, to John the Baptist, to the disciples.[123] Thus the whole life of Jesus Christ will make manifest "how God anointed Jesus of Nazareth with the Holy Spirit and with power."[124]

437

II.   . . . BORN OF THE VIRGIN MARY

487   What the Catholic faith believes about Mary is based on what it believes about Christ, and what it teaches about Mary illumines in turn its faith in Christ.

963

---

119 *Gal* 4:4.   120 *Col* 2:9.   121 *Lk* 1:34–35 (Gk.).   122 Cf. *Jn* 16:14–15.   123 Cf. *Mt* 1:20; 2:1–12; *Lk* 1:35; 2:8–20; *Jn* 1:31–34; 2:11.   124 *Acts* 10:38.

Mary's predestination

488 "God sent forth his Son," but to prepare a body for him,[125] he wanted the free cooperation of a creature. For this, from all eternity God chose for the mother of his Son a daughter of Israel, a young Jewish woman of Nazareth in Galilee, "a virgin betrothed to a man whose name was Joseph, of the house of David; and the virgin's name was Mary":[126]

> The Father of mercies willed that the Incarnation should be preceded by assent on the part of the predestined mother, so that just as a woman had a share in the coming of death, so also should a woman contribute to the coming of life.[127]

489 Throughout the Old Covenant the mission of many holy women *prepared* for that of Mary. At the very beginning there was Eve; despite her disobedience, she receives the promise of a posterity that will be victorious over the evil one, as well as the promise that she will be the mother of all the living.[128] By virtue of this promise, Sarah conceives a son in spite of her old age.[129] Against all human expectation God chooses those who were considered powerless and weak to show forth his faithfulness to his promises: Hannah, the mother of Samuel; Deborah; Ruth; Judith and Esther; and many other women.[130] Mary "stands out among the poor and humble of the Lord, who confidently hope for and receive salvation from him. After a long period of waiting the times are fulfilled in her, the exalted Daughter of Sion, and the new plan of salvation is established."[131]

722
410
145

64

The Immaculate Conception

490 To become the mother of the Savior, Mary "was enriched by God with gifts appropriate to such a role."[132] The angel Gabriel at the moment of the annunciation salutes her as "full of grace."[133] In fact, in order for Mary to be able to give the free assent of her faith

2676, 2853

---

125 *Gal* 4:4; *Heb* 10:5. 126 *Lk* 1:26–27. 127 *LG* 56; cf. *LG* 61. 128 Cf. *Gen* 3:15, 20. 129 Cf. *Gen* 18:10–14; 21:1–2. 130 Cf. *1 Cor* 1:17; *1 Sam* 1. 131 *LG* 55. 132 *LG* 56. 133 *Lk* 1:28.

to the announcement of her vocation, it was necessary
2001 that she be wholly borne by God's grace.

491   Through the centuries the Church has become
ever more aware that Mary, "full of grace" through
411 God,[134] was redeemed from the moment of her conception. That is what the dogma of the Immaculate Conception confesses, as Pope Pius IX proclaimed in 1854:

> The most Blessed Virgin Mary was, from the first
> moment of her conception, by a singular grace and
> privilege of almighty God and by virtue of the mer-
> its of Jesus Christ, Savior of the human race, pre-
> served immune from all stain of original sin.[135]

492   The "splendor of an entirely unique holiness" by
which Mary is "enriched from the first instant of her
conception" comes wholly from Christ: she is "redeemed, in a more exalted fashion, by reason of the
2011 merits of her Son."[136] The Father blessed Mary more
1077 than any other created person "in Christ with every
spiritual blessing in the heavenly places" and chose her
"in Christ before the foundation of the world, to be
holy and blameless before him in love."[137]

493   The Fathers of the Eastern tradition call the
Mother of God "the All-Holy" *(Panagia)* and celebrate
her as "free from any stain of sin, as though fashioned
by the Holy Spirit and formed as a new creature."[138] By
the grace of God Mary remained free of every personal
sin her whole life long.

"Let it be done to me according to your word . . ."

494   At the announcement that she would give birth
to "the Son of the Most High" without knowing man,
by the power of the Holy Spirit, Mary responded with
2617 the obedience of faith, certain that "with God nothing
148 will be impossible": "Behold, I am the handmaid of the
Lord; let it be [done] to me according to your word."[139]
Thus, giving her consent to God's word, Mary becomes

134 *Lk* 1:28.   135 Pius IX, *Ineffabilis Deus,* 1854: DS 2803.   136 *LG* 53, 56.
137 Cf. *Eph* 1:3–4.   138 *LG* 56.   139 *Lk* 1:28–38; cf. *Rom* 1:5.

the mother of Jesus. Espousing the divine will for salvation wholeheartedly, without a single sin to restrain her, she gave herself entirely to the person and to the work of her Son; she did so in order to serve the mystery of redemption with him and dependent on him, by God's grace:[140]

968

> As St. Irenaeus says, "Being obedient she became the cause of salvation for herself and for the whole human race."[141] Hence not a few of the early Fathers gladly assert . . . : "The knot of Eve's disobedience was untied by Mary's obedience: what the virgin Eve bound through her disbelief, Mary loosened by her faith."[142] Comparing her with Eve, they call Mary "the Mother of the living" and frequently claim: "Death through Eve, life through Mary."[143]

726

Mary's divine motherhood

495 Called in the Gospels "the mother of Jesus," Mary is acclaimed by Elizabeth, at the prompting of the Spirit and even before the birth of her son, as "the mother of my Lord."[144] In fact, the One whom she conceived as man by the Holy Spirit, who truly became her Son according to the flesh, was none other than the Father's eternal Son, the second person of the Holy Trinity. Hence the Church confesses that Mary is truly "Mother of God" *(Theo-tokos)*.[145]

466, 2677

Mary's virginity

496 From the first formulations of her faith, the Church has confessed that Jesus was conceived solely by the power of the Holy Spirit in the womb of the Virgin Mary, affirming also the corporeal aspect of this event: Jesus was conceived "by the Holy Spirit without human seed."[146] The Fathers see in the virginal conception the sign that it truly was the Son of God who came in a humanity like our own. Thus St. Ignatius of Antioch at the beginning of the second century says:

---

140 Cf. *LG* 56.   **141** St. Irenaeus, *Adv. haeres.* 3, 22, 4: PG 7/1, 959A.   **142** St. Irenaeus, *Adv. haeres.* 3, 22, 4: PG 7/1, 959A.   **143** *LG* 56; Epiphanius, *Haer.* 78, 18: PG 42, 728CD–729AB; St. Jerome, *Ep.* 22, 21: PL 22, 408.   **144** *Lk* 1:43; *Jn* 2:1; 19:25; cf. *Mt* 13:55; *et al.*   **145** Council of Ephesus (431): DS 251.
146 Council of the Lateran (649): DS 503; cf. DS 10–64.

> You are firmly convinced about our Lord, who is truly of the race of David according to the flesh, Son of God according to the will and power of God, truly born of a virgin, . . . he was truly nailed to a tree for us in his flesh under Pontius Pilate . . . he truly suffered, as he is also truly risen.[147]

497   The gospel accounts understand the virginal conception of Jesus as a divine work that surpasses all human understanding and possibility:[148] "That which is conceived in her is of the Holy Spirit," said the angel to Joseph about Mary his fiancée.[149] The Church sees here the fulfillment of the divine promise given through the prophet Isaiah: "Behold, a virgin shall conceive and bear a son."[150]

498   People are sometimes troubled by the silence of St. Mark's Gospel and the New Testament Epistles about Jesus' virginal conception. Some might wonder if we were merely dealing with legends or theological constructs not claiming to be history. To this we must respond: Faith in the virginal conception of Jesus met with the lively opposition, mockery, or incomprehension of non-believers, Jews and pagans alike;[151] so it could hardly have been motivated by pagan mythology or by some adaptation to the ideas of the age. The meaning of this event is accessible only to 90 faith, which understands in it the "connection of these mysteries with one another"[152] in the totality of Christ's mysteries, from his Incarnation to his Passover. St. Ignatius of Antioch already bears witness to this connection: "Mary's virginity and giving birth, and even the Lord's death es- 2717 caped the notice of the prince of this world: these three mysteries worthy of proclamation were accomplished in God's silence."[153]

Mary—"ever-virgin"

499   The deepening of faith in the virginal motherhood led the Church to confess Mary's real and perpetual virginity even in the act of giving birth to the Son of

---

147 St. Ignatius of Antioch, *Ad Smyrn.* 1–2: Apostolic Fathers, ed. J. B. Lightfoot (London: Macmillan, 1889) II/2, 289–293; SCh 10, 154–156; cf. *Rom* 1:3; *Jn* 1:13.   148 Cf. *Mt* 1:18–25; *Lk* 1:26–38.   149 *Mt* 1:20.   150 *Isa* 7:14 in the LXX, quoted in *Mt* 1:23 (Gk.).   151 Cf. St. Justin, *Dial.,* 99, 7: PG 6, 708–709; Origen, *Contra Celsum* 1, 32, 69: PG 11, 720–721; *et al.*   152 *Dei Filius* 4: DS 3016.   153 St. Ignatius of Antioch, *Ad Eph.* 19, 1: AF II/2, 76–80; SCh 10, 88; cf. *1 Cor* 2:8.

God made man.[154] In fact, Christ's birth "did not diminish his mother's virginal integrity but sanctified it."[155] And so the liturgy of the Church celebrates Mary as *Aeiparthenos,* the "Ever-virgin."[156]

500   Against this doctrine the objection is sometimes raised that the Bible mentions brothers and sisters of Jesus.[157] The Church has always understood these passages as not referring to other children of the Virgin Mary. In fact James and Joseph, "brothers of Jesus," are the sons of another Mary, a disciple of Christ, whom St. Matthew significantly calls "the other Mary."[158] They are close relations of Jesus, according to an Old Testament expression.[159]

501   Jesus is Mary's only son, but her spiritual motherhood extends to all men whom indeed he came to save: "The Son whom she brought forth is he whom God placed as the first-born among many brethren, that is, the faithful in whose generation and formulation she cooperates with a mother's love."[160] 969 970

Mary's virginal motherhood in God's plan

502   The eyes of faith can discover in the context of the whole of Revelation the mysterious reasons why God in his saving plan wanted his Son to be born of a virgin. These reasons touch both on the person of Christ and his redemptive mission, and on the welcome Mary gave that mission on behalf of all men. 90

503   Mary's virginity manifests God's absolute initiative in the Incarnation. Jesus has only God as Father. "He was never estranged from the Father because of the human nature which he assumed. . . . He is naturally Son of the Father as to his divinity and naturally son of his mother as to his humanity, but properly Son of the Father in both natures."[161] 422

504   Jesus is conceived by the Holy Spirit in the Virgin Mary's womb because he is the New Adam, who inaugurates the new creation: "The first man was from the earth, a man of dust; the second man is from heaven."[162] From his 359

---

154 Cf. DS 291; 294; 427; 442; 503; 571; 1880.   155 LG 57.   156 Cf. LG 52.
157 Cf. Mk 3:31–35; 6:3; 1 Cor 9:5; Gal 1:19.   158 Mt 13:55; 28:1; cf. Mt 27:56.   159 Cf. Gen 13:8; 14:16; 29:15; etc.   160 LG 63; cf. Jn 19:26–27; Rom 8:29; Rev 12:17.   161 Council of Friuli (796): DS 619; cf. Lk 2:48–49.   162 1 Cor 15:45, 47.

conception, Christ's humanity is filled with the Holy Spirit, for God "gives him the Spirit without measure."[163] From "his fullness" as the head of redeemed humanity "we have all received, grace upon grace."[164]

505   By his virginal conception, Jesus, the New Adam, ushers in *the new birth* of children adopted in the Holy Spirit through faith. "How can this be?"[165] Participation in 1265 the divine life arises "not of blood nor of the will of the flesh nor of the will of man, but of God."[166] The acceptance of this life is virginal because it is entirely the Spirit's gift to man. The spousal character of the human vocation in relation to God[167] is fulfilled perfectly in Mary's virginal motherhood.

506   Mary is a virgin because her virginity is *the sign of* 148 *her faith* "unadulterated by any doubt," and of her undivided gift of herself to God's will.[168] It is her faith that en-1814 ables her to become the mother of the Savior: "Mary is more blessed because she embraces faith in Christ than because she conceives the flesh of Christ."[169]

507   At once virgin and mother, Mary is the symbol and the most perfect realization of the Church: "the Church indeed . . . by receiving the word of God in faith becomes 967 herself a mother. By preaching and Baptism she brings forth sons, who are conceived by the Holy Spirit and born of God, to a new and immortal life. She herself is a virgin, who keeps in its entirety and purity the faith she pledged to 149 her spouse."[170]

IN BRIEF

508   From among the descendants of Eve, God chose the Virgin Mary to be the mother of his Son. "Full of grace," Mary is "the most excellent fruit of redemption" (*SC* 103): from the first instant of her conception, she was totally preserved from the stain of original sin and she remained pure from all personal sin throughout her life.

509   Mary is truly "Mother of God" since she is the mother of the eternal Son of God made man, who is God himself.

---

163 *Jn* 3:34. 164 *Jn* 1:16; cf. *Col* 1:18. 165 *Lk* 1:34; cf. *Jn* 3:9. 166 *Jn* 1:13. 167 Cf. *2 Cor* 11:2. 168 *LG* 63; cf. *1 Cor* 7:34–35. 169 St. Augustine, *De virg.*, 3: PL 40, 398. 170 *LG* 64; cf. 63.

510   Mary "remained a virgin in conceiving her Son, a virgin in giving birth to him, a virgin in carrying him, a virgin in nursing him at her breast, always a virgin" (St. Augustine, *Serm.* 186, 1: PL 38, 999): with her whole being she is "the handmaid of the Lord" (*Lk* 1:38).

511   The Virgin Mary "cooperated through free faith and obedience in human salvation" (*LG* 56). She uttered her yes "in the name of all human nature" (St. Thomas Aquinas, *STh* III, 30, 1). By her obedience she became the new Eve, mother of the living.

Paragraph 3. The Mysteries of Christ's Life

512   Concerning Christ's life the Creed speaks only about the mysteries of the Incarnation (conception and birth) and Paschal mystery (passion, crucifixion, death, burial, descent into hell, resurrection, and ascension). It says nothing explicitly about the mysteries of Jesus' hidden or public life, but the articles of faith concerning his Incarnation and Passover do shed light on the *whole* of   1163 his earthly life. "All that Jesus did and taught, from the beginning until the day when he was taken up to heaven,"[171] is to be seen in the light of the mysteries of Christmas and Easter.

513   According to circumstances catechesis will make use of all the richness of the mysteries of Jesus. Here it is enough merely to indicate some elements common to all the mysteries of Christ's life (I), in order then to   426, 561 sketch the principal mysteries of Jesus' hidden (II) and public (III) life.

I.   CHRIST'S WHOLE LIFE IS MYSTERY

514   Many things about Jesus of interest to human curiosity do not figure in the Gospels. Almost nothing is said about his hidden life at Nazareth, and even a great

---

171 *Acts* 1:1–2.

part of his public life is not recounted.[172] What is written in the Gospels was set down there "so that you may believe that Jesus is the Christ, the Son of God, and that believing you may have life in his name."[173]

515   The Gospels were written by men who were among the first to have the faith[174] and wanted to share it with others. Having known in faith who Jesus is, they could see and make others see the traces of his mystery in all his earthly life. From the swaddling clothes of his birth to the vinegar of his Passion and the shroud of his Resurrection, everything in Jesus' life was a sign of his mystery.[175] His deeds, miracles, and words all revealed that "in him the whole fullness of deity dwells bodily."[176] His humanity appeared as "sacrament," that is, the sign and instrument, of his divinity and of the salvation he brings: what was visible in his earthly life leads to the invisible mystery of his divine sonship and redemptive mission.

126

609, 774

477

Characteristics common to Jesus' mysteries

516   Christ's whole earthly life—his words and deeds, his silences and sufferings, indeed his manner of being and speaking—is *Revelation* of the Father. Jesus can say: "Whoever has seen me has seen the Father," and the Father can say: "This is my Son, my Chosen; listen to him!"[177] Because our Lord became man in order to do his Father's will, even the least characteristics of his mysteries manifest "God's love . . . among us."[178]

65

2708

517   Christ's whole life is a mystery of *redemption*. Redemption comes to us above all through the blood of his cross,[179] but this mystery is at work throughout Christ's entire life:

606

1115

—already in his Incarnation through which by becoming poor he enriches us with his poverty;[180]

172 Cf. *Jn* 20:30.   173 *Jn* 20:31.   174 Cf. *Mk* 1:1; *Jn* 21:24.   175 Cf. *Lk* 2:7; *Mt* 27:48; *Jn* 20:7.   176 *Col* 2:9.   177 *Jn* 14:9; *Lk* 9:35; cf. *Mt* 17:5; *Mk* 9:7 ("my beloved Son").   178 *1 Jn* 4:9.   179 Cf. *Eph* 1:7; *Col* 1:13–14; *1 Pet* 1:18–19.   180 Cf. *2 Cor* 8:9.

—in his hidden life which by his submission atones for our disobedience;[181]

—in his word which purifies its hearers;[182]

—in his healings and exorcisms by which "he took our infirmities and bore our diseases";[183]

—and in his Resurrection by which he justifies us.[184]

518   Christ's whole life is a mystery of recapitulation. All Jesus did, said, and suffered had for its aim restoring fallen man to his original vocation:

> When Christ became incarnate and was made man, he recapitulated in himself the long history of mankind and procured for us a 'short cut' to salvation, so that what we had lost in Adam, that is, being in the image and likeness of God, we might recover in Christ Jesus.[185] For this reason Christ experienced all the stages of life, thereby giving communion with God to all men.[186]

668, 2748

Our communion in the mysteries of Jesus

519   All Christ's riches "are for every individual and are everybody's property."[187] Christ did not live his life for himself but *for us,* from his Incarnation "for us men *793* and for our salvation" to his death "for our sins" and Resurrection "for our justification."[188] He is still "our *602* advocate with the Father," who "always lives to make intercession" for us.[189] He remains ever "in the presence of God on our behalf, bringing before him all that he *1085* lived and suffered for us."[190]

520   In all of his life Jesus presents himself as *our model.* He is "the perfect man,"[191] who invites us to become his disciples and follow him. In humbling himself, *459, 359* he has given us an example to imitate, through his prayer he draws us to pray, and by his poverty he calls *2607* us to accept freely the privation and persecutions that may come our way.[192]

---

181 Cf. *Lk* 2:51.   182 Cf. *Jn* 15:3.   183 *Mt* 8:17; cf. *Isa* 53:4.   184 Cf. *Rom* 4:25.   185 St. Irenaeus, *Adv. haeres.* 3, 18, 1: PG 7/1, 932.   186 St. Irenaeus, *Adv. haeres.* 3, 18, 7: PG 7/1, 937; cf. 2, 22, 4.   187 John Paul II, *RH* 11.   188 *1 Cor* 15:3; *Rom* 4:25.   189 *1 Jn* 2:1; *Heb* 7:25.   190 *Heb* 9:24.   191 *GS* 38; cf. *Rom* 15:5; *Phil* 2:5.   192 Cf. *Jn* 13:15; *Lk* 11:1; *Mt* 5:11-12.

2715 **521**   Christ enables us *to live in him* all that he himself lived, and *he lives it in us.* "By his Incarnation, he, the Son of God, has in a certain way united himself
1391 with each man."[193] We are called only to become one with him, for he enables us as the members of his Body to share in what he lived for us in his flesh as our model:

> We must continue to accomplish in ourselves the stages of Jesus' life and his mysteries and often to beg him to perfect and realize them in us and in his whole Church. . . . For it is the plan of the Son of God to make us and the whole Church partake in his mysteries and to extend them to and continue them in us and in his whole Church. This is his plan for fulfilling his mysteries in us.[194]

II.   THE MYSTERIES OF JESUS' INFANCY AND HIDDEN LIFE

The preparations

522   The coming of God's Son to earth is an event of such immensity that God willed to prepare for it over
711, 762 centuries. He makes everything converge on Christ: all the rituals and sacrifices, figures and symbols of the "First Covenant."[195] He announces him through the mouths of the prophets who succeeded one another in Israel. Moreover, he awakens in the hearts of the pagans a dim expectation of this coming.

523   *St. John the Baptist* is the Lord's immediate precursor or forerunner, sent to prepare his way.[196] "Prophet of the Most High," John surpasses all the
717-720 prophets, of whom he is the last.[197] He inaugurates the Gospel, already from his mother's womb welcomes the coming of Christ, and rejoices in being "the friend of the bridegroom," whom he points out as "the Lamb of God, who takes away the sin of the world."[198] Going before Jesus "in the spirit and power of Elijah," John

---

193 *GS* 22 § 2.   194 St. John Eudes, *LH,* Week 33, Friday, OR.   195 *Heb* 9:15.
196 Cf. *Acts* 13:24; *Mt* 3:3.   197 *Lk* 1:76; cf. 7:26; *Mt* 11:13.   198 *Jn* 1:29; cf.
Acts 1:22; *Lk* 1:41; 16:16; *Jn* 3:29.

bears witness to Christ in his preaching, by his Baptism of conversion, and through his martyrdom.[199]

524   When the Church celebrates *the liturgy of Advent* each year, she makes present this ancient expectancy of the Messiah, for by sharing in the long preparation for the Savior's first coming, the faithful renew their ardent desire for his second coming.[200] By celebrating the precursor's birth and martyrdom, the Church unites herself to his desire: "He must increase, but I must decrease."[201]

1171

The Christmas mystery

525   Jesus was born in a humble stable, into a poor family.[202] Simple shepherds were the first witnesses to this event. In this poverty heaven's glory was made manifest.[203] The Church never tires of singing the glory of this night:

437
2443

> The Virgin today brings into the world the Eternal
> And the earth offers a cave to the Inaccessible.
> The angels and shepherds praise him
> And the magi advance with the star,
> For you are born for us,
> Little Child, God eternal![204]

526   To become a child in relation to God is the condition for entering the kingdom.[205] For this, we must humble ourselves and become little. Even more: to become "children of God" we must be "born from above" or "born of God."[206] Only when Christ is formed in us will the mystery of Christmas be fulfilled in us.[207] Christmas is the mystery of this "marvelous exchange":

> O marvelous exchange! Man's Creator has become man, born of the Virgin. We have been made sharers in the divinity of Christ who humbled himself to share our humanity.[208]

460

---

199 *Lk* 1:17; cf. *Mk* 6:17–29.   200 Cf. *Rev* 22:17.   201 *Jn* 3:30.   202 Cf. *Lk* 2:6–7.   203 Cf. *Lk* 2:8–20.   204 *Kontakion* of Romanos the Melodist.   205 Cf. *Mt* 18:3–4.   206 *Jn* 3:7; 1:13; 1:12; cf. *Mt* 23:12.   207 Cf. *Gal* 4:19.   208 *LH*, Antiphon I of Evening Prayer for January 1st.

The mysteries of Jesus' infancy

527   Jesus' *circumcision,* on the eighth day after his birth,[209] is the sign of his incorporation into Abraham's descendants, into the people of the covenant. It is the sign of his submission to the Law[210] and his deputation
580 to Israel's worship, in which he will participate through-
1214 out his life. This sign prefigures that "circumcision of Christ" which is Baptism.[211]

528   The *Epiphany* is the manifestation of Jesus as Messiah of Israel, Son of God and Savior of the world. The great feast of Epiphany celebrates the adoration of
439 Jesus by the wise men *(magi)* from the East, together with his baptism in the Jordan and the wedding feast at Cana in Galilee.[212] In the magi, representatives of the neighboring pagan religions, the Gospel sees the first-fruits of the nations, who welcome the good news of salvation through the Incarnation. The magi's coming to Jerusalem in order to pay homage to the king of the Jews shows that they seek in Israel, in the messianic light of the star of David, the one who will be king of the nations.[213] Their coming means that pagans can dis-cover Jesus and worship him as Son of God and Savior of the world only by turning toward the Jews and re-ceiving from them the messianic promise as contained in
711-716 the Old Testament.[214] The Epiphany shows that "the full
122 number of the nations" now takes its "place in the fam-ily of the patriarchs," and acquires *Israelitica dignitas*[215] (are made "worthy of the heritage of Israel").

529   The *presentation of Jesus in the temple* shows him to be the firstborn Son who belongs to the Lord.[216] With Simeon and Anna, all Israel awaits its *encounter*
583 with the Savior—the name given to this event in the
439 Byzantine tradition. Jesus is recognized as the long-expected Messiah, the "light to the nations" and the "glory of Israel," but also "a sign that is spoken

---

209 Cf. *Lk* 2:21.   210 Cf. *Gal* 4:4.   211 Cf. *Col* 2:11–13.   212 *Mt* 2:1; cf. *LH,* Epiphany, Evening Prayer II, Antiphon at the Canticle of Mary.   213 Cf. *Mt* 2:2; *Num* 24:17–19; *Rev* 22:16.   214 Cf. *Jn* 4:22; *Mt* 2:4–6.   215 St. Leo the Great, *Sermo 3 in epiphania Domini* 1–3,5: PL 54, 242; *LH,* Epiphany, OR; *Roman Missal,* Easter Vigil 26, Prayer after the third reading.   216 Cf. *Lk* 2:22–39; *Ex* 13:2, 12–13.

against." The sword of sorrow predicted for Mary an- 614
nounces Christ's perfect and unique oblation on the
cross that will impart the salvation God had "prepared
in the presence of all peoples."

530   The *flight into Egypt* and the massacre of the in-
nocents[217] make manifest the opposition of darkness to
the light: "He came to his own home, and his own people received him not."[218] Christ's whole life was lived
under the sign of persecution. His own share it with 574
him.[219] Jesus' departure from Egypt recalls the exodus
and presents him as the definitive liberator of God's
people.[220]

The mysteries of Jesus' hidden life

531   During the greater part of his life Jesus shared
the condition of the vast majority of human beings: a
daily life spent without evident greatness, a life of man-
ual labor. His religious life was that of a Jew obedient
to the law of God,[221] a life in the community. From this 2427
whole period it is revealed to us that Jesus was "obedient" to his parents and that he "increased in wisdom
and in stature, and in favor with God and man."[222]

532   Jesus' obedience to his mother and legal father
fulfills the fourth commandment perfectly and was the
temporal image of his filial obedience to his Father in 2214-2220
heaven. The everyday obedience of Jesus to Joseph and
Mary both announced and anticipated the obedience of
Holy Thursday: "Not my will. . . ."[223] The obedience of
Christ in the daily routine of his hidden life was already 612
inaugurating his work of restoring what the disobedience of Adam had destroyed.[224]

533   The hidden life at Nazareth allows everyone to
enter into fellowship with Jesus by the most ordinary
events of daily life:

> The home of Nazareth is the school where we be-
> gin to understand the life of Jesus—the school of

---

217 Cf. *Mt* 2:13–18.   218 *Jn* 1:11.   219 Cf. *Jn* 15:20.   220 Cf. *Mt* 2:15; *Hos*
11:1.   221 Cf. *Gal* 4:4.   222 *Lk* 2:51–52.   223 *Lk* 22:42.   224 Cf. *Rom* 5:19.

the Gospel. First, then, a lesson of silence. May es-
2712   teem for *silence,* that admirable and indispensable
condition of mind, revive in us . . . A lesson on *family life.* May Nazareth teach us what family life is,
its communion of love, its austere and simple
beauty, and its sacred and inviolable character . . .
2204   A lesson of *work.* Nazareth, home of the "Carpenter's Son," in you I would choose to understand and
proclaim the severe and redeeming law of human
work. . . . To conclude, I want to greet all the
workers of the world, holding up to them their
2427   great pattern, their brother who is God.[225]

534   The *finding of Jesus in the temple* is the only
event that breaks the silence of the Gospels about the
hidden years of Jesus.[226] Here Jesus lets us catch a
583   glimpse of the mystery of his total consecration to a
2599   mission that flows from his divine sonship: "Did you
not know that I must be about my Father's work?"[227]
Mary and Joseph did not understand these words, but
they accepted them in faith. Mary "kept all these things
964   in her heart" during the years Jesus remained hidden in
the silence of an ordinary life.

III.   THE MYSTERIES OF JESUS' PUBLIC LIFE

The baptism of Jesus

535   Jesus' public life begins with his baptism by John
in the Jordan.[228] John preaches "a baptism of repentance
719-720 for the forgiveness of sins."[229] A crowd of sinners[230]—tax
collectors and soldiers, Pharisees and Sadducees, and
prostitutes—come to be baptized by him. "Then Jesus
appears." The Baptist hesitates, but Jesus insists and receives baptism. Then the Holy Spirit, in the form of a
701   dove, comes upon Jesus and a voice from heaven proclaims, "This is my beloved Son."[231] This is the mani-
438   festation ("Epiphany") of Jesus as Messiah of Israel and
Son of God.

536   The baptism of Jesus is on his part the accep-

---

225 Paul VI at Nazareth, January 5, 1964: *LH,* Feast of the Holy Family, OR.
226 Cf. *Lk* 2:41–52.   227 *Lk* 2:49 alt.   228 Cf. *Lk* 3:23; *Acts* 1:22.   229 *Lk*
3:3.   230 Cf. *Lk* 3:10–14; *Mt* 3:7; 21:32.   231 *Mt* 3:13–17.

tance and inauguration of his mission as God's suffering Servant. He allows himself to be numbered among sinners; he is already "the Lamb of God, who takes away the sin of the world."[232] Already he is anticipating the "baptism" of his bloody death.[233] Already he is coming to "fulfill all righteousness," that is, he is submitting himself entirely to his Father's will: out of love he consents to this baptism of death for the remission of our sins.[234] The Father's voice responds to the Son's acceptance, proclaiming his entire delight in his Son.[235] The Spirit whom Jesus possessed in fullness from his conception comes to "rest on him."[236] Jesus will be the source of the Spirit for all mankind. At his baptism "the heavens were opened"[237]—the heavens that Adam's sin had closed—and the waters were sanctified by the descent of Jesus and the Spirit, a prelude to the new creation.

606

1224

444

727
739

537   Through Baptism the Christian is sacramentally assimilated to Jesus, who in his own baptism anticipates his death and resurrection. The Christian must enter into this mystery of humble self-abasement and repentance, go down into the water with Jesus in order to rise with him, be reborn of water and the Spirit so as to become the Father's beloved son in the Son and "walk in newness of life":[238]

1262

> Let us be buried with Christ by Baptism to rise with him; let us go down with him to be raised with him; and let us rise with him to be glorified with him.[239]

628

> Everything that happened to Christ lets us know that, after the bath of water, the Holy Spirit swoops down upon us from high heaven and that, adopted by the Father's voice, we become sons of God.[240]

---

232 *Jn* 1:29; cf. *Isa* 53:12.   233 Cf. *Mk* 10:38; *Lk* 12:50.   234 *Mt* 3:15; cf. 26:39.   235 Cf. *Lk* 3:22; *Isa* 42:1.   236 *Jn* 1:32–33; cf. *Isa* 11:2.   237 *Mt* 3:16. 238 *Rom* 6:4.   239 St. Gregory of Nazianzus, *Oratio*. 40, 9: PG 36, 369. 240 St. Hilary of Poitiers, *In Matth*. 2, 5: PL 9, 927.

Jesus' temptations

538   The Gospels speak of a time of solitude for Jesus in the desert immediately after his baptism by John. Driven by the Spirit into the desert, Jesus remains there for forty days without eating; he lives among wild beasts, and angels minister to him.[241] At the end of this time Satan tempts him three times, seeking to compromise his
394 filial attitude toward God. Jesus rebuffs these attacks,
518 which recapitulate the temptations of Adam in Paradise and of Israel in the desert, and the devil leaves him "until an opportune time."[242]

397 **539**   The evangelists indicate the salvific meaning of this mysterious event: Jesus is the new Adam who remained faithful just where the first Adam had given in to temptation. Jesus fulfills Israel's vocation perfectly: in contrast to those who had once provoked God during forty years in the desert, Christ reveals himself as God's
385 Servant, totally obedient to the divine will. In this, Jesus is the devil's conqueror: he "binds the strong man" to take back his plunder.[243] Jesus' victory over the tempter
609 in the desert anticipates victory at the Passion, the supreme act of obedience of his filial love for the Father.

540   Jesus' temptation reveals the way in which the
2119 Son of God is Messiah, contrary to the way Satan proposes to him and the way men wish to attribute to
519, 2849 him.[244] This is why Christ vanquished the Tempter *for us:* "For we have not a high priest who is unable to sympathize with our weaknesses, but one who in every respect has been tested as we are, yet without sinning."[245] By the solemn forty days of *Lent* the Church unites her-
1438 self each year to the mystery of Jesus in the desert.

"The Kingdom of God is at hand"

541   "Now after John was arrested, Jesus came into Galilee, preaching the gospel of God, and saying: 'The time is fulfilled, and the kingdom of God is at hand: re-
2816 pent, and believe in the gospel.' "[246] "To carry out the

---

241 Cf. *Mk* 1:12–13.   242 *Lk* 4:13.   243 Cf. *Ps* 95:10; *Mk* 3:27.   244 Cf. *Mt* 16:21–23.   245 *Heb* 4:15.   246 *Mk* 1:14–15.

will of the Father Christ inaugurated the kingdom of heaven on earth."[247] Now the Father's will is "to raise up men to share in his own divine life."[248] He does this by gathering men around his Son Jesus Christ. This gathering is the Church, "on earth the seed and beginning of that kingdom."[249]

763
669, 768
865

542 Christ stands at the heart of this gathering of men into the "family of God." By his word, through signs that manifest the reign of God, and by sending out his disciples, Jesus calls all people to come together around him. But above all in the great Paschal mystery—his death on the cross and his Resurrection—he would accomplish the coming of his kingdom. "And I, when I am lifted up from the earth, will draw all men to myself." Into this union with Christ all men are called.[250]

2233

789

The proclamation of the Kingdom of God

543 *Everyone* is called to enter the kingdom. First announced to the children of Israel, this messianic kingdom is intended to accept men of all nations.[251] To enter it, one must first accept Jesus' word:

764

> The word of the Lord is compared to a seed which is sown in a field; those who hear it with faith and are numbered among the little flock of Christ have truly received the kingdom. Then, by its own power, the seed sprouts and grows until the harvest.[252]

544 The kingdom belongs *to the poor and lowly,* which means those who have accepted it with humble hearts. Jesus is sent to "preach good news to the poor";[253] he declares them blessed, for "theirs is the kingdom of heaven."[254] To them—the "little ones"—the Father is pleased to reveal what remains hidden from the wise and the learned.[255] Jesus shares the life of the poor, from the cradle to the cross; he experiences hunger, thirst, and privation.[256] Jesus identifies himself

709
2443
2546

---

247 *LG* 3. 248 *LG* 2. 249 *LG* 5. 250 *Jn* 12:32; cf. *LG* 3. 251 Cf. *Mt* 8:11; 10:5–7; 28:19. 252 *LG* 5; cf. *Mk* 4:14, 26–29; *Lk* 12:32. 253 *Lk* 4:18; cf. 7:22. 254 *Mt* 5:3. 255 Cf. *Mt* 11:25. 256 Cf. *Mt* 21:18; *Mk* 2:23–26; *Jn* 4:6–7; 19:28; *Lk* 9:58.

with the poor of every kind and makes active love toward them the condition for entering his kingdom.[257]

545   Jesus invites *sinners* to the table of the kingdom: "I came not to call the righteous, but sinners."[258] He invites them to that conversion without which one cannot enter the kingdom, but shows them in word and deed his Father's boundless mercy for them and the vast "joy in heaven over one sinner who repents."[259] The supreme proof of his love will be the sacrifice of his own life "for the forgiveness of sins."[260]

1443

588, 1846
1439

546   Jesus' invitation to enter his kingdom comes in the form of *parables,* a characteristic feature of his teaching.[261] Through his parables he invites people to the feast of the kingdom, but he also asks for a radical choice: to gain the kingdom, one must give everything.[262] Words are not enough; deeds are required.[263] The parables are like mirrors for man: will he be hard soil or good earth for the word?[264] What use has he made of the talents he has received?[265] Jesus and the presence of the kingdom in this world are secretly at the heart of the parables. One must enter the kingdom, that is, become a disciple of Christ, in order to "know the secrets of the kingdom of heaven."[266] For those who stay "outside," everything remains enigmatic.[267]

2613

542

The signs of the Kingdom of God

547   Jesus accompanies his words with many "mighty works and wonders and signs," which manifest that the kingdom is present in him and attest that he was the promised Messiah.[268]

670, 439

548   The signs worked by Jesus attest that the Father has sent him. They invite belief in him.[269] To those who turn to him in faith, he grants what they ask.[270] So miracles strengthen faith in the One who does his Father's works; they bear witness that he is the Son of God.[271]

156, 2616

257 Cf. *Mt* 25:31–46.   258 *Mk* 2:17; cf. *1 Tim* 1:15.   259 *Lk* 15:7; cf. 7:11–32.
260 *Mt* 26:28.   261 Cf. *Mk* 4:33–34.   262 Cf. *Mt* 13:44–45; 22:1–14.   263 Cf.
Mt 21:28–32.   264 Cf. *Mt* 13:3–9.   265 Cf. *Mt* 25:14–30.   266 *Mt* 13:11.
267 *Mk* 4:11; cf. *Mt* 13:10–15.   268 *Acts* 2:22; cf. *Lk* 7:18–23.   269 Cf. *Jn*
5:36; 10:25, 38.   270 Cf. *Mk* 5:25–34; 10:52; etc.   271 Cf. *Jn* 10:31–38.

But his miracles can also be occasions for "offense";[272] they are not intended to satisfy people's curiosity or desire for magic. Despite his evident miracles some people reject Jesus; he is even accused of acting by the power of demons.[273]

549 By freeing some individuals from the earthly evils of hunger, injustice, illness, and death,[274] Jesus performed messianic signs. Nevertheless he did not come to abolish all evils here below,[275] but to free men from the gravest slavery, sin, which thwarts them in their vocation as God's sons and causes all forms of human bondage.[276]

550 The coming of God's kingdom means the defeat of Satan's: "If it is by the Spirit of God that I cast out demons, then the kingdom of God has come upon you."[277] Jesus' *exorcisms* free some individuals from the domination of demons. They anticipate Jesus' great victory over "the ruler of this world."[278] The kingdom of God will be definitively established through Christ's cross: "God reigned from the wood."[279]

"The keys of the kingdom"

551 From the beginning of his public life Jesus chose certain men, twelve in number, to be with him and to participate in his mission.[280] He gives the Twelve a share in his authority and "sent them out to preach the kingdom of God and to heal."[281] They remain associated for ever with Christ's kingdom, for through them he directs the Church:

> As my Father appointed a kingdom for me, so do I appoint for you that you may eat and drink at my table in my kingdom, and sit on thrones judging the twelve tribes of Israel.[282]

552 Simon Peter holds the first place in the college of the Twelve;[283] Jesus entrusted a unique mission to him.

---

272 *Mt* 11:6.   273 Cf. *Jn* 11:47–48; *Mk* 3:22.   274 Cf. *Jn* 6:5–15; *Lk* 19:8; *Mt* 11:5.   275 Cf. *Lk* 12:13–14; *Jn* 18:36.   276 Cf. *Jn* 8:34–36.   277 *Mt* 12:26, 28. 278 *Jn* 12:31; cf. *Lk* 8:26–39.   279 *LH*, Lent, Holy Week, Evening Prayer, Hymn *Vexilla Regis:* "*Regnavit a ligno Deus.*"   280 Cf. *Mk* 3:13–19.   281 *Lk* 9:2. 282 *Lk* 22:29–30.   283 Cf. *Mk* 3:16; 9:2; *Lk* 24:34; *1 Cor* 15:5.

880 Through a revelation from the Father, Peter had con-
153, 442 fessed: "You are the Christ, the Son of the living God."
Our Lord then declared to him: "You are Peter, and on
this rock I will build my Church, and the gates of Hades
will not prevail against it."[284] Christ, the "living
stone,"[285] thus assures his Church, built on Peter, of victory over the powers of death. Because of the faith he
confessed Peter will remain the unshakeable rock of the
Church. His mission will be to keep this faith from
424 every lapse and to strengthen his brothers in it.[286]

553   Jesus entrusted a specific authority to Peter: "I
will give you the keys of the kingdom of heaven, and
881 whatever you bind on earth shall be bound in heaven,
and whatever you loose on earth shall be loosed in
heaven."[287] The "power of the keys" designates authority to govern the house of God, which is the Church. Jesus, the Good Shepherd, confirmed this mandate after
1445 his Resurrection: "Feed my sheep."[288] The power to
"bind and loose" connotes the authority to absolve sins,
to pronounce doctrinal judgments, and to make disciplinary decisions in the Church. Jesus entrusted this authority to the Church through the ministry of the apos-
641, 881 tles[289] and in particular through the ministry of Peter, the
only one to whom he specifically entrusted the keys of
the kingdom.

A foretaste of the Kingdom: the Transfiguration

554   From the day Peter confessed that Jesus is the
Christ, the Son of the living God, the Master "began to
show his disciples that he must go to Jerusalem and suffer many things . . . and be killed, and on the third day
be raised."[290] Peter scorns this prediction, nor do the
others understand it any better than he.[291] In this context the mysterious episode of Jesus' Transfiguration
takes place on a high mountain,[292] before three witnesses
697, 2600 chosen by himself: Peter, James, and John. Jesus' face
and clothes become dazzling with light, and Moses and

---

284 *Mt* 16:18.   285 *1 Pet* 2:4.   286 Cf. *Lk* 22:32.   287 *Mt* 16:19.   288 *Jn*
21:15–17; cf. 10:11.   289 Cf. *Mt* 18:18.   290 *Mt* 16:21.   291 Cf. *Mt* 16:22–23;
Mt 17:23; *Lk* 9:45.   292 Cf. *Mt* 17:1–8 and parallels; *2 Pet* 1:16–18.

Elijah appear, speaking "of his departure, which he was to accomplish at Jerusalem."[293] A cloud covers him and a voice from heaven says: "This is my Son, my Chosen; listen to him!"[294]   *440*

555   For a moment Jesus discloses his divine glory, confirming Peter's confession. He also reveals that he will have to go by the way of the cross at Jerusalem in order to "enter into his glory."[295] Moses and Elijah had *2576, 2583* seen God's glory on the Mountain; the Law and the Prophets had announced the Messiah's sufferings.[296] Christ's Passion is the will of the Father: the Son acts as God's servant;[297] the cloud indicates the presence of the *257* Holy Spirit. "The whole Trinity appeared: the Father in the voice; the Son in the man; the Spirit in the shining cloud."[298]

> You were transfigured on the mountain, and your disciples, as much as they were capable of it, beheld your glory, O Christ our God, so that when they should see you crucified they would understand that your Passion was voluntary, and proclaim to the world that you truly are the splendor of the Father.[299]

556   On the threshold of the public life: the baptism; on the threshold of the Passover: the Transfiguration. Jesus' baptism proclaimed "the mystery of the first regeneration," namely, our Baptism; the Transfiguration "is the sacrament of the second regeneration": our own Resurrection.[300] From now on we share in the Lord's Resurrection through the Spirit who acts in the sacraments of the Body of Christ. The Transfiguration gives *1003* us a foretaste of Christ's glorious coming, when he "will change our lowly body to be like his glorious body."[301] But it also recalls that "it is through many persecutions that we must enter the kingdom of God":[302]

> Peter did not yet understand this when he wanted to remain with Christ on the mountain. It has been

---

293 *Lk* 9:31. 294 *Lk* 9:35. 295 *Lk* 24:26. 296 Cf. *Lk* 24:27. 297 Cf. *Isa* 42:1. 298 St. Thomas Aquinas, *STh* III, 45, 4 *ad* 2. 299 Byzantine Liturgy, Feast of the Transfiguration, *Kontakion*. 300 St. Thomas Aquinas, *STh* III, 45, 4, *ad* 2. 301 *Phil* 3:21. 302 *Acts* 14:22.

reserved for you, Peter, but for after death. For now, Jesus says: "Go down to toil on earth, to serve on earth, to be scorned and crucified on earth. Life goes down to be killed; Bread goes down to suffer hunger; the Way goes down to be exhausted on his journey; the Spring goes down to suffer thirst; and you refuse to suffer?"[303]

Jesus' ascent to Jerusalem

557   "When the days drew near for him to be taken up [Jesus] set his face to go to Jerusalem."[304] By this decision he indicated that he was going up to Jerusalem prepared to die there. Three times he had announced his Passion and Resurrection; now, heading toward Jerusalem, Jesus says: "It cannot be that a prophet should perish away from Jerusalem."[305]

558   Jesus recalls the martyrdom of the prophets who had been put to death in Jerusalem. Nevertheless he persists in calling Jerusalem to gather around him: "How often would I have gathered your children together as a hen gathers her brood under her wings, and you would not!"[306] When Jerusalem comes into view he weeps over her and expresses once again his heart's desire: "Would that even today you knew the things that make for peace! But now they are hid from your eyes."[307]

Jesus' messianic entrance into Jerusalem

559   How will Jerusalem welcome her Messiah? Although Jesus had always refused popular attempts to make him king, he chooses the time and prepares the details for his messianic entry into the city of "his father David."[308] Acclaimed as son of David, as the one who brings salvation *(Hosanna* means "Save!" or "Give salvation!"), the "King of glory" enters his City "riding on an ass."[309] Jesus conquers the Daughter of Zion, a figure of his Church, neither by ruse nor by violence, but by the humility that bears witness to the truth.[310] And so

---

303 St. Augustine, *Sermo* 78, 6: PL 38, 492–493; cf. *Lk* 9:33.   304 *Lk* 9:51; cf. *Jn* 13:1.   305 *Lk* 13:33; cf. *Mk* 8:31–33; 9:31–32; 10:32–34.   306 *Mt* 23:37. 307 *Lk* 19:41–42.   308 *Lk* 1:32; cf. *Mt* 21:1–11; *Jn* 6:15.   309 *Ps* 24:7–10; *Zech* 9:9.   310 Cf. *Jn* 18:37.

the subjects of his kingdom on that day are children and God's poor, who acclaim him as had the angels when they announced him to the shepherds.[311] Their acclamation, "Blessed be he who comes in the name of the LORD,"[312] is taken up by the Church in the *"Sanctus"* of the Eucharistic liturgy that introduces the memorial of the Lord's Passover.

333

1352

560   *Jesus' entry into Jerusalem* manifested the coming of the kingdom that the King-Messiah was going to accomplish by the Passover of his Death and Resurrection. It is with the celebration of that entry on Palm Sunday that the Church's liturgy solemnly opens Holy Week.

550, 2816

IN BRIEF

561   "The whole of Christ's life was a continual teaching: his silences, his miracles, his gestures, his prayer, his love for people, his special affection for the little and the poor, his acceptance of the total sacrifice on the Cross for the redemption of the world, and his Resurrection are the actualization of his word and the fulfillment of Revelation" (John Paul II, *CT* 9).

562   Christ's disciples are to conform themselves to him until he is formed in them (cf. *Gal* 4:19). "For this reason we, who have been made like to him, who have died with him and risen with him, are taken up into the mysteries of his life, until we reign together with him" (*LG* 7 § 4).

563   No one, whether shepherd or wise man, can approach God here below except by kneeling before the manger at Bethlehem and adoring him hidden in the weakness of a new-born child.

564   By his obedience to Mary and Joseph, as well as by his humble work during the long years in

---

311 Cf. *Mt* 21:15–16; cf. *Ps* 8:3; *Lk* 19:38; 2:14.   312 Cf. *Ps* 118:26.

Nazareth, Jesus gives us the example of holiness in the daily life of family and work.

565 From the beginning of his public life, at his baptism, Jesus is the "Servant," wholly consecrated to the redemptive work that he will accomplish by the "baptism" of his Passion.

566 The temptation in the desert shows Jesus, the humble Messiah, who triumphs over Satan by his total adherence to the plan of salvation willed by the Father.

567 The Kingdom of heaven was inaugurated on earth by Christ. "This kingdom shone out before men in the word, in the works, and in the presence of Christ" (*LG* 5). The Church is the seed and beginning of this kingdom. Her keys are entrusted to Peter.

568 Christ's Transfiguration aims at strengthening the apostles' faith in anticipation of his Passion: the ascent onto the "high mountain" prepares for the ascent to Calvary. Christ, Head of the Church, manifests what his Body contains and radiates in the sacraments: "the hope of glory" (*Col* 1:27; cf. St. Leo the Great, *Sermo* 51, 3: PL 54, 310c).

569 Jesus went up to Jerusalem voluntarily, knowing well that there he would die a violent death because of the opposition of sinners (cf. *Heb* 12:3).

570 Jesus' entry into Jerusalem manifests the coming of the kingdom that the Messiah-King, welcomed into his city by children and the humble of heart, is going to accomplish by the Passover of his Death and Resurrection.

ARTICLE 4
"JESUS CHRIST SUFFERED UNDER PONTIUS PILATE, WAS CRUCIFIED, DIED, AND WAS BURIED"

571   The Paschal mystery of Christ's cross and Resurrection stands at the center of the Good News that the apostles, and the Church following them, are to proclaim to the world. God's saving plan was accomplished "once for all"[313] by the redemptive death of his Son Jesus Christ.   1067

572   The Church remains faithful to the interpretation of "all the Scriptures" that Jesus gave both before and after his Passover: "Was it not necessary that the Christ should suffer these things and enter into his glory?"[314] Jesus' sufferings took their historical, concrete form from the fact that he was "rejected by the elders and the chief priests and the scribes," who handed "him to the Gentiles to be mocked and scourged and crucified."[315]   599

573   Faith can therefore try to examine the circumstances of Jesus' death, faithfully handed on by the Gospels[316] and illuminated by other historical sources, the better to understand the meaning of the Redemption.   158

Paragraph 1. Jesus and Israel

574   From the beginning of Jesus' public ministry, certain Pharisees and partisans of Herod together with priests and scribes agreed together to destroy him.[317] Because of certain of his acts—expelling demons, forgiving sins, healing on the sabbath day, his novel interpretation of the precepts of the Law regarding purity, and his familiarity with tax collectors and public sinners[318]—some ill-intentioned persons suspected Jesus of demonic possession.[319] He is accused of blasphemy and false   530   591

---

313 *Heb* 9:26.   314 *Lk* 24:26–27, 44–45.   315 *Mk* 8:31; *Mt* 20:19.   316 Cf. *DV* 19.   317 Cf. *Mk* 3:6; 14:1.   318 Cf. *Mt* 12:24; *Mk* 2:7, 14–17; 3:1–6; 7:14–23.   319 Cf. *Mk* 3:22; *Jn* 8:48; 10:20.

prophecy, religious crimes which the Law punished with death by stoning.[320]

575   Many of Jesus' deeds and words constituted a "sign of contradiction,"[321] but more so for the religious authorities in Jerusalem, whom the Gospel according to John often calls simply "the Jews,"[322] than for the ordinary People of God.[323] To be sure, Christ's relations with the Pharisees were not exclusively polemical. Some Pharisees warned him of the danger he was courting;[324] Jesus praises some of them, like the scribe of *Mark* 12:34, and dines several times at their homes.[325] Jesus endorses some of the teachings imparted by this religious elite of God's people: the resurrection of the dead,[326] certain forms of piety (almsgiving, fasting, and prayer),[327] the custom of addressing God as Father, and the centrality of the commandment to love God and neighbor.[328]

993

576   In the eyes of many in Israel, Jesus seems to be acting against essential institutions of the Chosen People:

—submission to the whole of the Law in its written commandments and, for the Pharisees, in the interpretation of oral tradition;

—the centrality of the Temple at Jerusalem as the holy place where God's presence dwells in a special way;

—faith in the one God whose glory no man can share.

I.   JESUS AND THE LAW

577   At the beginning of the Sermon on the Mount Jesus issued a solemn warning in which he presented God's law, given on Sinai during the first covenant, in light of the grace of the New Covenant:

1965

> Do not think that I have come to abolish the law or the prophets: I have come not to abolish but to fulfill. For truly I tell you, until heaven and earth pass away, not one letter, not one stroke of a letter, will pass from the law, until all is accomplished. Therefore, whoever breaks one of the least of these com-

1967

---

320 Cf. *Mk* 2:7; *Jn* 5:18; *Jn* 7:12; 7:52; 8:59; 10:31, 33.   321 *Lk* 2:34.   322 Cf. *Jn* 1:19; 2:18; 5:10; 7:13; 9:22; 18:12; 19:38; 20:19.   323 *Jn* 7:48–49.   324 Cf. *Lk* 13:31.   325 Cf. *Lk* 7:36; 14:1.   326 Cf. *Mt* 22:23–34; *Lk* 20:39.   327 Cf. *Mt* 6:18.   328 Cf. *Mk* 12:28–34.

mandments, and teaches others to do the same, will be called least in the kingdom of heaven; but whoever does them and teaches them will be called great in the kingdom of heaven.[329]

578 Jesus, Israel's Messiah and therefore the greatest in the kingdom of heaven, was to fulfill the Law by keeping it in its all-embracing detail—according to his own words, down to "the least of these commandments."[330] He is in fact the only one who could keep it perfectly.[331] On their own admission the Jews were never able to observe the Law in its entirety without violating the least of its precepts.[332] This is why every year on the Day of Atonement the children of Israel ask God's forgiveness for their transgressions of the Law. The Law indeed makes up one inseparable whole, and St. James recalls, "Whoever keeps the whole law but fails in one point has become guilty of all of it."[333]

1953

579 This principle of integral observance of the Law not only in letter but in spirit was dear to the Pharisees. By giving Israel this principle they had led many Jews of Jesus' time to an extreme religious zeal.[334] This zeal, were it not to lapse into "hypocritical" casuistry,[335] could only prepare the People for the unprecedented intervention of God through the perfect fulfillment of the Law by the only Righteous One in place of all sinners.[336]

580 The perfect fulfillment of the Law could be the work of none but the divine legislator, born subject to the Law in the person of the Son.[337] In Jesus, the Law no longer appears engraved on tables of stone but "upon the heart" of the Servant who becomes "a covenant to the people," because he will "faithfully bring forth justice."[338] Jesus fulfills the Law to the point of taking upon himself "the curse of the Law" incurred by those who do not "abide by the things written in the book of the Law, and do them," for his death took place to redeem them "from the transgressions under the first covenant."[339]

527

---

329 Mt 5:17–19. 330 Mt 5:19. 331 Cf. Jn 8:46. 332 Cf. Jn 7:19; Acts 13:38–41; 15:10. 333 Jas 2:10; cf. Gal 3:10; 5:3. 334 Cf. Rom 10:2. 335 Cf. Mt 15:3–7, Lk 11:39–54. 336 Cf. Isa 53:11; Heb 9:15. 337 Cf. Gal 4:4. 338 Jer 31:33; Isa 42:3, 6. 339 Gal 3:13; 3:10; Heb 9:15.

581   The Jewish people and their spiritual leaders viewed Jesus as a rabbi.[340] He often argued within the framework of rabbinical interpretation of the Law.[341] Yet Jesus could not help but offend the teachers of the Law, for he was not content to propose his interpretation alongside theirs but taught the people "as one who had authority, and not as their scribes."[342] In Jesus, the same Word of God, that had resounded on Mount Sinai to give the written Law to Moses, made itself heard anew on the Mount of the Beatitudes.[343] Jesus did not abolish the Law but fulfilled it by giving its ultimate interpretation in a divine way: "You have heard that it was said to the men of old. . . . But I say to you. . . ."[344] With this same divine authority, he disavowed certain human traditions of the Pharisees that were "making void the word of God."[345]

582   Going even further, Jesus perfects the dietary law, so important in Jewish daily life, by revealing its pedagogical meaning through a divine interpretation: "Whatever goes into a man from outside cannot defile him . . . (Thus he declared all foods clean.). What comes out of a man is what defiles a man. For from within, out of the heart of man, come evil thoughts. . . ."[346] In presenting with divine authority the definitive interpretation of the Law, Jesus found himself confronted by certain teachers of the Law who did not accept his interpretation of the Law, guaranteed though it was by the divine signs that accompanied it.[347] This was the case especially with the sabbath laws, for he recalls often with rabbinical arguments, that the sabbath rest is not violated by serving God and neighbor,[348] which his own healings did.

II.   Jesus and the Temple

583   Like the prophets before him Jesus expressed the deepest respect for the Temple in Jerusalem. It was in the Temple that Joseph and Mary presented him forty days after his birth.[349] At the age of twelve he decided to remain in the Temple to remind his parents that he must be about his Father's business.[350] He went there each year during his hidden life at least for Passover.[351] His

---

340 Cf. *Jn* 11:28; 3:2; *Mt* 22:23–24, 34–36.   341 Cf. *Mt* 12:5; 9:12; *Mk* 2:23–27; *Lk* 6:6–9; *Jn* 7:22–23.   342 *Mt* 7:28–29.   343 Cf. *Mt* 5:1.   344 *Mt* 5:33–34.   345 *Mk* 7:13; cf. 3:8.   346 *Mk* 7:18–21; cf. *Gal* 3:24.   347 Cf. *Jn* 5:36; 10:25, 37–38; 12:37.   348 Cf. *Num* 28:9; *Mt* 12:5; *Mk* 2:25–27; *Lk* 13:15–16; 14:3–4; *Jn* 7:22–24.   349 *Lk* 2:22–39.   350 Cf. *Lk* 2:46–49.   351 Cf. *Lk* 2:41.

public ministry itself was patterned by his pilgrimages to Jerusalem for the great Jewish feasts.[352]

584   Jesus went up to the Temple as the privileged place of encounter with God. For him, the Temple was the dwelling of his Father, a house of prayer, and he was angered that its outer court had become a place of commerce.[353] He drove merchants out of it because of jealous love for his Father: "You shall not make my Father's house a house of trade. His disciples remembered that it was written, 'Zeal for your house will consume me.' "[354] After his Resurrection his apostles retained their reverence for the Temple.[355]   2599

585   On the threshold of his Passion Jesus announced the coming destruction of this splendid building, of which there would not remain "one stone upon another."[356] By doing so, he announced a sign of the last days, which were to begin with his own Passover.[357] But this prophecy would be distorted in its telling by false witnesses during his interrogation at the high priest's house and would be thrown back at him as an insult when he was nailed to the cross.[358]

586   Far from having been hostile to the Temple, where he gave the essential part of his teaching, Jesus was willing to pay the temple-tax, associating with him Peter, whom he had just made the foundation of his future Church.[359] He even identified himself with the Temple by presenting himself as God's definitive dwelling-place among men.[360] Therefore his being put to bodily death[361] presaged the destruction of the Temple, which would manifest the dawning of a new age in the history of salvation: "The hour is coming when neither on this mountain nor in Jerusalem will you worship the Father."[362]   797   1179

---

352 Cf. *Jn* 2:13–14; 5:1, 14; 7:1, 10, 14; 8:2; 10:22–23.   353 Cf. *Mt* 21:13.
354 *Jn* 2:16–17; cf. *Ps* 69:10.   355 Cf. *Acts* 2:46; 3:1; 5:20, 21; etc.   356 Cf. *Mt* 24:1–2.   357 Cf. *Mt* 24:3; *Lk* 13:35.   358 Cf. *Mk* 14:57–58; *Mt* 27:39–40.
359 Cf. *Mt* 8:4; 16:18; 17:24–27; *Lk* 17:14; *Jn* 4:22; 18:20.   360 Cf. *Jn* 2:21; *Mt* 12:6.   361 Cf. *Jn* 2:18–22.   362 *Jn* 4:21; cf. *Jn* 4:23–24; *Mt* 27:51; *Heb* 9:11; *Rev* 21:22.

III.   Jesus and Israel's Faith in the One God and Savior

587   If the Law and the Jerusalem Temple could be occasions of opposition to Jesus by Israel's religious authorities, his role in the redemption of sins, the divine work par excellence, was the true stumbling-block for them.[363]

588   Jesus scandalized the Pharisees by eating with tax collectors and sinners as familiarly as with themselves.[364] Against those among them "who trusted in themselves that they were righteous and despised others," Jesus affirmed: "I have not come to call the righteous, but sinners to repentance."[365] He went further by proclaiming before the Pharisees that, since sin is universal, those who pretend not to need salvation are blind to themselves.[366]

545

589   Jesus gave scandal above all when he identified his merciful conduct toward sinners with God's own attitude toward them.[367] He went so far as to hint that by sharing the table of sinners he was admitting them to the messianic banquet.[368] But it was most especially by forgiving sins that Jesus placed the religious authorities of Israel on the horns of a dilemma. Were they not entitled to demand in consternation, "Who can forgive sins but God alone?"[369] By forgiving sins Jesus either is blaspheming as a man who made himself God's equal or is speaking the truth, and his person really does make present and reveal God's name.[370]

431, 1441

432

590   Only the divine identity of Jesus' person can justify so absolute a claim as "He who is not with me is against me"; and his saying that there was in him "something greater than Jonah, . . . greater than Solomon," something "greater than the Temple"; his reminder that David had called the Messiah his Lord,[371]

---

363 Cf. Lk 2:34; 20:17–18; Ps 118:22.   364 Cf. Lk 5:30; 7:36; 11:37; 14:1.
365 Lk 18:9; 5:32; cf. Jn 7:49; 9:34.   366 Cf. Jn 8:33–36; 9:40–41.   367 Cf. Mt 9:13; Hos 6:6.   368 Cf. Lk 15:1–2, 22–32.   369 Mk 2:7.   370 Cf. Jn 5:18; 10:33; 17:6, 26.   371 Cf. Mt 12:6, 30, 36, 37, 41–42.

and his affirmations, "Before Abraham was, I AM"; and
even "I and the Father are one."[372]   *253*

591   Jesus asked the religious authorities of Jerusalem
to believe in him because of the Father's works which he
accomplished.[373] But such an act of faith must go
through a mysterious death to self, for a new "birth
from above" under the influence of divine grace.[374] Such *526*
a demand for conversion in the face of so surprising a
fulfillment of the promises[375] allows one to understand
the Sanhedrin's tragic misunderstanding of Jesus: they
judged that he deserved the death sentence as a blasphemer.[376] The members of the Sanhedrin were thus acting at the same time out of "ignorance" and the "hard-
ness" of their "unbelief."[377]   *574*

IN BRIEF

592   Jesus did not abolish the Law of Sinai, but rather
       fulfilled it (cf. *Mt* 5:17–19) with such perfection
       (cf. *Jn* 8:46) that he revealed its ultimate mean-
       ing (cf. *Mt* 5:33) and redeemed the transgres-
       sions against it (cf. *Heb* 9:15).

593   Jesus venerated the Temple by going up to it for
       the Jewish feasts of pilgrimage, and with a jeal-
       ous love he loved this dwelling of God among
       men. The Temple prefigures his own mystery.
       When he announces its destruction, it is as a
       manifestation of his own execution and of the
       entry into a new age in the history of salvation,
       when his Body would be the definitive Temple.

594   Jesus performed acts, such as pardoning sins,
       that manifested him to be the Savior God himself
       (cf. *Jn* 5:16–18). Certain Jews, who did not rec-
       ognize God made man (cf. *Jn* 1:14), saw in him
       only a man who made himself God (*Jn* 10:33),
       and judged him as a blasphemer.

---

372 *Jn* 8:58; 10:30.   373 *Jn* 10:36–38.   374 Cf. *Jn* 3:7; 6:44.   375 Cf. *Isa* 53:1.
376 Cf. *Mk* 3:6; *Mt* 26:64–66.   377 Cf. *Lk* 23:34; *Acts* 3:17–18; *Mk* 3:5; *Rom*
11:25, 20.

Paragraph 2. Jesus Died Crucified

I.   THE TRIAL OF JESUS

Divisions among the Jewish authorities concerning Jesus

595   Among the religious authorities of Jerusalem, not only were the Pharisee Nicodemus and the prominent Joseph of Arimathea both secret disciples of Jesus, but there was also long-standing dissension about him, so much so that St. John says of these authorities on the very eve of Christ's Passion, "many . . . believed in him," though very imperfectly.[378] This is not surprising, if one recalls that on the day after Pentecost "a great many of the priests were obedient to the faith" and "some believers . . . belonged to the party of the Pharisees," to the point that St. James could tell St. Paul, "How many thousands there are among the Jews of those who have believed; and they are all zealous for the Law."[379]

596   The religious authorities in Jerusalem were not unanimous about what stance to take toward Jesus.[380] The Pharisees threatened to excommunicate his followers.[381] To those who feared that "everyone will believe in him, and the Romans will come and destroy both our holy place and our nation," the high priest Caiaphas replied by prophesying: "It is expedient for you that one man should die for the people, and that the whole nation should not perish."[382] The Sanhedrin, having declared Jesus deserving of death as a blasphemer but having lost the right to put anyone to death, hands him over to the Romans, accusing him of political revolt, a charge that puts him in the same category as Barabbas who had been accused of sedition.[383] The high priests also threatened Pilate politically so that he would condemn Jesus to death.[384]

1753

Jews are not collectively responsible for Jesus' death

597   The historical complexity of Jesus' trial is apparent in the Gospel accounts. The personal sin of the participants (Judas, the Sanhedrin, Pilate) is known to God alone. Hence we cannot lay responsibility for the trial on the Jews in Jerusalem as a whole, despite the outcry

---

378 *Jn* 12:42; cf. 7:50; 9:16–17; 10:19–21; 19:38–39.   379 *Acts* 6:7; 15:5; 21:20.
380 Cf. *Jn* 9:16; *Jn* 10:19.   381 Cf. *Jn* 9:22.   382 *Jn* 11:48–50.   383 Cf. *Mt* 26:66; *Jn* 18:31; *Lk* 23:2, 19.   384 Cf. *Jn* 19:12, 15, 21.

of a manipulated crowd and the global reproaches contained in the apostles' calls to conversion after Pentecost.[385] Jesus himself, in forgiving them on the cross, and 1735 Peter in following suit, both accept "the ignorance" of the Jews of Jerusalem and even of their leaders.[386] Still less can we extend responsibility to other Jews of different times and places, based merely on the crowd's cry: "His blood be on us and on our children!" a formula for ratifying a judicial sentence.[387] As the Church declared at the Second Vatican Council:

> ... [N]either all Jews indiscriminately at that time, nor Jews today, can be charged with the crimes committed during his Passion. . . . [T]he Jews 839 should not be spoken of as rejected or accursed as if this followed from holy Scripture.[388]

All sinners were the authors of Christ's Passion

598   In her Magisterial teaching of the faith and in the witness of her saints, the Church has never forgotten that "sinners were the authors and the ministers of all the sufferings that the divine Redeemer endured."[389] Taking into account the fact that our sins affect Christ himself,[390] the Church does not hesitate to impute to Christians the gravest responsibility for the torments inflicted upon Jesus, a responsibility with which they have all too often burdened the Jews alone:

> We must regard as guilty all those who continue to 1851 relapse into their sins. Since our sins made the Lord Christ suffer the torment of the cross, those who plunge themselves into disorders and crimes crucify the Son of God anew in their hearts (for he is in them) and hold him up to contempt. And it can be seen that our crime in this case is greater in us than in the Jews. As for them, according to the witness of the Apostle, "None of the rulers of this age understood this; for if they had, they would not have crucified the Lord of glory." We, however, profess to know him. And when we deny him by our deeds, we in some way seem to lay violent hands on him.[391]

---

385 Cf. *Mk* 15:11; *Acts* 2:23, 36; 3:13–14; 4:10; 5:30; 7:52; 10:39; 13:27–28; 1 *Thess* 2:14–15.   386 Cf. *Lk* 23:34; *Acts* 3:17.   387 *Mt* 27:25; cf. *Acts* 5:28; 18:6.   388 *NA* 4.   389 *Roman Catechism* I, 5, 11; cf. *Heb* 12:3.   390 Cf. *Mt* 25:45; *Acts* 9:4–5.   391 *Roman Catechism* I, 5, 11; cf. *Heb* 6:6; 1 *Cor* 2:8.

> Nor did demons crucify him; it is you who have crucified him and crucify him still, when you delight in your vices and sins.[392]

II.   CHRIST'S REDEMPTIVE DEATH IN GOD'S PLAN OF SALVATION

"Jesus handed over according to the definite plan of God"

599   Jesus' violent death was not the result of chance in an unfortunate coincidence of circumstances, but is *517* part of the mystery of God's plan, as St. Peter explains to the Jews of Jerusalem in his first sermon on Pentecost: "This Jesus [was] delivered up according to the definite plan and foreknowledge of God."[393] This Biblical language does not mean that those who handed him over were merely passive players in a scenario written in advance by God.[394]

600   To God, all moments of time are present in their immediacy. When therefore he establishes his eternal plan of "predestination," he includes in it each person's free response to his grace: "In this city, in fact, both Herod and Pontius Pilate, with the Gentiles and the peoples of Israel, gathered together against your holy servant Jesus, whom you anointed, to do whatever your hand and your plan had predestined to take place."[395] For the sake of accomplishing his plan of sal-*312* vation, God permitted the acts that flowed from their blindness.[396]

"He died for our sins in accordance with the Scriptures"

601   The Scriptures had foretold this divine plan of salvation through the putting to death of "the righteous one, my Servant" as a mystery of universal redemption, that is, as the ransom that would free men from the slavery of sin.[397] Citing a confession of faith that he himself had "received," St. Paul professes that "Christ died

---

392 St. Francis of Assisi, *Admonitio* 5, 3.   393 *Acts* 2:23.   394 Cf. *Acts* 3:13.
395 *Acts* 4:27–28; cf. *Ps* 2:1–2.   396 Cf. *Mt* 26:54; *Jn* 18:36; 19:11; *Acts* 3:17–18.   397 *Isa* 53:11; cf. 53:12; *Jn* 8:34–36; *Acts* 3:14.

for our sins in accordance with the scriptures."[398] In particular Jesus' redemptive death fulfills Isaiah's prophecy 652 of the suffering Servant.[399] Indeed Jesus himself explained the meaning of his life and death in the light of God's suffering Servant.[400] After his Resurrection he 713 gave this interpretation of the Scriptures to the disciples at Emmaus, and then to the apostles.[401]

"For our sake God made him to be sin"

602 Consequently, St. Peter can formulate the apostolic faith in the divine plan of salvation in this way: "You were ransomed from the futile ways inherited from your fathers . . . with the precious blood of Christ, like that of a lamb without blemish or spot. He was destined before the foundation of the world but was made manifest at the end of the times for your sake."[402] Man's sins, following on original sin, are punishable by death.[403] By sending his own Son in the form of a slave, 400 in the form of a fallen humanity, on account of sin, God 519 "made him to be sin who knew no sin, so that in him we might become the righteousness of God."[404]

603 Jesus did not experience reprobation as if he himself had sinned.[405] But in the redeeming love that always united him to the Father, he assumed us in the state of our waywardness of sin, to the point that he could say in our name from the cross: "My God, my God, why have you forsaken me?"[406] Having thus established him in solidarity with us sinners, God "did 2572 not spare his own Son but gave him up for us all," so that we might be "reconciled to God by the death of his Son."[407]

God takes the initiative of universal redeeming love

604 By giving up his own Son for our sins, God manifests that his plan for us is one of benevolent love, prior

---

398 *1 Cor* 15:3; cf. also *Acts* 3:18; 7:52; 13:29; 26:22–23.   399 Cf. *Isa* 53:7–8 and *Acts* 8:32–35.   400 Cf. *Mt* 20:28.   401 Cf. *Lk* 24:25–27, 44–45.   402 *1 Pet* 1:18–20.   403 Cf. *Rom* 5:12; *1 Cor* 15:56.   404 *2 Cor* 5:21; cf. *Phil* 2:7; *Rom* 8:3.   405 Cf. *Jn* 8:46.   406 *Mk* 15:34; *Ps* 22:2; cf. *Jn* 8:29.   407 *Rom* 8:32, 5:10.

to any merit on our part: "In this is love, not that we
211, 2009 loved God but that he loved us and sent his Son to be
1825 the expiation for our sins."[408] God "shows his love for
us in that while we were yet sinners Christ died for
us."[409]

605   At the end of the parable of the lost sheep Jesus
recalled that God's love excludes no one: "So it is not
the will of your Father who is in heaven that one of
these little ones should perish."[410] He affirms that he
came "to give his life as a ransom for many"; this last
term is not restrictive, but contrasts the whole of hu-
402 manity with the unique person of the redeemer who
hands himself over to save us.[411] The Church, following
the apostles, teaches that Christ died for all men without exception: "There is not, never has been, and never
will be a single human being for whom Christ did not
634, 2793 suffer."[412]

III.   CHRIST OFFERED HIMSELF TO HIS FATHER FOR OUR SINS

Christ's whole life is an offering to the Father

606   The Son of God, who came down "from heaven,
not to do [his] own will, but the will of him who sent
[him],"[413] said on coming into the world, "Lo, I have
517 come to do your will, O God." "And by that will we
have been sanctified through the offering of the body of
Jesus Christ once for all."[414] From the first moment of
his Incarnation the Son embraces the Father's plan of divine salvation in his redemptive mission: "My food is to
do the will of him who sent me, and to accomplish his
work."[415] The sacrifice of Jesus "for the sins of the
536 whole world"[416] expresses his loving communion with
the Father. "The Father loves me, because I lay down
my life," said the Lord, "[for] I do as the Father has
commanded me, so that the world may know that I love
the Father."[417]

---

408 *1 Jn* 4:10; 4:19.   409 *Rom* 5:8.   410 *Mt* 18:14.   411 *Mt* 20:28; cf. *Rom*
5:18–19.   412 Council of Quiercy (853): DS 624; cf. *2 Cor* 5:15; *1 Jn* 2:2.   **413**
Jn 6:38.   414 *Heb* 10:5–10.   415 *Jn* 4:34.   416 *1 Jn* 2:2.   417 *Jn* 10:17; 14:31.

607   The desire to embrace his Father's plan of redeeming love inspired Jesus' whole life,[418] for his redemptive passion was the very reason for his Incarnation. And so he asked, "And what shall I say? 'Father, save me from this hour'? No, for this purpose I have come to this hour."[419] And again, "Shall I not drink the cup which the Father has given me?"[420] From the cross, just before "It is finished," he said, "I thirst."[421]

457

"The Lamb who takes away the sin of the world"

608   After agreeing to baptize him along with the sinners, John the Baptist looked at Jesus and pointed him out as the "Lamb of God, who takes away the sin of the world."[422] By doing so, he reveals that Jesus is at the same time the suffering Servant who silently allows himself to be led to the slaughter and who bears the sin of the multitudes, and also the Paschal Lamb, the symbol of Israel's redemption at the first Passover.[423] Christ's whole life expresses his mission: "to serve and to give his life as a ransom for many."[424]

523

517

Jesus freely embraced the Father's redeeming love

609   By embracing in his human heart the Father's love for men, Jesus "loved them to the end," for "greater love has no man than this, that a man lay down his life for his friends."[425] In suffering and death his humanity became the free and perfect instrument of his divine love which desires the salvation of men.[426] Indeed, out of love for his Father and for men, whom the Father wants to save, Jesus freely accepted his Passion and death: "No one takes [my life] from me, but I lay it down of my own accord."[427] Hence the sovereign freedom of God's Son as he went out to his death.[428]

478

515

272, 539

418 Cf. *Lk* 12:50; 22:15; *Mt* 16:21–23.   419 *Jn* 12:27.   420 *Jn* 18:11.   421 *Jn* 19:30; 19:28.   422 *Jn* 1:29; cf. *Lk* 3:21; *Mt* 3:14–15; *Jn* 1:36.   423 *Isa* 53:7, 12; cf. *Jer* 11:19; *Ex* 12:3–14; *Jn* 19:36; *1 Cor* 5:7.   424 *Mk* 10:45.   425 *Jn* 13:1; 15:13.   426 Cf. *Heb* 2:10, 17–18; 4:15; 5:7–9.   427 *Jn* 10:18.   428 Cf. *Jn* 18:4–6; *Mt* 26:53.

At the Last Supper Jesus anticipated the free offering of his life

610   Jesus gave the supreme expression of his free offering of himself at the meal shared with the twelve Apostles "on the night he was betrayed."[429] On the eve of his Passion, while still free, Jesus transformed this Last Supper with the apostles into the memorial of his voluntary offering to the Father for the salvation of men: "This is my body which is given for you." "This is my blood of the covenant, which is poured out for many for the forgiveness of sins."[430]

611   The Eucharist that Christ institutes at that moment will be the memorial of his sacrifice.[431] Jesus includes the apostles in his own offering and bids them perpetuate it.[432] By doing so, the Lord institutes his apostles as priests of the New Covenant: "For their sakes I sanctify myself, so that they also may be sanctified in truth."[433]

The agony at Gethsemani

612   The cup of the New Covenant, which Jesus anticipated when he offered himself at the Last Supper, is afterwards accepted by him from his Father's hands in his agony in the garden at Gethsemani,[434] making himself "obedient unto death." Jesus prays: "My Father, if it be possible, let this cup pass from me. . . ."[435] Thus he expresses the horror that death represented for his human nature. Like ours, his human nature is destined for eternal life; but unlike ours, it is perfectly exempt from sin, the cause of death.[436] Above all, his human nature has been assumed by the divine person of the "Author of life," the "Living One."[437] By accepting in his human will that the Father's will be done, he accepts his death as redemptive, for "he himself bore our sins in his body on the tree."[438]

---

429 *Roman Missal*, EP 111; cf. *Mt* 26:20; *1 Cor* 11:23.   430 *Lk* 22:19; *Mt* 26:28; cf. *1 Cor* 5:7.   431 *1 Cor* 11:25.   432 Cf. *Lk* 22:19.   433 *Jn* 17:19; cf. Council of Trent: DS 1752; 1764.   434 Cf. *Mt* 26:42; *Lk* 22:20.   435 *Phil* 2:8; *Mt* 26:39; cf. *Heb* 5:7–8.   436 Cf. *Rom* 5:12; *Heb* 4:15.   437 Cf. *Acts* 3:15; *Rev* 1:17; *Jn* 1:4; 5:26.   438 *1 Pet* 2:24; cf. *Mt* 26:42.

Christ's death is the unique and definitive sacrifice

613 Christ's death is both the *Paschal sacrifice* that accomplishes the definitive redemption of men, through "the Lamb of God, who takes away the sin of the world,"[439] and the *sacrifice of the New Covenant,* which restores man to communion with God by reconciling him to God through the "blood of the covenant, which was poured out for many for the forgiveness of sins."[440]

1366
2009

614 This sacrifice of Christ is unique; it completes and surpasses all other sacrifices.[441] First, it is a gift from God the Father himself, for the Father handed his Son over to sinners in order to reconcile us with himself. At the same time it is the offering of the Son of God made man, who in freedom and love offered his life to his Father through the Holy Spirit in reparation for our disobedience.[442]

529, 1330
2100

Jesus substitutes his obedience for our disobedience

615 "For as by one man's disobedience many were made sinners, so by one man's obedience many will be made righteous."[443] By his obedience unto death, Jesus accomplished the substitution of the suffering Servant, who "makes himself an *offering for sin,*" when "he bore the sin of many," and who "shall make many to be accounted righteous," for "he shall bear their iniquities."[444] Jesus atoned for our faults and made satisfaction for our sins to the Father.[445]

1850

433

411

Jesus consummates his sacrifice on the Cross

616 It is love "to the end"[446] that confers on Christ's sacrifice its value as redemption and reparation, as atonement and satisfaction. He knew and loved us all when he offered his life.[447] Now "the love of Christ controls us, because we are convinced that one has died for

478

---

439 *Jn* 1:29; cf. 8:34–36; *1 Cor* 5:7; *1 Pet* 1:19.   440 *Mt* 26:28; cf. *Ex* 24:8; *Lev* 16:15–16; *1 Cor* 11:25.   441 Cf. *Heb* 10:10.   442 Cf. *Jn* 10:17–18, 15:13; *Heb* 9:14; *1 Jn* 4:10.   443 *Rom* 5:19.   444 *Isa* 53:10–12.   445 Cf. Council of Trent (1547): DS 1529.   446 *Jn* 13:1.   447 Cf. *Gal* 2:20; *Eph* 5:2, 25.

all; therefore all have died."[448] No man, not even the holiest, was ever able to take on himself the sins of all men and offer himself as a sacrifice for all. The existence in Christ of the divine person of the Son, who at once surpasses and embraces all human persons and constitutes himself as the Head of all mankind, makes possible his redemptive sacrifice *for all*.

468
519

617   The Council of Trent emphasizes the unique character of Christ's sacrifice as "the source of eternal salvation"[449] and teaches that "his most holy Passion on the wood of the cross merited justification for us."[450] And the Church venerates his cross as it sings: "Hail, O Cross, our only hope."[451]

1992
1235

Our participation in Christ's sacrifice

618   The cross is the unique sacrifice of Christ, the "one mediator between God and men."[452] But because in his incarnate divine person he has in some way united himself to every man, "the possibility of being made partners, in a way known to God, in the paschal mystery" is offered to all men.[453] He calls his disciples to "take up [their] cross and follow [him],"[454] for "Christ also suffered for [us], leaving [us] an example so that [we] should follow in his steps."[455] In fact Jesus desires to associate with his redeeming sacrifice those who were to be its first beneficiaries.[456] This is achieved supremely in the case of his mother, who was associated more intimately than any other person in the mystery of his redemptive suffering.[457]

1368, 1460
307, 2100

964

> Apart from the cross there is no other ladder by which we may get to heaven.[458]

IN BRIEF

619   "Christ died for our sins in accordance with the scriptures" (*1 Cor* 15:3).

---

448 *2 Cor* 5:14.   449 *Heb* 5:9.   450 Council of Trent: DS 1529.   451 *LH,* Lent, Holy Week, Evening Prayer, Hymn *Vexilla regis.*   452 *1 Tim* 2:5.   453 *GS* 22 § 5; cf. § 2.   454 *Mt* 16:24.   455 *1 Pet* 2:21.   456 Cf. *Mk* 10:39; *Jn* 21:18–19; *Col* 1:24.   457 Cf. *Lk* 2:35.   458 St. Rose of Lima, cf. P. Hansen, *Vita mirabilis* (Louvain, 1668).

620 Our salvation flows from God's initiative of love for us, because "he loved us and sent his Son to be the expiation for our sins" (*1 Jn* 4:10). "God was in Christ reconciling the world to himself" (*2 Cor* 5:19).

621 Jesus freely offered himself for our salvation. Beforehand, during the Last Supper, he both symbolized this offering and made it really present: "This is my body which is given for you" (*Lk* 22:19).

622 The redemption won by Christ consists in this, that he came "to give his life as a ransom for many" (*Mt* 20:28), that is, he "loved [his own] to the end" (*Jn* 13:1), so that they might be "ransomed from the futile ways inherited from [their] fathers" (*1 Pet* 1:18).

623 By his loving obedience to the Father, "unto death, even death on a cross" (*Phil* 2:8), Jesus fulfills the atoning mission (cf. *Isa* 53:10) of the suffering Servant, who will "make many righteous; and he shall bear their iniquities" (*Isa* 53:11; cf. *Rom* 5:19).

Paragraph 3. Jesus Christ Was Buried

624 "By the grace of God" Jesus tasted death "for every one."[459] In his plan of salvation, God ordained that his Son should not only "die for our sins"[460] but should also "taste death," experience the condition of death, the separation of his soul from his body, between 1005, 362 the time he expired on the cross and the time he was raised from the dead. The state of the dead Christ is the mystery of the tomb and the descent into hell. It is the mystery of Holy Saturday, when Christ, lying in the tomb,[461] reveals God's great sabbath rest[462] after the fulfillment[463] of man's salvation, which brings peace 349 to the whole universe.[464]

---

459 *Heb* 2:9.   460 *1 Cor* 15:3.   461 Cf. *Jn* 19:42.   462 Cf. *Heb* 4:7–9.
463 Cf. *Jn* 19:30.   464 Cf. *Col* 1:18–20.

Christ in the tomb in his body

625   Christ's stay in the tomb constitutes the real link
between his passible state before Easter and his glorious
and risen state today. The same person of the "Living
One" can say, "I died, and behold I am alive for ever-
more":[465]

> God [the Son] did not impede death from separat-
> ing his soul from his body according to the neces-
> sary order of nature, but has reunited them to one
> another in the Resurrection, *so that he himself*
> *might be, in his person, the meeting point for death*
> *and life,* by arresting in himself the decomposition
> of nature produced by death and so becoming the
> source of reunion for the separated parts.[466]

626   Since the "Author of life" who was killed[467] is the
470, 650 same "living one [who has] risen,"[468] the divine person of
the Son of God necessarily continued to possess his hu-
man soul and body, separated from each other by death:

> By the fact that at Christ's death his soul was sepa-
> rated from his flesh, his one person is not itself di-
> vided into two persons; for the human body and
> soul of Christ have existed in the same way from
> the beginning of his earthly existence, in the divine
> person of the Word; and in death, although sepa-
> rated from each other, both remained with one and
> the same person of the Word.[469]

"You will not let your Holy One see corruption"

627   Christ's death was a real death in that it put an
end to his earthly human existence. But because of the
union his body retained with the person of the Son, his
1009 was not a mortal corpse like others, for "divine power
1683 preserved Christ's body from corruption."[470] Both of
these statements can be said of Christ: "He was cut off
out of the land of the living,"[471] and "My flesh will
dwell in hope. For you will not abandon my soul to
Hades, nor let your Holy One see corruption."[472] Jesus'
Resurrection "on the third day" was the proof of this,

---

465 *Rev* 1:18.   466 St. Gregory of Nyssa, *Orat. catech.,* 16: PG 45, 52D.
467 *Acts* 3:15.   468 *Lk* 24:5–6.   469 St. John Damascene, *De fide orth.,* 3, 27:
PG 94, 1098A.   470 St. Thomas Aquinas, *STh* III, 51, 3.   471 *Isa* 53:8.
472 *Acts* 2:26–27; cf. *Ps* 16:9–10.

for bodily decay was held to begin on the fourth day after death.[473]

"Buried with Christ . . ."

628   Baptism, the original and full sign of which is immersion, efficaciously signifies the descent into the tomb by the Christian who dies to sin with Christ in order to live a new life. "We were buried therefore with him by baptism into death, so that as Christ was raised from the dead by the glory of the Father, we too might walk in newness of life."[474]

537

1214

IN BRIEF

629   To the benefit of every man, Jesus Christ tasted death (cf. *Heb* 2:9). It is truly the Son of God made man who died and was buried.

630   During Christ's period in the tomb, his divine person continued to assume both his soul and his body, although they were separated from each other by death. For this reason the dead Christ's body "saw no corruption" (*Acts* 13:37).

ARTICLE 5
"HE DESCENDED INTO HELL. ON THE THIRD DAY HE ROSE AGAIN"

631   Jesus "descended into the lower parts of the earth. He who descended is he who also ascended far above all the heavens."[475] The Apostles' Creed confesses in the same article Christ's descent into hell and his Resurrection from the dead on the third day, because in his Passover it was precisely out of the depths of death that he made life spring forth:

> Christ, that Morning Star, who came back from the dead,
> and shed his peaceful light on all mankind,

---

473 Cf. *1 Cor* 15:4; *Lk* 24:46; *Mt* 12:40; *Jon* 2:1; *Hos* 6:2; cf. *Jn* 11:39.
474 *Rom* 6:4; cf. *Col* 2:12; *Eph* 5:26.   475 *Eph* 4:9–10.

your Son who lives and reigns for ever and ever.
Amen.[476]

Paragraph 1. Christ Descended into Hell

632   The frequent New Testament affirmations that
Jesus was "raised from the dead" presuppose that the
crucified one sojourned in the realm of the dead prior to
his resurrection.[477] This was the first meaning given in
the apostolic preaching to Christ's descent into hell: that
Jesus, like all men, experienced death and in his soul
joined the others in the realm of the dead. But he descended there as Savior, proclaiming the Good News to
the spirits imprisoned there.[478]

633   Scripture calls the abode of the dead, to which
the dead Christ went down, "hell"—*Sheol* in Hebrew
or *Hades* in Greek—because those who are there are deprived of the vision of God.[479] Such is the case for all the
dead, whether evil or righteous, while they await the redeemer: which does not mean that their lot is identical,
as Jesus shows through the parable of the poor man
Lazarus who was received into "Abraham's bosom":[480]
"It is precisely these holy souls, who awaited their Savior in Abraham's bosom, whom Christ the Lord deliv-
1033 ered when he descended into hell."[481] Jesus did not descend into hell to deliver the damned, nor to destroy the
hell of damnation, but to free the just who had gone before him.[482]

634   "The gospel was preached even to the dead."[483]
The descent into hell brings the Gospel message of salvation to complete fulfillment. This is the last phase of Jesus'
messianic mission, a phase which is condensed in time but
vast in its real significance: the spread of Christ's redemptive work to all men of all times and all places, for all who
605 are saved have been made sharers in the redemption.

---

476 *Roman Missal,* Easter Vigil 18, *Exsultet.*   477 *Acts* 3:15; *Rom* 8:11; *1 Cor*
15:20; cf. *Heb* 13:20.   478 Cf. *1 Pet* 3:18–19.   479 Cf. *Phil* 2:10; *Acts* 2:24; *Rev*
1:18; *Eph* 4:9; *Pss* 6:6; 88:11–13.   480 Cf. *Ps* 89:49; *1 Sam* 28:19; *Ezek*
32:17–32; *Lk* 16:22–26.   481 *Roman Catechism* I, 6, 3.   482 Cf. Council of
Rome (745): DS 587; Benedict XII, *Cum dudum* (1341): DS 1011; Clement VI,
Super quibusdam (1351): DS 1077; Council of Toledo IV (625): DS 485; *Mt*
27:52–53.   483 *1 Pet* 4:6.

635   Christ went down into the depths of death so that "the dead will hear the voice of the Son of God, and those who hear will live."[484] Jesus, "the Author of life," by dying destroyed "him who has the power of death, that is, the devil, and [delivered] all those who through fear of death were subject to lifelong bondage."[485] Henceforth the risen Christ holds "the keys of Death and Hades," so that "at the name of Jesus every knee should bow, in heaven and on earth and under the earth."[486]

> Today a great silence reigns on earth, a great silence and a great stillness. A great silence because the King is asleep. The earth trembled and is still because God has fallen asleep in the flesh and he has raised up all who have slept ever since the world began. . . . He has gone to search for Adam, our first father, as for a lost sheep. Greatly desiring to visit those who live in darkness and in the shadow of death, he has gone to free from sorrow Adam in his bonds and Eve, captive with him—He who is both their God and the son of Eve. . . . "I am your God, who for your sake have become your son. . . . I order you, O sleeper, to awake. I did not create you to be a prisoner in hell. Rise from the dead, for I am the life of the dead."[487]

IN BRIEF

636   By the expression "He descended into hell," the Apostles' Creed confesses that Jesus did really die and through his death for us conquered death and the devil "who has the power of death" (*Heb* 2:14).

637   In his human soul united to his divine person, the dead Christ went down to the realm of the dead. He opened heaven's gates for the just who had gone before him.

---

484 *Jn* 5:25; cf. *Mt* 12:40; *Rom* 10:7; *Eph* 4:9.   485 *Heb* 2:14–15; cf. *Acts* 3:15.
486 *Rev* 1:18; *Phil* 2:10.   487 Ancient Homily for Holy Saturday: PG 43, 440A, 452C; *LH,* Holy Saturday, OR.

Paragraph 2. On the Third Day He Rose from the Dead

638 "We bring you the good news that what God promised to the fathers, this day he has fulfilled to us their children by raising Jesus."[488] The Resurrection of Jesus is the crowning truth of our faith in Christ, a faith believed and lived as the central truth by the first Christian community; handed on as fundamental by Tradition; established by the documents of the New Testament; and preached as an essential part of the Paschal mystery along with the cross:

> Christ is risen from the dead!
> Dying, he conquered death;
> To the dead, he has given life.[489]

I.   THE HISTORICAL AND TRANSCENDENT EVENT

639 The mystery of Christ's resurrection is a real event, with manifestations that were historically verified, as the New Testament bears witness. In about a.d. 56, St. Paul could already write to the Corinthians: "I delivered to you as of first importance what I also received, that Christ died for our sins in accordance with the scriptures, and that he was buried, that he was raised on the third day in accordance with the scriptures, and that he appeared to Cephas, then to the Twelve . . ."[490] The Apostle speaks here of the living tradition of the Resurrection which he had learned after his conversion at the gates of Damascus.[491]

The empty tomb

640 "Why do you seek the living among the dead? He is not here, but has risen."[492] The first element we encounter in the framework of the Easter events is the empty tomb. In itself it is not a direct proof of Resurrection; the absence of Christ's body from the tomb could be explained otherwise.[493] Nonetheless the empty

---

488 *Acts* 13:32–33.   489 Byzantine Liturgy, Troparion of Easter.   490 *1 Cor* 15:3–4.   491 Cf. *Acts* 9:3–18.   492 *Lk* 24:5–6.   493 Cf. *Jn* 20:13; *Mt* 28:11–15.

tomb was still an essential sign for all. Its discovery by the disciples was the first step toward recognizing the very fact of the Resurrection. This was the case, first with the holy women, and then with Peter.[494] The disciple "whom Jesus loved" affirmed that when he entered the empty tomb and discovered "the linen cloths lying there," "he saw and believed."[495] This suggests that he realized from the empty tomb's condition that the absence of Jesus' body could not have been of human doing and that Jesus had not simply returned to earthly life as had been the case with Lazarus.[496]

999

The appearances of the Risen One

641   Mary Magdalene and the holy women who came to finish anointing the body of Jesus, which had been buried in haste because the Sabbath began on the evening of Good Friday, were the first to encounter the Risen One.[497] Thus the women were the first messengers of Christ's Resurrection for the apostles themselves.[498] They were the next to whom Jesus appears: first Peter, then the Twelve. Peter had been called to strengthen the faith of his brothers,[499] and so sees the Risen One before them; it is on the basis of his testimony that the community exclaims: "The Lord has risen indeed, and has appeared to Simon!"[500]

553

448

642   Everything that happened during those Paschal days involves each of the apostles—and Peter in particular—in the building of the new era begun on Easter morning. As witnesses of the Risen One, they remain the foundation stones of his Church. The faith of the first community of believers is based on the witness of concrete men known to the Christians and for the most part still living among them. Peter and the Twelve are the primary "witnesses to his Resurrection," but they are not the only ones—Paul speaks clearly of more than five hundred persons to whom Jesus appeared on a single occasion and also of James and of all the apostles.[501]

659, 881

860

---

494 Cf. *Lk* 24:3, 12, 22–23.   495 *Jn* 20:2, 6, 8.   496 Cf. *Jn* 11:44; 20:5–7.
497 *Mk* 16:1; *Lk* 24:1; *Jn* 19:31, 42.   498 Cf. *Lk* 24:9–10; *Mt* 28:9–10; *Jn* 20:11–18.   499 Cf. *1 Cor* 15:5; *Lk* 22:31–32.   500 *Lk* 24:34, 36.   501 *1 Cor* 15:4–8; cf. *Acts* 1:22.

643   Given all these testimonies, Christ's Resurrection cannot be interpreted as something outside the physical order, and it is impossible not to acknowledge it as an historical fact. It is clear from the facts that the disciples' faith was drastically put to the test by their master's Passion and death on the cross, which he had foretold.[502] The shock provoked by the Passion was so great that at least some of the disciples did not at once believe in the news of the Resurrection. Far from showing us a community seized by a mystical exaltation, the Gospels present us with disciples demoralized ("looking sad"[503]) and frightened. For they had not believed the holy women returning from the tomb and had regarded their words as an "idle tale."[504] When Jesus reveals himself to the Eleven on Easter evening, "he upbraided them for their unbelief and hardness of heart, because they had not believed those who saw him after he had risen."[505]

644   Even when faced with the reality of the risen Jesus the disciples are still doubtful, so impossible did the thing seem: they thought they were seeing a ghost. "In their joy they were still disbelieving and still wondering."[506] Thomas will also experience the test of doubt and St. Matthew relates that during the risen Lord's last appearance in Galilee "some doubted."[507] Therefore the hypothesis that the Resurrection was produced by the apostles' faith (or credulity) will not hold up. On the contrary their faith in the Resurrection was born, under the action of divine grace, from their direct experience of the reality of the risen Jesus.

The condition of Christ's risen humanity

645   By means of touch and the sharing of a meal, the risen Jesus establishes direct contact with his disciples. He invites them in this way to recognize that he is not a ghost and above all to verify that the risen body in which he appears to them is the same body that had been tortured and crucified, for it still bears the traces of his passion.[508] Yet at the same time this authentic, real body possesses the new properties of a glorious body: not limited by space and time but able to be present how and when he wills; for Christ's humanity can no longer be confined to earth and belongs henceforth only

999

---

502 Cf. *Lk* 22:31–32.   503 *Lk* 24:17; cf. *Jn* 20:19.   504 *Lk* 24:11; cf. *Mk* 16:11, 13.   505 *Mk* 16:14.   506 *Lk* 24:38–41.   507 Cf. *Jn* 20:24–27; *Mt* 28:17. 508 Cf. *Lk* 24:30, 39–40, 41–43; *Jn* 20:20, 27; 21:9, 13–15.

to the Father's divine realm.[509] For this reason too the risen Jesus enjoys the sovereign freedom of appearing as he wishes: in the guise of a gardener or in other forms familiar to his disciples, precisely to awaken their faith.[510]

646   Christ's Resurrection was not a return to earthly life, as was the case with the raisings from the dead that he had performed before Easter: Jairus' daughter, the young man of Naim, Lazarus. These actions were miraculous events, but the persons miraculously raised returned by Jesus' power to ordinary earthly life. At some particular moment they would die again. Christ's Resurrection is essentially different. In his risen body he passes from the state of death to another life beyond time and space. At Jesus' Resurrection his body is filled with the power of the Holy Spirit: he shares the divine life in his glorious state, so that St. Paul can say that Christ is "the man of heaven."[511]

934
549

The Resurrection as transcendent event

647   O truly blessed Night, sings the Exsultet of the Easter Vigil, which alone deserved to know the time and the hour when Christ rose from the realm of the dead![512] But no one was an eyewitness to Christ's Resurrection and no evangelist describes it. No one can say how it came about physically. Still less was its innermost essence, his passing over to another life, perceptible to the senses. Although the Resurrection was an historical event that could be verified by the sign of the empty tomb and by the reality of the apostles' encounters with the risen Christ, still it remains at the very heart of the mystery of faith as something that transcends and surpasses history. This is why the risen Christ does not reveal himself to the world, but to his disciples, "to those who came up with him from Galilee to Jerusalem, who are now his witnesses to the people."[513]

1000

---

509 Cf. *Mt* 28:9, 16–17; *Lk* 24:15, 36; *Jn* 20:14, 17, 19, 26; 21:4.   510 Cf. *Mk* 16:12; *Jn* 20:14–16; 21:4, 7.   511 Cf. *1 Cor* 15:35–50.   512 *"O vere beata nox, quae sola meruit scire tempus et horam, in qua Christus ab inferis resurrexit!"* 513 *Acts* 13:31; cf. *Jn* 14:22.

II. THE RESURRECTION—A WORK OF THE HOLY TRINITY

648   Christ's Resurrection is an object of faith in that it is a transcendent intervention of God himself in creation and history. In it the three divine persons act together as one, and manifest their own proper characteristics. The Father's power "raised up" Christ his Son and by doing so perfectly introduced his Son's humanity, including his body, into the Trinity. Jesus is conclusively revealed as "Son of God in power according to the Spirit of holiness by his Resurrection from the dead."[514] St. Paul insists on the manifestation of God's power[515] through the working of the Spirit who gave life to Jesus' dead humanity and called it to the glorious state of Lordship.

649   As for the Son, he effects his own Resurrection by virtue of his divine power. Jesus announces that the Son of man will have to suffer much, die, and then rise.[516] Elsewhere he affirms explicitly: "I lay down my life, that I may take it again. . . . I have power to lay it down, and I have power to take it again."[517] "We believe that Jesus died and rose again."[518]

650   The Fathers contemplate the Resurrection from the perspective of the divine person of Christ who remained united to his soul and body, even when these were separated from each other by death: "By the unity of the divine nature, which remains present in each of the two components of man, these are reunited. For as death is produced by the separation of the human components, so Resurrection is achieved by the union of the two."[519]

III. THE MEANING AND SAVING SIGNIFICANCE OF THE RESURRECTION

651   "If Christ has not been raised, then our preaching is in vain and your faith is in vain."[520] The Resur-

---

514 *Rom* 1:3–4; cf. *Acts* 2:24.   515 Cf. *Rom* 6:4; *2 Cor* 13:4; *Phil* 3:10; *Eph* 1:19–22; *Heb* 7:16.   516 Cf. *Mk* 8:31; 9:9–31; 10:34.   517 *Jn* 10:17–18. 518 *1 Thess* 4:14.   519 St. Gregory of Nyssa, *In Christi res. orat.* 1: PG 46:617B; cf. also DS 325; 359; 369.   520 *1 Cor* 15:14.

rection above all constitutes the confirmation of all
Christ's works and teachings. All truths, even those
most inaccessible to human reason, find their justifi- 129
cation if Christ by his Resurrection has given the defin- 274
itive proof of his divine authority, which he had
promised.

652 Christ's Resurrection is the fulfillment of the
promises both of the Old Testament and of Jesus him- 994, 601
self during his earthly life.[521] The phrase "in accordance
with the Scriptures"[522] indicates that Christ's Resurrection fulfilled these predictions.

653 The truth of Jesus' divinity is confirmed by his 445
Resurrection. He had said: "When you have lifted up
the Son of man, then you will know that I am he."[523]
The Resurrection of the crucified one shows that he was
truly "I Am," the Son of God and God himself. So St.
Paul could declare to the Jews: "What God promised to
the fathers, this he has fulfilled to us their children by
raising Jesus; as also it is written in the second psalm,
'You are my Son, today I have begotten you.' "[524]
Christ's Resurrection is closely linked to the Incarnation
of God's Son and is its fulfillment in accordance with
God's eternal plan. 461, 422

654 The Paschal mystery has two aspects: by his
death, Christ liberates us from sin; by his Resurrection,
he opens for us the way to a new life. This new life is
above all justification that reinstates us in God's grace,
"so that as Christ was raised from the dead by the glory 1987
of the Father, we too might walk in newness of life."[525]
Justification consists in both victory over the death
caused by sin and a new participation in grace.[526] It
brings about filial adoption so that men become Christ's
brethren, as Jesus himself called his disciples after his 1996
Resurrection: "Go and tell my brethren."[527] We are
brethren not by nature, but by the gift of grace, because
that adoptive filiation gains us a real share in the life of

521 Cf. *Mt* 28:6; *Mk* 16:7; *Lk* 24:6–7, 26–27, 44–48. 522 Cf. *1 Cor* 15:3–4; cf.
the Nicene Creed. 523 *Jn* 8:28. 524 *Acts* 13:32–34; cf. *Ps* 2:7. 525 *Rom* 6:4;
cf. 4:25. 526 Cf. *Eph* 2:4–5; *1 Pet* 1:3. 527 *Mt* 28:10; *Jn* 20:17.

the only Son, which was fully revealed in his Resurrection.

655 Finally, Christ's Resurrection—and the risen Christ himself—is the principle and source of our future
989 resurrection: "Christ has been raised from the dead, the first fruits of those who have fallen asleep. . . . For as in Adam all die, so also in Christ shall all be made alive."[528] The risen Christ lives in the hearts of his faithful while they await that fulfillment. In Christ, Christians "have tasted . . . the powers of the age to come"[529]
1002 and their lives are swept up by Christ into the heart of divine life, so that they may "live no longer for themselves but for him who for their sake died and was raised."[530]

IN BRIEF

656 Faith in the Resurrection has as its object an event which is historically attested to by the disciples, who really encountered the Risen One. At the same time, this event is mysteriously transcendent insofar as it is the entry of Christ's humanity into the glory of God.

657 The empty tomb and the linen cloths lying there signify in themselves that by God's power Christ's body had escaped the bonds of death and corruption. They prepared the disciples to encounter the Risen Lord.

658 Christ, "the first-born from the dead" (*Col* 1:18), is the principle of our own resurrection, even now by the justification of our souls (cf. *Rom* 6:4), and one day by the new life he will impart to our bodies (cf. *Rom* 8:11).

---

528 1 Cor 15:20–22.   529 Heb 6:5.   530 2 Cor 5:15; cf. Col 3:1–3.

ARTICLE 6
"HE ASCENDED INTO HEAVEN AND IS SEATED AT THE RIGHT HAND OF THE FATHER"

659   "So then the Lord Jesus, after he had spoken to them, was taken up into heaven, and sat down at the right hand of God."[531] Christ's body was glorified at the moment of his Resurrection, as proved by the new and supernatural properties it subsequently and perma- 645 nently enjoys.[532] But during the forty days when he eats and drinks familiarly with his disciples and teaches them about the kingdom, his glory remains veiled under the appearance of ordinary humanity.[533] Jesus' final apparition ends with the irreversible entry of his humanity into divine glory, symbolized by the cloud and by 66 heaven, where he is seated from that time forward at 697 God's right hand.[534] Only in a wholly exceptional and 642 unique way would Jesus show himself to Paul "as to one untimely born," in a last apparition that established him as an apostle.[535]

660   The veiled character of the glory of the Risen One during this time is intimated in his mysterious words to Mary Magdalene: "I have not yet ascended to the Father; but go to my brethren and say to them, I am ascending to my Father and your Father, to my God and your God."[536] This indicates a difference in manifestation between the glory of the risen Christ and that of the Christ exalted to the Father's right hand, a transition marked by the historical and transcendent event of the Ascension.

661   This final stage stays closely linked to the first, that is, to his descent from heaven in the Incarnation. Only the one who "came from the Father" can return to 461 the Father: Christ Jesus.[537] "No one has ascended into heaven but he who descended from heaven, the Son of

---

531 *Mk* 16:19.   532 Cf. *Lk* 24:31; *Jn* 20:19, 26.   533 Cf. *Acts* 1:3; 10:41; *Mk* 16:12; *Lk* 24:15; *Jn* 20:14–15; 21:4.   534 Cf. *Acts* 1:9; 2:33; 7:56; *Lk* 9:34–35; 24:51; *Ex* 13:22; *Mk* 16:19; *Ps* 110:1.   535 *1 Cor* 15:8; cf. 9:1; *Gal* 1:16.   536 *Jn* 20:17.   537 Cf. *Jn* 16:28.

man."[538] Left to its own natural powers humanity does not have access to the "Father's house," to God's life 792 and happiness.[539] Only Christ can open to man such access that we, his members, might have confidence that we too shall go where he, our Head and our Source, has preceded us.[540]

662 "And I, when I am lifted up from the earth, will draw all men to myself."[541] The lifting up of Jesus on the cross signifies and announces his lifting up by his Ascension into heaven, and indeed begins it. Jesus Christ, 1545 the one priest of the new and eternal Covenant, "entered, not into a sanctuary made by human hands . . . but into heaven itself, now to appear in the presence of God on our behalf."[542] There Christ permanently exercises his priesthood, for he "always lives to make intercession" for "those who draw near to God through him."[543] As "high priest of the good things to come" he 1137 is the center and the principal actor of the liturgy that honors the Father in heaven.[544]

663 Henceforth Christ is *seated at the right hand of the Father:* "By 'the Father's right hand' we understand the glory and honor of divinity, where he who exists as Son of God before all ages, indeed as God, of one being with the Father, is seated bodily after he became incar-648 nate and his flesh was glorified."[545]

664 Being seated at the Father's right hand signifies the inauguration of the Messiah's kingdom, the fulfillment 541 of the prophet Daniel's vision concerning the Son of man: "To him was given dominion and glory and kingdom, that all peoples, nations, and languages should serve him; his dominion is an everlasting dominion, which shall not pass away, and his kingdom one that shall not be destroyed."[546] After this event the apostles became witnesses of the "kingdom [that] will have no end."[547]

---

538 *Jn* 3:13; cf. *Eph* 4:8–10.   539 *Jn* 14:2.   540 *Roman Missal,* Preface of the Ascension: *"sed ut illuc confideremus, sua membra, nos subsequi quo ipse, caput nostrum principiumque, praecessit."*   541 *Jn* 12:32.   542 *Heb* 9:24.   543 *Heb* 7:25.   544 *Heb* 9:11; cf. *Rev* 4:6–11.   545 St. John Damascene, *De fide orth.,* 4, 2: PG 94, 1104C.   546 *Dan* 7:14.   547 Nicene Creed.

IN BRIEF

665   Christ's ascension marks the definitive entrance of Jesus' humanity into God's heavenly domain, whence he will come again (cf. *Acts* 1:11); this humanity in the meantime hides him from the eyes of men (cf. *Col* 3:3).

666   Jesus Christ, the head of the Church, precedes us into the Father's glorious kingdom so that we, the members of his Body, may live in the hope of one day being with him for ever.

667   Jesus Christ, having entered the sanctuary of heaven once and for all, intercedes constantly for us as the mediator who assures us of the permanent outpouring of the Holy Spirit.

ARTICLE 7
"FROM THENCE HE WILL COME AGAIN TO JUDGE THE LIVING AND THE DEAD"

I.   HE WILL COME AGAIN IN GLORY

Christ already reigns through the Church . . .

668   "Christ died and lived again, that he might be Lord both of the dead and of the living."[548] Christ's Ascension into heaven signifies his participation, in his humanity, in God's power and authority. Jesus Christ is Lord: he possesses all power in heaven and on earth. He is "far above all rule and authority and power and dominion," for the Father "has put all things under his feet."[549] Christ is Lord of the cosmos and of history. In him human history and indeed all creation are "set forth" and transcendently fulfilled.[550]   450   518

669   As Lord, Christ is also head of the Church, which is his Body.[551] Taken up to heaven and glorified after he had thus fully accomplished his mission, Christ

---

548 *Rom* 14:9.   549 *Eph* 1:20–22.   550 *Eph* 1:10; cf. *Eph* 4:10; *1 Cor* 15:24, 27–28.   551 Cf. *Eph* 1:22.

792, 1088 dwells on earth in his Church. The redemption is the source of the authority that Christ, by virtue of the Holy
541 Spirit, exercises over the Church. "The kingdom of Christ [is] already present in mystery," "on earth, the seed and the beginning of the kingdom."[552]

670   Since the Ascension God's plan has entered into its fulfillment. We are already at "the last hour."[553] "Already the final age of the world is with us, and the re-
1042 newal of the world is irrevocably under way; it is even now anticipated in a certain real way, for the Church on earth is endowed already with a sanctity that is real but
825 imperfect."[554] Christ's kingdom already manifests its
547 presence through the miraculous signs that attend its proclamation by the Church.[555]

. . . until all things are subjected to him

671   Though already present in his Church, Christ's reign is nevertheless yet to be fulfilled "with power and great glory" by the king's return to earth.[556] This reign is still under attack by the evil powers, even though they have been defeated definitively by Christ's Passover.[557]
1043 Until everything is subject to him, "until there be realized new heavens and a new earth in which justice
769, 773 dwells, the pilgrim Church, in her sacraments and institutions, which belong to this present age, carries the mark of this world which will pass, and she herself takes her place among the creatures which groan and travail yet and await the revelation of the sons of
1043, 2046 God."[558] That is why Christians pray, above all in the Eucharist, to hasten Christ's return by saying to him:[559]
2817 *Marana tha!* "Our Lord, come!"[560]

672   Before his Ascension Christ affirmed that the hour had not yet come for the glorious establishment of the messianic kingdom awaited by Israel[561] which, according to the prophets, was to bring all men the defin-

552 LG 3; 5; cf. Eph 4:11–13.   553 1 Jn 2:18; cf. 1 Pet 4:7.   554 LG 48 § 3; cf. 1 Cor 10:11.   555 Cf. Mk 16:17–18, 20.   556 Lk 21:27; cf. Mt 25:31.   557 Cf. 2 Thess 2:7.   558 LG 48 § 3; cf. 2 Pet 3:13; Rom 8:19–22; 1 Cor 15:28.   559 Cf. 1 Cor 11:26; 2 Pet 3:11–12.   560 1 Cor 16:22; Rev 22:17, 20.   561 Cf. Acts 1:6–7.

itive order of justice, love, and peace.[562] According to the Lord, the present time is the time of the Spirit and of witness, but also a time still marked by "distress"   732 and the trial of evil which does not spare the Church[563] and ushers in the struggles of the last days. It is a time   2612 of waiting and watching.[564]

The glorious advent of Christ, the hope of Israel

673   Since the Ascension Christ's coming in glory has been imminent,[565] even though "it is not for you to know times or seasons which the Father has fixed by his   1040, 1048 own authority."[566] This eschatological coming could be accomplished at any moment, even if both it and the final trial that will precede it are "delayed."[567]

674   The glorious Messiah's coming is suspended at every moment of history until his recognition by "all Israel," for "a hardening has come upon part of Israel" in their "unbelief" toward Jesus.[568] St. Peter says to the Jews of Jerusalem after Pentecost: "Repent therefore, and turn again, that your sins may be blotted out, that times of refreshing may come from the presence of the Lord, and that he may send the Christ appointed for you, Jesus, whom heaven must receive until the time for establishing all that God spoke by the mouth of his holy prophets from of old."[569] St. Paul echoes him: "For if their rejection means the reconciliation of the world, what will their acceptance mean but life from the dead?"[570] The "full inclusion" of the Jews in the Mes-   840 siah's salvation, in the wake of "the full number of the Gentiles,"[571] will enable the People of God to achieve "the measure of the stature of the fullness of Christ," in   58 which "God may be all in all."[572]

The Church's ultimate trial

675   Before Christ's second coming the Church must pass through a final trial that will shake the faith of

---

562 Cf. *Isa* 11:1–9.   563 Cf. *Acts* 1:8; *1 Cor* 7:26; *Eph* 5:16; *1 Pet* 4:17.
564 Cf. *Mt* 25:1, 13; *Mk* 13:33–37; *1 Jn* 2:18; 4:3; *1 Tim* 4:1.   565 Cf. *Rev* 22:20.   566 *Acts* 1:7; cf. *Mk* 13:32.   567 Cf. *Mt* 24:44; *1 Thess* 5:2; *2 Thess* 2:3–12.   568 *Rom* 11:20–26; cf. *Mt* 23:39.   569 *Acts* 3:19–21.   570 *Rom* 11:15.   571 *Rom* 11:12, 25; cf. *Lk* 21:24.   572 *Eph* 4:13; *1 Cor* 15:28.

769 many believers.[573] The persecution that accompanies her pilgrimage on earth[574] will unveil the "mystery of iniquity" in the form of a religious deception offering men an apparent solution to their problems at the price of apostasy from the truth. The supreme religious deception is that of the Antichrist, a pseudo-messianism by which man glorifies himself in place of God and of his Messiah come in the flesh.[575]

676   The Antichrist's deception already begins to take shape in the world every time the claim is made to realize within history that messianic hope which can only be realized beyond history through the eschatalogical judgment. The Church has rejected even modified forms of this falsification of the kingdom to come under the name of millenarianism,[576] especially the "intrinsically perverse" 2425 political form of a secular messianism.[577]

677   The Church will enter the glory of the kingdom only through this final Passover, when she will follow 1340 her Lord in his death and Resurrection.[578] The kingdom will be fulfilled, then, not by a historic triumph of the Church through a progressive ascendancy, but only by God's victory over the final unleashing of evil, which 2853 will cause his Bride to come down from heaven.[579] God's triumph over the revolt of evil will take the form of the Last Judgment after the final cosmic upheaval of this passing world.[580]

1038-1041 ## II.   TO JUDGE THE LIVING AND THE DEAD

678   Following in the steps of the prophets and John the Baptist, Jesus announced the judgment of the Last 1470 Day in his preaching.[581] Then will the conduct of each one and the secrets of hearts be brought to light.[582] Then will the culpable unbelief that counted the offer of God's grace as nothing be condemned.[583] Our attitude about our neighbor will disclose acceptance or refusal

---

573 Cf. *Lk* 18:8; *Mt* 24:12.   574 Cf. *Lk* 21:12; *Jn* 15:19–20.   575 Cf. *2 Thess* 2:4–12; *1 Thess* 5:2–3; *2 Jn* 7; *1 Jn* 2:18, 22.   576 Cf. DS 3839.   577 Pius XI, *Divini Redemptoris*, condemning the "false mysticism" of this "counterfeit of the redemption of the lowly"; cf. *GS* 20–21.   578 Cf. *Rev* 19:1–9.   579 Cf. *Rev* 13:8; 20:7–10; 21:2–4.   580 Cf. *Rev* 20:12; *2 Pet* 3:12–13.   581 Cf. *Dan* 7:10; *Joel* 3–4; *Mal* 3:19; *Mt* 3:7–12.   582 Cf. *Mk* 12:38–40; *Lk* 12:1–3; *Jn* 3:20–21; *Rom* 2:16; *1 Cor* 4:5.   583 Cf. *Mt* 11:20–24; 12:41–42.

of grace and divine love.[584] On the last day Jesus will say: "Truly I say to you, as you did it to one of the least of these my brethren, you did it to me."[585]

679   Christ is Lord of eternal life. Full right to pass definitive judgment on the works and hearts of men belongs to him as redeemer of the world. He "acquired" this right by his cross. The Father has given "all judgment to the Son."[586] Yet the Son did not come to judge,   *1021* but to save and to give the life he has in himself.[587] By rejecting grace in this life, one already judges oneself, receives according to one's works, and can even condemn oneself for all eternity by rejecting the Spirit of love.[588]

IN BRIEF

680   Christ the Lord already reigns through the Church, but all the things of this world are not yet subjected to him. The triumph of Christ's kingdom will not come about without one last assault by the powers of evil.

681   On Judgment Day at the end of the world, Christ will come in glory to achieve the definitive triumph of good over evil which, like the wheat and the tares, have grown up together in the course of history.

682   When he comes at the end of time to judge the living and the dead, the glorious Christ will reveal the secret disposition of hearts and will render to each man according to his works and according to his acceptance or refusal of grace.

---

584 Cf. *Mt* 5:22; 7:1–5.   585 *Mt* 25:40.   586 *Jn* 5:22; cf. 5:27; *Mt* 25:31; *Acts* 10:42; 17:31; *2 Tim* 4:1.   587 Cf. *Jn* 3:17; 5:26.   588 Cf. *Jn* 3:18; 12:48; *Mt* 12:32; *1 Cor* 3:12–15; *Heb* 6:4–6; 10:26–31.

CHAPTER THREE
I BELIEVE IN THE HOLY SPIRIT

683   "No one can say 'Jesus is Lord' except by the Holy Spirit."[1] "God has sent the Spirit of his Son into our hearts, crying, '*Abba!* Father!' "[2] This knowledge of faith is possible only in the Holy Spirit: to be in touch with Christ, we must first have been touched by the Holy Spirit. He comes to meet us and kindles faith in us. By virtue of our Baptism, the first sacrament of the faith, the Holy Spirit in the Church communicates to us, intimately and personally, the life that originates in the Father and is offered to us in the Son.

> Baptism gives us the grace of new birth in God the Father, through his Son, in the Holy Spirit. For those who bear God's Spirit are led to the Word, that is, to the Son, and the Son presents them to the Father, and the Father confers incorruptibility on them. And it is impossible to see God's Son without the Spirit, and no one can approach the Father without the Son, for the knowledge of the Father is the Son, and the knowledge of God's Son is obtained through the Holy Spirit.[3]

684   Through his grace, the Holy Spirit is the first to awaken faith in us and to communicate to us the new life, which is to "know the Father and the one whom he has sent, Jesus Christ."[4] But the Spirit is the last of the persons of the Holy Trinity to be revealed. St. Gregory of Nazianzus, the Theologian, explains this progression in terms of the pedagogy of divine "condescension":

> The Old Testament proclaimed the Father clearly, but the Son more obscurely. The New Testament revealed the Son and gave us a glimpse of the divinity of the Spirit. Now the Spirit dwells among us and grants us a clearer vision of himself. It was not prudent, when the divinity of the Father had not yet been confessed, to proclaim the Son openly and, when the divinity of the Son was not yet admitted, to add the Holy Spirit as an extra burden, to speak somewhat daringly. . . . By advancing and progress-

margin references: 424, 2670 · 152 · 249 · 236

---

1 *1 Cor* 12:3.   2 *Gal* 4:6.   3 St. Irenæus, *Dem. ap.* 7: SCh 62, 41–42.   4 *Jn* 17:3.

ing "from glory to glory," the light of the Trinity will shine in ever more brilliant rays.[5]

685   To believe in the Holy Spirit is to profess that the Holy Spirit is one of the persons of the Holy Trinity, consubstantial with the Father and the Son: "with the Father and the Son he is worshipped and glorified."[6] For this reason, the divine mystery of the Holy Spirit was already treated in the context of Trinitarian "theology." Here, however, we have to do with the Holy Spirit only in the divine "economy." 236

686   The Holy Spirit is at work with the Father and the Son from the beginning to the completion of the plan for our salvation. But in these "end times," ushered in by the Son's redeeming Incarnation, the Spirit is revealed and given, recognized and welcomed as a person. 258 Now can this divine plan, accomplished in Christ, the firstborn and head of the new creation, be embodied in mankind by the outpouring of the Spirit: as the Church, the communion of saints, the forgiveness of sins, the resurrection of the body, and the life everlasting.

Article 8
"I BELIEVE IN THE HOLY SPIRIT"

687   "No one comprehends the thoughts of God except the Spirit of God."[7] Now God's Spirit, who reveals God, makes known to us Christ, his Word, his living Utterance, but the Spirit does not speak of himself. The 243 Spirit who "has spoken through the prophets" makes us hear the Father's Word, but we do not hear the Spirit himself. We know him only in the movement by which he reveals the Word to us and disposes us to welcome him in faith. The Spirit of truth who "unveils" Christ to us "will not speak on his own."[8] Such properly divine self-effacement explains why "the world cannot receive [him], because it neither sees him nor knows him,"

---

5 St. Gregory of Nazianzus, *Oratio theol.*, 5, 26 (= *Oratio* 31, 26): PG 36, 161–163.   6 Nicene Creed; see above, par. 465.   7 1 *Cor* 2:11.   8 *Jn* 16:13.

while those who believe in Christ know the Spirit because he dwells with them.[9]

688   The Church, a communion living in the faith of the apostles which she transmits, is the place where we know the Holy Spirit:

—in the Scriptures he inspired;

—in the Tradition, to which the Church Fathers are always timely witnesses;

—in the Church's Magisterium, which he assists;

—in the sacramental liturgy, through its words and symbols, in which the Holy Spirit puts us into communion with Christ;

—in prayer, wherein he intercedes for us;

—in the charisms and ministries by which the Church is built up;

—in the signs of apostolic and missionary life;

—in the witness of saints through whom he manifests his holiness and continues the work of salvation.

I.   THE JOINT MISSION OF THE SON AND THE SPIRIT

689   The One whom the Father has sent into our hearts, the Spirit of his Son, is truly God.[10] Consubstantial with the Father and the Son, the Spirit is inseparable from them, in both the inner life of the Trinity and his gift of love for the world. In adoring the Holy Trinity, life-giving, consubstantial, and indivisible, the Church's faith also professes the distinction of persons. When the Father sends his Word, he always sends his Breath. In their joint mission, the Son and the Holy Spirit are distinct but inseparable. To be sure, it is Christ who is seen, the visible image of the invisible God, but it is the Spirit who reveals him.

690   Jesus is Christ, "anointed," because the Spirit is

---

9 *Jn* 14:17.   10 Cf. *Gal* 4:6.

his anointing, and everything that occurs from the Incarnation on derives from this fullness.[11] When Christ is finally glorified,[12] he can in turn send the Spirit from his place with the Father to those who believe in him: he communicates to them his glory,[13] that is, the Holy Spirit who glorifies him.[14] From that time on, this joint mission will be manifested in the children adopted by the Father in the Body of his Son: the mission of the Spirit of adoption is to unite them to Christ and make them live in him: *436* *788*

> The notion of anointing suggests . . . that there is no distance between the Son and the Spirit. Indeed, just as between the surface of the body and the anointing with oil neither reason nor sensation recognizes any intermediary, so the contact of the Son with the Spirit is immediate, so that anyone who would make contact with the Son by faith must first encounter the oil by contact. In fact there is no part that is not covered by the Holy Spirit. That is why the confession of the Son's Lordship is made in the Holy Spirit by those who receive him, the Spirit coming from all sides to those who approach the Son in faith.[15] *448*

II.   THE NAME, TITLES, AND SYMBOLS OF THE HOLY SPIRIT

The proper name of the Holy Spirit

691   "Holy Spirit" is the proper name of the one whom we adore and glorify with the Father and the Son. The Church has received this name from the Lord and professes it in the Baptism of her new children.[16]

> The term "Spirit" translates the Hebrew word *ruah,* which, in its primary sense, means breath, air, wind. Jesus indeed uses the sensory image of the wind to suggest to Nicodemus the transcendent newness of him who is personally God's breath, the divine Spirit.[17] On the other hand, "Spirit" and "Holy" are divine attributes common to the three divine persons. By joining the two terms, Scripture,

---

11 Cf. *Jn* 3:34.   12 *Jn* 7:39.   13 Cf. *Jn* 17:22.   14 Cf. *Jn* 16:14.   15 St. Gregory of Nyssa, *De Spiritu Sancto,* 16: PG 45, 1321A–B.   16 Cf. *Mt* 28:19.   17 *Jn* 3:5–8.

liturgy, and theological language designate the inexpressible person of the Holy Spirit, without any possible equivocation with other uses of the terms "spirit" and "holy."

Titles of the Holy Spirit

692   When he proclaims and promises the coming of the Holy Spirit, Jesus calls him the "Paraclete," literally, "he who is called to one's side," *ad-vocatus*.[18] "Para-

1433 clete" is commonly translated by "consoler," and Jesus is the first consoler.[19] The Lord also called the Holy Spirit "the Spirit of truth."[20]

693   Besides the proper name of "Holy Spirit," which is most frequently used in the *Acts of the Apostles* and in the Epistles, we also find in St. Paul the titles: the Spirit of the promise,[21] the Spirit of adoption,[22] the Spirit of Christ,[23] the Spirit of the Lord,[24] and the Spirit of God[25]—and, in St. Peter, the Spirit of glory.[26]

Symbols of the Holy Spirit

694   *Water.* The symbolism of water signifies the Holy Spirit's action in Baptism, since after the invocation of the Holy Spirit it becomes the efficacious sacramental sign of

1218 new birth: just as the gestation of our first birth took place in water, so the water of Baptism truly signifies that our birth into the divine life is given to us in the Holy Spirit. As "by one Spirit we were all baptized," so we are also "made to drink of one Spirit."[27] Thus the Spirit is also personally the living water welling up from Christ crucified[28] as its

2652 source and welling up in us to eternal life.[29]

695   *Anointing.* The symbolism of anointing with oil also signifies the Holy Spirit,[30] to the point of becoming a synonym for the Holy Spirit. In Christian initiation, anoint-

1293 ing is the sacramental sign of Confirmation, called "chrismation" in the Churches of the East. Its full force can be grasped only in relation to the primary anointing accomplished by the Holy Spirit, that of Jesus. Christ (in Hebrew

436 *"messiah"*) means the one "anointed" by God's Spirit. There were several anointed ones of the Lord in the Old

18 *Jn* 14:16, 26; 15:26; 16:7.   19 Cf. *1 Jn* 2:1.   20 *Jn* 16:13.   21 Cf. *Gal* 3:14; *Eph* 1:13.   22 *Rom* 8:15; *Gal* 4:6.   23 *Rom* 8:9.   24 *2 Cor* 3:17.   25 *Rom* 8:9, 14; 15:19; *1 Cor* 6:11; 7:40.   26 *1 Pet* 4:14.   27 *1 Cor* 12:13.   28 *Jn* 19:34; *1 Jn* 5:8.   29 Cf. *Jn* 4:10–14; 7:38; *Ex* 17:1–6; *Isa* 55:1; *Zech* 14:8; *1 Cor* 10:4; *Rev* 21:6; 22:17.   30 Cf. *1 Jn* 2:20:27; *2 Cor* 1:21.

Covenant, pre-eminently King David.[31] But Jesus is God's Anointed in a unique way: the humanity the Son assumed was entirely anointed by the Holy Spirit. The Holy Spirit established him as "Christ."[32] The Virgin Mary conceived Christ by the Holy Spirit who, through the angel, proclaimed him the Christ at his birth, and prompted Simeon to come to the temple to see the Christ of the Lord.[33] The Spirit filled Christ and the power of the Spirit went out from him in his acts of healing and of saving.[34] Finally, it was the Spirit who raised Jesus from the dead.[35] Now, fully established as "Christ" in his humanity victorious over death, Jesus pours out the Holy Spirit abundantly until "the saints" constitute—in their union with the humanity of the Son of God—that perfect man "to the measure of the stature of the fullness of Christ":[36] "the whole Christ," in St. Augustine's expression. *1504* *794*

696   *Fire.* While water signifies birth and the fruitfulness of life given in the Holy Spirit, fire symbolizes the transforming energy of the Holy Spirit's actions. The prayer of the prophet Elijah, who "arose like fire" and whose "word burned like a torch," brought down fire from heaven on the sacrifice on Mount Carmel.[37] This event was a "figure" of the fire of the Holy Spirit, who transforms what he touches. John the Baptist, who goes "before [the Lord] in the spirit and power of Elijah," proclaims Christ as the one who "will baptize you with the Holy Spirit and with fire."[38] Jesus will say of the Spirit: "I came to cast fire upon the earth; and would that it were already kindled!"[39] In the form of tongues "as of fire," the Holy Spirit rests on the disciples on the morning of Pentecost and fills them with himself.[40] The spiritual tradition has retained this symbolism of fire as one of the most expressive images of the Holy Spirit's actions.[41] "Do not quench the Spirit."[42] *1127* *2586* *718*

697   *Cloud and light.* These two images occur together in the manifestations of the Holy Spirit. In the theophanies of the Old Testament, the cloud, now obscure, now luminous, reveals the living and saving God, while veiling the transcendence of his glory—with Moses on Mount Sinai,[43] at the tent of meeting,[44] and during the wandering in the

---

31 Cf. *Ex* 30:22–32; *1 Sam* 16:13.   32 Cf. *Lk* 4:18–19; *Isa* 61:1.   33 Cf. *Lk* 2:11, 26–27.   34 Cf. *Lk* 4:1; 6:19; 8:46.   35 Cf. *Rom* 1:4; 8:11.   36 *Eph* 4:13; cf. *Acts* 2:36.   37 *Sir* 48:1; cf. *1 Kings* 18:38–39.   38 *Lk* 1:17; 3:16.   39 *Lk* 12:49.   40 *Acts* 2:3–4.   41 Cf. St. John of the Cross, *The Living Flame of Love,* in *The Collected Works of St. John of the Cross,* tr. K. Kavanaugh, OCD, and O. Rodriguez, OCD (Washington DC: Institute of Carmelite Studies, 1979), 577 ff.   42 *1 Thess* 5:19.   43 Cf. *Ex* 24:15–18.   44 Cf. *Ex* 33:9–10.

desert,[45] and with Solomon at the dedication of the Temple.[46] In the Holy Spirit, Christ fulfills these figures. The
484 Spirit comes upon the Virgin Mary and "overshadows" her, so that she might conceive and give birth to Jesus.[47] On the
554 mountain of Transfiguration, the Spirit in the "cloud came and overshadowed" Jesus, Moses and Elijah, Peter, James and John, and "a voice came out of the cloud, saying, 'This is my Son, my Chosen; listen to him!' "[48] Finally, the cloud took Jesus out of the sight of the disciples on the day of his ascension and will reveal him as Son of man in glory on the
659 day of his final coming.[49]

698   *The seal* is a symbol close to that of anointing. "The Father has set his seal" on Christ and also seals us in him.[50] Because this seal indicates the indelible effect of the
1295-1296 anointing with the Holy Spirit in the sacraments of Baptism, Confirmation, and Holy Orders, the image of the seal *(sphragis)* has been used in some theological traditions to
1121 express the indelible "character" imprinted by these three unrepeatable sacraments.

292 **699**   *The hand.* Jesus heals the sick and blesses little children by laying hands on them.[51] In his name the apostles
1288 will do the same.[52] Even more pointedly, it is by the Apos-
1300, tles' imposition of hands that the Holy Spirit is given.[53] The
1573, *Letter to the Hebrews* lists the imposition of hands among
1668 the "fundamental elements" of its teaching.[54] The Church has kept this sign of the all-powerful outpouring of the Holy Spirit in its sacramental epicleses.

700   *The finger.* "It is by the finger of God that [Jesus] cast out demons."[55] If God's law was written on tablets of
2056 stone "by the finger of God," then the "letter from Christ" entrusted to the care of the apostles, is written "with the Spirit of the living God, not on tablets of stone, but on tablets of human hearts."[56] The hymn *Veni Creator Spiritus* invokes the Holy Spirit as the *"finger of the Father's right hand."*[57]

1219 **701**   *The dove.* At the end of the flood, whose symbolism refers to Baptism, a dove released by Noah returns with a fresh olive-tree branch in its beak as a sign that the earth
535 was again habitable.[58] When Christ comes up from the wa-

---

45 Cf. *Ex* 40:36–38; *1 Cor* 10:1–2.   46 Cf. *1 Kings* 8:10–12.   47 *Lk* 1:35.
48 *Lk* 9:34–35.   49 Cf. *Acts* 1:9; cf. *Lk* 21:27.   50 *Jn* 6:27; cf. *2 Cor* 1:22; *Eph*
1:13; 4:30.   51 Cf. *Mk* 6:5; 8:23; 10:16.   52 Cf. *Mk* 16:18; *Acts* 5:12; 14:3.
53 Cf. *Acts* 8:17–19; 13:3; 19:6.   54 Cf. *Heb* 6:2.   55 *Lk* 11:20.   56 *Ex* 31:18;
2 Cor 3:3.   57 *LH*, Easter Season after Ascension, Hymn at Vespers: *digitus paternae dexterae.*   58 Cf. *Gen* 8:8–12.

ter of his baptism, the Holy Spirit, in the form of a dove, comes down upon him and remains with him.[59] The Spirit comes down and remains in the purified hearts of the baptized. In certain churches, the Eucharist is reserved in a metal receptacle in the form of a dove *(columbarium)* suspended above the altar. Christian iconography traditionally uses a dove to suggest the Spirit.

III.   GOD'S SPIRIT AND WORD IN THE TIME OF THE PROMISES

702   From the beginning until "the fullness of time,"[60] the joint mission of the Father's Word and Spirit remains *hidden,* but it is at work. God's Spirit prepares   122
for the time of the Messiah. Neither is fully revealed but both are already promised, to be watched for and welcomed at their manifestation. So, for this reason, when the Church reads the Old Testament, she searches there for what the Spirit, "who has spoken through the prophets," wants to tell us about Christ.[61]   107

> By "prophets" the faith of the Church here under-   243
> stands all whom the Holy Spirit inspired in the composition of the sacred books, both of the Old and the New Testaments. Jewish tradition distinguishes first the Law (the five first books or Pentateuch), then the Prophets (our historical and prophetic books) and finally the Writings (especially the wisdom literature, in particular the Psalms).[62]

In creation

703   The Word of God and his Breath are at the ori-   292
gin of the being and life of every creature:[63]

> It belongs to the Holy Spirit to rule, sanctify, and   291
> animate creation, for he is God, consubstantial with the Father and the Son.... Power over life pertains to the Spirit, for being God he preserves creation in the Father through the Son.[64]

704   "God fashioned man with his own hands [that is, the Son and the Holy Spirit] and impressed his own form on the flesh he had fashioned, in such a way that even what was visible might bear the divine form."[65]   356

---

59 Cf. *Mt* 3:16 and parallels.   60 *Gal* 4:4.   61 Cf. *2 Cor* 3:14; *Jn* 5:39, 46.
62 Cf. *Lk* 24:44.   63 Cf. *Pss* 33:6; 104:30; *Gen* 1:2; 2:7; *Eccl* 3:20–21; *Ezek* 37:10.   64 Byzantine liturgy, Sundays of the second mode, *Troparion* of Morning Prayer.   65 St. Irenæus, *Dem ap.* 11:SCh 62, 48–49.

The Spirit of the promise

410 **705**   Disfigured by sin and death, man remains "in
the image of God," in the image of the Son, but is de-
2809 prived "of the glory of God,"[66] of his "likeness." The
promise made to Abraham inaugurates the economy of
salvation, at the culmination of which the Son himself
will assume that "image"[67] and restore it in the Father's
"likeness" by giving it again its Glory, the Spirit who is
"the giver of life."

706   Against all human hope, God promises descendants to Abraham, as the fruit of faith and of the power
of the Holy Spirit.[68] In Abraham's progeny all the na-
60 tions of the earth will be blessed. This progeny will be
Christ himself,[69] in whom the outpouring of the Holy
Spirit will "gather into one the children of God who are
scattered abroad."[70] God commits himself by his own
solemn oath to giving his beloved Son and "the
promised Holy Spirit . . . [who is] the guarantee of our
inheritance until we acquire possession of it."[71]

In Theophanies and the Law

707   Theophanies (manifestations of God) light up
the way of the promise, from the patriarchs to Moses
and from Joshua to the visions that inaugurated the
missions of the great prophets. Christian tradition has
always recognized that God's Word allowed himself to
be seen and heard in these theophanies, in which the
cloud of the Holy Spirit both revealed him and con-
cealed him in its shadow.

708   This divine pedagogy appears especially in the
gift of the Law.[72] God gave the letter of the Law as a
1961-1964 "pedagogue" to lead his people towards Christ.[73] But
the Law's powerlessness to save man deprived of the di-
122 vine "likeness," along with the growing awareness of sin
2585 that it imparts,[74] enkindles a desire for the Holy Spirit.
The lamentations of the Psalms bear witness to this.

---

66 *Rom* 3:23.   67 Cf. *Jn* 1:14; *Phil* 2:7.   68 Cf. *Gen* 18:1–15; *Lk* 1:26–38,
54–55; *Jn* 1:12–13; *Rom* 4:16–21.   69 Cf. *Gen* 12:3; *Gal* 3:16.   70 Cf. *Jn* 11:52.
71 *Eph* 1:13–14; cf. *Gen* 22:17–19; *Lk* 1:73; *Jn* 3:16; *Rom* 8:32; *Gal* 3:14.
72 Cf. *Ex* 19–20; *Deut* 1–11; 29–30.   73 *Gal* 3:24.   74 Cf. *Rom* 3:20.

In the Kingdom and the Exile

709 The Law, the sign of God's promise and cove- 2579
nant, ought to have governed the hearts and institutions
of that people to whom Abraham's faith gave birth. "If
you will obey my voice and keep my covenant, . . . you
shall be to me a kingdom of priests and a holy nation."[75] 544
But after David, Israel gave in to the temptation of becoming a kingdom like other nations. The Kingdom,
however, the object of the promise made to David,[76]
would be the work of the Holy Spirit; it would belong
to the poor according to the Spirit.

710 The forgetting of the Law and the infidelity to
the covenant end in death: it is the Exile, apparently the
failure of the promises, which is in fact the mysterious
fidelity of the Savior God and the beginning of a
promised restoration, but according to the Spirit. The
People of God had to suffer this purification.[77] In God's
plan, the Exile already stands in the shadow of the
Cross, and the Remnant of the poor that returns from
the Exile is one of the most transparent prefigurations
of the Church.

Expectation of the Messiah and his Spirit

711 "Behold, I am doing a new thing."[78] Two
prophetic lines were to develop, one leading to the ex- 64
pectation of the Messiah, the other pointing to the announcement of a new Spirit. They converge in the small 522
Remnant, the people of the poor, who await in hope the
"consolation of Israel" and "the redemption of
Jerusalem."[79]

We have seen earlier how Jesus fulfills the prophecies concerning himself. We limit ourselves here to those in
which the relationship of the Messiah and his Spirit appears more clearly.

712 The characteristics of the awaited *Messiah* begin to
appear in the "Book of Emmanuel" ("Isaiah said this when
he saw his glory,"[80] speaking of Christ), especially in the 439
first two verses of *Isaiah* 11:

---

75 *Ex* 19:5–6; Cf. *1 Pet* 2:9.   76 Cf. *2 Sam* 7; *Ps* 89; *Lk* 1:32–33.   77 Cf. *Lk*
24:26.   78 *Isa* 43:19.   79 Cf. *Zeph* 2:3; *Lk* 2:25, 38.   80 *Jn* 12:41; cf. *Isa*
6–12.

There shall come forth a shoot from the stump of
Jesse,
and a branch shall grow out of his roots.
And the Spirit of the LORD shall rest upon him,
the spirit of wisdom and understanding,
the spirit of counsel and might,
the spirit of knowledge and the fear of the LORD.[81]

713   The Messiah's characteristics are revealed above
all in the "Servant songs."[82] These songs proclaim the
meaning of Jesus' Passion and show how he will pour
out the Holy Spirit to give life to the many: not as an
601 outsider, but by embracing our "form as slave."[83] Taking our death upon himself, he can communicate to us
his own Spirit of life.

714   This is why Christ inaugurates the proclamation
of the Good News by making his own the following
passage from Isaiah:[84]

The Spirit of the LORD God is upon me,
because the LORD has anointed me
to bring good tidings to the afflicted;
he has sent me to bind up the broken hearted,
to proclaim liberty to the captives
and the opening of the prison to those who are
bound;
to proclaim the year of the LORD's favor.

715   The prophetic texts that directly concern the
sending of the Holy Spirit are oracles by which God
speaks to the heart of his people in the language of the
214 promise, with the accents of "love and fidelity."[85] St. Peter will proclaim their fulfillment on the morning of
Pentecost.[86] According to these promises, at the "end
time" the Lord's Spirit will renew the hearts of men, en-
graving a new law in them. He will gather and reconcile
the scattered and divided peoples; he will transform the
1965 first creation, and God will dwell there with men in
peace.

---

81 *Isa* 11:1–2.   82 Cf. *Isa* 42:1–9; cf. *Mt* 12:18–21; *Jn* 1:32–34; then cf. *Isa*
49:1–6; cf. *Mt* 3:17; *Lk* 2:32; finally cf. *Isa* 50:4–10 and *Isa* 52:13–53:12.
83 *Phil* 2:7.   84 *Isa* 61:1–2; cf. *Lk* 4:18–19.   85 Cf. *Ezek* 11:19; 36:25–28;
37:1–14; *Jer* 31:31–34; and cf. *Joel* 3:1–5.   86 Cf. *Acts* 2:17–21.

716   The People of the "poor"[87]—those who, humble and meek, rely solely on their God's mysterious plans, who await the justice, not of men but of the Messiah—are in the end the great achievement of the Holy Spirit's hidden mission during the time of the promises that prepare for Christ's coming. It is this quality of heart, purified and enlightened by the Spirit, which is expressed in the Psalms. In these poor, the Spirit is making ready "a people prepared for the Lord."[88]   *368*

IV.   THE SPIRIT OF CHRIST IN THE FULLNESS OF TIME

John, precursor, prophet, and baptist

717   "There was a man sent from God, whose name was John."[89] John was "filled with the Holy Spirit even from his mother's womb"[90] by Christ himself, whom the Virgin Mary had just conceived by the Holy Spirit. *523* Mary's visitation to Elizabeth thus became a visit from God to his people.[91]

718   John is "Elijah [who] must come."[92] The fire of the Spirit dwells in him and makes him the forerunner of the coming Lord. In John, the precursor, the Holy Spirit completes the work of "[making] ready a people *696* prepared for the Lord."[93]

719   John the Baptist is "more than a prophet."[94] In him, the Holy Spirit concludes his speaking through the prophets. John completes the cycle of prophets begun by Elijah.[95] He proclaims the imminence of the consolation of Israel; he is the "voice" of the Consoler who is coming.[96] As the Spirit of truth will also do, John "came to bear witness to the light."[97] In John's sight, the Spirit *2684* thus brings to completion the careful search of the prophets and fulfills the longing of the angels.[98] "He on whom you see the Spirit descend and remain, this is he who baptizes with the Holy Spirit. And I have seen and

---

87 Cf. *Zeph* 2:3; *Pss* 22:27; 34:3; *Isa* 49:13; 61:1; etc.   88 *Lk* 1:17.   89 *Jn* 1:6.
90 *Lk* 1:15, 41.   91 Cf. *Lk* 1:68.   92 *Mt* 17:10–13; cf. *Lk* 1:78.   93 *Lk* 1:17.
94 *Lk* 7:26.   95 Cf. *Mt* 11:13–14.   96 *Jn* 1:23; cf. *Isa* 40:1–3.   97 *Jn* 1:7; cf. *Jn* 15:26; 5:35.   98 Cf. *1 Pet* 1:10–12.

have borne witness that this is the Son of God. . . . Be-
536 hold, the Lamb of God."[99]

720   Finally, with John the Baptist, the Holy Spirit begins the restoration to man of "the divine likeness," pre-
535 figuring what he would achieve with and in Christ.
John's baptism was for repentance; baptism in water
and the Spirit will be a new birth.[100]

"Rejoice, you who are full of grace"

721   Mary, the all-holy ever-virgin Mother of God, is
the masterwork of the mission of the Son and the Spirit
in the fullness of time. For the first time in the plan of
salvation and because his Spirit had prepared her, the
484 Father found the *dwelling place* where his Son and his
Spirit could dwell among men. In this sense the
Church's Tradition has often read the most beautiful
texts on wisdom in relation to Mary.[101] Mary is acclaimed and represented in the liturgy as the "Seat of
Wisdom."

In her, the "wonders of God" that the Spirit was
to fulfill in Christ and the Church began to be manifested:

489 **722**   The Holy Spirit *prepared* Mary by his grace. It
was fitting that the mother of him in whom "the whole
fullness of deity dwells bodily"[102] should herself be "full
of grace." She was, by sheer grace, conceived without
sin as the most humble of creatures, the most capable
of welcoming the inexpressible gift of the Almighty. It
was quite correct for the angel Gabriel to greet her as
2676 the "Daughter of Zion": "Rejoice."[103] It is the thanksgiving of the whole People of God, and thus of the
Church, which Mary in her canticle[104] lifts up to the Father in the Holy Spirit while carrying within her the
eternal Son.

723   In Mary, the Holy Spirit *fulfills* the plan of the
Father's loving goodness. With and through the Holy
485 Spirit, the Virgin conceives and gives birth to the Son of

---

99 *Jn* 1:33–36.   100 Cf. *Jn* 3:5.   101 Cf. *Prov* 8:1–9:6; *Sir* 24.   102 *Col* 2:9.
103 Cf. *Zeph* 3:14; *Zech* 2:14.   104 Cf. *Lk* 1:46–55.

God. By the Holy Spirit's power and her faith, her virginity became uniquely fruitful.[105]   *506*

724   In Mary, the Holy Spirit *manifests* the Son of the Father, now become the Son of the Virgin. She is the burning bush of the definitive theophany. Filled with the Holy Spirit she makes the Word visible in the humility of his flesh. It is to the poor and the first representatives   *963* of the gentiles that she makes him known.[106]

725   Finally, through Mary, the Holy Spirit begins to bring men, the objects of God's merciful love,[107] *into communion* with Christ. And the humble are always the first to accept him: shepherds, magi, Simeon and Anna,   *208, 2619* the bride and groom at Cana, and the first disciples.

726   At the end of this mission of the Spirit, Mary became the Woman, the new Eve ("mother of the living"), the mother of the "whole Christ."[108] As such, she was   *494, 2618* present with the Twelve, who "with one accord devoted themselves to prayer,"[109] at the dawn of the "end time" which the Spirit was to inaugurate on the morning of Pentecost with the manifestation of the Church.

Christ Jesus

727   The entire mission of the Son and the Holy Spirit, in the fullness of time, is contained in this: that the Son is the one anointed by the Father's Spirit since   *438, 695* his Incarnation—Jesus is the Christ, the Messiah.   *536*

Everything in the second chapter of the Creed is to be read in this light. Christ's whole work is in fact a joint mission of the Son and the Holy Spirit. Here, we shall mention only what has to do with Jesus' promise of the Holy Spirit and the gift of him by the glorified Lord.

728   Jesus does not reveal the Holy Spirit fully, until he himself has been glorified through his Death and Resurrection. Nevertheless, little by little he alludes to him even in his teaching of the multitudes, as when he reveals that his own flesh will be food for the life of the

---

105 Cf. *Lk* 1:26–38; *Rom* 4:18–21; *Gal* 4:26–28.   106 Cf. *Lk* 1:15–19; *Mt* 2:11.
107 Cf. *Lk* 2:14.   108 Cf. *Jn* 19:25–27.   109 *Acts* 1:14.

world.[110] He also alludes to the Spirit in speaking to Nicodemus,[111] to the Samaritan woman,[112] and to those who take part in the feast of Tabernacles.[113] To his disciples he speaks openly of the Spirit in connection with 2615 prayer[114] and with the witness they will have to bear.[115]

729   Only when the hour has arrived for his glorification does Jesus *promise* the coming of the Holy Spirit, since his Death and Resurrection will fulfill the promise made to the fathers.[116] The Spirit of truth, the other Paraclete, will be given by the Father in answer to Jesus' prayer; he will be sent by the Father in Jesus' name; and Jesus will send him from the Father's side, since he comes from the Father. The Holy Spirit will come and we shall know him; he will be with us for ever; he will remain with us. The Spirit will teach us everything, remind us of all that Christ said to us and bear witness to him. The Holy Spirit will lead us into all truth and will glorify Christ. He will prove the world wrong about sin, 388, 1433 righteousness, and judgment.

730   At last Jesus' hour arrives:[117] he commends his spirit into the Father's hands[118] at the very moment when by his death he conquers death, so that, "raised from the dead by the glory of the Father,"[119] he might immediately *give* the Holy Spirit by "breathing" on his disciples.[120] From this hour onward, the mission of Christ and the Spirit becomes the mission of the Church: "As 850 the Father has sent me, even so I send you."[121]

V.   THE SPIRIT AND THE CHURCH IN THE LAST DAYS

Pentecost

731   On the day of Pentecost when the seven weeks of Easter had come to an end, Christ's Passover is fulfilled 2623, 767 in the outpouring of the Holy Spirit, manifested, given,

---

110 Cf. *Jn* 6:27, 51, 62–63.   111 Cf. *Jn* 3:5–8.   112 Cf. *Jn* 4:10, 14, 23–24. 113 Cf. *Jn* 7:37–39.   114 Cf. *Lk* 11:13.   115 Cf. *Mt* 10:19–20.   116 Cf. *Jn* 14:16–17, 26; 15:26; 16:7–15; 17:26.   117 Cf. *Jn* 13:1; 17:1.   118 Cf. *Lk* 23:46; *Jn* 19:30.   119 *Rom* 6:4.   120 Cf. *Jn* 20:22.   121 *Jn* 20:21; cf. *Mt* 28:19; *Lk* 24:47–48; *Acts* 1:8.

and communicated as a divine person: of his fullness, Christ, the Lord, pours out the Spirit in abundance.[122]   *1302*

732   On that day, the Holy Trinity is fully revealed. Since that day, the Kingdom announced by Christ has been open to those who believe in him: in the humility of the flesh and in faith, they already share in the com-   *244* munion of the Holy Trinity. By his coming, which never ceases, the Holy Spirit causes the world to enter into the   *672* "last days," the time of the Church, the Kingdom already inherited though not yet consummated.

> We have seen the true Light, we have received the heavenly Spirit, we have found the true faith: we adore the indivisible Trinity, who has saved us.[123]

The Holy Spirit—God's gift
733   "God is Love"[124] and love is his first gift, containing all others. "God's love has been poured into our   *218* hearts through the Holy Spirit who has been given to us."[125]

734   Because we are dead or at least wounded through sin, the first effect of the gift of love is the forgiveness of our sins. The communion of the Holy   *1987* Spirit[126] in the Church restores to the baptized the divine likeness lost through sin.

735   He, then, gives us the "pledge" or "first fruits" of our inheritance: the very life of the Holy Trinity,   *1822* which is to love as "God [has] loved us."[127] This love (the "charity" of *1 Cor* 13) is the source of the new life in Christ, made possible because we have received "power" from the Holy Spirit.[128]

736   By this power of the Spirit, God's children can bear much fruit. He who has grafted us onto the true vine will make us bear "the fruit of the Spirit: . . . love,   *1832* joy, peace, patience, kindness, goodness, faithfulness, gentleness, self-control."[129] "We live by the Spirit"; the

---

122 Cf. *Acts* 2:33–36.   123 Byzantine liturgy, Pentecost, Vespers, *Troparion*, repeated after communion.   124 *1 Jn* 4:8, 16.   125 *Rom* 5:5.   126 *2 Cor* 13:14. 127 *1 Jn* 4:11–12; cf. *Rom* 8:23; *2 Cor* 1:21.   128 *Acts* 1:8; cf. *1 Cor* 13. 129 *Gal* 5:22–23.

more we renounce ourselves, the more we "walk by the Spirit."[130]

> Through the Holy Spirit we are restored to paradise, led back to the Kingdom of heaven, and adopted as children, given confidence to call God "Father" and to share in Christ's grace, called children of light and given a share in eternal glory.[131]

The Holy Spirit and the Church

787-798   737   The mission of Christ and the Holy Spirit is brought to completion in the Church, which is the Body of Christ and the Temple of the Holy Spirit. This joint mission henceforth brings Christ's faithful to share in his communion with the Father in the Holy Spirit. The 1093-1109 Spirit *prepares* men and goes out to them with his grace, in order to draw them to Christ. The Spirit *manifests* the risen Lord to them, recalls his word to them and opens their minds to the understanding of his Death and Resurrection. He *makes present* the mystery of Christ, supremely in the Eucharist, in order to reconcile them, to *bring them into communion* with God, that they may "bear much fruit."[132]

738   Thus the Church's mission is not an addition to that of Christ and the Holy Spirit, but is its sacrament: in her whole being and in all her members, the Church 850, 777 is sent to announce, bear witness, make present, and spread the mystery of the communion of the Holy Trinity (the topic of the next article):

> All of us who have received one and the same Spirit, that is, the Holy Spirit, are in a sense blended together with one another and with God. For if Christ, together with the Father's and his own Spirit, comes to dwell in each of us, though we are many, still the Spirit is one and undivided. He binds together the spirits of each and every one of us, ... and makes all appear as one in him. For just as the power of Christ's sacred flesh unites those in whom it dwells into one body, I think that in the same way

---

130 *Gal* 5:25; cf. *Mt* 16:24–26.   131 St. Basil, *De Spiritu Sancto*, 15, 36: PG 32, 132.   132 *Jn* 15:8, 16.

the one and undivided Spirit of God, who dwells in all, leads all into spiritual unity.[133]

739   Because the Holy Spirit is the anointing of Christ, it is Christ who, as the head of the Body, pours out the Spirit among his members to nourish, heal, and organize them in their mutual functions, to give them life, send them to bear witness, and associate them to his self-offering to the Father and to his intercession for the whole world. Through the Church's sacraments, Christ communicates his Holy and sanctifying Spirit to the members of his Body. (This will be the topic of Part Two of the Catechism.)

1076

740   These "mighty works of God," offered to believers in the sacraments of the Church, bear their fruit in the new life in Christ, according to the Spirit. (This will be the topic of Part Three.)

741   "The Spirit helps us in our weakness; for we do not know how to pray as we ought, but the Spirit himself intercedes with sighs too deep for words."[134] The Holy Spirit, the artisan of God's works, is the master of prayer. (This will be the topic of Part Four.)

IN BRIEF

742   "Because you are sons, God has sent the Spirit of his Son into our hearts, crying, 'Abba! Father!' " (*Gal* 4:6).

743   From the beginning to the end of time, whenever God sends his Son, he always sends his Spirit: their mission is conjoined and inseparable.

744   In the fullness of time the Holy Spirit completes in Mary all the preparations for Christ's coming among the People of God. By the action of the Holy Spirit in her, the Father gives the world Emmanuel, "God-with-us" (*Mt* 1:23).

745   The Son of God was consecrated as Christ (Mes-

---

133 St. Cyril of Alexandria, *In Jo. ev.,* 11, 11: PG 74, 561.   134 *Rom* 8:26.

siah) by the anointing of the Holy Spirit at his
Incarnation (cf. *Ps* 2:6–7).

746   By his Death and his Resurrection, Jesus is constituted in glory as Lord and Christ (cf. *Acts*
2:36). From his fullness, he poured out the Holy
Spirit on the apostles and the Church.

747   The Holy Spirit, whom Christ the head pours
out on his members, builds, animates, and sanctifies the Church. She is the sacrament of the
Holy Trinity's communion with men.

ARTICLE 9
"I BELIEVE IN THE HOLY CATHOLIC CHURCH"

748   "Christ is the light of humanity; and it is, accordingly, the heart-felt desire of this sacred Council,
being gathered together in the Holy Spirit, that, by proclaiming his Gospel to every creature, it may bring to all
men that light of Christ which shines out visibly from
the Church."[135] These words open the Second Vatican
Council's *Dogmatic Constitution on the Church*. By
choosing this starting point, the Council demonstrates
that the article of faith about the Church depends entirely on the articles concerning Christ Jesus. The
Church has no other light than Christ's; according to a
favorite image of the Church Fathers, the Church is like
the moon, all its light reflected from the sun.

749   The article concerning the Church also depends
entirely on the article about the Holy Spirit, which immediately precedes it. "Indeed, having shown that the
Spirit is the source and giver of all holiness, we now
confess that it is he who has endowed the Church with
holiness."[136] The Church is, in a phrase used by the Fathers, the place "where the Spirit flourishes."[137]

750   To believe that the Church is "holy" and

---

135 *LG* 1; cf. *Mk* 16:15.   136 *Roman Catechism* I, 10, 1.   137 St. Hippolytus,
Trad. Ap. 35:SCh 11, 118.

"catholic," and that she is "one" and "apostolic" (as the Nicene Creed adds), is inseparable from belief in God, the Father, the Son, and the Holy Spirit. In the Apostles' Creed we profess "one Holy Church" *(Credo ... Ecclesiam),* and not to believe *in* the Church, so as not to confuse God with his works and to attribute clearly to God's goodness *all* the gifts he has bestowed on his Church.[138]

811

169

Paragraph 1. The Church in God's Plan

I. NAMES AND IMAGES OF THE CHURCH

751 The word "Church" (Latin *ecclesia,* from the Greek *ek-ka-lein,* to "call out of") means a convocation or an assembly. It designates the assemblies of the people, usually for a religious purpose.[139] *Ekklesia* is used frequently in the Greek Old Testament for the assembly of the Chosen People before God, above all for their assembly on Mount Sinai where Israel received the Law and was established by God as his holy people.[140] By calling itself "Church," the first community of Christian believers recognized itself as heir to that assembly. In the Church, God is "calling together" his people from all the ends of the earth. The equivalent Greek term *Kyriake,* from which the English word *Church* and the German *Kirche* are derived, means "what belongs to the Lord."

752 In Christian usage, the word "church" designates the liturgical assembly,[141] but also the local community[142] or the whole universal community of believers.[143] These three meanings are inseparable. "The Church" is the People that God gathers in the whole world. She exists in local communities and is made real as a liturgical, above all a Eucharistic, assembly. She draws her life from the word and the Body of Christ and so herself becomes Christ's Body.

1140, 832

830

---

138 *Roman Catechism* I, 10, 22.   139 Cf. *Acts* 19:39.   140 Cf. *Ex* 19.   141 Cf. *1 Cor* 11:18; 14:19, 28, 34, 35.   142 Cf. *1 Cor* 1:2; 16:1.   143 Cf. *1 Cor* 15:9; *Gal* 1:13; *Phil* 3:6.

Symbols of the Church

753   In Scripture, we find a host of interrelated images and figures through which Revelation speaks of the inexhaustible mystery of the Church. The images taken from the Old Testament are variations on a profound theme: the People of God. In the New Testament, all
781, 789   these images find a new center because Christ has become the head of this people, which henceforth is his Body.[144] Around this center are grouped images taken "from the life of the shepherd or from cultivation of the land, from the art of building or from family life and marriage."[145]

857   754   "The Church is, accordingly, a *sheepfold,* the sole and necessary gateway to which is Christ. It is also the flock of which God himself foretold that he would be the shepherd, and whose sheep, even though governed by human shepherds, are unfailingly nourished and led by Christ himself, the Good Shepherd and Prince of Shepherds, who gave his life for his sheep.[146]

755   "The Church is a *cultivated field,* the tillage of God. On that land the ancient olive tree grows whose holy roots were the prophets and in which the reconciliation of Jews and Gentiles has been brought about and will be brought about again. That land, like a choice vineyard, has been planted by the heavenly cultivator. Yet the true vine is Christ who gives life and fruitfulness to the branches, that is, to us, who through the Church remain in Christ, with-
795   out whom we can do nothing.[147]

756   "Often, too, the Church is called the *building* of God. The Lord compared himself to the stone which the
797   builders rejected, but which was made into the cornerstone. On this foundation the Church is built by the apostles and from it the Church receives solidity and unity. This edifice has many names to describe it: the house of God in
857   which his *family* dwells; the household of God in the Spirit; the dwelling-place of God among men; and, especially, the holy *temple.* This temple, symbolized in places of worship built out of stone, is praised by the Fathers and, not without reason, is compared in the liturgy to the Holy City, the
1045   New Jerusalem. As living stones we here on earth are built

---

144 Cf. *Eph* 1:22; *Col* 1:18; *LG* 9.   145 *LG* 6.   146 *LG* 6; cf. *Jn* 10:1–10; *Isa* 40:11; *Ezek* 34:11–31; *Jn* 10:11; *1 Pet* 5:4; *Jn* 10:11–16.   147 *LG* 6; cf. *1 Cor* 3:9; *Rom* 11:13–26; *Mt* 21:33–43 and parallels; *Isa* 5:1–7; *Jn* 15:1–5.

into it. It is this holy city that is seen by John as it comes down out of heaven from God when the world is made anew, prepared like a bride adorned for her husband.[148]

757 "The Church, further, which is called 'that   *507, 796* Jerusalem which is above' and 'our mother', is described as the spotless spouse of the spotless lamb. It is she whom Christ 'loved and for whom he delivered himself up that he might sanctify her.' It is she whom he unites to himself by   *1616* an unbreakable alliance, and whom he constantly 'nourishes and cherishes.' "[149]

II.   THE CHURCH'S ORIGIN, FOUNDATION, AND MISSION

758   We begin our investigation of the Church's mys-   *257* tery by meditating on her origin in the Holy Trinity's plan and her progressive realization in history.

A plan born in the Father's heart

759   "The eternal Father, in accordance with the utterly gratuitous and mysterious design of his wisdom and goodness, created the whole universe and chose to raise up men to share in his own divine life,"[150] to which   *293* he calls all men in his Son. "The Father . . . determined to call together in a holy Church those who should believe in Christ."[151] This "family of God" is gradually   *1655* formed and takes shape during the stages of human history, in keeping with the Father's plan. In fact, "already present in figure at the beginning of the world, this Church was prepared in marvellous fashion in the history of the people of Israel and the old Alliance. Established in this last age of the world and made manifest in the outpouring of the Spirit, it will be brought to glorious completion at the end of time."[152]

---

148 *LG* 6; cf. *1 Cor* 3:9; *Mt* 21:42 and parallels; *Acts* 4:11; *1 Pet* 2:7; *Ps* 118:22; *1 Cor* 3:11; *1 Tim* 3:15; *Eph* 2:19–22; *Rev* 21:3; *1 Pet* 2:5; *Rev* 21:1–2.   149 *LG* 6; cf. *Gal* 4:26; *Rev* 12:17; 19:7; 21:2, 9; 22:17; *Eph* 5:25–26, 29.   150 *LG* 2. 151 *LG* 2.   152 *LG* 2.

The Church—foreshadowed from the world's beginning

760   Christians of the first centuries said, "The world was created for the sake of the Church."[153] God created the world for the sake of communion with his divine

294 life, a communion brought about by the "convocation" of men in Christ, and this "convocation" is the Church. The Church is the goal of all things,[154] and God permitted such painful upheavals as the angels' fall and man's sin only as occasions and means for displaying all the

309 power of his arm and the whole measure of the love he wanted to give the world:

> Just as God's will is creation and is called "the world," so his intention is the salvation of men, and it is called "the Church."[155]

The Church—prepared for in the Old Covenant

761   The gathering together of the People of God began at the moment when sin destroyed the communion of men with God, and that of men among themselves. The gathering together of the Church is, as it were,

55 God's reaction to the chaos provoked by sin. This re-unification is achieved secretly in the heart of all peoples: "In every nation anyone who fears him and does what is right is acceptable" to God.[156]

762   The remote *preparation* for this gathering together of the People of God begins when he calls Abraham and promises that he will become the father of a

122, 522 great people.[157] Its immediate preparation begins with

60 Israel's election as the People of God. By this election, Israel is to be the sign of the future gathering of all nations.[158] But the prophets accuse Israel of breaking the covenant and behaving like a prostitute. They announce

64 a new and eternal covenant. "Christ instituted this New Covenant."[159]

---

153 *Pastor Hermæ*, Vision 2, 4, 1: PG 2, 899; cf. Aristides, *Apol.* 16, 6; St. Justin, *Apol.* 2, 7: PG 6, 456; Tertullian, *Apol.* 31, 3;32, 1: PL 1, 508–509.   **154** Cf. St. Epiphanius, *Panarion* 1, 1, 5: PG 41, 181C.   **155** Clement of Alex., *Pæd.* 1, 6, 27:PG 8, 281.   **156** *Acts* 10:35; cf. *LG* 9; 13; 16.   **157** Cf. *Gen* 12:2; 15:5–6.   **158** Cf. *Ex* 19:5–6; *Deut* 7:6; *Isa* 2:2–5; *Mic* 4:1–4.   **159** *LG* 9; cf. *Hos* 1; *Isa* 1:2–4; *Jer* 2; 31:31–34; *Isa* 55:3.

The Church—instituted by Christ Jesus

763   It was the Son's task to accomplish the Father's plan of salvation in the fullness of time. Its accomplishment was the reason for his being sent.[160] "The Lord Jesus inaugurated his Church by preaching the Good News, that is, the coming of the Reign of God, promised over the ages in the scriptures."[161] To fulfill the Father's will, Christ ushered in the Kingdom of heaven on earth. The Church "is the Reign of Christ already present in mystery."[162]

541

764   "This Kingdom shines out before men in the word, in the works and in the presence of Christ."[163] To welcome Jesus' word is to welcome "the Kingdom itself."[164] The seed and beginning of the Kingdom are the "little flock" of those whom Jesus came to gather around him, the flock whose shepherd he is.[165] They form Jesus' true family.[166] To those whom he thus gathered around him, he taught a new "way of acting" and a prayer of their own.[167]

543

1691

2558

765   The Lord Jesus endowed his community with a structure that will remain until the Kingdom is fully achieved. Before all else there is the choice of the Twelve with Peter as their head.[168] Representing the twelve tribes of Israel, they are the foundation stones of the new Jerusalem.[169] The Twelve and the other disciples share in Christ's mission and his power, but also in his lot.[170] By all his actions, Christ prepares and builds his Church.

610

551

766   The Church is born primarily of Christ's total self-giving for our salvation, anticipated in the institution of the Eucharist and fulfilled on the cross. "The origin and growth of the Church are symbolized by the blood and water which flowed from the open side of the crucified Jesus."[171] "For it was from the side of Christ as he slept the sleep of death upon the cross that there came forth the 'wondrous sacrament of the whole Church.' "[172] As Eve was formed from the sleeping

813, 860

1340

617

478

---

160 Cf. *LG* 3; *AG* 3.   161 *LG* 5.   162 *LG* 3.   163 *LG* 5.   164 *LG* 5.   165 *Lk* 12:32; cf. *Mt* 10:16; 26:31; *Jn* 10:1–21.   166 Cf. *Mt* 12:49.   167 Cf. *Mt* 5–6. 168 Cf. *Mk* 3:14–15.   169 Cf. *Mt* 19:28; *Lk* 22:30; *Rev* 21:12–14.   170 Cf. *Mk* 6:7; *Lk* 10:1–2; *Mt* 10:25; *Jn* 15:20.   171 *LG* 3; cf. *Jn* 19:34.   172 *SC* 5.

Adam's side, so the Church was born from the pierced heart of Christ hanging dead on the cross.[173]

The Church—revealed by the Holy Spirit

767   "When the work which the Father gave the Son to do on earth was accomplished, the Holy Spirit was
731   sent on the day of Pentecost in order that he might continually sanctify the Church."[174] Then "the Church was openly displayed to the crowds and the spread of the Gospel among the nations, through preaching, was begun."[175] As the "convocation" of all men for salvation,
849   the Church in her very nature is missionary, sent by Christ to all the nations to make disciples of them.[176]

768   So that she can fulfill her mission, the Holy Spirit "bestows upon [the Church] varied hierarchic and charismatic gifts, and in this way directs her."[177] "Henceforward the Church, endowed with the gifts of her founder and faithfully observing his precepts of charity, humility and self-denial, receives the mission of proclaiming and establishing among all peoples the Kingdom of Christ and of God, and she is on earth
541   the seed and the beginning of that kingdom."[178]

The Church—perfected in glory

769   "The Church . . . will receive its perfection only in the glory of heaven,"[179] at the time of Christ's glorious return. Until that day, "the Church progresses on her
671, 2818   pilgrimage amidst this world's persecutions and God's consolations."[180] Here below she knows that she is in exile far from the Lord, and longs for the full coming of
675   the Kingdom, when she will "be united in glory with her king."[181] The Church, and through her the world, will not be perfected in glory without great trials. Only then will "all the just from the time of Adam, 'from Abel, the just one, to the last of the elect,' . . . be gathered together
1045   in the universal Church in the Father's presence."[182]

---

173 Cf. St. Ambrose, *In Luc.* 2, 85–89: PL 15, 1666–1668.   174 *LG* 4; cf. *Jn* 17:4.   175 *AG* 4.   176 Cf. *Mt* 28:19–20; *AG* 2; 5–6.   177 *LG* 4.   178 *LG* 5. 179 *LG* 48.   180 St. Augustine, *De civ. Dei*, 18, 51: PL 41, 614; cf. *LG* 8. 181 *LG* 5; cf. 6; *2 Cor* 5:6.   182 *LG* 2.

III. THE MYSTERY OF THE CHURCH

770   The Church is in history, but at the same time she transcends it. It is only "with the eyes of faith"[183] that one can see her in her visible reality and at the same time in her spiritual reality as bearer of divine life.   812

The Church—both visible and spiritual

771   "The one mediator, Christ, established and ever 827 sustains here on earth his holy Church, the community of faith, hope, and charity, as a visible organization through which he communicates truth and grace to all men."[184] The Church is at the same time:

—a "society structured with hierarchical organs and the 1880 mystical body of Christ;

—the visible society and the spiritual community;

—the earthly Church and the Church endowed with 954 heavenly riches."[185]

These dimensions together constitute "one complex reality which comes together from a human and a divine element":[186]

> The Church is essentially both human and divine, visible but endowed with invisible realities, zealous in action and dedicated to contemplation, present in the world, but as a pilgrim, so constituted that in her the human is directed toward and subordinated to the divine, the visible to the invisible, action to contemplation, and this present world to that city yet to come, the object of our quest.[187]

> Oh humility! O sublimity! Both tabernacle of cedar and sanctuary of God; earthly dwelling and celestial palace; house of clay and royal hall; body of death and temple of light; and at last both object of scorn to the proud and bride of Christ! She is black but beautiful, O daughters of Jerusalem, for even if the labor and pain of her long exile may have discolored her, yet heaven's beauty has adorned her.[188]

---

183 *Roman Catechism* I, 10, 20.   184 *LG* 8 § 1.   185 *LG* 8.   186 *LG* 8.
187 *SC* 2; cf. *Heb* 13:14.   188 St. Bernard of Clairvaux, *In Cant. Sermo* 27:14: PL 183:920D.

The Church—mystery of men's union with God

518   **772**   It is in the Church that Christ fulfills and reveals
his own mystery as the purpose of God's plan: "to unite
796   all things in him."[189] St. Paul calls the nuptial union of
Christ and the Church "a great mystery." Because she is
united to Christ as to her bridegroom, she becomes a
mystery in her turn.[190] Contemplating this mystery in
her, Paul exclaims: "Christ in you, the hope of glory."[191]

773   In the Church this communion of men with God,
in the "love [that] never ends," is the purpose which
governs everything in her that is a sacramental means,
tied to this passing world.[192] "[The Church's] structure
671   is totally ordered to the holiness of Christ's members.
And holiness is measured according to the 'great mystery' in which the Bride responds with the gift of love to
972   the gift of the Bridegroom."[193] Mary goes before us all
in the holiness that is the Church's mystery as "the bride
without spot or wrinkle."[194] This is why the "Marian"
dimension of the Church precedes the "Petrine."[195]

The universal Sacrament of Salvation

774   The Greek word *mysterion* was translated into
Latin by two terms: *mysterium* and *sacramentum*. In later
usage the term *sacramentum* emphasizes the visible sign of
1075   the hidden reality of salvation which was indicated by the
term *mysterium*. In this sense, Christ himself is the mystery
of salvation: "For there is no other mystery of God, except
Christ."[196] The saving work of his holy and sanctifying humanity is the sacrament of salvation, which is revealed and
active in the Church's sacraments (which the Eastern
Churches also call "the holy mysteries"). The seven sacra-
515   ments are the signs and instruments by which the Holy
2014   Spirit spreads the grace of Christ the head throughout the
1116   Church which is his Body. The Church, then, both contains
and communicates the invisible grace she signifies. It is in
this analogical sense, that the Church is called a "sacrament."

775   "The Church, in Christ, is like a sacrament—a
sign and instrument, that is, of communion with God

---

189 *Eph* 1:10.   190 *Eph* 5:32; 3:9–11; 5:25–27.   191 *Col* 1:27.   192 *1 Cor*
13:8; cf. *LG* 48.   193 John Paul II, *MD* 27.   194 *Eph* 5:27.   195 Cf. John Paul
II, *MD* 27.   196 St. Augustine, *Ep* 187, 11, 34: PL 33, 846.

and of unity among all men."[197] The Church's first purpose is to be the sacrament of the *inner union of men with God*. Because men's communion with one another is rooted in that union with God, the Church is also the sacrament of the *unity of the human race*. In her, this unity is already begun, since she gathers men "from every nation, from all tribes and peoples and tongues";[198] at the same time, the Church is the "sign and instrument" of the full realization of the unity yet to come.

360

776   As sacrament, the Church is Christ's instrument. "She is taken up by him also as the instrument for the salvation of all," "the universal sacrament of salvation," by which Christ is "at once manifesting and actualizing the mystery of God's love for men."[199] The Church "is the visible plan of God's love for humanity," because God desires "that the whole human race may become one People of God, form one Body of Christ, and be built up into one temple of the Holy Spirit."[200]

1088

IN BRIEF

777   The word "Church" means "convocation." It designates the assembly of those whom God's Word "convokes," i.e., gathers together to form the People of God, and who themselves, nourished with the Body of Christ, become the Body of Christ.

778   The Church is both the means and the goal of God's plan: prefigured in creation, prepared for in the Old Covenant, founded by the words and actions of Jesus Christ, fulfilled by his redeeming cross and his Resurrection, the Church has been manifested as the mystery of salvation by the outpouring of the Holy Spirit. She will be perfected in the glory of heaven as the assembly of all the redeemed of the earth (cf. *Rev* 14:4).

779   The Church is both visible and spiritual, a hierarchical society and the Mystical Body of Christ.

---

197 *LG* 1.   198 *Rev* 7:9.   199 *LG* 9 § 2, 48 § 2; GS 45 § 1.   200 Paul VI, June 22, 1973; AG 7 § 2; cf. *LG* 17.

She is one, yet formed of two components, human and divine. That is her mystery, which only faith can accept.

780   The Church in this world is the sacrament of salvation, the sign and the instrument of the communion of God and men.

Paragraph 2. The Church—People of God, Body of Christ, Temple of the Holy Spirit

I.   THE CHURCH—PEOPLE OF GOD
781   "At all times and in every race, anyone who fears God and does what is right has been acceptable to him. He has, however, willed to make men holy and save them, not as individuals without any bond or link between them, but rather to make them into a people who might acknowledge him and serve him in holiness. He therefore chose the Israelite race to be his own people and established a covenant with it. He gradually instructed this people. . . . All these things, however, happened as a preparation for and figure of that new and perfect covenant which was to be ratified in Christ . . . the New Covenant in his blood; he called together a race made up of Jews and Gentiles which would be one, not according to the flesh, but in the Spirit."[201]

Characteristics of the People of God
871 782   The People of God is marked by characteristics that clearly distinguish it from all other religious, ethnic, political, or cultural groups found in history:

2787 —It is the People *of* God: God is not the property of any one people. But he acquired a people for himself from those who previously were not a people: "a chosen race, a royal priesthood, a holy nation."[202]

1267 —One becomes a *member* of this people not by a physical birth, but by being "born anew," a birth "of water

---

201 *LG* 9; cf. *Acts* 10:35; *1 Cor* 11:25.   202 *1 Pet* 2:9.

and the Spirit,"[203] that is, by faith in Christ, and Baptism.

—This People has for its Head Jesus the Christ (the anointed, the Messiah). Because the same anointing, the Holy Spirit, flows from the head into the body, this is "the messianic people." 695

—"The *status* of this people is that of the dignity and freedom of the sons of God, in whose hearts the Holy Spirit dwells as in a temple." 1741

—"Its *law* is the new commandment to love as Christ loved us."[204] This is the "new" law of the Holy Spirit.[205] 1972

—Its *mission* is to be salt of the earth and light of the world.[206] This people is "a most sure seed of unity, hope, and salvation for the whole human race." 849

—Its *destiny,* finally, "is the Kingdom of God which has been begun by God himself on earth and which must be further extended until it has been brought to perfection by him at the end of time."[207] 769

A priestly, prophetic, and royal people
783   Jesus Christ is the one whom the Father anointed with the Holy Spirit and established as priest, prophet, and king. The whole People of God participates in these three offices of Christ and bears the responsibilities for mission and service that flow from them.[208] 436 873

784   On entering the People of God through faith and Baptism, one receives a share in this people's unique, *priestly* vocation: "Christ the Lord, high priest taken from among men, has made this new people 'a kingdom of priests to God, his Father.' The baptized, by regeneration and the anointing of the Holy Spirit, are *consecrated* to be a spiritual house and a holy priesthood."[209] 1268 1546

785   "The holy People of God shares also in Christ's *prophetic* office," above all in the supernatural sense of

---

203 *Jn* 3:3–5.   204 Cf. *Jn* 13:34.   205 *Rom* 8:2; *Gal* 5:25.   206 Cf. *Mt* 5:13–16.   207 *LG* 9 § 2.   208 Cf. John Paul II, *RH* 18–21.   209 *LG* 10; cf. *Heb* 5:1–5; *Rev* 1:6.

faith that belongs to the whole People, lay and clergy,
92 when it "unfailingly adheres to this faith . . . once for all
delivered to the saints,"[210] and when it deepens its understanding and becomes Christ's witness in the midst
of this world.

786   Finally, the People of God shares in the *royal* office of Christ. He exercises his kingship by drawing all
men to himself through his death and Resurrection.[211]
Christ, King and Lord of the universe, made himself the
servant of all, for he came "not to be served but to
serve, and to give his life as a ransom for many."[212] For
the Christian, "to reign is to serve him," particularly
when serving "the poor and the suffering, in whom the
2449 Church recognizes the image of her poor and suffering
founder."[213] The People of God fulfills its royal dignity
by a life in keeping with its vocation to serve with
2443 Christ.

> The sign of the cross makes kings of all those re-
> born in Christ and the anointing of the Holy Spirit
> consecrates them as priests, so that, apart from the
> particular service of our ministry, all spiritual and
> rational Christians are recognized as members of
> this royal race and sharers in Christ's priestly office.
> What, indeed, is as royal for a soul as to govern the
> body in obedience to God? And what is as priestly
> as to dedicate a pure conscience to the Lord and to
> offer the spotless offerings of devotion on the altar
> of the heart?[214]

II.   THE CHURCH—BODY OF CHRIST

The Church is communion with Jesus

787   From the beginning, Jesus associated his disciples with his own life, revealed the mystery of the Kingdom to them, and gave them a share in his mission, joy,
and sufferings.[215] Jesus spoke of a still more intimate
communion between him and those who would follow
755 him: "Abide in me, and I in you. . . . I am the vine, you

---

210 *LG* 12; cf. *Jude* 3.   211 Cf. *Jn* 12:32.   212 *Mt* 20:28.   213 *LG* 8; cf. 36.
214 St. Leo the Great, *Sermo* 4, 1: PL 54, 149.   215 Cf. *Mk* 1:16–20; 3:13–19;
Mt 13:10–17; *Lk* 10:17–20; 22:28–30.

are the branches."[216] And he proclaimed a mysterious and real communion between his own body and ours: "He who eats my flesh and drinks my blood abides in me, and I in him."[217]

788   When his visible presence was taken from them, Jesus did not leave his disciples orphans. He promised to remain with them until the end of time; he sent them his Spirit.[218] As a result communion with Jesus has become, in a way, more intense: "By communicating his Spirit, *690* Christ mystically constitutes as his body those brothers of his who are called together from every nation."[219]

789   The comparison of the Church with the body casts light on the intimate bond between Christ and his Church. Not only is she gathered *around him;* she is united *in him,* in his body. Three aspects of the Church *521* as the Body of Christ are to be more specifically noted: the unity of all her members with each other as a result of their union with Christ; Christ as head of the Body; and the Church as bride of Christ.

"One Body"

790   Believers who respond to God's word and become members of Christ's Body, become intimately united with him: "In that body the life of Christ is communicated to those who believe, and who, through the *947* sacraments, are united in a hidden and real way to Christ in his Passion and glorification."[220] This is especially true of Baptism, which unites us to Christ's death *1227* and Resurrection, and the Eucharist, by which "really *1329* sharing in the body of the Lord, . . . we are taken up into communion with him and with one another."[221]

791   The body's unity does not do away with the diversity of its members: "In the building up of Christ's Body there is engaged a diversity of members and func- *814* tions. There is only one Spirit who, according to his own richness and the needs of the ministries, gives his *1937*

---

216 *Jn* 15:4–5. 217 *Jn* 6:56. 218 Cf. *Jn* 14:18; 20:22; *Mt* 28:20; *Acts* 2:33.
219 *LG* 7. 220 *LG* 7. 221 *LG* 7; cf. *Rom* 6:4–5; *1 Cor* 12:13.

different gifts for the welfare of the Church."[222] The unity of the Mystical Body produces and stimulates charity among the faithful: "From this it follows that if one member suffers anything, all the members suffer with him, and if one member is honored, all the members together rejoice."[223] Finally, the unity of the Mystical Body triumphs over all human divisions: "For as many of you as were baptized into Christ have put on Christ. There is neither Jew nor Greek, there is neither slave nor free, there is neither male nor female; for you are all one in Christ Jesus."[224]

"Christ is the Head of this Body"

669, 1119   **792**   Christ "is the head of the body, the Church."[225] He is the principle of creation and redemption. Raised to the Father's glory, "in everything he [is] preeminent,"[226] especially in the Church, through whom he extends his reign over all things.

661   **793**   *Christ unites us with his Passover:* all his members must strive to resemble him, "until Christ be
519   formed" in them.[227] "For this reason we . . . are taken up into the mysteries of his life, . . . associated with his sufferings as the body with its head, suffering with him, that with him we may be glorified."[228]

794   *Christ provides for our growth:* to make us grow toward him, our head,[229] he provides in his Body, the Church, the gifts and assistance by which we help one
872   another along the way of salvation.

795   Christ and his Church thus together make up the "whole Christ" *(Christus totus)*. The Church is one
695   with Christ. The saints are acutely aware of this unity:

> Let us rejoice then and give thanks that we have become not only Christians, but Christ himself. Do you understand and grasp, brethren, God's grace toward us? Marvel and rejoice: we have become Christ. For if he is the head, we are the members; he

---

222 *LG* 7 § 3.   223 *LG* 7 § 3; cf. 1 *Cor* 12:26.   224 *Gal* 3:27–28.   225 *Col* 1:18.   226 *Col* 1:18.   227 *Gal* 4:19.   228 *LG* 7 § 4; cf. *Phil* 3:21; *Rom* 8:17. 229 Cf. *Col* 2:19; *Eph* 4:11–16.

and we together are the whole man. . . . The fullness of Christ then is the head and the members. But what does "head and members" mean? Christ and the Church.[230]

Our redeemer has shown himself to be one person with the holy Church whom he has taken to himself.[231]

Head and members form as it were one and the same mystical person.[232] *1474*

A reply of St. Joan of Arc to her judges sums up the faith of the holy doctors and the good sense of the believer: "About Jesus Christ and the Church, I simply know they're just one thing, and we shouldn't complicate the matter."[233]

The Church is the Bride of Christ

796 The unity of Christ and the Church, head and members of one Body, also implies the distinction of the two within a personal relationship. This aspect is often expressed by the image of bridegroom and bride. The *757* theme of Christ as Bridegroom of the Church was prepared for by the prophets and announced by John the Baptist.[234] The Lord referred to himself as the "bride- *219* groom."[235] The Apostle speaks of the whole Church and of each of the faithful, members of his Body, as a bride "betrothed" to Christ the Lord so as to become but one spirit with him.[236] The Church is the spotless bride of the *772* spotless Lamb.[237] "Christ loved the Church and gave *1602* himself up for her, that he might sanctify her."[238] He has joined her with himself in an everlasting covenant and never stops caring for her as for his own body:[239] *1616*

> This is the whole Christ, head and body, one formed from many . . . whether the head or members speak, it is Christ who speaks. He speaks in his role as the head *(ex persona capitis)* and in his role as body *(ex persona corporis)*. What does this mean? "The two will become one flesh. This is a

---

230 St. Augustine, *In Jo. ev.* 21, 8: PL 35, 1568.   231 Pope St. Gregory the Great, *Moralia in Job, præf.,* 14: PL 75, 525A.   232 St. Thomas Aquinas, *STh* III, 48, 2.   233 Acts of the Trial of Joan of Arc.   234 *Jn* 3:29.   235 *Mk* 2:19. 236 Cf. *Mt* 22:1–14; 25:1–13; 1 *Cor* 6:15–17; 2 *Cor* 11:2.   237 Cf. *Rev* 22:17; *Eph* 1:4; 5:27.   238 *Eph* 5:25–26.   239 Cf. *Eph* 5:29.

great mystery, and I am applying it to Christ and the Church."[240] And the Lord himself says in the Gospel: "So they are no longer two, but one flesh."[241] They are, in fact, two different persons, yet they are one in the conjugal union, ... *as head, he calls himself the bridegroom, as body, he calls himself "bride."*[242]

III.   THE CHURCH IS THE TEMPLE OF THE HOLY SPIRIT

797   "What the soul is to the human body, the Holy Spirit is to the Body of Christ, which is the Church."[243]

813   "To this Spirit of Christ, as an invisible principle, is to be ascribed the fact that all the parts of the body are joined one with the other and with their exalted head; for the whole Spirit of Christ is in the head, the whole Spirit is in the body, and the whole Spirit is in each of the members."[244] The Holy Spirit makes the Church

586   "the temple of the living God":[245]

> Indeed, it is to the Church herself that the "Gift of God" has been entrusted. ... In it is in her that communion with Christ has been deposited, that is to say: the Holy Spirit, the pledge of incorruptibility, the strengthening of our faith and the ladder of our ascent to God. ... For where the Church is, there also is God's Spirit; where God's Spirit is, there is the Church and every grace.[246]

798   The Holy Spirit is "the principle of every vital and truly saving action in each part of the Body."[247] He

737   works in many ways to build up the whole Body in charity:[248] by God's Word "which is able to build you up";[249] by Baptism, through which he forms Christ's

1091-1109   Body;[250] by the sacraments, which give growth and healing to Christ's members; by "the grace of the apostles, which holds first place among his gifts";[251] by the virtues, which make us act according to what is good; finally, by the many special graces (called "charisms"),

---

240 *Eph* 5:31–32.   241 *Mt* 19:6.   242 St. Augustine, *En. in Ps.* 74:4: PL 36, 948–949.   243 St. Augustine, *Sermo* 267, 4: PL 38, 1231D.   244 Pius XII, encyclical, *Mystici Corporis*: DS 3808.   245 *2 Cor* 6:16; cf. *1 Cor* 3:16–17; *Eph* 2:21.   246 St. Irenaeus, *Adv. haeres.* 3, 24, 1:PG 7/1, 966.   247 Pius XII, encyclical, *Mystici Corporis*: DS 3808.   248 Cf. *Eph* 4:16.   249 *Acts* 20:32. 250 Cf. *1 Cor* 12:13.   251 *LG* 7 § 2.

by which he makes the faithful "fit and ready to undertake various tasks and offices for the renewal and building up of the Church."[252]   791

Charisms

799   Whether extraordinary or simple and humble, charisms are graces of the Holy Spirit which directly or indirectly benefit the Church, ordered as they are to her building up, to the good of men, and to the needs of the world.   951, 2003

800   Charisms are to be accepted with gratitude by the person who receives them and by all members of the Church as well. They are a wonderfully rich grace for the apostolic vitality and for the holiness of the entire Body of Christ, provided they really are genuine gifts of the Holy Spirit and are used in full conformity with authentic promptings of this same Spirit, that is, in keeping with charity, the true measure of all charisms.[253]

801   It is in this sense that discernment of charisms is always necessary. No charism is exempt from being referred and submitted to the Church's shepherds. "Their office [is] not indeed to extinguish the Spirit, but to test all things and hold fast to what is good,"[254] so that all the diverse and complementary charisms work together "for the common good."[255]   894

1905

IN BRIEF

802   Christ Jesus "gave himself for us to redeem us from all iniquity and to purify for himself a people of his own" (*Titus* 2:14).

803   "You are a chosen race, a royal priesthood, a holy nation, God's own people" (*1 Pet* 2:9).

804   One enters into the People of God by faith and Baptism. "All men are called to belong to the new People of God" (*LG* 13), so that, in Christ, "men may form one family and one People of God" (*AG* 1).

---

252 *LG* 12 § 2; cf. *AA* 3.   253 Cf. *1 Cor* 13.   254 *LG* 12; cf. 30; *1 Thess* 5:12, 19–21; John Paul II, *Christifideles Laici*, 24.   255 *1 Cor* 12:7.

805   The Church is the Body of Christ. Through the Spirit and his action in the sacraments, above all the Eucharist, Christ, who once was dead and is now risen, establishes the community of believers as his own Body.

806   In the unity of this Body, there is a diversity of members and functions. All members are linked to one another, especially to those who are suffering, to the poor and persecuted.

807   The Church is this Body of which Christ is the head: she lives from him, in him, and for him; he lives with her and in her.

808   The Church is the Bride of Christ: he loved her and handed himself over for her. He has purified her by his blood and made her the fruitful mother of all God's children.

809   The Church is the Temple of the Holy Spirit. The Spirit is the soul, as it were, of the Mystical Body, the source of its life, of its unity in diversity, and of the riches of its gifts and charisms.

810   "Hence the universal Church is seen to be 'a people brought into unity from the unity of the Father, the Son, and the Holy Spirit' " (*LG* 4 citing St. Cyprian, *De Dom. orat.* 23: PL 4, 553).

Paragraph 3. The Church Is One, Holy, Catholic, and Apostolic

811   "This is the sole Church of Christ, which in the Creed we profess to be one, holy, catholic and apostolic."[256] These four characteristics, inseparably linked with each other,[257] indicate essential features of the Church and her mission. The Church does not possess them of herself; it is Christ who, through the Holy Spirit, makes his Church one, holy, catholic, and apostolic, and it is he who calls her to realize each of these qualities.

750

832, 865

---

256 *LG* 8.   257 Cf. DS 2888.

812   Only faith can recognize that the Church possesses these properties from her divine source. But their historical manifestations are signs that also speak clearly to human reason. As the First Vatican Council *156, 770* noted, the "Church herself, with her marvellous propagation, eminent holiness, and inexhaustible fruitfulness in everything good, her catholic unity and invincible stability, is a great and perpetual motive of credibility and an irrefutable witness of her divine mission."[258]

I.   THE CHURCH IS ONE

"The sacred mystery of the Church's unity" (UR 2)

813   *The Church is one because of her source:* "the highest exemplar and source of this mystery is the unity, in the Trinity of Persons, of one God, the Father and the Son in the Holy Spirit."[259] The Church is one *because of* *172* *her founder:* for "the Word made flesh, the prince of *766* peace, reconciled all men to God by the cross, . . . restoring the unity of all in one people and one body."[260] *797* The Church is one *because of her "soul":* "It is the Holy Spirit, dwelling in those who believe and pervading and ruling over the entire Church, who brings about that wonderful communion of the faithful and joins them together so intimately in Christ that he is the principle of the Church's unity."[261] Unity is of the essence of the Church:

> What an astonishing mystery! There is one Father of the universe, one Logos of the universe, and also one Holy Spirit, everywhere one and the same; there is also one virgin become mother, and I should like to call her "Church."[262]

814   From the beginning, this one Church has been marked by a great *diversity* which comes from both the variety of God's gifts and the diversity of those who receive them. Within the unity of the People of God, a *791, 873* multiplicity of peoples and cultures is gathered together.

---

258 Vatican Council I, *Dei Filius* 3: DS 3013.   259 UR 2 § 5.   260 GS 78 § 3.
261 *UR* 2 § 2.   262 St. Clement of Alexandria, *Paed.* 1, 6, 42: PG 8, 300.

1202 Among the Church's members, there are different gifts, offices, conditions, and ways of life. "Holding a rightful place in the communion of the Church there are also particular Churches that retain their own traditions."[263] The great richness of such diversity is not opposed to

832 the Church's unity. Yet sin and the burden of its consequences constantly threaten the gift of unity. And so the Apostle has to exhort Christians to "maintain the unity of the Spirit in the bond of peace."[264]

1827 **815** What are these bonds of unity? Above all, charity "binds everything together in perfect harmony."[265]

830, 837 But the unity of the pilgrim Church is also assured by

173 visible bonds of communion:

—profession of one faith received from the Apostles;

—common celebration of divine worship, especially of the sacraments;

—apostolic succession through the sacrament of Holy Orders, maintaining the fraternal concord of God's family.[266]

816 "The sole Church of Christ [is that] which our Savior, after his Resurrection, entrusted to Peter's pastoral care, commissioning him and the other apostles to extend and rule it. . . . This Church, constituted and organized as a society in the present world, subsists in *(subsistit in)* the Catholic Church, which is governed by the successor of Peter and by the bishops in communion with him."[267]

830 The Second Vatican Council's *Decree on Ecumenism* explains: "For it is through Christ's Catholic Church alone, which is the universal help toward salvation, that the fullness of the means of salvation can be obtained. It was to the apostolic college alone, of which Peter is the head, that we believe that our Lord entrusted all the blessings of the New Covenant, in order to establish on earth the one Body of Christ into which all those should

---

263 *LG* 13 § 2.   264 *Eph* 4:3.   265 *Col* 3:14.   266 Cf. *UR* 2; *LG* 14; CIC, can. 205.   267 *LG* 8 § 2.

be fully incorporated who belong in any way to the People of God."[268]

Wounds to unity

817 In fact, "in this one and only Church of God from its very beginnings there arose certain rifts, which the Apostle strongly censures as damnable. But in subsequent centuries much more serious dissensions appeared and large communities became separated from full communion with the Catholic Church—for which, often enough, men of both sides were to blame."[269] The ruptures that wound the unity of Christ's Body—here we must distinguish heresy, apostasy, and schism[270]—do not occur without human sin:

2089

> Where there are sins, there are also divisions, schisms, heresies, and disputes. Where there is virtue, however, there also are harmony and unity, from which arise the one heart and one soul of all believers.[271]

818 "However, one cannot charge with the sin of the separation those who at present are born into these communities [that resulted from such separation] and in them are brought up in the faith of Christ, and the Catholic Church accepts them with respect and affection as brothers. . . . All who have been justified by faith in Baptism are incorporated into Christ; they therefore have a right to be called Christians, and with good reason are accepted as brothers in the Lord by the children of the Catholic Church."[272]

1271

819 "Furthermore, many elements of sanctification and of truth"[273] are found outside the visible confines of the Catholic Church: "the written Word of God; the life of grace; faith, hope, and charity, with the other interior gifts of the Holy Spirit, as well as visible elements."[274] Christ's Spirit uses these Churches and ecclesial communities as means of salvation, whose power derives from the fullness of grace and truth that Christ has en-

---

268 UR 3 § 5.   269 UR 3 § 1.   270 Cf. CIC, can. 751.   271 Origen, *Hom. in Ezech.* 9, 1: PG 13, 732.   272 UR 3 § 1.   273 LG 8 § 2.   274 UR 3 § 2; cf. LG 15.

trusted to the Catholic Church. All these blessings come from Christ and lead to him,[275] and are in themselves calls to "Catholic unity."[276]

Toward unity

820   "Christ bestowed unity on his Church from the beginning. This unity, we believe, subsists in the Catholic Church as something she can never lose, and we hope that it will continue to increase until the end of time."[277] Christ always gives his Church the gift of unity, but the Church must always pray and work to maintain, reinforce, and perfect the unity that Christ wills for her.

2748   This is why Jesus himself prayed at the hour of his Passion, and does not cease praying to his Father, for the unity of his disciples: "That they may all be one. As you, Father, are in me and I am in you, may they also be one in us, . . . so that the world may know that you have sent me."[278] The desire to recover the unity of all Christians is a gift of Christ and a call of the Holy Spirit.[279]

821   Certain things are required in order to respond adequately to this call:

—a permanent *renewal* of the Church in greater fidelity to her vocation; such renewal is the driving-force of the movement toward unity;[280]

827   —*conversion of heart* as the faithful "try to live holier lives according to the Gospel";[281] for it is the unfaithfulness of the members to Christ's gift which causes divisions;

2791   —*prayer in common,* because "change of heart and holiness of life, along with public and private prayer for the unity of Christians, should be regarded as the soul of the whole ecumenical movement, and merits the name 'spiritual ecumenism;' "[282]

—*fraternal knowledge of each other;*[283]

—*ecumenical formation* of the faithful and especially of priests;[284]

—*dialogue* among theologians and meetings among Christians of the different churches and communities;[285]

---

275 Cf. UR 3.   276 Cf. LG 8.   277 UR 4 § 3.   278 *Jn* 17:21; cf. *Heb* 7:25.
279 Cf. UR 1.   280 Cf. UR 6.   281 UR 7 § 3.   282 UR 8 § 1.   283 Cf. UR 9.
284 Cf. UR 10.   285 Cf. UR 4; 9; 11.

—*collaboration* among Christians in various areas of service to mankind.[286] "Human service" is the idiomatic phrase.

822   Concern for achieving unity "involves the whole Church, faithful and clergy alike."[287] But we must realize "that this holy objective—the reconciliation of all Christians in the unity of the one and only Church of Christ—transcends human powers and gifts." That is why we place all our hope "in the prayer of Christ for the Church, in the love of the Father for us, and in the power of the Holy Spirit."[288]

II.   THE CHURCH IS HOLY

823   "The Church . . . is held, as a matter of faith, to be unfailingly holy. This is because Christ, the Son of God, who with the Father and the Spirit is hailed as 'alone holy,' loved the Church as his Bride, giving himself up for her so as to sanctify her; he joined her to himself as his body and endowed her with the gift of the Holy Spirit for the glory of God."[289] The Church, then, is "the holy People of God,"[290] and her members are called "saints."[291]

*(margin: 459, 796)*

*(margin: 946)*

824   United with Christ, the Church is sanctified by him; through him and with him she becomes sanctifying. "All the activities of the Church are directed, as toward their end, to the sanctification of men in Christ and the glorification of God."[292] It is in the Church that "the fullness of the means of salvation"[293] has been deposited. It is in her that "by the grace of God we acquire holiness."[294]

*(margin: 816)*

825   "The Church on earth is endowed already with a sanctity that is real though imperfect."[295] In her members perfect holiness is something yet to be acquired: "Strengthened by so many and such great means of salvation, all the faithful, whatever their condition or state—though each in his own way—are called by the

*(margin: 670)*

*(margin: 2013)*

---

286 Cf. UR 12.   287 UR 5.   288 UR 24 § 2.   289 LG 39; cf. Eph 5:25–26.
290 LG 12.   291 Acts 9:13; 1 Cor 6:1; 16:1.   292 SC 10.   293 UR 3 § 5.
294 LG 48.   295 LG 48 § 3.

Lord to that perfection of sanctity by which the Father himself is perfect."[296]

1827, **826**   Charity is the soul of the holiness to which all
2658   are called: it "governs, shapes, and perfects all the means of sanctification."[297]

864

If the Church was a body composed of different members, it couldn't lack the noblest of all; *it must have a Heart, and a Heart BURNING WITH LOVE.* And I realized that *this love alone* was the true motive force which enabled the other members of the Church to act; if it ceased to function, the Apostles would forget to preach the gospel, the Martyrs would refuse to shed their blood. LOVE, IN FACT, IS THE VOCATION WHICH INCLUDES ALL OTHERS; IT'S A UNIVERSE OF ITS OWN, COMPRISING ALL TIME AND SPACE—IT'S ETERNAL![298]

827   "Christ, 'holy, innocent, and undefiled,' knew nothing of sin, but came only to expiate the sins of the people. The Church, however, clasping sinners to her
1425-1429   bosom, at once holy and always in need of purification,
821   follows constantly the path of penance and renewal."[299] All members of the Church, including her ministers, must acknowledge that they are sinners.[300] In everyone, the weeds of sin will still be mixed with the good wheat of the Gospel until the end of time.[301] Hence the Church gathers sinners already caught up in Christ's salvation but still on the way to holiness:

The Church is therefore holy, though having sinners in her midst, because she herself has no other life but the life of grace. If they live her life, her members are sanctified; if they move away from her life, they fall into sins and disorders that prevent the radiation of her sanctity. This is why she suffers and does penance for those offenses, of which she has the power to free her children through the blood of Christ and the gift of the Holy Spirit.[302]

---

296 *LG* 11 § 3.   297 *LG* 42.   298 St. Thérèse of Lisieux, *Autobiography of a Saint,* tr. Ronald Knox (London: Harvill, 1958) 235.   299 *LG* 8 § 3; cf. UR 3; 6; *Heb* 2:17; 7:26; *2 Cor* 5:21.   300 Cf. *1 Jn* 1:8–10.   301 Cf. *Mt* 13:24–30. 302 Paul VI, *CPG* § 19.

828 By *canonizing* some of the faithful, i.e., by solemnly proclaiming that they practiced heroic virtue and lived in fidelity to God's grace, the Church recognizes the power of the Spirit of holiness within her and sustains the hope of believers by proposing the saints to them as models and intercessors.[303] "The saints have always been the source and origin of renewal in the most difficult moments in the Church's history."[304] Indeed, "holiness is the hidden source and infallible measure of her apostolic activity and missionary zeal."[305]

1173

2045

829 "But while in the most Blessed Virgin the Church has already reached that perfection whereby she exists without spot or wrinkle, the faithful still strive to conquer sin and increase in holiness. And so they turn their eyes to Mary":[306] in her, the Church is already the "all-holy."

1172

972

III.   THE CHURCH IS CATHOLIC

What does "catholic" mean?

830 The word "catholic" means "universal," in the sense of "according to the totality" or "in keeping with the whole." The Church is catholic in a double sense:

First, the Church is catholic because Christ is present in her. "Where there is Christ Jesus, there is the Catholic Church."[307] In her subsists the fullness of Christ's body united with its head; this implies that she receives from him "the fullness of the means of salvation"[308] which he has willed: correct and complete confession of faith, full sacramental life, and ordained ministry in apostolic succession. The Church was, in this fundamental sense, catholic on the day of Pentecost[309] and will always be so until the day of the Parousia.

795

815-816

831 Secondly, the Church is catholic because she has been sent out by Christ on a mission to the whole of the human race:[310]

849

---

303 Cf. *LG* 40; 48–51.   304 John Paul II, *CL* 16, 3.   305 *CL* 17, 3.   306 *LG* 65; cf. *Eph* 5:26–27.   307 St. Ignatius of Antioch, *Ad Smyrn.* 8, 2: *Apostolic Fathers,* II/2, 311.   308 *UR* 3; *AG* 6; *Eph* 1:22–23.   309 Cf. *AG* 4.   310 Cf. *Mt* 28:19.

360

518

All men are called to belong to the new People of God. This People, therefore, while remaining one and only one, is to be spread throughout the whole world and to all ages in order that the design of God's will may be fulfilled: he made human nature one in the beginning and has decreed that all his children who were scattered should be finally gathered together as one.... The character of universality which adorns the People of God is a gift from the Lord himself whereby the Catholic Church ceaselessly and efficaciously seeks for the return of all humanity and all its goods, under Christ the Head in the unity of his Spirit.[311]

Each particular Church is "catholic"

814
811

832   "The Church of Christ is really present in all legitimately organized local groups of the faithful, which, in so far as they are united to their pastors, are also quite appropriately called Churches in the New Testament.... In them the faithful are gathered together through the preaching of the Gospel of Christ, and the mystery of the Lord's Supper is celebrated.... In these communities, though they may often be small and poor, or existing in the diaspora, Christ is present, through whose power and influence the One, Holy, Catholic, and Apostolic Church is constituted."[312]

886

833   The phrase "particular church," which is the diocese (or eparchy), refers to a community of the Christian faithful in communion of faith and sacraments with their bishop ordained in apostolic succession.[313] These particular Churches "are constituted after the model of the universal Church; it is in these and formed out of them that the one and unique Catholic Church exists."[314]

882, 1369

834   Particular Churches are fully catholic through their communion with one of them, the Church of Rome "which presides in charity."[315] "For with this church, by reason of its pre-eminence, the whole Church, that is the faithful everywhere, must necessar-

---

311 *LG* 13 §§ 1–2; cf. *Jn* 11:52.   312 *LG* 26.   313 Cf. *CD* 11; CIC, cann. 368–369.   314 *LG* 23.   315 St. Ignatius of Antioch, *Ad Rom.* 1, 1: *Apostolic Fathers,* II/2, 192; cf. *LG* 13.

ily be in accord."[316] Indeed, "from the incarnate Word's descent to us, all Christian churches everywhere have held and hold the great Church that is here [at Rome] to be their only basis and foundation since, according to the Savior's promise, the gates of hell have never prevailed against her."[317]

835   "Let us be very careful not to conceive of the universal Church as the simple sum, or . . . the more or less anomalous federation of essentially different particular churches. In the mind of the Lord the Church is universal by vocation and mission, but when she puts down her roots in a variety of cultural, social, and human terrains, she takes on different external expressions and appearances in each part of the world."[318] The rich variety of ecclesiastical disciplines, liturgical rites, and theological and spiritual heritages proper to the local churches "unified in a common effort, shows all the more resplendently the catholicity of the undivided Church."[319]

1202

Who belongs to the Catholic Church?

836   "All men are called to this catholic unity of the People of God. . . . And to it, in different ways, belong or are ordered: the Catholic faithful, others who believe in Christ, and finally all mankind, called by God's grace to salvation."[320]

831

837   "Fully incorporated into the society of the Church are those who, possessing the Spirit of Christ, accept all the means of salvation given to the Church together with her entire organization, and who—by the bonds constituted by the profession of faith, the sacraments, ecclesiastical government, and communion—are joined in the visible structure of the Church of Christ, who rules her through the Supreme Pontiff and the bishops. Even though incorporated into the Church, one who does not however persevere in charity is not saved. He remains indeed in the bosom of the Church, but 'in body' not 'in heart.' "[321]

771
815

882

838   "The Church knows that she is joined in many

---

316 St. Irenaeus, *Adv. haeres.* 3, 3, 2: PG 7/1, 849; cf. Vatican Council I: DS 3057.   317 St. Maximus the Confessor, *Opuscula theo.*: PG 91:137–140.   318 Paul VI, *EN* 62.   319 *LG* 23.   320 *LG* 13.   321 *LG* 14.

ways to the baptized who are honored by the name of Christian, but do not profess the Catholic faith in its en-
818 tirety or have not preserved unity or communion under the successor of Peter."[322] Those "who believe in Christ and have been properly baptized are put in a certain, although imperfect, communion with the Catholic
1271 Church."[323] *With the Orthodox Churches,* this communion is so profound "that it lacks little to attain the fullness that would permit a common celebration of the
1399 Lord's Eucharist."[324]

The Church and non-Christians

856 839   "Those who have not yet received the Gospel are related to the People of God in various ways."[325]

The relationship of the Church with the Jewish People. When she delves into her own mystery, the Church, the People of God in the New Covenant, discovers her link with the Jewish People,[326] "the first to
63 hear the Word of God."[327] The Jewish faith, unlike other
147 non-Christian religions, is already a response to God's revelation in the Old Covenant. To the Jews "belong the sonship, the glory, the covenants, the giving of the law, the worship, and the promises; to them belong the patriarchs, and of their race, according to the flesh, is the Christ";[328] "for the gifts and the call of God are irrevocable."[329]

840   And when one considers the future, God's People of the Old Covenant and the new People of God tend towards
674 similar goals: expectation of the coming (or the return) of the Messiah. But one awaits the return of the Messiah who died and rose from the dead and is recognized as Lord and Son of God; the other awaits the coming of a Messiah, whose features remain hidden till the end of time; and the latter waiting is accompanied by the drama of not knowing
597 or of misunderstanding Christ Jesus.

841   *The Church's relationship with the Muslims.* "The plan of salvation also includes those who acknowledge the Creator, in the first place amongst whom are

---

322 *LG* 15.   323 *UR* 3.   324 Paul VI, Discourse, December 14, 1975; cf. *UR* 13–18.   325 *LG* 16.   326 Cf. *NA* 4.   327 *Roman Missal,* Good Friday 13: General Intercessions, VI.   328 *Rom* 9:4–5.   329 *Rom* 11:29.

the Muslims; these profess to hold the faith of Abraham, and together with us they adore the one, merciful God, mankind's judge on the last day."[330]

842 *The Church's bond with non-Christian religions* is in the first place the common origin and end of the human race:

360

> All nations form but one community. This is so because all stem from the one stock which God created to people the entire earth, and also because all share a common destiny, namely God. His providence, evident goodness, and saving designs extend to all against the day when the elect are gathered together in the holy city. . . .[331]

843 The Catholic Church recognizes in other religions that search, among shadows and images, for the God who is unknown yet near since he gives life and breath and all things and wants all men to be saved. Thus, the Church considers all goodness and truth found in these religions as "a preparation for the Gospel and given by him who enlightens all men that they may at length have life."[332]

28
856

844 In their religious behavior, however, men also display the limits and errors that disfigure the image of God in them:

29

> Very often, deceived by the Evil One, men have become vain in their reasonings, and have exchanged the truth of God for a lie, and served the creature rather than the Creator. Or else, living and dying in this world without God, they are exposed to ultimate despair.[333]

845 To reunite all his children, scattered and led astray by sin, the Father willed to call the whole of humanity together into his Son's Church. The Church is the place where humanity must rediscover its unity and salvation. The Church is "the world reconciled." She is that bark which "in the full sail of the Lord's cross, by the breath of the Holy Spirit, navigates safely in this world." According to another image dear to the Church

30
953

---

330 *LG* 16; cf. *NA* 3. 331 *NA* 1. 332 *LG* 16; cf. *NA* 2; *EN* 53. 333 *LG* 16; cf. *Rom* 1:21, 25.

1219 Fathers, she is prefigured by Noah's ark, which alone saves from the flood.[334]

"Outside the Church there is no salvation"

846   How are we to understand this affirmation, often repeated by the Church Fathers?[335] Re-formulated positively, it means that all salvation comes from Christ the Head through the Church which is his Body:

> Basing itself on Scripture and Tradition, the Council teaches that the Church, a pilgrim now on earth, is necessary for salvation: the one Christ is the mediator and the way of salvation; he is present to us in his body which is the Church. He himself explicitly asserted the necessity of faith and Baptism, and thereby affirmed at the same time the necessity of the Church which men enter through Baptism as through a door. Hence they could not be saved who, knowing that the Catholic Church was founded as necessary by God through Christ, would refuse either to enter it or to remain in it.[336]

161, 1257

847   This affirmation is not aimed at those who, through no fault of their own, do not know Christ and his Church:

> Those who, through no fault of their own, do not know the Gospel of Christ or his Church, but who nevertheless seek God with a sincere heart, and, moved by grace, try in their actions to do his will as they know it through the dictates of their conscience—those too may achieve eternal salvation.[337]

848   "Although in ways known to himself God can lead those who, through no fault of their own, are ignorant of the Gospel, to that faith without which it is impossible to please him, the Church still has the obligation and also the sacred right to evangelize all men."[338]

1260

---

334 St. Augustine, *Serm.* 96, 7, 9: PL 38, 588; St. Ambrose, *De virg.* 18, 118: PL 16, 297B; cf. already *1 Pet* 3:20–21.   335 Cf. Cyprian, *Ep.* 73.21: PL 3, 1169; *De unit.*: PL 4, 509–536.   336 *LG* 14; cf. *Mk* 16:16; *Jn* 3:5.   337 *LG* 16; cf. DS 3866-3872.   338 *AG* 7; cf. *Heb* 11:6; *1 Cor* 9:16.

Mission—a requirement of the Church's catholicity

849   *The missionary mandate.* "Having been divinely sent to the nations that she might be 'the universal sacrament of salvation,' the Church, in obedience to the command of her founder and because it is demanded by her own essential universality, strives to preach the Gospel to all men":[339] "Go therefore and make disciples of all nations, baptizing them in the name of the Father and of the Son and of the Holy Spirit, teaching them to observe all that I have commanded you; and Lo, I am with you always, until the close of the age."[340]   738, 767

850   *The origin and purpose of mission.* The Lord's missionary mandate is ultimately grounded in the eternal love of the Most Holy Trinity: "The Church on earth is by her nature missionary since, according to the plan of the Father, she has as her origin the mission of the Son and the Holy Spirit."[341] The ultimate purpose of mission is none other than to make men share in the communion between the Father and the Son in their Spirit of love.[342]   257, 730

851   *Missionary motivation.* It is from God's love for all men that the Church in every age receives both the obligation and the vigor of her missionary dynamism, "for the love of Christ urges us on."[343] Indeed, God "desires all men to be saved and to come to the knowledge of the truth";[344] that is, God wills the salvation of everyone through the knowledge of the truth. Salvation is found in the truth. Those who obey the prompting of the Spirit of truth are already on the way of salvation. But the Church, to whom this truth has been entrusted, must go out to meet their desire, so as to bring them the truth. Because she believes in God's universal plan of salvation, the Church must be missionary.   221, 429, 74, 217, 2104, 890

852   *Missionary paths.* The Holy Spirit is the protagonist, "the principal agent of the whole of the Church's   2044

339 *AG* 1; cf. *Mt* 16:15.   340 *Mt* 28:19–20.   341 *AG* 2.   342 Cf. John Paul II, *RMiss* 23.   343 *2 Cor* 5:14; cf. *AA* 6; *RMiss* 11.   344 *1 Tim* 2:4.

mission."[345] It is he who leads the Church on her mis-
2473 sionary paths. "This mission continues and, in the
course of history, unfolds the mission of Christ, who
was sent to evangelize the poor; so the Church, urged
on by the Spirit of Christ, must walk the road Christ
himself walked, a way of poverty and obedience, of service and self-sacrifice even to death, a death from which
he emerged victorious by his resurrection."[346] So it is
that "the blood of martyrs is the seed of Christians."[347]

853   On her pilgrimage, the Church has also experienced
the "discrepancy existing between the message she proclaims and the human weakness of those to whom the
Gospel has been entrusted."[348] Only by taking the "way of
penance and renewal," the "narrow way of the cross," can
1428 the People of God extend Christ's reign.[349] For "just as
Christ carried out the work of redemption in poverty and
oppression, so the Church is called to follow the same path
2443 if she is to communicate the fruits of salvation to men."[350]

854   By her very mission, "the Church . . . travels the
same journey as all humanity and shares the same earthly
lot with the world: she is to be a leaven and, as it were, the
soul of human society in its renewal by Christ and transformation into the family of God."[351] Missionary endeavor
requires *patience*. It begins with the proclamation of the
Gospel to peoples and groups who do not yet believe in
2105 Christ,[352] continues with the establishment of Christian
communities that are "a sign of God's presence in the
world,"[353] and leads to the foundation of local churches.[354]
1204 It must involve a process of inculturation if the Gospel is to
take flesh in each people's culture.[355] There will be times of
defeat. "With regard to individuals, groups, and peoples it
is only by degrees that [the Church] touches and penetrates
them, and so receives them into a fullness which is
Catholic."[356]

855   The Church's mission stimulates efforts *towards
Christian unity*.[357] Indeed, "divisions among Christians pre-
821 vent the Church from realizing in practice the fullness of
catholicity proper to her in those of her sons who, though
joined to her by Baptism, are yet separated from full communion with her. Furthermore, the Church herself finds it

---

345 John Paul II, *RMiss* 21.   346 *AG* 5.   347 Tertullian, *Apol.* 50, 13: PL 1,
603.   348 *GS* 43 § 6.   349 *LG* 8 § 3; 15; *AG* 1 § 3; cf. *RMiss* 12–20.   350 *LG*
8 § 3.   351 *GS* 40 § 2.   352 Cf. *RMiss* 42–47.   353 *AG* 15 § 1.   354 Cf.
RMiss 48–49.   355 Cf. *RMiss* 52–54.   356 *AG* 6 § 2.   357 Cf. *RMiss* 50.

more difficult to express in actual life her full catholicity in all its aspects."[358]

856   The missionary task implies a *respectful dialogue* with those who do not yet accept the Gospel.[359] Believers can profit from this dialogue by learning to appreciate better "those elements of truth and grace which are found 839
among peoples, and which are, as it were, a secret presence of God."[360] They proclaim the Good News to those who do not know it, in order to consolidate, complete, and raise up the truth and the goodness that God has distributed among men and nations, and to purify them from error and evil 843
"for the glory of God, the confusion of the demon, and the happiness of man."[361]

IV.   THE CHURCH IS APOSTOLIC
857   The Church is apostolic because she is founded 75
on the apostles, in three ways:

—she was and remains built on "the foundation of the Apostles,"[362] the witnesses chosen and sent on mission by Christ himself;[363]

—with the help of the Spirit dwelling in her, the Church 171
keeps and hands on the teaching,[364] the "good deposit," the salutary words she has heard from the apostles;[365]

—she continues to be taught, sanctified, and guided by the apostles until Christ's return, through their successors in pastoral office: the college of bishops, "assisted by priests, in union with the successor of Peter, the 880
Church's supreme pastor":[366]   1575

> You are the eternal Shepherd
> who never leaves his flock untended.
> Through the apostles
> you watch over us and protect us always.
> You made them shepherds of the flock
> to share in the work of your Son. . . .[367]

The Apostles' mission
858   Jesus is the Father's Emissary. From the beginning of his ministry, he "called to him those whom he

---

358 *UR* 4 § 8.   359 Cf. *RMiss* 55.   360 *AG* 9.   361 *AG* 9.   362 *Eph* 2:20; *Rev* 21:14.   363 Cf. *Mt* 28:16–20; *Acts* 1:8; *1 Cor* 9:1; 15:7–8; *Gal* 1:1; etc.   364 Cf. *Acts* 2:42.   365 Cf. *2 Tim* 1:13–14.   366 *AG* 5.   367 *Roman Missal*, Preface of the Apostles I.

desired; . . . . And he appointed twelve, whom also he
551 named apostles, to be with him, and to be sent out to
preach."[368] From then on, they would also be his "emissaries" (Greek *apostoloi*). In them, Christ continues his
own mission: "As the Father has sent me, even so I send
you."[369] The apostles' ministry is the continuation of his
425, 1086 mission; Jesus said to the Twelve: "he who receives you
receives me."[370]

859 Jesus unites them to the mission he received from
the Father. As "the Son can do nothing of his own accord," but receives everything from the Father who sent
him, so those whom Jesus sends can do nothing apart
from him,[371] from whom they received both the mandate
for their mission and the power to carry it out. Christ's
apostles knew that they were called by God as "minis-
876 ters of a new covenant," "servants of God," "ambas-
sadors for Christ," "servants of Christ and stewards of
the mysteries of God."[372]

860 In the office of the apostles there is one aspect
that cannot be transmitted: to be the chosen witnesses
of the Lord's Resurrection and so the foundation stones
of the Church. But their office also has a permanent as-
642 pect. Christ promised to remain with them always. The
divine mission entrusted by Jesus to them "will continue
to the end of time, since the Gospel they handed on is
765 the lasting source of all life for the Church. Therefore,
1087 . . . the apostles took care to appoint successors."[373]

The bishops—successors of the apostles

861 "In order that the mission entrusted to them
might be continued after their death, [the apostles] consigned, by will and testament, as it were, to their imme-
77 diate collaborators the duty of completing and consoli-
dating the work they had begun, urging them to tend to
the whole flock, in which the Holy Spirit had appointed
them to shepherd the Church of God. They accordingly
1087 designated such men and then made the ruling that like-

---

368 Mk 3:13–14.   369 Jn 20:21; cf. 13:20; 17:18.   370 Mt 10:40; cf. Lk 10:16.
371 Jn 5:19, 30; cf. Jn 15:5.   372 2 Cor 3:6; 6:4; 5:20; 1 Cor 4:1.   373 LG 20;
cf. Mt 28:20.

wise on their death other proven men should take over their ministry."[374]

862 "Just as the office which the Lord confided to Peter alone, as first of the apostles, destined to be transmitted to his successors, is a permanent one, so also endures the office, which the apostles received, of shepherding the Church, a charge destined to be exercised without interruption by the sacred order of bishops."[375] Hence the Church teaches that "the bishops have by divine institution taken the place of the apostles as pastors of the Church, in such wise that whoever listens to them is listening to Christ and whoever despises them despises Christ and him who sent Christ."[376]

880

1556

The apostolate
863 The whole Church is apostolic, in that she remains, through the successors of St. Peter and the other apostles, in communion of faith and life with her origin: and in that she is "sent out" into the whole world. All members of the Church share in this mission, though in various ways. "The Christian vocation is, of its nature, a vocation to the apostolate as well." Indeed, we call an apostolate "every activity of the Mystical Body" that aims "to spread the Kingdom of Christ over all the earth."[377]

900

2472

864 "Christ, sent by the Father, is the source of the Church's whole apostolate"; thus the fruitfulness of apostolate for ordained ministers as well as for lay people clearly depends on their vital union with Christ.[378] In keeping with their vocations, the demands of the times and the various gifts of the Holy Spirit, the apostolate assumes the most varied forms. But charity, drawn from the Eucharist above all, is always "as it were, the soul of the whole apostolate."[379]

828

824

1324

865 The Church is ultimately *one, holy, catholic, and apostolic* in her deepest and ultimate identity, because it is in her that "the Kingdom of heaven," the "Reign of

811

---

374 *LG* 20; cf. *Acts* 20:28; St. Clement of Rome, *Ad Cor.* 42, 44: PG 1, 291–300.
375 *LG* 20 § 2.   376 *LG* 20 § 2.   377 *AA* 2.   378 *AA* 4; cf. *Jn* 15:5.
379 *AA* 3.

541 God,"[380] already exists and will be fulfilled at the end of time. The kingdom has come in the person of Christ and grows mysteriously in the hearts of those incorporated into him, until its full eschatological manifestation. Then all those he has redeemed and made "holy and blameless before him in love,"[381] will be gathered together as the one People of God, the "Bride of the Lamb,"[382] "the holy city Jerusalem coming down out of heaven from God, having the glory of God."[383] For "the wall of the city had twelve foundations, and on them the twelve names of the *twelve apostles of the Lamb.*"[384]

IN BRIEF

866   The Church is one: she acknowledges one Lord, confesses one faith, is born of one Baptism, forms only one Body, is given life by the one Spirit, for the sake of one hope (cf. *Eph* 4:3–5), at whose fulfillment all divisions will be overcome.

867   The Church is holy: the Most Holy God is her author; Christ, her bridegroom, gave himself up to make her holy; the Spirit of holiness gives her life. Since she still includes sinners, she is "the sinless one made up of sinners." Her holiness shines in the saints; in Mary she is already all-holy.

868   The Church is catholic: she proclaims the fullness of the faith. She bears in herself and administers the totality of the means of salvation. She is sent out to all peoples. She speaks to all men. She encompasses all times. She is "missionary of her very nature" (*AG* 2).

869   The Church is apostolic. She is built on a lasting foundation: "the twelve apostles of the Lamb" (*Rev* 21:14). She is indestructible (cf. *Mt* 16:18). She is upheld infallibly in the truth: Christ governs her through Peter and the other apostles,

---

380 *Rev* 19:6.   381 *Eph* 1:4.   382 *Rev* 21:9.   383 *Rev* 21:10–11.   384 *Rev* 21:14.

who are present in their successors, the Pope and the college of bishops.

870   "The sole Church of Christ which in the Creed we profess to be one, holy, catholic, and apostolic, . . . subsists in the Catholic Church, which is governed by the successor of Peter and by the bishops in communion with him. Nevertheless, many elements of sanctification and of truth are found outside its visible confines" (*LG* 8).

Paragraph 4. Christ's Faithful— Hierarchy, Laity, Consecrated Life

871   "The Christian faithful are those who, inasmuch as they have been incorporated in Christ through Baptism, have been constituted as the people of God; for this reason, since they have become sharers in Christ's priestly, prophetic, and royal office in their own manner, they are called to exercise the mission which God has entrusted to the Church to fulfill in the world, in accord with the condition proper to each one."[385]

1268-1269

782-786

872   "In virtue of their rebirth in Christ there exists among all the Christian faithful a true equality with regard to dignity and the activity whereby all cooperate in the building up of the Body of Christ in accord with each one's own condition and function."[386]

1934

794

873   The very differences which the Lord has willed to put between the members of his body serve its unity and mission. For "in the Church there is diversity of ministry but unity of mission. To the apostles and their successors Christ has entrusted the office of teaching, sanctifying, and governing in his name and by his power. But the laity are made to share in the priestly, prophetical, and kingly office of Christ; they have therefore, in the Church and in the world, their own assignment in the mission of the whole People of God."[387] Finally, "from both groups [hierarchy and laity] there exist Christian faithful who are consecrated to God in

814, 1937

---

385 CIC, can. 204 § 1; cf. *LG* 31.   386 CIC, can. 208; cf. *LG* 32.   387 *AA* 2.

their own special manner and serve the salvific mission of the Church through the profession of the evangelical counsels."[388]

I.   THE HIERARCHICAL CONSTITUTION OF THE CHURCH

Why the ecclesial ministry?

874   Christ is himself the source of ministry in the Church. He instituted the Church. He gave her author-
1544 ity and mission, orientation and goal:

> In order to shepherd the People of God and to in-crease its numbers without cease, Christ the Lord set up in his Church a variety of offices which aim at the good of the whole body. The holders of of-fice, who are invested with a sacred power, are, in fact, dedicated to promoting the interests of their brethren, so that all who belong to the People of God . . . may attain to salvation.[389]

875   "How are they to believe in him of whom they have never heard? And how are they to hear without a preacher? And how can men preach unless they are
166 sent?"[390] No one—no individual and no community—can proclaim the Gospel to himself: "Faith comes from what is heard."[391] No one can give himself the mandate and the mission to proclaim the Gospel. The one sent by the Lord does not speak and act on his own authority, but by virtue of Christ's authority; not as a member of the community, but speaking to it in the name of Christ. No one can bestow grace on himself; it must be given and offered. This fact presupposes ministers of grace, authorized and empowered by Christ. From him, they receive the mission and faculty ("the sacred power") to
1548 act *in persona Christi Capitis*. The ministry in which Christ's emissaries do and give by God's grace what they
1536 cannot do and give by their own powers, is called a "sacrament" by the Church's tradition. Indeed, the min-istry of the Church is conferred by a special sacrament.

---

388 CIC, can. 207 § 2.   389 *LG* 18.   390 *Rom* 10:14–15.
391 *Rom* 10:17.

876   Intrinsically linked to the sacramental nature of ecclesial ministry is *its character as service*. Entirely dependent on Christ who gives mission and authority, ministers are truly "slaves of Christ,"[392] in the image of him who freely took "the form of a slave" for us.[393] Because the word and grace of which they are ministers are not their own, but are given to them by Christ for the sake of others, they must freely become the slaves of all.[394]

1551

427

877   Likewise, it belongs to the sacramental nature of ecclesial ministry that it have a *collegial character*. In fact, from the beginning of his ministry, the Lord Jesus instituted the Twelve as "the seeds of the new Israel and the beginning of the sacred hierarchy."[395] Chosen together, they were also sent out together, and their fraternal unity would be at the service of the fraternal communion of all the faithful: they would reflect and witness to the communion of the divine persons.[396] For this reason every bishop exercises his ministry from within the episcopal college, in communion with the bishop of Rome, the successor of St. Peter and head of the college. So also priests exercise their ministry from within the *presbyterium* of the diocese, under the direction of their bishop.

1559

878   Finally, it belongs to the sacramental nature of ecclesial ministry that it have a *personal character*. Although Christ's ministers act in communion with one another, they also always act in a personal way. Each one is called personally: "You, follow me"[397] in order to be a personal witness within the common mission, to bear personal responsibility before him who gives the mission, acting "in his person" and for other persons: "I baptize you in the name of the Father and of the Son and of the Holy Spirit . . ."; "I absolve you. . . ."

1484

879   Sacramental ministry in the Church, then, is at once a collegial and a personal service, exercised in the name of Christ. This is evidenced by the bonds between

392 Cf. *Rom* 1:1.   393 *Phil* 2:7.   394 Cf. *1 Cor* 9:19.   395 *AG* 5.   396 Cf. *Jn* 17:21–23.   397 *Jn* 21:22; Cf. *Mt* 4:19–21; *Jn* 1:4.

the episcopal college and its head, the successor of St. Peter, and in the relationship between the bishop's pastoral responsibility for his particular church and the common solicitude of the episcopal college for the universal Church.

The episcopal college and its head, the Pope

880   When Christ instituted the Twelve, "he constituted [them] in the form of a college or permanent assembly, at the head of which he placed Peter, chosen 552, 862 from among them."[398] Just as "by the Lord's institution, St. Peter and the rest of the apostles constitute a single apostolic college, so in like fashion the Roman Pontiff, Peter's successor, and the bishops, the successors of the apostles, are related with and united to one another."[399]

881   The Lord made Simon alone, whom he named Peter, the "rock" of his Church. He gave him the keys of his Church and instituted him shepherd of the whole 553 flock.[400] "The office of binding and loosing which was given to Peter was also assigned to the college of apostles united to its head."[401] This pastoral office of Peter and the other apostles belongs to the Church's very 642 foundation and is continued by the bishops under the primacy of the Pope.

882   The *Pope,* Bishop of Rome and Peter's successor, "is the perpetual and visible source and foundation of the unity both of the bishops and of the whole company 834, 1369 of the faithful."[402] "For the Roman Pontiff, by reason of 837 his office as Vicar of Christ, and as pastor of the entire Church has full, supreme, and universal power over the whole Church, a power which he can always exercise unhindered."[403]

883   "The *college or body of bishops* has no authority unless united with the Roman Pontiff, Peter's successor, as its head." As such, this college has "supreme and full authority over the universal Church; but this power

---

398 *LG* 19; cf. *Lk* 6:13; *Jn* 21:15–17.   399 *LG* 22; cf. CIC, can. 330.   400 Cf. *Mt* 16:18–19; *Jn* 21:15–17.   401 *LG* 22 § 2.   402 *LG* 23.   403 *LG* 22; cf. CD 2, 9.

cannot be exercised without the agreement of the Roman Pontiff."[404]

884 "The college of bishops exercises power over the universal Church in a solemn manner in an ecumenical council."[405] But "there never is an ecumenical council which is not confirmed or at least recognized as such by Peter's successor."[406]

885 "This college, in so far as it is composed of many members, is the expression of the variety and universality of the People of God; and of the unity of the flock of Christ, in so far as it is assembled under one head."[407]

886 "The individual *bishops* are the visible source and foundation of unity in their own particular Churches."[408] As such, they "exercise their pastoral office over the portion of the People of God assigned to them,"[409] assisted by priests and deacons. But, as a member of the episcopal college, each bishop shares in the concern for all the Churches.[410] The bishops exercise this care first "by ruling well their own Churches as portions of the universal Church," and so contributing "to the welfare of the whole Mystical Body, which, from another point of view, is a corporate body of Churches."[411] They extend it especially to the poor,[412] to those persecuted for the faith, as well as to missionaries who are working throughout the world.

887 Neighboring particular Churches who share the same culture form ecclesiastical provinces or larger groupings called patriarchates or regions.[413] The bishops of these groupings can meet in synods or provincial councils. "In a like fashion, the episcopal conferences at the present time are in a position to contribute in many and fruitful ways to the concrete realization of the collegiate spirit."[414]

The teaching office

888 Bishops, with priests as co-workers, have as their first task "to preach the Gospel of God to all men," in

1560
833

2448

85-87,
2032-2040

---
404 *LG* 22; cf. CIC, can. 336.   405 CIC, can. 337 § 1.   406 *LG* 22.   407 *LG* 22.   408 *LG* 23.   409 *LG* 23.   410 Cf. *CD* 3.   411 *LG* 23.   412 Cf. *Gal* 2:10. 413 Cf. *Apostolic Constitutions* 34.   414 *LG* 23 § 3.

2068 keeping with the Lord's command.[415] They are "heralds of faith, who draw new disciples to Christ; they are authentic teachers" of the apostolic faith "endowed with the authority of Christ."[416]

889   In order to preserve the Church in the purity of the faith handed on by the apostles, Christ who is the Truth willed to confer on her a share in his own infalli-
92 bility. By a "supernatural sense of faith" the People of God, under the guidance of the Church's living Magisterium, "unfailingly adheres to this faith."[417]

890   The mission of the Magisterium is linked to the definitive nature of the covenant established by God with his people in Christ. It is this Magisterium's task to preserve God's people from deviations and defections
851 and to guarantee them the objective possibility of professing the true faith without error. Thus, the pastoral duty of the Magisterium is aimed at seeing to it that the People of God abides in the truth that liberates. To fulfill this service, Christ endowed the Church's shepherds with the charism of infallibility in matters of faith and
1785 morals. The exercise of this charism takes several forms:

891   "The Roman Pontiff, head of the college of bishops, enjoys this infallibility in virtue of his office, when, as supreme pastor and teacher of all the faithful—who confirms his brethren in the faith—he proclaims by a definitive act a doctrine pertaining to faith or morals. . . . The infallibility promised to the Church is also present in the body of bishops when, together with Peter's successor, they exercise the supreme Magisterium," above all in an Ecumenical Council.[418] When the Church through its supreme Magisterium proposes a doctrine "for belief as being divinely revealed,"[419] and as the teaching of Christ, the definitions "must be adhered to with the obedience of faith."[420] This infallibility extends as far as the deposit of divine Revelation itself.[421]

892   Divine assistance is also given to the successors of the apostles, teaching in communion with the succes-

---

415 *PO* 4; cf. *Mk* 16:15.   416 *LG* 25.   417 *LG* 12; cf. *DV* 10.   418 *LG* 25; cf. Vatican Council I: DS 3074.   419 *DV* 10 § 2.   420 *LG* 25 § 2.   421 Cf. *LG* 25.

sor of Peter, and, in a particular way, to the bishop of Rome, pastor of the whole Church, when, without arriving at an infallible definition and without pronouncing in a "definitive manner," they propose in the exercise of the ordinary Magisterium a teaching that leads to better understanding of Revelation in matters of faith and morals. To this ordinary teaching the faithful "are to adhere to it with religious assent"[422] which, though distinct from the assent of faith, is nonetheless an extension of it.

The sanctifying office

893   The bishop is "the steward of the grace of the supreme priesthood,"[423] especially in the Eucharist which he offers personally or whose offering he assures through the priests, his co-workers. The Eucharist is the center of the life of the particular Church. The bishop and priests sanctify the Church by their prayer and work, by their ministry of the word and of the sacraments. They sanctify her by their example, "not as domineering over those in your charge but being examples to the flock."[424] Thus, "together with the flock entrusted to them, they may attain to eternal life."[425]   *1561*

The governing office

894   "The bishops, as vicars and legates of Christ, govern the particular Churches assigned to them by their counsels, exhortations, and example, but over and above that also by the authority and sacred power" which indeed they ought to exercise so as to edify, in the spirit of service which is that of their Master.[426]   *801*

895   "The power which they exercise personally in the name of Christ, is proper, ordinary, and immediate, although its exercise is ultimately controlled by the supreme authority of the Church."[427] But the bishops should not be thought of as vicars of the Pope. His ordinary and immediate authority over the whole Church does not annul, but on the contrary confirms and defends that of the bishops. Their authority must be exer-   *1558*

---

422 *LG* 25.   423 *LG* 26.   424 *1 Pet* 5:3.   425 *LG* 26 § 3.   426 *LG* 27; cf. *Lk* 22:26–27.   427 *LG* 27.

cised in communion with the whole Church under the guidance of the Pope.

896   The Good Shepherd ought to be the model and "form" of the bishop's pastoral office. Conscious of his own weaknesses, "the bishop . . . can have compassion for those who are ignorant and erring. He should not *1550* refuse to listen to his subjects whose welfare he promotes as of his very own children. . . . The faithful . . . should be closely attached to the bishop as the Church is to Jesus Christ, and as Jesus Christ is to the Father":[428]

> Let all follow the bishop, as Jesus Christ follows his Father, and the college of presbyters as the apostles; respect the deacons as you do God's law. Let no one do anything concerning the Church in separation from the bishop.[429]

II.   THE LAY FAITHFUL

897   "The term 'laity' is here understood to mean all the faithful except those in Holy Orders and those who belong to a religious state approved by the Church. *873* That is, the faithful, who by Baptism are incorporated into Christ and integrated into the People of God, are made sharers in their particular way in the priestly, prophetic, and kingly office of Christ, and have their own part to play in the mission of the whole Christian people in the Church and in the world."[430]

The vocation of lay people

898   "By reason of their special vocation it belongs to the laity to seek the kingdom of God by engaging in temporal affairs and directing them according to God's *2105* will. . . . It pertains to them in a special way so to illuminate and order all temporal things with which they are closely associated that these may always be effected and grow according to Christ and may be to the glory of the Creator and Redeemer."[431]

899   The initiative of lay Christians is necessary especially when the matter involves discovering or inventing

---

428 *LG* 27 § 2.   429 St. Ignatius of Antioch, *Ad Smyrn.* 8, 1: *Apostolic Fathers,* II/2, 309.   430 *LG* 31.   431 *LG* 31 § 2.

the means for permeating social, political, and eco- 2442
nomic realities with the demands of Christian doctrine
and life. This initiative is a normal element of the life of
the Church:

> Lay believers are in the front line of Church life; for
> them the Church is the animating principle of hu-
> man society. Therefore, they in particular ought to
> have an ever-clearer consciousness not only of be-
> longing to the Church, but of being the Church,
> that is to say, the community of the faithful on
> earth under the leadership of the Pope, the common
> Head, and of the bishops in communion with him.
> They are the Church.[432]

900   Since, like all the faithful, lay Christians are entrusted by God with the apostolate by virtue of their
Baptism and Confirmation, they have the right and
duty, individually or grouped in associations, to work   863
so that the divine message of salvation may be known
and accepted by all men throughout the earth. This duty
is the more pressing when it is only through them that
men can hear the Gospel and know Christ. Their activity in ecclesial communities is so necessary that, for the
most part, the apostolate of the pastors cannot be fully
effective without it.[433]

The participation of lay people in Christ's priestly office

901   "Hence the laity, dedicated as they are to Christ
and anointed by the Holy Spirit, are marvellously called
and prepared so that even richer fruits of the Spirit may   784, 1268
be produced in them. For all their works, prayers, and
apostolic undertakings, family and married life, daily
work, relaxation of mind and body, if they are accomplished in the Spirit—indeed even the hardships of life if
patiently born—all these become spiritual sacrifices acceptable to God through Jesus Christ. In the celebration
of the Eucharist these may most fittingly be offered to
the Father along with the body of the Lord. And so,
worshipping everywhere by their holy actions, the laity

---

432 Pius XII, Discourse, February 20, 1946: AAS 38 (1946) 149; quoted by John
Paul II, *CL* 9.   433 Cf. *LG* 33.

358 consecrate the world itself to God, everywhere offering worship by the holiness of their lives."[434]

902 In a very special way, parents share in the office of sanctifying "by leading a conjugal life in the Christian spirit and by seeing to the Christian education of their children."[435]

903 Lay people who possess the required qualities can be admitted permanently to the ministries of lector and acolyte.[436] When the necessity of the Church warrants it *1143* and when ministers are lacking, lay persons, even if they are not lectors or acolytes, can also supply for certain of their offices, namely, to exercise the ministry of the word, to preside over liturgical prayers, to confer Baptism, and to distribute Holy Communion in accord with the prescriptions of law."[437]

Participation in Christ's prophetic office

904 "Christ . . . fulfills this prophetic office, not only *785* by the hierarchy . . . but also by the laity. He accordingly both establishes them as witnesses and provides *92* them with the sense of the faith [*sensus fidei*] and the grace of the word"[438]

> To teach in order to lead others to faith is the task of every preacher and of each believer.[439]

2044 **905** Lay people also fulfill their prophetic mission by evangelization, "that is, the proclamation of Christ by word and the testimony of life." For lay people, "this evangelization . . . acquires a specific property and peculiar efficacy because it is accomplished in the ordinary circumstances of the world."[440]

> This witness of life, however, is not the sole element in the apostolate; the true apostle is on the lookout for occasions of announcing Christ by word, either *2472* to unbelievers . . . or to the faithful.[441]

2495 **906** Lay people who are capable and trained may also collaborate in catechetical formation, in teaching the sacred sciences, and in use of the communications media.[442]

---

434 *LG* 34; cf. *LG* 10; *1 Pet* 2:5.   435 CIC, can. 835 § 4.   436 Cf. CIC, can. 230 § 1.   437 CIC, can. 230 § 3.   438 *LG* 35.   439 St. Thomas Aquinas, *STh.* III, 71, 4 *ad* 3.   440 *LG* 35 § 1, § 2.   441 *AA* 6 § 3; cf. *AG* 15.   442 Cf. CIC, cann. 229; 774; 776; 780; 823 § 1.

907   "In accord with the knowledge, competence, and preeminence which they possess, [lay people] have the right and even at times a duty to manifest to the sacred pastors their opinion on matters which pertain to the good of the Church, and they have a right to make their opinion known to the other Christian faithful, with due regard to the integrity of faith and morals and reverence toward their pastors, and with consideration for the common good and the dignity of persons."[443]

Participation in Christ's kingly office

908   By his obedience unto death,[444] Christ communicated to his disciples the gift of royal freedom, so that they might "by the self-abnegation of a holy life, overcome the reign of sin in themselves":[445]   786

> That man is rightly called a king who makes his own body an obedient subject and, by governing himself with suitable rigor, refuses to let his passions breed rebellion in his soul, for he exercises a kind of royal power over himself. And because he knows how to rule his own person as king, so too does he sit as its judge. He will not let himself be imprisoned by sin, or thrown headlong into wickedness.[446]

909   "Moreover, by uniting their forces let the laity so remedy the institutions and conditions of the world when the latter are an inducement to sin, that these may be conformed to the norms of justice, favoring rather than hindering the practice of virtue. By so doing they will impregnate culture and human works with a moral value."[447]   1887

910   "The laity can also feel called, or be in fact called, to cooperate with their pastors in the service of the ecclesial community, for the sake of its growth and life. This can be done through the exercise of different kinds of ministries according to the grace and charisms which the Lord has been pleased to bestow on them."[448]   799

911   In the Church, "lay members of the Christian faithful can cooperate in the exercise of this power [of gover-

---

443 CIC, can. 212 § 3.   444 Cf. *Phil* 2:8–9.   445 *LG* 36.   446 St. Ambrose, *Psal.* 118:14:30: PL 15:1476.   447 *LG* 36 § 3.   448 Paul VI, *EN* 73.

nance] in accord with the norm of law."[449] And so the Church provides for their presence at particular councils, diocesan synods, pastoral councils; the exercise in solidum of the pastoral care of a parish, collaboration in finance committees, and participation in ecclesiastical tribunals, etc.[450]

912   The faithful should "distinguish carefully between the rights and the duties which they have as belonging to the Church and those which fall to them as

2245   members of the human society. They will strive to unite the two harmoniously, remembering that in every temporal affair they are to be guided by a Christian conscience, since no human activity, even of the temporal order, can be withdrawn from God's dominion."[451]

913   "Thus, every person, through these gifts given to him, is at once the witness and the living instrument of the mission of the Church itself 'according to the measure of Christ's bestowal.' "[452]

III.   THE CONSECRATED LIFE

914   "The state of life which is constituted by the profession of the evangelical counsels, while not entering into the hierarchical structure of the Church, belongs

2103   undeniably to her life and holiness."[453]

Evangelical counsels, consecrated life

915   Christ proposes the evangelical counsels, in their great variety, to every disciple. The perfection of charity, to which all the faithful are called, entails for those who

1973-1974   freely follow the call to consecrated life the obligation of practicing chastity in celibacy for the sake of the Kingdom, poverty and obedience. It is the *profession* of these counsels, within a permanent state of life recognized by the Church, that characterizes the life consecrated to God.[454]

916   The religious state is thus one way of experiencing a "more intimate" consecration, rooted in Baptism

2687   and dedicated totally to God.[455] In the consecrated life,

---

449 CIC, can. 129 § 2.   450 Cf. CIC, cann. 443 § 4; 463 §§ 1 and 2; 492 § 1; 511; 517 § 2; 536; 1421 § 2.   451 *LG* 36 § 4.   452 *LG* 33 § 2; cf. *Eph* 4:7. 453 *LG* 44 § 4.   454 Cf. *LG* 42–43; *PC* 1.   455 Cf. *PC* 5.

Christ's faithful, moved by the Holy Spirit, propose to follow Christ more nearly, to give themselves to God who is loved above all and, pursuing the perfection of charity in the service of the Kingdom, to signify and proclaim in the Church the glory of the world to come.[456]

933

One great tree, with many branches
917 "From the God-given seed of the counsels a wonderful and wide-spreading tree has grown up in the field of the Lord, branching out into various forms of the religious life lived in solitude or in community. Different religious families have come into existence in which spiritual resources are multiplied for the progress in holiness of their members and for the good of the entire Body of Christ."[457]

2684

918 From the very beginning of the Church there were men and women who set out to follow Christ with greater liberty, and to imitate him more closely, by practicing the evangelical counsels. They led lives dedicated to God, each in his own way. Many of them, under the inspiration of the Holy Spirit, became hermits or founded religious families. These the Church, by virtue of her authority, gladly accepted and approved.[458]

919 Bishops will always strive to discern new gifts of consecrated life granted to the Church by the Holy Spirit; the approval of new forms of consecrated life is reserved to the Apostolic See.[459]

The eremitic life
920 Without always professing the three evangelical counsels publicly, hermits "devote their life to the praise of God and salvation of the world through a stricter separation from the world, the silence of solitude and assiduous prayer and penance."[460]

921 They manifest to everyone the interior aspect of the mystery of the Church, that is, personal intimacy with Christ. Hidden from the eyes of men, the life of the

2719

---

456 Cf. CIC, can. 573. 457 LG 43. 458 PC 1. 459 Cf. CIC, can. 605.
460 CIC, can. 603 § 1.

hermit is a silent preaching of the Lord, to whom he has surrendered his life simply because he is everything to 2015 him. Here is a particular call to find in the desert, in the thick of spiritual battle, the glory of the Crucified One.

Consecrated virgins

922   From apostolic times Christian virgins, called by the Lord to cling only to him with greater freedom of heart, body, and spirit, have decided with the Church's 1618-1620 approval to live in a state of virginity "for the sake of the Kingdom of heaven."[461]

923   "Virgins who, committed to the holy plan of following Christ more closely, are consecrated to God by the diocesan bishop according to the approved liturgical 1537 rite, are betrothed mystically to Christ, the Son of God, and are dedicated to the service of the Church."[462] By this 1672 solemn rite (Consecratio Virginum), the virgin is "constituted . . . a sacred person, a transcendent sign of the Church's love for Christ, and an eschatological image of this heavenly Bride of Christ and of the life to come."[463]

924   "As with other forms of consecrated life," the order of virgins establishes the woman living in the world (or the nun) in prayer, penance, service of her brethren, and apostolic activity, according to the state of life and spiritual gifts given to her.[464] Consecrated virgins can form themselves into associations to observe their commitment more faithfully.[465]

Religious life

925   Religious life was born in the East during the first centuries of Christianity. Lived within institutes canonically erected by the Church, it is distinguished 1672 from other forms of consecrated life by its liturgical character, public profession of the evangelical counsels, fraternal life led in common, and witness given to the union of Christ with the Church.[466]

---

461 Mt 19:12; cf. 1 Cor 7:34–36.   462 CIC, can. 604 § 1.   463 Ordo Consecrationis Virginum, Praenotanda 1.   464 Cf. CIC, can. 604 § 1; OCV Praenotanda 2.   465 Cf. CIC, can. 604 § 2.   466 Cf. CIC, cann. 607; 573; UR 15.

926   Religious life derives from the mystery of the Church. It is a gift she has received from her Lord, a gift she offers as a stable way of life to the faithful called by God to profess the counsels. Thus, the Church can both show forth Christ and acknowledge herself to be the Savior's bride. Religious life in its various forms is called 796 to signify the very charity of God in the language of our time.

927   All religious, whether exempt or not, take their place among the collaborators of the diocesan bishop in his pastoral duty.[467] From the outset of the work of evangelization, the missionary "planting" and expansion of 854 the Church require the presence of the religious life in all its forms.[468] "History witnesses to the outstanding service rendered by religious families in the propagation of the faith and in the formation of new Churches: from the ancient monastic institutions to the medieval orders, all the way to the more recent congregations."[469]

Secular institutes

928   "A secular institute is an institute of consecrated life in which the Christian faithful living in the world strive for the perfection of charity and work for the sanctification of the world especially from within."[470]

929   By a "life perfectly and entirely consecrated to [such] sanctification," the members of these institutes share in the Church's task of evangelization, "in the world and from within the world," where their presence 901 acts as "leaven in the world."[471] "Their witness of a Christian life" aims "to order temporal things according to God and inform the world with the power of the gospel." They commit themselves to the evangelical counsels by sacred bonds and observe among themselves the communion and fellowship appropriate to their "particular secular way of life."[472]

---

467 Cf. CD 33–35; CIC, can. 591.   468 Cf. AG 18; 40.   469 John Paul II, *RMiss* 69.   470 CIC, can. 710.   471 Pius XII, *Provida Mater;* cf. PC 11.   472 Cf. CIC, can. 713 § 2.

Societies of apostolic life

930 Alongside the different forms of consecrated life are "societies of apostolic life whose members without religious vows pursue the particular apostolic purpose of their society, and lead a life as brothers or sisters in common according to a particular manner of life, strive for the perfection of charity through the observance of the constitutions. Among these there are societies in which the members embrace the evangelical counsels" according to their constitutions.[473]

Consecration and mission: proclaiming the King who is coming

931 Already dedicated to him through Baptism, the person who surrenders himself to the God he loves above all else thereby consecrates himself more intimately to God's service and to the good of the Church. By this state of life consecrated to God, the Church manifests Christ and shows us how the Holy Spirit acts so wonderfully in her. And so the first mission of those who profess the evangelical counsels is to live out their consecration. Moreover, "since members of institutes of consecrated life dedicate themselves through their consecration to the service of the Church they are obliged in a special manner to engage in missionary work, in accord with the character of the institute."[474]

932 In the Church, which is like the sacrament—the sign and instrument—of God's own life, the consecrated life is seen as a special sign of the mystery of redemp-
775 tion. To follow and imitate Christ more nearly and to manifest more clearly his self-emptying is to be more deeply present to one's contemporaries, in the heart of Christ. For those who are on this "narrower" path encourage their brethren by their example, and bear striking witness "that the world cannot be transfigured and offered to God without the spirit of the Beatitudes."[475]

672 **933** Whether their witness is public, as in the religious state, or less public, or even secret, Christ's com-

---

473 Cf. CIC, can. 731 §§ 1 and 2.   474 CIC, can. 783; cf. *RM* 69.   475 *LG* 31 § 2.

ing remains for all those consecrated both the origin and rising sun of their life: 672

> For the People of God has here no lasting city, . . .   769
> [and this state] reveals more clearly to all believers
> the heavenly goods which are already present in
> this age, witnessing to the new and eternal life
> which we have acquired through the redemptive
> work of Christ and preluding our future resurrec-
> tion and the glory of the heavenly kingdom.[476]

IN BRIEF

934   "Among the Christian faithful by divine institution there exist in the Church sacred ministers,
who are also called clerics in law, and other
Christian faithful who are also called laity." In
both groups there are those Christian faithful
who, professing the evangelical counsels, are
consecrated to God and so serve the Church's
saving mission (cf. CIC, can. 207 § 1, 2).

935   To proclaim the faith and to plant his reign,
Christ sends his apostles and their successors. He
gives them a share in his own mission. From him
they receive the power to act in his person.

936   The Lord made St. Peter the visible foundation
of his Church. He entrusted the keys of the
Church to him. The bishop of the Church of
Rome, successor to St. Peter, is "head of the college of bishops, the Vicar of Christ and Pastor of
the universal Church on earth" (CIC, can. 331).

937   The Pope enjoys, by divine institution, "supreme, full, immediate, and universal power in
the care of souls" (CD 2).

938   The Bishops, established by the Holy Spirit, succeed the apostles. They are "the visible source
and foundation of unity in their own particular
Churches" (LG 23).

939   Helped by the priests, their co-workers, and by
the deacons, the bishops have the duty of au-

---

476 *LG* 44 § 3.

thentically teaching the faith, celebrating divine worship, above all the Eucharist, and guiding their Churches as true pastors. Their responsibility also includes concern for all the Churches, with and under the Pope.

940   "The characteristic of the lay state being a life led in the midst of the world and of secular affairs, lay people are called by God to make of their apostolate, through the vigor of their Christian spirit, a leaven in the world" (*AA* 2 § 2).

941   Lay people share in Christ's priesthood: ever more united with him, they exhibit the grace of Baptism and Confirmation in all dimensions of their personal, family, social, and ecclesial lives, and so fulfill the call to holiness addressed to all the baptized.

942   By virtue of their prophetic mission, lay people "are called . . . to be witnesses to Christ in all circumstances and at the very heart of the community of mankind" (*GS* 43 § 4).

943   By virtue of their kingly mission, lay people have the power to uproot the rule of sin within themselves and in the world, by their self-denial and holiness of life (cf. *LG* 36).

944   The life consecrated to God is characterized by the public profession of the evangelical counsels of poverty, chastity, and obedience, in a stable state of life recognized by the Church.

945   Already destined for him through Baptism, the person who surrenders himself to the God he loves above all else thereby consecrates himself more intimately to God's service and to the good of the whole Church.

1474-1477 Paragraph 5. The Communion of Saints
946   After confessing "the holy catholic Church," the Apostles' Creed adds "the communion of saints." In a

certain sense this article is a further explanation of the
preceding: "What is the Church if not the assembly of 823
all the saints?"[477] The communion of saints is the
Church.

947 "Since all the faithful form one body, the good of
each is communicated to the others. . . . We must therefore believe that there exists a communion of goods in
the Church. But the most important member is Christ,
since he is the head. . . . Therefore, the riches of Christ 790
are communicated to all the members, through the
sacraments."[478] "As this Church is governed by one and
the same Spirit, all the goods she has received necessarily become a common fund."[479]

948 The term "communion of saints" therefore has
two closely linked meanings: communion "in holy
things *(sancta)*" and "among holy persons *(sancti)*." 1331

> *Sancta sanctis!* ("God's holy gifts for God's holy
> people") is proclaimed by the celebrant in most
> Eastern liturgies during the elevation of the holy
> Gifts before the distribution of communion. The
> faithful *(sancti)* are fed by Christ's holy body and
> blood *(sancta)* to grow in the communion of the
> Holy Spirit *(koinonia)* and to communicate it to the
> world.

I.   COMMUNION IN SPIRITUAL GOODS
949 In the primitive community of Jerusalem, the
disciples "devoted themselves to the apostles' teaching
and fellowship, to the breaking of the bread and the
prayers."[480]

> *Communion in the faith.* The faith of the faith- 185
> ful is the faith of the Church, received from the apostles.
> Faith is a treasure of life which is enriched by being
> shared.

950 *Communion of the sacraments.* "The fruit of all
the sacraments belongs to all the faithful. All the sacra- 1130
ments are sacred links uniting the faithful with one another and binding them to Jesus Christ, and above all

---

477 Nicetas, *Expl. symb.* 10: PL 52:871B.   478 St. Thomas Aquinas, *Symb.*, 10.
479 *Roman Catechism* I, 10, 24.   480 *Acts* 2:42.

Baptism, the gate by which we enter into the Church. The communion of saints must be understood as the communion of the sacraments. . . . The name 'commu-
1331 nion' can be applied to all of them, for they unite us to God. . . . But this name is better suited to the Eucharist than to any other, because it is primarily the Eucharist that brings this communion about."[481]

951   *Communion of charisms.* Within the commu-nion of the Church, the Holy Spirit "distributes special
799 graces among the faithful of every rank" for the build-ing up of the Church.[482] Now, "to each is given the man-ifestation of the Spirit for the common good."[483]

952   *"They had everything in common."*[484] "Every-thing the true Christian has is to be regarded as a good
2402 possessed in common with everyone else. All Christians should be ready and eager to come to the help of the needy . . . and of their neighbors in want."[485] A Christ-ian is a steward of the Lord's goods.[486]

953   *Communion in charity.* In the sanctorum com-
1827 munio, "None of us lives to himself, and none of us dies to himself."[487] "If one member suffers, all suffer to-gether; if one member is honored, all rejoice together. Now you are the body of Christ and individually mem-
2011 bers of it."[488] "Charity does not insist on its own way."[489] In this solidarity with all men, living or dead,
845, 1469 which is founded on the communion of saints, the least of our acts done in charity redounds to the profit of all. Every sin harms this communion.

II.   THE COMMUNION OF THE CHURCH OF HEAVEN AND EARTH

954   *The three states of the Church.* "When the Lord comes in glory, and all his angels with him, death will
771 be no more and all things will be subject to him. But at the present time some of his disciples are pilgrims on
1031 earth. Others have died and are being purified, while

---

481 *Roman Catechism* I, 10, 24.   482 *LG* 12 § 2.   483 *1 Cor* 12:7.   484 *Acts* 4:32.   485 *Roman Catechism* I, 10, 27.   486 Cf. *Lk* 16:1, 3.   487 *Rom* 14:7. 488 *1 Cor* 12:26–27.   489 *1 Cor* 13:5; cf. 10:24.

still others are in glory, contemplating 'in full light, God   *1023*
himself triune and one, exactly as he is' ":[490]

> All of us, however, in varying degrees and in differ-
> ent ways share in the same charity towards God
> and our neighbours, and we all sing the one hymn
> of glory to our God. All, indeed, who are of Christ
> and who have his Spirit form one Church and in
> Christ cleave together.[491]

955 "So it is that the union of the wayfarers with the
brethren who sleep in the peace of Christ is in no way
interrupted, but on the contrary, according to the constant faith of the Church, this union is reinforced by an
exchange of spiritual goods."[492]

956 *The intercession of the saints.* "Being more
closely united to Christ, those who dwell in heaven fix
the whole Church more firmly in holiness. . . . [T]hey   *1370*
do not cease to intercede with the Father for us, as they   *2682*
proffer the merits which they acquired on earth through
the one mediator between God and men, Christ Jesus.
. . . So by their fraternal concern is our weakness greatly
helped."[493]

> Do not weep, for I shall be more useful to you after
> my death and I shall help you then more effectively
> than during my life.[494]

> I want to spend my heaven in doing good on
> earth.[495]

957 *Communion with the saints.* "It is not merely by
the title of example that we cherish the memory of those
in heaven; we seek, rather, that by this devotion to the exercise of fraternal charity the union of the whole Church   *1173*
in the Spirit may be strengthened. Exactly as Christian
communion among our fellow pilgrims brings us closer
to Christ, so our communion with the saints joins us to
Christ, from whom as from its fountain and head issues
all grace, and the life of the People of God itself"[496]:

---

490 *LG* 49; cf. *Mt* 25:31; *1 Cor* 15:26–27; Council of Florence (1439): DS 1305.
491 *LG* 49; cf. *Eph* 4:16.   492 *LG* 49.   493 *LG* 49; cf. *1 Tim* 2:5.   494 St.
Dominic, dying, to his brothers.   495 St. Thérèse of Lisieux, *The Final
Conversations*, tr. John Clarke (Washington: ICS, 1977), 102.   496 *LG* 50; cf.
Eph 4:1–6.

We worship Christ as God's Son; we love the martyrs as the Lord's disciples and imitators, and
rightly so because of their matchless devotion towards their king and master. May we also be their
companions and fellow disciples![497]

958   *Communion with the dead.* "In full conscious-
1371   ness of this communion of the whole Mystical Body of
1032, 1689 Jesus Christ, the Church in its pilgrim members, from
the very earliest days of the Christian religion, has honored with great respect the memory of the dead; and
'because it is a holy and a wholesome thought to pray
for the dead that they may be loosed from their sins' she
offers her suffrages for them."[498] Our prayer for them is
capable not only of helping them, but also of making
their intercession for us effective.

959   *In the one family of God.* "For if we continue to
love one another and to join in praising the Most Holy
1027   Trinity—all of us who are sons of God and form one
family in Christ—we will be faithful to the deepest vocation of the Church."[499]

IN BRIEF

960   The Church is a "communion of saints": this expression refers first to the "holy things" *(sancta),*
above all the Eucharist, by which "the unity of
believers, who form one body in Christ, is both
represented and brought about" *(LG* 3).

961   The term "communion of saints" refers also to
the communion of "holy persons" *(sancti)* in
Christ who "died for all," so that what each one
does or suffers in and for Christ bears fruit for
all.

962   "We believe in the communion of all the faithful
of Christ, those who are pilgrims on earth, the
dead who are being purified, and the blessed in
heaven, all together forming one Church; and we
believe that in this communion, the merciful love

---

497 *Martyrium Polycarpi,* 17: *Apostolic Fathers* II/3, 396.   498 *LG* 50; cf. 2
Macc 12:45.   499 *LG* 51; cf. *Heb* 3:6.

of God and his saints is always [attentive] to our prayers" (Paul VI, *CPG* § 30).

Paragraph 6. Mary—Mother of Christ, Mother of the Church

963   Since the Virgin Mary's role in the mystery of Christ and the Spirit has been treated, it is fitting now to consider her place in the mystery of the Church. "The Virgin Mary . . . is acknowledged and honored as being truly the Mother of God and of the redeemer. . . . She is 'clearly the mother of the members of Christ' . . . since she has by her charity joined in bringing about the birth of believers in the Church, who are members of its head."[500] "Mary, Mother of Christ, Mother of the Church."[501]

484-507,
721-726

I.   MARY'S MOTHERHOOD WITH REGARD TO THE CHURCH

Wholly united with her Son . . .

964   Mary's role in the Church is inseparable from her union with Christ and flows directly from it. "This union of the mother with the Son in the work of salvation is made manifest from the time of Christ's virginal conception up to his death";[502] it is made manifest above all at the hour of his Passion:

> Thus the Blessed Virgin advanced in her pilgrimage of faith, and faithfully persevered in her union with her Son unto the cross. There she stood, in keeping with the divine plan, enduring with her only begotten Son the intensity of his suffering, joining herself with his sacrifice in her mother's heart, and lovingly consenting to the immolation of this victim, born of her: to be given, by the same Christ Jesus dying on the cross, as a mother to his disciple, with these words: "Woman, behold your son."[503]

534

618

965   After her Son's Ascension, Mary "aided the beginnings of the Church by her prayers."[504] In her associ-

---

[500] *LG* 53; cf. St. Augustine, *De virg.* 6: PL 40, 399.   [501] Paul VI, Discourse, November 21, 1964.   [502] *LG* 57.   [503] *LG* 58; cf. *Jn* 19:26–27.   [504] *LG* 69.

ation with the apostles and several women, "we also see Mary by her prayers imploring the gift of the Spirit, who had already overshadowed her in the Annunciation."[505]

... also in her Assumption

966 "Finally the Immaculate Virgin, preserved free from all stain of original sin, when the course of her earthly life was finished, was taken up body and soul into heavenly glory, and exalted by the Lord as Queen over all things, so that she might be the more fully conformed to her Son, the Lord of lords and conqueror of sin and death."[506] The Assumption of the Blessed Virgin is a singular participation in her Son's Resurrection and an anticipation of the resurrection of other Christians:

> In giving birth you kept your virginity; in your Dormition you did not leave the world, O Mother of God, but were joined to the source of Life. You conceived the living God and, by your prayers, will deliver our souls from death.[507]

... she is our Mother in the order of grace

967 By her complete adherence to the Father's will, to his Son's redemptive work, and to every prompting of the Holy Spirit, the Virgin Mary is the Church's model of faith and charity. Thus she is a "preeminent and . . . wholly unique member of the Church"; indeed, she is the "exemplary realization" *(typus)*[508] of the Church.

968 Her role in relation to the Church and to all humanity goes still further. "In a wholly singular way she cooperated by her obedience, faith, hope, and burning charity in the Savior's work of restoring supernatural life to souls. For this reason she is a mother to us in the order of grace."[509]

969 "This motherhood of Mary in the order of grace continues uninterruptedly from the consent which she loyally gave at the Annunciation and which she sustained without wavering beneath the cross, until the

---

505 *LG* 59.   506 *LG* 59; cf. Pius XII, *Munificentissimus Deus* (1950): DS 3903; cf. *Rev* 19:16.   507 Byzantine Liturgy, *Troparion,* Feast of the Dormition, August 15th.   508 *LG* 53; 63.   509 *LG* 61.

eternal fulfilment of all the elect. Taken up to heaven she did not lay aside this saving office but by her manifold intercession continues to bring us the gifts of eternal salvation. . . . Therefore the Blessed Virgin is invoked in the Church under the titles of Advocate, Helper, Benefactress, and Mediatrix."[510]

970   "Mary's function as mother of men in no way obscures or diminishes this unique mediation of Christ, but rather shows its power. But the Blessed Virgin's salutary influence on men . . . flows forth from the superabundance of the merits of Christ, rests on his mediation, depends entirely on it, and draws all its power from it."[511] "No creature could ever be counted along with the Incarnate Word and Redeemer; but just as the priesthood of Christ is shared in various ways both by his ministers and the faithful, and as the one goodness of God is radiated in different ways among his creatures, so also the unique mediation of the Redeemer does not exclude but rather gives rise to a manifold cooperation which is but a sharing in this one source."[512]

II.   DEVOTION TO THE BLESSED VIRGIN

971   *"All generations will call me blessed"*: "The Church's devotion to the Blessed Virgin is intrinsic to Christian worship."[513] The Church rightly honors "the Blessed Virgin with special devotion. From the most ancient times the Blessed Virgin has been honored with the title of 'Mother of God,' to whose protection the faithful fly in all their dangers and needs. . . . This very special devotion . . . differs essentially from the adoration which is given to the incarnate Word and equally to the Father and the Holy Spirit, and greatly fosters this adoration."[514] The liturgical feasts dedicated to the Mother of God and Marian prayer, such as the rosary, an "epitome of the whole Gospel," express this devotion to the Virgin Mary.[515]

III.   MARY—ESCHATOLOGICAL ICON OF THE CHURCH

972   After speaking of the Church, her origin, mission, and destiny, we can find no better way to conclude

Marginal references: 1370, 2008, 1545, 308, 2673-2679, 1172, 2678

---

510 *LG* 62.   511 *LG* 60.   512 *LG* 62.   513 *Lk* 1:48; Paul VI, *MC* 56.
514 *LG* 66.   515 Cf. Paul VI, *MC* 42; *SC* 103.

than by looking to Mary. In her we contemplate what the Church already is in her mystery on her own "pil-
773   grimage of faith," and what she will be in the homeland at the end of her journey. There, "in the glory of the Most Holy and Undivided Trinity," "in the communion
829   of all the saints,"[516] the Church is awaited by the one she venerates as Mother of her Lord and as her own mother.

2853

> In the meantime the Mother of Jesus, in the glory which she possesses in body and soul in heaven, is the image and beginning of the Church as it is to be perfected in the world to come. Likewise she shines forth on earth, until the day of the Lord shall come, a sign of certain hope and comfort to the pilgrim People of God.[517]

IN BRIEF

973   By pronouncing her "fiat" at the Annunciation and giving her consent to the Incarnation, Mary was already collaborating with the whole work her Son was to accomplish. She is mother wherever he is Savior and head of the Mystical Body.

974   The Most Blessed Virgin Mary, when the course of her earthly life was completed, was taken up body and soul into the glory of heaven, where she already shares in the glory of her Son's Resurrection, anticipating the resurrection of all members of his Body.

975   "We believe that the Holy Mother of God, the new Eve, Mother of the Church, continues in heaven to exercise her maternal role on behalf of the members of Christ" (Paul VI, *CPG* § 15).

Article 10
"I BELIEVE IN THE FORGIVENESS OF SINS"

976   The Apostle's Creed associates faith in the forgiveness of sins not only with faith in the Holy Spirit,

---

516 *LG* 69.   517 *LG* 68; cf. 2 *Pet* 3:10.

but also with faith in the Church and in the communion of saints. It was when he gave the Holy Spirit to his apostles that the risen Christ conferred on them his own divine power to forgive sins: "Receive the Holy Spirit. If you forgive the sins of any, they are forgiven; if you retain the sins of any, they are retained."[518]

> (Part Two of the catechism will deal explicitly with the forgiveness of sins through Baptism, the sacrament of Penance, and the other sacraments, especially the Eucharist. Here it will suffice to suggest some basic facts briefly.)

I.   One Baptism for the Forgiveness of Sins   1263

977   Our Lord tied the forgiveness of sins to faith and Baptism: "Go into all the world and preach the gospel to the whole creation. He who believes and is baptized will be saved."[519] Baptism is the first and chief sacrament of forgiveness of sins because it unites us with Christ, who died for our sins and rose for our justification, so that "we too might walk in newness of life."[520]

978   "When we made our first profession of faith while receiving the holy Baptism that cleansed us, the forgiveness we received then was so full and complete that there remained in us absolutely nothing left to efface, neither original sin nor offenses committed by our own will, nor was there left any penalty to suffer in order to expiate them. . . . Yet the grace of Baptism delivers no one from all the weakness of nature. On the contrary, we must still combat the movements of   1264 concupiscence that never cease leading us into evil."[521]

979   In this battle against our inclination towards evil, who could be brave and watchful enough to escape every wound of sin? "If the Church has the power to forgive sins, then Baptism cannot be her only means of using the keys of the Kingdom of heaven received from Jesus Christ. The Church must be able to forgive all   1446 penitents their offenses, even if they should sin until the last moment of their lives."[522]

---

518 *Jn* 20:22–23.   519 *Mk* 16:15–16.   520 *Rom* 6:4; cf. 4:25.   521 *Roman Catechism* I, 11, 3.   522 *Roman Catechism* I, 11, 4.

980   It is through the sacrament of Penance that the baptized can be reconciled with God and with the Church:

1422-1484

> Penance has rightly been called by the holy Fathers "a laborious kind of baptism." This sacrament of Penance is necessary for salvation for those who have fallen after Baptism, just as Baptism is necessary for salvation for those who have not yet been reborn.[523]

II.   THE POWER OF THE KEYS

981   After his Resurrection, Christ sent his apostles "so that repentance and forgiveness of sins should be preached in his name to all nations."[524] The apostles and their successors carry out this "ministry of reconciliation," not only by announcing to men God's forgiveness merited for us by Christ, and calling them to conversion and faith; but also by communicating to them the forgiveness of sins in Baptism, and reconciling them with God and with the Church through the power of the keys, received from Christ.[525]

1444

553

> [The Church] has received the keys of the Kingdom of heaven so that, in her, sins may be forgiven through Christ's blood and the Holy Spirit's action. In this Church, the soul dead through sin comes back to life in order to live with Christ, whose grace has saved us.[526]

982   There is no offense, however serious, that the Church cannot forgive. "There is no one, however wicked and guilty, who may not confidently hope for forgiveness, provided his repentance is honest."[527] Christ who died for all men desires that in his Church the gates of forgiveness should always be open to anyone who turns away from sin.[528]

1463

605

983   Catechesis strives to awaken and nourish in the faithful faith in the incomparable greatness of the risen Christ's gift to his Church: the mission and the power to

1442

---

523 Council of Trent (1551): DS 1672; cf. St. Gregory of Nazianzus, *Oratio* 39, 17: PG 36, 356.   524 *Lk* 24:47.   525 *2 Cor* 5:18.   526 St. Augustine, *Sermo* 214, 11: PL 38, 1071–1072.   527 *Roman Catechism* I, 11, 5.   528 Cf. *Mt* 18:21–22.

forgive sins through the ministry of the apostles and their successors:

> The Lord wills that his disciples possess a tremen- 1465
> dous power: that his lowly servants accomplish in
> his name all that he did when he was on earth.[529]

> Priests have received from God a power that he has
> given neither to angels nor to archangels. . . . God
> above confirms what priests do here below.[530]

> Were there no forgiveness of sins in the Church,
> there would be no hope of life to come or eternal
> liberation. Let us thank God who has given his
> Church such a gift.[531]

IN BRIEF

984 The Creed links "the forgiveness of sins" with its profession of faith in the Holy Spirit, for the risen Christ entrusted to the apostles the power to forgive sins when he gave them the Holy Spirit.

985 Baptism is the first and chief sacrament of the forgiveness of sins: it unites us to Christ, who died and rose, and gives us the Holy Spirit.

986 By Christ's will, the Church possesses the power to forgive the sins of the baptized and exercises it through bishops and priests normally in the sacrament of Penance.

987 "In the forgiveness of sins, both priests and sacraments are instruments which our Lord Jesus Christ, the only author and liberal giver of salvation, wills to use in order to efface our sins and give us the grace of justification" (*Roman Catechism*, I, 11, 6).

ARTICLE 11
"I BELIEVE IN THE RESURRECTION OF THE BODY"

988 The Christian Creed—the profession of our faith in God, the Father, the Son, and the Holy Spirit, and in

---

529 Cf. St. Ambrose, *De poenit.* I, 15: PL 16, 490. 530 St. John Chrysostom, *De sac.* 3, 5: PG 48, 643. 531 St. Augustine, *Sermo* 213, 8: PL 38,1064.

God's creative, saving, and sanctifying action—culminates in the proclamation of the resurrection of the dead on the last day and in life everlasting.

989   We firmly believe, and hence we hope that, just as Christ is truly risen from the dead and lives for ever, *655* so after death the righteous will live for ever with the *648* risen Christ and he will raise them up on the last day.[532] Our resurrection, like his own, will be the work of the Most Holy Trinity:

> If the Spirit of him who raised Jesus from the dead dwells in you, he who raised Christ Jesus from the dead will give life to your mortal bodies also through his Spirit who dwells in you.[533]

990   The term "flesh" refers to man in his state of weakness and mortality.[534] The "resurrection of the flesh" (the literal formulation of the Apostles' Creed) means not only that the immortal soul will live on after death, but that *364* even our "mortal body" will come to life again.[535]

991   Belief in the resurrection of the dead has been an essential element of the Christian faith from its begin-*638* nings. "The confidence of Christians is the resurrection of the dead; believing this we live."[536]

> How can some of you say that there is no resurrection of the dead? But if there is no resurrection of the dead, then Christ has not been raised; if Christ has not been raised, then our preaching is in vain and your faith is in vain. . . . But in fact Christ has been raised from the dead, the first fruits of those who have fallen asleep.[537]

I.   CHRIST'S RESURRECTION AND OURS

The progressive revelation of the Resurrection

992   God revealed the resurrection of the dead to his people progressively. Hope in the bodily resurrection of the dead established itself as a consequence intrinsic to faith in God as creator of the whole man, soul and body. The creator of heaven and earth is also the one

---

532 Cf. *Jn* 6:39–40.   533 *Rom* 8:11; cf. *1 Thess* 4:14; *1 Cor* 6:14; *2 Cor* 4:14; *Phil* 3:10–11.   534 Cf. *Gen* 6:3; *Ps* 56:5; *Isa* 40:6.   535 *Rom* 8:11. 536 Tertullian, *De res.* 1, 1: PL 2, 841.   537 *1 Cor* 15:12–14.

who faithfully maintains his covenant with Abraham
and his posterity. It was in this double perspective that 297
faith in the resurrection came to be expressed. In their
trials, the Maccabean martyrs confessed:

> The King of the universe will raise us up to an ever-
> lasting renewal of life, because we have died for his
> laws.[538] One cannot but choose to die at the hands
> of men and to cherish the hope that God gives of
> being raised again by him.[539]

993   The Pharisees and many of the Lord's contemporaries hoped for the resurrection. Jesus teaches it
firmly. To the Sadducees who deny it he answers, "Is 575
not this why you are wrong, that you know neither the
scriptures nor the power of God?"[540] Faith in the resurrection rests on faith in God who "is not God of the
dead, but of the living."[541]   205

994   But there is more. Jesus links faith in the resurrection to his own person: "I am the Resurrection and
the life."[542] It is Jesus himself who on the last day will
raise up those who have believed in him, who have eaten
his body and drunk his blood.[543] Already now in this
present life he gives a sign and pledge of this by restoring some of the dead to life,[544] announcing thereby his 646
own Resurrection, though it was to be of another order.
He speaks of this unique event as the "sign of Jonah,"[545]
the sign of the temple: he announces that he will be put
to death but rise thereafter on the third day.[546]

995   To be a witness to Christ is to be a "witness to his 860
Resurrection," to "[have eaten and drunk] with him af- 655
ter he rose from the dead."[547] Encounters with the risen
Christ characterize the Christian hope of resurrection.
We shall rise like Christ, with him, and through him.

996   From the beginning, Christian faith in the resurrection has met with incomprehension and opposition.[548] "On no point does the Christian faith encounter 643

---

538 *2 Macc* 7:9.   539 *2 Macc* 7:14; cf. 7:29; *Dan* 12:1–13.   540 *Mk* 12:24; cf.
Jn 11:24; *Acts* 23:6.   541 *Mk* 12:27.   542 *Jn* 11:25.   543 Cf. *Jn* 5:24–25; 6:40,
54.   544 Cf. *Mk* 5:21–42; *Lk* 7:11–17; *Jn* 11.   545 *Mt* 12:39.   546 Cf. *Mk*
10:34; *Jn* 2:19–22.   547 *Acts* 1:22; 10:41; cf. 4:33.   548 Cf. *Acts* 17:32; *1 Cor*
15:12–13.

more opposition than on the resurrection of the body."[549] It is very commonly accepted that the life of the human person continues in a spiritual fashion after death. But how can we believe that this body, so clearly mortal, could rise to everlasting life?

How do the dead rise?

997   *What is "rising"?* In death, the separation of the soul from the body, the human body decays and the soul goes to meet God, while awaiting its reunion with its *366* glorified body. God, in his almighty power, will definitively grant incorruptible life to our bodies by reuniting them with our souls, through the power of Jesus' Resurrection.

998   *Who will rise?* All the dead will rise, "those who have done good, to the resurrection of life, and those *1038* who have done evil, to the resurrection of judgment."[550]

999   *How?* Christ is raised with his own body: "See my hands and my feet, that it is I myself";[551] but he did not return to an earthly life. So, in him, "all of them will rise again with their own bodies which they now bear," *640* but Christ "will change our lowly body to be like his *645* glorious body," into a "spiritual body":[552]

> But someone will ask, "How are the dead raised? With what kind of body do they come?" You foolish man! What you sow does not come to life unless it dies. And what you sow is not the body which is to be, but a bare kernel. . . . What is sown is perishable, what is raised is imperishable. . . . The dead will be raised imperishable. . . . For this perishable nature must put on the imperishable, and this mortal nature must put on immortality.[553]

1000   This "how" exceeds our imagination and understanding; it is accessible only to faith. Yet our participation in the Eucharist already gives us a foretaste of *647* Christ's transfiguration of our bodies:

---

549 St. Augustine, *En. in Ps.* 88, 5: PL 37, 1134.   550 *Jn* 5:29; cf. *Dan* 12:2.
551 *Lk* 24:39.   552 Lateran Council IV (1215): DS 801; *Phil* 3:21; *1 Cor* 15:44.
553 *1 Cor* 15:35–37, 42, 52, 53.

> Just as bread that comes from the earth, after God's 1405
> blessing has been invoked upon it, is no longer or-
> dinary bread, but Eucharist, formed of two things,
> the one earthly and the other heavenly: so too our
> bodies, which partake of the Eucharist, are no
> longer corruptible, but possess the hope of resur-
> rection.[554]

1001 *When?* Definitively "at the last day," "at the end 1038
of the world."[555] Indeed, the resurrection of the dead is 673
closely associated with Christ's Parousia:

> For the Lord himself will descend from heaven,
> with a cry of command, with the archangel's call,
> and with the sound of the trumpet of God. And the
> dead in Christ will rise first.[556]

Risen with Christ

1002 Christ will raise us up "on the last day"; but it is
also true that, in a certain way, we have already risen
with Christ. For, by virtue of the Holy Spirit, Christian
life is already now on earth a participation in the death 655
and Resurrection of Christ:

> And you were buried with him in Baptism, in which
> you were also raised with him through faith in the
> working of God, who raised him from the dead. . . .
> If then you have been raised with Christ, seek the
> things that are above, where Christ is, seated at the
> right hand of God.[557]

1003 United with Christ by Baptism, believers already
truly participate in the heavenly life of the risen Christ,
but this life remains "hidden with Christ in God."[558] 1227
The Father has already "raised us up with him, and
made us sit with him in the heavenly places in Christ Je- 2796
sus."[559] Nourished with his body in the Eucharist, we already belong to the Body of Christ. When we rise on the
last day we "also will appear with him in glory."[560]

1004 In expectation of that day, the believer's body
and soul already participate in the dignity of belonging
to Christ. This dignity entails the demand that he 364

---

554 St. Irenaeus, *Adv. haeres.* 4, 18, 4–5: PG 7/1, 1028–1029.   555 *Jn* 6: 39–40,
44, 54; 11:24; *LG* 48 § 3.   556 *1 Thess* 4:16.   557 *Col* 2:12; 3:1.   558 *Col* 3:3;
cf. *Phil* 3:20.   559 *Eph* 2:6.   560 *Col* 3:4.

1397 should treat with respect his own body, but also the body of every other person, especially the suffering:

> The body [is meant] for the Lord, and the Lord for the body. And God raised the Lord and will also raise us up by his power. Do you not know that your bodies are members of Christ?. . . . You are not your own; . . . . So glorify God in your body.[561]

II.   DYING IN CHRIST JESUS

1005 To rise with Christ, we must die with Christ: we must "be away from the body and at home with the Lord."[562] In that "departure" which is death the soul is separated from the body.[563] It will be reunited with the 650 body on the day of resurrection of the dead.[564]

Death

1006 "It is in regard to death that man's condition is most shrouded in doubt."[565] In a sense bodily death is natural, but for faith it is in fact "the wages of sin."[566] For those who die in Christ's grace it is a participation in the death of the Lord, so that they can also share his Resurrection.[567]

1007 *Death is the end of earthly life.* Our lives are measured by time, in the course of which we change, grow old and, as with all living beings on earth, death seems like the normal end of life. That aspect of death lends urgency to our lives: remembering our mortality helps us realize that we have only a limited time in which to bring our lives to fulfillment:

> Remember also your Creator in the days of your youth, . . . before the dust returns to the earth as it was, and the spirit returns to God who gave it.[568]

1008 *Death is a consequence of sin.* The Church's Magisterium, as authentic interpreter of the affirmations of Scripture and Tradition, teaches that death entered the world on account of man's sin.[569] Even though

561 1 Cor 6:13–15, 19–20.   562 2 Cor 5:8.   563 Cf. Phil 1:23.   564 Cf. Paul VI, CPG § 28.   565 GS 18.   566 Rom 6:23; cf. Gen 2:17.   567 Cf. Rom 6:3–9; Phil 3:10–11.   568 Eccl 12:1, 7.   569 Cf. Gen 2:17; 3:3; 3:19; Wis 1:13; Rom 5:12; 6:23; DS 1511.

man's nature is mortal, God had destined him not to 401 die. Death was therefore contrary to the plans of God the Creator and entered the world as a consequence of sin.[570] "Bodily death, from which man would have been immune had he not sinned" is thus "the last enemy" of 376 man left to be conquered.[571]

1009 *Death is transformed by Christ.* Jesus, the Son of God, also himself suffered the death that is part of the human condition. Yet, despite his anguish as he faced death, he accepted it in an act of complete and free sub- 612 mission to his Father's will.[572] The obedience of Jesus has transformed the curse of death into a blessing.[573]

The meaning of Christian death   1681-1690

1010 Because of Christ, Christian death has a positive meaning: "For to me to live is Christ, and to die is gain."[574] "The saying is sure: if we have died with him, we will also live with him."[575] What is essentially new about Christian death is this: through Baptism, the Christian has already "died with Christ" sacramentally, in order to live a new life; and if we die in Christ's grace, 1220 physical death completes this "dying with Christ" and so completes our incorporation into him in his redeeming act:

> It is better for me to die in *(eis)* Christ Jesus than to reign over the ends of the earth. Him it is I seek— who died for us. Him it is I desire—who rose for us. I am on the point of giving birth. . . . Let me receive pure light; when I shall have arrived there, then shall I be a man.[576]

1011 In death, God calls man to himself. Therefore the Christian can experience a desire for death like St. Paul's: "My desire is to depart and be with Christ."[577] He can transform his own death into an act of obedience and love towards the Father, after the example of 1025 Christ:[578]

---

570 Cf. *Wis* 2:23–24. 571 *GS* 18 § 2; cf. *1 Cor* 15:26. 572 Cf. *Mk* 14:33–34; *Heb* 5:7–8. 573 Cf. *Rom* 5:19–21. 574 *Phil* 1:21. 575 *2 Tim* 2:11. 576 St. Ignatius of Antioch, *Ad Rom.*, 6, 1–2; *Apostolic Fathers*, II/2, 217–220. 577 *Phil* 1:23. 578 Cf. *Lk* 23:46.

> My earthly desire has been crucified; . . . there is
> living water in me, water that murmurs and says
> within me: Come to the Father.[579]

> I want to see God and, in order to see him, I must
> die.[580]

> I am not dying; I am entering life.[581]

1012 The Christian vision of death receives privileged
expression in the liturgy of the Church.[582]

> Lord, for your faithful people life is changed, not
> ended.
> When the body of our earthly dwelling lies in
> death
> we gain an everlasting dwelling place in heaven.[583]

1013 Death is the end of man's earthly pilgrimage, of
the time of grace and mercy which God offers him so as
to work out his earthly life in keeping with the divine
plan, and to decide his ultimate destiny. When "the single course of our earthly life" is completed,[584] we shall
not return to other earthly lives: "It is appointed for men
to die once."[585] There is no "reincarnation" after death.

1014 The Church encourages us to prepare ourselves
for the hour of our death. In the litany of the saints, for
instance, she has us pray: "From a sudden and unfore-
seen death, deliver us, O Lord";[586] to ask the Mother of
God to intercede for us "at the hour of our death" in the
Hail Mary; and to entrust ourselves to St. Joseph, the
2676-2677 patron of a happy death.

> Every action of yours, every thought, should be
> those of one who expects to die before the day is
> out. Death would have no great terrors for you if
> you had a quiet conscience. . . . Then why not keep
> clear of sin instead of running away from death? If
> you aren't fit to face death today, it's very unlikely
> you will be tomorrow. . . .[587]

> Praised are you, my Lord, for our sister bodily
> Death,

---

579 St. Ignatius of Antioch, *Ad Rom.,* 6, 1–2: *Apostolic Fathers,* II/2, 223–224.
580 St. Teresa of Avila, *Life,* chap. 1.   581 St. Thérèse of Lisieux, *The Last
Conversations.*   582 Cf. *1 Thess* 4:13–14.   583 *Roman* Missal, Preface of
Christian Death I.   584 *LG* 48 § 3.   585 *Heb* 9:27.   586 *Roman Missal,* Litany
of the Saints.   587 *The Imitation of Christ,* 1, 23, 1.

from whom no living man can escape.
Woe on those who will die in mortal sin!
Blessed are they who will be found
in your most holy will,
for the second death will not harm them.[588]

IN BRIEF

1015   "The flesh is the hinge of salvation" (Tertullian, *De res.* 8, 2: PL 2, 852). We believe in God who is creator of the flesh; we believe in the Word made flesh in order to redeem the flesh; we believe in the resurrection of the flesh, the fulfillment of both the creation and the redemption of the flesh.

1016   By death the soul is separated from the body, but in the resurrection God will give incorruptible life to our body, transformed by reunion with our soul. Just as Christ is risen and lives for ever, so all of us will rise at the last day.

1017   "We believe in the true resurrection of this flesh that we now possess" (Council of Lyons II: DS 854). We sow a corruptible body in the tomb, but he raises up an incorruptible body, a "spiritual body" (cf. *1 Cor* 15:42–44).

1018   As a consequence of original sin, man must suffer "bodily death, from which man would have been immune had he not sinned" (*GS* § 18).

1019   Jesus, the Son of God, freely suffered death for us in complete and free submission to the will of God, his Father. By his death he has conquered death, and so opened the possibility of salvation to all men.

ARTICLE 12
"I BELIEVE IN LIFE EVERLASTING"

1020   The Christian who unites his own death to that of Jesus views it as a step towards him and an entrance   *1523-1525*

---

588 St. Francis of Assisi, *Canticle of the Creatures.*

into everlasting life. When the Church for the last time speaks Christ's words of pardon and absolution over the dying Christian, seals him for the last time with a strengthening anointing, and gives him Christ in viaticum as nourishment for the journey, she speaks with gentle assurance:

> Go forth, Christian soul, from this world
> in the name of God the almighty Father,
> who created you,
> in the name of Jesus Christ, the Son of the living
> God,
> who suffered for you,
> in the name of the Holy Spirit,
> who was poured out upon you.
> Go forth, faithful Christian!
>
> May you live in peace this day,
> may your home be with God in Zion,
> with Mary, the virgin Mother of God,
> with Joseph, and all the angels and saints. . . .
>
> May you return to [your Creator]
> who formed you from the dust of the earth.
> May holy Mary, the angels, and all the saints
> come to meet you as you go forth from this
> life. . . .
> May you see your Redeemer face to face. . . .[589]

2677, 336

I.   THE PARTICULAR JUDGMENT

1021 Death puts an end to human life as the time open to either accepting or rejecting the divine grace manifested in Christ.[590] The New Testament speaks of judgment primarily in its aspect of the final encounter with Christ in his second coming, but also repeatedly affirms that each will be rewarded immediately after death in accordance with his works and faith. The parable of the poor man Lazarus and the words of Christ on the cross to the good thief, as well as other New Testament texts speak of a final destiny of the soul—a destiny which can be different for some and for others.[591]

679

1022 Each man receives his eternal retribution in his

---

589 *OCF,* Prayer of Commendation.   590 Cf. *2 Tim* 1:9–10.   591 Cf. *Lk* 16:22; 23:43; *Mt* 16:26; *2 Cor* 5:8; *Phil* 1:23; *Heb* 9:27; 12:23.

immortal soul at the very moment of his death, in a par- 393
ticular judgment that refers his life to Christ: either
entrance into the blessedness of heaven—through a purification[592] or immediately,[593]—or immediate and everlasting damnation.[594]

> At the evening of life, we shall be judged on our
> love.[595]   1470

II. HEAVEN

1023 Those who die in God's grace and friendship and
are perfectly purified live for ever with Christ. They are 954
like God for ever, for they "see him as he is," face to
face:[596]

> By virtue of our apostolic authority, we define the
> following: According to the general disposition of
> God, the souls of all the saints . . . and other faith-
> ful who died after receiving Christ's holy Baptism
> (provided they were not in need of purification
> when they died, . . . or, if they then did need or will
> need some purification, when they have been puri-
> fied after death, . . .) already before they take up
> their bodies again and before the general judg-
> ment—and this since the Ascension of our Lord and
> Savior Jesus Christ into heaven—have been, are
> and will be in heaven, in the heavenly Kingdom and
> celestial paradise with Christ, joined to the com-
> pany of the holy angels. Since the Passion and death
> of our Lord Jesus Christ, these souls have seen and
> do see the divine essence with an intuitive vision,
> and even face to face, without the mediation of any
> creature.[597]

1024 This perfect life with the Most Holy Trinity—
this communion of life and love with the Trinity, with
the Virgin Mary, the angels and all the blessed—is called
"heaven." Heaven is the ultimate end and fulfillment of 260, 326
the deepest human longings, the state of supreme, de- 2794, 1718
finitive happiness.

---

592 Cf. Council of Lyons II (1274): DS 857–858; Council of Florence (1439): DS
1304–1306; Council of Trent (1563): DS 1820.   593 Cf. Benedict XII, *Benedictus
Deus* (1336): DS 1000–1001; John XXII, *Ne super his* (1334): DS 990.   594 Cf.
Benedict XII, *Benedictus Deus* (1336): DS 1002.   595 St. John of the Cross,
Dichos 64.   596 *1 Jn* 3:2; cf. *1 Cor* 13:12; *Rev* 22:4.   597 Benedict XII,
Benedictus Deus (1336): DS 1000; cf. *LG* 49.

1025 To live in heaven is "to be with Christ." The
1011 elect live "in Christ,"[598] but they retain, or rather find,
their true identity, their own name.[599]

> For life is to be with Christ; where Christ is, there
> is life, there is the kingdom.[600]

1026 By his death and Resurrection, Jesus Christ has
"opened" heaven to us. The life of the blessed consists
in the full and perfect possession of the fruits of the redemption accomplished by Christ. He makes partners in
his heavenly glorification those who have believed in
793 him and remained faithful to his will. Heaven is the
blessed community of all who are perfectly incorporated into Christ.

1027 This mystery of blessed communion with God
and all who are in Christ is beyond all understanding
and description. Scripture speaks of it in images: life,
959, 1720 light, peace, wedding feast, wine of the kingdom, the Father's house, the heavenly Jerusalem, paradise: "no eye
has seen, nor ear heard, nor the heart of man conceived,
what God has prepared for those who love him."[601]

1028 Because of his transcendence, God cannot be
seen as he is, unless he himself opens up his mystery to
1722, 163 man's immediate contemplation and gives him the capacity for it. The Church calls this contemplation of
God in his heavenly glory "the beatific vision":

> How great will your glory and happiness be, to be
> allowed to see God, to be honored with sharing the
> joy of salvation and eternal light with Christ your
> Lord and God, . . . to delight in the joy of immor-
> tality in the Kingdom of heaven with the righteous
> and God's friends.[602]

956 **1029** In the glory of heaven the blessed continue joy-
668 fully to fulfill God's will in relation to other men and to
all creation. Already they reign with Christ; with him
"they shall reign for ever and ever."[603]

---

598 *Phil* 1:23; cf. *Jn* 14:3; *1 Thess* 4:17.   599 Cf. *Rev* 2:17.   600 St. Ambrose,
In Luc., 10, 121: PL 15, 1834A.   601 *1 Cor* 2:9.   602 St. Cyprian, *Ep.* 58,
10, 1: CSEL 3/2, 665.   603 *Rev* 22:5; cf. *Mt* 25:21, 23.

III.   THE FINAL PURIFICATION, OR PURGATORY

1030   All who die in God's grace and friendship, but still imperfectly purified, are indeed assured of their eternal salvation; but after death they undergo purification, so as to achieve the holiness necessary to enter the joy of heaven.

1031   The Church gives the name *Purgatory* to this final purification of the elect, which is entirely different   *954, 1472* from the punishment of the damned.[604] The Church formulated her doctrine of faith on Purgatory especially at the Councils of Florence and Trent. The tradition of the Church, by reference to certain texts of Scripture, speaks of a cleansing fire:[605]

> As for certain lesser faults, we must believe that, before the Final Judgment, there is a purifying fire. He who is truth says that whoever utters blasphemy against the Holy Spirit will be pardoned neither in this age nor in the age to come. From this sentence we understand that certain offenses can be forgiven in this age, but certain others in the age to come.[606]

1032   This teaching is also based on the practice of prayer for the dead, already mentioned in Sacred Scripture: "Therefore [Judas Maccabeus] made atonement   *958* for the dead, that they might be delivered from their sin."[607] From the beginning the Church has honored the   *1371* memory of the dead and offered prayers in suffrage for them, above all the Eucharistic sacrifice, so that, thus   *1479* purified, they may attain the beatific vision of God.[608] The Church also commends almsgiving, indulgences, and works of penance undertaken on behalf of the dead:

> Let us help and commemorate them. If Job's sons were purified by their father's sacrifice, why would we doubt that our offerings for the dead bring them some consolation? Let us not hesitate to help those who have died and to offer our prayers for them.[609]

---

604 Cf. Council of Florence (1439): DS 1304; Council of Trent (1563): DS 1820; (1547): 1580; see also Benedict XII, *Benedictus Deus* (1336): DS 1000.   605 Cf. *1 Cor* 3:15; *1 Pet* 1:7.   606 St. Gregory the Great, *Dial.* 4, 39: PL 77, 396; cf. *Mt* 12:31.   607 *2 Macc* 12:46.   608 Cf. Council of Lyons II (1274): DS 856. 609 St. John Chrysostom, *Hom. in 1 Cor.* 41, 5: PG 61, 361; cf. *Job* 1:5.

IV.   HELL

1033 We cannot be united with God unless we freely choose to love him. But we cannot love God if we sin gravely against him, against our neighbor or against ourselves: "He who does not love remains in death. Anyone who hates his brother is a murderer, and you know that no murderer has eternal life abiding in him."[610] Our

1861 Lord warns us that we shall be separated from him if we
393 fail to meet the serious needs of the poor and the little
633 ones who are his brethren.[611] To die in mortal sin without repenting and accepting God's merciful love means remaining separated from him for ever by our own free choice. This state of definitive self-exclusion from communion with God and the blessed is called "hell."

1034 Jesus often speaks of "Gehenna," of "the unquenchable fire" reserved for those who to the end of their lives refuse to believe and be converted, where both soul and body can be lost.[612] Jesus solemnly proclaims that he "will send his angels, and they will gather . . . all evil doers, and throw them into the furnace of fire,"[613] and that he will pronounce the condemnation: "Depart from me, you cursed, into the eternal fire!"[614]

1035 The teaching of the Church affirms the existence of hell and its eternity. Immediately after death the souls of those who die in a state of mortal sin descend into hell, where they suffer the punishments of hell, "eternal fire."[615] The chief punishment of hell is eternal separa-
393 tion from God, in whom alone man can possess the life and happiness for which he was created and for which he longs.

1036 The affirmations of Sacred Scripture and the teachings of the Church on the subject of hell are a *call to the responsibility* incumbent upon man to make use
1734 of his freedom in view of his eternal destiny. They are at
1428 the same time an urgent *call to conversion:* "Enter by the narrow gate; for the gate is wide and the way is easy,

---

610 *1 Jn* 3:14–15.   611 Cf. *Mt* 25:31–46.   612 Cf. *Mt* 5:22, 29; 10:28; 13:42, 50; *Mk* 9:43–48.   613 *Mt* 13:41–42.   614 *Mt* 25:41.   615 Cf. DS 76; 409; 411; 801; 858; 1002; 1351; 1575; Paul VI, *CPG* § 12.

that leads to destruction, and those who enter by it are many. For the gate is narrow and the way is hard, that leads to life, and those who find it are few."[616]

> Since we know neither the day nor the hour, we should follow the advice of the Lord and watch constantly so that, when the single course of our earthly life is completed, we may merit to enter with him into the marriage feast and be numbered among the blessed, and not, like the wicked and slothful servants, be ordered to depart into the eternal fire, into the outer darkness where "men will weep and gnash their teeth."[617]

1037 God predestines no one to go to hell;[618] for this, a willful turning away from God (a mortal sin) is necessary, and persistence in it until the end. In the Eucharistic liturgy and in the daily prayers of her faithful, the Church implores the mercy of God, who does not want "any to perish, but all to come to repentance":[619]

162

1014, 1821

> Father, accept this offering
> from your whole family.
> Grant us your peace in this life,
> save us from final damnation,
> and count us among those you have chosen.[620]

V. THE LAST JUDGMENT

678-679

1038 The resurrection of all the dead, "of both the just and the unjust,"[621] will precede the Last Judgment. This will be "the hour when all who are in the tombs will hear [the Son of man's] voice and come forth, those who have done good, to the resurrection of life, and those who have done evil, to the resurrection of judgment."[622] Then Christ will come "in his glory, and all the angels with him. . . . Before him will be gathered all the nations, and he will separate them one from another as a shepherd separates the sheep from the goats, and he will place the sheep at his right hand, but the goats at the left. . . . And they will go away into eternal punishment, but the righteous into eternal life."[623]

1001, 998

---

616 *Mt* 7:13–14.   617 *LG* 48 § 3; *Mt* 22:13; cf. *Heb* 9:27; *Mt* 25:13, 26, 30, 31–46.   618 Cf. Council of Orange II (529): DS 397; Council of Trent (1547):1567.   619 *2 Pet* 3:9.   620 *Roman Missal*, EP I (Roman Canon) 88.
621 *Acts* 24:15.   622 *Jn* 5:28–29.   623 *Mt* 25:31, 32, 46.

1039   In the presence of Christ, who is Truth itself, the truth of each man's relationship with God will be laid bare.[624] The Last Judgment will reveal even to its furthest consequences the good each person has done or 678 failed to do during his earthly life:

> All that the wicked do is recorded, and they do not know. When "our God comes, he does not keep silence." . . . he will turn towards those at his left hand: . . . "I placed my poor little ones on earth for you. I as their head was seated in heaven at the right hand of my Father—but on earth my members were suffering, my members on earth were in need. If you gave anything to my members, what you gave would reach their Head. Would that you had known that my little ones were in need when I placed them on earth for you and appointed them your stewards to bring your good works into my treasury. But you have placed nothing in their hands; therefore you have found nothing in my presence."[625]

1040   The Last Judgment will come when Christ returns in glory. Only the Father knows the day and the hour; only he determines the moment of its coming. 637 Then through his Son Jesus Christ he will pronounce the final word on all history. We shall know the ultimate meaning of the whole work of creation and of the entire economy of salvation and understand the marvellous ways by which his Providence led everything towards its 314 final end. The Last Judgment will reveal that God's justice triumphs over all the injustices committed by his creatures and that God's love is stronger than death.[626]

1041   The message of the Last Judgment calls men to conversion while God is still giving them "the acceptable time, . . . the day of salvation."[627] It inspires a holy 1432 fear of God and commits them to the justice of the Kingdom of God. It proclaims the "blessed hope" of the Lord's return, when he will come "to be glorified in his saints, and to be marvelled at in all who have believed."[628]

---

624 Cf. *Jn* 12:49.   625 St. Augustine, *Sermo* 18, 4: PL 38, 130–131; cf. *Ps* 50:3.
626 Cf. *Song* 8:6.   627 *2 Cor* 6:2.   628 *Titus* 2:13; *2 Thess* 1:10.

VI. **THE HOPE OF THE NEW HEAVEN AND THE**   *2854*
     NEW EARTH

1042 At the end of time, the Kingdom of God will
come in its fullness. After the universal judgment, the
righteous will reign for ever with Christ, glorified in   *769*
body and soul. The universe itself will be renewed: *670*

> The Church . . . will receive her perfection only in
> the glory of heaven, when will come the time of the
> renewal of all things. At that time, together with the   *310*
> human race, the universe itself, which is so closely
> related to man and which attains its destiny through
> him, will be perfectly re-established in Christ.[629]

1043 Sacred Scripture calls this mysterious renewal,
which will transform humanity and the world, "new
heavens and a new earth."[630] It will be the definitive re-   *671*
alization of God's plan to bring under a single head "all   *280, 518*
things in [Christ], things in heaven and things on
earth."[631]

1044 In this new universe, the heavenly Jerusalem, God
will have his dwelling among men.[632] "He will wipe away
every tear from their eyes, and death shall be no more,
neither shall there be mourning nor crying nor pain any
more, for the former things have passed away."[633]

1045 *For man,* this consummation will be the final realization of the unity of the human race, which God
willed from creation and of which the pilgrim Church
has been "in the nature of sacrament."[634] Those who are   *775*
united with Christ will form the community of the redeemed, "the holy city" of God, "the Bride, the wife of   *1404*
the Lamb."[635] She will not be wounded any longer by
sin, stains, self-love, that destroy or wound the earthly
community.[636] The beatific vision, in which God opens
himself in an inexhaustible way to the elect, will be the
ever-flowing well-spring of happiness, peace, and mutual communion.

1046 *For the cosmos,* Revelation affirms the profound
common destiny of the material world and man:

---

629 *LG* 48; cf. *Acts* 3:21; *Eph* 1:10; *Col* 1:20; *2 Pet* 3:10–13.   630 *2 Pet* 3:13;
cf. *Rev* 21:1.   631 *Eph* 1:10.   632 Cf. *Rev* 21:5.   633 *Rev* 21:4.   634 Cf. *LG*
1.   635 *Rev* 21:2, 9.   636 Cf. *Rev* 21:27.

349   For the creation waits with eager longing for the revealing of the sons of God . . . in hope because the creation itself will be set free from its bondage to decay. . . . We know that the whole creation has been groaning in travail together until now; and not only the creation, but we ourselves, who have the first fruits of the Spirit, groan inwardly as we wait for adoption as sons, the redemption of our bodies.[637]

1047   The visible universe, then, is itself destined to be transformed, "so that the world itself, restored to its original state, facing no further obstacles, should be at the service of the just," sharing their glorification in the risen Jesus Christ.[638]

1048   *"We know neither the moment of the consummation* of the earth and of man, nor the way in which the universe will be transformed. The form of this
673   world, distorted by sin, is passing away, and we are taught that God is preparing a new dwelling and a new earth in which righteousness dwells, in which happiness will fill and surpass all the desires of peace arising in the hearts of men."[639]

1049   "Far from diminishing our concern to develop this earth, the expectancy of a new earth should spur us on, for it is here that the body of a new human family grows, foreshadowing in some way the age which is to come. That is why, although we must be careful to distinguish earthly progress clearly from the increase of the
2820   kingdom of Christ, such progress is of vital concern to the kingdom of God, insofar as it can contribute to the better ordering of human society."[640]

1050   "When we have spread on earth the fruits of our nature and our enterprise . . . according to the com-
1709   mand of the Lord and in his Spirit, we will find them once again, cleansed this time from the stain of sin, illuminated and transfigured, when Christ presents to his
260   Father an eternal and universal kingdom."[641] God will then be "all in all" in eternal life:[642]

---

637 *Rom* 8:19–23.   638 St. Irenaeus, *Adv. haeres.* 5, 32, 1: PG 7/2, 210.
639 GS 39 § 1.   640 GS 39 § 2.   641 GS 39 § 3.   642 *1 Cor* 5:28.

True and subsistent life consists in this: the Father, through the Son and in the Holy Spirit, pouring out his heavenly gifts on all things without exception. Thanks to his mercy, we too, men that we are, have received the inalienable promise of eternal life.[643]

IN BRIEF

1051 Every man receives his eternal recompense in his immortal soul from the moment of his death in a particular judgment by Christ, the judge of the living and the dead.

1052 "We believe that the souls of all who die in Christ's grace . . . are the People of God beyond death. On the day of resurrection, death will be definitively conquered, when these souls will be reunited with their bodies" (Paul VI, *CPG* § 28).

1053 "We believe that the multitude of those gathered around Jesus and Mary in Paradise forms the Church of heaven, where in eternal blessedness they see God as he is and where they are also, to various degrees, associated with the holy angels in the divine governance exercised by Christ in glory, by interceding for us and helping our weakness by their fraternal concern" (Paul VI, *CPG* § 29).

1054 Those who die in God's grace and friendship imperfectly purified, although they are assured of their eternal salvation, undergo a purification after death, so as to achieve the holiness necessary to enter the joy of God.

1055 By virtue of the "communion of saints," the Church commends the dead to God's mercy and offers her prayers, especially the holy sacrifice of the Eucharist, on their behalf.

1056 Following the example of Christ, the Church warns the faithful of the "sad and lamentable reality of eternal death" (*GCD* 69), also called "hell."

---

643 St. Cyril of Jerusalem, *Catech. illum.* 18, 29: PG 33, 1049.

1057 Hell's principal punishment consists of eternal separation from God in whom alone man can have the life and happiness for which he was created and for which he longs.

1058 The Church prays that no one should be lost: "Lord, let me never be parted from you." If it is true that no one can save himself, it is also true that God "desires all men to be saved" (*1 Tim* 2:4), and that for him "all things are possible" (*Mt* 19:26).

1059 "The holy Roman Church firmly believes and confesses that on the Day of Judgment all men will appear in their own bodies before Christ's tribunal to render an account of their own deeds" (Council of Lyons II [1274]: DS 859; cf. DS 1549).

1060 At the end of time, the Kingdom of God will come in its fullness. Then the just will reign with Christ for ever, glorified in body and soul, and the material universe itself will be transformed. God will then be "all in all" (*1 Cor* 15:28), in eternal life.

"AMEN"

1061 The Creed, like the last book of the Bible,[644] ends with the Hebrew word amen. This word frequently concludes prayers in the New Testament. The Church likewise ends her prayers with "Amen."

2856

1062 In Hebrew, amen comes from the same root as the word "believe." This root expresses solidity, trustworthiness, faithfulness. And so we can understand why "Amen" may express both God's faithfulness towards us and our trust in him.

214

1063 In the book of the prophet Isaiah, we find the expression "God of truth" (literally "God of the Amen"), that is, the God who is faithful to his promises: "He

215

---

644 Cf. *Rev* 22:21.

who blesses himself in the land shall bless himself by the God of truth [amen]."[645] Our Lord often used the word "Amen," sometimes repeated,[646] to emphasize the trust- *156* worthiness of his teaching, his authority founded on God's truth.

1064 Thus the Creed's final "Amen" repeats and confirms its first words: "I believe." To believe is to say "Amen" to God's words, promises and commandments; *197, 2101* to entrust oneself completely to him who is the "Amen" of infinite love and perfect faithfulness. The Christian's everyday life will then be the "Amen" to the "I believe" of our baptismal profession of faith:

> May your Creed be for you as a mirror. Look at yourself in it, to see if you believe everything you say you believe. And rejoice in your faith each day.[647]

1065 Jesus Christ himself is the "Amen."[648] He is the definitive "Amen" of the Father's love for us. He takes up and completes our "Amen" to the Father: "For all the promises of God find their Yes in him. That is why we utter the Amen through him, to the glory of God":[649]

> Through him, with him, in him
> in the unity of the Holy Spirit,
> all glory and honor is yours,
> almighty Father,
> God, for ever and ever.
> AMEN.

645 *Isa* 65:16.   646 Cf. *Mt* 6:2, 5, 16; *Jn* 5:19.   647 St. Augustine, *Sermo* 58, 11, 13: PL 38, 399.   648 *Rev* 3:14.   649 2 *Cor* 1:20.

PART TWO
THE CELEBRATION OF THE CHRISTIAN MYSTERY

Why the liturgy?

1066 In the Symbol of the faith the Church confesses the mystery of the Holy Trinity and of the plan of God's "good pleasure" for all creation: the Father accomplishes the "mystery of his will" by giving his beloved *50* Son and his Holy Spirit for the salvation of the world and for the glory of his name.[1] Such is the mystery of Christ, revealed and fulfilled in history according to the wisely ordered plan that St. Paul calls the "plan of the mystery"[2] and the patristic tradition will call the "econ- *236* omy of the Word incarnate" or the "economy of salvation."

1067 "The wonderful works of God among the people of the Old Testament were but a prelude to the work of Christ the Lord in redeeming mankind and giving perfect glory to God. He accomplished this work principally by the Paschal mystery of his blessed Passion, Resurrection from the dead, and glorious Ascension, whereby 'dying he destroyed our death, rising he restored our life.' For it was from the side of Christ as he slept the sleep of death upon the cross that there came forth 'the wondrous sacrament of the whole Church.' "[3] For this reason, the Church celebrates in the liturgy above all the Paschal mystery by which Christ accomplished the work of our salvation. *571*

1068 It is this mystery of Christ that the Church proclaims and celebrates in her liturgy so that the faithful may live from it and bear witness to it in the world:

> For it is in the liturgy, especially in the divine sacrifice of the Eucharist, that "the work of our redemption is accomplished," and it is through the liturgy especially that the faithful are enabled to ex-

---

1 *Eph* 1:9. 2 *Eph* 3:9; cf. 3:4. 3 *SC* 5 § 2; cf. St. Augustine, *En. in Ps.* 138, 2: PL 37, 1784–1785.

press in their lives and manifest to others the mystery of Christ and the real nature of the true Church.[4]

What does the word liturgy mean?

1069 The word "liturgy" originally meant a "public work" or a "service in the name of/on behalf of the people." In Christian tradition it means the participation of the People of God in "the work of God."[5] Through the liturgy Christ, our redeemer and high priest, continues the work of our redemption in, with, and through his Church.

1070 In the New Testament the word "liturgy" refers not only to the celebration of divine worship but also to the proclamation of the Gospel and to active charity.[6] In all of these situations it is a question of the service of God and neighbor. In a liturgical celebration the Church is servant in the image of her Lord, the one *"leitourgos"*;[7] she shares in Christ's priesthood (worship), which is both prophetic (proclamation) and kingly (service of charity):

783

> The liturgy then is rightly seen as an exercise of the priestly office of Jesus Christ. It involves the presentation of man's sanctification under the guise of signs perceptible by the senses and its accomplishment in ways appropriate to each of these signs. In it full public worship is performed by the Mystical Body of Jesus Christ, that is, by the Head and his members. From this it follows that every liturgical celebration, because it is an action of Christ the priest and of his Body which is the Church, is a sacred action surpassing all others. No other action of the Church can equal its efficacy by the same title and to the same degree.[8]

Liturgy as source of life

1071 As the work of Christ liturgy is also an action of his *Church*. It makes the Church present and manifests her as the visible sign of the communion in Christ be-

---

4 SC 2. 5 Cf. *Jn* 17:4. 6 Cf. *Lk* 1:23; *Acts* 13:2; *Rom* 15:16, 27; 2 *Cor* 9:12; *Phil* 2:14–17, 25, 30. 7 Cf. *Heb* 8:2, 6. 8 SC 7 § 2–3.

tween God and men. It engages the faithful in the new life of the community and involves the "conscious, active, and fruitful participation" of everyone.[9]

1692

1072 "The sacred liturgy does not exhaust the entire activity of the Church":[10] it must be preceded by evangelization, faith, and conversion. It can then produce its fruits in the lives of the faithful: new life in the Spirit, involvement in the mission of the Church, and service to her unity.

Prayer and liturgy

1073 The liturgy is also a participation in Christ's own prayer addressed to the Father in the Holy Spirit. In the liturgy, all Christian prayer finds its source and goal. Through the liturgy the inner man is rooted and grounded in "the great love with which [the Father] loved us" in his beloved Son.[11] It is the same "marvelous work of God" that is lived and internalized by all prayer, "at all times in the Spirit."[12]

2558

Catechesis and liturgy

1074 "The liturgy is the summit toward which the activity of the Church is directed; it is also the font from which all her power flows."[13] It is therefore the privileged place for catechizing the People of God. "Catechesis is intrinsically linked with the whole of liturgical and sacramental activity, for it is in the sacraments, especially in the Eucharist, that Christ Jesus works in fullness for the transformation of men."[14]

1075 Liturgical catechesis aims to initiate people into the mystery of Christ (It is "mystagogy.") by proceeding from the visible to the invisible, from the sign to the thing signified, from the "sacraments" to the "mysteries." Such catechesis is to be presented by local and regional catechisms. This Catechism, which aims to serve the whole Church in all the diversity of her rites and cultures,[15] will present what is fundamental and common

426

774

---

9 SC 11. 10 SC 9. 11 *Eph* 2:4; 3:16–17. 12 *Eph* 6:18. 13 SC 10. 14 John Paul II, *CT* 23. 15 Cf. SC 3–4.

to the whole Church in the liturgy as mystery and as celebration *(Section One),* and then the seven sacraments
and the sacramentals *(Section Two).*

SECTION ONE
THE SACRAMENTAL ECONOMY

1076 The Church was made manifest to the world on
the day of Pentecost by the outpouring of the Holy
Spirit.[1] The gift of the Spirit ushers in a new era in the
"dispensation of the mystery"—the age of the Church,
during which Christ manifests, makes present, and com-
739 municates his work of salvation through the liturgy of
his Church, "until he comes."[2] In this age of the Church
Christ now lives and acts in and with his Church, in a
new way appropriate to this new age. He acts through
the sacraments in what the common Tradition of the
East and the West calls "the sacramental economy"; this
is the communication (or "dispensation") of the fruits
of Christ's Paschal mystery in the celebration of the
Church's "sacramental" liturgy.

It is therefore important first to explain this
"sacramental dispensation" *(chapter one).* The nature
and essential features of liturgical celebration will then
appear more clearly *(chapter two).*

---

1 Cf. *SC* 6; *LG* 2.   2 1 *Cor* 11:26.

CHAPTER ONE
THE PASCHAL MYSTERY IN THE AGE OF THE CHURCH

ARTICLE 1
THE LITURGY—WORK OF THE HOLY TRINITY

I. THE FATHER—SOURCE AND GOAL OF THE LITURGY

1077 "Blessed be the God and Father of our Lord Jesus Christ, who has blessed us in Christ with every spiritual blessing in the heavenly places, even as he chose us in him before the foundation of the world, that we should be holy and blameless before him. He destined us before him in love to be his sons through Jesus Christ, according to the purpose of his will, to the praise of his glorious grace which he freely bestowed on us in the Beloved."[3] 492

1078 Blessing is a divine and life-giving action, the source of which is the Father; his blessing is both word and gift.[4] When applied to man, the word "blessing" means adoration and surrender to his Creator in thanksgiving. 2626

1079 From the beginning until the end of time the whole of God's work is a *blessing*. From the liturgical poem of the first creation to the canticles of the heavenly Jerusalem, the inspired authors proclaim the plan of salvation as one vast divine blessing.

1080 From the very beginning God blessed all living beings, especially man and woman. The covenant with Noah and with all living things renewed this blessing of fruitfulness despite man's sin which had brought a curse on the ground. But with Abraham, the divine blessing entered into human history which was moving toward death, to redirect it toward life, toward its

---

3 Eph 1:3–6.   4 *eu-logia, bene-dictio.*

source. By the faith of "the father of all believers," who embraced the blessing, the history of salvation is inaugurated.

1081 The divine blessings were made manifest in astonishing and saving events: the birth of Isaac, the escape from Egypt (Passover and Exodus), the gift of the promised land, the election of David, the presence of God in the Temple, the purifying exile, and return of a "small remnant." The Law, the Prophets, and the Psalms, interwoven in the liturgy of the Chosen People, recall these divine blessings and at the same time respond to them with blessings of praise and thanksgiving.

1082 In the Church's liturgy the divine blessing is fully revealed and communicated. The Father is acknowledged and adored as the source and the end of all the blessings of creation and salvation. In his Word who became incarnate, died, and rose for us, he fills us with his blessings. Through his Word, he pours into our hearts the Gift that contains all gifts, the Holy Spirit.

2627 **1083** The dual dimension of the Christian liturgy as a response of faith and love to the spiritual blessings the Father bestows on us is thus evident. On the one hand, the Church, united with her Lord and "in the Holy Spirit,"[5] blesses the Father "for his inexpressible gift"[6] in her adoration, praise, and thanksgiving. On the other hand, until the consummation of God's plan, the Church never ceases to present to the Father the offer-
1360 ing of his own gifts and to beg him to send the Holy Spirit upon that offering, upon herself, upon the faithful, and upon the whole world, so that through communion in the death and resurrection of Christ the Priest, and by the power of the Spirit, these divine blessings will bring forth the fruits of life "to the praise of his glorious grace."[7]

---

5 *Lk* 10:21.   6 *2 Cor* 9:15.   7 *Eph* 1:6.

II. Christ's Work in the Liturgy

Christ glorified . . .

1084 "Seated at the right hand of the Father" and 662 pouring out the Holy Spirit on his Body which is the Church, Christ now acts through the sacraments he instituted to communicate his grace. The sacraments are perceptible signs (words and actions) accessible to our 1127 human nature. By the action of Christ and the power of the Holy Spirit they make present efficaciously the grace that they signify.

1085 In the liturgy of the Church, it is principally his own Paschal mystery that Christ signifies and makes present. During his earthly life Jesus announced his Paschal mystery by his teaching and anticipated it by his actions. When his Hour comes, he lives out the unique event of history which does not pass away: Jesus dies, is buried, rises from the dead, and is seated at the right hand of the Father "once for all."[8] His Paschal mystery is a real event that occurred in our history, but it is unique: all other historical events happen once, and then they pass away, swallowed up in the past. The Paschal mystery of Christ, by contrast, cannot remain only in the past, because by his death he destroyed 519 death, and all that Christ is—all that he did and suffered for all men—participates in the divine eternity, and so transcends all times while being made present in them all. The event of the Cross and Resurrection *abides* and 1165 draws everything toward life.

. . . from the time of the Church of the Apostles . . .

1086 "Accordingly, just as Christ was sent by the Fa- 858 ther so also he sent the apostles, filled with the Holy Spirit. This he did so that they might preach the Gospel to every creature and proclaim that the Son of God by his death and resurrection had freed us from the power of Satan and from death and brought us into the Kingdom of his Father. But he also willed that the work of

---

8 *Rom* 6:10; *Heb* 7:27; 9:12; cf. *Jn* 13:1; 17:1.

salvation which they preached should be set in train through the sacrifice and sacraments, around which the entire liturgical life revolves."⁹

861 **1087** Thus the risen Christ, by giving the Holy Spirit 1536 to the apostles, entrusted to them his power of sanctifying:¹⁰ they became sacramental signs of Christ. By the power of the same Holy Spirit they entrusted this power to their successors. This "apostolic succession" structures the whole liturgical life of the Church and is itself sacramental, handed on by the sacrament of Holy Orders.

... is present in the earthly liturgy ...

1088 "To accomplish so great a work"—the dispensation or communication of his work of salvation— "Christ is always present in his Church, especially in her 776 liturgical celebrations. He is present in the Sacrifice of 669 the Mass not only in the person of his minister, 'the same now offering, through the ministry of priests, who formerly offered himself on the cross,' but especially in the Eucharistic species. By his power he is present in the 1373 sacraments so that when anybody baptizes, it is really Christ himself who baptizes. He is present in his word since it is he himself who speaks when the holy Scriptures are read in the Church. Lastly, he is present when the Church prays and sings, for he has promised 'where two or three are gathered together in my name there am I in the midst of them.' "¹¹

1089 "Christ, indeed, always associates the Church with himself in this great work in which God is perfectly glorified and men are sanctified. The Church is his 796 beloved Bride who calls to her Lord and through him offers worship to the eternal Father."¹²

... which participates in the liturgy of heaven

1137-1139 **1090** "In the earthly liturgy we share in a foretaste of that heavenly liturgy which is celebrated in the Holy City of Jerusalem toward which we journey as pilgrims,

---

9 *SC* 6.   10 Cf. *Jn* 20:21–23.   11 *SC* 7; *Mt* 18:20.   12 *SC* 7.

where Christ is sitting at the right hand of God, Minister of the sanctuary and of the true tabernacle. With all the warriors of the heavenly army we sing a hymn of glory to the Lord; venerating the memory of the saints, we hope for some part and fellowship with them; we eagerly await the Savior, our Lord Jesus Christ, until he, our life, shall appear and we too will appear with him in glory."[13]

III.   THE HOLY SPIRIT AND THE CHURCH IN THE LITURGY

1091 In the liturgy the Holy Spirit is teacher of the faith of the People of God and artisan of "God's masterpieces," the sacraments of the New Covenant. The   798
desire and work of the Spirit in the heart of the Church is that we may live from the life of the risen Christ. When the Spirit encounters in us the response of faith which he has aroused in us, he brings about genuine cooperation. Through it, the liturgy becomes the common work of the Holy Spirit and the Church.

1092 In this sacramental dispensation of Christ's mystery the Holy Spirit acts in the same way as at other times in the economy of salvation: he prepares the   737
Church to encounter her Lord; he recalls and makes Christ manifest to the faith of the assembly. By his transforming power, he makes the mystery of Christ present here and now. Finally the Spirit of communion unites the Church to the life and mission of Christ.

The Holy Spirit prepares for the reception of Christ

1093 In the sacramental economy the Holy Spirit fulfills what was prefigured in *the Old Covenant*. Since Christ's Church was "prepared in marvellous fashion in   762
the history of the people of Israel and in the Old Covenant,"[14] the Church's liturgy has retained certain elements of the worship of the Old Covenant as integral and irreplaceable, adopting them as her own:

---

13 *SC* 8; cf. *LG* 50.   14 *LG* 2.

121 —notably, reading the Old Testament;

2585 —praying the Psalms;

1081 —above all, recalling the saving events and significant realities which have found their fulfillment in the mystery of Christ (promise and covenant, Exodus and Passover, kingdom and temple, exile and return).

128-130 **1094** It is on this harmony of the two Testaments that the Paschal catechesis of the Lord is built,[15] and then, that of the Apostles and the Fathers of the Church. This catechesis unveils what lay hidden under the letter of the Old Testament: the mystery of Christ. It is called "typological" because it reveals the newness of Christ on the basis of the "figures" (types) which announce him in the deeds, words, and symbols of the first covenant. By this re-reading in the Spirit of Truth, starting from Christ, the figures are unveiled.[16] Thus the flood and Noah's ark prefigured salvation by Baptism,[17] as did the cloud and the crossing of the Red Sea. Water from the rock was the figure of the spiritual gifts of Christ, and manna in the desert prefigured the Eucharist, "the true bread from heaven."[18]

1095 For this reason the Church, especially during Advent and Lent and above all at the Easter Vigil, re-reads and re-lives the great events of salvation history in
281 the "today" of her liturgy. But this also demands that catechesis help the faithful to open themselves to this
117 spiritual understanding of the economy of salvation as the Church's liturgy reveals it and enables us to live it.

1096 *Jewish liturgy and Christian liturgy.* A better knowledge of the Jewish people's faith and religious life as professed and lived even now can help our better understanding of certain aspects of Christian liturgy. For both Jews and Christians Sacred Scripture is an essential part of their respective liturgies: in the proclamation of the Word of God, the response to this word, prayer of praise and intercession for the living and the dead, invocation of God's mercy. In its characteristic structure the Liturgy of the

---

15 Cf. *DV* 14–16; *Lk* 24:13–49.   16 Cf. *2 Cor* 3:14–16.   17 Cf. *1 Pet* 3:21.
18 *Jn* 6:32; cf. *1 Cor* 10:1–6.

Word originates in Jewish prayer. The Liturgy of the Hours and other liturgical texts and formularies, as well as those of our most venerable prayers, including the Lord's Prayer, have parallels in Jewish prayer. The Eucharistic Prayers also draw their inspiration from the Jewish tradition. The relationship between Jewish liturgy and Christian liturgy, but also their differences in content, are particularly evident in the great feasts of the liturgical year, such as Passover. Christians and Jews both celebrate the Passover. For Jews, it is the Passover of history, tending toward the future; for Christians, it is the Passover fulfilled in the death and Resurrection of Christ, though always in expectation of its definitive consummation.   *1174* *1352* *840*

1097 In the *liturgy of the New Covenant* every liturgical action, especially the celebration of the Eucharist and the sacraments, is an encounter between Christ and the Church. The liturgical assembly derives its unity from the "communion of the Holy Spirit" who gathers the children of God into the one Body of Christ. This assembly transcends racial, cultural, social—indeed, all human affinities.

1098 The assembly should *prepare* itself to encounter its Lord and to become "a people well disposed." The preparation of hearts is the joint work of the Holy Spirit and the assembly, especially of its ministers. The grace of the Holy Spirit seeks to awaken faith, conversion of heart, and adherence to the Father's will. These dispositions are the precondition both for the reception of other graces conferred in the celebration itself and the fruits of new life which the celebration is intended to produce afterward.   *1430*

The Holy Spirit recalls the mystery of Christ

1099 The Spirit and the Church cooperate to manifest Christ and his work of salvation in the liturgy. Primarily in the Eucharist, and by analogy in the other sacraments, the liturgy is the *memorial* of the mystery of salvation. The Holy Spirit is the Church's living memory.[19]   *91*

---

19 Cf. *Jn* 14:26.

1134 **1100** *The Word of God.* The Holy Spirit first recalls the meaning of the salvation event to the liturgical assembly by giving life to the Word of God, which is proclaimed so that it may be received and lived:

103, 131   In the celebration of the liturgy, Sacred Scripture is extremely important. From it come the lessons that are read and explained in the homily and the psalms that are sung. It is from the Scriptures that the prayers, collects, and hymns draw their inspiration and their force, and that actions and signs derive their meaning.[20]

117 **1101** The Holy Spirit gives a spiritual understanding of the Word of God to those who read or hear it, according to the dispositions of their hearts. By means of the words, actions, and symbols that form the structure of a celebration, the Spirit puts both the faithful and the ministers into a living relationship with Christ, the Word and Image of the Father, so that they can live out the meaning of what they hear, contemplate, and do in the celebration.

1102 "By the saving word of God, faith . . . is nourished in the hearts of believers. By this faith then the congregation of the faithful begins and grows."[21] The proclamation does not stop with a teaching; it elicits the *response of faith* as consent and commitment, directed

143 at the covenant between God and his people. Once again it is the Holy Spirit who gives the grace of faith, strengthens it and makes it grow in the community. The liturgical assembly is first of all a communion in faith.

1362 **1103** *Anamnesis.* The liturgical celebration always refers to God's saving interventions in history. "The economy of Revelation is realized by deeds and words which are intrinsically bound up with each other. . . . [T]he words for their part proclaim the works and bring to light the mystery they contain."[22] In the Liturgy of the Word the Holy Spirit "recalls" to the assembly all that Christ has done for us. In keeping with the nature of liturgical actions and the ritual traditions of the

---

20 *SC* 24.   21 *PO* 4.   22 *DV* 2.

churches, the celebration "makes a remembrance" of the marvelous works of God in an anamnesis which may be more or less developed. The Holy Spirit who thus awakens the memory of the Church then inspires thanksgiving and praise *(doxology).*

The Holy Spirit makes present the mystery of Christ

1104 Christian liturgy not only recalls the events that saved us but actualizes them, makes them present. The Paschal mystery of Christ is celebrated, not repeated. It is the celebrations that are repeated, and in each celebration there is an outpouring of the Holy Spirit that makes the unique mystery present.   *1085*

1105 The *Epiclesis* ("invocation upon") is the intercession in which the priest begs the Father to send the Holy Spirit, the Sanctifier, so that the offerings may become the body and blood of Christ and that the faithful, by receiving them, may themselves become a living offering to God.[23]   *1153*

1106 Together with the anamnesis, the epiclesis is at the heart of each sacramental celebration, most especially of the Eucharist:

> You ask how the bread becomes the Body of Christ, and the wine . . . the Blood of Christ. I shall tell you: the Holy Spirit comes upon them and accomplishes what surpasses every word and thought. . . . Let it be enough for you to understand that it is by the Holy Spirit, just as it was of the Holy Virgin and by the Holy Spirit that the Lord, through and in himself, took flesh.[24]   *1375*

1107 The Holy Spirit's transforming power in the liturgy hastens the coming of the kingdom and the consummation of the mystery of salvation. While we wait in hope he causes us really to anticipate the fullness of communion with the Holy Trinity. Sent by the Father who hears the epiclesis of the Church, the Spirit gives   *2816*

---

23 Cf. *Rom* 12:1.   24 St. John Damascene, *De fide orth.* 4, 13: PG 94, 1145A.

life to those who accept him and is, even now, the "guarantee" of their inheritance.[25]

The communion of the Holy Spirit

1108 In every liturgical action the Holy Spirit is sent in order to bring us into communion with Christ and so to form his Body. The Holy Spirit is like the sap of the Father's vine which bears fruit on its branches.[26] The most intimate cooperation of the Holy Spirit and the Church is achieved in the liturgy. The Spirit, who is the Spirit of communion, abides indefectibly in the Church. For this reason the Church is the great sacrament of divine communion which gathers God's scattered children together. Communion with the Holy Trinity and fraternal communion are inseparably the fruit of the Spirit in the liturgy.[27]

1109 The epiclesis is also a prayer for the full effect of the assembly's communion with the mystery of Christ. "The grace of the Lord Jesus Christ and the love of God and the fellowship of the Holy Spirit"[28] have to remain with us always and bear fruit beyond the Eucharistic celebration. The Church therefore asks the Father to send the Holy Spirit to make the lives of the faithful a living sacrifice to God by their spiritual transformation into the image of Christ, by concern for the Church's unity, and by taking part in her mission through the witness and service of charity.

IN BRIEF

1110 In the liturgy of the Church, God the Father is blessed and adored as the source of all the blessings of creation and salvation with which he has blessed us in his Son, in order to give us the Spirit of filial adoption.

1111 Christ's work in the liturgy is sacramental: because his mystery of salvation is made present there by the power of his Holy Spirit; because his

---

25 Cf. *Eph* 1:14; *2 Cor* 1:22.   26 Cf. *Jn* 15:1–17; *Gal* 5:22.   27 Cf. *1 Jn* 1:3–7.
28 *2 Cor* 13:13.

Body, which is the Church, is like a sacrament (sign and instrument) in which the Holy Spirit dispenses the mystery of salvation; and because through her liturgical actions the pilgrim Church already participates, as by a foretaste, in the heavenly liturgy.

1112 The mission of the Holy Spirit in the liturgy of the Church is to prepare the assembly to encounter Christ; to recall and manifest Christ to the faith of the assembly; to make the saving work of Christ present and active by his transforming power; and to make the gift of communion bear fruit in the Church.

ARTICLE 2
THE PASCHAL MYSTERY IN THE CHURCH'S SACRAMENTS

1113 The whole liturgical life of the Church revolves *1210* around the Eucharistic sacrifice and the sacraments.[29] There are seven sacraments in the Church: Baptism, Confirmation or Chrismation, Eucharist, Penance, Anointing of the Sick, Holy Orders, and Matrimony.[30] This article will discuss what is common to the Church's seven sacraments from a doctrinal point of view. What is common to them in terms of their celebration will be presented in the second chapter, and what is distinctive about each will be the topic of the *Section Two*.

I.   THE SACRAMENTS OF CHRIST
1114 "Adhering to the teaching of the Holy Scriptures, to the apostolic traditions, and to the consensus ... of the Fathers," we profess that "the sacraments of the new law were ... all instituted by Jesus Christ our Lord."[31]

1115 Jesus' words and actions during his hidden life

---

29 Cf. *SC* 6.   30 Cf. Council of Lyons II (1274) DS 860; Council of Florence (1439): DS 1310; Council of Trent (1547): DS 1601.   31 Council of Trent (1547): DS 1600–1601.

and public ministry were already salvific, for they anticipated the power of his Paschal mystery. They announced and prepared what he was going to give the
512–560 Church when all was accomplished. The mysteries of
Christ's life are the foundations of what he would
henceforth dispense in the sacraments, through the ministers of his Church, for "what was visible in our Savior
has passed over into his mysteries."[32]

1504 **1116** Sacraments are "powers that come forth" from
774 the Body of Christ,[33] which is ever-living and life-giving.
They are actions of the Holy Spirit at work in his Body,
the Church. They are "the masterworks of God" in the
new and everlasting covenant.

II.   THE SACRAMENTS OF THE CHURCH

120 **1117** As she has done for the canon of Sacred Scripture and for the doctrine of the faith, the Church, by the
power of the Spirit who guides her "into all truth," has
gradually recognized this treasure received from Christ
and, as the faithful steward of God's mysteries, has
determined its "dispensation."[34] Thus the Church has
discerned over the centuries that among liturgical celebrations there are seven that are, in the strict sense
of the term, sacraments instituted by the Lord.

1118 The sacraments are "of the Church" in the double sense that they are "by her" and "for her." They are
"by the Church," for she is the sacrament of Christ's action at work in her through the mission of the Holy
1396 Spirit. They are "for the Church" in the sense that "the
sacraments make the Church,"[35] since they manifest and
communicate to men, above all in the Eucharist, the
mystery of communion with the God who is love, One
in three persons.

792 **1119** Forming "as it were, one mystical person" with
Christ the head, the Church acts in the sacraments as
"an organically structured priestly community."[36]

---

32 St. Leo the Great, *Sermo.* 74, 2: PL 54, 398.   33 Cf. *Lk* 5:17; 6:19; 8:46.
34 *Jn* 16:13; cf. *Mt* 13:52; *1 Cor* 4:1.   35 St. Augustine, *De civ. Dei*, 22, 17: PL
41, 779; cf. St. Thomas Aquinas, *STh* III, 64, 2 *ad* 3.   36 *LG* 11; cf. Pius XII,
Mystici Corporis (1943).

Through Baptism and Confirmation the priestly people is enabled to celebrate the liturgy, while those of the faithful "who have received Holy Orders, are appointed to nourish the Church with the word and grace of God in the name of Christ."[37]

1120 The ordained ministry or *ministerial* priesthood is at the service of the baptismal priesthood.[38] The ordained priesthood guarantees that it really is Christ who acts in the sacraments through the Holy Spirit for the Church. The saving mission entrusted by the Father to his incarnate Son was committed to the apostles and through them to their successors: they receive the Spirit of Jesus to act in his name and in his person.[39] The ordained minister is the sacramental bond that ties the liturgical action to what the apostles said and did and, through them, to the words and actions of Christ, the source and foundation of the sacraments.

1547

1121 The three sacraments of Baptism, Confirmation, and Holy Orders confer, in addition to grace, a sacramental *character* or "seal" by which the Christian shares in Christ's priesthood and is made a member of the Church according to different states and functions. This configuration to Christ and to the Church, brought about by the Spirit, is indelible;[40] it remains for ever in the Christian as a positive disposition for grace, a promise and guarantee of divine protection, and as a vocation to divine worship and to the service of the Church. Therefore these sacraments can never be repeated.

1272, 1304
1582

III. THE SACRAMENTS OF FAITH

1122 Christ sent his apostles so that "repentance and forgiveness of sins should be preached in his name to all nations."[41] "Go therefore and make disciples of all nations, baptizing them in the name of the Father and of the Son and of the Holy Spirit."[42] The mission to baptize, and so the sacramental mission, is implied in the

---

37 *LG* 11 § 2.   38 Cf. *LG* 10 § 2.   39 Cf. *Jn* 20:21–23; *Lk* 24:47; *Mt* 28:18–20.
40 Cf. Council of Trent (1547): DS 1609.   41 *Lk* 24:47.   42 *Mt* 28:19.

849 mission to evangelize, because the sacrament is pre-
1236 pared for by *the word of God and by the faith* which is
     assent to this word:

> The People of God is formed into one in the first
> place by the Word of the living God.... The
> preaching of the Word is required for the sacra-
> mental ministry itself, since the sacraments are
> sacraments of faith, drawing their origin and nour-
> ishment from the Word.[43]

1123 "The purpose of the sacraments is to sanctify
men, to build up the Body of Christ and, finally, to give
worship to God. Because they are signs they also instruct. They not only presuppose faith, but by words
1154 and objects they also nourish, strengthen, and express
it. That is why they are called 'sacraments *of faith*.' "[44]

166 **1124** The Church's faith precedes the faith of the believer who is invited to adhere to it. When the Church
celebrates the sacraments, she confesses the faith received from the apostles—whence the ancient saying:
1327 *lex orandi, lex credendi* (or: *legem credendi lex statuat
supplicandi,* according to Prosper of Aquitaine [5th
78   cent.]).[45] The law of prayer is the law of faith: the
Church believes as she prays. Liturgy is a constitutive element of the holy and living Tradition.[46]

1205 **1125** For this reason no sacramental rite may be modified or manipulated at the will of the minister or the
community. Even the supreme authority in the Church
may not change the liturgy arbitrarily, but only in the
obedience of faith and with religious respect for the
mystery of the liturgy.

1126 Likewise, since the sacraments express and develop the communion of faith in the Church, the *lex
815 orandi* is one of the essential criteria of the dialogue that
seeks to restore the unity of Christians.[47]

---

43 *PO* 4 §§ 1, 2.   44 *SC* 59.   45 *Ep.* 8.   46 Cf. *DV* 8.   47 Cf. *UR* 2; 15.

IV. THE SACRAMENTS OF SALVATION

1127 Celebrated worthily in faith, the sacraments confer the grace that they signify.[48] They are *efficacious* because in them Christ himself is at work: it is he who baptizes, he who acts in his sacraments in order to communicate the grace that each sacrament signifies. The Father always hears the prayer of his Son's Church which, in the epiclesis of each sacrament, expresses her faith in the power of the Spirit. As fire transforms into itself everything it touches, so the Holy Spirit transforms into the divine life whatever is subjected to his power.

1084

1105

696

1128 This is the meaning of the Church's affirmation[49] that the sacraments act *ex opere operato* (literally: "by the very fact of the action's being performed"), i.e., by virtue of the saving work of Christ, accomplished once for all. It follows that "the sacrament is not wrought by the righteousness of either the celebrant or the recipient, but by the power of God."[50] From the moment that a sacrament is celebrated in accordance with the intention of the Church, the power of Christ and his Spirit acts in and through it, independently of the personal holiness of the minister. Nevertheless, the fruits of the sacraments also depend on the disposition of the one who receives them.

1584

1129 The Church affirms that for believers the sacraments of the New Covenant are *necessary for salvation*.[51] "Sacramental grace" is the grace of the Holy Spirit, given by Christ and proper to each sacrament. The Spirit heals and transforms those who receive him by conforming them to the Son of God. The fruit of the sacramental life is that the Spirit of adoption makes the faithful partakers in the divine nature[52] by uniting them in a living union with the only Son, the Savior.

1257

2003

460

---

48 Cf. Council of Trent (1547): DS 1605; DS 1606.   49 Cf. Council of Trent (1547): DS 1608.   50 St. Thomas Aquinas, *STh* III, 68, 8.   51 Cf. Council of Trent (1547): DS 1604.   52 Cf. *2 Pet* 1:4.

V.   THE SACRAMENTS OF ETERNAL LIFE

1130 The Church celebrates the mystery of her Lord "until he comes," when God will be "everything to everyone."[53] Since the apostolic age the liturgy has been drawn toward its goal by the Spirit's groaning in the Church: *Marana tha!*[54] The liturgy thus shares in Jesus' desire: "I have earnestly desired to eat this Passover with you . . . until it is fulfilled in the kingdom of God."[55] In the sacraments of Christ the Church already receives the guarantee of her inheritance and even now shares in everlasting life, while "awaiting our blessed hope, the appearing of the glory of our great God and Savior Christ Jesus."[56] The "Spirit and the Bride say, 'Come . . . Come, Lord Jesus!' "[57]

> St. Thomas sums up the various aspects of sacramental signs: "Therefore a sacrament is a sign that commemorates what precedes it—Christ's Passion; demonstrates what is accomplished in us through Christ's Passion—grace; and prefigures what that Passion pledges to us—future glory."[58]

IN BRIEF

1131 The sacraments are efficacious signs of grace, instituted by Christ and entrusted to the Church, by which divine life is dispensed to us. The visible rites by which the sacraments are celebrated signify and make present the graces proper to each sacrament. They bear fruit in those who receive them with the required dispositions.

1132 The Church celebrates the sacraments as a priestly community structured by the baptismal priesthood and the priesthood of ordained ministers.

1133 The Holy Spirit prepares the faithful for the sacraments by the Word of God and the faith which welcomes that word in well-disposed hearts. Thus the sacraments strengthen faith and express it.

---

53 *1 Cor* 11:26; 15:28.   54 *1 Cor* 16:22.   55 *Lk* 22:15.   56 *Titus* 2:13.
57 *Rev* 22:17, 20.   58 St. Thomas Aquinas, *STh* III, 60, 3.

1134 The fruit of sacramental life is both personal and ecclesial. For every one of the faithful on the one hand, this fruit is life for God in Christ Jesus; for the Church, on the other, it is an increase in charity and in her mission of witness.

CHAPTER TWO
THE SACRAMENTAL CELEBRATION OF THE PASCHAL MYSTERY

1135 The catechesis of the liturgy entails first of all an understanding of the sacramental economy (Chapter One). In this light, the innovation of its *celebration* is revealed. This chapter will therefore treat of the celebration of the sacraments of the Church. It will consider that which, through the diversity of liturgical traditions, is common to the celebration of the seven sacraments. What is proper to each will be treated later. This fundamental catechesis on the sacramental celebrations responds to the first questions posed by the faithful regarding this subject:

—Who celebrates the liturgy?

—How is the liturgy celebrated?

—When is the liturgy celebrated?

—Where is the liturgy celebrated?

ARTICLE 1
CELEBRATING THE CHURCH'S LITURGY

I. WHO CELEBRATES?

1136 Liturgy is an "action" of the *whole Christ (Christus totus)*. Those who even now celebrate it without signs are already in the heavenly liturgy, where celebration is wholly communion and feast.

795
1090

2642 ## The celebrants of the heavenly liturgy

1137 The book of *Revelation* of St. John, read in the Church's liturgy, first reveals to us, "A throne stood in heaven, with one seated on the throne": "the Lord God."[1] It then shows the Lamb, "standing, as though it had been slain": Christ crucified and risen, the one high priest of the true sanctuary, the same one "who offers
662 and is offered, who gives and is given."[2] Finally it presents "the river of the water of life . . . flowing from the throne of God and of the Lamb," one of the most beautiful symbols of the Holy Spirit.[3]

1138 "Recapitulated in Christ," these are the ones who take part in the service of the praise of God and the
335 fulfillment of his plan: the heavenly powers, all creation (the four living beings), the servants of the Old and New Covenants (the twenty-four elders), the new People of God (the one hundred and forty-four thousand),[4] especially the martyrs "slain for the word of God," and the
1370 all-holy Mother of God (the Woman), the Bride of the Lamb,[5] and finally "a great multitude which no one could number, from every nation, from all tribes, and peoples and tongues."[6]

1139 It is in this eternal liturgy that the Spirit and the Church enable us to participate whenever we celebrate the mystery of salvation in the sacraments.

The celebrants of the sacramental liturgy

752, 1348 **1140** It is the whole *community*, the Body of Christ united with its Head, that celebrates. "Liturgical services are not private functions but are celebrations of the Church which is 'the sacrament of unity,' namely, the holy people united and organized under the authority of the bishops. Therefore, liturgical services pertain to the whole Body of the Church. They manifest it, and have effects upon it. But they touch individual members of the Church in different ways, depending on their or-

---

1 *Rev* 4:2, 8; *Isa* 6:1; cf. *Ezek* 1:26–28.   **2** *Rev* 5:6; *Liturgy of St. John Chrysostom*, Anaphora; cf. *Jn* 1:29; *Heb* 4:14–15; 10:19–21.   **3** *Rev* 22:1; cf. 21:6; *Jn* 4:10–14.   **4** Cf. *Rev* 4–5; 7:1–8; 14:1; *Isa* 6:2–3.   **5** *Rev* 6:9–11; *Rev* 21:9; cf. 12.   **6** *Rev* 7:9.

ders, their role in the liturgical services, and their actual participation in them."[7] For this reason, "rites which are meant to be celebrated in common, with the faithful   *1372* present and actively participating, should as far as possible be celebrated in that way rather than by an individual and quasi-privately."[8]

1141 The celebrating assembly is the community of the baptized who, "by regeneration and the anointing of the Holy Spirit, are consecrated to be a spiritual house and a holy priesthood, that . . . they may offer spiritual sacrifices."[9] This "common priesthood" is that of Christ   *1120* the sole priest, in which all his members participate:[10]

> Mother Church earnestly desires that all the faithful should be led to that full, conscious, and active participation in liturgical celebrations which is demanded by the very nature of the liturgy, and to which the Christian people, "a chosen race, a royal priesthood, a holy nation, a redeemed people," have a right and an obligation by reason of their Baptism.[11]

1268

1142 But "the members do not all have the same function."[12] Certain members are called by God, in and through the Church, to a special service of the community. These servants are chosen and consecrated by the sacrament of Holy Orders, by which the Holy Spirit enables them to act in the person of Christ the head, for the service of all the members of the Church.[13] The ordained minister is, as it were, an "icon" of Christ the   *1549* priest. Since it is in the Eucharist that the sacrament of the Church is made fully visible, it is in his presiding at the Eucharist that the bishop's ministry is most evident, as well as, in communion with him, the ministry of   *1561* priests and deacons.

1143 For the purpose of assisting the work of the common priesthood of the faithful, other *particular ministries* also exist, not consecrated by the sacrament of Holy Orders; their functions are determined by the   *903*

---

7 *SC* 26.   8 *SC* 27.   9 *LG* 10; cf. *1 Pet* 2:4–5.   10 Cf. *LG* 10; 34; *PO* 2.
11 *SC* 14; cf. *1 Pet* 2:9; 2:4–5.   12 *Rom* 12:4.   13 Cf. *PO* 2; 15.

bishops, in accord with liturgical traditions and pastoral needs. "Servers, readers, commentators, and members 1672 of the choir also exercise a genuine liturgical function."[14]

1144 In the celebration of the sacraments it is thus the whole assembly that is *leitourgos*, each according to his function, but in the "unity of the Spirit" who acts in all. "In liturgical celebrations each person, minister or layman, who has an office to perform, should carry out *all* and *only* those parts which pertain to his office by the nature of the rite and the norms of the liturgy."[15]

II.   HOW IS THE LITURGY CELEBRATED?

1333-1340 **Signs and symbols**

53 **1145** A sacramental celebration is woven from signs and symbols. In keeping with the divine pedagogy of salvation, their meaning is rooted in the work of creation and in human culture, specified by the events of the Old Covenant and fully revealed in the person and work of Christ.

1146 *Signs of the human world.* In human life, signs and symbols occupy an important place. As a being at once body and spirit, man expresses and perceives spir-362, 2702 itual realities through physical signs and symbols. As a social being, man needs signs and symbols to communicate with others, through language, gestures, and actions. The same holds true for his relationship with 1879 God.

299 **1147** God speaks to man through the visible creation. The material cosmos is so presented to man's intelligence that he can read there traces of its Creator.[16] Light and darkness, wind and fire, water and earth, the tree and its fruit speak of God and symbolize both his greatness and his nearness.

1148 Inasmuch as they are creatures, these perceptible realities can become means of expressing the action of

---

14 *SC* 29.   15 *SC* 28.   16 Cf. *Wis* 13:1; *Rom* 1:19 f.; *Acts* 14:17.

God who sanctifies men, and the action of men who offer worship to God. The same is true of signs and symbols taken from the social life of man: washing and anointing, breaking bread and sharing the cup can express the sanctifying presence of God and man's gratitude toward his Creator.

1149 The great religions of mankind witness, often 843 impressively, to this cosmic and symbolic meaning of religious rites. The liturgy of the Church presupposes, integrates and sanctifies elements from creation and human culture, conferring on them the dignity of signs of grace, of the new creation in Jesus Christ.

1150 *Signs of the covenant.* The Chosen People re- 1334 ceived from God distinctive signs and symbols that marked its liturgical life. These are no longer solely celebrations of cosmic cycles and social gestures, but signs of the covenant, symbols of God's mighty deeds for his people. Among these liturgical signs from the Old Covenant are circumcision, anointing and consecration of kings and priests, laying on of hands, sacrifices, and above all the Passover. The Church sees in these signs a prefiguring of the sacraments of the New Covenant.

1151 *Signs taken up by Christ.* In his preaching the 1335 Lord Jesus often makes use of the signs of creation to make known the mysteries of the Kingdom of God.[17] He performs healings and illustrates his preaching with physical signs or symbolic gestures.[18] He gives new meaning to the deeds and signs of the Old Covenant, above all to the Exodus and the Passover,[19] for he himself is the meaning of all these signs.

1152 *Sacramental signs.* Since Pentecost, it is through the sacramental signs of his Church that the Holy Spirit carries on the work of sanctification. The sacraments of the Church do not abolish but purify and integrate all the richness of the signs and symbols of the cosmos and of social life. Further, they fulfill the types and figures of the Old Covenant, signify and make actively present the

---

17 Cf. *Lk* 8:10.   18 Cf. *Jn* 9:6; *Mk* 7:33 ff.; 8:22 ff.   19 Cf. *Lk* 9:31; 22:7–20.

salvation wrought by Christ, and prefigure and anticipate the glory of heaven.

Words and actions

1153 A sacramental celebration is a meeting of God's
children with their Father, in Christ and the Holy Spirit;
53   this meeting takes the form of a dialogue, through actions and words. Admittedly, the symbolic actions are
already a language, but the Word of God and the response of faith have to accompany and give life to them,
so that the seed of the Kingdom can bear its fruit in
good soil. The liturgical actions signify what the Word
of God expresses: both his free initiative and his people's response of faith.

1100   **1154** The *liturgy of the Word* is an integral part of
sacramental celebrations. To nourish the faith of believers, the signs which accompany the Word of God should
103   be emphasized: the book of the Word (a lectionary or a
book of the Gospels), its veneration (procession, incense, candles), the place of its proclamation (lectern or
ambo), its audible and intelligible reading, the minister's
homily which extends its proclamation, and the responses of the assembly (acclamations, meditation
psalms, litanies, and profession of faith).

1155 The liturgical word and action are inseparable
1127   both insofar as they are signs and instruction and insofar as they accomplish what they signify. When the Holy
Spirit awakens faith, he not only gives an understanding
of the Word of God, but through the sacraments also
makes present the "wonders" of God which it proclaims. The Spirit makes present and communicates the
Father's work, fulfilled by the beloved Son.

Singing and music

1156 "The musical tradition of the universal Church
is a treasure of inestimable value, greater even than that
of any other art. The main reason for this pre-eminence
is that, as a combination of sacred music and words, it
forms a necessary or integral part of solemn liturgy."[20]

---

20 *SC* 112.

The composition and singing of inspired psalms, often accompanied by musical instruments, were already closely linked to the liturgical celebrations of the Old Covenant. The Church continues and develops this tradition: "Address ... one another in psalms and hymns and spiritual songs, singing and making melody to the Lord with all your heart." "He who sings prays twice."[21]

1157 Song and music fulfill their function as signs in a manner all the more significant when they are "more closely connected ... with the liturgical action,"[22] according to three principal criteria: beauty expressive of prayer, the unanimous participation of the assembly at the designated moments, and the solemn character of the celebration. In this way they participate in the purpose of the liturgical words and actions: the glory of God and the sanctification of the faithful:[23]

> How I wept, deeply moved by your hymns, songs, and the voices that echoed through your Church! What emotion I experienced in them! Those sounds flowed into my ears, distilling the truth in my heart. A feeling of devotion surged within me, and tears streamed down my face—tears that did me good.[24]

1158 The harmony of signs (song, music, words, and actions) is all the more expressive and fruitful when expressed in the *cultural richness* of the People of God who celebrate.[25] Hence "religious singing by the faithful is to be intelligently fostered so that in devotions and sacred exercises as well as in liturgical services," in conformity with the Church's norms, "the voices of the faithful may be heard." But "the texts intended to be sung must always be in conformity with Catholic doctrine. Indeed they should be drawn chiefly from the Sacred Scripture and from liturgical sources."[26]

*(margin references: 2502, 1201, 1674)*

---

21 *Eph* 5:19; St. Augustine, *En. in Ps.* 72, 1: PL 36, 914; cf. *Col* 3:16.   22 *SC* 112 § 3.   23 Cf. *SC* 112.   24 St. Augustine, *Conf.* 9, 6, 14: PL 32, 769–770. 25 Cf. *SC* 119.   26 *SC* 118; 121.

476-477 **Holy images**

2129-2132 **1159** The sacred image, the liturgical icon, principally represents *Christ*. It cannot represent the invisible and incomprehensible God, but the incarnation of the Son of God has ushered in a new "economy" of images:

> Previously God, who has neither a body nor a face, absolutely could not be represented by an image. But now that he has made himself visible in the flesh and has lived with men, I can make an image of what I have seen of God . . . and contemplate the glory of the Lord, his face unveiled.[27]

1160 Christian iconography expresses in images the same Gospel message that Scripture communicates by words. Image and word illuminate each other:

> We declare that we preserve intact all the written and unwritten traditions of the Church which have been entrusted to us. One of these traditions consists in the production of representational artwork, which accords with the history of the preaching of the Gospel. For it confirms that the incarnation of the Word of God was real and not imaginary, and to our benefit as well, for realities that illustrate each other undoubtedly reflect each other's meaning.[28]

1161 All the signs in the liturgical celebrations are related to Christ: as are sacred images of the holy Mother of God and of the saints as well. They truly signify Christ, who is glorified in them. They make manifest the "cloud of witnesses"[29] who continue to participate in the salvation of the world and to whom we are united, above all in sacramental celebrations. Through their icons, it is man "in the image of God," finally transfigured "into his likeness,"[30] who is revealed to our faith. So too are the angels, who also are recapitulated in Christ:

> Following the divinely inspired teaching of our holy Fathers and the tradition of the Catholic Church (for we know that this tradition comes from the

---

27 St. John Damascene, *De imag.* 1, 16: PG 96:1245–1248.   28 Council of Nicaea II (787): COD 111.   29 *Heb* 12:1.   30 Cf. *Rom* 8:29; *1 Jn* 3:2.

Holy Spirit who dwells in her) we rightly define with full certainty and correctness that, like the figure of the precious and life-giving cross, venerable and holy images of our Lord and God and Savior, Jesus Christ, our inviolate Lady, the holy Mother of God, and the venerated angels, all the saints and the just, whether painted or made of mosaic or another suitable material, are to be exhibited in the holy churches of God, on sacred vessels and vestments, walls and panels, in houses and on streets.[31]

1162 "The beauty of the images moves me to contemplation, as a meadow delights the eyes and subtly infuses the soul with the glory of God."[32] Similarly, the contemplation of sacred icons, united with meditation on the Word of God and the singing of liturgical hymns, enters into the harmony of the signs of celebration so that the mystery celebrated is imprinted in the heart's memory and is then expressed in the new life of the faithful. 2502

III.   When Is the Liturgy Celebrated?

Liturgical seasons

1163 "Holy Mother Church believes that she should celebrate the saving work of her divine Spouse in a sacred commemoration on certain days throughout the course of the year. Once each week, on the day which she has called the Lord's Day, she keeps the memory of the Lord's resurrection. She also celebrates it once every year, together with his blessed Passion, at Easter, that most solemn of all feasts. In the course of the year, moreover, she unfolds the whole mystery of Christ. . . . 512 Thus recalling the mysteries of the redemption, she opens up to the faithful the riches of her Lord's powers and merits, so that these are in some way made present in every age; the faithful lay hold of them and are filled with saving grace."[33]

1164 From the time of the Mosaic law, the People of God have observed fixed feasts, beginning with

---

31 Council of Nicaea II: DS 600.   32 St. John Damascene, *De imag.* 1, 27: PG 94, 1268A, B.   33 SC 102.

Passover, to commemorate the astonishing actions of the Savior God, to give him thanks for them, to perpetuate their remembrance, and to teach new generations to conform their conduct to them. In the age of the Church, between the Passover of Christ already accomplished once for all, and its consummation in the kingdom of God, the liturgy celebrated on fixed days bears the imprint of the newness of the mystery of Christ.

2659-2836 **1165** When the Church celebrates the mystery of Christ, there is a word that marks her prayer: "Today!"—a word echoing the prayer her Lord taught her and the call of the Holy Spirit.[34] This "today" of the living God which man is called to enter is "the hour" of Jesus' Passover, which reaches across and underlies all
1085 history:

> Life extends over all beings and fills them with unlimited light; the Orient of orients pervades the universe, and he who was "before the daystar" and before the heavenly bodies, immortal and vast, the great Christ, shines over all beings more brightly than the sun. Therefore a day of long, eternal light is ushered in for us who believe in him, a day which is never blotted out: the mystical Passover.[35]

2174-2188 **The Lord's day**

1166 "By a tradition handed down from the apostles which took its origin from the very day of Christ's Resurrection, the Church celebrates the Paschal mystery every seventh day, which day is appropriately called the
1343 Lord's Day or Sunday."[36] The day of Christ's Resurrection is both the first day of the week, the memorial of the first day of creation, and the "eighth day," on which Christ after his "rest" on the great sabbath inaugurates the "day that the Lord has made," the "day that knows no evening."[37] The Lord's Supper is its center, for there the whole community of the faithful encounters the risen Lord who invites them to his banquet:[38]

---

34 Cf. *Mt* 6:11; *Heb* 3:7–4:11; *Ps* 95:7.   35 St. Hippolytus, *De pasch.* 1–2: SCh 27, 117.   36 *SC* 106.   37 Byzantine liturgy.   38 Cf. *Jn* 21:12; *Lk* 24:30.

The Lord's day, the day of Resurrection, the day of Christians, is our day. It is called the Lord's day because on it the Lord rose victorious to the Father. If pagans call it the "day of the sun," we willingly agree, for today the light of the world is raised, today is revealed the sun of justice with healing in his rays.[39]

1167 Sunday is the pre-eminent day for the liturgical assembly, when the faithful gather "to listen to the word of God and take part in the Eucharist, thus calling to mind the Passion, Resurrection, and glory of the Lord Jesus, and giving thanks to God who 'has begotten them again, by the resurrection of Jesus Christ from the dead' unto a living hope":[40]

When we ponder, O Christ, the marvels accomplished on this day, the Sunday of your holy resurrection, we say: "Blessed is Sunday, for on it began creation . . . the world's salvation . . . the renewal of the human race. . . . On Sunday heaven and earth rejoiced and the whole universe was filled with light. Blessed is Sunday, for on it were opened the gates of paradise so that Adam and all the exiles might enter it without fear.[41]

The liturgical year

1168 Beginning with the Easter Triduum as its source of light, the new age of the Resurrection fills the whole liturgical year with its brilliance. Gradually, on either side of this source, the year is transfigured by the liturgy. It really is a "year of the Lord's favor."[42] The economy of salvation is at work within the framework of time, but since its fulfillment in the Passover of Jesus and the outpouring of the Holy Spirit, the culmination of history is anticipated "as a foretaste," and the kingdom of God enters into our time. 2698

1169 Therefore *Easter* is not simply one feast among others, but the "Feast of feasts," the "Solemnity of solemnities," just as the Eucharist is the "Sacrament of 1330

39 St. Jerome, *Pasch.*: CCL 78, 550.   **40** SC 106.   **41** Fanqîth, *The Syriac Office of Antioch,* vol. VI, first part of Summer, 193 B.   **42** *Lk* 4:19.

sacraments" (the Great Sacrament). St. Athanasius calls Easter "the Great Sunday"[43] and the Eastern Churches call Holy Week "the Great Week." The mystery of the
560 Resurrection, in which Christ crushed death, permeates with its powerful energy our old time, until all is subjected to him.

1170 At the Council of Nicaea in 325, all the Churches agreed that Easter, the Christian Passover, should be celebrated on the Sunday following the first full moon (14 Nisan) after the vernal equinox. The reform of the Western calendar, called "Gregorian" after Pope Gregory XIII (1582), caused a discrepancy of several days with the Eastern calendar. Today, the Western and Eastern Churches are seeking an agreement in order once again to celebrate the day of the Lord's Resurrection on a common date.

1171 In the liturgical year the various aspects of the one Paschal mystery unfold. This is also the case with the cycle of feasts surrounding the mystery of the incarnation (Annunciation, Christmas, Epiphany). They
524 commemorate the beginning of our salvation and communicate to us the first fruits of the Paschal mystery.

The sanctoral in the liturgical year
1172 "In celebrating this annual cycle of the mysteries of Christ, Holy Church honors the Blessed Mary,
971 Mother of God, with a special love. She is inseparably
2030 linked with the saving work of her Son. In her the Church admires and exalts the most excellent fruit of redemption and joyfully contemplates, as in a faultless image, that which she herself desires and hopes wholly to be."[44]

957 **1173** When the Church keeps the memorials of martyrs and other saints during the annual cycle, she proclaims the Paschal mystery in those "who have suffered and have been glorified with Christ. She proposes them to the faithful as examples who draw all men to the Father through Christ, and through their merits she begs for God's favors."[45]

---

43 St. Athanasius *(ad 329) ep. fest.* 1: PG 24, 1366.   44 *SC* 103.   45 *SC* 104; cf. *SC* 108, 111.

The Liturgy of the Hours

1174 The mystery of Christ, his Incarnation and Passover, which we celebrate in the Eucharist especially at the Sunday assembly, permeates and transfigures the time of each day, through the celebration of the Liturgy of the Hours, "the divine office."[46] This celebration, faithful to the apostolic exhortations to "pray constantly," is "so devised that the whole course of the day and night is made holy by the praise of God."[47] In this "public prayer of the Church,"[48] the faithful (clergy, religious, and lay people) exercise the royal priesthood of the baptized. Celebrated in "the form approved" by the Church, the Liturgy of the Hours "is truly the voice of the Bride herself addressed to her Bridegroom. It is the very prayer which Christ himself together with his Body addresses to the Father."[49]

2698

1175 The Liturgy of the Hours is intended to become the prayer of the whole People of God. In it Christ himself "continues his priestly work through his Church."[50] His members participate according to their own place in the Church and the circumstances of their lives: priests devoted to the pastoral ministry, because they are called to remain diligent in prayer and the service of the word; religious, by the charism of their consecrated lives; all the faithful as much as possible: "Pastors of souls should see to it that the principal hours, especially Vespers, are celebrated in common in church on Sundays and on the more solemn feasts. The laity, too, are encouraged to recite the divine office, either with the priests, or among themselves, or even individually."[51]

1176 The celebration of the Liturgy of the Hours demands not only harmonizing the voice with the praying heart, but also a deeper "understanding of the liturgy and of the Bible, especially of the Psalms."[52]

2700

1177 The hymns and litanies of the Liturgy of the Hours integrate the prayer of the psalms into the age of the Church, expressing the symbolism of the time of day, the liturgical season, or the feast being celebrated. Moreover, the reading from the Word of God at each

2586

---

46 Cf. *SC*, ch. IV, 83–101.   47 *SC* 84; *1 Thess* 5:17; *Eph* 6:18.   48 *SC* 98.
49 *SC* 84.   50 *SC* 83.   51 *SC* 100; cf. 86; 96; 98; *PO* 5.   52 *SC* 90.

Hour (with the subsequent responses or *troparia)* and readings from the Fathers and spiritual masters at certain Hours, reveal more deeply the meaning of the mystery being celebrated, assist in understanding the psalms, and prepare for silent prayer. The *lectio divina,* where the Word of God is so read and meditated that it becomes prayer, is thus rooted in the liturgical celebration.

1178 The Liturgy of the Hours, which is like an extension of the Eucharistic celebration, does not exclude but rather in a complementary way calls forth the various devotions of the People of God, especially adora-

1378 tion and worship of the Blessed Sacrament.

IV.   WHERE IS THE LITURGY CELEBRATED?

1179 The worship "in Spirit and in truth"[53] of the New Covenant is not tied exclusively to any one place. The whole earth is sacred and entrusted to the children of men. What matters above all is that, when the faithful assemble in the same place, they are the "living stones," gathered to be "built into a spiritual house."[54]

586 For the Body of the risen Christ is the spiritual temple from which the source of living water springs forth: incorporated into Christ by the Holy Spirit, "we are the temple of the living God."[55]

2106 **1180** When the exercise of religious liberty is not thwarted,[56] Christians construct buildings for divine worship. These visible churches are not simply gathering places but signify and make visible the Church living in this place, the dwelling of God with men reconciled and united in Christ.

2691 **1181** A church, "a house of prayer in which the Eucharist is celebrated and reserved, where the faithful assemble, and where is worshipped the presence of the Son of God our Savior, offered for us on the sacrificial altar for the help and consolation of the faithful—this house ought to be in good taste and a worthy place for

---

53 *Jn* 4:24.   54 1 *Pet* 2:4-5.   55 2 *Cor* 6:16.   56 Cf. *DH* 4.

prayer and sacred ceremonial."[57] In this "house of God" the truth and the harmony of the signs that make it up should show Christ to be present and active in this place.[58]

1182 The *altar* of the New Covenant is the Lord's   617, 1383
Cross,[59] from which the sacraments of the Paschal mystery flow. On the altar, which is the center of the church, the sacrifice of the Cross is made present under sacramental signs. The altar is also the table of the Lord, to which the People of God are invited.[60] In certain Eastern liturgies, the altar is also the symbol of the tomb (Christ truly died and is truly risen).

1183 The *tabernacle* is to be situated "in churches in a   1379
most worthy place with the greatest honor."[61] The dignity,   2120
placing, and security of the Eucharistic tabernacle should foster adoration before the Lord really present in the Blessed Sacrament of the altar.[62]

    The *sacred chrism (myron),* used in anointings as   1241
the sacramental sign of the seal of the gift of the Holy Spirit, is traditionally reserved and venerated in a secure place in the sanctuary. The oil of catechumens and the oil of the sick may also be placed there.

1184 The *chair (cathedra)* of the bishop or the priest "should express his office of presiding over the assembly and of directing prayer."[63]

    The *lectern (ambo):* "The dignity of the Word of   103
God requires the church to have a suitable place for an- nouncing his message so that the attention of the people may be easily directed to that place during the liturgy of the Word."[64]

1185 The gathering of the People of God begins with Baptism; a church must have a place for the celebration of *Baptism* (baptistry) and for fostering remembrance of the baptismal promises (holy water font).

    The renewal of the baptismal life requires *penance.* A church, then, must lend itself to the expression of repen- tance and the reception of forgiveness, which requires an appropriate place to receive penitents.

    A church must also be a space that invites us to the   2717
recollection and silent prayer that extend and internalize the great prayer of the Eucharist.

---

57 *PO* 5; cf. *SC* 122–127.   58 Cf. *SC* 7.   59 Cf. *Heb* 13:10.   60 Cf. GIRM 259.
61 Paul VI, *Mysterium Fidei:* AAS (1965) 771.   62 Cf. *SC* 128.   63 GIRM 271.
64 GIRM 272.

1186 Finally, the church has an eschatological significance. To enter into the house of God, we must cross a
1130 *threshold,* which symbolizes passing from the world wounded by sin to the world of the new Life to which all men are called. The visible church is a symbol of the Father's house toward which the People of God is journeying and where the Father "will wipe every tear from their eyes."[65] Also for this reason, the Church is the house of *all* God's children, open and welcoming.

IN BRIEF

1187 The liturgy is the work of the whole Christ, head and body. Our high priest celebrates it unceasingly in the heavenly liturgy, with the holy Mother of God, the apostles, all the saints, and the multitude of those who have already entered the kingdom.

1188 In a liturgical celebration, the whole assembly is *leitourgos,* each member according to his own function. The baptismal priesthood is that of the whole Body of Christ. But some of the faithful are ordained through the sacrament of Holy Orders to represent Christ as head of the Body.

1189 The liturgical celebration involves signs and symbols relating to creation (candles, water, fire), human life (washing, anointing, breaking bread), and the history of salvation (the rites of the Passover). Integrated into the world of faith and taken up by the power of the Holy Spirit, these cosmic elements, human rituals, and gestures of remembrance of God become bearers of the saving and sanctifying action of Christ.

1190 The Liturgy of the Word is an integral part of the celebration. The meaning of the celebration is expressed by the Word of God which is proclaimed and by the response of faith to it.

---

65 *Rev* 21:4.

1191   Song and music are closely connected with the liturgical action. The criteria for their proper use are the beauty expressive of prayer, the unanimous participation of the assembly, and the sacred character of the celebration.

1192   Sacred images in our churches and homes are intended to awaken and nourish our faith in the mystery of Christ. Through the icon of Christ and his works of salvation, it is he whom we adore. Through sacred images of the holy Mother of God, of the angels and of the saints, we venerate the persons represented.

1193   Sunday, the "Lord's Day," is the principal day for the celebration of the Eucharist because it is the day of the Resurrection. It is the pre-eminent day of the liturgical assembly, the day of the Christian family, and the day of joy and rest from work. Sunday is "the foundation and kernel of the whole liturgical year" (*SC* 106).

1194   The Church, "in the course of the year, . . . unfolds the whole mystery of Christ from his Incarnation and Nativity through his Ascension, to Pentecost and the expectation of the blessed hope of the coming of the Lord" (*SC* 102 § 2).

1195   By keeping the memorials of the saints—first of all the holy Mother of God, then the apostles, the martyrs, and other saints—on fixed days of the liturgical year, the Church on earth shows that she is united with the liturgy of heaven. She gives glory to Christ for having accomplished his salvation in his glorified members; their example encourages her on her way to the Father.

1196   The faithful who celebrate the Liturgy of the Hours are united to Christ our high priest, by the prayer of the Psalms, meditation on the Word of God, and canticles and blessings, in order to be joined with his unceasing and universal prayer that gives glory to the Father and implores the gift of the Holy Spirit on the whole world.

1197 Christ is the true temple of God, "the place where his glory dwells"; by the grace of God, Christians also become temples of the Holy Spirit, living stones out of which the Church is built.

1198 In its earthly state the Church needs places where the community can gather together. Our visible churches, holy places, are images of the holy city, the heavenly Jerusalem, toward which we are making our way on pilgrimage.

1199 It is in these churches that the Church celebrates public worship to the glory of the Holy Trinity, hears the word of God and sings his praise, lifts up her prayer, and offers the sacrifice of Christ sacramentally present in the midst of the assembly. These churches are also places of recollection and personal prayer.

Article 2
LITURGICAL DIVERSITY AND THE UNITY OF THE MYSTERY

Liturgical traditions and the catholicity of the Church

1200 From the first community of Jerusalem until the parousia, it is the same Paschal mystery that the Churches of God, faithful to the apostolic faith, celebrate in every place. The mystery celebrated in the liturgy is one, but the forms of its celebration are diverse.

2625

1201 The mystery of Christ is so unfathomably rich that it cannot be exhausted by its expression in any single liturgical tradition. The history of the blossoming and development of these rites witnesses to a remarkable complementarity. When the Churches lived their

2663

respective liturgical traditions in the communion of the faith and the sacraments of the faith, they enriched one another and grew in fidelity to Tradition and to the common mission of the whole Church.[66] *1158*

1202 The diverse liturgical traditions have arisen by very reason of the Church's mission. Churches of the same geographical and cultural area came to celebrate the mystery of Christ through particular expressions characterized by the culture: in the tradition of the "deposit of faith,"[67] in liturgical symbolism, in the organization of fraternal communion, in the theological understanding of the mysteries, and in various forms of holiness. Through the liturgical life of a local church, Christ, the light and salvation of all peoples, is made manifest to the particular people and culture to which that Church is sent and in which she is rooted. The Church is catholic, capable of integrating into her unity, while purifying them, all the authentic riches of cultures.[68] *814   1674   835   1937*

1203 The liturgical traditions or rites presently in use in the Church are the Latin (principally the Roman rite, but also the rites of certain local churches, such as the Ambrosian rite, or those of certain religious orders) and the Byzantine, Alexandrian or Coptic, Syriac, Armenian, Maronite, and Chaldean rites. In "faithful obedience to tradition, the sacred Council declares that Holy Mother Church holds all lawfully recognized rites to be of equal right and dignity, and that she wishes to preserve them in the future and to foster them in every way."[69]

Liturgy and culture

1204 The celebration of the liturgy, therefore, should correspond to the genius and culture of the different peoples.[70] In order that the mystery of Christ be "made known to all the nations . . . to bring about the obedience of faith,"[71] it must be proclaimed, celebrated, and lived in all cultures in such a way that they themselves are not abolished by it, but redeemed and fulfilled:[72] It *2684   854, 1232*

---

66 Cf. Paul VI, *EN* 63–64.   67 *2 Tim* 1:14 (Vulg.).   68 Cf. *LG* 23; *UR* 4.
69 *SC* 4.   70 Cf. *SC* 37–40.   71 *Rom* 16:26.   72 Cf. *CT* 53.

2527 is with and through their own human culture, assumed and transfigured by Christ, that the multitude of God's children has access to the Father, in order to glorify him in the one Spirit.

1125 **1205** "In the liturgy, above all that of the sacraments, there is an *immutable part,* a part that is divinely instituted and of which the Church is the guardian, and parts that *can be changed,* which the Church has the power and on occasion also the duty to adapt to the cultures of recently evangelized peoples."[73]

1206 "Liturgical diversity can be a source of enrichment, but it can also provoke tensions, mutual misunderstandings, and even schisms. In this matter it is clear that diversity must not damage unity. It must express only fidelity to the common faith, to the sacramental signs that the Church has received from Christ, and to hierarchical communion. Cultural adaptation also requires a conversion of heart and even, where necessary, a breaking with ancestral customs incompatible with the Catholic faith."[74]

IN BRIEF

1207 It is fitting that liturgical celebration tends to express itself in the culture of the people where the Church finds herself, though without being submissive to it. Moreover, the liturgy itself generates cultures and shapes them.

1208 The diverse liturgical traditions or rites, legitimately recognized, manifest the catholicity of the Church, because they signify and communicate the same mystery of Christ.

1209 The criterion that assures unity amid the diversity of liturgical traditions is fidelity to apostolic Tradition, i.e., the communion in the faith and the sacraments received from the apostles, a

---

73 John Paul II, *Vicesimus quintus annus,* 16; cf. SC 21.   74 John Paul II, *Vicesimus quintus annus,* 16.

communion that is both signified and guaranteed by apostolic succession.

SECTION TWO
THE SEVEN SACRAMENTS
OF THE CHURCH

1210 Christ instituted the sacraments of the new law. 1113 There are seven: Baptism, Confirmation (or Chrismation), the Eucharist, Penance, the Anointing of the Sick, Holy Orders, and Matrimony. The seven sacraments touch all the stages and all the important moments of Christian life:[1] they give birth and increase, healing and mission to the Christian's life of faith. There is thus a certain resemblance between the stages of natural life and the stages of the spiritual life.

1211 Following this analogy, the *first chapter* will expound the three sacraments of Christian initiation; the *second,* the sacraments of healing; and the *third,* the sacraments at the service of communion and the mission of the faithful. This order, while not the only one possible, does allow one to see that the sacraments form an organic whole in which each particular sacrament has its own vital place. In this organic whole, the Eucharist occupies a unique place as the "Sacrament of sacraments": "all the other sacraments are ordered to it as to 1374 their end."[2]

CHAPTER ONE
THE SACRAMENTS OF
CHRISTIAN INITIATION

1212 The sacraments of Christian initiation—Baptism, Confirmation, and the Eucharist—lay the *foundations* of every Christian life. "The sharing in the divine nature given to men through the grace of Christ bears a certain likeness to the origin, development, and nourishing of natural life. The faithful are born anew by Baptism, strengthened by the sacrament of Confirma-

---

1 Cf. St. Thomas Aquinas, *STh* III, 65, 1.   2 St. Thomas Aquinas, *STh* III, 65, 3.

tion, and receive in the Eucharist the food of eternal life. By means of these sacraments of Christian initiation, they thus receive in increasing measure the treasures of the divine life and advance toward the perfection of charity."[3]

ARTICLE 1
THE SACRAMENT OF BAPTISM

1213   Holy Baptism is the basis of the whole Christian life, the gateway to life in the Spirit (*vitae spiritualis ianua*),[4] and the door which gives access to the other sacraments. Through Baptism we are freed from sin and reborn as sons of God; we become members of Christ, are incorporated into the Church and made sharers in her mission: "Baptism is the sacrament of regeneration through water in the word."[5]

I.   WHAT IS THIS SACRAMENT CALLED?

1214   This sacrament is called *Baptism,* after the central rite by which it is carried out: to baptize (Greek *baptizein*) means to "plunge" or "immerse"; the "plunge" into the water symbolizes the catechumen's
628 burial into Christ's death, from which he rises up by resurrection with him, as "a new creature."[6]

1215   This sacrament is also called *"the washing of regeneration and renewal by the Holy Spirit,"* for it signifies and actually brings about the birth of water and the
1257 Spirit without which no one "can enter the kingdom of God."[7]

1216   "This bath is called *enlightenment,* because those who receive this [catechetical] instruction are enlightened in their understanding. . . ."[8] Having received in Baptism the Word, "the true light that enlightens every man," the person baptized has been "enlight-

---

3 Paul VI, apostolic constitution, *Divinae consortium naturae:* AAS 63 (1971) 657; cf. RCIA Introduction 1–2.   4 Cf. Council of Florence: DS 1314: *vitae spiritualis ianua.*   5 *Roman Catechism* II, 2, 5; cf. Council of Florence: DS 1314; CIC, cann. 204 § 1; 849; CCEO, can. 675 § 1.   6 *2 Cor* 5:17; *Gal* 6:15; cf. *Rom* 6:3–4; *Col* 2:12.   7 *Titus* 3:5; *Jn* 3:5.   8 St. Justin, *Apol.* 1, 61, 12: PG 6, 421.

ened," he becomes a "son of light," indeed, he becomes 1243
"light" himself:[9]

> Baptism is God's most beautiful and magnificent
> gift. . . . We call it gift, grace, anointing, enlighten-
> ment, garment of immortality, bath of rebirth, seal,
> and most precious gift. It is called *gift* because it is
> conferred on those who bring nothing of their own;
> *grace* since it is given even to the guilty; *Baptism* be-
> cause sin is buried in the water; *anointing* for it is
> priestly and royal as are those who are anointed; *en-
> lightenment* because it radiates light; *clothing* since
> it veils our shame; *bath* because it washes; and *seal*
> as it is our guard and the sign of God's Lordship.[10]

II.   BAPTISM IN THE ECONOMY OF SALVATION

Prefigurations of Baptism in the Old Covenant

1217 In the liturgy of the Easter Vigil, during the
blessing of the baptismal water, the Church solemnly
commemorates the great events in salvation history that
already prefigured the mystery of Baptism:

> Father, you give us grace through sacramental
> signs,
> which tell us of the wonders of your unseen
> power.
>
> In Baptism we use your gift of water,
> which you have made a rich symbol
> of the grace you give us in this sacrament.[11]

1218 Since the beginning of the world, water, so hum- 344
ble and wonderful a creature, has been the source of life 694
and fruitfulness. Sacred Scripture sees it as "overshadowed" by the Spirit of God:[12]

> At the very dawn of creation
> your Spirit breathed on the waters,
> making them the wellspring of all holiness.[13]

1219 The Church has seen in Noah's ark a prefiguring 701, 845
of salvation by Baptism, for by it "a few, that is, eight
persons, were saved through water":[14]

---

9 *Jn* 1:9; *1 Thess* 5:5; *Heb* 10:32; *Eph* 5:8.   10 St. Gregory of Nazianzus, *Oratio*
40, 3–4: PG 36, 361C.   11 *Roman Missal,* Easter Vigil 42: Blessing of Water.
12 Cf. *Gen* 1:2.   13 *Roman Missal,* Easter Vigil 42: Blessing of Water.   14 *1 Pet*
3:20.

The waters of the great flood
you made a sign of the waters of Baptism,
that make an end of sin and a new beginning of
goodness.[15]

1220 If water springing up from the earth symbolizes life, the water of the sea is a symbol of death and so can represent the mystery of the cross. By this symbolism *1010* Baptism signifies communion with Christ's death.

1221 But above all, the crossing of the Red Sea, literally the liberation of Israel from the slavery of Egypt, announces the liberation wrought by Baptism:

You freed the children of Abraham from the slavery of Pharaoh, bringing them dry-shod through the waters of the Red Sea, to be an image of the people set free in Baptism.[16]

1222 Finally, Baptism is prefigured in the crossing of the Jordan River by which the People of God received the gift of the land promised to Abraham's descendants, an image of eternal life. The promise of this blessed inheritance is fulfilled in the New Covenant.

Christ's Baptism

1223 All the Old Covenant prefigurations find their fulfillment in Christ Jesus. He begins his public life after having himself baptized by St. John the Baptist in the Jordan.[17] After his resurrection Christ gives this mission to his apostles: "Go therefore and make disciples of all nations, baptizing them in the name of the Father and *232* of the Son and of the Holy Spirit, teaching them to observe all that I have commanded you."[18]

536 **1224** Our Lord voluntarily submitted himself to the baptism of St. John, intended for sinners, in order to "fulfill all righteousness."[19] Jesus' gesture is a manifestation of his self-emptying.[20] The Spirit who had hov-

---

15 *Roman Missal*, Easter Vigil 42: Blessing of Water.   16 *Roman Missal*, Easter Vigil 42: Blessing of Water: "Abrahae filios per mare Rubrum sicco vestigio transire fecisti, ut plebs, a Pharaonis servitute liberata, populum baptizatorum præfiguraret."   17 Cf. *Mt* 3:13.   18 *Mt* 28:19–20; cf. *Mk* 16:15–16.   19 *Mt* 3:15.   20 Cf. *Phil* 2:7.

ered over the waters of the first creation descended then on the Christ as a prelude of the new creation, and the Father revealed Jesus as his "beloved Son."[21]

1225 In his Passover Christ opened to all men the fountain of Baptism. He had already spoken of his Passion, which he was to suffer in Jerusalem, as a "Baptism" with which he had to be baptized.[22] The blood and water that flowed from the pierced side of the crucified Jesus are types of Baptism and the Eucharist, the sacraments of new life.[23] From then on, it is possible "to be born of water and the Spirit"[24] in order to enter the Kingdom of God.

766

> See where you are baptized, see where Baptism comes from, if not from the cross of Christ, from his death. There is the whole mystery: he died for you. In him you are redeemed, in him you are saved.[25]

Baptism in the Church

1226 From the very day of Pentecost the Church has celebrated and administered holy Baptism. Indeed St. Peter declares to the crowd astounded by his preaching: "Repent, and be baptized every one of you in the name of Jesus Christ for the forgiveness of your sins; and you shall receive the gift of the Holy Spirit."[26] The apostles and their collaborators offer Baptism to anyone who believed in Jesus: Jews, the God-fearing, pagans.[27] Always, Baptism is seen as connected with faith: "Believe in the Lord Jesus, and you will be saved, you and your household," St. Paul declared to his jailer in Philippi. And the narrative continues, the jailer "was baptized at once, with all his family."[28]

849

1227 According to the Apostle Paul, the believer enters through Baptism into communion with Christ's death, is buried with him, and rises with him:

790

> Do you not know that all of us who have been baptized into Christ Jesus were baptized into his death?

---

21 *Mt* 3:16–17. 22 *Mk* 10:38; cf. *Lk* 12:50. 23 Cf. *Jn* 19:34; *1 Jn* 5:6–8.
24 Cf. *Jn* 3:5. 25 St. Ambrose, *De sacr.* 2, 2, 6: PL 16, 444; cf. *Jn* 3:5. 26 *Acts* 2:38. 27 Cf. *Acts* 2:41; 8:12–13; 10:48; 16:15. 28 *Acts* 16:31–33.

We were buried therefore with him by baptism into death, so that as Christ was raised from the dead by the glory of the Father, we too might walk in newness of life.[29]

The baptized have "put on Christ."[30] Through the Holy Spirit, Baptism is a bath that purifies, justifies, and sanctifies.[31]

1228 Hence Baptism is a bath of water in which the "imperishable seed" of the Word of God produces its life-giving effect.[32] St. Augustine says of Baptism: "The word is brought to the material element, and it becomes a sacrament."[33]

III. HOW IS THE SACRAMENT OF BAPTISM CELEBRATED?

Christian Initiation

1229 From the time of the apostles, becoming a Christian has been accomplished by a journey and initiation in several stages. This journey can be covered rapidly or slowly, but certain essential elements will always have to be present: proclamation of the Word, acceptance of the Gospel entailing conversion, profession of faith, Baptism itself, the outpouring of the Holy Spirit, and admission to Eucharistic communion.

1230 This initiation has varied greatly through the centuries according to circumstances. In the first centuries of the Church, Christian initiation saw considerable development. A long period of *catechumenate* included a series of preparatory rites, which were liturgical landmarks along the path of catechumenal preparation and culminated in the celebration of the sacraments of Christian initiation.

1248

1231 Where infant Baptism has become the form in which this sacrament is usually celebrated, it has become a single act encapsulating the preparatory stages of Christian initiation in a very abridged way. By its very nature infant Baptism requires a *post-baptismal catechumenate*. Not only is there a need for instruction after Baptism, but also

---

29 *Rom* 6:3–4; cf. *Col* 2:12.   30 *Gal* 3:27.   31 Cf. *1 Cor* 6:11; 12:13.   32 *1 Pet* 1:23; cf. *Eph* 5:26.   33 St. Augustine, *In Jo. ev.* 80, 3: PL 35, 1840.

for the necessary flowering of baptismal grace in personal 13
growth. The *catechism* has its proper place here.

1232 The second Vatican Council restored for the Latin
Church "the catechumenate for adults, comprising several
distinct steps."[34] The rites for these stages are to be found
in the *Rite of Christian Initiation of Adults (RCIA)*.[35] The
Council also gives permission that: "In mission countries,
in addition to what is furnished by the Christian tradition,
those elements of initiation rites may be admitted which are 1204
already in use among some peoples insofar as they can be
adapted to the Christian ritual."[36]

1233 Today in all the rites, Latin and Eastern, the Christian initiation of adults begins with their entry into the catechumenate and reaches its culmination in a single celebration of the three sacraments of initiation: Baptism,
Confirmation, and the Eucharist.[37] In the Eastern rites the
Christian initiation of infants also begins with Baptism followed immediately by Confirmation and the Eucharist,
while in the Roman rite it is followed by years of catechesis
before being completed later by Confirmation and the Eucharist, the summit of their Christian initiation.[38]

The mystagogy of the celebration

1234 The meaning and grace of the sacrament of Baptism are clearly seen in the rites of its celebration. By following the gestures and words of this celebration with
attentive participation, the faithful are initiated into the
riches this sacrament signifies and actually brings about
in each newly baptized person.

1235 The *sign of the cross,* on the threshold of the cel- 617
ebration, marks with the imprint of Christ the one who
is going to belong to him and signifies the grace of the 2157
redemption Christ won for us by his cross.

1236 The proclamation of the Word of God enlightens
the candidates and the assembly with the revealed truth
and elicits the response of faith, which is inseparable 1122
from Baptism. Indeed Baptism is "the sacrament of
faith" in a particular way, since it is the sacramental entry into the life of faith.

---

34 *SC* 64.   35 Cf. RCIA (1972).   36 *SC* 65; cf. *SC* 37–40.   37 Cf. AG 14; CIC,
cann. 851; 865; 866.   38 Cf. CIC, cann. 851, 2°; 868.

1237 Since Baptism signifies liberation from sin and from its instigator the devil, one or more *exorcisms* are
1673 pronounced over the candidate. The celebrant then anoints him with the oil of catechumens, or lays his hands on him, and he explicitly renounces Satan. Thus
189 prepared, he is able to *confess the faith of the Church,* to which he will be "entrusted" by Baptism.[39]

1217 **1238** The *baptismal water* is consecrated by a prayer of epiclesis (either at this moment or at the Easter Vigil). The Church asks God that through his Son the power of the Holy Spirit may be sent upon the water, so that those who will be baptized in it may be "born of water and the Spirit."[40]

1214 **1239** The *essential rite* of the sacrament follows: *Baptism* properly speaking. It signifies and actually brings about death to sin and entry into the life of the Most Holy Trinity through configuration to the Paschal mystery of Christ. Baptism is performed in the most expressive way by triple immersion in the baptismal water. However, from ancient times it has also been able to be conferred by pouring the water three times over the candidate's head.

1240 In the Latin Church this triple infusion is accompanied by the minister's words: "N., I baptize you in the name of the Father, and of the Son, and of the Holy Spirit." In the Eastern liturgies the catechumen turns toward the East and the priest says: "The servant of God, N., is baptized in the name of the Father, and of the Son, and of the Holy Spirit." At the invocation of each person of the Most Holy Trinity, the priest immerses the candidate in the water and raises him up again.

1294, 1574 **1241** The *anointing with sacred chrism,* perfumed oil consecrated by the bishop, signifies the gift of the Holy Spirit to the newly baptized, who has become a Christian, that is, one "anointed" by the Holy Spirit, incorporated into Christ who is anointed priest, prophet, and
783 king.[41]

1242 In the liturgy of the Eastern Churches, the post-

---

39 Cf. *Rom* 6:17.   40 *Jn* 3:5.   41 Cf. RBC 62.

baptismal anointing is the sacrament of Chrismation (Confirmation). In the Roman liturgy the post-baptismal anointing announces a second anointing with sacred chrism to be conferred later by the bishop—Confirmation, which will as it were "confirm" and complete the baptismal anointing. *1291*

1243 The white garment symbolizes that the person baptized has "put on Christ,"[42] has risen with Christ. The *candle,* lit from the Easter candle, signifies that Christ has enlightened the neophyte. In him the baptized are "the light of the world."[43] *1216*

The newly baptized is now, in the only Son, a child of God entitled to say the prayer of the children of God: "Our Father." *2769*

1244 *First Holy Communion.* Having become a child of God clothed with the wedding garment, the neophyte is admitted "to the marriage supper of the Lamb"[44] and receives the food of the new life, the body and blood of Christ. The Eastern Churches maintain a lively awareness of the unity of Christian initiation by giving Holy Communion to all the newly baptized and confirmed, even little children, recalling the Lord's words: "Let the children come to me, do not hinder them."[45] The Latin Church, which reserves admission to Holy Communion to those who have attained the age of reason, expresses the orientation of Baptism to the Eucharist by having the newly baptized child brought to the altar for the praying of the Our Father. *1292*

1245 The *solemn blessing* concludes the celebration of Baptism. At the Baptism of newborns the blessing of the mother occupies a special place.

IV. WHO CAN RECEIVE BAPTISM?
1246 "Every person not yet baptized and only such a person is able to be baptized."[46]

---

42 *Gal* 3:27. 43 *Mt* 5:14; cf. *Phil* 2:15. 44 *Rev* 19:9. 45 *Mk* 10:14. 46 CIC, can. 864; cf. CCEO, can. 679.

The Baptism of adults

1247 Since the beginning of the Church, adult Baptism is the common practice where the proclamation of the Gospel is still new. The catechumenate (preparation for Baptism) therefore occupies an important place. This initiation into Christian faith and life should dispose the catechumen to receive the gift of God in Baptism, Confirmation, and the Eucharist.

1230   **1248** The catechumenate, or formation of catechumens, aims at bringing their conversion and faith to maturity, in response to the divine initiative and in union with an ecclesial community. The catechumenate is to be "a formation in the whole Christian life ... during which the disciples will be joined to Christ their teacher. The catechumens should be properly initiated into the mystery of salvation and the practice of the evangelical virtues, and they should be introduced into the life of faith, liturgy, and charity of the People of God by successive sacred rites."[47]

1259   **1249** Catechumens "are already joined to the Church, they are already of the household of Christ, and are quite frequently already living a life of faith, hope, and charity."[48] "With love and solicitude mother Church already embraces them as her own."[49]

The Baptism of infants

403   **1250** Born with a fallen human nature and tainted by original sin, children also have need of the new birth in Baptism to be freed from the power of darkness and brought into the realm of the freedom of the children of God, to which all men are called.[50] The sheer gratu-
1996   itousness of the grace of salvation is particularly manifest in infant Baptism. The Church and the parents would deny a child the priceless grace of becoming a child of God were they not to confer Baptism shortly after birth.[51]

---

47 *AG* 14; cf. RCIA 19; 98.   48 *AG* 14 § 5.   49 *LG* 14 § 3; cf. CIC, cann. 206; 788 § 3.   50 Cf. Council of Trent (1546): DS 1514; cf. *Col* 1:12–14.   51 Cf. CIC, can. 867; CCEO, cann. 681; 686, 1.

1251 Christian parents will recognize that this practice also accords with their role as nurturers of the life that God has entrusted to them.[52]

1252 The practice of infant Baptism is an immemorial tradition of the Church. There is explicit testimony to this practice from the second century on, and it is quite possible that, from the beginning of the apostolic preaching, when whole "households" received baptism, infants may also have been baptized.[53]

Faith and Baptism

1253 Baptism is the sacrament of faith.[54] But faith needs the community of believers. It is only within the faith of the Church that each of the faithful can believe. The faith required for Baptism is not a perfect and mature faith, but a beginning that is called to develop. The catechumen or the godparent is asked: "What do you ask of God's Church?" The response is: "Faith!"   *1123*   *168*

1254 For all the baptized, children or adults, faith must grow *after* Baptism. For this reason the Church celebrates each year at the Easter Vigil the renewal of baptismal promises. Preparation for Baptism leads only to the threshold of new life. Baptism is the source of that new life in Christ from which the entire Christian life springs forth.   *2101*

1255 For the grace of Baptism to unfold, the parents' help is important. So too is the role of the *godfather* and *godmother,* who must be firm believers, able and ready to help the newly baptized—child or adult—on the road of Christian life.[55] Their task is a truly ecclesial function (*officium*).[56] The whole ecclesial community bears some responsibility for the development and safeguarding of the grace given at Baptism.   *1311*

---

52 Cf. *LG* 11; 41; *GS* 48; CIC, can. 868.   53 Cf. *Acts* 16:15, 33; 18:8; *1 Cor* 1:16; CDF, instruction, *Pastoralis actio:* AAS 72 (1980) 1137–1156.   54 Cf. *Mk* 16:16.   55 Cf. CIC, cann. 872–874.   56 Cf. *SC* 67.

V.   WHO CAN BAPTIZE?

1256   The ordinary ministers of Baptism are the bishop and priest and, in the Latin Church, also the deacon.[57] In case of necessity, any person, even someone not baptized, can baptize, if he has the required intention. The intention required is to will to do what the Church does when she baptizes, and to apply the Trinitarian baptismal formula. The Church finds the reason for this possibility in the universal saving will of God and the necessity of Baptism for salvation.[58]

1752

VI.   THE NECESSITY OF BAPTISM

1129   **1257**   The Lord himself affirms that Baptism is necessary for salvation.[59] He also commands his disciples to proclaim the Gospel to all nations and to baptize them.[60] Baptism is necessary for salvation for those to whom the Gospel has been proclaimed and who have *161, 846* had the possibility of asking for this sacrament.[61] The Church does not know of any means other than Baptism that assures entry into eternal beatitude; this is why she takes care not to neglect the mission she has received from the Lord to see that all who can be baptized are "reborn of water and the Spirit." *God has bound salvation to the sacrament of Baptism, but he himself is not bound by his sacraments.*

1258   The Church has always held the firm conviction that those who suffer death for the sake of the faith without having received Baptism are baptized by their death for and with Christ. This *Baptism of blood,* like *2473* the *desire for Baptism,* brings about the fruits of Baptism without being a sacrament.

1249   **1259**   For *catechumens* who die before their Baptism, their explicit desire to receive it, together with repentance for their sins, and charity, assures them the salvation that they were not able to receive through the sacrament.

---

57 Cf. CIC, can. 861 § 1; CCEO, can. 677 § 1.   58 Cf. *1 Tim* 2:4.   59 Cf. *Jn* 3:5.   60 Cf. *Mt* 28:19–20; cf. Council of Trent (1547) DS 1618; *LG* 14; *AG* 5. 61 Cf. *Mk* 16:16.

1260 "Since Christ died for all, and since all men are in fact called to one and the same destiny, which is divine, we must hold that the Holy Spirit offers to all the possibility of being made partakers, in a way known to God, of the Paschal mystery."[62] Every man who is igno- 848
rant of the Gospel of Christ and of his Church, but seeks the truth and does the will of God in accordance with his understanding of it, can be saved. It may be supposed that such persons would have *desired Baptism explicitly* if they had known its necessity.

1261 As regards *children who have died without Baptism,* the Church can only entrust them to the mercy of God, as she does in her funeral rites for them. Indeed, the great mercy of God who desires that all men should be saved, and Jesus' tenderness toward children which caused him to say: "Let the children come to me, do not hinder them,"[63] allow us to hope that there is a way of salvation for children who have died without Baptism. All the more urgent is the Church's call not to prevent 1250
little children coming to Christ through the gift of holy Baptism.

VII. THE GRACE OF BAPTISM

1262 The different effects of Baptism are signified by 1234
the perceptible elements of the sacramental rite. Immersion in water symbolizes not only death and purification, but also regeneration and renewal. Thus the two principal effects are purification from sins and new birth in the Holy Spirit.[64]

For the forgiveness of sins . . .

1263 By Baptism *all sins* are forgiven, original sin and 977
all personal sins, as well as all punishment for sin.[65] In 1425
those who have been reborn nothing remains that would impede their entry into the Kingdom of God, neither Adam's sin, nor personal sin, nor the consequences of sin, the gravest of which is separation from God.

1264 Yet certain temporal consequences of sin remain

---

62 GS 22 § 5; cf. LG 16; AG 7.   63 Mk 10:14; cf. 1 Tim 2:4.   64 Cf. Acts 2:38; Jn 3:5.   65 Cf. Council of Florence (1439): DS 1316.

in the baptized, such as suffering, illness, death, and such frailties inherent in life as weaknesses of character, and so on, as well as an inclination to sin that Tradition calls *concupiscence,* or metaphorically, "the tinder for sin" *(fomes peccati);* since concupiscence "is left for us to wrestle with, it cannot harm those who do not consent but manfully resist it by the grace of Jesus Christ."[66] Indeed, "an athlete is not crowned unless he competes according to the rules."[67]

975, 2514
1426

405

"A new creature"

505
460
1265 Baptism not only purifies from all sins, but also makes the neophyte "a new creature," an adopted son of God, who has become a "partaker of the divine nature,"[68] member of Christ and co-heir with him,[69] and a temple of the Holy Spirit.[70]

1266 The Most Holy Trinity gives the baptized sanctifying grace, the grace of *justification:*

1992 —enabling them to believe in God, to hope in him, and to love him through the theological virtues;

1812 —giving them the power to live and act under the prompting of the Holy Spirit through the gifts of the Holy Spirit;

1831 —allowing them to grow in goodness through the moral virtues.

1810   Thus the whole organism of the Christian's supernatural life has its roots in Baptism.

Incorporated into the Church, the Body of Christ

782 **1267** Baptism makes us members of the Body of Christ: "Therefore ... we are members one of another."[71] Baptism incorporates us *into the Church.* From the baptismal fonts is born the one People of God of the New Covenant, which transcends all the natural or human limits of nations, cultures, races, and sexes: "For by one Spirit we were all baptized into one body."[72]

---

66 Council of Trent (1546): DS 1515.   67 *2 Tim* 2:5.   68 *2 Cor* 5:17; *2 Pet* 1:4; cf. *Gal* 4:5–7.   69 Cf. *1 Cor* 6:15; 12:27; *Rom* 8:17.   70 Cf. *1 Cor* 6:19.
71 *Eph* 4:25.   72 *1 Cor* 12:13.

1268 The baptized have become "living stones" to be "built into a spiritual house, to be a holy priesthood."[73] By Baptism they share in the priesthood of Christ, in his prophetic and royal mission. They are "a chosen race, a royal priesthood, a holy nation, God's own people, that [they] may declare the wonderful deeds of him who called [them] out of darkness into his marvelous light."[74] *Baptism gives a share in the common priesthood of all believers.*

1141

784

1269 Having become a member of the Church, the person baptized belongs no longer to himself, but to him who died and rose for us.[75] From now on, he is called to be subject to others, to serve them in the communion of the Church, and to "obey and submit" to the Church's leaders,[76] holding them in respect and affection.[77] Just as Baptism is the source of responsibilities and duties, the baptized person also enjoys rights within the Church: to receive the sacraments, to be nourished with the Word of God and to be sustained by the other spiritual helps of the Church.[78]

871

1270 "Reborn as sons of God, [the baptized] must profess before men the faith they have received from God through the Church" and participate in the apostolic and missionary activity of the People of God.[79]

The sacramental bond of the unity of Christians

1271 Baptism constitutes the foundation of communion among all Christians, including those who are not yet in full communion with the Catholic Church: "For men who believe in Christ and have been properly baptized are put in some, though imperfect, communion with the Catholic Church. Justified by faith in Baptism, [they] are incorporated into Christ; they therefore have a right to be called Christians, and with good reason are accepted as brothers by the children of the Catholic Church."[80] "Baptism therefore constitutes *the sacra-*

---

73 *1 Pet* 2:5. 74 *1 Pet* 2:9. 75 Cf. *1 Cor* 6:19; *2 Cor* 5:15. 76 *Heb* 13:17.
77 Cf. *Eph* 5:21; *1 Cor* 16:15–16; *1 Thess* 5:12–13; *Jn* 13:12–15. 78 Cf. *LG* 37;
CIC, cann. 208–223; CCEO, can. 675:2. 79 *LG* 11; cf. *LG* 17; *AG* 7; 23.
80 *UR* 3.

mental bond of unity existing among all who through it are reborn."[81]

An indelible spiritual mark . . .

1272 Incorporated into Christ by Baptism, the person baptized is configured to Christ. Baptism seals the Christian with the indelible spiritual mark *(character)* of his belonging to Christ. No sin can erase this mark, even if sin prevents Baptism from bearing the fruits of salvation.[82] Given once for all, Baptism cannot be repeated.

1273 Incorporated into the Church by Baptism, the faithful have received the sacramental character that consecrates them for Christian religious worship.[83] The baptismal seal enables and commits Christians to serve God by a vital participation in the holy liturgy of the Church and to exercise their baptismal priesthood by the witness of holy lives and practical charity.[84]

1274 The Holy Spirit has marked us with the *seal of the Lord ("Dominicus character")* "for the day of redemption."[85] "Baptism indeed is the seal of eternal life."[86] The faithful Christian who has "kept the seal" until the end, remaining faithful to the demands of his Baptism, will be able to depart this life "marked with the sign of faith,"[87] with his baptismal faith, in expectation of the blessed vision of God—the consummation of faith—and in the hope of resurrection.

197
2016

IN BRIEF

1275 Christian initiation is accomplished by three sacraments together: Baptism which is the beginning of new life; Confirmation which is its strengthening; and the Eucharist which nourishes the disciple with Christ's Body and Blood for his transformation in Christ.

1276 "Go therefore and make disciples of all nations,

81 *UR* 22 § 2.   82 Cf. *Rom* 8:29; Council of Trent (1547): DS 1609–1619.
83 Cf. *LG* 11.   84 Cf. *LG* 10.   85 St. Augustine, *Ep.* 98, 5: PL 33, 362; *Eph* 4:30; cf. 1:13–14; 2 *Cor* 1:21–22.   86 St. Irenaeus, *Dem ap.* 3: SCh 62, 32.
87 *Roman Missal*, EP I (Roman Canon) 97.

baptizing them in the name of the Father and of the Son and of the Holy Spirit, teaching them to observe all that I have commanded you" (*Mt* 28:19–20).

1277   Baptism is birth into the new life in Christ. In accordance with the Lord's will, it is necessary for salvation, as is the Church herself, which we enter by Baptism.

1278   The essential rite of Baptism consists in immersing the candidate in water or pouring water on his head, while pronouncing the invocation of the Most Holy Trinity: the Father, the Son, and the Holy Spirit.

1279   The fruit of Baptism, or baptismal grace, is a rich reality that includes forgiveness of original sin and all personal sins, birth into the new life by which man becomes an adoptive son of the Father, a member of Christ and a temple of the Holy Spirit. By this very fact the person baptized is incorporated into the Church, the Body of Christ, and made a sharer in the priesthood of Christ.

1280   Baptism imprints on the soul an indelible spiritual sign, the character, which consecrates the baptized person for Christian worship. Because of the character Baptism cannot be repeated (cf. DS 1609 and DS 1624).

1281   Those who die for the faith, those who are catechumens, and all those who, without knowing of the Church but acting under the inspiration of grace, seek God sincerely and strive to fulfill his will, are saved even if they have not been baptized (cf. *LG* 16).

1282   Since the earliest times, Baptism has been administered to children, for it is a grace and a gift of God that does not presuppose any human merit; children are baptized in the faith of the

Church. Entry into Christian life gives access to true freedom.

1283   With respect to children who have died without Baptism, the liturgy of the Church invites us to trust in God's mercy and to pray for their salvation.

1284   In case of necessity, any person can baptize provided that he have the intention of doing that which the Church does and provided that he pours water on the candidate's head while saying: "I baptize you in the name of the Father, and of the Son, and of the Holy Spirit."

ARTICLE 2
THE SACRAMENT OF CONFIRMATION

1285   Baptism, the Eucharist, and the sacrament of Confirmation together constitute the "sacraments of Christian initiation," whose unity must be safeguarded. It must be explained to the faithful that the reception of the sacrament of Confirmation is necessary for the completion of baptismal grace.[88] For "by the sacrament of Confirmation, [the baptized] are more perfectly bound to the Church and are enriched with a special strength of the Holy Spirit. Hence they are, as true witnesses of Christ, more strictly obliged to spread and defend the faith by word and deed."[89]

I.   CONFIRMATION IN THE ECONOMY OF SALVATION

1286   In the Old Testament the prophets announced that the Spirit of the Lord would rest on the hoped-for Messiah for his saving mission.[90] The descent of the Holy Spirit on Jesus at his baptism by John was the sign that this was he who was to come, the Messiah, the Son of God.[91] He was conceived of the Holy Spirit; his whole

702-716

---

88 Cf. *Roman Ritual*, Rite of Confirmation *(OC)*, Introduction 1.   89 *LG* 11; cf. *OC*, Introduction 2.   90 Cf. *Isa* 11:2; 61:1; *Lk* 4:16–22.   91 Cf. *Mt* 3:13–17; *Jn* 1:33–34.

life and his whole mission are carried out in total communion with the Holy Spirit whom the Father gives him "without measure."[92]

1287 This fullness of the Spirit was not to remain uniquely the Messiah's, but was to be communicated to *the whole messianic people.*[93] On several occasions 739 Christ promised this outpouring of the Spirit,[94] a promise which he fulfilled first on Easter Sunday and then more strikingly at Pentecost.[95] Filled with the Holy Spirit the apostles began to proclaim "the mighty works of God," and Peter declared this outpouring of the Spirit to be the sign of the messianic age.[96] Those who believed in the apostolic preaching and were baptized received the gift of the Holy Spirit in their turn.[97]

1288 "From that time on the apostles, in fulfillment of Christ's will, imparted to the newly baptized by the laying on of hands the gift of the Spirit that completes the grace of Baptism. For this reason in the *Letter to the Hebrews* the doctrine concerning Baptism and the 699 laying on of hands is listed among the first elements of Christian instruction. The imposition of hands is rightly recognized by the Catholic tradition as the origin of the sacrament of Confirmation, which in a certain way perpetuates the grace of Pentecost in the Church."[98]

1289 Very early, the better to signify the gift of the Holy Spirit, an anointing with perfumed oil *(chrism)* 695 was added to the laying on of hands. This anointing highlights the name "Christian," which means "anointed" and derives from that of Christ himself whom God "anointed with the Holy Spirit."[99] This rite 436 of anointing has continued ever since, in both East and West. For this reason the Eastern Churches call this sacrament *Chrismation*, anointing with chrism, or *myron* which means "chrism." In the West, *Confirmation* 1297 suggests both the ratification of Baptism, thus complet-

---

92 *Jn* 3:34.   93 Cf. *Ezek* 36:25–27; *Joel* 3:1–2.   94 Cf. *Lk* 12:12; *Jn* 3:5–8; 7:37–39; 16:7–15; *Acts* 1:8.   95 Cf. *Jn* 20:22; *Acts* 2:1–4.   96 *Acts* 2:11; cf. 2:17–18.   97 Cf. *Acts* 2:38.   98 Paul VI, *Divinae consortium naturae*, 659; cf. *Acts* 8:15–17; 19:5–6; *Heb* 6:2.   99 *Acts* 10:38.

ing Christian initiation, and the strengthening of baptismal grace—both fruits of the Holy Spirit.

Two traditions: East and West

1290 In the first centuries Confirmation generally comprised one single celebration with Baptism, forming with it a "double sacrament," according to the expression of St. Cyprian. Among other reasons, the multiplication of infant baptisms all through the year, the increase of rural parishes, and the growth of dioceses often prevented the bishop from being present at all baptismal celebrations. In the West the desire to reserve the completion of Baptism to the bishop caused the temporal separation of the two sacraments. The East has kept them united, so that Confirmation is con-

1233 ferred by the priest who baptizes. But he can do so only with the "myron" consecrated by a bishop.[100]

1242 **1291** A custom of the Roman Church facilitated the development of the Western practice: a double anointing with sacred chrism after Baptism. The first anointing of the neophyte on coming out of the baptismal bath was performed by the priest; it was completed by a second anointing on the forehead of the newly baptized by the bishop.[101] The first anointing with sacred chrism, by the priest, has remained attached to the baptismal rite; it signifies the participation of the one baptized in the prophetic, priestly, and kingly offices of Christ. If Baptism is conferred on an adult, there is only one post-baptismal anointing, that of Confirmation.

1244 **1292** The practice of the Eastern Churches gives greater emphasis to the unity of Christian initiation. That of the Latin Church more clearly expresses the communion of the new Christian with the bishop as guarantor and servant of the unity, catholicity and apostolicity of his Church, and hence the connection with the apostolic origins of Christ's Church.

II. THE SIGNS AND THE RITE OF CONFIRMATION

1293 In treating the rite of Confirmation, it is fitting to consider the sign of *anointing* and what it signifies and imprints: a spiritual *seal*.

695   Anointing, in Biblical and other ancient symbol-

---

100 Cf. CCEO, can. 695 § 1; 696 § 1.   101 Cf. St. Hippolytus, *Trad. Ap.* 21: SCh 11, 80–95.

ism, is rich in meaning: oil is a sign of abundance and joy;[102] it cleanses (anointing before and after a bath) and limbers (the anointing of athletes and wrestlers); oil is a sign of healing, since it is soothing to bruises and wounds;[103] and it makes radiant with beauty, health, and strength.

1294 Anointing with oil has all these meanings in the sacramental life. The pre-baptismal anointing with the oil of catechumens signifies cleansing and strengthening; the anointing of the sick expresses healing and comfort. The post-baptismal anointing with sacred chrism in Confirmation and ordination is the sign of consecration. By Confirmation Christians, that is, those who are anointed, share more completely in the mission of Jesus Christ and the fullness of the Holy Spirit with which he is filled, so that their lives may give off "the aroma of Christ."[104] *1152*

1295 By this anointing the confirmand receives the "mark," the *seal* of the Holy Spirit. A seal is a symbol of a person, a sign of personal authority, or ownership of an object.[105] Hence soldiers were marked with their leader's seal and slaves with their master's. A seal authenticates a juridical act or document and occasionally makes it secret.[106] *698*

1296 Christ himself declared that he was marked with his Father's seal.[107] Christians are also marked with a seal: "It is God who establishes us with you in Christ and has commissioned us; he has put his seal on us and given us his Spirit in our hearts as a guarantee."[108] This seal of the Holy Spirit marks our total belonging to Christ, our enrollment in his service for ever, as well as the promise of divine protection in the great eschatological trial.[109] *1121*

---

102 Cf. *Deut* 11:14; *Pss* 23:5; 104:15.   103 Cf. *Isa* 1:6; *Lk* 10:34.   104 *2 Cor* 2:15.   105 Cf. *Gen* 38:18; 41:42; *Deut* 32:34; *CT* 8:6.   106 Cf. *1 Kings* 21:8; *Jer* 32:10; *Isa* 29:11.   107 Cf. *Jn* 6:27.   108 *2 Cor* 1:21–22; cf. *Eph* 1:13; 4, 30. 109 Cf. *Rev* 7:2–3; 9:4; *Ezek* 9:4–6.

The celebration of Confirmation

1183   **1297** *The consecration of the sacred chrism* is an important action that precedes the celebration of Confirmation, but is in a certain way a part of it. It is the bishop who, in the course of the Chrism Mass of Holy Thursday, consecrates the sacred chrism for his whole
1241   diocese. In some Eastern Churches this consecration is even reserved to the patriarch:

> The Syriac liturgy of Antioch expresses the epiclesis for the consecration of the sacred chrism (myron) in this way: "[Father . . . send your Holy Spirit] on us and on this oil which is before us and consecrate it, so that it may be for all who are anointed and marked with it holy myron, priestly myron, royal myron, anointing with gladness, clothing with light, a cloak of salvation, a spiritual gift, the sanctification of souls and bodies, imperishable happiness, the indelible seal, a buckler of faith, and a fearsome helmet against all the works of the adversary."

1298 When Confirmation is celebrated separately from Baptism, as is the case in the Roman Rite, the Liturgy of Confirmation begins with the renewal of baptismal promises and the profession of faith by the confirmands. This clearly shows that Confirmation follows Baptism.[110] When adults are baptized, they immediately receive Confirmation and participate in the Eucharist.[111]

1299 In the Roman Rite the bishop extends his hands over the whole group of the confirmands. Since the time of the apostles this gesture has signified the gift of the Spirit. The bishop invokes the outpouring of the Spirit in these words:

> All-powerful God, Father of our Lord Jesus Christ,
> by water and the Holy Spirit
> you freed your sons and daughters from sin
> and gave them new life.
> Send your Holy Spirit upon them

---

110 Cf. *SC* 71.   111 Cf. CIC, can. 866.

to be their helper and guide.
Give them the spirit of wisdom and
understanding,
the spirit of right judgment and courage,
the spirit of knowledge and reverence.
Fill them with the spirit of wonder and awe in
your presence.
We ask this through Christ our Lord.[112]   *1831*

1300   The *essential rite* of the sacrament follows. In the Latin rite, "the sacrament of Confirmation is conferred through the anointing with chrism on the forehead, which is done by the laying on of the hand, and through the words: *'Accipe signaculum doni Spiritus Sancti'* [Be *699* sealed with the Gift of the Holy Spirit.]."[113] In the Eastern Churches, after a prayer of epiclesis the more significant parts of the body are anointed with myron: forehead, eyes, nose, ears, lips, breast, back, hands, and feet. Each anointing is accompanied by the formula: "The seal of the gift that is the Holy Spirit."

1301   The sign of peace that concludes the rite of the sacrament signifies and demonstrates ecclesial communion with the bishop and with all the faithful.[114]

III.   THE EFFECTS OF CONFIRMATION

1302   It is evident from its celebration that the effect of the sacrament of Confirmation is the full outpouring of the Holy Spirit as once granted to the apostles on the *731* day of Pentecost.

1303   From this fact, Confirmation brings an increase *1262-1274* and deepening of baptismal grace:

—it roots us more deeply in the divine filiation which makes us cry, "Abba! Father!";[115]

—it unites us more firmly to Christ;

—it increases the gifts of the Holy Spirit in us;

—it renders our bond with the Church more perfect;[116]

---

112 OC 25.   113 Paul VI, apostolic constitution, *Divinae consortium naturae*, 663.   114 Cf. St. Hippolytus, *Trad. Ap.* 21: SCh 11, 80–95.   115 *Rom* 8:15. 116 Cf. *LG* 11.

—it gives us a special strength of the Holy Spirit to
2044 spread and defend the faith by word and action as true
witnesses of Christ, to confess the name of Christ
boldly, and never to be ashamed of the Cross:[117]

> Recall then that you have received the spiritual seal,
> the spirit of wisdom and understanding, the spirit
> of right judgment and courage, the spirit of knowl-
> edge and reverence, the spirit of holy fear in God's
> presence. Guard what you have received. God the
> Father has marked you with his sign; Christ the
> Lord has confirmed you and has placed his pledge,
> the Spirit, in your hearts.[118]

1121 **1304** Like Baptism which it completes, Confirmation
is given only once, for it too imprints on the soul an *indelible spiritual mark,* the "character," which is the sign
that Jesus Christ has marked a Christian with the seal of
his Spirit by clothing him with power from on high so
that he may be his witness.[119]

1268 **1305** This "character" perfects the common priesthood of the faithful, received in Baptism, and "the confirmed person receives the power to profess faith in
Christ publicly and as it were officially *(quasi ex offi-
cio)*."[120]

IV.   WHO CAN RECEIVE THIS SACRAMENT?

1306 Every baptized person not yet confirmed can and
should receive the sacrament of Confirmation.[121] Since
1212 Baptism, Confirmation, and Eucharist form a unity, it
follows that "the faithful are obliged to receive this
sacrament at the appropriate time,"[122] for without Confirmation and Eucharist, Baptism is certainly valid and
efficacious, but Christian initiation remains incomplete.

1307 The Latin tradition gives "the age of discretion"
as the reference point for receiving Confirmation. But in
danger of death children should be confirmed even if
they have not yet attained the age of discretion.[123]

---

117 Cf. Council of Florence (1439): DS 1319; *LG* 11; 12.   118 St. Ambrose, De
myst. 7, 42: PL 16, 402–403.   119 Cf. Council of Trent (1547): DS 1609; *Lk*
24:48–49.   120 St. Thomas Aquinas, *STh III,* 72, 5, *ad* 2.   121 Cf. CIC, can.
889 § 1.   122 CIC, can. 890.   123 Cf. CIC, cann. 891; 883, 3°.

1308 Although Confirmation is sometimes called the "sacrament of Christian maturity," we must not confuse adult faith with the adult age of natural growth, nor forget that the baptismal grace is a grace of free, un- merited election and does not need "ratification" to be- come effective. St. Thomas reminds us of this: *1250*

> Age of body does not determine age of soul. Even in childhood man can attain spiritual maturity: as the book of *Wisdom* says: "For old age is not hon- ored for length of time, or measured by number of years." Many children, through the strength of the Holy Spirit they have received, have bravely fought for Christ even to the shedding of their blood.[124]

1309 *Preparation* for Confirmation should aim at leading the Christian toward a more intimate union with Christ and a more lively familiarity with the Holy Spirit—his actions, his gifts, and his biddings—in order to be more capable of assuming the apostolic responsi- bilities of Christian life. To this end catechesis for Con- firmation should strive to awaken a sense of belonging to the Church of Jesus Christ, the universal Church as well as the parish community. The latter bears special responsibility for the preparation of confirmands.[125]

1310 To receive Confirmation one must be in a state of grace. One should receive the sacrament of Penance in order to be cleansed for the gift of the Holy Spirit.   *2670* More intense prayer should prepare one to receive the strength and graces of the Holy Spirit with docility and readiness to act.[126]

1311 Candidates for Confirmation, as for Baptism, fittingly seek the spiritual help of a *sponsor*. To empha- size the unity of the two sacraments, it is appropriate   *1255* that this be one of the baptismal godparents.[127]

---

124 St. Thomas Aquinas, *STh* III, 72, 8, *ad* 2; cf. *Wis* 4:8.   125 Cf. OC Introduction 3.   126 Cf. *Acts* 1:14.   127 Cf. OC Introduction 5; 6; CIC, can. 893 §§ 1–2.

V.   THE MINISTER OF CONFIRMATION

1233 **1312** The *original minister* of Confirmation is the bishop.[128]

In the East, ordinarily the priest who baptizes also immediately confers Confirmation in one and the same celebration. But he does so with sacred chrism consecrated by the patriarch or the bishop, thus expressing the apostolic unity of the Church whose bonds are strengthened by the sacrament of Confirmation. In the Latin Church, the same discipline applies to the Baptism of adults or to the reception into full communion with the Church of a person baptized in another Christian community that does not have valid Confirmation.[129]

1290 **1313** In the Latin Rite, the ordinary minister of Confirmation is the bishop.[130] Although the bishop may for grave reasons concede to priests the faculty of administering Confirmation,[131] it is appropriate from the very meaning of the sacrament that he should confer it himself, mindful that the celebration of Confirmation has been temporally separated from Baptism for this reason. Bishops are the successors of the apostles. They have received the fullness of the sacrament of Holy Orders. The administration of this sacrament by them demonstrates clearly that its effect is to unite those who receive it more closely to the Church, to her apostolic origins, and *1285* to her mission of bearing witness to Christ.

1307 **1314** If a Christian is in danger of death, any priest should give him Confirmation.[132] Indeed the Church desires that none of her children, even the youngest, should depart this world without having been perfected by the Holy Spirit with the gift of Christ's fullness.

IN BRIEF

1315 "Now when the apostles at Jerusalem heard that Samaria had received the word of God, they sent to them Peter and John, who came down and

---

128 Cf. *LG* 26.   129 Cf. CIC, can. 883 § 2.   130 Cf. CIC, can. 882.   131 Cf. CIC, can. 884 § 2.   132 Cf. CIC, can. 883 § 3.

prayed for them that they might receive the Holy Spirit; for it had not yet fallen on any of them, but they had only been baptized in the name of the Lord Jesus. Then they laid their hands on them and they received the Holy Spirit" (*Acts* 8:14–17).

1316   Confirmation perfects Baptismal grace; it is the sacrament which gives the Holy Spirit in order to root us more deeply in the divine filiation, incorporate us more firmly into Christ, strengthen our bond with the Church, associate us more closely with her mission, and help us bear witness to the Christian faith in words accompanied by deeds.

1317   Confirmation, like Baptism, imprints a spiritual mark or indelible character on the Christian's soul; for this reason one can receive this sacrament only once in one's life.

1318   In the East this sacrament is administered immediately after Baptism and is followed by participation in the Eucharist; this tradition highlights the unity of the three sacraments of Christian initiation. In the Latin Church this sacrament is administered when the age of reason has been reached, and its celebration is ordinarily reserved to the bishop, thus signifying that this sacrament strengthens the ecclesial bond.

1319   A candidate for Confirmation who has attained the age of reason must profess the faith, be in the state of grace, have the intention of receiving the sacrament, and be prepared to assume the role of disciple and witness to Christ, both within the ecclesial community and in temporal affairs.

1320   The essential rite of Confirmation is anointing the forehead of the baptized with sacred chrism (in the East other sense-organs as well), together with the laying on of the minister's hand and the words: *"Accipe signaculum doni Spiritus Sancti"* (Be sealed with the Gift of the Holy Spirit.) in the

Roman Rite, or "The seal of the gift that is the Holy Spirit" in the Byzantine rite.

1321 When Confirmation is celebrated separately from Baptism, its connection with Baptism is expressed, among other ways, by the renewal of baptismal promises. The celebration of Confirmation during the Eucharist helps underline the unity of the sacraments of Christian initiation.

ARTICLE 3
THE SACRAMENT OF THE EUCHARIST

1212 **1322** The holy Eucharist completes Christian initiation. Those who have been raised to the dignity of the royal priesthood by Baptism and configured more deeply to Christ by Confirmation participate with the whole community in the Lord's own sacrifice by means of the Eucharist.

1323 "At the Last Supper, on the night he was betrayed, our Savior instituted the Eucharistic sacrifice of his Body and Blood. This he did in order to perpetuate the sacrifice of the cross throughout the ages until he should come again, and so to entrust to his beloved Spouse, the Church, a memorial of his death and resurrection: a sacrament of love, a sign of unity, a bond of *1402* charity, a Paschal banquet 'in which Christ is consumed, the mind is filled with grace, and a pledge of future glory is given to us.' "[133]

I.   THE EUCHARIST—SOURCE AND SUMMIT OF ECCLESIAL LIFE

864 **1324** The Eucharist is "the source and summit of the Christian life."[134] "The other sacraments, and indeed all ecclesiastical ministries and works of the apostolate, are bound up with the Eucharist and are oriented toward it. For in the blessed Eucharist is contained the whole spir-

---

133 *SC* 47.   134 *LG* 11.

itual good of the Church, namely Christ himself, our Pasch."[135]

1325 "The Eucharist is the efficacious sign and sublime cause of that communion in the divine life and that unity of the People of God by which the Church is kept in being. It is the culmination both of God's action sanctifying the world in Christ and of the worship men offer to Christ and through him to the Father in the Holy Spirit."[136]   775

1326 Finally, by the Eucharistic celebration we already unite ourselves with the heavenly liturgy and anticipate eternal life, when God will be all in all.[137]   1090

1327 In brief, the Eucharist is the sum and summary of our faith: "Our way of thinking is attuned to the Eucharist, and the Eucharist in turn confirms our way of thinking."[138]   1124

II.   WHAT IS THIS SACRAMENT CALLED?

1328 The inexhaustible richness of this sacrament is expressed in the different names we give it. Each name evokes certain aspects of it. It is called:

Eucharist, because it is an action of thanksgiving to God. The Greek words *eucharistein*[139] and *eulogein*[140] recall the Jewish blessings that proclaim—especially during a meal—God's works: creation, redemption, and sanctification.   2637 1082 1359

1329 The Lord's Supper, because of its connection with the supper which the Lord took with his disciples on the eve of his Passion and because it anticipates the wedding feast of the Lamb in the heavenly Jerusalem.[141]   1382

The *Breaking of Bread,* because Jesus used this rite, part of a Jewish meal, when as master of the table he blessed and distributed the bread,[142] above all at the Last Supper.[143] It is by this action that his disciples will

---

135 PO 5.   136 Congregation of Rites, instruction, *Eucharisticum mysterium,* 6.
137 Cf. *1 Cor* 15:28.   138 St. Irenaeus, *Adv. haeres.* 4, 18, 5: PG 7/1, 1028.
139 Cf. *Lk* 22:19; *1 Cor* 11:24.   140 Cf. *Mt* 26:26; *Mk* 14:22.   141 Cf. *1 Cor* 11:20; *Rev* 19:9.   142 Cf. *Mt* 14:19; 15:36; *Mk* 8:6, 19.   143 Cf. *Mt* 26:26; *1 Cor* 11:24.

recognize him after his Resurrection,[144] and it is this expression that the first Christians will use to designate

790 their Eucharistic assemblies;[145] by doing so they signified that all who eat the one broken bread, Christ, enter into communion with him and form but one body in him.[146]

1348 The *Eucharistic assembly (synaxis)*, because the Eucharist is celebrated amid the assembly of the faithful, the visible expression of the Church.[147]

1341 **1330** The *memorial* of the Lord's Passion and Resurrection.

The *Holy Sacrifice*, because it makes present the one sacrifice of Christ the Savior and includes the Church's offering. The terms *holy sacrifice of the Mass,* *"sacrifice of praise," spiritual sacrifice, pure and holy*

614, 2643 *sacrifice* are also used,[148] since it completes and surpasses all the sacrifices of the Old Covenant.

The *Holy and Divine Liturgy*, because the Church's whole liturgy finds its center and most intense expression in the celebration of this sacrament; in the same sense we also call its celebration the *Sacred Mys-*

1169 *teries.* We speak of the *Most Blessed Sacrament* because it is the Sacrament of sacraments. The Eucharistic species reserved in the tabernacle are designated by this same name.

950 **1331** *Holy Communion*, because by this sacrament we unite ourselves to Christ, who makes us sharers in his Body and Blood to form a single body.[149] We also call it:

948 *the holy things (ta hagia; sancta)*[150]—the first meaning of the phrase "communion of saints" in the Apostles'

1405 Creed—*the bread of angels, bread from heaven, medicine of immortality,*[151] *viaticum. . . .*

1332 *Holy Mass (Missa)*, because the liturgy in which the mystery of salvation is accomplished concludes with the sending forth *(missio)* of the faithful, so that they

849 may fulfill God's will in their daily lives.

---

144 Cf. *Lk* 24:13–35.   145 Cf. *Acts* 2:42, 46; 20:7, 11.   146 Cf. *1 Cor* 10:16–17.   147 Cf. *1 Cor* 11:17–34.   148 *Heb* 13:15; cf. *1 Pet* 2:5; *Ps* 116:13, 17; *Mal* 1:11.   149 Cf. *1 Cor* 10:16–17.   150 *Apostolic Constitutions* 8, 13, 12: PG 1, 1108; *Didache* 9, 5; 10:6: SCh 248, 176–178.   151 St. Ignatius of Antioch, *Ad Eph.* 20, 2: SCh 10, 76.

III.   THE EUCHARIST IN THE ECONOMY OF SALVATION

The signs of bread and wine

1333 At the heart of the Eucharistic celebration are *1350* the bread and wine that, by the words of Christ and the invocation of the Holy Spirit, become Christ's Body and Blood. Faithful to the Lord's command the Church continues to do, in his memory and until his glorious return, what he did on the eve of his Passion: "He took bread. . . ." "He took the cup filled with wine. . . ." The signs of bread and wine become, in a way surpassing understanding, the Body and Blood of Christ; they continue also to signify the goodness of creation. Thus in the Offertory we give thanks to the Creator for bread and wine,[152] fruit of the "work of human hands," but *1147* above all as "fruit of the earth" and "of the vine"—gifts of the Creator. The Church sees in the gesture of the *1148* king-priest Melchizedek, who "brought out bread and wine," a prefiguring of her own offering.[153]

1334 In the Old Covenant bread and wine were of- *1150* fered in sacrifice among the first fruits of the earth as a sign of grateful acknowledgment to the Creator. But they also received a new significance in the context of the Exodus: the unleavened bread that Israel eats every year at *1363* Passover commemorates the haste of the departure that liberated them from Egypt; the remembrance of the manna in the desert will always recall to Israel that it lives by the bread of the Word of God;[154] their daily bread is the fruit of the promised land, the pledge of God's faithfulness to his promises. The "cup of blessing"[155] at the end of the Jewish Passover meal adds to the festive joy of wine an eschatological dimension: the messianic expectation of the rebuilding of Jerusalem. When Jesus instituted the Eucharist, he gave a new and definitive meaning to the blessing of the bread and the cup.

1335 The miracles of the multiplication of the loaves, *1151*

---

152 Cf. *Ps* 104:13–15.   153 *Gen* 14:18; cf. *Roman Missal*, EP I (Roman Canon) 95.   154 Cf. *Deut* 8:3.   155 *1 Cor* 10:16.

when the Lord says the blessing, breaks and distributes the loaves through his disciples to feed the multitude, prefigure the superabundance of this unique bread of his Eucharist.[156] The sign of water turned into wine at Cana already announces the Hour of Jesus' glorification. It makes manifest the fulfillment of the wedding feast in the Father's kingdom, where the faithful will drink the new wine that has become the Blood of Christ.[157]

1336 The first announcement of the Eucharist divided the disciples, just as the announcement of the Passion scandalized them: "This is a hard saying; who can listen to it?"[158] The Eucharist and the Cross are stumbling blocks. It is the same mystery and it never ceases to be an occasion of division. "Will you also go away?":[159] the Lord's question echoes through the ages, as a loving invitation to discover that only he has "the words of eternal life"[160] and that to receive in faith the gift of his Eucharist is to receive the Lord himself.

1327

The institution of the Eucharist

610 **1337** The Lord, having loved those who were his own, loved them to the end. Knowing that the hour had come to leave this world and return to the Father, in the course of a meal he washed their feet and gave them the commandment of love.[161] In order to leave them a pledge of this love, in order never to depart from his own and to make them sharers in his Passover, he instituted the Eucharist as the memorial of his death and Resurrection, and commanded his apostles to celebrate it until his return; "thereby he constituted them priests

611 of the New Testament."[162]

1338 The three synoptic Gospels and St. Paul have handed on to us the account of the institution of the Eucharist; St. John, for his part, reports the words of Jesus in the synagogue of Capernaum that prepare for the institution of the Eucharist: Christ calls himself the bread of life, come down from heaven.[163]

---

156 Cf. *Mt* 14:13–21; 15:32–39.   157 Cf. *Jn* 2:11; *Mk* 14:25.   158 *Jn* 6:60.
159 *Jn* 6:67.   160 *Jn* 6:68.   161 Cf. *Jn* 13:1–17; 34–35.   162 Council of Trent
(1562): DS 1740.   163 Cf. *Jn* 6.

1339 Jesus chose the time of Passover to fulfill what *1169* he had announced at Capernaum: giving his disciples his Body and his Blood:

> Then came the day of Unleavened Bread, on which the passover lamb had to be sacrificed. So Jesus sent Peter and John, saying, "Go and prepare the passover meal for us, that we may eat it. . . ." They went . . . and prepared the passover. And when the hour came, he sat at table, and the apostles with him. And he said to them, "I have earnestly desired to eat this passover with you before I suffer; for I tell you I shall not eat it again until it is fulfilled in the kingdom of God.". . . . And he took bread, and when he had given thanks he broke it and gave it to them, saying, "This is my body which is given for you. Do this in remembrance of me." And likewise the cup after supper, saying, "This cup which is poured out for you is the New Covenant in my blood."[164]

1340 By celebrating the Last Supper with his apostles in the course of the Passover meal, Jesus gave the Jewish Passover its definitive meaning. Jesus' passing over *1151* to his father by his death and Resurrection, the new Passover, is anticipated in the Supper and celebrated in the Eucharist, which fulfills the Jewish Passover and anticipates the final Passover of the Church in the glory of *677* the kingdom.

"Do this in memory of me"

1341 The command of Jesus to repeat his actions and *611* words "until he comes" does not only ask us to remember Jesus and what he did. It is directed at the liturgical celebration, by the apostles and their successors, of the *memorial* of Christ, of his life, of his death, of his Res- *1363* urrection, and of his intercession in the presence of the Father.[165]

1342 From the beginning the Church has been faithful *2624* to the Lord's command. Of the Church of Jerusalem it is written:

---

164 *Lk* 22:7–20; cf. *Mt* 26:17–29; *Mk* 14:12–25; *1 Cor* 11:23–26.   165 Cf. *1 Cor* 11:26.

> They devoted themselves to the apostles' teaching
> and fellowship, to the breaking of bread and the
> prayers. . . . Day by day, attending the temple to-
> gether and breaking bread in their homes, they par-
> took of food with glad and generous hearts.[166]

1166, **1343** It was above all on "the first day of the week,"
2177 Sunday, the day of Jesus' resurrection, that the
Christians met "to break bread."[167] From that time
on down to our own day the celebration of the Eucharist has been continued so that today we encounter
it everywhere in the Church with the same fundamental structure. It remains the center of the Church's
life.

1404 **1344** Thus from celebration to celebration, as they
proclaim the Paschal mystery of Jesus "until he comes,"
the pilgrim People of God advances, "following the narrow way of the cross,"[168] toward the heavenly banquet,
when all the elect will be seated at the table of the kingdom.

IV.   THE LITURGICAL CELEBRATION
OF THE EUCHARIST

The Mass of all ages

1345 As early as the second century we have the witness of St. Justin Martyr for the basic lines of the order
of the Eucharistic celebration. They have stayed the
same until our own day for all the great liturgical families. St. Justin wrote to the pagan emperor Antoninus
Pius (138–161) around the year 155, explaining what
Christians did:

> On the day we call the day of the sun, all who dwell
> in the city or country gather in the same place.

> The memoirs of the apostles and the writings of the
> prophets are read, as much as time permits.

> When the reader has finished, he who presides over
> those gathered admonishes and challenges them to
> imitate these beautiful things.

---

166 *Acts* 2:42, 46.   167 *Acts* 20:7.   168 *AG* 1; cf. *1 Cor* 11:26.

Then we all rise together and offer prayers* for ourselves . . . and for all others, wherever they may be, so that we may be found righteous by our life and actions, and faithful to the commandments, so as to obtain eternal salvation.

When the prayers are concluded we exchange the kiss.

Then someone brings bread and a cup of water and wine mixed together to him who presides over the brethren.

He takes them and offers praise and glory to the Father of the universe, through the name of the Son and of the Holy Spirit and for a considerable time he gives thanks (in Greek: *eucharistian*) that we have been judged worthy of these gifts.

When he has concluded the prayers and thanksgivings, all present give voice to an acclamation by saying: "Amen."

When he who presides has given thanks and the people have responded, those whom we call deacons give to those present the "eucharisted" bread, wine and water and take them to those who are absent.[169]

1346 The liturgy of the Eucharist unfolds according to a fundamental structure which has been preserved throughout the centuries down to our own day. It displays two great parts that form a fundamental unity:

—the gathering, the liturgy of the Word, with readings, homily, and general intercessions;

—the liturgy of the Eucharist, with the presentation of the bread and wine, the consecratory thanksgiving, and communion.

The liturgy of the Word and liturgy of the Eucharist together form "one single act of worship";[170] the Eucharistic table set for us is the table both of the Word of God and of the Body of the Lord.[171]

---

169 St. Justin, *Apol.* 1, 65–67: PG 6, 428–429; the text before the asterisk (*) is from chap. 67.   170 *SC* 56.   171 Cf. *DV* 21.

1347 Is this not the same movement as the Paschal meal of the risen Jesus with his disciples? Walking with them he explained the Scriptures to them; sitting with them at table "he took bread, blessed and broke it, and gave it to them."[172]

The movement of the celebration

1348 *All gather together.* Christians come together in one place for the Eucharistic assembly. At its head is
1140 Christ himself, the principal agent of the Eucharist. He is high priest of the New Covenant; it is he himself who presides invisibly over every Eucharistic celebration. It is in representing him that the bishop or priest acting *in*
1548 *the person of Christ the head (in persona Christi capitis)* presides over the assembly, speaks after the readings, receives the offerings, and says the Eucharistic Prayer. *All* have their own active parts to play in the celebration, each in his own way: readers, those who bring up the offerings, those who give communion, and the whole people whose "Amen" manifests their participation.

1184 1349 The *Liturgy of the Word* includes "the writings of the prophets," that is, the Old Testament, and "the memoirs of the apostles" (their letters and the Gospels). After the homily, which is an exhortation to accept this Word as what it truly is, the Word of God,[173] and to put it into practice, come the intercessions for all men, according to the Apostle's words: "I urge that supplications, prayers, intercessions, and thanksgivings be made for all men, for kings, and all who are in high positions."[174]

1350 The *presentation of the offerings* (the Offertory). Then, sometimes in procession, the bread and wine are brought to the altar; they will be offered by the priest in the name of Christ in the Eucharistic sacrifice in which they will become his body and blood. It is the very action of Christ at the Last Supper—"taking the bread and a cup." "The Church alone offers this pure oblation

---

172 Cf. *Lk* 24:13–35.   173 Cf. *1 Thess* 2:13.   174 *1 Tim* 2:1–2.

to the Creator, when she offers what comes forth from his creation with thanksgiving."[175] The presentation of the offerings at the altar takes up the gesture of Melchizedek and commits the Creator's gifts into the hands of Christ who, in his sacrifice, brings to perfection all human attempts to offer sacrifices.

1359

614

1351 From the very beginning Christians have brought, along with the bread and wine for the Eucharist, gifts to share with those in need. This custom of the *collection,* ever appropriate, is inspired by the example of Christ who became poor to make us rich:[176]

1397

2186

> Those who are well off, and who are also willing, give as each chooses. What is gathered is given to him who presides to assist orphans and widows, those whom illness or any other cause has deprived of resources, prisoners, immigrants and, in a word, all who are in need.[177]

1352 The *anaphora:* with the Eucharistic Prayer—the prayer of thanksgiving and consecration—we come to the heart and summit of the celebration:

In the *preface,* the Church gives thanks to the Father, through Christ, in the Holy Spirit, for all his works: creation, redemption, and sanctification. The whole community thus joins in the unending praise that the Church in heaven, the angels and all the saints, sing to the thrice-holy God.

559

1353 In the *epiclesis,* the Church asks the Father to send his Holy Spirit (or the power of his blessing[178]) on the bread and wine, so that by his power they may become the body and blood of Jesus Christ and so that those who take part in the Eucharist may be one body and one spirit (some liturgical traditions put the epiclesis after the anamnesis).

1105

In the *institution narrative,* the power of the words and the action of Christ, and the power of the Holy Spirit, make sacramentally present under the species of bread and wine Christ's body and blood, his sacrifice offered on the cross once for all.

1375

---

175 St. Irenaeus, *Adv. haeres.* 4, 18, 4: PG 7/1, 1027; cf. *Mal* 1:11.   176 Cf. *1 Cor* 16:1; *2 Cor* 8:9.   177 St. Justin, *Apol.* 1, 67: PG 6, 429.   178 Cf. *Roman Missal,* EP I (Roman Canon) 90.

1103 **1354** In the *anamnesis* that follows, the Church calls to mind the Passion, resurrection, and glorious return of Christ Jesus; she presents to the Father the offering of his Son which reconciles us with him.

In the *intercessions,* the Church indicates that the *954* Eucharist is celebrated in communion with the whole Church in heaven and on earth, the living and the dead, and in communion with the pastors of the Church, the Pope, the diocesan bishop, his presbyterium and his deacons, and all the bishops of the whole world together with their Churches.

1382 **1355** In the communion, preceded by the Lord's prayer and the breaking of the bread, the faithful receive "the bread of heaven" and "the cup of salvation," the body and blood of Christ who offered himself "for the life of the world":[179]

1327
> Because this bread and wine have been made Eucharist ("eucharisted," according to an ancient expression), "we call this food *Eucharist,* and no one may take part in it unless he believes that what we teach is true, has received baptism for the forgiveness of sins and new birth, and lives in keeping with what Christ taught."[180]

V.   THE SACRAMENTAL SACRIFICE: THANKSGIVING, MEMORIAL, PRESENCE

1356 If from the beginning Christians have celebrated the Eucharist and in a form whose substance has not changed despite the great diversity of times and liturgies, it is because we know ourselves to be bound by the command the Lord gave on the eve of his Passion: "Do this in remembrance of me."[181]

1357 We carry out this command of the Lord by celebrating the *memorial of his sacrifice.* In so doing, *we offer to the Father* what he has himself given us: the gifts of his creation, bread and wine which, by the power of the Holy Spirit and by the words of Christ, have become the body and blood of Christ. Christ is thus really and mysteriously made *present.*

---

179 *Jn* 6:51.   180 St. Justin, *Apol.* 1, 66, 1–2: PG 6, 428.   181 *1 Cor* 11:24–25.

1358 We must therefore consider the Eucharist as:

—thanksgiving and praise to the *Father;*

—the sacrificial memorial of *Christ* and his Body;

—the presence of Christ by the power of his word and of his *Spirit.*

Thanksgiving and praise to the Father

1359 The Eucharist, the sacrament of our salvation accomplished by Christ on the cross, is also a sacrifice *293* of praise in thanksgiving for the work of creation. In the Eucharistic sacrifice the whole of creation loved by God is presented to the Father through the death and the Resurrection of Christ. Through Christ the Church can offer the sacrifice of praise in thanksgiving for all that God has made good, beautiful, and just in creation and in humanity.

1360 The Eucharist is a sacrifice of thanksgiving to the *1083* Father, a blessing by which the Church expresses her gratitude to God for all his benefits, for all that he has accomplished through creation, redemption, and sanctification. Eucharist means first of all "thanksgiving."

1361 The Eucharist is also the sacrifice of praise by which the Church sings the glory of God in the name of all creation. This sacrifice of praise is possible only through Christ: he unites the faithful to his person, to *294* his praise, and to his intercession, so that the sacrifice of praise to the Father is offered *through* Christ and *with* him, to be accepted *in* him.

The sacrificial memorial of Christ and of his Body, the Church

1362 The Eucharist is the memorial of Christ's Passover, the making present and the sacramental offering of his unique sacrifice, in the liturgy of the Church which is his Body. In all the Eucharistic Prayers we find after the words of institution a prayer called the *anamnesis* or memorial. *1103*

1363 In the sense of Sacred Scripture the *memorial* is *1099* not merely the recollection of past events but the proclamation of the mighty works wrought by God for men.[182] In the liturgical celebration of these events, they become in a certain way present and real. This is how Israel understands its liberation from Egypt: every time Passover is celebrated, the Exodus events are made present to the memory of believers so that they may conform their lives to them.

1364 In the New Testament, the memorial takes on new meaning. When the Church celebrates the Eucharist, she commemorates Christ's Passover, and it is

611
made present: the sacrifice Christ offered once for all on
1085
the cross remains ever present.[183] "As often as the sacrifice of the Cross by which 'Christ our Pasch has been sacrificed' is celebrated on the altar, the work of our redemption is carried out."[184]

2100 **1365** Because it is the memorial of Christ's Passover, the Eucharist is also a sacrifice. The sacrificial character of the Eucharist is manifested in the very words of institution: "This is my body which is given for you" and "This cup which is poured out for you is the New Covenant in my blood."[185] In the Eucharist Christ gives us the very body which he gave up for us on the cross, the very blood which he "poured out for many for the

1846
forgiveness of sins."[186]

613 **1366** The Eucharist is thus a sacrifice because it *re-presents* (makes present) the sacrifice of the cross, because it is its *memorial* and because it *applies* its fruit:

> [Christ], our Lord and God, was once and for all to offer himself to God the Father by his death on the altar of the cross, to accomplish there an everlasting redemption. But because his priesthood was not to end with his death, at the Last Supper "on the night when he was betrayed," [he wanted] to leave to his beloved spouse the Church a visible sacrifice (as the nature of man demands) by which the bloody sacrifice which he was to accomplish once

182 Cf. *Ex* 13:3. 183 Cf. *Heb* 7:25–27. 184 *LG* 3; cf. *1 Cor* 5:7. 185 *Lk* 22:19–20. 186 *Mt* 26:28.

for all on the cross would be re-presented, its memory perpetuated until the end of the world, and its salutary power be applied to the forgiveness of the sins we daily commit.[187]

1367 The sacrifice of Christ and the sacrifice of the Eucharist are *one single sacrifice:* "The victim is one and the same: the same now offers through the ministry of priests, who then offered himself on the cross; only the manner of offering is different." "In this divine sacrifice which is celebrated in the Mass, the same Christ who offered himself once in a bloody manner on the altar of the cross is contained and is offered in an unbloody manner."[188]

1545

1368 *The Eucharist is also the sacrifice of the Church.* The Church which is the Body of Christ participates in the offering of her Head. With him, she herself is offered whole and entire. She unites herself to his intercession with the Father for all men. In the Eucharist the sacrifice of Christ becomes also the sacrifice of the members of his Body. The lives of the faithful, their praise, sufferings, prayer, and work, are united with those of Christ and with his total offering, and so acquire a new value. Christ's sacrifice present on the altar makes it possible for all generations of Christians to be united with his offering.

618

2031

1109

In the catacombs the Church is often represented as a woman in prayer, arms outstretched in the praying position. Like Christ who stretched out his arms on the cross, through him, with him, and in him, she offers herself and intercedes for all men.

1369 *The whole Church is united with the offering and intercession of Christ.* Since he has the ministry of Peter in the Church, the *Pope* is associated with every celebration of the Eucharist, wherein he is named as the sign and servant of the unity of the universal Church. The *bishop* of the place is always responsible for the Eucharist, even when a *priest* presides; the bishop's name is mentioned to signify his presidency over the particu-

834, 882

1561, 1566

---

187 Council of Trent (1562): DS 1740; cf. *1 Cor* 11:23; *Heb* 7:24, 27.
188 Council of Trent (1562): DS 1743; cf. *Heb* 9:14, 27.

lar Church, in the midst of his presbyterium and with the assistance of *deacons*. The community intercedes also for all ministers who, for it and with it, offer the Eucharistic sacrifice:

> Let only that Eucharist be regarded as legitimate, which is celebrated under [the presidency of] the bishop or him to whom he has entrusted it.[189]

> Through the ministry of priests the spiritual sacrifice of the faithful is completed in union with the sacrifice of Christ the only Mediator, which in the Eucharist is offered through the priests' hands in the name of the whole Church in an unbloody and sacramental manner until the Lord himself comes.[190]

1370 To the offering of Christ are united not only the members still here on earth, but also those already *in the glory of heaven*. In communion with and commemorating the Blessed Virgin Mary and all the saints, the Church offers the Eucharistic sacrifice. In the Eucharist the Church is as it were at the foot of the cross with Mary, united with the offering and intercession of Christ.

956
969

1371 The Eucharistic sacrifice is also offered for *the faithful departed* who "have died in Christ but are not yet wholly purified,"[191] so that they may be able to enter into the light and peace of Christ:

958, 1689
1032

> Put this body anywhere! Don't trouble yourselves about it! I simply ask you to remember me at the Lord's altar wherever you are.[192]

> Then, we pray [in the anaphora] for the holy fathers and bishops who have fallen asleep, and in general for all who have fallen asleep before us, in the belief that it is a great benefit to the souls on whose behalf the supplication is offered, while the holy and tremendous Victim is present. . . . By offering to God our supplications for those who have fallen asleep, if they have sinned, we . . . offer Christ sacrificed for the sins of all, and so render fa-

---

189 St. Ignatius of Antioch, *Ad Smyrn.* 8:1; SCh 10, 138.   190 *PO* 2 § 4.
191 Council of Trent (1562): DS 1743.   192 St. Monica, before her death, to her sons, St. Augustine and his brother; *Conf.* 9, 11, 27: PL 32, 775.

vorable, for them and for us, the God who loves man.[193]

1372 St. Augustine admirably summed up this doctrine that moves us to an ever more complete participation in our Redeemer's sacrifice which we celebrate in the Eucharist:

1140

> This wholly redeemed city, the assembly and society of the saints, is offered to God as a universal sacrifice by the high priest who in the form of a slave went so far as to offer himself for us in his Passion, to make us the Body of so great a head. . . . Such is the sacrifice of Christians: "we who are many are one Body in Christ." The Church continues to reproduce this sacrifice in the sacrament of the altar so well-known to believers wherein it is evident to them that in what she offers she herself is offered.[194]

The presence of Christ by the power of his word and the Holy Spirit

1373 "Christ Jesus, who died, yes, who was raised from the dead, who is at the right hand of God, who indeed intercedes for us," is present in many ways to his Church:[195] in his word, in his Church's prayer, "where two or three are gathered in my name,"[196] in the poor, the sick, and the imprisoned,[197] in the sacraments of which he is the author, in the sacrifice of the Mass, and in the person of the minister. But "he is present . . . most *especially in the Eucharistic species.*"[198]

1088

1374 The mode of Christ's presence under the Eucharistic species is unique. It raises the Eucharist above all the sacraments as "the perfection of the spiritual life and the end to which all the sacraments tend."[199] In the most blessed sacrament of the Eucharist "the body and blood, together with the soul and divinity, of our Lord Jesus Christ and, therefore, *the whole Christ is truly, really, and substantially* contained."[200] "This presence is

1211

---

193 St. Cyril of Jerusalem, *Catech. myst.* 5, 9. 10: PG 33, 1116–1117.   194 St. Augustine, *De civ. Dei*, 10, 6: PL 41, 283; cf. *Rom* 12:5.   195 *Rom* 8:34; cf. *LG* 48.   196 *Mt* 18:20.   197 Cf. *Mt* 25:31–46.   198 *SC* 7.   199 St. Thomas Aquinas, *STh* III, 73, 3c.   200 Council of Trent (1551): DS 1651.

called 'real'—by which is not intended to exclude the other types of presence as if they could not be 'real' too, but because it is presence in the fullest sense: that is to say, it is a *substantial* presence by which Christ, God and man, makes himself wholly and entirely present."[201]

1375 It is by the conversion of the bread and wine into Christ's body and blood that Christ becomes present in this sacrament. The Church Fathers strongly affirmed

1105 the faith of the Church in the efficacy of the Word of Christ and of the action of the Holy Spirit to bring about this conversion. Thus St. John Chrysostom declares:

> It is not man that causes the things offered to become the Body and Blood of Christ, but he who was crucified for us, Christ himself. The priest, in the role of Christ, pronounces these words, but
1128 their power and grace are God's. This is my body, he says. This word transforms the things offered.[202]

And St. Ambrose says about this conversion:

> Be convinced that this is not what nature has formed, but what the blessing has consecrated. The power of the blessing prevails over that of nature, because by the blessing nature itself is changed. . . . Could not Christ's word, which can make from
298 nothing what did not exist, change existing things into what they were not before? It is no less a feat to give things their original nature than to change their nature.[203]

1376 The Council of Trent summarizes the Catholic faith by declaring: "Because Christ our Redeemer said that it was truly his body that he was offering under the species of bread, it has always been the conviction of the Church of God, and this holy Council now declares again, that by the consecration of the bread and wine there takes place a change of the whole substance of the bread into the substance of the body of Christ our Lord and of the whole substance of the wine into the substance of his blood. This change the holy Catholic

201 Paul VI, *MF* 39.   202 St. John Chrysostom, *prod. Jud.* 1:6: PG 49, 380.
203 St. Ambrose, *De myst.* 9, 50; 52: PL 16, 405–407.

Church has fittingly and properly called transubstantiation."[204]

1377 The Eucharistic presence of Christ begins at the moment of the consecration and endures as long as the Eucharistic species subsist. Christ is present whole and entire in each of the species and whole and entire in each of their parts, in such a way that the breaking of the bread does not divide Christ.[205]

1378 *Worship of the Eucharist.* In the liturgy of the Mass we express our faith in the real presence of Christ under the species of bread and wine by, among other ways, genuflecting or bowing deeply as a sign of adoration of the Lord. "The Catholic Church has always offered and still offers to the sacrament of the Eucharist the cult of adoration, not only during Mass, but also outside of it, reserving the consecrated hosts with the utmost care, exposing them to the solemn veneration of the faithful, and carrying them in procession."[206]

1178

103
2628

1379 The tabernacle was first intended for the reservation of the Eucharist in a worthy place so that it could be brought to the sick and those absent, outside of Mass. As faith in the real presence of Christ in his Eucharist deepened, the Church became conscious of the meaning of silent adoration of the Lord present under the Eucharistic species. It is for this reason that the tabernacle should be located in an especially worthy place in the church and should be constructed in such a way that it emphasizes and manifests the truth of the real presence of Christ in the Blessed Sacrament.

1183

2691

1380 It is highly fitting that Christ should have wanted to remain present to his Church in this unique way. Since Christ was about to take his departure from his own in his visible form, he wanted to give us his sacramental presence; since he was about to offer himself on the cross to save us, he wanted us to have the memorial of the love with which he loved us "to the end,"[207] even to the giving of his life. In his Eucharistic

669

---

204 Council of Trent (1551): DS 1642; cf. *Mt* 26:26 ff.; *Mk* 14:22 ff.; *Lk* 22:19 ff.; *1 Cor* 11:24 ff. 205 Cf. Council of Trent: DS 1641. 206 Paul VI, *MF* 56. 207 *Jn* 13:1.

presence he remains mysteriously in our midst as the
478 one who loved us and gave himself up for us,[208] and he
remains under signs that express and communicate this
love:

> The Church and the world have a great need for
> Eucharistic worship. Jesus awaits us in this sacra-
> ment of love. Let us not refuse the time to go to
2715   meet him in adoration, in contemplation full of
> faith, and open to making amends for the serious
> offenses and crimes of the world. Let our adoration
> never cease.[209]

1381 "That in this sacrament are the true Body of
Christ and his true Blood is something that 'cannot be
156 apprehended by the senses,' says St. Thomas, 'but *only*
215 *by faith*, which relies on divine authority.' For this reason, in a commentary on *Luke* 22:19 ('This is my body
which is given for you.'), St. Cyril says: 'Do not doubt
whether this is true, but rather receive the words of
the Savior in faith, for since he is the truth, he cannot
lie.' "[210]

> Godhead here in hiding, whom I do adore
> Masked by these bare shadows, shape and nothing
> more,
> See, Lord, at thy service low lies here a heart
> Lost, all lost in wonder at the God thou art.
>
> Seeing, touching, tasting are in thee deceived;
> How says trusty hearing? that shall be believed;
> What God's Son has told me, take for truth I do;
> Truth himself speaks truly or there's nothing
> true.[211]

VI. The Paschal Banquet

1382 The Mass is at the same time, and inseparably,
the sacrificial memorial in which the sacrifice of the
cross is perpetuated and the sacred banquet of communion with the Lord's body and blood. But the celebration of the Eucharistic sacrifice is wholly directed to-

---

208 Cf. *Gal* 2:20.   209 John Paul II, *Dominicae cenae*, 3.   210 St. Thomas
Aquinas, *STh* III, 75, 1; cf. Paul VI, *MF* 18; St. Cyril of Alexandria, *In Luc.* 22,
19: PG 72, 912; cf. Paul VI, *MF* 18.   211 St. Thomas Aquinas (attr.), *Adoro te
devote;* tr. Gerard Manley Hopkins.

ward the intimate union of the faithful with Christ through communion. To receive communion is to receive Christ himself who has offered himself for us. *950*

1383 *The altar,* around which the Church is gathered *1182* in the celebration of the Eucharist, represents the two aspects of the same mystery: the altar of the sacrifice and the table of the Lord. This is all the more so since the Christian altar is the symbol of Christ himself, present in the midst of the assembly of his faithful, both as the victim offered for our reconciliation and as food from heaven who is giving himself to us. "For what is the altar of Christ if not the image of the Body of Christ?"[212] asks St. Ambrose. He says elsewhere, "The altar represents the body [of Christ] and the Body of Christ is on the altar."[213] The liturgy expresses this unity of sacrifice and communion in many prayers. Thus the Roman Church prays in its anaphora:

> We entreat you, almighty God,
> that by the hands of your holy Angel
> this offering may be borne to your altar in heaven
> in the sight of your divine majesty,
> so that as we receive in communion at this altar
> the most holy Body and Blood of your Son,
> we may be filled with every heavenly blessing and
> grace.[214]

"Take this and eat it, all of you": communion

1384 The Lord addresses an invitation to us, urging us *2835* to receive him in the sacrament of the Eucharist: "Truly, I say to you, unless you eat the flesh of the Son of man and drink his blood, you have no life in you."[215]

1385 To respond to this invitation we must *prepare ourselves* for so great and so holy a moment. St. Paul urges us to examine our conscience: "Whoever, therefore, eats the bread or drinks the cup of the Lord in an

---

212 St. Ambrose, *De Sacr.* 5, 2, 7: PL 16, 447C. 213 St. Ambrose, *De Sacr.* 4, 2, 7: PL 16, 437D. 214 *Roman Missal,* EP I (Roman Canon) 96: Supplices te rogamus, omnipotens Deus: iube hæc perferri per manus sancti Angeli tui in sublime altare tuum, in conspectu divinae maiestatis tuae: ut, quotquot ex hac altaris participatione sacrosanctum Filii Corpus et Sanguinem sumpserimus, omni benedictione cælesti et gratia repleamur. 215 *Jn* 6:53.

unworthy manner will be guilty of profaning the body and blood of the Lord. Let a man examine himself, and so eat of the bread and drink of the cup. For any one who eats and drinks without discerning the body eats

1457 and drinks judgment upon himself."[216] Anyone conscious of a grave sin must receive the sacrament of Reconciliation before coming to communion.

1386 Before so great a sacrament, the faithful can only echo humbly and with ardent faith the words of the Centurion: *"Domine, non sum dignus ut intres sub tectum meum, sed tantum dic verbo, et sanabitur anima mea"* ("Lord, I am not worthy that you should enter under my roof, but only say the word and my soul will be healed.").[217] And in the Divine Liturgy of St. John Chrysostom the faithful pray in the same spirit:

732   O Son of God, bring me into communion today with your mystical supper. I shall not tell your enemies the secret, nor kiss you with Judas' kiss. But like the good thief I cry, "Jesus, remember me when you come into your kingdom."

1387 To prepare for worthy reception of this sacrament, the faithful should observe the fast required in their

2043 Church.[218] Bodily demeanor (gestures, clothing) ought to convey the respect, solemnity, and joy of this moment when Christ becomes our guest.

1388 It is in keeping with the very meaning of the Eucharist that the faithful, if they have the required dispositions, *receive communion each time* they participate in the Mass.[219] As the Second Vatican Council says: "That more perfect form of participation in the Mass whereby the faithful, after the priest's communion, receive the Lord's Body from the same sacrifice, is warmly recommended."[220]

2042 **1389** The Church obliges the faithful "to take part in the Divine Liturgy on Sundays and feast days" and, prepared by the sacrament of Reconciliation, to receive the Eucharist at least once a year, if possible during the

---

216 1 Cor 11:27–29. 217 *Roman Missal,* response to the invitation to communion; cf. *Mt* 8:8. 218 Cf. CIC, can. 919. 219 Cf. CIC, can. 917; AAS 76 (1984) 746–747. 220 *SC* 55.

Easter season.[221] But the Church strongly encourages the faithful to receive the holy Eucharist on Sundays and feast days, or more often still, even daily.

2837

1390 Since Christ is sacramentally present under each of the species, communion under the species of bread alone makes it possible to receive all the fruit of Eucharistic grace. For pastoral reasons this manner of receiving communion has been legitimately established as the most common form in the Latin rite. But "the sign of communion is more complete when given under both kinds, since in that form the sign of the Eucharistic meal appears more clearly."[222] This is the usual form of receiving communion in the Eastern rites.

The fruits of Holy Communion

1391 *Holy Communion augments our union with Christ.* The principal fruit of receiving the Eucharist in Holy Communion is an intimate union with Christ Jesus. Indeed, the Lord said: "He who eats my flesh and drinks my blood abides in me, and I in him."[223] Life in Christ has its foundation in the Eucharistic banquet: "As the living Father sent me, and I live because of the Father, so he who eats me will live because of me."[224]

460

521

> On the feasts of the Lord, when the faithful receive the Body of the Son, they proclaim to one another the Good News that the first fruits of life have been given, as when the angel said to Mary Magdalene, "Christ is risen!" Now too are life and resurrection conferred on whoever receives Christ.[225]

1392 What material food produces in our bodily life, Holy Communion wonderfully achieves in our spiritual life. Communion with the flesh of the risen Christ, a flesh "given life and giving life through the Holy Spirit,"[226] preserves, increases, and renews the life of grace received at Baptism. This growth in Christian life needs the nourishment of Eucharistic Communion, the bread for our pilgrimage until the moment of death, when it will be given to us as viaticum.

1212

1524

---

221 OE 15; CIC, can. 920.   222 GIRM 240.   223 *Jn* 6:56.   224 *Jn* 6:57.
225 Fanqîth, Syriac Office of Antioch, Vol. I, Commun., 237 a-b.   226 PO 5.

1393 *Holy Communion separates us from sin.* The body of Christ we receive in Holy Communion is "given up for us," and the blood we drink "shed for the many for the forgiveness of sins." For this reason the Eu-

613 charist cannot unite us to Christ without at the same time cleansing us from past sins and preserving us from future sins:

> For as often as we eat this bread and drink the cup, we proclaim the death of the Lord. If we proclaim the Lord's death, we proclaim the forgiveness of sins. If, as often as his blood is poured out, it is poured for the forgiveness of sins, I should always receive it, so that it may always forgive my sins. Because I always sin, I should always have a remedy.[227]

1394 As bodily nourishment restores lost strength, so the Eucharist strengthens our charity, which tends to be

1863 weakened in daily life; and this living charity *wipes*
1436 *away venial sins.*[228] By giving himself to us Christ revives our love and enables us to break our disordered attachments to creatures and root ourselves in him:

> Since Christ died for us out of love, when we celebrate the memorial of his death at the moment of sacrifice we ask that love may be granted to us by the coming of the Holy Spirit. We humbly pray that in the strength of this love by which Christ willed to die for us, we, by receiving the gift of the Holy Spirit, may be able to consider the world as crucified for us, and to be ourselves as crucified to the world. . . . Having received the gift of love, let us die to sin and live for God.[229]

1395 By the same charity that it enkindles in us, the Eucharist *preserves us from future mortal sins.* The

1855 more we share the life of Christ and progress in his friendship, the more difficult it is to break away from him by mortal sin. The Eucharist is not ordered to the forgiveness of mortal sins—that is proper to the sacra-

1446 ment of Reconciliation. The Eucharist is properly the

---

227 St. Ambrose, *De Sacr.* 4, 6, 28: PL 16, 446; cf. *1 Cor* 11:26. 228 Cf. Council of Trent (1551): DS 1638. 229 St. Fulgentius of Ruspe, *Contra Fab.* 28, 16–19: CCL 19A, 813–814.

sacrament of those who are in full communion with the Church.

1396 *The unity of the Mystical Body: the Eucharist* 1118
makes the Church. Those who receive the Eucharist are united more closely to Christ. Through it Christ unites them to all the faithful in one body—the Church. Communion renews, strengthens, and deepens this incorporation into the Church, already achieved by Baptism. In Baptism we have been called to form but one body.[230]
The Eucharist fulfills this call: "The cup of blessing 1267 which we bless, is it not a participation in the blood of Christ? The bread which we break, is it not a participation in the body of Christ? Because there is one bread, we who are many are one body, for we all partake of the one bread:"[231]

790

> If you are the body and members of Christ, then it
> is your sacrament that is placed on the table of the 1064
> Lord; it is your sacrament that you receive. To that
> which you are you respond "Amen" ("yes, it is
> true!") and by responding to it you assent to it. For
> you hear the words, "the Body of Christ" and re-
> spond "Amen." Be then a member of the Body of
> Christ that your *Amen* may be true.[232]

1397 *The Eucharist commits us to the poor.* To receive
in truth the Body and Blood of Christ given up for us, 2449
we must recognize Christ in the poorest, his brethren:

> You have tasted the Blood of the Lord, yet you do
> not recognize your brother, ... You dishonor this
> table when you do not judge worthy of sharing
> your food someone judged worthy to take part in
> this meal. . . . God freed you from all your sins and
> invited you here, but you have not become more
> merciful.[233]

1398 *The Eucharist and the unity of Christians.* Before the greatness of this mystery St. Augustine exclaims, "*O sacrament of devotion! O sign of unity! O
bond of charity!*"[234] The more painful the experience of 817

---

230 Cf. *1 Cor* 12:13. 231 *1 Cor* 10:16–17. 232 St. Augustine, *Sermo* 272: PL
38, 1247. 233 St. John Chrysostom, *Hom. in 1 Cor.* 27, 4: PG 61, 229–230; cf.
Mt 25:40. 234 St. Augustine, *In Jo. ev.* 26, 13: PL 35, 1613; cf. SC 47.

the divisions in the Church which break the common participation in the table of the Lord, the more urgent are our prayers to the Lord that the time of complete unity among all who believe in him may return.

838 **1399** The Eastern churches that are not in full communion with the Catholic Church celebrate the Eucharist with great love. "These Churches, although separated from us, yet possess true sacraments, above all—by apostolic succession—the priesthood and the Eucharist, whereby they are still joined to us in closest intimacy." A certain communion *in sacris,* and so in the Eucharist, "given suitable circumstances and the approval of Church authority, is not merely possible but is encouraged."[235]

1400 Ecclesial communities derived from the Reformation and separated from the Catholic Church, "have not preserved the proper reality of the Eucharistic mystery in its fullness, especially because of the absence of the sacrament of Holy Orders."[236] It is for this reason that Eucharis-

1536 tic intercommunion with these communities is not possible for the Catholic Church. However these ecclesial communities, "when they commemorate the Lord's death and resurrection in the Holy Supper ... profess that it signifies life in communion with Christ and await his coming in glory."[237]

1483 **1401** When, in the Ordinary's judgment, a grave necessity arises, Catholic ministers may give the sacraments of Eucharist, Penance, and Anointing of the Sick to other Christians not in full communion with the Catholic Church, who ask for them of their own will, provided they

1385 give evidence of holding the Catholic faith regarding these sacraments and possess the required dispositions.[238]

VII. THE EUCHARIST—"PLEDGE OF THE GLORY TO COME"

1402 In an ancient prayer the Church acclaims the mystery of the Eucharist: "O sacred banquet in which Christ is received as food, the memory of his Passion is

1323 renewed, the soul is filled with grace and a pledge of the life to come is given to us." If the Eucharist is the memorial of the Passover of the Lord Jesus, if by our communion at the altar we are filled "with every heavenly

---

235 *UR* 15 § 2; cf. CIC, can. 844 § 3.   236 *UR* 22 § 3.   237 *UR* 22 § 3.
238 Cf. CIC, can. 844 § 4.

blessing and grace,"[239] then the Eucharist is also an anticipation of the heavenly glory.

1130

1403 At the Last Supper the Lord himself directed his disciples' attention toward the fulfillment of the Passover in the kingdom of God: "I tell you I shall not drink again of this fruit of the vine until that day when I drink it new with you in my Father's kingdom."[240] Whenever the Church celebrates the Eucharist she remembers this promise and turns her gaze "to him who is to come." In her prayer she calls for his coming: "*Marana tha!*" "Come, Lord Jesus!"[241] "May your grace come and this world pass away!"[242]

671

1404 The Church knows that the Lord comes even now in his Eucharist and that he is there in our midst. However, his presence is veiled. Therefore we celebrate the Eucharist "awaiting the blessed hope and the coming of our Savior, Jesus Christ,"[243] asking "to share in your glory when every tear will be wiped away. On that day we shall see you, our God, as you are. We shall become like you and praise you for ever through Christ our Lord."[244]

1041
1028

1405 There is no surer pledge or clearer sign of this great hope in the new heavens and new earth "in which righteousness dwells,"[245] than the Eucharist. Every time this mystery is celebrated, "the work of our redemption is carried on" and we "break the one bread that provides the medicine of immortality, the antidote for death, and the food that makes us live for ever in Jesus Christ."[246]

1042

1000

IN BRIEF

1406 Jesus said: "I am the living bread that came down from heaven; if any one eats of this bread, he will live for ever; . . . he who eats my flesh

---

239 *Roman Missal*, EP I (Roman Canon) 96: *Supplices te rogamus.*   240 *Mt* 26:29; cf. *Lk* 22:18; *Mk* 14:25.   241 *Rev* 1:4; 22:20; *1 Cor* 16:22.   242 *Didache* 10, 6: SCh 248, 180.   243 *Roman Missal* 126, embolism after the Our Father: *expectantes beatam spem et adventum Salvatoris nostri Jesu Christi*; cf. *Titus* 2:13. 244 EP III 116: prayer for the dead.   245 *2 Pet* 3:13.   246 *LG* 3; St. Ignatius of Antioch, *Ad Eph.* 20, 2: SCh 10, 76.

and drinks my blood has eternal life and ...
abides in me, and I in him" (*Jn* 6:51, 54, 56).

1407   The Eucharist is the heart and the summit of the
Church's life, for in it Christ associates his
Church and all her members with his sacrifice of
praise and thanksgiving offered once for all on
the cross to his Father; by this sacrifice he pours
out the graces of salvation on his Body which is
the Church.

1408   The Eucharistic celebration always includes: the
proclamation of the Word of God; thanksgiving
to God the Father for all his benefits, above all
the gift of his Son; the consecration of bread and
wine; and participation in the liturgical banquet
by receiving the Lord's body and blood. These
elements constitute one single act of worship.

1409   The Eucharist is the memorial of Christ's
Passover, that is, of the work of salvation accomplished by the life, death, and resurrection of
Christ, a work made present by the liturgical action.

1410   It is Christ himself, the eternal high priest of the
New Covenant who, acting through the ministry
of the priests, offers the Eucharistic sacrifice.
And it is the same Christ, really present under
the species of bread and wine, who is the offering of the Eucharistic sacrifice.

1411   Only validly ordained priests can preside at the
Eucharist and consecrate the bread and the wine
so that they become the Body and Blood of the
Lord.

1412   The essential signs of the Eucharistic sacrament
are wheat bread and grape wine, on which the
blessing of the Holy Spirit is invoked and the
priest pronounces the words of consecration
spoken by Jesus during the Last Supper: "This is
my body which will be given up for you. ...
This is the cup of my blood. ..."

1413 By the consecration the transubstantiation of the bread and wine into the Body and Blood of Christ is brought about. Under the consecrated species of bread and wine Christ himself, living and glorious, is present in a true, real, and substantial manner: his Body and his Blood, with his soul and his divinity (cf. Council of Trent: DS 1640; 1651).

1414 As sacrifice, the Eucharist is also offered in reparation for the sins of the living and the dead and to obtain spiritual or temporal benefits from God.

1415 Anyone who desires to receive Christ in Eucharistic communion must be in the state of grace. Anyone aware of having sinned mortally must not receive communion without having received absolution in the sacrament of penance.

1416 Communion with the Body and Blood of Christ increases the communicant's union with the Lord, forgives his venial sins, and preserves him from grave sins. Since receiving this sacrament strengthens the bonds of charity between the communicant and Christ, it also reinforces the unity of the Church as the Mystical Body of Christ.

1417 The Church warmly recommends that the faithful receive Holy Communion each time they participate in the celebration of the Eucharist; she obliges them to do so at least once a year.

1418 Because Christ himself is present in the sacrament of the altar, he is to be honored with the worship of adoration. "To visit the Blessed Sacrament is . . . a proof of gratitude, an expression of love, and a duty of adoration toward Christ our Lord" (Paul VI, *MF* 66).

1419 Having passed from this world to the Father, Christ gives us in the Eucharist the pledge of glory with him. Participation in the Holy Sacri-

fice identifies us with his Heart, sustains our
strength along the pilgrimage of this life, makes
us long for eternal life, and unites us even now
to the Church in heaven, the Blessed Virgin
Mary, and all the saints.

CHAPTER TWO
THE SACRAMENTS OF HEALING

1420 Through the sacraments of Christian initiation,
man receives the new life of Christ. Now we carry this
life "in earthen vessels," and it remains "hidden with
Christ in God."[1] We are still in our "earthly tent," subject to suffering, illness, and death.[2] This new life as a
child of God can be weakened and even lost by sin.

1421 The Lord Jesus Christ, physician of our souls
and bodies, who forgave the sins of the paralytic and restored him to bodily health,[3] has willed that his Church
continue, in the power of the Holy Spirit, his work of
healing and salvation, even among her own members.
This is the purpose of the two sacraments of healing: the
sacrament of Penance and the sacrament of Anointing
of the Sick.

ARTICLE 4
THE SACRAMENT OF PENANCE
AND RECONCILIATION

980 **1422** "Those who approach the sacrament of Penance
obtain pardon from God's mercy for the offense committed against him, and are, at the same time, reconciled with the Church which they have wounded by
their sins and which by charity, by example, and by
prayer labors for their conversion."[4]

I.   WHAT IS THIS SACRAMENT CALLED?

1989 **1423** It is called the *sacrament of conversion* because
it makes sacramentally present Jesus' call to conversion,

---

1 2 *Cor* 4:7; *Col* 3:3.   2 2 *Cor* 5:1.   3 Cf. *Mk* 2:1–12.   4 *LG* 11 § 2.

the first step in returning to the Father[5] from whom one has strayed by sin.

It is called the *sacrament of Penance,* since it 1440 consecrates the Christian sinner's personal and ecclesial steps of conversion, penance, and satisfaction.

1424 It is called the *sacrament of confession,* since the 1456 disclosure or confession of sins to a priest is an essential element of this sacrament. In a profound sense it is also a "confession"—acknowledgment and praise—of the holiness of God and of his mercy toward sinful man.

It is called the *sacrament of forgiveness,* since by 1449 the priest's sacramental absolution God grants the penitent "pardon and peace."[6]

It is called the *sacrament of Reconciliation,* be- 1442 cause it imparts to the sinner the love of God who reconciles: "Be reconciled to God."[7] He who lives by God's merciful love is ready to respond to the Lord's call: "Go; first be reconciled to your brother."[8]

II.   WHY A SACRAMENT OF RECONCILIATION AFTER BAPTISM?

1425 "You were washed, you were sanctified, you 1263 were justified in the name of the Lord Jesus Christ and in the Spirit of our God."[9] One must appreciate the magnitude of the gift God has given us in the sacraments of Christian initiation in order to grasp the degree to which sin is excluded for him who has "put on Christ."[10] But the apostle John also says: "If we say we have no sin, we deceive ourselves, and the truth is not in us."[11] And the Lord himself taught us to pray: "Forgive us our trespasses,"[12] linking our forgiveness of one an- 2838 other's offenses to the forgiveness of our sins that God will grant us.

1426 *Conversion* to Christ, the new birth of Baptism, the gift of the Holy Spirit and the Body and Blood of Christ received as food have made us "holy and without blemish," just as the Church herself, the Bride of Christ,

---

5 Cf. *Mk* 1:15; *Lk* 15:18. 6 *OP* 46: formula of absolution. 7 2 *Cor* 5:20.
8 *Mt* 5:24. 9 1 *Cor* 6:11. 10 *Gal* 3:27. 11 1 *Jn* 1:8. 12 Cf. *Lk* 11:4; *Mt* 6:12.

is "holy and without blemish."[13] Nevertheless the new life received in Christian initiation has not abolished the frailty and weakness of human nature, nor the inclina- tion to sin that tradition calls *concupiscence,* which re- mains in the baptized such that with the help of the grace of Christ they may prove themselves in the strug- gle of Christian life.[14] This is the struggle of *conversion* directed toward holiness and eternal life to which the Lord never ceases to call us.[15]

405, 978
1264

III.   THE CONVERSION OF THE BAPTIZED

541   **1427**   Jesus calls to conversion. This call is an essential part of the proclamation of the kingdom: "The time is fulfilled, and the kingdom of God is at hand; repent, and believe in the gospel."[16] In the Church's preaching this call is addressed first to those who do not yet know Christ and his Gospel. Also, Baptism is the principal place for the first and fundamental conversion. It is by faith in the Gospel and by Baptism[17] that one renounces evil and gains salvation, that is, the forgiveness of all sins and the gift of new life.

1226

1428   Christ's call to conversion continues to resound in the lives of Christians. This *second conversion* is an uninterrupted task for the whole Church who, "clasp- ing sinners to her bosom, [is] at once holy and always in need of purification, [and] follows constantly the path of penance and renewal."[18] This endeavor of con- version is not just a human work. It is the movement of a "contrite heart," drawn and moved by grace to respond to the merciful love of God who loved us first.[19]

1036

853

1996

1429   St. Peter's conversion after he had denied his master three times bears witness to this. Jesus' look of infinite mercy drew tears of repentance from Peter and, after the Lord's resurrection, a threefold affirmation of love for him.[20] The second conversion also has a *com-*

---

13 *Eph* 1:4; 5:27.   14 Cf. Council of Trent (1546): DS 1515.   15 Cf. Council of Trent (1547): DS 1545; *LG* 40.   16 *Mk* 1:15.   17 Cf. *Acts* 2:38.   18 *LG* 8 § 3.
19 *Ps* 51:17; cf. *Jn* 6:44; 12:32; *1 Jn* 4:10.   20 Cf. *Lk* 22:61; *Jn* 21:15–17.

munitarian dimension, as is clear in the Lord's call to a whole Church: "Repent!"[21]

> St. Ambrose says of the two conversions that, in the Church, "there are water and tears: the water of Baptism and the tears of repentance."[22]

IV. INTERIOR PENANCE

1430 Jesus' call to conversion and penance, like that of the prophets before him, does not aim first at outward works, "sackcloth and ashes," fasting and mortification, but at the *conversion of the heart, interior conversion*. Without this, such penances remain sterile and false; however, interior conversion urges expression in visible signs, gestures and works of penance.[23]   *1098*

1431 Interior repentance is a radical reorientation of our whole life, a return, a conversion to God with all our heart, an end of sin, a turning away from evil, with repugnance toward the evil actions we have committed. At the same time it entails the desire and resolution to change one's life, with hope in God's mercy and trust in the help of his grace. This conversion of heart is accompanied by a salutary pain and sadness which the Fathers called *animi cruciatus* (affliction of spirit) and *compunctio cordis* (repentance of heart).[24]   *1451*

368

1432 The human heart is heavy and hardened. God must give man a new heart.[25] Conversion is first of all a work of the grace of God who makes our hearts return to him: "Restore us to thyself, O LORD, that we may be restored!"[26] God gives us the strength to begin anew. It is in discovering the greatness of God's love that our heart is shaken by the horror and weight of sin and begins to fear offending God by sin and being separated from him. The human heart is converted by looking upon him whom our sins have pierced:[27]   *1989*

---

21 *Rev* 2:5, 16.   22 St. Ambrose, *ep.* 41, 12: PL 16, 1116.   23 Cf. *Joel* 2:12–13; *Isa* 1:16–17; *Mt* 6:1–6; 16–18.   24 Cf. Council of Trent (1551): DS 1676–1678; 1705; cf. *Roman Catechism*, II, V, 4.   25 Cf. *Ezek* 36:26–27.   26 *Lam* 5:21. 27 Cf. *Jn* 19:37; *Zech* 12:10.

> Let us fix our eyes on Christ's blood and understand how precious it is to his Father, for, poured out for our salvation, it has brought to the whole world the grace of repentance.[28]

729 **1433** Since Easter, the Holy Spirit has proved "the world wrong about sin,"[29] i.e., proved that the world has not believed in him whom the Father has sent. But this same Spirit who brings sin to light is also the Con- *692, 1848* soler who gives the human heart grace for repentance and conversion.[30]

V.   THE MANY FORMS OF PENANCE IN CHRISTIAN LIFE

1969 **1434** The interior penance of the Christian can be expressed in many and various ways. Scripture and the Fathers insist above all on three forms, *fasting, prayer,* and *almsgiving,*[31] which express conversion in relation to oneself, to God, and to others. Alongside the radical purification brought about by Baptism or martyrdom they cite as means of obtaining forgiveness of sins: efforts at reconciliation with one's neighbor, tears of repentance, concern for the salvation of one's neighbor, the intercession of the saints, and the practice of charity "which covers a multitude of sins."[32]

1435 Conversion is accomplished in daily life by gestures of reconciliation, concern for the poor, the exercise and defense of justice and right,[33] by the admission of faults to one's brethren, fraternal correction, revision of life, examination of conscience, spiritual direction, acceptance of suffering, endurance of persecution for the sake of righteousness. Taking up one's cross each day and following Jesus is the surest way of penance.[34]

1436 *Eucharist and Penance.* Daily conversion and penance find their source and nourishment in the Eucharist, for in it is made present the sacrifice of Christ which has reconciled us with God. Through the Eucharist those who live from the life of Christ are fed and strengthened. "It is a remedy to free us from our daily faults and to *1394* preserve us from mortal sins."[35]

---

28 St. Clement of Rome, *Ad Cor.* 7, 4: PG 1, 224.   29 Cf. *Jn* 16:8–9.   30 Cf. *Jn* 15:26; *Acts* 2:36–38; John Paul II, *DeV* 27–48.   31 Cf. *Tob* 12:8; *Mt* 6:1–18. 32 *1 Pet* 4:8; cf. *Jas* 5:20.   33 Cf. *Am* 5:24; *Isa* 1:17.   34 Cf. *Lk* 9:23. 35 Council of Trent (1551): DS 1638.

1437 Reading Sacred Scripture, praying the Liturgy of the Hours and the Our Father—every sincere act of worship or devotion revives the spirit of conversion and repentance within us and contributes to the forgiveness of our sins.

1438 *The seasons and days of penance* in the course of the liturgical year (Lent, and each Friday in memory of the death of the Lord) are intense moments of the Church's penitential practice.[36] These times are particularly appropriate for spiritual exercises, penitential liturgies, pilgrimages as signs of penance, voluntary self-denial such as fasting and almsgiving, and fraternal sharing (charitable and missionary works). *540*

2043

1439 *The process of conversion and repentance* was described by Jesus in the parable of the prodigal son, the center of which is the merciful father:[37] the fascination of illusory freedom, the abandonment of the father's house; the extreme misery in which the son finds himself after squandering his fortune; his deep humiliation at finding himself obliged to feed swine, and still worse, at wanting to feed on the husks the pigs ate; his reflection on all he has lost; his repentance and decision to declare himself guilty before his father; the journey back; the father's generous welcome; the father's joy—all these are characteristic of the process of conversion. The beautiful robe, the ring, and the festive banquet are symbols of that new life—pure, worthy, and joyful—of anyone who returns to God and to the bosom of his family, which is the Church. Only the heart of Christ who knows the depths of his Father's love could reveal to us the abyss of his mercy in so simple and beautiful a way. *545*

VI. THE SACRAMENT OF PENANCE AND RECONCILIATION

1440 Sin is before all else an offense against God, a rupture of communion with him. At the same time it damages communion with the Church. For this reason conversion entails both God's forgiveness and reconciliation with the Church, which are expressed and accomplished liturgically by the sacrament of Penance and Reconciliation.[38] *1850*

---

36 Cf. SC 109–110; CIC, cann. 1249–1253; CCEO, cann. 880–883.   37 Cf. *Lk* 15:11–24.   38 Cf. *LG* 11.

Only God forgives sin

270, 431   **1441**   Only God forgives sins.[39] Since he is the Son of God, Jesus says of himself, "The Son of man has authority on earth to forgive sins" and exercises this di-
589   vine power: "Your sins are forgiven."[40] Further, by virtue of his divine authority he gives this power to men to exercise in his name.[41]

1442   Christ has willed that in her prayer and life and action his whole Church should be the sign and instrument of the forgiveness and reconciliation that he acquired for us at the price of his blood. But he entrusted the exercise of the power of absolution to the apostolic
983   ministry which he charged with the "ministry of reconciliation."[42] The apostle is sent out "on behalf of Christ" with "God making his appeal" through him and pleading: "Be reconciled to God."[43]

Reconciliation with the Church

1443   During his public life Jesus not only forgave sins, but also made plain the effect of this forgiveness: he reintegrated forgiven sinners into the community of the People of God from which sin had alienated or even
545   excluded them. A remarkable sign of this is the fact that Jesus receives sinners at his table, a gesture that expresses in an astonishing way both God's forgiveness and the return to the bosom of the People of God.[44]

981   **1444**   In imparting to his apostles his own power to forgive sins the Lord also gives them the authority to reconcile sinners with the Church. This ecclesial dimension of their task is expressed most notably in Christ's solemn words to Simon Peter: "I will give you the keys of the kingdom of heaven, and whatever you bind on earth shall be bound in heaven, and whatever you loose on earth shall be loosed in heaven."[45] "The office of binding and loosing which was given to Peter was also assigned to the college of the apostles united to its head."[46]

---

39 Cf. *Mk* 2:7.   40 *Mk* 2:5, 10; *Lk* 7:48.   41 Cf. *Jn* 20:21-23.   42 2 *Cor* 5:18.
43 2 *Cor* 5:20.   44 Cf. *Lk* 15; 19:9.   45 *Mt* 16:19; cf. *Mt* 18:18; 28:16-20.
46 *LG* 22 § 2.

1445 The words *bind and loose* mean: whomever you 553 exclude from your communion, will be excluded from communion with God; whomever you receive anew into your communion, God will welcome back into his. *Reconciliation with the Church is inseparable from reconciliation with God.*

The sacrament of forgiveness

1446 Christ instituted the sacrament of Penance for all 979 sinful members of his Church: above all for those who, since Baptism, have fallen into grave sin, and have thus 1856 lost their baptismal grace and wounded ecclesial communion. It is to them that the sacrament of Penance offers a new possibility to convert and to recover the grace of justification. The Fathers of the Church present this 1990 sacrament as "the second plank [of salvation] after the shipwreck which is the loss of grace."[47]

1447 Over the centuries the concrete form in which the Church has exercised this power received from the Lord has varied considerably. During the first centuries the reconciliation of Christians who had committed particularly grave sins after their Baptism (for example, idolatry, murder, or adultery) was tied to a very rigorous discipline, according to which penitents had to do public penance for their sins, often for years, before receiving reconciliation. To this "order of penitents" (which concerned only certain grave sins), one was only rarely admitted and in certain regions only once in a lifetime. During the seventh century Irish missionaries, inspired by the Eastern monastic tradition, took to continental Europe the "private" practice of penance, which does not require public and prolonged completion of penitential works before reconciliation with the Church. From that time on, the sacrament has been performed in secret between penitent and priest. This new practice envisioned the possibility of repetition and so opened the way to a regular frequenting of this sacrament. It allowed the forgiveness of grave sins and venial sins to be integrated into one sacramental celebration. In its main lines this is the form of penance that the Church has practiced down to our day.

1448 Beneath the changes in discipline and celebration

---

47 Tertullian, *De Pænit.* 4, 2: PL 1, 1343; cf. Council of Trent (1547): DS 1542.

that this sacrament has undergone over the centuries, the same *fundamental structure* is to be discerned. It comprises two equally essential elements: on the one hand, the acts of the man who undergoes conversion through the action of the Holy Spirit: namely, contrition, confession, and satisfaction; on the other, God's action through the intervention of the Church. The Church, who through the bishop and his priests forgives sins in the name of Jesus Christ and determines the manner of satisfaction, also prays for the sinner and does penance with him. Thus the sinner is healed and re-established in ecclesial communion.

1481 **1449** The formula of absolution used in the Latin Church expresses the essential elements of this sacrament: the Father of mercies is the source of all forgiveness. He effects the reconciliation of sinners through the
234 Passover of his Son and the gift of his Spirit, through the prayer and ministry of the Church:

> God, the Father of mercies,
> through the death and the resurrection of his Son
> has reconciled the world to himself
> and sent the Holy Spirit among us
> for the forgiveness of sins;
> through the ministry of the Church
> may God give you pardon and peace,
> and I absolve you from your sins
> in the name of the Father, and of the Son, and of the Holy Spirit.[48]

VII. The Acts of the Penitent
1450 "Penance requires . . . the sinner to endure all things willingly, be contrite of heart, confess with the lips, and practice complete humility and fruitful satisfaction."[49]

Contrition
1451 Among the penitent's acts contrition occupies first place. Contrition is "sorrow of the soul and detes-

---

48 *OP* 46: formula of absolution.   49 *Roman Catechism* II, V, 21; cf. Council of Trent (1551): DS 1673.

tation for the sin committed, together with the resolution not to sin again."[50]

431

1452 When it arises from a love by which God is loved above all else, contrition is called "perfect" (contrition of charity). Such contrition remits venial sins; it also obtains forgiveness of mortal sins if it includes the firm resolution to have recourse to sacramental confession as soon as possible.[51]

1822

1453 The contrition called "imperfect" (or "attrition") is also a gift of God, a prompting of the Holy Spirit. It is born of the consideration of sin's ugliness or the fear of eternal damnation and the other penalties threatening the sinner (contrition of fear). Such a stirring of conscience can initiate an interior process which, under the prompting of grace, will be brought to completion by sacramental absolution. By itself however, imperfect contrition cannot obtain the forgiveness of grave sins, but it disposes one to obtain forgiveness in the sacrament of Penance.[52]

1454 The reception of this sacrament ought to be prepared for by an *examination of conscience* made in the light of the Word of God. The passages best suited to this can be found in the moral catechesis of the Gospels and the apostolic Letters, such as the Sermon on the Mount and the apostolic teachings.[53]

The confession of sins

1455 The confession (or disclosure) of sins, even from a simply human point of view, frees us and facilitates our reconciliation with others. Through such an admission man looks squarely at the sins he is guilty of, takes responsibility for them, and thereby opens himself again to God and to the communion of the Church in order to make a new future possible.

1424

1734

1456 Confession to a priest is an essential part of the sacrament of Penance: "All mortal sins of which penitents after a diligent self-examination are conscious

---

50 Council of Trent (1551): DS 1676.   51 Cf. Council of Trent (1551): DS 1677. 52 Cf. Council of Trent (1551): DS 1678; 1705.   53 Cf. *Mt* 5–7; *Rom* 12–15; *1 Cor* 12–13; *Gal* 5; *Eph* 4–6; etc.

1855   must be recounted by them in confession, even if they
are most secret and have been committed against the
last two precepts of the Decalogue; for these sins sometimes wound the soul more grievously and are more
dangerous than those which are committed openly."[54]

1505
When Christ's faithful strive to confess all the sins
that they can remember, they undoubtedly place all
of them before the divine mercy for pardon. But
those who fail to do so and knowingly withhold
some, place nothing before the divine goodness for
remission through the mediation of the priest, "for
if the sick person is too ashamed to show his
wound to the doctor, the medicine cannot heal
what it does not know."[55]

2042   **1457**   According to the Church's command, "after having
attained the age of discretion, each of the faithful is bound
by an obligation faithfully to confess serious sins at least
once a year."[56] Anyone who is aware of having committed
a mortal sin must not receive Holy Communion, even if he
1385   experiences deep contrition, without having first received
sacramental absolution, unless he has a grave reason for receiving Communion and there is no possibility of going to
confession.[57] Children must go to the sacrament of Penance
before receiving Holy Communion for the first time.[58]

1458   Without being strictly necessary, confession of
everyday faults (venial sins) is nevertheless strongly recommended by the Church.[59] Indeed the regular confes-
1783   sion of our venial sins helps us form our conscience,
fight against evil tendencies, let ourselves be healed by
Christ and progress in the life of the Spirit. By receiving
more frequently through this sacrament the gift of the
Father's mercy, we are spurred to be merciful as he is
merciful:[60]

Whoever confesses his sins . . . is already working
with God. God indicts your sins; if you also indict
them, you are joined with God. Man and sinner
are, so to speak, two realities: when you hear

---

54 Council of Trent (1551): DS 1680 (ND 1626); cf. *Ex* 20:17; *Mt* 5:28.
55 Council of Trent (1551): DS 1680 (ND 1626); cf. St. Jerome, *In Eccl.* 10, 11:
PL 23:1096.   56 Cf. CIC, can. 989; Council of Trent (1551): DS 1683; DS 1708.
57 Cf. Council of Trent (1551): DS 1647; 1661; CIC, can. 916; CCEO, can. 711.
58 Cf. CIC, can. 914.   59 Cf. Council of Trent: DS 1680; CIC, can. 988 § 2.
60 Cf. *Lk* 6:36.

"man"—this is what God has made; when you hear "sinner"—this is what man himself has made. Destroy what you have made, so that God may save what he has made.... When you begin to abhor what you have made, it is then that your good works are beginning, since you are accusing yourself of your evil works. The beginning of good works is the confession of evil works. You do the truth and come to the light.[61]   2468

Satisfaction

1459 Many sins wrong our neighbor. One must do what is possible in order to repair the harm (e.g., return stolen goods, restore the reputation of someone slandered, pay compensation for injuries). Simple justice requires as much. But sin also injures and weakens the sinner himself, as well as his relationships with God and neighbor. Absolution takes away sin, but it does not remedy all the disorders sin has caused.[62] Raised up from sin, the sinner must still recover his full spiritual health by doing something more to make amends for the sin: he must "make satisfaction for" or "expiate" his sins. This satisfaction is also called "penance."   2412   2487   1473

1460 The *penance* the confessor imposes must take into account the penitent's personal situation and must seek his spiritual good. It must correspond as far as possible with the gravity and nature of the sins committed. It can consist of prayer, an offering, works of mercy, service of neighbor, voluntary self-denial, sacrifices, and above all the patient acceptance of the cross we must bear. Such penances help configure us to Christ, who alone expiated our sins once for all. They allow us to become co-heirs with the risen Christ, "provided we suffer with him."[63]   2447   618

> The satisfaction that we make for our sins, however, is not so much ours as though it were not done through Jesus Christ. We who can do nothing our-

---

61 St. Augustine, *In Jo. ev.* 12, 13: PL 35, 1491.   **62** Cf. Council of Trent (1551): DS 1712.   **63** *Rom* 8:17; *Rom* 3:25; *1 Jn* 2:1–2; cf. Council of Trent (1551): DS 1690.

selves, as if just by ourselves, can do all things with the cooperation of "him who strengthens" us. Thus man has nothing of which to boast, but all our boasting is in Christ . . . in whom we make satisfaction by bringing forth "fruits that befit repentance." These fruits have their efficacy from him, by him they are offered to the Father, and through him they are accepted by the Father.[64]

2011

VIII. THE MINISTER OF THIS SACRAMENT

981 **1461** Since Christ entrusted to his apostles the ministry of reconciliation,[65] bishops who are their successors, and priests, the bishops' collaborators, continue to exercise this ministry. Indeed bishops and priests, by virtue of the sacrament of Holy Orders, have the power to forgive all sins "in the name of the Father, and of the Son, and of the Holy Spirit."

1462 Forgiveness of sins brings reconciliation with God, but also with the Church. Since ancient times the bishop, visible head of a particular Church, has thus *886* rightfully been considered to be the one who principally has the power and ministry of reconciliation: he is the *1567* moderator of the penitential discipline.[66] Priests, his collaborators, exercise it to the extent that they have received the commission either from their bishop (or religious superior) or the Pope, according to the law of the Church.[67]

1463 Certain particularly grave sins incur excommunication, the most severe ecclesiastical penalty, which impedes the reception of the sacraments and the exercise of certain ecclesiastical acts, and for which absolution consequently cannot be granted, according to canon law, except by the Pope, the bishop of the place or priests authorized by them.[68] In danger of death any priest, even if deprived of faculties for hearing confessions, can absolve from every *982* sin and excommunication.[69]

1464 Priests must encourage the faithful to come to

---

64 Council of Trent (1551): DS 1691; cf. *Phil* 4:13; *1 Cor* 1:31; *2 Cor* 10:17; *Gal* 6:14; *Lk* 3:8.   65 Cf. *Jn* 20:23; *2 Cor* 5:18.   66 Cf. *LG* 26 § 3.   67 Cf. CIC, cann. 844; 967–969; 972; CCEO, can. 722 §§ 3–4.   68 Cf. CIC, cann. 1331; 1354–1357; CCEO, can. 1431; 1434; 1420.   69 Cf. CIC, can. 976; CCEO, can. 725.

the sacrament of Penance and must make themselves available to celebrate this sacrament each time Christians reasonably ask for it.[70]

1465 When he celebrates the sacrament of Penance, the priest is fulfilling the ministry of the Good Shepherd who seeks the lost sheep, of the Good Samaritan who binds up wounds, of the Father who awaits the prodigal son and welcomes him on his return, and of the just and impartial judge whose judgment is both just and merciful. The priest is the sign and the instrument of God's merciful love for the sinner.

983

1466 The confessor is not the master of God's forgiveness, but its servant. The minister of this sacrament should unite himself to the intention and charity of Christ.[71] He should have a proven knowledge of Christian behavior, experience of human affairs, respect and sensitivity toward the one who has fallen; he must love the truth, be faithful to the Magisterium of the Church, and lead the penitent with patience toward healing and full maturity. He must pray and do penance for his penitent, entrusting him to the Lord's mercy.

1551

2690

1467 Given the delicacy and greatness of this ministry and the respect due to persons, the Church declares that every priest who hears confessions is bound under very severe penalties to keep absolute secrecy regarding the sins that his penitents have confessed to him. He can make no use of knowledge that confession gives him about penitents' lives.[72] This secret, which admits of no exceptions, is called the "sacramental seal," because what the penitent has made known to the priest remains "sealed" by the sacrament.

2490

IX. THE EFFECTS OF THIS SACRAMENT

1468 "The whole power of the sacrament of Penance consists in restoring us to God's grace and joining us with him in an intimate friendship."[73] Reconciliation with God is thus the purpose and effect of this sacra-

---

70 Cf. CIC, can. 986; CCEO, can. 735; PO 13.   71 Cf. PO 13.   72 Cf. CIC, can. 1388 § 1; CCEO, can. 1456.   73 *Roman Catechism*, II, V, 18.

ment. For those who receive the sacrament of Penance with contrite heart and religious disposition, reconciliation "is usually followed by peace and serenity of con-

2305 science with strong spiritual consolation."[74] Indeed the sacrament of Reconciliation with God brings about a true "spiritual resurrection," restoration of the dignity and blessings of the life of the children of God, of which the most precious is friendship with God.[75]

953 **1469** This sacrament *reconciles us with the Church.* Sin damages or even breaks fraternal communion. The sacrament of Penance repairs or restores it. In this sense it does not simply heal the one restored to ecclesial communion, but has also a revitalizing effect on the life of the Church which suffered from the sin of one of her members.[76] Re-established or strengthened in the communion of saints, the sinner is made stronger by the exchange of spiritual goods among all the living members of the Body of Christ, whether still on pilgrimage or al-

949 ready in the heavenly homeland:[77]

> It must be recalled that . . . this reconciliation with God leads, as it were, to other reconciliations, which repair the other breaches caused by sin. The forgiven penitent is reconciled with himself in his inmost being, where he regains his innermost truth. He is reconciled with his brethren whom he has in some way offended and wounded. He is reconciled with the Church. He is reconciled with all creation.[78]

1470 In this sacrament, the sinner, placing himself before the merciful judgment of God, *anticipates* in a certain way *the judgment* to which he will be subjected at

678, 1039 the end of his earthly life. For it is now, in this life, that we are offered the choice between life and death, and it is only by the road of conversion that we can enter the Kingdom, from which one is excluded by grave sin.[79] In converting to Christ through penance and faith, the sinner passes from death to life and "does not come into judgment."[80]

---

74 Council of Trent (1551): DS 1674.   75 Cf. *Lk* 15:32.   76 Cf. *1 Cor* 12:26.
77 Cf. *LG* 48–50.   78 John Paul II, *RP* 31, 5.   79 Cf. *1 Cor* 5:11; *Gal* 5:19–21; *Rev* 22:15.   80 *Jn* 5:24.

X.   INDULGENCES

1471 The doctrine and practice of indulgences in the Church are closely linked to the effects of the sacrament of Penance.

What is an indulgence?

"An indulgence is a remission before God of the temporal punishment due to sins whose guilt has already been forgiven, which the faithful Christian who is duly disposed gains under certain prescribed conditions through the action of the Church which, as the minister of redemption, dispenses and applies with authority the treasury of the satisfactions of Christ and the saints."[81]

"An indulgence is partial or plenary according as it removes either part or all of the temporal punishment due to sin."[82] Indulgences may be applied to the living or the dead.

The punishments of sin

1472 To understand this doctrine and practice of the Church, it is necessary to understand that sin has *a double consequence*. Grave sin deprives us of communion with God and therefore makes us incapable of eternal life, the privation of which is called the "eternal punishment" of sin. On the other hand every sin, even venial, entails an unhealthy attachment to creatures, which must be purified either here on earth, or after death in the state called Purgatory. This purification frees one from what is called the "temporal punishment" of sin. These two punishments must not be conceived of as a kind of vengeance inflicted by God from without, but as following from the very nature of sin. A conversion which proceeds from a fervent charity can attain the complete purification of the sinner in such a way that no punishment would remain.[83]

1473 The forgiveness of sin and restoration of communion with God entail the remission of the eternal punishment of sin, but temporal punishment of sin remains. While patiently bearing sufferings and trials of all kinds, when the day comes, serenely facing death, the Christian must strive to accept this temporal punishment of sin as a grace. He should strive by works of mercy and charity, as well as by prayer and the various practices of penance, to

1861

1031

2447

---

81 Paul VI, apostolic constitution, *Indulgentiarum doctrina,* Norm 1.
82 *Indulgentiarum doctrina,* Norm 2; cf. Norm 3.   83 Cf. Council of Trent (1551): DS 1712–1713; (1563): 1820.

put off completely the "old man" and to put on the "new man."[84]

In the Communion of Saints

946-959 **1474** The Christian who seeks to purify himself of his sin and to become holy with the help of God's grace is not alone. "The life of each of God's children is joined in Christ and through Christ in a wonderful way to the life of all the other Christian brethren in the supernatural unity of the 795 Mystical Body of Christ, as in a single mystical person."[85]

1475 In the communion of saints, "a perennial link of charity exists between the faithful who have already reached their heavenly home, those who are expiating their sins in purgatory and those who are still pilgrims on earth. Between them there is, too, an abundant exchange of all good things."[86] In this wonderful exchange, the holiness of one profits others, well beyond the harm that the sin of one could cause others. Thus recourse to the communion of saints lets the contrite sinner be more promptly and efficaciously purified of the punishments for sin.

1476 We also call these spiritual goods of the communion of saints the *Church's treasury,* which is "not the sum total of the material goods which have accumulated during the course of the centuries. On the contrary the 'treasury of the Church' is the infinite value, which can never be exhausted, which Christ's merits have before God. They were 617 offered so that the whole of mankind could be set free from sin and attain communion with the Father. In Christ, the Redeemer himself, the satisfactions and merits of his Redemption exist and find their efficacy."[87]

969 **1477** "This treasury includes as well the prayers and good works of the Blessed Virgin Mary. They are truly immense, unfathomable, and even pristine in their value before God. In the treasury, too, are the prayers and good works of all the saints, all those who have followed in the footsteps of Christ the Lord and by his grace have made their lives holy and carried out the mission the Father entrusted to them. In this way they attained their own salvation and at the same time cooperated in saving their brothers in the unity of the Mystical Body."[88]

---

84 *Eph* 4:22, 24.   85 *Indulgentiarum doctrina,* 5.   86 *Indulgentiarum doctrina,*
5.   87 *Indulgentiarum doctrina,* 5.   88 *Indulgentiarum doctrina,* 5.

Obtaining indulgence from God through the Church

1478 An indulgence is obtained through the Church   *981*
who, by virtue of the power of binding and loosing granted
her by Christ Jesus, intervenes in favor of individual Christians and opens for them the treasury of the merits of
Christ and the saints to obtain from the Father of mercies
the remission of the temporal punishments due for their
sins. Thus the Church does not want simply to come to the
aid of these Christians, but also to spur them to works of
devotion, penance, and charity.[89]

1479 Since the faithful departed now being purified are   *1032*
also members of the same communion of saints, one way we
can help them is to obtain indulgences for them, so that the
temporal punishments due for their sins may be remitted.

XI.   THE CELEBRATION OF THE SACRAMENT OF PENANCE

1480 Like all the sacraments, Penance is a liturgical
action. The elements of the celebration are ordinarily
these: a greeting and blessing from the priest, reading
the word of God to illuminate the conscience and elicit
contrition, and an exhortation to repentance; the confession, which acknowledges sins and makes them
known to the priest; the imposition and acceptance of a
penance; the priest's absolution; a prayer of thanksgiving and praise and dismissal with the blessing of the
priest.

1481 The Byzantine Liturgy recognizes several formulas   *1449*
of absolution, in the form of invocation, which admirably
express the mystery of forgiveness: "May the same God,
who through the Prophet Nathan forgave David when he
confessed his sins, who forgave Peter when he wept bitterly,
the prostitute when she washed his feet with her tears, the
Pharisee, and the prodigal son, through me, a sinner, forgive you both in this life and in the next and enable you to
appear before his awe-inspiring tribunal without condemnation, he who is blessed for ever and ever. Amen."

1482 The sacrament of Penance can also take place in the
framework of a *communal celebration* in which we prepare
ourselves together for confession and give thanks together

---

89 Cf. *Indulgentiarum doctrina,* 5.

for the forgiveness received. Here, the personal confession of sins and individual absolution are inserted into a liturgy of the word of God with readings and a homily, an examination of conscience conducted in common, a communal request for forgiveness, the Our Father and a thanksgiving in common. This communal celebration expresses more clearly the ecclesial character of penance. However, regardless of its manner of celebration the sacrament of Penance is always, by its very nature, a liturgical action, and therefore an ecclesial and public action.[90]

1140

1401   **1483**   In case of grave necessity recourse may be had to a *communal celebration of reconciliation with general confession and general absolution.* Grave necessity of this sort can arise when there is imminent danger of death without sufficient time for the priest or priests to hear each penitent's confession. Grave necessity can also exist when, given the number of penitents, there are not enough confessors to hear individual confessions properly in a reasonable time, so that the penitents through no fault of their own would be deprived of sacramental grace or Holy Communion for a long time. In this case, for the absolution to be valid the faithful must have the intention of individually confessing their sins in the time required.[91] The diocesan bishop is the judge of whether or not the conditions required for general absolution exist.[92] A large gathering of the faithful on the occasion of major feasts or pilgrimages does not constitute a case of grave necessity.[93]

1484   "Individual, integral confession and absolution remain the only ordinary way for the faithful to reconcile themselves with God and the Church, unless physical or moral impossibility excuses from this kind of confession."[94] There are profound reasons for this. Christ is at work in each of the sacraments. He personally addresses every sinner: "My son, your sins are forgiven."[95] He is the physician tending each one of the sick who need him to cure them.[96] He raises them up and reintegrates them into fraternal communion. Personal confession is thus the form most expressive of reconciliation with God and with the Church.

878

90 Cf. *SC* 26–27.   91 Cf. CIC, can. 962 § 1.   92 Cf. CIC, can. 961 § 2.   93 Cf. CIC, can. 961 § 1.   94 *OP* 31.   95 *Mk* 2:5.   96 Cf. *Mk* 2:17.

IN BRIEF

1485 "On the evening of that day, the first day of the week," Jesus showed himself to his apostles. "He breathed on them, and said to them: 'Receive the Holy Spirit. If you forgive the sins of any, they are forgiven; if you retain the sins of any, they are retained' " (*Jn* 20:19, 22–23).

1486 The forgiveness of sins committed after Baptism is conferred by a particular sacrament called the sacrament of conversion, confession, penance, or reconciliation.

1487 The sinner wounds God's honor and love, his own human dignity as a man called to be a son of God, and the spiritual well-being of the Church, of which each Christian ought to be a living stone.

1488 To the eyes of faith no evil is graver than sin and nothing has worse consequences for sinners themselves, for the Church, and for the whole world.

1489 To return to communion with God after having lost it through sin is a process born of the grace of God who is rich in mercy and solicitous for the salvation of men. One must ask for this precious gift for oneself and for others.

1490 The movement of return to God, called conversion and repentance, entails sorrow for and abhorrence of sins committed, and the firm purpose of sinning no more in the future. Conversion touches the past and the future and is nourished by hope in God's mercy.

1491 The sacrament of Penance is a whole consisting in three actions of the penitent and the priest's absolution. The penitent's acts are repentance, confession or disclosure of sins to the priest, and the intention to make reparation and do works of reparation.

1492 Repentance (also called contrition) must be inspired by motives that arise from faith. If repentance arises from love of charity for God, it is called "perfect" contrition; if it is founded on other motives, it is called "imperfect."

1493 One who desires to obtain reconciliation with God and with the Church, must confess to a priest all the unconfessed grave sins he remembers after having carefully examined his conscience. The confession of venial faults, without being necessary in itself, is nevertheless strongly recommended by the Church.

1494 The confessor proposes the performance of certain acts of "satisfaction" or "penance" to be performed by the penitent in order to repair the harm caused by sin and to re-establish habits befitting a disciple of Christ.

1495 Only priests who have received the faculty of absolving from the authority of the Church can forgive sins in the name of Christ.

1496 The spiritual effects of the sacrament of Penance are:

—reconciliation with God by which the penitent recovers grace;

—reconciliation with the Church;

—remission of the eternal punishment incurred by mortal sins;

—remission, at least in part, of temporal punishments resulting from sin;

—peace and serenity of conscience, and spiritual consolation;

—an increase of spiritual strength for the Christian battle.

1497 Individual and integral confession of grave sins followed by absolution remains the only ordinary means of reconciliation with God and with the Church.

1498   Through indulgences the faithful can obtain the remission of temporal punishment resulting from sin for themselves and also for the souls in Purgatory.

ARTICLE 5
THE ANOINTING OF THE SICK

1499   "By the sacred anointing of the sick and the prayer of the priests the whole Church commends those who are ill to the suffering and glorified Lord, that he may raise them up and save them. And indeed she exhorts them to contribute to the good of the People of God by freely uniting themselves to the Passion and death of Christ."[97]

I.   ITS FOUNDATIONS IN THE ECONOMY OF SALVATION

Illness in human life
1500   Illness and suffering have always been among the gravest problems confronted in human life. In illness, man experiences his powerlessness, his limitations, and his finitude. Every illness can make us glimpse death.

1006

1501   Illness can lead to anguish, self-absorption, sometimes even despair and revolt against God. It can also make a person more mature, helping him discern in his life what is not essential so that he can turn toward that which is. Very often illness provokes a search for God and a return to him.

The sick person before God
1502   The man of the Old Testament lives his sickness in the presence of God. It is before God that he laments his illness, and it is of God, Master of life and death,

---

97 LG 11; cf. *Jas* 5:14–16; *Rom* 8:17; *Col* 1:24; *2 Tim* 2:11–12; *1 Pet* 4:13.

that he implores healing.[98] Illness becomes a way to conversion; God's forgiveness initiates the healing.[99] It is the experience of Israel that illness is mysteriously linked to *164* sin and evil, and that faithfulness to God according to *376* his law restores life: "For I am the Lord, your healer."[100] The prophet intuits that suffering can also have a redemptive meaning for the sins of others.[101] Finally Isaiah announces that God will usher in a time for Zion when he will pardon every offense and heal every illness.[102]

Christ the physician

549 **1503** Christ's compassion toward the sick and his many healings of every kind of infirmity are a resplendent sign that "God has visited his people"[103] and that the Kingdom of God is close at hand. Jesus has the power not only to heal, but also to forgive sins;[104] he has come to heal the whole man, soul and body; he is the *1421* physician the sick have need of.[105] His compassion toward all who suffer goes so far that he identifies himself with them: "I was sick and you visited me."[106] His preferential love for the sick has not ceased through the centuries to draw the very special attention of Christians *2288* toward all those who suffer in body and soul. It is the source of tireless efforts to comfort them.

1504 Often Jesus asks the sick to believe.[107] He makes use of signs to heal: spittle and the laying on of hands,[108] mud and washing.[109] The sick try to touch him, "for *695* power came forth from him and healed them all."[110] And so in the sacraments Christ continues to "touch" *1116* us in order to heal us.

1505 Moved by so much suffering Christ not only allows himself to be touched by the sick, but he makes their miseries his own: "He took our infirmities and bore our diseases."[111] But he did not heal all the sick. His healings were signs of the coming of the Kingdom

---

98 Cf. *Pss* 6:3; 38; *Isa* 38.   99 Cf. *Pss* 32:5; 38:5; 39:9, 12; 107:20; cf. *Mk* 2:5–12.   100 *Ex* 15:26.   101 Cf. *Isa* 53:11.   102 Cf. *Isa* 33:24.   103 *Lk* 7:16; cf. *Mt* 4:24.   104 Cf. *Mk* 2:5–12.   105 Cf. *Mk* 2:17.   106 *Mt* 25:36.   107 Cf. *Mk* 5:34, 36; 9:23.   108 Cf. *Mk* 7:32–36; 8:22–25.   109 Cf. *Jn* 9:6–7.   110 *Lk* 6:19; cf. *Mk* 1:41; 3:10; 6:56.   111 *Mt* 8:17; cf. *Isa* 53:4.

of God. They announced a more radical healing: the victory over sin and death through his Passover. On the cross Christ took upon himself the whole weight of evil and took away the "sin of the world,"[112] of which illness is only a consequence. By his passion and death on the cross Christ has given a new meaning to suffering: it can henceforth configure us to him and unite us with his redemptive Passion. 440

307

"Heal the sick . . ."

1506 Christ invites his disciples to follow him by taking up their cross in their turn.[113] By following him they acquire a new outlook on illness and the sick. Jesus associates them with his own life of poverty and service. He makes them share in his ministry of compassion and healing: "So they went out and preached that men should repent. And they cast out many demons, and anointed with oil many that were sick and healed them."[114] 859

1507 The risen Lord renews this mission ("In my name . . . they will lay their hands on the sick, and they will recover."[115]) and confirms it through the signs that the Church performs by invoking his name.[116] These signs demonstrate in a special way that Jesus is truly "God who saves."[117] 430

1508 The Holy Spirit gives to some a special charism of healing[118] so as to make manifest the power of the grace of the risen Lord. But even the most intense prayers do not always obtain the healing of all illnesses. Thus St. Paul must learn from the Lord that "my grace is sufficient for you, for my power is made perfect in weakness," and that the sufferings to be endured can mean that "in my flesh I complete what is lacking in Christ's afflictions for the sake of his Body, that is, the Church."[119] 798

618

1509 "Heal the sick!"[120] The Church has received this

---

112 *Jn* 1:29; cf. *Isa* 53:4–6.   113 Cf. *Mt* 10:38.   114 *Mk* 6:12–13.   115 *Mk* 16:17–18.   116 Cf. *Acts* 9:34; 14:3.   117 Cf. *Mt* 1:21; *Acts* 4:12.   118 Cf. *1 Cor* 12:9, 28, 30.   119 *2 Cor* 12:9; *Col* 1:24.   120 *Mt* 10:8.

charge from the Lord and strives to carry it out by taking care of the sick as well as by accompanying them with her prayer of intercession. She believes in the life-giving presence of Christ, the physician of souls and bodies. This presence is particularly active through the sacraments, and in an altogether special way through the Eucharist, the bread that gives eternal life and that St. Paul suggests is connected with bodily health.[121]

1510 However, the apostolic Church has its own rite for the sick, attested to by St. James: "Is any among you sick? Let him call for the elders *[presbyters]* of the Church and let them pray over him, anointing him with oil in the name of the Lord; and the prayer of faith will save the sick man, and the Lord will raise him up; and if he has committed sins, he will be forgiven."[122] Tradition has recognized in this rite one of the seven sacraments.[123]

A sacrament of the sick

1511 The Church believes and confesses that among the seven sacraments there is one especially intended to strengthen those who are being tried by illness, the Anointing of the Sick:

> This sacred anointing of the sick was instituted by Christ our Lord as a true and proper sacrament of the New Testament. It is alluded to indeed by Mark, but is recommended to the faithful and promulgated by James the apostle and brother of the Lord.[124]

1512 From ancient times in the liturgical traditions of both East and West, we have testimonies to the practice of anointings of the sick with blessed oil. Over the centuries the Anointing of the Sick was conferred more and more exclusively on those at the point of death. Because of this it received the name "Extreme Unction." Notwithstanding this evolution the liturgy has never failed to beg the Lord that the sick person may recover his health if it would be conducive to his salvation.[125]

---

121 Cf. *Jn* 6:54, 58; *1 Cor* 11:30.   **122** *Jas* 5:14–15.   **123** Cf. Council of Constantinople II (553): DS 216; Council of Florence (1439): 1324–1325; Council of Trent (1551) 1695–1696; 1716–1717.   **124** Council of Trent (1551): DS 1695; cf. *Mk* 6:13; *Jas* 5:14–15.   **125** Cf. Council of Trent (1551): DS 1696.

1513 The Apostolic Constitution *Sacram unctionem infirmorum,*[126] following upon the Second Vatican Council,[127] established that henceforth, in the Roman Rite, the following be observed:

> The sacrament of Anointing of the Sick is given to those who are seriously ill by anointing them on the forehead and hands with duly blessed oil—pressed from olives or from other plants—saying, only once: "Through this holy anointing may the Lord in his love and mercy help you with the grace of the Holy Spirit. May the Lord who frees you from sin save you and raise you up."[128]

II. WHO RECEIVES AND WHO ADMINISTERS THIS SACRAMENT?

In case of grave illness . . .

1514 The Anointing of the Sick "is not a sacrament for those only who are at the point of death. Hence, as soon as anyone of the faithful begins to be in danger of death from sickness or old age, the fitting time for him to receive this sacrament has certainly already arrived."[129]

1515 If a sick person who received this anointing recovers his health, he can in the case of another grave illness receive this sacrament again. If during the same illness the person's condition becomes more serious, the sacrament may be repeated. It is fitting to receive the Anointing of the Sick just prior to a serious operation. The same holds for the elderly whose frailty becomes more pronounced.

". . . let him call for the presbyters of the Church"

1516 Only priests (bishops and presbyters) are ministers of the Anointing of the Sick.[130] It is the duty of pastors to instruct the faithful on the benefits of this sacra-

---

126 Paul VI, apostolic constitution, *Sacram unctionem infirmorum,* November 30, 1972.   127 Cf. SC 73.   128 Cf. CIC, can. 847 § 1.   129 SC 73; cf. CIC, cann. 1004 § 1; 1005; 1007; CCEO, can. 738.   130 Cf. Council of Trent (1551): DS 1697; 1719; CIC, can. 1003; CCEO, can. 739 § 1.

ment. The faithful should encourage the sick to call for a priest to receive this sacrament. The sick should prepare themselves to receive it with good dispositions, assisted by their pastor and the whole ecclesial community, which is invited to surround the sick in a special way through their prayers and fraternal attention.

III.   HOW IS THIS SACRAMENT CELEBRATED?

1140   **1517**   Like all the sacraments the Anointing of the Sick is a liturgical and communal celebration,[131] whether it takes place in the family home, a hospital or church, for a single sick person or a whole group of sick persons. It is very fitting to celebrate it within the Eucharist, the memorial of the Lord's Passover. If circumstances suggest it, the celebration of the sacrament can be preceded by the sacrament of Penance and followed by the sacrament of the Eucharist. As the sacrament of Christ's Passover the Eucharist should always be the last sacrament of the earthly journey, the "viaticum" for "passing

1524   over" to eternal life.

1518   Word and sacrament form an indivisible whole. The Liturgy of the Word, preceded by an act of repentance, opens the celebration. The words of Christ, the witness of the apostles, awaken the faith of the sick person and of the community to ask the Lord for the strength of his Spirit.

1519   The celebration of the sacrament includes the following principal elements: the "priests of the Church"[132]—in silence—lay hands on the sick; they pray over them in the faith of the Church[133]—this is the epiclesis proper to this sacrament; they then anoint them with oil blessed, if possible, by the bishop.

These liturgical actions indicate what grace this sacrament confers upon the sick.

---

131 Cf. SC 27.   132 Jas 5:14.   133 Cf. Jas 5:15.

IV. THE EFFECTS OF THE CELEBRATION OF THIS SACRAMENT

1520 *A particular gift of the Holy Spirit.* The first *733* grace of this sacrament is one of strengthening, peace and courage to overcome the difficulties that go with the condition of serious illness or the frailty of old age. This grace is a gift of the Holy Spirit, who renews trust and faith in God and strengthens against the temptations of the evil one, the temptation to discouragement and anguish in the face of death.[134] This assistance from the Lord by the power of his Spirit is meant to lead the sick person to healing of the soul, but also of the body if such is God's will.[135] Furthermore, "if he has committed sins, he will be forgiven."[136]

1521 *Union with the passion of Christ.* By the grace of this sacrament the sick person receives the strength and the gift of uniting himself more closely to Christ's Passion: in a certain way he is *consecrated* to bear fruit by *1535* configuration to the Savior's redemptive Passion. Suffering, a consequence of original sin, acquires a new meaning; it becomes a participation in the saving work of Jesus. *1499*

1522 An *ecclesial grace.* The sick who receive this sacrament, "by freely uniting themselves to the passion and death of Christ," "contribute to the good of the People of God."[137] By celebrating this sacrament the Church, in the communion of saints, intercedes for the benefit of the sick person, and he, for his part, *953* through the grace of this sacrament, contributes to the sanctification of the Church and to the good of all men for whom the Church suffers and offers herself through Christ to God the Father.

1523 A *preparation for the final journey.* If the sacra- *1020* ment of anointing of the sick is given to all who suffer from serious illness and infirmity, even more rightly is it given to those at the point of departing this life; so it is also called *sacramentum exeuntium* (the sacrament of

---

134 Cf. *Heb* 2:15. 135 Cf. Council of Florence (1439): DS 1325. 136 *Jas* 5:15; cf. Council of Trent (1551): DS 1717. 137 *LG* 11 § 2.

those departing).[138] The Anointing of the Sick completes our conformity to the death and Resurrection of Christ, just as Baptism began it. It completes the holy anointings that mark the whole Christian life: that of Baptism which sealed the new life in us, and that of Confirmation which strengthened us for the combat of this life.

1294
1020 This last anointing fortifies the end of our earthly life like a solid rampart for the final struggles before entering the Father's house.[139]

V.   VIATICUM, THE LAST SACRAMENT OF THE CHRISTIAN

1392 1524 In addition to the Anointing of the Sick, the Church offers those who are about to leave this life the Eucharist as viaticum. Communion in the body and blood of Christ, received at this moment of "passing over" to the Father, has a particular significance and importance. It is the seed of eternal life and the power of resurrection, according to the words of the Lord: "He who eats my flesh and drinks my blood has eternal life, and I will raise him up at the last day."[140] The sacrament of Christ once dead and now risen, the Eucharist is here the sacrament of passing over from death to life, from this world to the Father.[141]

1680 1525 Thus, just as the sacraments of Baptism, Confirmation, and the Eucharist form a unity called "the sacraments of Christian initiation," so too it can be said that Penance, the Anointing of the Sick and the Eucharist as viaticum constitute at the end of Christian life "the sacraments that prepare for our heavenly homeland" or the sacraments that complete the earthly pil-
2299 grimage.

IN BRIEF

1526 "Is any among you sick? Let him call for the presbyters of the Church, and let them pray over him, anointing him with oil in the name of the

---

138 Council of Trent (1551): DS 1698.   139 Council of Trent (1551): DS 1694.
140 *Jn* 6:54.   141 Cf. *Jn* 13:1.

Lord; and the prayer of faith will save the sick man, and the Lord will raise him up; and if he has committed sins, he will be forgiven" (*Jas* 5:14–15).

1527   The sacrament of Anointing of the Sick has as its purpose the conferral of a special grace on the Christian experiencing the difficulties inherent in the condition of grave illness or old age.

1528   The proper time for receiving this holy anointing has certainly arrived when the believer begins to be in danger of death because of illness or old age.

1529   Each time a Christian falls seriously ill, he may receive the Anointing of the Sick, and also when, after he has received it, the illness worsens.

1530   Only priests (presbyters and bishops) can give the sacrament of the Anointing of the Sick, using oil blessed by the bishop, or if necessary by the celebrating presbyter himself.

1531   The celebration of the Anointing of the Sick consists essentially in the anointing of the forehead and hands of the sick person (in the Roman Rite) or of other parts of the body (in the Eastern rite), the anointing being accompanied by the liturgical prayer of the celebrant asking for the special grace of this sacrament.

1532   The special grace of the sacrament of the Anointing of the Sick has as its effects:

—the uniting of the sick person to the passion of Christ, for his own good and that of the whole Church;

—the strengthening, peace, and courage to endure in a Christian manner the sufferings of illness or old age;

—the forgiveness of sins, if the sick person was not able to obtain it through the sacrament of Penance;

—the restoration of health, if it is conducive to the salvation of his soul;

—the preparation for passing over to eternal life.

Chapter Three
The Sacraments at the Service of Communion

1212   **1533** Baptism, Confirmation, and Eucharist are sacraments of Christian initiation. They ground the common vocation of all Christ's disciples, a vocation to holiness and to the mission of evangelizing the world. They confer the graces needed for the life according to the Spirit during this life as pilgrims on the march towards the homeland.

1534 Two other sacraments, Holy Orders and Matrimony, are directed towards the salvation of others; if they contribute as well to personal salvation, it is through service to others that they do so. They confer a particular mission in the Church and serve to build up the People of God.

784   **1535** Through these sacraments those already *consecrated* by Baptism and Confirmation¹ for the common priesthood of all the faithful can receive particular *consecrations*. Those who receive the sacrament of Holy Orders are *consecrated* in Christ's name "to feed the Church by the word and grace of God."² On their part, "Christian spouses are fortified and, as it were, *consecrated* for the duties and dignity of their state by a special sacrament."³

---

1 Cf. *LG* 10.   2 *LG* 11 § 2.   3 *GS* 48 § 2.

ARTICLE 6
THE SACRAMENT OF HOLY ORDERS

1536 Holy Orders is the sacrament through which the mission entrusted by Christ to his apostles continues to be exercised in the Church until the end of time: thus it is the sacrament of apostolic ministry. It includes three degrees: episcopate, presbyterate, and diaconate.

860

(On the institution and mission of the apostolic ministry by Christ, see above, no. 874 ff. Here only the sacramental means by which this ministry is handed on will be treated.)

I.   WHY IS THIS SACRAMENT CALLED "ORDERS"?

1537 The word *order* in Roman antiquity designated an established civil body, especially a governing body. *Ordinatio* means incorporation into an *ordo*. In the Church there are established bodies which Tradition, not without a basis in Sacred Scripture,[4] has since ancient times called *taxeis* (Greek) or *ordines*. And so the liturgy speaks of the *ordo episcoporum,* the *ordo presbyterorum,* the *ordo diaconorum*. Other groups also receive this name of *ordo:* catechumens, virgins, spouses, widows, ...

923, 1631

1538 Integration into one of these bodies in the Church was accomplished by a rite called *ordinatio,* a religious and liturgical act which was a consecration, a blessing or a sacrament. Today the word *"ordination"* is reserved for the sacramental act which integrates a man into the order of bishops, presbyters, or deacons, and goes beyond a simple *election, designation, delegation,* or *institution* by the community, for it confers a gift of the Holy Spirit that permits the exercise of a "sacred power" *(sacra potestas)*[5] which can come only from Christ himself through his Church. Ordination is also called *consecratio,* for it is a setting apart and an investiture by Christ himself for his Church.

875

---

4 Cf. *Heb* 5:6; 7:11; *Ps* 110:4.   5 Cf. *LG* 10.

699 The *laying on of hands* by the bishop, with the consecratory prayer, constitutes the visible sign of this ordination.

II.   THE SACRAMENT OF HOLY ORDERS IN THE ECONOMY OF SALVATION

The priesthood of the Old Covenant

1539 The chosen people was constituted by God as "a kingdom of priests and a holy nation."[6] But within the people of Israel, God chose one of the twelve tribes, that of Levi, and set it apart for liturgical service; God himself is its inheritance.[7] A special rite consecrated the beginnings of the priesthood of the Old Covenant. The priests are "appointed to act on behalf of men in relation to God, to offer gifts and sacrifices for sins."[8]

2099 1540 Instituted to proclaim the Word of God and to restore communion with God by sacrifices and prayer,[9] this priesthood nevertheless remains powerless to bring about salvation, needing to repeat its sacrifices ceaselessly and being unable to achieve a definitive sanctification, which only the sacrifice of Christ would accomplish.[10]

1541 The liturgy of the Church, however, sees in the priesthood of Aaron and the service of the Levites, as in the institution of the seventy elders,[11] a prefiguring of the ordained ministry of the New Covenant. Thus in the Latin Rite the Church prays in the consecratory preface of the ordination of bishops:

> God the Father of our Lord Jesus Christ, . . .
> by your gracious word
> you have established the plan of your Church.
>
> From the beginning,
> you chose the descendants of Abraham to be your holy nation.
> You established rulers and priests,

---

6 *Ex* 19:6; cf. *Isa* 61:6.   7 Cf. *Num* 1:48–53; *Josh* 13:33.   8 *Heb* 5:1; cf. *Ex* 29:1–30; *Lev* 8.   9 Cf. *Mal* 2:7–9.   10 Cf. *Heb* 5:3; 7:27; 10:1–4.   11 Cf. *Num* 11:24–25.

and did not leave your sanctuary without
ministers to serve you. . . .[12]

1542   At the ordination of priests, the Church prays:

Lord, holy Father, . . .
when you had appointed high priests to rule your
people,
you chose other men next to them in rank and
dignity
to be with them and to help them in their task. . . .

you extended the spirit of Moses to seventy wise
men. . . .
You shared among the sons of Aaron
the fullness of their father's power.[13]

1543   In the consecratory prayer for ordination of deacons, the Church confesses:

Almighty God . . . ,
You make the Church, Christ's body,
grow to its full stature as a new and greater
temple.
You enrich it with every kind of grace
and perfect it with a diversity of members
to serve the whole body in a wonderful pattern of
unity

You established a threefold ministry of worship
and service,
for the glory of your name.
As ministers of your tabernacle you chose the sons
of Levi
and gave them your blessing as their everlasting
inheritance.[14]

The one priesthood of Christ

1544   Everything that the priesthood of the Old
Covenant prefigured finds its fulfillment in Christ Jesus,
the "one mediator between God and men."[15] The Christian tradition considers Melchizedek, "priest of God
Most High," as a prefiguration of the priesthood of   874

---

12 *Roman Pontifical,* Ordination of Bishops 26, Prayer of Consecration.
13 *Roman Pontifical,* Ordination of Priests 22, Prayer of Consecration.
14 *Roman Pontifical,* Ordination of Deacons 21, Prayer of Consecration.
15 1 Tim 2:5.

Christ, the unique "high priest after the order of Melchizedek";[16] "holy, blameless, unstained,"[17] "by a single offering he has perfected for all time those who are sanctified,"[18] that is, by the unique sacrifice of the cross.

1367   **1545** The redemptive sacrifice of Christ is unique, accomplished once for all; yet it is made present in the Eucharistic sacrifice of the Church. The same is true of the 662 one priesthood of Christ; it is made present through the ministerial priesthood without diminishing the uniqueness of Christ's priesthood: "Only Christ is the true priest, the others being only his ministers."[19]

Two participations in the one priesthood of Christ

1546 Christ, high priest and unique mediator, has made of the Church "a kingdom, priests for his God and Father."[20] The whole community of believers is, as such, priestly. The faithful exercise their baptismal priesthood through their participation, each according 1268 to his own vocation, in Christ's mission as priest, prophet, and king. Through the sacraments of Baptism and Confirmation the faithful are "consecrated to be . . . a holy priesthood."[21]

1142   **1547** The ministerial or hierarchical priesthood of bishops and priests, and the common priesthood of all the faithful participate, "each in its own proper way, in the one priesthood of Christ." While being "ordered one to another," they differ essentially.[22] In what sense? While the common priesthood of the faithful is exercised by the unfolding of baptismal grace—a life of faith, hope, and charity, a life according to the Spirit—, the ministerial priesthood is at the service of the common priesthood. It is directed at the unfolding of the 1120 baptismal grace of all Christians. The ministerial priesthood is a *means* by which Christ unceasingly builds up

---

16 *Heb* 5:10; cf. 6:20; *Gen* 14:18.   17 *Heb* 7:26.   18 *Heb* 10:14.   19 St. Thomas Aquinas, *Hebr* 8, 4.   20 *Rev* 1:6; cf. *Rev* 5:9–10; *1 Pet* 2:5, 9.   21 *LG* 10 § 1.   22 *LG* 10 § 2.

and leads his Church. For this reason it is transmitted by its own sacrament, the sacrament of Holy Orders.

In the person of Christ the Head . . .

1548 In the ecclesial service of the ordained minister, it is Christ himself who is present to his Church as Head of his Body, Shepherd of his flock, high priest of the redemptive sacrifice, Teacher of Truth. This is what the Church means by saying that the priest, by virtue of the sacrament of Holy Orders, acts *in persona Christi Capitis*:[23]

> It is the same priest, Christ Jesus, whose sacred person his minister truly represents. Now the minister, by reason of the sacerdotal consecration which he has received, is truly made like to the high priest and possesses the authority to act in the power and place of the person of Christ himself *(virtute ac persona ipsius Christi).*[24]

> Christ is the source of all priesthood: the priest of the old law was a figure of Christ, and the priest of the new law acts in the person of Christ.[25]

1549 Through the ordained ministry, especially that of bishops and priests, the presence of Christ as head of the Church is made visible in the midst of the community of believers.[26] In the beautiful expression of St. Ignatius of Antioch, the bishop is *typos tou Patros:* he is like the living image of God the Father.[27]

1550 This presence of Christ in the minister is not to be understood as if the latter were preserved from all human weaknesses, the spirit of domination, error, even sin. The power of the Holy Spirit does not guarantee all acts of ministers in the same way. While this guarantee extends to the sacraments, so that even the minister's sin cannot impede the fruit of grace, in many other acts the minister leaves human traces that are not always signs of fidelity to the Gospel and consequently can harm the apostolic fruitfulness of the Church.

875
792

1142

896

1128

1584

---

23 Cf. *LG* 10; 28; *SC* 33; *CD* 11; *PO* 2; 6.   24 Pius XII, encyclical, *Mediator Dei:* AAS, 39 (1947) 548.   25 St. Thomas Aquinas, *STh* III, 22, 4c.   26 Cf. *LG* 21.   27 St. Ignatius of Antioch, *Ad Trall.* 3, 1: SCh 10, 96; cf. *Ad Magn.* 6, 1: SCh 10, 82–84.

1551 This priesthood is ministerial. "That office . . . which the Lord committed to the pastors of his people, is in the strict sense of the term a *service.*"[28] It is entirely
876 related to Christ and to men. It depends entirely on Christ and on his unique priesthood; it has been instituted for the good of men and the communion of the Church. The sacrament of Holy Orders communicates a
1538 "sacred power" which is none other than that of Christ. The exercise of this authority must therefore be mea-
608 sured against the model of Christ, who by love made himself the least and the servant of all.[29] "The Lord said clearly that concern for his flock was proof of love for him."[30]

. . . "in the name of the whole Church"

1552 The ministerial priesthood has the task not only of representing Christ—Head of the Church—before the assembly of the faithful, but also of acting in the name of the whole Church when presenting to God the prayer of the Church, and above all when offering the Eucharistic sacrifice.[31]

1553 "In the name of the *whole* Church" does not mean that priests are the delegates of the community. The prayer and offering of the Church are inseparable from the prayer and offering of Christ, her head; it is always the case that Christ worships in and through his Church. The whole Church, the Body of Christ, prays and offers herself "through him, with him, in him," in
795 the unity of the Holy Spirit, to God the Father. The whole Body, *caput et membra,* prays and offers itself, and therefore those who in the Body are especially his ministers are called ministers not only of Christ, but also of the Church. It is because the ministerial priesthood represents Christ that it can represent the Church.

---

28 *LG* 24.   29 Cf. *Mk* 10:43–45; *1 Pet* 5:3.   30 St. John Chrysostom, *De sac.* 2, 4: PG 48, 636; cf. *Jn* 21:15–17.   31 Cf. *SC* 33N; *LG* 10.

III.   THE THREE DEGREES OF THE SACRAMENT OF HOLY ORDERS

1554 "The divinely instituted ecclesiastical ministry is exercised in different degrees by those who even from ancient times have been called bishops, priests, and deacons."[32] Catholic doctrine, expressed in the liturgy, the Magisterium, and the constant practice of the Church, recognizes that there are two degrees of ministerial participation in the priesthood of Christ: the episcopacy and the presbyterate. The diaconate is intended to help and serve them. For this reason the term *sacerdos* in current usage denotes bishops and priests but not deacons. Yet Catholic doctrine teaches that the degrees of priestly participation (episcopate and presbyterate) and the degree of service (diaconate) are all three conferred by a sacramental act called "ordination," that is, by the sacrament of Holy Orders:

1536

1538

> Let everyone revere the deacons as Jesus Christ, the bishop as the image of the Father, and the presbyters as the senate of God and the assembly of the apostles. For without them one cannot speak of the Church.[33]

Episcopal ordination—fullness of the sacrament of Holy Orders

1555 "Amongst those various offices which have been exercised in the Church from the earliest times the chief place, according to the witness of tradition, is held by the function of those who, through their appointment to the dignity and responsibility of bishop, and in virtue consequently of the unbroken succession going back to the beginning, are regarded as transmitters of the apostolic line."[34]

861

1556 To fulfill their exalted mission, "the apostles were endowed by Christ with a special outpouring of the Holy Spirit coming upon them, and by the imposition of hands they passed on to their auxiliaries the gift of the Spirit, which is transmitted down to our day through episcopal consecration."[35]

862

---

32 *LG* 28. 33 St. Ignatius of Antioch, *Ad Trall.* 3, 1: SCh 10, 96. 34 *LG* 20.
35 *LG* 21; cf. *Acts* 1:8; 2:4; *Jn* 20:22–23; *1 Tim* 4:14; *2 Tim* 1:6–7.

1557 The Second Vatican Council "teaches ... that *the fullness of the sacrament of Holy Orders* is conferred by episcopal consecration, that fullness namely which, both in the liturgical tradition of the Church and the language of the Fathers of the Church, is called the high priesthood, the acme *(summa)* of the sacred ministry."[36]

895   **1558** "Episcopal consecration confers, together with the office of sanctifying, also the offices of teaching and ruling.... In fact ... by the imposition of hands and

1121   through the words of the consecration, the grace of the Holy Spirit is given, and a sacred character is impressed in such wise that bishops, in an eminent and visible manner, take the place of Christ himself, teacher, shepherd, and priest, and act as his representative *(in Eius persona agant)*."[37] "By virtue, therefore, of the Holy Spirit who has been given to them, bishops have been constituted true and authentic teachers of the faith and have been made pontiffs and pastors."[38]

1559 "One is constituted a member of the episcopal body in virtue of the sacramental consecration and by the hierarchical communion with the head and members of the college."[39] The character and *collegial nature* of the episcopal order are evidenced among other ways

877   by the Church's ancient practice which calls for several bishops to participate in the consecration of a new bishop.[40] In our day, the lawful ordination of a bishop requires a special intervention of the Bishop of Rome,

882   because he is the supreme visible bond of the communion of the particular Churches in the one Church and the guarantor of their freedom.

833   **1560** As Christ's vicar, each bishop has the pastoral care of the particular Church entrusted to him, but at the same time he bears collegially with all his brothers in the episcopacy the *solicitude for all the Churches:*

886   "Though each bishop is the lawful pastor only of the portion of the flock entrusted to his care, as a legitimate

---

36 *LG* 21 § 2.   37 *LG* 21.   38 *CD* 2 § 2.   39 *LG* 22.   40 Cf. *LG* 22.

successor of the apostles he is, by divine institution and precept, responsible with the other bishops for the apostolic mission of the Church."[41]

1561 The above considerations explain why the Eucharist celebrated by the bishop has a quite special significance as an expression of the Church gathered around the altar, with the one who represents Christ, the Good Shepherd and Head of his Church, presiding.[42]

The ordination of priests—co-workers of the bishops

1562 "Christ, whom the Father hallowed and sent into the world, has, through his apostles, made their successors, the bishops namely, sharers in his consecration and mission; and these, in their turn, duly entrusted in varying degrees various members of the Church with the office of their ministry."[43] "The function of the bishops' ministry was handed over in a subordinate degree to priests so that they might be appointed in the order of the priesthood and be *co-workers of the episcopal order* for the proper fulfillment of the apostolic mission that had been entrusted to it by Christ."[44]

1563 "Because it is joined with the episcopal order the office of priests shares in the authority by which Christ himself builds up and sanctifies and rules his Body. Hence the priesthood of priests, while presupposing the sacraments of initiation, is nevertheless conferred by its own particular sacrament. Through that sacrament priests by the anointing of the Holy Spirit are signed with a special character and so are configured to Christ the priest in such a way that they are able to act in the person of Christ the head."[45]

1564 "Whilst not having the supreme degree of the pontifical office, and notwithstanding the fact that they depend on the bishops in the exercise of their own proper power, the priests are for all that associated with

1369

1121

---

41 Pius XII, *Fidei donum:* AAS 49 (1957) 237; cf. *LG* 23; *CD* 4; 36; 37; *AG* 5; 6; 38. 42 Cf. *SC* 41; *LG* 26. 43 *LG* 28; cf. *Jn* 10:36. 44 *PO* 2 § 2. 45 *PO* 2.

them by reason of their sacerdotal dignity; and in virtue of the sacrament of Holy Orders, after the image of Christ, the supreme and eternal priest, they are consecrated in order to preach the Gospel and shepherd the faithful as well as to celebrate divine worship *as true*
611 *priests of the New Testament.*"[46]

1565 Through the sacrament of Holy Orders priests share in the universal dimensions of the mission that Christ entrusted to the apostles. The spiritual gift they
849 have received in ordination prepares them, not for a limited and restricted mission, "but for the fullest, in fact the universal mission of salvation 'to the end of the earth,' "[47] "prepared in spirit to preach the Gospel everywhere."[48]

1369 **1566** "It is in the Eucharistic cult or in the *Eucharistic assembly* of the faithful *(synaxis)* that they exercise in a supreme degree their sacred office; there, acting in the person of Christ and proclaiming his mystery, they unite the votive offerings of the faithful to the sacrifice of Christ their head, and in the sacrifice of the Mass they make present again and apply, until the coming of the Lord, the unique sacrifice of the New Testament, that namely of Christ offering himself once for all a spotless
611 victim to the Father."[49] From this unique sacrifice their whole priestly ministry draws its strength.[50]

1462 **1567** "The priests, prudent cooperators of the episcopal college and its support and instrument, called to the service of the People of God, constitute, together with their bishop, a unique sacerdotal college *(presbyterium)* dedicated, it is true, to a variety of distinct duties. In each local assembly of the faithful they represent, in a
2179 certain sense, the bishop, with whom they are associated in all trust and generosity; in part they take upon themselves his duties and solicitude and in their daily toils discharge them."[51] Priests can exercise their min-

---

46 *LG* 28; cf. *Heb* 5:1–10; 7:24; 9:11–28; Innocent I, *Epist. ad Decentium:* PL 20, 554 A; St. Gregory of Nazianzus, *Oratio* 2, 22: PG 35, 432B.   47 *PO* 10; *OT* 20; cf. *Acts* 1:8.   48 *OT* 20.   49 *LG* 28; cf. *1 Cor* 11:26.   50 Cf. *PO* 2. 51 *LG* 28 § 2.

istry only in dependence on the bishop and in communion with him. The promise of obedience they make to the bishop at the moment of ordination and the kiss of peace from him at the end of the ordination liturgy mean that the bishop considers them his co-workers, his sons, his brothers and his friends, and that they in return owe him love and obedience.

1568 "All priests, who are constituted in the order of priesthood by the sacrament of Order, are bound together by an intimate sacramental brotherhood, but in a special way they form one priestly body in the diocese to which they are attached under their own bishop. . . ."[52] The unity of the presbyterium finds liturgical expression in the custom of the presbyters' imposing hands, after the bishop, during the rite of ordination.

1537

The ordination of deacons—"in order to serve"

1569 "At a lower level of the hierarchy are to be found deacons, who receive the imposition of hands 'not unto the priesthood, but unto the ministry.' "[53] At an ordination to the diaconate only the bishop lays hands on the candidate, thus signifying the deacon's special attachment to the bishop in the tasks of his "diakonia."[54]

1570 Deacons share in Christ's mission and grace in a special way.[55] The sacrament of Holy Orders marks them with an *imprint* ("character") which cannot be removed and which configures them to Christ, who made himself the "deacon" or servant of all.[56] Among other tasks, it is the task of deacons to assist the bishop and priests in the celebration of the divine mysteries, above all the Eucharist, in the distribution of Holy Communion, in assisting at and blessing marriages, in the proclamation of the Gospel and preaching, in presiding over funerals, and in dedicating themselves to the various ministries of charity.[57]

1121

---

52 *PO* 8.   53 *LG* 29; cf. *CD* 15.   54 Cf. St. Hippolytus, *Trad. ap.* 8: SCh 11, 58–62.   55 Cf. *LG* 41; *AA* 16.   56 Cf. *Mk* 10:45; *Lk* 22:27; St. Polycarp, *Ad Phil.* 5, 2: SCh 10, 182.   57 Cf. *LG* 29; *SC* 35 § 4; *AG* 16.

1571 Since the Second Vatican Council the Latin Church
has restored the diaconate "as a proper and permanent
rank of the hierarchy,"[58] while the Churches of the East had
always maintained it. This *permanent diaconate,* which can
be conferred on married men, constitutes an important en-
1579 richment for the Church's mission. Indeed it is appropriate
and useful that men who carry out a truly diaconal ministry in the Church, whether in its liturgical and pastoral
life or whether in its social and charitable works, should
"be strengthened by the imposition of hands which has
come down from the apostles. They would be more closely
bound to the altar and their ministry would be made more
fruitful through the sacramental grace of the diaconate."[59]

IV. THE CELEBRATION OF THIS SACRAMENT

1572 Given the importance that the ordination of a
bishop, a priest, or a deacon has for the life of the particular Church, its celebration calls for as many of the
faithful as possible to take part. It should take place
preferably on Sunday, in the cathedral, with solemnity
appropriate to the occasion. All three ordinations, of
the bishop, of the priest, and of the deacon, follow the
same movement. Their proper place is within the Eucharistic liturgy.

1573 The *essential rite* of the sacrament of Holy Orders for all three degrees consists in the bishop's imposition of hands on the head of the ordinand and in the
699 bishop's specific consecratory prayer asking God for the
1585 outpouring of the Holy Spirit and his gifts proper to
the ministry to which the candidate is being ordained.[60]

1574 As in all the sacraments additional rites surround
the celebration. Varying greatly among the different liturgical traditions, these rites have in common the expression of
the multiple aspects of sacramental grace. Thus in the Latin
Church, the initial rites—presentation and election of the
ordinand, instruction by the bishop, examination of the
candidate, litany of the saints—attest that the choice of
the candidate is made in keeping with the practice of the
Church and prepare for the solemn act of consecration, after which several rites symbolically express and complete

---

58 LG 29 § 2.   59 AG 16 § 6.   60 Cf. Pius XII, apostolic constitution,
Sacramentum Ordinis: DS *3858.*

the mystery accomplished: for bishop and priest, an anointing with holy chrism, a sign of the special anointing of the Holy Spirit who makes their ministry fruitful; giving the book of the Gospels, the ring, the miter, and the crosier to the bishop as the sign of his apostolic mission to proclaim the Word of God, of his fidelity to the Church, the bride of Christ, and his office as shepherd of the Lord's flock; presentation to the priest of the paten and chalice, "the offering of the holy people" which he is called to present to God; giving the book of the Gospels to the deacon who has just received the mission to proclaim the Gospel of Christ.

1294

796

V.   WHO CAN CONFER THIS SACRAMENT?

1575   Christ himself chose the apostles and gave them a share in his mission and authority. Raised to the Father's right hand, he has not forsaken his flock but he keeps it under his constant protection through the apostles, and guides it still through these same pastors who continue his work today.[61] Thus, it is Christ whose gift it is that some be apostles, others pastors. He continues to act through the bishops.[62]

857

1576   Since the sacrament of Holy Orders is the sacrament of the apostolic ministry, it is for the bishops as the successors of the apostles to hand on the "gift of the Spirit,"[63] the "apostolic line."[64] Validly ordained bishops, i.e., those who are in the line of apostolic succession, validly confer the three degrees of the sacrament of Holy Orders.[65]

1536

VI.   WHO CAN RECEIVE THIS SACRAMENT?

1577   "Only a baptized man *(vir)* validly receives sacred ordination."[66] The Lord Jesus chose men *(viri)* to form the college of the twelve apostles, and the apostles did the same when they chose collaborators to succeed them in their ministry.[67] The college of bishops, with whom the priests are united in the priesthood, makes the college of the twelve an ever-present and ever-active

551

861

862

---

61 Cf. *Roman Missal*, Preface of the Apostles I.   62 Cf. *LG* 21; Eph 4:11.
63 *LG* 21 § 2.   64 *LG* 20.   65 Cf. DS 794 and Cf. DS 802; CIC, can. 1012;
CCEO, can. 744; 747.   66 CIC, can. 1024.   67 Cf. *Mk* 3:14–19; *Lk* 6:12–16;
1 Tim 3:1–13; *2 Tim* 1:6; *Titus* 1:5–9; St. Clement of Rome, *Ad Cor.* 42, 4; 44, 3:
PG 1, 292–293; 300.

reality until Christ's return. The Church recognizes herself to be bound by this choice made by the Lord himself. For this reason the ordination of women is not possible.[68]

1578 No one has a *right* to receive the sacrament of
Holy Orders. Indeed no one claims this office for himself; he is called to it by God.[69] Anyone who thinks he
recognizes the signs of God's call to the ordained ministry must humbly submit his desire to the authority of
the Church, who has the responsibility and right to call
someone to receive orders. Like every grace this sacrament can be *received* only as an unmerited gift.

2121

1579 All the ordained ministers of the Latin Church,
with the exception of permanent deacons, are normally
chosen from among men of faith who live a celibate life
and who intend to remain *celibate* "for the sake of the
kingdom of heaven."[70] Called to consecrate themselves
with undivided heart to the Lord and to "the affairs of
the Lord,"[71] they give themselves entirely to God and to
men. Celibacy is a sign of this new life to the service of
which the Church's minister is consecrated; accepted
with a joyous heart celibacy radiantly proclaims the
Reign of God.[72]

1618

2233

1580 In the Eastern Churches a different discipline has
been in force for many centuries: while bishops are chosen solely from among celibates, married men can be ordained as deacons and priests. This practice has long
been considered legitimate; these priests exercise a fruitful ministry within their communities.[73] Moreover,
priestly celibacy is held in great honor in the Eastern
Churches and many priests have freely chosen it for the
sake of the Kingdom of God. In the East as in the West
a man who has already received the sacrament of Holy
Orders can no longer marry.

---

68 Cf. John Paul II, *MD* 26–27; CDF, declaration, *Inter insigniores:* AAS 69
(1977) 98–116.   69 Cf. *Heb* 5:4.   70 *Mt* 19:12.   71 1 *Cor* 7:32.   72 Cf. *PO*
16.   73 Cf. *PO* 16.

VII. THE EFFECTS OF THE SACRAMENT OF HOLY ORDERS

The indelible character

1581 This sacrament configures the recipient to Christ by a special grace of the Holy Spirit, so that he may serve as Christ's instrument for his Church. By ordination one is enabled to act as a representative of Christ, Head of the Church, in his triple office of priest, prophet, and king. *1548*

1582 As in the case of Baptism and Confirmation this share in Christ's office is granted once for all. The sacrament of Holy Orders, like the other two, confers an *indelible spiritual character* and cannot be repeated or conferred temporarily.[74] *1121*

1583 It is true that someone validly ordained can, for a just reason, be discharged from the obligations and functions linked to ordination, or can be forbidden to exercise them; but he cannot become a layman again in the strict sense,[75] because the character imprinted by ordination is for ever. The vocation and mission received on the day of his ordination mark him permanently.

1584 Since it is ultimately Christ who acts and effects salvation through the ordained minister, the unworthiness of the latter does not prevent Christ from acting.[76] St. Augustine states this forcefully: *1128*

> As for the proud minister, he is to be ranked with the devil. Christ's gift is not thereby profaned: what flows through him keeps its purity, and what passes through him remains clear and reaches the fertile earth. . . . The spiritual power of the sacrament is indeed comparable to light: those to be enlightened receive it in its purity, and if it should pass through defiled beings, it is not itself defiled.[77] *1550*

---

74 Cf. Council of Trent: DS 1767; *LG* 21; 28; 29; *PO* 2.   75 Cf. CIC, cann. 290–293; 1336 § 1 3°, 5°; 1338 § 2; Council of Trent: DS 1774.   76 Cf. Council of Trent: DS 1612; DS 1154.   77 St. Augustine, *In Jo. ev.* 5, 15: PL 35, 1422.

The grace of the Holy Spirit

1585 The grace of the Holy Spirit proper to this sacrament is configuration to Christ as Priest, Teacher, and Pastor, of whom the ordained is made a minister.

1586 For the bishop, this is first of all a grace of strength ("the governing spirit": Prayer of Episcopal Consecration in the Latin rite):[78] the grace to guide and defend his Church with strength and prudence as a father and pastor, with gratuitous love for all and a preferential love for the poor, the sick, and the needy. This grace impels him to proclaim the Gospel to all, to be the model for his flock, to go before it on the way of sanctification by identifying himself in the Eucharist with Christ the priest and victim, not fearing to give his life for his sheep:

2448

1558

> Father, you know all hearts.
> You have chosen your servant for the office of bishop.
> May he be a shepherd to your holy flock,
> and a high priest blameless in your sight,
> ministering to you night and day;
> may he always gain the blessing of your favor
> and offer the gifts of your holy Church.
> Through the Spirit who gives the grace of high priesthood
> grant him the power
> to forgive sins as you have commanded,
> to assign ministries as you have decreed,
> and to loose from every bond by the authority which you
> gave to your apostles.
> May he be pleasing to you by his gentleness and purity of heart,
> presenting a fragrant offering to you,
> through Jesus Christ, your Son. . . .[79]

1564 **1587** The spiritual gift conferred by presbyteral ordination is expressed by this prayer of the Byzantine Rite. The bishop, while laying on his hand, says among other things:

---

78 Cf. *Roman Pontifical,* Ordination of Bishops 26, Prayer of Consecration; cf. CD 13; 16.   79 *Roman Pontifical,* Ordination of Bishops 26, Prayer of Consecration; cf. St. Hippolytus, *Trad. ap.* 3: SCh 11, 44–46.

Lord, fill with the gift of the Holy Spirit
him whom you have deigned to raise to the rank
of the priesthood,
that he may be worthy to stand without reproach
before your altar,
to proclaim the Gospel of your kingdom,
to fulfill the ministry of your word of truth,
to offer you spiritual gifts and sacrifices,
to renew your people by the bath of rebirth;
so that he may go out to meet
our great God and Savior Jesus Christ, your only
Son,
on the day of his second coming,
and may receive from your vast goodness
the recompense for a faithful administration of his
order.[80]

1588 With regard to deacons, "strengthened by sacra- 1569
mental grace they are dedicated to the People of God, in
conjunction with the bishop and his body of priests, in
the service *(diakonia)* of the liturgy, of the Gospel, and
of works of charity."[81]

1589 Before the grandeur of the priestly grace and
office, the holy doctors felt an urgent call to conversion in order to conform their whole lives to him
whose sacrament had made them ministers. Thus St.
Gregory of Nazianzus, as a very young priest, ex-
claimed:

> We must begin by purifying ourselves before puri-
> fying others; we must be instructed to be able to in-
> struct, become light to illuminate, draw close to
> God to bring him close to others, be sanctified to
> sanctify, lead by the hand and counsel prudently. I
> know whose ministers we are, where we find our-
> selves and to where we strive. I know God's great-
> ness and man's weakness, but also his potential.
> [Who then is the priest? He is] the defender
> of truth, who stands with angels, gives glory with
> archangels, causes sacrifices to rise to the al-tar on
> high, shares Christ's priesthood, refashions cre-
> ation, restores it in God's image, recreates it for the 460

---

80 Byzantine Liturgy, *Euchologion.*   81 LG 29.

world on high and, even greater, is divinized and divinizes.[82]

And the holy Curé of Ars: "The priest continues the work of redemption on earth. . . . If we really understood the priest on earth, we would die not of fright but of love. . . . The Priesthood is the love of the heart of Jesus."[83]

1551

IN BRIEF

1590   St. Paul said to his disciple Timothy: "I remind you to rekindle the gift of God that is within you through the laying on of my hands" (2 *Tim* 1:6), and "If any one aspires to the office of bishop, he desires a noble task." (1 *Tim* 3:1) To Titus he said: "This is why I left you in Crete, that you amend what was defective, and appoint presbyters in every town, as I directed you" (*Titus* 1:5).

1591   The whole Church is a priestly people. Through Baptism all the faithful share in the priesthood of Christ. This participation is called the "common priesthood of the faithful." Based on this common priesthood and ordered to its service, there exists another participation in the mission of Christ: the ministry conferred by the sacrament of Holy Orders, where the task is to serve in the name and in the person of Christ the Head in the midst of the community.

1592   The ministerial priesthood differs in essence from the common priesthood of the faithful because it confers a sacred power for the service of the faithful. The ordained ministers exercise their service for the People of God by teaching (*munus docendi*), divine worship (*munus liturgicum*), and pastoral governance (*munus regendi*).

---

82 St. Gregory of Nazianzus, *Oratio* 2, 71, 74, 73: PG 35, 480–481.   83 St. John Vianney, quoted in B. Nodet, *Jean-Marie Vianney, Curé d'Ars*, 100.

1593   Since the beginning, the ordained ministry has been conferred and exercised in three degrees: that of bishops, that of presbyters, and that of deacons. The ministries conferred by ordination are irreplaceable for the organic structure of the Church: without the bishop, presbyters, and deacons, one cannot speak of the Church (cf. St. Ignatius of Antioch, *Ad Trall.* 3,1).

1594   The bishop receives the fullness of the sacrament of Holy Orders, which integrates him into the episcopal college and makes him the visible head of the particular Church entrusted to him. As successors of the apostles and members of the college, the bishops share in the apostolic responsibility and mission of the whole Church under the authority of the Pope, successor of St. Peter.

1595   Priests are united with the bishops in sacerdotal dignity and at the same time depend on them in the exercise of their pastoral functions; they are called to be the bishops' prudent co-workers. They form around their bishop the presbyterium which bears responsibility with him for the particular Church. They receive from the bishop the charge of a parish community or a determinate ecclesial office.

1596   Deacons are ministers ordained for tasks of service of the Church; they do not receive the ministerial priesthood, but ordination confers on them important functions in the ministry of the word, divine worship, pastoral governance, and the service of charity, tasks which they must carry out under the pastoral authority of their bishop.

1597   The sacrament of Holy Orders is conferred by the laying on of hands followed by a solemn prayer of consecration asking God to grant the ordinand the graces of the Holy Spirit required for his ministry. Ordination imprints an indelible sacramental character.

1598 The Church confers the sacrament of Holy Orders only on baptized men *(viri),* whose suitability for the exercise of the ministry has been duly recognized. Church authority alone has the responsibility and right to call someone to receive the sacrament of Holy Orders.

1599 In the Latin Church the sacrament of Holy Orders for the presbyterate is normally conferred only on candidates who are ready to embrace celibacy freely and who publicly manifest their intention of staying celibate for the love of God's kingdom and the service of men.

1600 It is bishops who confer the sacrament of Holy Orders in the three degrees.

ARTICLE 7
THE SACRAMENT OF MATRIMONY

1601 "The matrimonial covenant, by which a man and a woman establish between themselves a partnership of the whole of life, is by its nature ordered toward the good of the spouses and the procreation and education of offspring; this covenant between baptized persons has been raised by Christ the Lord to the dignity of a sacrament."[84]

I.   MARRIAGE IN GOD'S PLAN

369   **1602** Sacred Scripture begins with the creation of man
769   and woman in the image and likeness of God and concludes with a vision of "the wedding-feast of the Lamb."[85] Scripture speaks throughout of marriage and its "mystery," its institution and the meaning God has given it, its origin and its end, its various realizations throughout the history of salvation, the difficulties aris-

---

84 CIC, can. 1055 § 1; cf. *GS* 48 § 1.   85 *Rev* 19:7, 9; cf. *Gen* 1:26–27.

ing from sin and its renewal "in the Lord" in the New Covenant of Christ and the Church.[86]

Marriage in the order of creation

1603 "The intimate community of life and love which constitutes the married state has been established by the Creator and endowed by him with its own proper laws. 371 . . . God himself is the author of marriage."[87] The vocation to marriage is written in the very nature of man and woman as they came from the hand of the Creator. Marriage is not a purely human institution despite the 2331 many variations it may have undergone through the centuries in different cultures, social structures, and spiritual attitudes. These differences should not cause us to forget its common and permanent characteristics. Although the dignity of this institution is not transparent everywhere with the same clarity,[88] some sense of the greatness of the matrimonial union exists in all cultures. "The well-being of the individual person and of both 2210 human and Christian society is closely bound up with the healthy state of conjugal and family life."[89]

1604 God who created man out of love also calls him to love—the fundamental and innate vocation of every human being. For man is created in the image and likeness of God who is himself love.[90] Since God created him man and woman, their mutual love becomes an image of the absolute and unfailing love with which God 355 loves man. It is good, very good, in the Creator's eyes. And this love which God blesses is intended to be fruitful and to be realized in the common work of watching over creation: "And God blessed them, and God said to them: 'Be fruitful and multiply, and fill the earth and subdue it.' "[91]

1605 Holy Scripture affirms that man and woman 372 were created for one another: "It is not good that the man should be alone."[92] The woman, "flesh of his flesh," i.e., his counterpart, his equal, his nearest in all

---

86 *1 Cor* 7:39; cf. *Eph* 5:31–32. 87 *GS* 48 § 1. 88 Cf. *GS* 47 § 2. 89 *GS* 47 § 1. 90 Cf. *Gen* 1:27; *1 Jn* 4:8, 16. 91 *Gen* 1:28; cf. 1:31. 92 *Gen* 2:18.

things, is given to him by God as a "helpmate"; she thus represents God from whom comes our help.[93] "Therefore a man leaves his father and his mother and cleaves to his wife, and they become one flesh."[94] The Lord himself shows that this signifies an unbreakable union
1614   of their two lives by recalling what the plan of the Creator had been "in the beginning": "So they are no longer two, but one flesh."[95]

Marriage under the regime of sin

1606 Every man experiences evil around him and within himself. This experience makes itself felt in the relationships between man and woman. Their union has always been threatened by discord, a spirit of domination, infidelity, jealousy, and conflicts that can escalate into hatred and separation. This disorder can manifest itself more or less acutely, and can be more or less overcome according to the circumstances of cultures, eras, and individuals, but it does seem to have a universal character.

1607 According to faith the disorder we notice so painfully does not stem from the *nature* of man and
1849   woman, nor from the nature of their relations, but from
    sin. As a break with God, the first sin had for its first
400   consequence the rupture of the original communion between man and woman. Their relations were distorted by mutual recriminations;[96] their mutual attraction, the Creator's own gift, changed into a relationship of domination and lust;[97] and the beautiful vocation of man and woman to be fruitful, multiply, and subdue the earth was burdened by the pain of childbirth and the toil of work.[98]

55   **1608** Nevertheless, the order of creation persists, though seriously disturbed. To heal the wounds of sin, man and woman need the help of the grace that God in his infinite mercy never refuses them.[99] Without his help man and woman cannot achieve the union of their lives for which God created them "in the beginning."

---

93 Cf. *Gen* 2:18–25.   94 *Gen* 2:24.   95 *Mt* 19:6.   96 Cf. *Gen* 3:12.   97 Cf. *Gen* 2:22; 3:16b.   98 Cf. *Gen* 1:28; 3:16–19.   99 Cf. *Gen* 3:21.

Marriage under the pedagogy of the Law

1609 In his mercy God has not forsaken sinful man. *410*
The punishments consequent upon sin, "pain in child-
bearing" and toil "in the sweat of your brow,"[100] also
embody remedies that limit the damaging effects of sin.
After the fall, marriage helps to overcome self-absorption, egoism, pursuit of one's own pleasure, and to open
oneself to the other, to mutual aid and to self-giving.

1610 Moral conscience concerning the unity and indissolubility of marriage developed under the pedagogy
of the old law. In the Old Testament the polygamy of *1963*
patriarchs and kings is not yet explicitly rejected. Nevertheless, the law given to Moses aims at protecting the *2387*
wife from arbitrary domination by the husband, even
though according to the Lord's words it still carries
traces of man's "hardness of heart" which was the reason Moses permitted men to divorce their wives.[101]

1611 Seeing God's covenant with Israel in the image of *219*
exclusive and faithful married love, the prophets pre- *2380*
pared the Chosen People's conscience for a deepened
understanding of the unity and indissolubility of mar- *2361*
riage.[102] The books of *Ruth* and *Tobit* bear moving witness to an elevated sense of marriage and to the fidelity
and tenderness of spouses. Tradition has always seen in
the *Song of Solomon* a unique expression of human
love, a pure reflection of God's love—a love "strong as
death" that "many waters cannot quench."[103]

Marriage in the Lord

1612 The nuptial covenant between God and his people Israel had prepared the way for the new and everlasting covenant in which the Son of God, by becoming *521*
incarnate and giving his life, has united to himself in a
certain way all mankind saved by him, thus preparing
for "the wedding-feast of the Lamb."[104]

1613 On the threshold of his public life Jesus performs

---

100 *Gen* 3:16, 19. 101 Cf. *Mt* 19:8; *Deut* 24:1. 102 Cf. *Hos* 1–3; *Isa* 54; 62;
Jer 2–3; 31; *Ezek* 16; 23; *Mal* 2:13–17. 103 *Song* 8:6–7. 104 *Rev* 19:7, 9; cf.
GS 22.

his first sign—at his mother's request—during a wedding feast.[105] The Church attaches great importance to Jesus' presence at the wedding at Cana. She sees in it the confirmation of the goodness of marriage and the proclamation that thenceforth marriage will be an efficacious sign of Christ's presence.

2336   **1614**   In his preaching Jesus unequivocally taught the original meaning of the union of man and woman as the Creator willed it from the beginning: permission given by Moses to divorce one's wife was a concession to the hardness of hearts.[106] The matrimonial union of man
2382   and woman is indissoluble: God himself has determined it: "what therefore God has joined together, let no man put asunder."[107]

2364   **1615**   This unequivocal insistence on the indissolubility of the marriage bond may have left some perplexed and could seem to be a demand impossible to realize. However, Jesus has not placed on spouses a burden impossible to bear, or too heavy—heavier than the Law of Moses.[108] By coming to restore the original order of creation disturbed by sin, he himself gives the strength and grace to live marriage in the new dimension of the Reign of God. It is by following Christ, renouncing themselves, and taking up their crosses that spouses will be able to "receive" the original meaning of marriage and live it with the help of Christ.[109] This grace of Christian marriage is a fruit of Christ's cross, the source of all
1642   Christian life.

1616   This is what the Apostle Paul makes clear when he says: "Husbands, love your wives, as Christ loved the church and gave himself up for her, that he might sanctify her," adding at once: "For this reason a man shall leave his father and mother and be joined to his wife, and the two shall become one. This is a great mystery, and I mean in reference to Christ and the Church."[110]

---

105 Cf. *Jn* 2:1-11.   106 Cf. *Mt* 19:8.   107 *Mt* 19:6.   108 Cf. *Mk* 8:34; *Mt* 11:29-30.   109 Cf. *Mt* 19:11.   110 *Eph* 5:25-26, 31-32; cf. *Gen* 2:24.

1617 The entire Christian life bears the mark of the spousal love of Christ and the Church. Already Baptism, the entry into the People of God, is a nuptial mystery; it is so to speak the nuptial bath[111] which precedes the wedding feast, the Eucharist. Christian marriage in its turn becomes an efficacious sign, the sacrament of the covenant of Christ and the Church. Since it signifies and communicates grace, marriage between baptized persons is a true sacrament of the New Covenant.[112]

796

Virginity for the sake of the Kingdom

1618 Christ is the center of all Christian life. The bond with him takes precedence over all other bonds, familial or social.[113] From the very beginning of the Church there have been men and women who have renounced the great good of marriage to follow the Lamb wherever he goes, to be intent on the things of the Lord, to seek to please him, and to go out to meet the Bridegroom who is coming.[114] Christ himself has invited certain persons to follow him in this way of life, of which he remains the model:

2232

1579

> "For there are eunuchs who have been so from birth, and there are eunuchs who have been made eunuchs by men, and there are eunuchs who have made themselves eunuchs for the sake of the kingdom of heaven. He who is able to receive this, let him receive it."[115]

1619 Virginity for the sake of the kingdom of heaven is an unfolding of baptismal grace, a powerful sign of the supremacy of the bond with Christ and of the ardent expectation of his return, a sign which also recalls that marriage is a reality of this present age which is passing away.[116]

922-924

1620 Both the sacrament of Matrimony and virginity for the Kingdom of God come from the Lord himself. It is he who gives them meaning and grants them the grace which is indispensable for living them out in conformity

---

111 Cf. *Eph* 5:26–27.   112 Cf. DS 1800; CIC, can. 1055 § 2.   113 Cf. *Lk* 14:26; *Mk* 10:28–31.   114 Cf. *Rev* 14:4; *1 Cor* 7:32; *Mt* 25:6.   115 *Mt* 19:12.   116 Cf. *Mk* 12:25; *1 Cor* 7:31.

with his will.[117] Esteem of virginity for the sake of the
2349 kingdom[118] and the Christian understanding of marriage
are inseparable, and they reinforce each other:

> Whoever denigrates marriage also diminishes the
> glory of virginity. Whoever praises it makes virgin-
> ity more admirable and resplendent. What appears
> good only in comparison with evil would not be
> truly good. The most excellent good is something
> even better than what is admitted to be good.[119]

II.   THE CELEBRATION OF MARRIAGE

1621   In the Latin Rite the celebration of marriage between two Catholic faithful normally takes place during
Holy Mass, because of the connection of all the sacraments with the Paschal mystery of Christ.[120] In the Eu-
1323 charist the memorial of the New Covenant is realized,
the New Covenant in which Christ has united himself
for ever to the Church, his beloved bride for whom he
gave himself up.[121] It is therefore fitting that the spouses
should seal their consent to give themselves to each
other through the offering of their own lives by uniting
it to the offering of Christ for his Church made present
in the Eucharistic sacrifice, and by receiving the Eu-
1368 charist so that, communicating in the same Body and
the same Blood of Christ, they may form but "one
body" in Christ.[122]

1622   "Inasmuch as it is a sacramental action of sanctification, the liturgical celebration of marriage . . .
must be, per se, valid, worthy, and fruitful."[123] It is
therefore appropriate for the bride and groom to prepare themselves for the celebration of their marriage by
1422 receiving the sacrament of penance.

1623   In the Latin Church, it is ordinarily understood
that the spouses, as ministers of Christ's grace, mutually
confer upon each other the sacrament of Matrimony by
expressing their consent before the Church. In the Eastern liturgies the minister of this sacrament (which is

---

117 Cf. *Mt* 19:3–12.   118 Cf. *LG* 42; *PC* 12; *OT* 10.   119 St. John Chrysostom,
De virg. 10, 1: PG 48, 540; cf. John Paul II, *FC* 16.   120 Cf. *SC* 61.   121 Cf.
LG 6.   122 Cf. *1 Cor* 10:17.   123 *FC* 67.

called "Crowning") is the priest or bishop who, after receiving the mutual consent of the spouses, successively crowns the bridegroom and the bride as a sign of the marriage covenant.

1624 The various liturgies abound in prayers of blessing and epiclesis asking God's grace and blessing on the new couple, especially the bride. In the epiclesis of this sacrament the spouses receive the Holy Spirit as the communion of love of Christ and the Church.[124] The Holy Spirit is the seal of their covenant, the ever-available source of their love and the strength to renew their fidelity. *736*

III. MATRIMONIAL CONSENT

1625 The parties to a marriage covenant are a baptized man and woman, free to contract marriage, who *1734* freely express their consent; "to be free" means:

—not being under constraint;

—not impeded by any natural or ecclesiastical law.

1626 The Church holds the exchange of consent between the spouses to be the indispensable element that "makes the marriage."[125] If consent is lacking there is no *2201* marriage.

1627 The consent consists in a "human act by which the partners mutually give themselves to each other": "I take you to be my wife"—"I take you to be my husband."[126] This consent that binds the spouses to each other finds its fulfillment in the two "becoming one flesh."[127]

1628 The consent must be an act of the will of each of *1735* the contracting parties, free of coercion or grave external fear.[128] No human power can substitute for this consent.[129] If this freedom is lacking the marriage is invalid.

1629 For this reason (or for other reasons that render the

---

124 Cf. *Eph* 5:32. 125 CIC, can. 1057 § 1. 126 *GS* 48 § 1; *OCM* 45; cf. CIC, can. 1057 § 2. 127 *Gen* 2:24; cf. *Mk* 10:8; *Eph* 5:31. 128 Cf. CIC, can. 1103. 129 Cf. CIC, can. 1057 § 1.

marriage null and void) the Church, after an examination of the situation by the competent ecclesiastical tribunal, can declare the nullity of a marriage, i.e., that the marriage never existed.[130] In this case the contracting parties are free to marry, provided the natural obligations of a previous union are discharged.[131]

1630 The priest (or deacon) who assists at the celebration of a marriage receives the consent of the spouses in the name of the Church and gives the blessing of the Church. The presence of the Church's minister (and also of the witnesses) visibly expresses the fact that marriage is an ecclesial reality.

1631 This is the reason why the Church normally requires that the faithful contract marriage according to the ecclesiastical form. Several reasons converge to explain this requirement:[132]

1069 —Sacramental marriage is a liturgical act. It is therefore appropriate that it should be celebrated in the public liturgy of the Church;

1537 —Marriage introduces one into an ecclesial *order,* and creates rights and duties in the Church between the spouses and towards their children;

—Since marriage is a state of life in the Church, certainty about it is necessary (hence the obligation to have witnesses);

2365 —The public character of the consent protects the "I do" once given and helps the spouses remain faithful to it.

1632 So that the "I do" of the spouses may be a free and responsible act and so that the marriage covenant may have solid and lasting human and Christian foundations, preparation for marriage is of prime importance.

2206 The example and teaching given by parents and families remain the special form of this preparation.

---

130 Cf. CIC, cann. 1095–1107.   131 Cf. CIC, can. 1071.   132 Cf. Council of Trent: DS 1813–1816; CIC, can. 1108.

The role of pastors and of the Christian community as the "family of God" is indispensable for the transmission of the human and Christian values of marriage and family,[133] and much more so in our era when many young people experience broken homes which no longer sufficiently assure this initiation:

> It is imperative to give suitable and timely instruction to young people, above all in the heart of their own families, about the dignity of married love, its role and its exercise, so that, having learned the value of chastity, they will be able at a suitable age to engage in honorable courtship and enter upon a marriage of their own.[134]

2350

Mixed marriages and disparity of cult

1633 In many countries the situation of a *mixed marriage* (marriage between a Catholic and a baptized non-Catholic) often arises. It requires particular attention on the part of couples and their pastors. A case of marriage with *disparity of cult* (between a Catholic and a non-baptized person) requires even greater circumspection.

1634 Difference of confession between the spouses does not constitute an insurmountable obstacle for marriage, when they succeed in placing in common what they have received from their respective communities, and learn from each other the way in which each lives in fidelity to Christ. But the difficulties of mixed marriages must not be underestimated. They arise from the fact that the separation of Christians has not yet been overcome. The spouses risk experiencing the tragedy of Christian disunity even in the heart of their own home. Disparity of cult can further aggravate these difficulties. Differences about faith and the very notion of marriage, but also different religious mentalities, can become sources of tension in marriage, especially as regards the education of children. The temptation to religious indifference can then arise.

817

1635 According to the law in force in the Latin Church, a mixed marriage needs for liceity the *express permission* of ecclesiastical authority.[135] In case of disparity of cult an *express dispensation* from this impediment is required for the validity of the marriage.[136] This permission or dispensation presupposes that both parties know and do not exclude the

---

133 Cf. CIC, can. 1063.   134 *GS* 49 § 3.   135 Cf. CIC, can. 1124.   136 Cf. CIC, can. 1086.

essential ends and properties of marriage and the obligations assumed by the Catholic party concerning the baptism and education of the children in the Catholic
Church.[137]

821 **1636** Through ecumenical dialogue Christian communities in many regions have been able to put into effect a
common pastoral practice for mixed marriages. Its task is
to help such couples live out their particular situation in the
light of faith, overcome the tensions between the couple's
obligations to each other and towards their ecclesial communities, and encourage the flowering of what is common
to them in faith and respect for what separates them.

1637 In marriages with disparity of cult the Catholic
spouse has a particular task: "For the unbelieving husband
is consecrated through his wife, and the unbelieving wife is
consecrated through her husband."[138] It is a great joy for
the Christian spouse and for the Church if this "consecration" should lead to the free conversion of the other spouse
to the Christian faith.[139] Sincere married love, the humble
and patient practice of the family virtues, and perseverance
in prayer can prepare the non-believing spouse to accept
the grace of conversion.

IV. THE EFFECTS OF THE SACRAMENT OF MATRIMONY

1638 "From a valid marriage arises *a bond* between
the spouses which by its very nature is perpetual and exclusive; furthermore, in a Christian marriage the
spouses are strengthened and, as it were, consecrated
for the duties and the dignity of their state *by a special
sacrament.* "[140]

The marriage bond

1639 The consent by which the spouses mutually give
and receive one another is sealed by God himself.[141]
From their covenant arises "an institution, confirmed
by the divine law, . . . even in the eyes of society."[142] The
covenant between the spouses is integrated into God's
covenant with man: "Authentic married love is caught
up into divine love."[143]

---

137 Cf. CIC, can. 1125.   138 *1 Cor* 7:14.   139 Cf. *1 Cor* 7:16.   140 Cf. CIC,
can. 1134.   141 Cf. *Mk* 10:9.   142 *GS* 48 § 1.   143 *GS* 48 § 2.

1640 Thus *the marriage bond* has been established by God himself in such a way that a marriage concluded and consummated between baptized persons can never be dissolved. This bond, which results from the free human act of the spouses and their consummation of the marriage, is a reality, henceforth irrevocable, and gives rise to a covenant guaranteed by God's fidelity. The Church does not have the power to contravene this disposition of divine wisdom.[144]

2365

The grace of the sacrament of Matrimony

1641 "By reason of their state in life and of their order, [Christian spouses] have their own special gifts in the People of God."[145] This grace proper to the sacrament of Matrimony is intended to perfect the couple's love and to strengthen their indissoluble unity. By this grace they "help one another to attain holiness in their married life and in welcoming and educating their children."[146]

1642 *Christis the source of this grace.* "Just as of old God encountered his people with a covenant of love and fidelity, so our Savior, the spouse of the Church, now encounters Christian spouses through the sacrament of Matrimony."[147] Christ dwells with them, gives them the strength to take up their crosses and so follow him, to rise again after they have fallen, to forgive one another, to bear one another's burdens, to "be subject to one another out of reverence for Christ,"[148] and to love one another with supernatural, tender, and fruitful love. In the joys of their love and family life he gives them here on earth a foretaste of the wedding feast of the Lamb:

1615
796

> How can I ever express the happiness of a marriage joined by the Church, strengthened by an offering, sealed by a blessing, announced by angels, and ratified by the Father? ... How wonderful the bond between two believers, now one in hope, one in desire, one in discipline, one in the same service! They are both children of one Father and servants of the

---

144 Cf. CIC, can. 1141. 145 *LG* 11 § 2. 146 *LG* 11 § 2; cf. *LG* 41. 147 *GS* 48 § 2. 148 *Eph* 5:21; cf. *Gal* 6:2.

same Master, undivided in spirit and flesh, truly two in one flesh. Where the flesh is one, one also is the spirit.[149]

V. THE GOODS AND REQUIREMENTS OF CONJUGAL LOVE

2361   **1643** "Conjugal love involves a totality, in which all the elements of the person enter—appeal of the body and instinct, power of feeling and affectivity, aspiration of the spirit and of will. It aims at a deeply personal unity, a unity that, beyond union in one flesh, leads to forming one heart and soul; it demands *indissolubility* and *faithfulness* in definitive mutual giving; and it is open to *fertility*. In a word it is a question of the normal characteristics of all natural conjugal love, but with a new significance which not only purifies and strengthens them, but raises them to the extent of making them the expression of specifically Christian values."[150]

The unity and indissolubility of marriage

1644 The love of the spouses requires, of its very nature, the unity and indissolubility of the spouses' community of persons, which embraces their entire life: "so they are no longer two, but one flesh."[151] They "are called to grow continually in their marriage communion through day-to-day fidelity to their marriage promise of total mutual self-giving."[152] This human communion is confirmed, purified, and completed by communion in Jesus Christ, given through the sacrament of Matrimony. It is deepened by lives of the common faith and by the Eucharist received together.

1645 "The unity of marriage, distinctly recognized by our Lord, is made clear in the equal personal dignity
369   which must be accorded to man and wife in mutual and unreserved affection."[153] *Polygamy* is contrary to conjugal love which is undivided and exclusive.[154]

---

149 Tertullian, *Ad uxorem.* 2, 8, 6–7: PL 1, 1412–1413; cf. FC 13.   150 FC 13.
151 *Mt* 19:6; cf. *Gen* 2:24.   152 FC 19.   153 GS 49 § 2.   154 Cf. FC 19.

The fidelity of conjugal love   2364-2365

1646 By its very nature conjugal love requires the inviolable fidelity of the spouses. This is the consequence of the gift of themselves which they make to each other. Love seeks to be definitive; it cannot be an arrangement "until further notice." The "intimate union of marriage, as a mutual giving of two persons, and the good of the children, demand total fidelity from the spouses and require an unbreakable union between them."[155]

1647 The deepest reason is found in the fidelity of God to his covenant, in that of Christ to his Church. Through the sacrament of Matrimony the spouses are enabled to represent this fidelity and witness to it. Through the sacrament, the indissolubility of marriage receives a new and deeper meaning.

1648 It can seem difficult, even impossible, to bind oneself for life to another human being. This makes it all the more important to proclaim the Good News that God loves us with a definitive and irrevocable love, that married couples share in this love, that it supports and sustains them, and that by their own faithfulness they can be witnesses to God's faithful love. Spouses who with God's grace give this witness, often in very difficult conditions, deserve the gratitude and support of the ecclesial community.[156]

1649 Yet there are some situations in which living together becomes practically impossible for a variety of reasons. In such cases the Church permits the physical *separation* of the couple and their living apart. The spouses do not cease to be husband and wife before God and so are not free to contract a new union. In this difficult situation, the best solution would be, if possible, reconciliation. The Christian community is called to help these persons live out their situation in a Christian manner and in fidelity to their marriage bond which remains indissoluble.[157]   2383

1650 Today there are numerous Catholics in many countries who have recourse to civil *divorce* and contract new civil unions. In fidelity to the words of Jesus Christ— "Whoever divorces his wife and marries another, commits   2384

---

155 *GS* 48 § 1.   156 Cf. *FC* 20.   157 Cf. *FC* 83; CIC, cann. 1151–1155.

adultery against her; and if she divorces her husband and marries another, she commits adultery"[158]—the Church maintains that a new union cannot be recognized as valid, if the first marriage was. If the divorced are remarried civilly, they find themselves in a situation that objectively contravenes God's law. Consequently, they cannot receive Eucharistic communion as long as this situation persists. For the same reason, they cannot exercise certain ecclesial responsibilities. Reconciliation through the sacrament of Penance can be granted only to those who have repented for having violated the sign of the covenant and of fidelity to Christ, and who are committed to living in complete continence.

1651 Toward Christians who live in this situation, and who often keep the faith and desire to bring up their children in a Christian manner, priests and the whole community must manifest an attentive solicitude, so that they do not consider themselves separated from the Church, in whose life they can and must participate as baptized persons:

> They should be encouraged to listen to the Word of God, to attend the Sacrifice of the Mass, to persevere in prayer, to contribute to works of charity and to community efforts for justice, to bring up their children in the Christian faith, to cultivate the spirit and practice of penance and thus implore, day by day, God's grace.[159]

2366-2367 **The openness to fertility**

1652 "By its very nature the institution of marriage and married love is ordered to the procreation and education of the offspring and it is in them that it finds its crowning glory."[160]

372

> Children are the supreme gift of marriage and contribute greatly to the good of the parents themselves. God himself said: "It is not good that man should be alone," and "from the beginning [he] made them male and female"; wishing to associate them in a special way in his own creative work, God blessed man and woman with the words: "Be fruitful and multiply." Hence, true married love and the whole structure of family life which results from it, without diminishment of the other ends of

---

158 *Mk* 10:11-12.   159 *FC* 84.   160 *GS* 48 § 1; 50.

marriage, are directed to disposing the spouses to cooperate valiantly with the love of the Creator and Savior, who through them will increase and enrich his family from day to day.[161]

1653 The fruitfulness of conjugal love extends to the fruits of the moral, spiritual, and supernatural life that parents hand on to their children by education. Parents are the principal and first educators of their children.[162] In this sense the fundamental task of marriage and family is to be at the service of life.[163]

2231

1654 Spouses to whom God has not granted children can nevertheless have a conjugal life full of meaning, in both human and Christian terms. Their marriage can radiate a fruitfulness of charity, of hospitality, and of sacrifice.

VI. THE DOMESTIC CHURCH

1655 Christ chose to be born and grow up in the bosom of the holy family of Joseph and Mary. The Church is nothing other than "the family of God." From the beginning, the core of the Church was often constituted by those who had become believers "together with all [their] household."[164] When they were converted, they desired that "their whole household" should also be saved.[165] These families who became believers were islands of Christian life in an unbelieving world.

759

1656 In our own time, in a world often alien and even hostile to faith, believing families are of primary importance as centers of living, radiant faith. For this reason the Second Vatican Council, using an ancient expression, calls the family the *Ecclesia domestica*.[166] It is in the bosom of the family that parents are "by word and example . . . the first heralds of the faith with regard to their children. They should encourage them in the vocation which is proper to each child, fostering with special care any religious vocation."[167]

2204

---

161 GS 50 § 1; cf. *Gen* 2:18; *Mt* 19:4; *Gen* 1:28.   162 Cf. GE 3.   163 Cf. FC 28.   164 Cf. *Acts* 18:8.   165 Cf. *Acts* 16:31; *Acts* 11:14.   166 LG 11; cf. FC 21.   167 LG 11.

1657 It is here that the father of the family, the mother, children, and all members of the family exercise the *priesthood of the baptized* in a privileged way "by the reception of the sacraments, prayer and thanksgiving, the witness of a holy life, and self-denial and active charity."[168] Thus the home is the first school of Christian life and "a school for human enrichment."[169] Here one learns endurance and the joy of work, fraternal love, generous—even repeated—forgiveness, and above all divine worship in prayer and the offering of one's life.

*margin: 1268*
*margin: 2214-2231*
margin: 2685

1658 We must also remember the great number of *single persons* who, because of the particular circumstances in which they have to live—often not of their choosing—are especially close to Jesus' heart and therefore deserve the special affection and active solicitude of the Church, especially of pastors. Many remain *without a human family,* often due to conditions of poverty. Some live their situation in the spirit of the Beatitudes, serving God and neighbor in exemplary fashion. The doors of homes, the "domestic churches," and of the great family which is the Church must be open to all of them. "No one is without a family in this world: the Church is a home and family for everyone, especially those who 'labor and are heavy laden.' "[170]

*margin: 2231*
*margin: 2233*

IN BRIEF

1659 St. Paul said: "Husbands, love your wives, as Christ loved the Church. . . . This is a great mystery, and I mean in reference to Christ and the Church" (*Eph* 5:25, 32).

1660 The marriage covenant, by which a man and a woman form with each other an intimate communion of life and love, has been founded and endowed with its own special laws by the Creator. By its very nature it is ordered to the good of the couple, as well as to the generation and education of children. Christ the Lord raised

---

168 *LG* 10.   169 *GS* 52 § 1.   170 *FC* 85; cf. *Mt* 11:28.

marriage between the baptized to the dignity of a sacrament (cf. CIC, can. 1055 § 1; cf. *GS* 48 § 1).

1661 The sacrament of Matrimony signifies the union of Christ and the Church. It gives spouses the grace to love each other with the love with which Christ has loved his Church; the grace of the sacrament thus perfects the human love of the spouses, strengthens their indissoluble unity, and sanctifies them on the way to eternal life (cf. Council of Trent: DS 1799).

1662 Marriage is based on the consent of the contracting parties, that is, on their will to give themselves, each to the other, mutually and definitively, in order to live a covenant of faithful and fruitful love.

1663 Since marriage establishes the couple in a public state of life in the Church, it is fitting that its celebration be public, in the framework of a liturgical celebration, before the priest (or a witness authorized by the Church), the witnesses, and the assembly of the faithful.

1664 Unity, indissolubility, and openness to fertility are essential to marriage. Polygamy is incompatible with the unity of marriage; divorce separates what God has joined together; the refusal of fertility turns married life away from its "supreme gift," the child (*GS* 50 §1).

1665 The remarriage of persons divorced from a living, lawful spouse contravenes the plan and law of God as taught by Christ. They are not separated from the Church, but they cannot receive Eucharistic communion. They will lead Christian lives especially by educating their children in the faith.

1666 The Christian home is the place where children receive the first proclamation of the faith. For this reason the family home is rightly called "the

domestic church," a community of grace and
prayer, a school of human virtues and of Christian charity.

CHAPTER FOUR
OTHER LITURGICAL CELEBRATIONS

ARTICLE 1
SACRAMENTALS

1667 "Holy Mother Church has, moreover, instituted
sacramentals. These are sacred signs which bear a resemblance to the sacraments. They signify effects, particularly of a spiritual nature, which are obtained
through the intercession of the Church. By them men
are disposed to receive the chief effect of the sacraments, and various occasions in life are rendered
holy."[171]

The characteristics of sacramentals
1668 Sacramentals are instituted for the sanctification
of certain ministries of the Church, certain states of
life, a great variety of circumstances in Christian life,
and the use of many things helpful to man. In accordance with bishops' pastoral decisions, they can also respond to the needs, culture, and special history of the
Christian people of a particular region or time. They always include a prayer, often accompanied by a specific
sign, such as the laying on of hands, the sign of the
cross, or the sprinkling of holy water (which recalls
Baptism).

699, 2157

1669 Sacramentals derive from the baptismal priesthood: every baptized person is called to be a "blessing,"
and to bless.[172] Hence lay people may preside at certain
blessings; the more a blessing concerns ecclesial and
sacramental life, the more is its administration reserved
to the ordained ministry (bishops, priests, or deacons).[173]

784
2626

---

171 *SC* 60; cf. CIC, can. 1166; CCEO, can. 867.   172 Cf. *Gen* 12:2; *Lk* 6:28;
Rom 12:14; *1 Pet* 3:9.   173 Cf. *SC* 79; CIC, can. 1168; *De Ben* 16, 18.

1670 Sacramentals do not confer the grace of the Holy   *1128*
Spirit in the way that the sacraments do, but by the
Church's prayer, they prepare us to receive grace and
dispose us to cooperate with it. "For well-disposed
members of the faithful, the liturgy of the sacraments   *2001*
and sacramentals sanctifies almost every event of their
lives with the divine grace which flows from the Paschal
mystery of the Passion, Death, and Resurrection of
Christ. From this source all sacraments and sacramentals draw their power. There is scarcely any proper use
of material things which cannot be thus directed toward
the sanctification of men and the praise of God."[174]

Various forms of sacramentals

1671 Among sacramentals *blessings* (of persons, meals,   *1078*
objects, and places) come first. Every blessing praises God
and prays for his gifts. In Christ, Christians are blessed by
God the Father "with every spiritual blessing."[175] This is
why the Church imparts blessings by invoking the name of
Jesus, usually while making the holy sign of the cross of
Christ.

1672 Certain blessings have a lasting importance because
they *consecrate* persons to God, or reserve objects and
places for liturgical use. Among those blessings which are
intended for persons—not to be confused with sacramental
ordination—are the blessing of the abbot or abbess of a
monastery, the consecration of virgins, the rite of religious   *923*
profession and the blessing of certain ministries of the   *925*
Church (readers, acolytes, catechists, etc.). The dedication   *903*
or blessing of a church or an altar, the blessing of holy oils,
vessels, and vestments, bells, etc., can be mentioned as examples of blessings that concern objects.

1673 When the Church asks publicly and authoritatively
in the name of Jesus Christ that a person or object be protected against the power of the Evil One and withdrawn   *395*
from his dominion, it is called *exorcism*. Jesus performed   *550*
exorcisms and from him the Church has received the power
and office of exorcizing.[176] In a simple form, exorcism is
performed at the celebration of Baptism. The solemn exor-   *1237*
cism, called "a major exorcism," can be performed only by
a priest and with the permission of the bishop. The priest
must proceed with prudence, strictly observing the rules es-

---

174 *SC* 61.   175 *Eph* 1:3.   176 Cf. *Mk* 1:25–26; 3:15; 6:7, 13; 16:17.

tablished by the Church. Exorcism is directed at the expulsion of demons or to the liberation from demonic possession through the spiritual authority which Jesus entrusted to his Church. Illness, especially psychological illness, is a very different matter; treating this is the concern of medical science. Therefore, before an exorcism is performed, it is important to ascertain that one is dealing with the presence of the Evil One, and not an illness.[177]

Popular piety

1674 Besides sacramental liturgy and sacramentals, catechesis must take into account the forms of piety and popular devotions among the faithful. The religious sense of the Christian people has always found expression in various forms of piety surrounding the Church's sacramental life, such as the veneration of relics, visits to sanctuaries, pilgrimages, processions, the stations of the cross, religious dances, the rosary, medals,[178] etc.

2688

2669, 2678

1675 These expressions of piety extend the liturgical life of the Church, but do not replace it. They "should be so drawn up that they harmonize with the liturgical seasons, accord with the sacred liturgy, are in some way derived from it and lead the people to it, since in fact the liturgy by its very nature is far superior to any of them."[179]

1676 Pastoral discernment is needed to sustain and support popular piety and, if necessary, to purify and correct the religious sense which underlies these devotions so that the faithful may advance in knowledge of the mystery of Christ.[180] Their exercise is subject to the care and judgment of the bishops and to the general norms of the Church.

426

> At its core the piety of the people is a storehouse of values that offers answers of Christian wisdom to the great questions of life. The Catholic wisdom of the people is capable of fashioning a vital synthesis. . . . It creatively combines the divine and the human, Christ and Mary, spirit and body, communion and institution, person and community, faith and homeland, intelligence and emotion. This wisdom is a Christian humanism that radically affirms the dignity of every person as a child of God, establishes a basic fraternity, teaches people to encounter

---

177 Cf. CIC, can. 1172.   178 Cf. Council of Nicæa II: DS 601; 603; Council of Trent: DS 1822.   179 SC 13 § 3.   180 Cf. John Paul II, CT 54.

nature and understand work, provides reasons for joy and humor even in the midst of a very hard life. For the people this wisdom is also a principle of discernment and an evangelical instinct through which they spontaneously sense when the Gospel is served in the Church and when it is emptied of its content and stifled by other interests.[181]

IN BRIEF

1677   Sacramentals are sacred signs instituted by the Church. They prepare men to receive the fruit of the sacraments and sanctify different circumstances of life.

1678   Among the sacramentals blessings occupy an important place. They include both praise of God for his works and gifts, and the Church's intercession for men that they may be able to use God's gifts according to the spirit of the Gospel.

1679   In addition to the liturgy, Christian life is nourished by various forms of popular piety, rooted in the different cultures. While carefully clarifying them in the light of faith, the Church fosters the forms of popular piety that express an evangelical instinct and a human wisdom and that enrich Christian life.

ARTICLE 2
CHRISTIAN FUNERALS

1680   All the sacraments, and principally those of   1525
Christian initiation, have as their goal the last Passover of the child of God which, through death, leads him into the life of the Kingdom. Then what he confessed in faith and hope will be fulfilled: "I look for the resurrection of the dead, and the life of the world to come."[182]

---

181 CELAM, Third General Conference (Puebla, 1979), Final Document, § 448 (tr. NCCB, 1979); cf. Paul VI, *EN* 48.   182 Niceno-Constantinopolitan Creed.

I.   THE CHRISTIAN'S LAST PASSOVER

1010-1014   **1681**   The Christian meaning of death is revealed in the light of the *Paschal mystery* of the death and resurrection of Christ in whom resides our only hope. The Christian who dies in Christ Jesus is "away from the body and at home with the Lord."[183]

1682   For the Christian the day of death inaugurates, *at the end of his sacramental life,* the fulfillment of his new birth begun at Baptism, the definitive "conformity" to "the image of the Son" conferred by the anointing of the Holy Spirit, and participation in the feast of the Kingdom which was anticipated in the Eucharist—even if final purifications are still necessary for him in order to be clothed with the nuptial garment.

1683   The Church who, as Mother, has borne the Christian sacramentally in her womb during his earthly pilgrimage, accompanies him at his journey's end, in or-
1020   der to surrender him "into the Father's hands." She offers to the Father, in Christ, the child of his grace, and she commits to the earth, in hope, the seed of the body
627   that will rise in glory.[184] This offering is fully celebrated in the Eucharistic sacrifice; the blessings before and after Mass are sacramentals.

II.   THE CELEBRATION OF FUNERALS

1684   The Christian funeral confers on the deceased neither a sacrament nor a sacramental, since he has "passed" beyond the sacramental economy. It is nonetheless a liturgical celebration of the Church.[185] The ministry of the Church aims at expressing efficacious communion with *the deceased,* at the participation in that communion of *the community* gathered for the funeral and at the proclamation of eternal life to the community.

1685   The different funeral rites express the *Paschal character* of Christian death and are in keeping with the situations and traditions of each region, even as to the color of the liturgical vestments worn.[186]

1686   The *Order of Christian Funerals (Ordo exsequiarum)* of the Roman liturgy gives three types of funeral

---

183 2 Cor 5:8.   184 Cf. 1 Cor 15:42–44.   185 Cf. SC 81–82.   186 Cf. SC 81.

celebrations, corresponding to the three places in which they are conducted (the home, the church, and the cemetery), and according to the importance attached to them by the family, local customs, the culture, and popular piety. This order of celebration is common to all the liturgical traditions and comprises four principal elements:

1687 *The greeting of the community.* A greeting of faith begins the celebration. Relatives and friends of the deceased are welcomed with a word of "consolation" (in the New Testament sense of the Holy Spirit's power in hope).[187] The community assembling in prayer also awaits the "words of eternal life." The death of a member of the community (or the anniversary of a death, or the seventh or fortieth day after death) is an event that should lead beyond the perspectives of "this world" and should draw the faithful into the true perspective of faith in the risen Christ.

1688 The liturgy of the Word during funerals demands very careful preparation because the assembly present for the funeral may include some faithful who rarely attend the liturgy, and friends of the deceased who are not Christians. The homily in particular must "avoid the literary genre of funeral eulogy"[188] and illumine the mystery of Christian death in the light of the risen Christ.

1689 *The Eucharistic Sacrifice.* When the celebration takes place in church, the Eucharist is the heart of the Paschal reality of Christian death.[189] In the Eucharist, the Church expresses her efficacious communion with the departed: offering to the Father in the Holy Spirit the sacrifice of the death and resurrection of Christ, she asks to purify his child of his sins and their consequences, and to admit him to the Paschal fullness of the table of the Kingdom.[190] It is by the Eucharist thus celebrated that the community of the faithful, especially the family of the deceased, learn to live in communion with the one who "has fallen asleep in the Lord," by communicating in the Body of Christ of which he is a living member and, then, by praying for him and with him.

1690 A *farewell* to the deceased is his final "commendation to God" by the Church. It is "the last farewell by which the Christian community greets one of its members before his body is brought to its tomb."[191] The Byzantine

1371

958

2300

---

187 Cf. 1 *Thess* 4:18.   188 OCF 41.   189 Cf. OCF 1.   190 Cf. OCF 57.
191 OCF 10.

tradition expresses this by the kiss of farewell to the deceased:

> By this final greeting "we sing for his departure from this life and separation from us, but also because there is a communion and a reunion. For even dead, we are not at all separated from one another, because we all run the same course and we will find one another again in the same place. We shall never be separated, for we live for Christ, and now we are united with Christ as we go toward him ... we shall all be together in Christ."[192]

---

192 St. Simeon of Thessalonica, *De ordine sepulturæ*. 336: PG 155, 684.

PART THREE
LIFE IN CHRIST

1691 "Christian, recognize your dignity and, now that you share in God's own nature, do not return to your former base condition by sinning. Remember who is your head and of whose body you are a member. Never *790* forget that you have been rescued from the power of darkness and brought into the light of the Kingdom of God."[1]

1692 The Symbol of the faith confesses the greatness of God's gifts to man in his work of creation, and even more in redemption and sanctification. What faith confesses, the sacraments communicate: by the sacraments of rebirth, Christians have become "children of God,"[2] "partakers of the divine nature."[3] Coming to see in the faith their new dignity, Christians are called to lead henceforth a life "worthy of the gospel of Christ."[4] They are made capable of doing so by the grace of Christ and the gifts of his Spirit, which they receive through the sacraments and through prayer.

1693 Christ Jesus always did what was pleasing to the *Father*,[5] and always lived in perfect communion with him. Likewise Christ's disciples are invited to live in the sight of the Father "who sees in secret,"[6] in order to become "perfect as your heavenly Father is perfect."[7]

1694 Incorporated into *Christ* by Baptism, Christians *1267* are "dead to sin and alive to God in Christ Jesus" and so participate in the life of the Risen Lord.[8] Following Christ and united with him,[9] Christians can strive to be "imitators of God as beloved children, and walk in love"[10] by conforming their thoughts, words and actions to the "mind . . . which is yours in Christ Jesus,"[11] and by following his example.[12]

---

1 St. Leo the Great, *Sermo 21 in nat. Dom.*, 3: PL 54, 192C. 2 *Jn* 1:12; *1 Jn* 3:1.
3 *2 Pet* 1:4. 4 *Phil* 1:27. 5 Cf. *Jn* 8:29. 6 *Mt* 6:6. 7 *Mt* 5:48. 8 *Rom* 6:11
and cf. 6:5; cf. *Col* 2:12. 9 Cf. *Jn* 15:5. 10 *Eph* 5:1-2. 11 *Phil* 2:5. 12 Cf.
Jn 13:12-16.

1695 "Justified in the name of the Lord Jesus Christ and in the Spirit of our God,"[13] "sanctified . . . [and] called to be saints,"[14] Christians have become the temple of the *Holy Spirit.*[15] This "Spirit of the Son" teaches them to pray to the Father[16] and, having become their life, prompts them to act so as to bear "the fruit of the Spirit"[17] by charity in action. Healing the wounds of sin, the Holy Spirit renews us interiorly through a spiritual transformation.[18] He enlightens and strengthens us to live as "children of light" through "all that is good and right and true."[19]

1696 The way of Christ "leads to life"; a contrary way "leads to destruction."[20] The Gospel parable of the *two ways* remains ever present in the catechesis of the Church; it shows the importance of moral decisions for our salvation: "There are two ways, the one of life, the other of death; but between the two, there is a great difference."[21]

1970

1697 *Catechesis* has to reveal in all clarity the joy and the demands of the way of Christ.[22] Catechesis for the "newness of life"[23] in him should be:

737 ff. —*a catechesis of the Holy Spirit,* the interior Master of life according to Christ, a gentle guest and friend who inspires, guides, corrects, and strengthens this life;

1938 ff. —*a catechesis of grace,* for it is by grace that we are saved and again it is by grace that our works can bear fruit for eternal life;

1716 ff. —*a catechesis of the beatitudes,* for the way of Christ is summed up in the beatitudes, the only path that leads to the eternal beatitude for which the human heart longs;

1846 ff. —*a catechesis of sin and forgiveness,* for unless man acknowledges that he is a sinner he cannot know the truth about himself, which is a condition for acting justly; and without the offer of forgiveness he would not be able to bear this truth;

---

13 *1 Cor* 6:11.   14 *1 Cor* 1:2   15 Cf. *1 Cor* 6:19.   16 Cf. *Gal* 4:6.   17 *Gal* 5:22, 25.   18 Cf. *Eph* 4:23.   19 *Eph* 5:8, 9.   20 *Mt* 7:13; cf. *Deut* 30:15–20. 21 *Didache* 1, 1:SCh 248, 140.   22 Cf. John Paul II, *CT* 29.   23 *Rom* 6:4.

—*a catechesis of the human virtues* which causes one to   *1803 ff.*
grasp the beauty and attraction of right dispositions towards goodness;

—*a catechesis of the Christian virtues* of faith, hope,   *1812 ff.*
and charity, generously inspired by the example of the
saints;

—*a catechesis of the twofold commandment of charity*   *2067 ff.*
set forth in the Decalogue;

—*an ecclesial catechesis,* for it is through the manifold   *946 ff.*
exchanges of "spiritual goods" in the "communion of
saints" that Christian life can grow, develop, and be
communicated.

1698 The first and last point of reference of this cate-   *426*
chesis will always be Jesus Christ himself, who is "the
way, and the truth, and the life."[24] It is by looking to
him in faith that Christ's faithful can hope that he himself fulfills his promises in them, and that, by loving him
with the same love with which he has loved them, they
may perform works in keeping with their dignity:

> I ask you to consider that our Lord Jesus Christ is
> your true head, and that you are one of his mem-
> bers. He belongs to you as the head belongs to its
> members; all that is his is yours: his spirit, his heart,
> his body and soul, and all his faculties. You must
> make use of all these as of your own, to serve,
> praise, love, and glorify God. You belong to him, as
> members belong to their head. And so he longs for
> you to use all that is in you, as if it were his own,
> for the service and glory of the Father.[25]

> For to me, to live is Christ.[26]

---

24 *Jn* 14:6. 25 St. John Eudes, *Tract. de admirabili corde Jesu,* 1, 5. 26 *Phil*
1:21.

SECTION ONE
MAN'S VOCATION
LIFE IN THE SPIRIT

1699 Life in the Holy Spirit fulfills the vocation of man *(chapter one)*. This life is made up of divine charity and human solidarity *(chapter two)*. It is graciously offered as salvation *(chapter three)*.

CHAPTER ONE
THE DIGNITY OF THE HUMAN PERSON

356 **1700** The dignity of the human person is rooted in his creation in the image and likeness of God *(article 1)*; it is fulfilled in his vocation to divine beatitude *(article 2)*. It is essential to a human being freely to direct himself to this fulfillment *(article 3)*. By his deliberate actions *(article 4)*, the human person does, or does not, conform to the good promised by God and attested by moral conscience *(article 5)*. Human beings make their own contribution to their interior growth; they make their whole sentient and spiritual lives into means of this growth *(article 6)*. With the help of grace they grow in virtue *(article 7)*, avoid sin, and if they sin they en-
1439 trust themselves as did the prodigal son[1] to the mercy of our Father in heaven *(article 8)*. In this way they attain to the perfection of charity.

ARTICLE 1
MAN: THE IMAGE OF GOD

359 **1701** "Christ, . . . in the very revelation of the mystery of the Father and of his love, makes man fully manifest to himself and brings to light his exalted vocation."[2] It is in Christ, "the image of the invisible God,"[3] that man has been created "in the image and likeness" of the Creator. It is in Christ, Redeemer and Savior, that the divine image, disfigured in man by the first sin, has been restored to its original beauty and ennobled by the grace of God.[4]

---

1 *Lk* 15:11–32.   **2** *GS* 22.   **3** *Col* 1:15; cf. 2 *Cor* 4:4.   **4** Cf. *GS* 22.

1702 The divine image is present in every man. It   *1878*
shines forth in the communion of persons, in the likeness of the union of the divine persons among themselves (cf. *chapter two*).

1703 Endowed with "a spiritual and immortal" soul,[5]   *363*
the human person is "the only creature on earth that
God has willed for its own sake."[6] From his conception,   *2258*
he is destined for eternal beatitude.

1704 The human person participates in the light and
power of the divine Spirit. By his reason, he is capable
of understanding the order of things established by the
Creator. By free will, he is capable of directing himself   *339*
toward his true good. He finds his perfection "in seeking and loving what is true and good."[7]   *30*

1705 By virtue of his soul and his spiritual powers of
intellect and will, man is endowed with freedom, an   *1730*
"outstanding manifestation of the divine image."[8]

1706 By his reason, man recognizes the voice of God
which urges him "to do what is good and avoid what is
evil."[9] Everyone is obliged to follow this law, which
makes itself heard in conscience and is fulfilled in the
love of God and of neighbor. Living a moral life bears   *1776*
witness to the dignity of the person.

1707 "Man, enticed by the Evil One, abused his freedom at the very beginning of history."[10] He succumbed
to temptation and did what was evil. He still desires the   *397*
good, but his nature bears the wound of original sin. He
is now inclined to evil and subject to error:

> Man is divided in himself. As a result, the whole life
> of men, both individual and social, shows itself to
> be a struggle, and a dramatic one, between good
> and evil, between light and darkness.[11]

1708 By his Passion, Christ delivered us from Satan   *617*
and from sin. He merited for us the new life in the Holy
Spirit. His grace restores what sin had damaged in us.

---

5 *GS* 14 § 2.   6 *GS* 24 § 3.   7 *GS* 15 § 2.   8 *GS* 17.   9 *GS* 16.   10 *GS* 13 § 1.
11 *GS* 13 § 2.

1265   **1709** He who believes in Christ becomes a son of God. This filial adoption transforms him by giving him the ability to follow the example of Christ. It makes him capable of acting rightly and doing good. In union with his Savior, the disciple attains the perfection of charity which is holiness. Having matured in grace, the moral

1050   life blossoms into eternal life in the glory of heaven.

IN BRIEF

1710 "Christ . . . makes man fully manifest to man himself and brings to light his exalted vocation" (*GS* 22 § 1).

1711 Endowed with a spiritual soul, with intellect and with free will, the human person is from his very conception ordered to God and destined for eternal beatitude. He pursues his perfection in "seeking and loving what is true and good" (*GS* 15 § 2).

1712 In man, true freedom is an "outstanding manifestation of the divine image" (*GS* 17).

1713 Man is obliged to follow the moral law, which urges him "to do what is good and avoid what is evil" (cf. *GS* 16). This law makes itself heard in his conscience.

1714 Man, having been wounded in his nature by original sin, is subject to error and inclined to evil in exercising his freedom.

1715 He who believes in Christ has new life in the Holy Spirit. The moral life, increased and brought to maturity in grace, is to reach its fulfillment in the glory of heaven.

ARTICLE 2
OUR VOCATION TO BEATITUDE

I.   THE BEATITUDES

1716 The Beatitudes are at the heart of Jesus' preaching. They take up the promises made to the chosen people since Abraham. The Beatitudes fulfill the promises by ordering them no longer merely to the possession of a territory, but to the Kingdom of heaven:

> Blessed are the poor in spirit, for theirs is the king-   2546
> dom of heaven.
> Blessed are those who mourn, for they shall be comforted.
> Blessed are the meek, for they shall inherit the earth.
> Blessed are those who hunger and thirst for righteousness, for they shall be satisfied.
> Blessed are the merciful, for they shall obtain mercy.
> Blessed are the pure in heart, for they shall see God.
> Blessed are the peacemakers, for they shall be called sons of God.
> Blessed are those who are persecuted for righteousness' sake,
> for theirs is the kingdom of heaven.
> Blessed are you when men revile you and persecute you
> and utter all kinds of evil against you falsely on my account.
> Rejoice and be glad,
> for your reward is great in heaven.[12]

1717 The Beatitudes depict the countenance of Jesus   459
Christ and portray his charity. They express the vocation of the faithful associated with the glory of his Passion and Resurrection; they shed light on the actions and attitudes characteristic of the Christian life; they are the paradoxical promises that sustain hope in the midst of tribulations; they proclaim the blessings and rewards

---

12 *Mt* 5:3–12.

1820 already secured, however dimly, for Christ's disciples; they have begun in the lives of the Virgin Mary and all the saints.

II.   THE DESIRE FOR HAPPINESS

27, 1024 **1718** The Beatitudes respond to the natural desire for happiness. This desire is of divine origin: God has placed it in the human heart in order to draw man to the One who alone can fulfill it:

> We all want to live happily; in the whole human race there is no one who does not assent to this proposition, even before it is fully articulated.[13]

2541
> How is it, then, that I seek you, Lord? Since in seeking you, my God, I seek a happy life, let me seek you so that my soul may live, for my body draws life from my soul and my soul draws life from you.[14]

> God alone satisfies.[15]

1950 **1719** The Beatitudes reveal the goal of human existence, the ultimate end of human acts: God calls us to his own beatitude. This vocation is addressed to each individual personally, but also to the Church as a whole, the new people made up of those who have accepted the promise and live from it in faith.

III.   CHRISTIAN BEATITUDE

1027 **1720** The New Testament uses several expressions to characterize the beatitude to which God calls man:

—the coming of the Kingdom of God;[16]

—the vision of God: "Blessed are the pure in heart, for they shall see God";[17]

—entering into the joy of the Lord;[18]

—entering into God's rest:[19]

---

13 St. Augustine, *De moribus eccl.* 1, 3, 4: PL 32, 1312. 14 St. Augustine, *Conf.* 10, 20: PL 32, 791. 15 St. Thomas Aquinas, *Expos. in symb. apost.* I. 16 Cf. *Mt* 4:17. 17 *Mt* 5:8; cf. *1 Jn* 2; *1 Cor* 13:12. 18 *Mt* 25:21–23. 19 Cf. *Heb* 4:7–11.

There we shall rest and see, we shall see and love,
we shall love and praise. Behold what will be at
the end without end. For what other end do we
have, if not to reach the kingdom which has no
end?[20]

1721 God put us in the world to know, to love, and to
serve him, and so to come to paradise. Beatitude makes
us "partakers of the divine nature" and of eternal life.[21]
With beatitude, man enters into the glory of Christ[22] and
into the joy of the Trinitarian life.   260

1722 Such beatitude surpasses the understanding
and powers of man. It comes from an entirely free
gift of God: whence it is called supernatural, as is 1028
the grace that disposes man to enter into the divine
joy.

"Blessed are the pure in heart, for they shall see
God." It is true, because of the greatness and inexpressible glory of God, that "man shall not see me
and live," for the Father cannot be grasped. But because of God's love and goodness toward us, and
because he can do all things, he goes so far as to
grant those who love him the privilege of seeing
him.... For "what is impossible for men is possi-
ble for God."[23]   294

1723 The beatitude we are promised confronts us with
decisive moral choices. It invites us to purify our hearts
of bad instincts and to seek the love of God above all 2519
else. It teaches us that true happiness is not found in
riches or well-being, in human fame or power, or in any
human achievement—however beneficial it may be—
such as science, technology, and art, or indeed in any
creature, but in God alone, the source of every good and
of all love: 227

All bow down before wealth. Wealth is that to
which the multitude of men pay an instinctive
homage. They measure happiness by wealth; and
by wealth they measure respectability.... It is a
homage resulting from a profound faith... that

---

20 St. Augustine, *De civ. Dei* 22, 30, 5: PL 41, 804.   21 2 *Pet* 1:4; cf. *Jn* 17:3.
22 Cf. *Rom* 8:18.   23 St. Irenaeus, *Adv. haeres.* 4, 20, 5: PG 7/1, 1034–1035.

with wealth he may do all things. Wealth is one idol of the day and notoriety is a second. . . . Notoriety, or the making of a noise in the world—it may be called "newspaper fame"—has come to be considered a great good in itself, and a ground of veneration.[24]

1724 The Decalogue, the Sermon on the Mount, and the apostolic catechesis describe for us the paths that lead to the Kingdom of heaven. Sustained by the grace of the Holy Spirit, we tread them, step by step, by everyday acts. By the working of the Word of Christ, we slowly bear fruit in the Church to the glory of God.[25]

IN BRIEF

1725 The Beatitudes take up and fulfill God's promises from Abraham on by ordering them to the Kingdom of heaven. They respond to the desire for happiness that God has placed in the human heart.

1726 The Beatitudes teach us the final end to which God calls us: the Kingdom, the vision of God, participation in the divine nature, eternal life, filiation, rest in God.

1727 The beatitude of eternal life is a gratuitous gift of God. It is supernatural, as is the grace that leads us there.

1728 The Beatitudes confront us with decisive choices concerning earthly goods; they purify our hearts in order to teach us to love God above all things.

1729 The beatitude of heaven sets the standards for discernment in the use of earthly goods in keeping with the law of God.

---

24 John Henry Cardinal Newman, "Saintliness the Standard of Christian Principle," in *Discourses to Mixed Congregations* (London: Longmans, Green and Co., 1906) V, 89–90.   25 Cf. the parable of the sower: *Mt* 13:3–23.

Article 3
MAN'S FREEDOM

1730 God created man a rational being, conferring on him the dignity of a person who can initiate and control his own actions. "God willed that man should be 'left in the hand of his own counsel,' so that he might of his own accord seek his Creator and freely attain his full and blessed perfection by cleaving to him."[26]   30

> Man is rational and therefore like God; he is created with free will and is master over his acts.[27]

I.   Freedom and Responsibility

1731 Freedom is the power, rooted in reason and will, to act or not to act, to do this or that, and so to perform deliberate actions on one's own responsibility. By free will one shapes one's own life. Human freedom is a force for growth and maturity in truth and goodness; it attains its perfection when directed toward God, our   172 beatitude.

1732 As long as freedom has not bound itself definitively to its ultimate good which is God, there is the   396 possibility of *choosing between good and evil,* and thus   1849 of growing in perfection or of failing and sinning. This freedom characterizes properly human acts. It is the basis of praise or blame, merit or reproach.   2006

1733 The more one does what is good, the freer one   1803 becomes. There is no true freedom except in the service of what is good and just. The choice to disobey and do evil is an abuse of freedom and leads to "the slavery of sin."[28]

1734 Freedom makes man *responsible* for his acts to   1036 the extent that they are voluntary. Progress in virtue, knowledge of the good, and ascesis enhance the mastery   1804 of the will over its acts.

1735 *Imputability* and responsibility for an action can

---

26 GS 17; Sir 15:14.   27 St. Irenaeus, *Adv. haeres.* 4, 4, 3: PG 7/1, 983.   28 Cf. Rom 6:17.

be diminished or even nullified by ignorance, inadvertence, duress, fear, habit, inordinate attachments, and
597 other psychological or social factors.

2568 **1736** Every act directly willed is imputable to its author:

> Thus the Lord asked Eve after the sin in the garden: "What is this that you have done?"[29] He asked Cain the same question.[30] The prophet Nathan questioned David in the same way after he committed adultery with the wife of Uriah and had him murdered.[31]

> An action can be indirectly voluntary when it results from negligence regarding something one should have known or done: for example, an accident arising from ignorance of traffic laws.

2263 **1737** An effect can be tolerated without being willed by its agent; for instance, a mother's exhaustion from tending her sick child. A bad effect is not imputable if it was not willed either as an end or as a means of an action, e.g., a death a person incurs in aiding someone in danger. For a bad effect to be imputable it must be foreseeable and the agent must have the possibility of avoiding it, as in the case of manslaughter caused by a drunken driver.

1738 Freedom is exercised in relationships between human beings. Every human person, created in the image of God, has the natural right to be recognized as a free and responsible being. All owe to each other this duty of respect. The *right to the exercise of freedom,* especially in moral and religious matters, is an inalienable
2106 requirement of the dignity of the human person. This right must be recognized and protected by civil authority within the limits of the common good and public or-
2109 der.[32]

II.   HUMAN FREEDOM IN THE ECONOMY OF SALVATION

387 **1739** *Freedom and sin.* Man's freedom is limited and fallible. In fact, man failed. He freely sinned. By refusing God's plan of love, he deceived himself and became a slave to sin. This first alienation engendered a multi-

---

29 *Gen* 3:13.   30 Cf. *Gen* 4:10.   31 Cf. *2 Sam* 12:7–15.   32 Cf. *DH* 2 § 7.

tude of others. From its outset, human history attests   *401*
the wretchedness and oppression born of the human
heart in consequence of the abuse of freedom.

1740 *Threats to freedom.* The exercise of freedom   *2108*
does not imply a right to say or do everything. It is false
to maintain that man, "the subject of this freedom," is
"an individual who is fully self-sufficient and whose
finality is the satisfaction of his own interests in the
enjoyment of earthly goods."[33] Moreover, the economic, social, political, and cultural conditions that are
needed for a just exercise of freedom are too often dis-
regarded or violated. Such situations of blindness and
injustice injure the moral life and involve the strong as   *1887*
well as the weak in the temptation to sin against charity. By deviating from the moral law man violates his
own freedom, becomes imprisoned within himself, dis-
rupts neighborly fellowship, and rebels against divine
truth.

1741 *Liberation and salvation.* By his glorious Cross
Christ has won salvation for all men. He redeemed
them from the sin that held them in bondage. "For free-
dom Christ has set us free."[34] In him we have commu-
nion with the "truth that makes us free."[35] The Holy   *782*
Spirit has been given to us and, as the Apostle teaches,
"Where the Spirit of the Lord is, there is freedom."[36]
Already we glory in the "liberty of the children of
God."[37]

1742 *Freedom and grace.* The grace of Christ is not in
the slightest way a rival of our freedom when this freedom accords with the sense of the true and the good
that God has put in the human heart. On the contrary,   *2002*
as Christian experience attests especially in prayer, the
more docile we are to the promptings of grace, the more
we grow in inner freedom and confidence during trials,
such as those we face in the pressures and constraints of
the outer world. By the working of grace the Holy Spirit   *1784*
educates us in spiritual freedom in order to make us free

---

33 CDF, instruction, *Libertatis conscientia* 13.   34 *Gal* 5:1.   35 Cf. *Jn* 8:32.
36 *2 Cor* 17.   37 *Rom* 8:21.

collaborators in his work in the Church and in the world:

> Almighty and merciful God,
> in your goodness take away from us all that is harmful,
> so that, made ready both in mind and body,
> we may freely accomplish your will.[38]

IN BRIEF

1743 "God willed that man should be left in the hand of his own counsel (cf. *Sir* 15:14), so that he might of his own accord seek his creator and freely attain his full and blessed perfection by cleaving to him" (*GS* 17 § 1).

1744 Freedom is the power to act or not to act, and so to perform deliberate acts of one's own. Freedom attains perfection in its acts when directed toward God, the sovereign Good.

1745 Freedom characterizes properly human acts. It makes the human being responsible for acts of which he is the voluntary agent. His deliberate acts properly belong to him.

1746 The imputability or responsibility for an action can be diminished or nullified by ignorance, duress, fear, and other psychological or social factors.

1747 The right to the exercise of freedom, especially in religious and moral matters, is an inalienable requirement of the dignity of man. But the exercise of freedom does not entail the putative right to say or do anything.

1748 "For freedom Christ has set us free" (*Gal* 5:1).

---

38 *Roman Missal*, 32nd Sunday, Opening Prayer: *Omnipotens et misericors Deus, universa nobis adversantia propitiatus exclude, ut, mente et corpore pariter expediti, quæ tua sunt liberis mentibus exsequamur.*

Article 4
THE MORALITY OF HUMAN ACTS

1749   Freedom makes man a moral subject. When he acts deliberately, man is, so to speak, the *father of his acts.* Human acts, that is, acts that are freely chosen in consequence of a judgment of conscience, can be   1732 morally evaluated. They are either good or evil.

I.   THE SOURCES OF MORALITY
1750   The morality of human acts depends on:

—the object chosen;

—the end in view or the intention;

—the circumstances of the action.

The object, the intention, and the circumstances make up the "sources," or constitutive elements, of the morality of human acts.

1751   The *object* chosen is a good toward which the will deliberately directs itself. It is the matter of a human act. The object chosen morally specifies the act of the will, insofar as reason recognizes and judges it to be or not to be in conformity with the true good. Objective norms of morality express the rational order of good and evil, attested to by conscience.   1794

1752   In contrast to the object, the *intention* resides in the acting subject. Because it lies at the voluntary source of an action and determines it by its end, intention is an element essential to the moral evaluation of an action. The end is the first goal of the intention and indicates the purpose pursued in the action. The intention is a   2520 movement of the will toward the end: it is concerned with the goal of the activity. It aims at the good anticipated from the action undertaken. Intention is not limited to directing individual actions, but can guide several actions toward one and the same purpose; it can orient one's whole life toward its ultimate end. For example, a service done with the end of helping one's neighbor can at the same time be inspired by the love of   1731

God as the ultimate end of all our actions. One and the same action can also be inspired by several intentions, such as performing a service in order to obtain a favor or to boast about it.

1753 A good intention (for example, that of helping one's neighbor) does not make behavior that is intrinsically disordered, such as lying and calumny, good or

2479 just. The end does not justify the means. Thus the condemnation of an innocent person cannot be justified as a legitimate means of saving the nation. On the other hand, an added bad intention (such as vainglory) makes

596 an act evil that, in and of itself, can be good (such as almsgiving).[39]

1754 The *circumstances,* including the consequences, are secondary elements of a moral act. They contribute to increasing or diminishing the moral goodness or evil of human acts (for example, the amount of a theft). They can also diminish or increase the agent's responsibility (such as acting out of a fear of death). Circumstances of themselves cannot change the moral quality

1735 of acts themselves; they can make neither good nor right an action that is in itself evil.

II.   GOOD ACTS AND EVIL ACTS

1755 A *morally good* act requires the goodness of the object, of the end, and of the circumstances together. An evil end corrupts the action, even if the object is good in itself (such as praying and fasting "in order to be seen by men").

The *object of the choice* can by itself vitiate an act in its entirety. There are some concrete acts—such as fornication—that it is always wrong to choose, because choosing them entails a disorder of the will, that is, a moral evil.

1756 It is therefore an error to judge the morality of human acts by considering only the intention that inspires them or the circumstances (environment, social

---

39 Cf. *Mt* 6:2–4.

pressure, duress or emergency, etc.) which supply their context. There are acts which, in and of themselves, independently of circumstances and intentions, are always gravely illicit by reason of their object; such as blasphemy and perjury, murder and adultery. One may not do evil so that good may result from it.

1789

IN BRIEF

1757 The object, the intention, and the circumstances make up the three "sources" of the morality of human acts.

1758 The object chosen morally specifies the act of willing accordingly as reason recognizes and judges it good or evil.

1759 "An evil action cannot be justified by reference to a good intention" (cf. St. Thomas Aquinas, *Dec. praec.* 6). The end does not justify the means.

1760 A morally good act requires the goodness of its object, of its end, and of its circumstances together.

1761 There are concrete acts that it is always wrong to choose, because their choice entails a disorder of the will, i.e., a moral evil. One may not do evil so that good may result from it.

Article 5
THE MORALITY OF THE PASSIONS

1762 The human person is ordered to beatitude by his deliberate acts: the passions or feelings he experiences can dispose him to it and contribute to it.

I. Passions

1763 The term "passions" belongs to the Christian patrimony. Feelings or passions are emotions or movements of the sensitive appetite that incline us to act or not to act in regard to something felt or imagined to be good or evil.

1764   The passions are natural components of the human psyche; they form the passageway and ensure the connection between the life of the senses and the life of the mind. Our Lord called man's heart the source from 368 which the passions spring.[40]

1765   There are many passions. The most fundamental passion is love, aroused by the attraction of the good. Love causes a desire for the absent good and the hope of obtaining it; this movement finds completion in the pleasure and joy of the good possessed. The apprehension of evil causes hatred, aversion, and fear of the impending evil; this movement ends in sadness at some present evil, or in the anger that resists it.

1766   "To love is to will the good of another."[41] All other affections have their source in this first movement 1704 of the human heart toward the good. Only the good can be loved.[42] Passions "are evil if love is evil and good if it is good."[43]

II.   Passions and Moral Life

1767   In themselves passions are neither good nor evil. They are morally qualified only to the extent that they 1860 effectively engage reason and will. Passions are said to be voluntary, "either because they are commanded by the will or because the will does not place obstacles in their way."[44] It belongs to the perfection of the moral or human good that the passions be governed by reason.[45]

1768   Strong feelings are not decisive for the morality or the holiness of persons; they are simply the inexhaustible reservoir of images and affections in which the moral life is expressed. Passions are morally good when they contribute to a good action, evil in the opposite case. The upright will orders the movements of the

---

40 Cf. *Mk* 7:21.   41 St. Thomas Aquinas, *STh* I-II, 26, 4, *corp. art.*   42 Cf. St. Augustine, *De Trin.*, 8, 3, 4: PL 42, 949–950.   43 St. Augustine, *De civ. Dei* 14, 7, 2: PL 41, 410.   44 St. Thomas Aquinas, *STh* I-II, 24, 1 *corp. art.*   45 Cf. St. Thomas Aquinas, *STh* I-II, 24, 3.

senses it appropriates to the good and to beatitude; an evil will succumbs to disordered passions and exacerbates them. Emotions and feelings can be taken up into the *virtues* or perverted by the *vices*.   1803, 1865

1769 In the Christian life, the Holy Spirit himself accomplishes his work by mobilizing the whole being, with all its sorrows, fears and sadness, as is visible in the Lord's agony and passion. In Christ human feelings are able to reach their consummation in charity and divine beatitude.

1770 Moral perfection consists in man's being moved to the good not by his will alone, but also by his sensitive appetite, as in the words of the psalm: "My heart   30
and flesh sing for joy to the living God."[46]

IN BRIEF

1771 The term "passions" refers to the affections or the feelings. By his emotions man intuits the good and suspects evil.

1772 The principal passions are love and hatred, desire and fear, joy, sadness, and anger.

1773 In the passions, as movements of the sensitive appetite, there is neither moral good nor evil. But insofar as they engage reason and will, there is moral good or evil in them.

1774 Emotions and feelings can be taken up in the virtues or perverted by the vices.

1775 The perfection of the moral good consists in man's being moved to the good not only by his will but also by his "heart."

---

46 *Ps* 84:2.

ARTICLE 6
MORAL CONSCIENCE

1776 "Deep within his conscience man discovers a law which he has not laid upon himself but which he must obey. Its voice, ever calling him to love and to do what *1954* is good and to avoid evil, sounds in his heart at the right moment.... For man has in his heart a law inscribed by God.... His conscience is man's most secret core and his sanctuary. There he is alone with God whose voice echoes in his depths."[47]

I.   THE JUDGMENT OF CONSCIENCE

1777 Moral conscience,[48] present at the heart of the person, enjoins him at the appropriate moment to do good and to avoid evil. It also judges particular choices, approving those that are good and denouncing those that are evil.[49] It bears witness to the authority of truth in reference to the supreme Good to which the human *1766* person is drawn, and it welcomes the commandments. When he listens to his conscience, the prudent man can *2071* hear God speaking.

1778 Conscience is a judgment of reason whereby the human person recognizes the moral quality of a concrete act that he is going to perform, is in the process of *1749* performing, or has already completed. In all he says and does, man is obliged to follow faithfully what he knows to be just and right. It is by the judgment of his conscience that man perceives and recognizes the prescriptions of the divine law:

> Conscience is a law of the mind; yet [Christians] would not grant that it is nothing more; I mean that it was not a dictate, nor conveyed the notion of responsibility, of duty, of a threat and a promise.... [Conscience] is a messenger of him, who, both in nature and in grace, speaks to us behind a veil, and teaches and rules us by his representatives. Conscience is the aboriginal Vicar of Christ.[50]

---

47 *GS* 16.   **48** Cf. *Rom* 2:14–16.   **49** Cf. *Rom* 1:32.   **50** John Henry Cardinal Newman, "Letter to the Duke of Norfolk," V, in *Certain Difficulties felt by Anglicans in Catholic Teaching* II (London: Longmans Green, 1885), 248.

1779 It is important for every person to be sufficiently present to himself in order to hear and follow the voice of his conscience. This requirement of *interiority* is all the more necessary as life often distracts us from any reflection, self-examination or introspection: *1886*

> Return to your conscience, question it. . . . Turn inward, brethren, and in everything you do, see God as your witness.[51]

1780 The dignity of the human person implies and requires *uprightness of moral conscience.* Conscience includes the perception of the principles of morality (synderesis); their application in the given circumstances by practical discernment of reasons and goods; and finally judgment about concrete acts yet to be performed or already performed. The truth about the moral good, stated in the law of reason, is recognized practically and concretely by the *prudent judgment* of conscience. We call that man prudent who chooses in conformity with this judgment. *1806*

1781 Conscience enables one to assume *responsibility* *1731* for the acts performed. If man commits evil, the just judgment of conscience can remain within him as the witness to the universal truth of the good, at the same time as the evil of his particular choice. The verdict of the judgment of conscience remains a pledge of hope and mercy. In attesting to the fault committed, it calls to mind the forgiveness that must be asked, the good that must still be practiced, and the virtue that must be constantly cultivated with the grace of God:

> We shall . . . reassure our hearts before him whenever our hearts condemn us; for God is greater than our hearts, and he knows everything.[52]

1782 Man has the right to act in conscience and in freedom so as personally to make moral decisions. "He must not be forced to act contrary to his conscience. Nor must he be prevented from acting according to his conscience, especially in religious matters."[53] *2106*

---

51 St. Augustine, *In ep Jo.* 8, 9: PL 35, 2041.   52 *1 Jn* 3:19–20.   53 *DH* 3 § 2.

II.   THE FORMATION OF CONSCIENCE

1783   Conscience must be informed and moral judgment enlightened. A well-formed conscience is upright and truthful. It formulates its judgments according to reason, in conformity with the true good willed by the wisdom of the Creator. The education of conscience is indispensable for human beings who are subjected to negative influences and tempted by sin to prefer their own judgment and to reject authoritative teachings.

2039

1784   The education of the conscience is a lifelong task. From the earliest years, it awakens the child to the knowledge and practice of the interior law recognized by conscience. Prudent education teaches virtue; it prevents or cures fear, selfishness and pride, resentment arising from guilt, and feelings of complacency, born of human weakness and faults. The education of the conscience guarantees freedom and engenders peace of heart.

1742

1785   In the formation of conscience the Word of God is the light for our path,[54] we must assimilate it in faith and prayer and put it into practice. We must also examine our conscience before the Lord's Cross. We are assisted by the gifts of the Holy Spirit, aided by the witness or advice of others and guided by the authoritative teaching of the Church.[55]

890

III.   TO CHOOSE IN ACCORD WITH CONSCIENCE

1786   Faced with a moral choice, conscience can make either a right judgment in accordance with reason and the divine law or, on the contrary, an erroneous judgment that departs from them.

1787   Man is sometimes confronted by situations that make moral judgments less assured and decision difficult. But he must always seriously seek what is right and good and discern the will of God expressed in divine law.

1955

1788   To this purpose, man strives to interpret the data

---

54 Cf. *Ps* 119:105.   55 Cf. *DH* 14.

of experience and the signs of the times assisted by the
virtue of prudence, by the advice of competent people, *1806*
and by the help of the Holy Spirit and his gifts.

1789 Some rules apply in every case:

—One may never do evil so that good may result from *1756*
it;

—the Golden Rule: "Whatever you wish that men *1970*
would do to you, do so to them."[56]

—charity always proceeds by way of respect for one's *1827*
neighbor and his conscience: "Thus sinning against
your brethren and wounding their conscience . . . you *1971*
sin against Christ."[57] Therefore "it is right not to . . . do
anything that makes your brother stumble."[58]

IV. ERRONEOUS JUDGMENT

1790 A human being must always obey the certain
judgment of his conscience. If he were deliberately to
act against it, he would condemn himself. Yet it can
happen that moral conscience remains in ignorance and
makes erroneous judgments about acts to be performed
or already committed.

1791 This ignorance can often be imputed to personal
responsibility. This is the case when a man "takes little
trouble to find out what is true and good, or when conscience is by degrees almost blinded through the habit
of committing sin."[59] In such cases, the person is culpa- *1704*
ble for the evil he commits.

1792 Ignorance of Christ and his Gospel, bad example *133*
given by others, enslavement to one's passions, assertion
of a mistaken notion of autonomy of conscience, rejection of the Church's authority and her teaching, lack of
conversion and of charity: these can be at the source of
errors of judgment in moral conduct.

1793 If—on the contrary—the ignorance is invincible, *1860*
or the moral subject is not responsible for his erroneous

---

56 *Mt* 7:12; cf. *Lk* 6:31; *Tob* 4:15.   57 1 *Cor* 8:12.   58 *Rom* 14:21.   59 *GS* 16.

judgment, the evil committed by the person cannot be imputed to him. It remains no less an evil, a privation, a disorder. One must therefore work to correct the errors of moral conscience.

1794 A good and pure conscience is enlightened by true faith, for charity proceeds at the same time "from a pure heart and a good conscience and sincere faith."[60]

1751   The more a correct conscience prevails, the more do persons and groups turn aside from blind choice and try to be guided by objective standards of moral conduct.[61]

IN BRIEF

1795 "Conscience is man's most secret core, and his sanctuary. There he is alone with God whose voice echoes in his depths" (*GS* 16).

1796 Conscience is a judgment of reason by which the human person recognizes the moral quality of a concrete act.

1797 For the man who has committed evil, the verdict of his conscience remains a pledge of conversion and of hope.

1798 A well-formed conscience is upright and truthful. It formulates its judgments according to reason, in conformity with the true good willed by the wisdom of the Creator. Everyone must avail himself of the means to form his conscience.

1799 Faced with a moral choice, conscience can make either a right judgment in accordance with reason and the divine law or, on the contrary, an erroneous judgment that departs from them.

1800 A human being must always obey the certain judgment of his conscience.

1801 Conscience can remain in ignorance or make er-

---

60 *1 Tim* 5; cf. 3:9; *2 Tim* 3; *1 Pet* 3:21; *Acts* 24:16.   61 *GS* 16.

roneous judgments. Such ignorance and errors are not always free of guilt.

1802   The Word of God is a light for our path. We must assimilate it in faith and prayer and put it into practice. This is how moral conscience is formed.

ARTICLE 7
THE VIRTUES

1803   "Whatever is true, whatever is honorable, whatever is just, whatever is pure, whatever is lovely, whatever is gracious, if there is any excellence, if there is anything worthy of praise, think about these things."[62]

A virtue is an habitual and firm disposition to do   *1733*
the good. It allows the person not only to perform good acts, but to give the best of himself. The virtuous person tends toward the good with all his sensory and spiritual powers; he pursues the good and chooses it in concrete   *1768*
actions.

The goal of a virtuous life is to become like God.[63]

I.   THE HUMAN VIRTUES
1804   *Human virtues* are firm attitudes, stable dispositions, habitual perfections of intellect and will that govern our actions, order our passions, and guide our conduct according to reason and faith. They make possible ease, self-mastery, and joy in leading a morally good   *2500*
life. The virtuous man is he who freely practices the good.

The moral virtues are acquired by human effort. They are the fruit and seed of morally good acts; they   *1827*
dispose all the powers of the human being for communion with divine love.

The cardinal virtues
1805   Four virtues play a pivotal role and accordingly are called "cardinal"; all the others are grouped around

---

62 *Phil* 4:8.   63 St. Gregory of Nyssa, *De beatitudinibus,* 1: PG 44, 1200D.

them. They are: prudence, justice, fortitude, and temperance. "If anyone loves righteousness, [Wisdom's] labors are virtues; for she teaches temperance and prudence, justice, and courage."[64] These virtues are praised under other names in many passages of Scripture.

1806 *Prudence* is the virtue that disposes practical reason to discern our true good in every circumstance and to choose the right means of achieving it; "the prudent man looks where he is going."[65] "Keep sane and sober for your prayers."[66] Prudence is "right reason in action," writes St. Thomas Aquinas, following Aristotle.[67]

1788 It is not to be confused with timidity or fear, nor with duplicity or dissimulation. It is called *auriga virtutum* (the charioteer of the virtues); it guides the other virtues by setting rule and measure. It is prudence that immediately guides the judgment of conscience. The prudent

1780 man determines and directs his conduct in accordance with this judgment. With the help of this virtue we apply moral principles to particular cases without error and overcome doubts about the good to achieve and the evil to avoid.

1807 *Justice* is the moral virtue that consists in the constant and firm will to give their due to God and neighbor. Justice toward God is called the "virtue of re-

2095 ligion." Justice toward men disposes one to respect the rights of each and to establish in human relationships the harmony that promotes equity with regard to per-

2401 sons and to the common good. The just man, often mentioned in the Sacred Scriptures, is distinguished by habitual right thinking and the uprightness of his conduct toward his neighbor. "You shall not be partial to the poor or defer to the great, but in righteousness shall you judge your neighbor."[68] "Masters, treat your slaves justly and fairly, knowing that you also have a Master in heaven."[69]

1808 *Fortitude* is the moral virtue that ensures firmness in difficulties and constancy in the pursuit of the

---

64 *Wis* 8:7.   65 *Prov* 14:15.   66 1 *Pet* 4:7.   67 St. Thomas Aquinas, *STh* II-II, 47, 2.   68 *Lev* 19:15.   69 *Col* 4:1.

good. It strengthens the resolve to resist temptations and to overcome obstacles in the moral life. The virtue of fortitude enables one to conquer fear, even fear of death, and to face trials and persecutions. It disposes 2848 one even to renounce and sacrifice his life in defense of a just cause. "The Lord is my strength and my song."[70] 2473 "In the world you have tribulation; but be of good cheer, I have overcome the world."[71]

1809 *Temperance* is the moral virtue that moderates the attraction of pleasures and provides balance in the use of created goods. It ensures the will's mastery over instincts and keeps desires within the limits of what is honorable. The temperate person directs the sensitive 2341 appetites toward what is good and maintains a healthy discretion: "Do not follow your inclination and strength, walking according to the desires of your heart."[72] Temperance is often praised in the Old Testament: "Do not follow your base desires, but restrain 2517 your appetites."[73] In the New Testament it is called "moderation" or "sobriety." We ought "to live sober, upright, and godly lives in this world."[74]

> To live well is nothing other than to love God with all one's heart, with all one's soul and with all one's efforts; from this it comes about that love is kept whole and uncorrupted (through temperance). No misfortune can disturb it (and this is fortitude). It obeys only [God] (and this is justice), and is careful in discerning things, so as not to be surprised by deceit or trickery (and this is prudence).[75]

The virtues and grace

1810 Human virtues acquired by education, by deliberate acts and by a perseverance ever-renewed in repeated efforts are purified and elevated by divine grace. 1266 With God's help, they forge character and give facility in the practice of the good. The virtuous man is happy to practice them.

1811 It is not easy for man, wounded by sin, to main-

---

70 *Ps* 118:14.   71 *Jn* 16:33.   72 *Sir* 5:2; cf. 37:27–31.   73 *Sir* 18:30.   74 *Titus* 2:12.   75 St. Augustine, *De moribus eccl.* 1, 25, 46: PL 32, 1330–1331.

tain moral balance. Christ's gift of salvation offers us
the grace necessary to persevere in the pursuit of the
2015 virtues. Everyone should always ask for this grace of
light and strength, frequent the sacraments, cooperate
with the Holy Spirit, and follow his calls to love what is
good and shun evil.

2086-2094, ## II.   THE THEOLOGICAL VIRTUES
2656-2658 **1812**   The human virtues are rooted in the theological
virtues, which adapt man's faculties for participation in
the divine nature:[76] for the theological virtues relate directly to God. They dispose Christians to live in a relationship with the Holy Trinity. They have the One and
1266 Triune God for their origin, motive, and object.

1813   The theological virtues are the foundation of
Christian moral activity; they animate it and give it its
special character. They inform and give life to all the
moral virtues. They are infused by God into the souls of
the faithful to make them capable of acting as his children and of meriting eternal life. They are the pledge of
the presence and action of the Holy Spirit in the faculties of the human being. There are three theological
2088 virtues: faith, hope, and charity.[77]

142-175 ### Faith
1814   Faith is the theological virtue by which we believe in God and believe all that he has said and revealed
to us, and that Holy Church proposes for our belief, be-
506 cause he is truth itself. By faith "man freely commits his
entire self to God."[78] For this reason the believer seeks
to know and do God's will. "The righteous shall live by
faith." Living faith "work[s] through charity."[79]

1815   The gift of faith remains in one who has not
sinned against it.[80] But "faith apart from works is
dead":[81] when it is deprived of hope and love, faith does
not fully unite the believer to Christ and does not make
him a living member of his Body.

---

76 Cf. 2 *Pet* 1:4.   77 Cf. 1 *Cor* 13:13.   78 *DV* 5.   79 *Rom* 1:17; *Gal* 5:6.
80 Cf. Council of Trent (1547): DS 1545.   81 *Jas* 2:26.

1816 The disciple of Christ must not only keep the 2471
faith and live on it, but also profess it, confidently bear
witness to it, and spread it: "All however must be prepared to confess Christ before men and to follow him
along the way of the Cross, amidst the persecutions
which the Church never lacks."[82] Service of and witness
to the faith are necessary for salvation: "So every one
who acknowledges me before men, I also will acknowledge before my Father who is in heaven; but whoever
denies me before men, I also will deny before my Father
who is in heaven."[83]

Hope

1817 Hope is the theological virtue by which we desire
the kingdom of heaven and eternal life as our happiness,
placing our trust in Christ's promises and relying not on 1024
our own strength, but on the help of the grace of the
Holy Spirit. "Let us hold fast the confession of our hope
without wavering, for he who promised is faithful."[84]
"The Holy Spirit . . . he poured out upon us richly
through Jesus Christ our Savior, so that we might be justified by his grace and become heirs in hope of eternal
life."[85]

1818 The virtue of hope responds to the aspiration to 27
happiness which God has placed in the heart of every
man; it takes up the hopes that inspire men's activities
and purifies them so as to order them to the Kingdom
of heaven; it keeps man from discouragement; it sustains him during times of abandonment; it opens up his
heart in expectation of eternal beatitude. Buoyed up by
hope, he is preserved from selfishness and led to the
happiness that flows from charity.

1819 Christian hope takes up and fulfills the hope of
the chosen people which has its origin and model in the
hope of Abraham, who was blessed abundantly by the
promises of God fulfilled in Isaac, and who was purified
by the test of the sacrifice.[86] "Hoping against hope, he 146

---

82 *LG* 42; cf. *DH* 14.   83 *Mt* 10:32–33.   84 *Heb* 10:23.   85 *Titus* 3:6–7.
86 Cf. *Gen* 17:4–8; 22:1–18.

believed, and thus became the father of many nations."[87]

1820   Christian hope unfolds from the beginning of Jesus' preaching in the proclamation of the beatitudes. The *beatitudes* raise our hope toward heaven as the new Promised Land; they trace the path that leads through the trials that await the disciples of Jesus. But through the merits of Jesus Christ and of his Passion, God keeps us in the "hope that does not disappoint."[88] Hope is the "sure and steadfast anchor of the soul . . . that enters . . . where Jesus has gone as a forerunner on our behalf."[89] Hope is also a weapon that protects us in the struggle of salvation: "Let us . . . put on the breastplate of faith and charity, and for a helmet the hope of salvation."[90] It affords us joy even under trial: "Rejoice in your hope, be patient in tribulation."[91] Hope is expressed and nourished in prayer, especially in the Our Father, the summary of everything that hope leads us to desire.

1821   We can therefore hope in the glory of heaven promised by God to those who love him and do his will.[92] In every circumstance, each one of us should hope, with the grace of God, to persevere "to the end"[93] and to obtain the joy of heaven, as God's eternal reward for the good works accomplished with the grace of Christ. In hope, the Church prays for "all men to be saved."[94] She longs to be united with Christ, her Bridegroom, in the glory of heaven:

> Hope, O my soul, hope. You know neither the day nor the hour. Watch carefully, for everything passes quickly, even though your impatience makes doubtful what is certain, and turns a very short time into a long one. Dream that the more you struggle, the more you prove the love that you bear your God, and the more you will rejoice one day with your Beloved, in a happiness and rapture that can never end.[95]

1716

2772

2016

1037

---

87 *Rom* 4:18.   88 *Rom* 5:5.   89 *Heb* 6:19–20.   90 *1 Thess* 5:8.   91 *Rom* 12:12.   92 Cf. *Rom* 8:28–30; *Mt* 7:21.   93 *Mt* 10:22; cf. Council of Trent: DS 1541.   94 *1 Tim* 2:4.   95 St. Teresa of Avila, *Excl.* 15:3.

Charity

1822 Charity is the theological virtue by which we 1723
love God above all things for his own sake, and our
neighbor as ourselves for the love of God.

1823 Jesus makes charity the *new commandment*.[96] By 1970
loving his own "to the end,"[97] he makes manifest the Father's love which he receives. By loving one another, the
disciples imitate the love of Jesus which they themselves
receive. Whence Jesus says: "As the Father has loved
me, so have I loved you; abide in my love." And again:
"This is my commandment, that you love one another
as I have loved you."[98]

1824 Fruit of the Spirit and fullness of the Law, char- 735
ity keeps the *commandments* of God and his Christ:
"Abide in my love. If you keep my commandments, you
will abide in my love."[99]

1825 Christ died out of love for us, while we were still 604
"enemies."[100] The Lord asks us to love as he does, even
our *enemies,* to make ourselves the neighbor of those
farthest away, and to love children and the poor as
Christ himself.[101]

> The Apostle Paul has given an incomparable depic-
> tion of charity: "charity is patient and kind, charity
> is not jealous or boastful; it is not arrogant or rude.
> Charity does not insist on its own way; it is not ir-
> ritable or resentful; it does not rejoice at wrong, but
> rejoices in the right. Charity bears all things, be-
> lieves all things, hopes all things, endures all
> things."[102]

1826 "If I . . . have not charity," says the Apostle, "I
am nothing." Whatever my privilege, service, or even
virtue, "if I . . . have not charity, I gain nothing."[103]
Charity is superior to all the virtues. It is the first of the
theological virtues: "So faith, hope, charity abide, these
three. But *the greatest of these is charity.*"[104]

1827 The practice of all the virtues is animated and in-

---

96 Cf. *Jn* 13:34. 97 *Jn* 13:1. 98 *Jn* 15:9, 12. 99 *Jn* 15:9–10; cf. *Mt* 22:40;
Rom 13:8–10. 100 *Rom* 5:10. 101 Cf. *Mt* 5:44; *Lk* 10:27–37; *Mk* 9:37; *Mt*
25:40, 45. 102 *1 Cor* 13:4–7. 103 *1 Cor* 13:1–4. 104 *1 Cor* 13:13.

spired by charity, which "binds everything together in
815 perfect harmony";[105] it is the *form of the virtues;* it ar-
ticulates and orders them among themselves; it is the
826 source and the goal of their Christian practice. Charity
upholds and purifies our human ability to love, and
raises it to the supernatural perfection of divine love.

1828 The practice of the moral life animated by charity gives to the Christian the spiritual freedom of the
1972 children of God. He no longer stands before God as a
slave, in servile fear, or as a mercenary looking for
wages, but as a son responding to the love of him who
"first loved us":[106]

> If we turn away from evil out of fear of punish-
> ment, we are in the position of slaves. If we pursue
> the enticement of wages, ... we resemble merce-
> naries. Finally if we obey for the sake of the good
> itself and out of love for him who commands ...
> we are in the position of children.[107]

1829 The *fruits* of charity are joy, peace, and mercy;
charity demands beneficence and fraternal correction; it
2540 is benevolence; it fosters reciprocity and remains disinterested and generous; it is friendship and communion:

> Love is itself the fulfillment of all our works. There
> is the goal; that is why we run: we run toward it,
> and once we reach it, in it we shall find rest.[108]

III.   THE GIFTS AND FRUITS OF THE HOLY SPIRIT

1830 The moral life of Christians is sustained by the
gifts of the Holy Spirit. These are permanent dispositions which make man docile in following the promptings of the Holy Spirit.

1831 The seven *gifts* of the Holy Spirit are wisdom,
understanding, counsel, fortitude, knowledge, piety,
and fear of the Lord. They belong in their fullness to
Christ, Son of David.[109] They complete and perfect the
1266, 1299 virtues of those who receive them. They make the faithful docile in readily obeying divine inspirations.

---

105 *Col* 3:14.   106 Cf. *1 Jn* 4:19.   107 St. Basil, *Reg. fus. tract., prol.* 3: PG 31,
896 B.   108 St. Augustine, *In ep. Jo.* 10, 4: PL 35, 2057.   109 Cf. *Isa* 11:1–2.

Let your good spirit lead me on a level path.[110]

For all who are led by the Spirit of God are sons of God . . . If children, then heirs, heirs of God and fellow heirs with Christ.[111]

1832 The *fruits* of the Spirit are perfections that the Holy Spirit forms in us as the first fruits of eternal glory. The tradition of the Church lists twelve of them: "charity, joy, peace, patience, kindness, goodness, generosity, gentleness, faithfulness, modesty, self-control, chastity."[112] *736*

IN BRIEF

1833 Virtue is a habitual and firm disposition to do good.

1834 The human virtues are stable dispositions of the intellect and the will that govern our acts, order our passions, and guide our conduct in accordance with reason and faith. They can be grouped around the four cardinal virtues: prudence, justice, fortitude, and temperance.

1835 Prudence disposes the practical reason to discern, in every circumstance, our true good and to choose the right means for achieving it.

1836 Justice consists in the firm and constant will to give God and neighbor their due.

1837 Fortitude ensures firmness in difficulties and constancy in the pursuit of the good.

1838 Temperance moderates the attraction of the pleasures of the senses and provides balance in the use of created goods.

1839 The moral virtues grow through education, deliberate acts, and perseverance in struggle. Divine grace purifies and elevates them.

1840 The theological virtues dispose Christians to live in a relationship with the Holy Trinity. They

---

110 *Ps* 143:10.   **111** *Rom* 8:14, 17.   **112** *Gal* 5:22–23 (Vulg.).

have God for their origin, their motive, and their object—God known by faith, God hoped in and loved for his own sake.

1841   There are three theological virtues: faith, hope, and charity. They inform all the moral virtues and give life to them.

1842   By faith, we believe in God and believe all that he has revealed to us and that Holy Church proposes for our belief.

1843   By hope we desire, and with steadfast trust await from God, eternal life and the graces to merit it.

1844   By charity, we love God above all things and our neighbor as ourselves for love of God. Charity, the form of all the virtues, "binds everything together in perfect harmony" (*Col* 3:14).

1845   The seven gifts of the Holy Spirit bestowed upon Christians are wisdom, understanding, counsel, fortitude, knowledge, piety, and fear of the Lord.

ARTICLE 8
SIN

I.   MERCY AND SIN

430   1846   The Gospel is the revelation in Jesus Christ of God's mercy to sinners.[113] The angel announced to Joseph: "You shall call his name Jesus, for he will save his people from their sins."[114] The same is true of the Eu-
1365   charist, the sacrament of redemption: "This is my blood of the covenant, which is poured out for many for the forgiveness of sins."[115]

387, 1455   1847   "God created us without us: but he did not will to save us without us."[116] To receive his mercy, we must admit our faults. "If we say we have no sin, we deceive ourselves, and the truth is not in us. If we confess our

---

113 Cf. *Lk* 15.   114 *Mt* 1:21.   115 *Mt* 26:28.   116 St. Augustine, *Sermo* 169, 11, 13: PL 38, 923.

sins, he is faithful and just, and will forgive our sins and cleanse us from all unrighteousness."[117]

1848 As St. Paul affirms, "Where sin increased, grace abounded all the more."[118] But to do its work grace must uncover sin so as to convert our hearts and bestow $_{385}$ on us "righteousness to eternal life through Jesus Christ our Lord."[119] Like a physician who probes the wound before treating it, God, by his Word and by his Spirit, casts a living light on sin:

> Conversion *requires convincing of sin;* it includes the interior judgment of conscience, and this, being a proof of the action of the Spirit of truth in man's inmost being, becomes at the same time the start of a new grant of grace and love: "Receive the Holy Spirit." Thus in this "convincing concerning sin" $_{1433}$ we discover *a double gift:* the gift of the truth of conscience and the gift of the certainty of redemption. The Spirit of truth is the Consoler.[120]

II. THE DEFINITION OF SIN

1849 Sin is an offense against reason, truth, and right $_{311}$ conscience; it is failure in genuine love for God and neighbor caused by a perverse attachment to certain goods. It wounds the nature of man and injures human solidarity. It has been defined as "an utterance, a deed, or a desire contrary to the eternal law."[121] $_{1952}$

1850 Sin is an offense against God: "Against you, you $_{1440}$ alone, have I sinned, and done that which is evil in your sight."[122] Sin sets itself against God's love for us and turns our hearts away from it. Like the first sin, it is dis- $_{397}$ obedience, a revolt against God through the will to become "like gods,"[123] knowing and determining good and evil. Sin is thus "love of oneself even to contempt of God."[124] In this proud self-exaltation, sin is diametrically opposed to the obedience of Jesus, which achieves our salvation.[125] $_{615}$

---

117 *1 Jn* 8–9.   118 *Rom* 5:20.   119 *Rom* 5:21.   120 John Paul II, *DeV* 31 § 2.
121 St. Augustine, *Contra Faustum* 22: PL 42, 418; St. Thomas Aquinas, *STh* I-II, 71, 6.   122 *Ps* 51:4.   123 *Gen* 3:5.   124 St. Augustine, *De civ. Dei* 14, 28: PL 41, 436.   125 Cf. *Phil* 2:6–9.

1851   It is precisely in the Passion, when the mercy of Christ is about to vanquish it, that sin most clearly manifests its violence and its many forms: unbelief, murderous hatred, shunning and mockery by the leaders and the people, Pilate's cowardice and the cruelty of the sol-

598   diers, Judas' betrayal—so bitter to Jesus, Peter's denial and the disciples' flight. However, at the very hour of

2746, 616   darkness, the hour of the prince of this world,[126] the sacrifice of Christ secretly becomes the source from which the forgiveness of our sins will pour forth inexhaustibly.

III.   THE DIFFERENT KINDS OF SINS

1852   There are a great many kinds of sins. Scripture provides several lists of them. The *Letter to the Galatians* contrasts the works of the flesh with the fruit of the Spirit: "Now the works of the flesh are plain: fornication, impurity, licentiousness, idolatry, sorcery, enmity, strife, jealousy, anger, selfishness, dissension, factions, envy, drunkenness, carousing, and the like. I warn you, as I warned you before, that those who do such things shall not inherit the Kingdom of God."[127]

1751   1853   Sins can be distinguished according to their objects, as can every human act; or according to the virtues they oppose, by excess or defect; or according to the commandments they violate. They can also be classed according to whether they concern God, neighbor, or oneself; they can

2067   be divided into spiritual and carnal sins, or again as sins in thought, word, deed, or omission. The root of sin is in the heart of man, in his free will, according to the teaching of the Lord: "For out of the heart come evil thoughts, murder,

368   adultery, fornication, theft, false witness, slander. These are what defile a man."[128] But in the heart also resides charity, the source of the good and pure works, which sin wounds.

IV.   THE GRAVITY OF SIN: MORTAL AND VENIAL SIN

1854   Sins are rightly evaluated according to their gravity. The distinction between mortal and venial sin, already evident in Scripture,[129] became part of the tradi-

---

126 Cf. *Jn* 14:30.   127 *Gal* 5:19–21; cf. *Rom* 1:28–32; *1 Cor* 9–10; *Eph* 5:3–5; *Col* 3:5–8; *1 Tim* 9–10; *2 Tim* 2–5.   128 *Mt* 15:19–20.   129 Cf. *1 Jn* 16–17.

tion of the Church. It is corroborated by human experience.

1855   *Mortal sin* destroys charity in the heart of man   *1395* by a grave violation of God's law; it turns man away from God, who is his ultimate end and his beatitude, by preferring an inferior good to him.

    Venial sin allows charity to subsist, even though it offends and wounds it.

1856   Mortal sin, by attacking the vital principle within us—that is, charity—necessitates a new initiative   *1446* of God's mercy and a conversion of heart which is normally accomplished within the setting of the sacrament of reconciliation:

> When the will sets itself upon something that is of its nature incompatible with the charity that orients man toward his ultimate end, then the sin is mortal by its very object . . . whether it contradicts the love of God, such as blasphemy or perjury, or the love of neighbor, such as homicide or adultery. . . . But when the sinner's will is set upon something that of its nature involves a disorder, but is not opposed to the love of God and neighbor, such as thoughtless chatter or immoderate laughter and the like, such sins are venial.[130]

1857   For a *sin* to be *mortal,* three conditions must together be met: "Mortal sin is sin whose object is grave matter and which is also committed with full knowledge and deliberate consent."[131]

1858   *Grave matter* is specified by the Ten Command-   *2072* ments, corresponding to the answer of Jesus to the rich young man: "Do not kill, Do not commit adultery, Do not steal, Do not bear false witness, Do not defraud, Honor your father and your mother."[132] The gravity of sins is more or less great: murder is graver than theft. One must also take into account who is wronged: violence against parents is in itself graver than violence   *2214* against a stranger.

---

130 St. Thomas Aquinas, *STh* I-II, 88, 2, *corp. art.*   131 *RP* 17 § 12.   132 *Mk* 10:19.

1734 **1859** Mortal sin requires *full knowledge* and *complete consent*. It presupposes knowledge of the sinful character of the act, of its opposition to God's law. It also implies a consent sufficiently deliberate to be a personal choice. Feigned ignorance and hardness of heart[133] do not diminish, but rather increase, the voluntary character of a sin.

1735 **1860** *Unintentional ignorance* can diminish or even remove the imputability of a grave offense. But no one is deemed to be ignorant of the principles of the moral law, which are written in the conscience of every man. The promptings of feelings and passions can also di-
1767 minish the voluntary and free character of the offense, as can external pressures or pathological disorders. Sin committed through malice, by deliberate choice of evil, is the gravest.

1742 **1861** Mortal sin is a radical possibility of human freedom, as is love itself. It results in the loss of charity and the privation of sanctifying grace, that is, of the state of grace. If it is not redeemed by repentance and God's forgiveness, it causes exclusion from Christ's kingdom and the eternal death of hell, for our freedom has the power
1033 to make choices for ever, with no turning back. However, although we can judge that an act is in itself a grave offense, we must entrust judgment of persons to the justice and mercy of God.

1862 One commits *venial sin* when, in a less serious matter, he does not observe the standard prescribed by the moral law, or when he disobeys the moral law in a grave matter, but without full knowledge or without complete consent.

1394 **1863** Venial sin weakens charity; it manifests a disordered affection for created goods; it impedes the soul's progress in the exercise of the virtues and the practice of the moral good; it merits temporal punishment. Deliberate and unrepented venial sin disposes us little by lit-
1472 tle to commit mortal sin. However venial sin does not

---

133 Cf. *Mk* 3:5–6; *Lk* 16:19–31.

set us in direct opposition to the will and friendship of God; it does not break the covenant with God. With God's grace it is humanly reparable. "Venial sin does not deprive the sinner of sanctifying grace, friendship with God, charity, and consequently eternal happiness."[134]

> While he is in the flesh, man cannot help but have at least some light sins. But do not despise these sins which we call "light": if you take them for light when you weigh them, tremble when you count them. A number of light objects makes a great mass; a number of drops fills a river; a number of grains makes a heap. What then is our hope? Above all, confession. . . .[135]

1864 "Whoever *blasphemes against the Holy Spirit* never has forgiveness, but is guilty of an eternal sin."[136] There are no limits to the mercy of God, but anyone who deliberately refuses to accept his mercy by repenting, rejects the forgiveness of his sins and the salvation offered by the Holy Spirit.[137] Such hardness of heart can lead to final impenitence and eternal loss.

2091

1037

V.   THE PROLIFERATION OF SIN

1865   Sin creates a proclivity to sin; it engenders vice by repetition of the same acts. This results in perverse inclinations which cloud conscience and corrupt the concrete judgment of good and evil. Thus sin tends to reproduce itself and reinforce itself, but it cannot destroy the moral sense at its root.

401

1768

1866   Vices can be classified according to the virtues they oppose, or also be linked to the *capital sins* which Christian experience has distinguished, following St. John Cassian and St. Gregory the Great. They are called "capital" because they engender other sins, other vices.[138] They are pride, avarice, envy, wrath, lust, gluttony, and sloth or acedia.

2539

1867   The catechetical tradition also recalls that there

2268

---

134 John Paul II, *RP* 17 § 9.   **135** St. Augustine, *In ep. Jo.* 1, 6: PL 35, 1982.
136 *Mk* 3:29; cf. *Mt* 12:32; *Lk* 12:10.   **137** Cf. John Paul II, *DeV* 46.   **138** Cf.
St. Gregory the Great, *Moralia in Job*, 31, 45: PL 76, 621A.

are *"sins that cry to heaven"*: the blood of Abel,[139] the sin of the Sodomites,[140] the cry of the people oppressed in Egypt,[141] the cry of the foreigner, the widow, and the orphan,[142] injustice to the wage earner.[143]

1868 Sin is a personal act. Moreover, we have a responsibility for the sins committed by others when *we*
1736 *cooperate in them:*

—by participating directly and voluntarily in them;

—by ordering, advising, praising, or approving them;

—by not disclosing or not hindering them when we have an obligation to do so;

—by protecting evil-doers.

1869 Thus sin makes men accomplices of one another and causes concupiscence, violence, and injustice to reign among them. Sins give rise to social situations and institutions that are contrary to the divine goodness.
408 "Structures of sin" are the expression and effect of per-
1887 sonal sins. They lead their victims to do evil in their turn. In an analogous sense, they constitute a "social sin."[144]

IN BRIEF

1870 "God has consigned all men to disobedience, that he may have mercy upon all" (*Rom* 11:32).

1871 Sin is an utterance, a deed, or a desire contrary to the eternal law (St. Augustine, *Faust* 22: PL 42, 418). It is an offense against God. It rises up against God in a disobedience contrary to the obedience of Christ.

1872 Sin is an act contrary to reason. It wounds man's nature and injures human solidarity.

1873 The root of all sins lies in man's heart. The kinds and the gravity of sins are determined principally by their objects.

---

139 Cf. *Gen* 4:10.   140 Cf. *Gen* 18:20; 19:13.   141 Cf. *Ex* 3:7–10.   142 Cf. *Ex* 20:20–22.   143 Cf. *Deut* 24:14–15; *Jas* 5:4.   144 John Paul II, *RP* 16.

1874 To choose deliberately—that is, both knowing it and willing it—something gravely contrary to the divine law and to the ultimate end of man is to commit a mortal sin. This destroys in us the charity without which eternal beatitude is impossible. Unrepented, it brings eternal death.

1875 Venial sin constitutes a moral disorder that is reparable by charity, which it allows to subsist in us.

1876 The repetition of sins—even venial ones—engenders vices, among which are the capital sins.

CHAPTER TWO
THE HUMAN COMMUNITY

1877 The vocation of humanity is to show forth the *355* image of God and to be transformed into the image of the Father's only Son. This vocation takes a personal form since each of us is called to enter into the divine beatitude; it also concerns the human community as a whole.

ARTICLE 1
THE PERSON AND SOCIETY

I.   THE COMMUNAL CHARACTER OF THE HUMAN VOCATION

1878 All men are called to the same end: God himself. There is a certain resemblance between the union of the *1702* divine persons and the fraternity that men are to establish among themselves in truth and love.[1] Love of neighbor is inseparable from love for God.

1879 The human person needs to live in society. Society *1936* is not for him an extraneous addition but a requirement of his nature. Through the exchange with others, mutual service and dialogue with his brethren, man develops his potential; he thus responds to his vocation.[2]

---

1 Cf. *GS* 24 § 3.   2 Cf. *GS* 25 § 1.

771 **1880** A *society* is a group of persons bound together organically by a principle of unity that goes beyond each one of them. As an assembly that is at once visible and spiritual, a society endures through time: it gathers up the past and prepares for the future. By means of society, each man is established as an "heir" and receives certain "talents" that enrich his identity and whose fruits he must develop.[3] He rightly owes loyalty to the communities of which he is part and respect to those in authority who have charge of the common good.

1881 Each community is defined by its purpose and consequently obeys specific rules; but "the *human per-*
1929 *son* . . . is and ought to be the principle, the subject and the end of all social institutions."[4]

1882 Certain societies, such as the family and the state, correspond more directly to the nature of man; they are necessary to him. To promote the participation of the greatest number in the life of a society, the creation of voluntary associations and institutions must be
1913 encouraged "on both national and international levels, which relate to economic and social goals, to cultural and recreational activities, to sport, to various professions, and to political affairs."[5] This *"socialization"* also expresses the natural tendency for human beings to associate with one another for the sake of attaining objectives that exceed individual capacities. It develops the qualities of the person, especially the sense of initiative and responsibility, and helps guarantee his rights.[6]

1883 Socialization also presents dangers. Excessive intervention by the state can threaten personal freedom and initiative. The teaching of the Church has elaborated the principle of *subsidiarity,* according to which "a community of a higher order should not interfere in the internal life of a community of a lower order, depriving the latter of its functions, but rather should sup-
2431 port it in case of need and help to co-ordinate its activ-

---

3 Cf. *Lk* 19:13, 15.   4 *GS* 25 § 1.   5 John XXIII, *MM* 60.   6 Cf. *GS* 25 § 2; *CA* 12.

ity with the activities of the rest of society, always with a view to the common good."[7]

1884 God has not willed to reserve to himself all exercise of power. He entrusts to every creature the functions it is capable of performing, according to the capacities of its own nature. This mode of governance ought to be followed in social life. The way God acts in governing the world, which bears witness to such great regard for human freedom, should inspire the wisdom of those who govern human communities. They should behave as ministers of divine providence. *307* *302*

1885 The principle of subsidiarity is opposed to all forms of collectivism. It sets limits for state intervention. It aims at harmonizing the relationships between individuals and societies. It tends toward the establishment of true international order.

II.   CONVERSION AND SOCIETY

1886 Society is essential to the fulfillment of the human vocation. To attain this aim, respect must be accorded to the just hierarchy of values, which "subordinates physical and instinctual dimensions to interior and spiritual ones:"[8] *1779*

> Human society must primarily be considered something pertaining to the spiritual. Through it, in the bright light of truth, men should share their knowledge, be able to exercise their rights and fulfill their obligations, be inspired to seek spiritual values; mutually derive genuine pleasure from the beautiful, of whatever order it be; always be readily disposed to *2500* pass on to others the best of their own cultural heritage; and eagerly strive to make their own the spiritual achievements of others. These benefits not only influence, but at the same time give aim and scope to all that has bearing on cultural expressions, economic, and social institutions, political movements and forms, laws, and all other structures by which society is outwardly established and constantly developed.[9]

---

7 *CA* 48 § 4; cf. Pius XI, *Quadragesimo anno* I, 184–186.   8 *CA* 36 § 2.
9 John XXIII, *PT* 36.

1887   The inversion of means and ends,[10] which results in giving the value of ultimate end to what is only a means for attaining it, or in viewing persons as mere means to that end, engenders unjust structures which "make Christian conduct in keeping with the commandments of the divine Law-giver difficult and almost impossible."[11]

909

1869

1888   It is necessary, then, to appeal to the spiritual and moral capacities of the human person and to the permanent need for his *inner conversion,* so as to obtain social changes that will really serve him. The acknowledged priority of the conversion of heart in no way eliminates but on the contrary imposes the obligation of bringing the appropriate remedies to institutions and living conditions when they are an inducement to sin, so that they conform to the norms of justice and advance the good rather than hinder it.[12]

407
1430

1889   Without the help of grace, men would not know how "to discern the often narrow path between the cowardice which gives in to evil, and the violence which under the illusion of fighting evil only makes it worse."[13] This is the path of charity, that is, of the love of God and of neighbor. Charity is the greatest social commandment. It respects others and their rights. It requires the practice of justice, and it alone makes us capable of it. Charity inspires a life of self-giving: "Whoever seeks to gain his life will lose it, but whoever loses his life will preserve it."[14]

1825

IN BRIEF

1890   There is a certain resemblance between the union of the divine persons and the fraternity that men ought to establish among themselves.

1891   The human person needs life in society in order to develop in accordance with his nature. Certain societies, such as the family and the

---

10 Cf. *CA* 41.   11 Pius XII, Address at Pentecost, June 1, 1941.   12 Cf. *LG* 36.
13 *CA* 25.   14 *Lk* 17:33.

state, correspond more directly to the nature of man.

1892 "The human person ... is and ought to be the principle, the subject, and the object of every social organization" (*GS* 25 § 1).

1893 Widespread participation in voluntary associations and institutions is to be encouraged.

1894 In accordance with the principle of subsidiarity, neither the state nor any larger society should substitute itself for the initiative and responsibility of individuals and intermediary bodies.

1895 Society ought to promote the exercise of virtue, not obstruct it. It should be animated by a just hierarchy of values.

1896 Where sin has perverted the social climate, it is necessary to call for the conversion of hearts and appeal to the grace of God. Charity urges just reforms. There is no solution to the social question apart from the Gospel (cf. *CA* 3, 5).

ARTICLE 2
PARTICIPATION IN SOCIAL LIFE

I.   AUTHORITY

1897 "Human society can be neither well-ordered nor prosperous unless it has some people invested with legitimate authority to preserve its institutions and to devote themselves as far as is necessary to work and care for the good of all."[15]

2234

By "authority" one means the quality by virtue of which persons or institutions make laws and give orders to men and expect obedience from them.

1898 Every human community needs an authority to govern it.[16] The foundation of such authority lies in human nature. It is necessary for the unity of the state. Its

---

15 John XXIII, *PT* 46.   16 Cf. Leo XIII, *Immortale Dei; Diuturnum illud.*

role is to ensure as far as possible the common good of the society.

2235   **1899** The authority required by the moral order derives from God: "Let every person be subject to the governing authorities. For there is no authority except from God, and those that exist have been instituted by God. Therefore he who resists the authorities resists what God has appointed, and those who resist will incur judgment."[17]

2238   **1900** The duty of obedience requires all to give due honor to authority and to treat those who are charged to exercise it with respect, and, insofar as it is deserved, with gratitude and good-will.

2240   Pope St. Clement of Rome provides the Church's most ancient prayer for political authorities:[18] "Grant to them, Lord, health, peace, concord, and stability, so that they may exercise without offense the sovereignty that you have given them. Master, heavenly King of the ages, you give glory, honor, and power over the things of earth to the sons of men. Direct, Lord, their counsel, following what is pleasing and acceptable in your sight, so that by exercising with devotion and in peace and gentleness the power that you have given to them, they may find favor with you."[19]

1901 If authority belongs to the order established by God, "the choice of the political regime and the appointment of rulers are left to the free decision of the citizens."[20]

            The diversity of political regimes is morally acceptable, provided they serve the legitimate good of the
2242   communities that adopt them. Regimes whose nature is contrary to the natural law, to the public order, and to the fundamental rights of persons cannot achieve the common good of the nations on which they have been imposed.

1930   **1902** Authority does not derive its moral legitimacy from itself. It must not behave in a despotic manner, but

---

17 *Rom* 13:1–2; cf. *1 Pet* 2:13–17.   18 Cf. as early as *1 Tim* 2:1–2.   19 St. Clement of Rome, *Ad Cor.* 61: SCh 167, 198–200.   20 *GS* 74 § 3.

must act for the common good as a "moral force based on freedom and a sense of responsibility":[21]

> A human law has the character of law to the extent [1951] that it accords with right reason, and thus derives from the eternal law. Insofar as it falls short of right reason it is said to be an unjust law, and thus has not so much the nature of law as of a kind of violence.[22]

1903 Authority is exercised legitimately only when it seeks the common good of the group concerned and if it employs morally licit means to attain it. If rulers were to enact unjust laws or take measures contrary to the moral order, such arrangements would not be binding [2242] in conscience. In such a case, "authority breaks down completely and results in shameful abuse."[23]

1904 "It is preferable that each power be balanced by other powers and by other spheres of responsibility which keep it within proper bounds. This is the principle of the 'rule of law,' in which the law is sovereign and not the arbitrary will of men."[24]

II. THE COMMON GOOD

1905 In keeping with the social nature of man, the good of each individual is necessarily related to the [801] common good, which in turn can be defined only in reference to the human person: [1881]

> Do not live entirely isolated, having retreated into yourselves, as if you were already justified, but gather instead to seek the common good together.[25]

1906 By common good is to be understood "the sum total of social conditions which allow people, either as groups or as individuals, to reach their fulfillment more fully and more easily."[26] The common good concerns the life of all. It calls for prudence from each, and even more from those who exercise the office of authority. It consists of *three essential elements:*

---

21 *GS* 74 § 2. 22 St. Thomas Aquinas, *STh* I-II, 93, 3, *ad* 2. 23 John XXIII, *PT* 51. 24 *CA* 44. 25 *Ep. Barnabae*, 4, 10: PG 2, 734. 26 *GS* 26 § 1; cf. *GS* 74 § 1.

1929 **1907** First, the common good presupposes *respect for the person* as such. In the name of the common good, public authorities are bound to respect the fundamental and inalienable rights of the human person. Society should permit each of its members to fulfill his vocation. In particular, the common good resides in the conditions for the exercise of the natural freedoms indispensable for the development of the human vocation, such as "the right to act according to a sound norm of conscience and to safeguard ... privacy, and rightful
2106 freedom also in matters of religion."[27]

1908 Second, the common good requires the *social well-being* and *development* of the group itself. Devel-
2441 opment is the epitome of all social duties. Certainly, it is the proper function of authority to arbitrate, in the name of the common good, between various particular interests; but it should make accessible to each what is needed to lead a truly human life: food, clothing, health, work, education and culture, suitable information, the right to establish a family, and so on.[28]

2304 **1909** Finally, the common good requires *peace,* that is, the stability and security of a just order. It presupposes that authority should ensure by morally acceptable means the *security* of society and its members. It is the
2310 basis of the right to legitimate personal and collective defense.

1910 Each human community possesses a common good which permits it to be recognized as such; it is in the *political community* that its most complete realiza-
2244 tion is found. It is the role of the state to defend and promote the common good of civil society, its citizens, and intermediate bodies.

1911 Human interdependence is increasing and gradually spreading throughout the world. The unity of the human family, embracing people who enjoy equal nat-
2438 ural dignity, implies a *universal common good.* This good calls for an organization of the community of na-

---

27 *GS* 26 § 2.   28 Cf. *GS* 26 § 2.

tions able to "provide for the different needs of men; this will involve the sphere of social life to which belong questions of food, hygiene, education, ... and certain situations arising here and there, as for example ... alleviating the miseries of refugees dispersed throughout the world, and assisting migrants and their families."[29]

1912 The common good is always oriented towards the progress of persons: "The order of things must be subordinate to the order of persons, and not the other *1881* way around."[30] This order is founded on truth, built up in justice, and animated by love.

III. RESPONSIBILITY AND PARTICIPATION

1913 "Participation" is the voluntary and generous engagement of a person in social interchange. It is necessary that all participate, each according to his position and role, in promoting the common good. This obligation is inherent in the dignity of the human person.

1914 Participation is achieved first of all by taking charge of the areas for which one assumes *personal responsibility:* by the care taken for the education of his *1734* family, by conscientious work, and so forth, man participates in the good of others and of society.[31]

1915 As far as possible citizens should take an active *2239* part in *public life.* The manner of this participation may vary from one country or culture to another. "One must pay tribute to those nations whose systems permit the largest possible number of the citizens to take part in public life in a climate of genuine freedom."[32]

1916 As with any ethical obligation, the participation of all in realizing the common good calls for a continually renewed *conversion* of the social partners. Fraud *1888* and other subterfuges, by which some people evade the constraints of the law and the prescriptions of societal obligation, must be firmly condemned because they are incompatible with the requirements of justice. Much *2409*

---

29 *GS* 84 § 2. 30 *GS* 26 § 3. 31 Cf. *CA* 43. 32 *GS* 31 § 3.

care should be taken to promote institutions that improve the conditions of human life.[33]

1917 It is incumbent on those who exercise authority
to strengthen the values that inspire the confidence of
the members of the group and encourage them to put
themselves at the service of others. Participation begins
with education and culture. "One is entitled to think
that the future of humanity is in the hands of those who
are capable of providing the generations to come with
1818 reasons for life and optimism."[34]

IN BRIEF

1918 "There is no authority except from God, and
those authorities that exist have been instituted
by God" (*Rom* 13:1).

1919 Every human community needs an authority in
order to endure and develop.

1920 "The political community and public authority
are based on human nature and therefore . . . belong to an order established by God" (*GS* 74 §
3).

1921 Authority is exercised legitimately if it is committed to the common good of society. To attain this it must employ morally acceptable
means.

1922 The diversity of political regimes is legitimate,
provided they contribute to the good of the community.

1923 Political authority must be exercised within the
limits of the moral order and must guarantee the
conditions for the exercise of freedom.

1924 The common good comprises "the sum total of
social conditions which allow people, either as
groups or as individuals, to reach their fulfillment more fully and more easily" (*GS* 26 § 1).

---

33 Cf. *GS* 30 § 1.   34 *GS* 31 § 3.

1925 The common good consists of three essential elements: respect for and promotion of the fundamental rights of the person; prosperity, or the development of the spiritual and temporal goods of society; the peace and security of the group and of its members.

1926 The dignity of the human person requires the pursuit of the common good. Everyone should be concerned to create and support institutions that improve the conditions of human life.

1927 It is the role of the state to defend and promote the common good of civil society. The common good of the whole human family calls for an organization of society on the international level.

ARTICLE 3
SOCIAL JUSTICE

1928 Society ensures social justice when it provides the conditions that allow associations or individuals to obtain what is their due, according to their nature and their vocation. Social justice is linked to the common good and the exercise of authority. *2832*

I. RESPECT FOR THE HUMAN PERSON

1929 Social justice can be obtained only in respecting *1881* the transcendent dignity of man. The person represents the ultimate end of society, which is ordered to him:

> What is at stake is the dignity of the human person, whose defense and promotion have been entrusted to us by the Creator, and to whom the men and women at every moment of history are strictly and responsibly in debt.[35]

1930 Respect for the human person entails respect for the rights that flow from his dignity as a creature. These rights are prior to society and must be recognized by it. *1700* They are the basis of the moral legitimacy of every au-

---

35 John Paul II, *SRS* 47.

1902 thority: by flouting them, or refusing to recognize them in its positive legislation, a society undermines its own moral legitimacy.[36] If it does not respect them, authority can rely only on force or violence to obtain obedience from its subjects. It is the Church's role to remind men of good will of these rights and to distinguish them from unwarranted or false claims.

1931 Respect for the human person proceeds by way
2212 of respect for the principle that "everyone should look upon his neighbor (without any exception) as 'another self,' above all bearing in mind his life and the means necessary for living it with dignity."[37] No legislation could by itself do away with the fears, prejudices, and attitudes of pride and selfishness which obstruct the es-
1825 tablishment of truly fraternal societies. Such behavior will cease only through the charity that finds in every man a "neighbor," a brother.

1932 The duty of making oneself a neighbor to others and actively serving them becomes even more urgent when it involves the disadvantaged, in whatever area this may be. "As you did it to one of the least of these
2449 my brethren, you did it to me."[38]

1933 This same duty extends to those who think or act differently from us. The teaching of Christ goes so far as to require the forgiveness of offenses. He extends the commandment of love, which is that of the New Law, to all enemies.[39] Liberation in the spirit of the
2303 Gospel is incompatible with hatred of one's enemy as a person, but not with hatred of the evil that he does as an enemy.

II.   EQUALITY AND DIFFERENCES AMONG MEN
1934 Created in the image of the one God and equally endowed with rational souls, all men have the same nature and the same origin. Redeemed by the sacrifice of Christ, all are called to participate in the same divine
225 beatitude: all therefore enjoy an equal dignity.

---

36 Cf. John XXIII, *PT* 65.   37 *GS* 27 § 1.   38 *Mt* 25:40.   39 Cf. *Mt* 5:43–44.

1935 The equality of men rests essentially on their dignity as persons and the rights that flow from it: *357*

> Every form of social or cultural discrimination in fundamental personal rights on the grounds of sex, race, color, social conditions, language, or religion must be curbed and eradicated as incompatible with God's design.[40]

1936 On coming into the world, man is not equipped   *1879* with everything he needs for developing his bodily and spiritual life. He needs others. Differences appear tied to age, physical abilities, intellectual or moral aptitudes, the benefits derived from social commerce, and the distribution of wealth.[41] The "talents" are not distributed equally.[42]

1937 These differences belong to God's plan, who   *340* wills that each receive what he needs from others, and that those endowed with particular "talents" share the   *791* benefits with those who need them. These differences   *1202* encourage and often oblige persons to practice generosity, kindness, and sharing of goods; they foster the mutual enrichment of cultures:

> I distribute the virtues quite diversely; I do not give all of them to each person, but some to one, some to others. . . . I shall give principally charity to one; justice to another; humility to this one, a living faith to that one. . . . And so I have given many gifts and graces, both spiritual and temporal, with such diversity that I have not given everything to one single person, so that you may be constrained to practice charity towards one another. . . . I have willed that one should need another and that all should be my ministers in distributing the graces and gifts they have received from me.[43]

1938 There exist also *sinful inequalities* that affect   *2437* millions of men and women. These are in open contradiction of the Gospel:

> Their equal dignity as persons demands that we strive for fairer and more humane conditions. Ex-   *2317*

---

40 *GS* 29 § 2.   41 Cf. *GS* 29 § 2.   42 Cf. *Mt* 25:14–30; *Lk* 19:11–27.   43 St. Catherine of Siena, *Dial.* I, 7.

cessive economic and social disparity between individuals and peoples of the one human race is a
source of scandal and militates against social justice, equity, human dignity, as well as social and international peace.[44]

III.   HUMAN SOLIDARITY

2213 **1939** The principle of solidarity, also articulated in
terms of "friendship" or "social charity," is a direct demand of human and Christian brotherhood.[45]

360

An error, "today abundantly widespread, is disregard for the law of human solidarity and charity, dictated and imposed both by our common
origin and by the equality in rational nature of
all men, whatever nation they belong to. This law
is sealed by the sacrifice of redemption offered
by Jesus Christ on the altar of the Cross to his
heavenly Father, on behalf of sinful humanity."[46]

2402 **1940** Solidarity is manifested in the first place by the
distribution of goods and remuneration for work. It
also presupposes the effort for a more just social order
where tensions are better able to be reduced and conflicts more readily settled by negotiation.

2317 **1941** Socio-economic problems can be resolved only
with the help of all the forms of solidarity: solidarity
of the poor among themselves, between rich and poor,
of workers among themselves, between employers and
employees in a business, solidarity among nations
and peoples. International solidarity is a requirement of
the moral order; world peace depends in part upon
this.

1942 The virtue of solidarity goes beyond material
goods. In spreading the spiritual goods of the faith, the
1887 Church has promoted, and often opened new paths for,
the development of temporal goods as well. And so
throughout the centuries has the Lord's saying been ver-

---

44 GS 29 § 3.   45 Cf. John Paul II, *SRS* 38–40; *CA* 10.   46 Pius XII, *Summi
pontificatus*, October 20, 1939; AAS 31 (1939) 423 ff.

ified: "Seek first his kingdom and his righteousness, and
all these things shall be yours as well":[47]   2632

> For two thousand years this sentiment has lived and
> endured in the soul of the Church, impelling souls
> then and now to the heroic charity of monastic
> farmers, liberators of slaves, healers of the sick, and
> messengers of faith, civilization, and science to all
> generations and all peoples for the sake of creating
> the social conditions capable of offering to every-
> one possible a life worthy of man and of a Christ-
> ian.[48]

IN BRIEF

1943   Society ensures social justice by providing the
conditions that allow associations and individuals to obtain their due.

1944   Respect for the human person considers the
other "another self." It presupposes respect for
the fundamental rights that flow from the dignity intrinsic of the person.

1945   The equality of men concerns their dignity as
persons and the rights that flow from it.

1946   The differences among persons belong to God's
plan, who wills that we should need one another.
These differences should encourage charity.

1947   The equal dignity of human persons requires the
effort to reduce excessive social and economic
inequalities. It gives urgency to the elimination
of sinful inequalities.

1948   Solidarity is an eminently Christian virtue. It
practices the sharing of spiritual goods even
more than material ones.

---

47 *Mt* 6:33.   48 Pius XII, Discourse, June 1, 1941.

CHAPTER THREE
GOD'S SALVATION: LAW AND GRACE

1949 Called to beatitude but wounded by sin, man stands in need of salvation from God. Divine help comes to him in Christ through the law that guides him and the grace that sustains him:

> Work out your own salvation with fear and trembling; for God is at work in you, both to will and to work for his good pleasure.[1]

ARTICLE 1
THE MORAL LAW

1950 The moral law is the work of divine Wisdom. Its biblical meaning can be defined as fatherly instruction,
53 God's pedagogy. It prescribes for man the ways, the rules of conduct that lead to the promised beatitude; it
1719 proscribes the ways of evil which turn him away from God and his love. It is at once firm in its precepts and, in its promises, worthy of love.

1951 Law is a rule of conduct enacted by competent authority for the sake of the common good. The moral law presupposes the rational order, established among creatures for their good and to serve their final end, by the power, wisdom, and goodness of the Creator. All law finds its first and ultimate truth in the eternal law.
295 Law is declared and established by reason as a partici-
306 pation in the providence of the living God, Creator and Redeemer of all. "Such an ordinance of reason is what one calls law."[2]

> Alone among all animate beings, man can boast of having been counted worthy to receive a law from God: as an animal endowed with reason, capable of understanding and discernment, he is to govern his
301 conduct by using his freedom and reason, in obedience to the One who has entrusted everything to him.[3]

---

1 *Phil* 2:12–13.   2 Leo XIII, *Libertas præstantissimum:* AAS 20 (1887/88), 597; cf. St. Thomas Aquinas, *STh* I-II, 90, 1.   3 Cf. Tertullian, *Adv. Marc,* 2, 4: PL 2, 288–289.

1952 There are different expressions of the moral law, all of them interrelated: eternal law—the source, in God, of all law; natural law; revealed law, comprising the Old Law and the New Law, or Law of the Gospel; finally, civil and ecclesiastical laws.

1953 The moral law finds its fullness and its unity in Christ. Jesus Christ is in person the way of perfection. He is the end of the law, for only he teaches and bestows the justice of God: "For Christ is the end of the law, that every one who has faith may be justified."[4]   *578*

I.   THE NATURAL MORAL LAW

1954 Man participates in the wisdom and goodness of the Creator who gives him mastery over his acts and the ability to govern himself with a view to the true and the good. The natural law expresses the original moral sense which enables man to discern by reason the good and the evil, the truth and the lie: *307*
1776

> The natural law is written and engraved in the soul of each and every man, because it is human reason ordaining him to do good and forbidding him to sin . . . But this command of human reason would not have the force of law if it were not the voice and interpreter of a higher reason to which our spirit and our freedom must be submitted.[5]

1955 The "divine and natural" law[6] shows man the way to follow so as to practice the good and attain his end. The natural law states the first and essential precepts which govern the moral life. It hinges upon the desire for God and submission to him, who is the source and judge of all that is good, as well as upon the sense that the other is one's equal. Its principal precepts are expressed in the Decalogue. This law is called "natural," not in reference to the nature of irrational beings, but because reason which decrees it properly belongs to human nature: *1787*
396
2070

> Where then are these rules written, if not in the book of that light we call the truth? In it is written

---

4 *Rom* 10:4.   5 Leo XIII, *Libertas præstantissimum,* 597.   6 GS 89 § 1.

every just law; from it the law passes into the heart of the man who does justice, not that it migrates into it, but that it places its imprint on it, like a seal on a ring that passes onto wax, without leaving the ring.[7]

The natural law is nothing other than the light of understanding placed in us by God; through it we know what we must do and what we must avoid. God has given this light or law at the creation.[8]

1956 The natural law, present in the heart of each man and established by reason, is universal in its precepts
2261 and its authority extends to all men. It expresses the dignity of the person and determines the basis for his fundamental rights and duties:

For there is a true law: right reason. It is in conformity with nature, is diffused among all men, and is immutable and eternal; its orders summon to duty; its prohibitions turn away from offense. . . . To replace it with a contrary law is a sacrilege; failure to apply even one of its provisions is forbidden; no one can abrogate it entirely.[9]

1957 Application of the natural law varies greatly; it can demand reflection that takes account of various conditions of life according to places, times, and circumstances. Nevertheless, in the diversity of cultures, the natural law remains as a rule that binds men among themselves and imposes on them, beyond the inevitable differences, common principles.

2072 **1958** The natural law is *immutable* and permanent throughout the variations of history;[10] it subsists under the flux of ideas and customs and supports their progress. The rules that express it remain substantially valid. Even when it is rejected in its very principles, it cannot be destroyed or removed from the heart of man. It always rises again in the life of individuals and societies:

---

7 St. Augustine, *De Trin.* 14, 15, 21: PL 42, 1052.   8 St. Thomas Aquinas, *Dec. præc.* I.   9 Cicero, *Rep.* III, 22, 33.   10 Cf. *GS* 10.

> Theft is surely punished by your law, O Lord, and
> by the law that is written in the human heart, the
> law that iniquity itself does not efface.[11]

1959   The natural law, the Creator's very good work,
provides the solid foundation on which man can build
the structure of moral rules to guide his choices. It also
provides the indispensable moral foundation for building the human community. Finally, it provides the nec-   *1879*
essary basis for the civil law with which it is connected,
whether by a reflection that draws conclusions from its
principles, or by additions of a positive and juridical nature.

1960   The precepts of natural law are not perceived by
everyone clearly and immediately. In the present situation sinful man needs grace and revelation so moral and   *2071*
religious truths may be known "by everyone with facil-   *37*
ity, with firm certainty and with no admixture of error."[12] The natural law provides revealed law and grace
with a foundation prepared by God and in accordance
with the work of the Spirit.

II.   THE OLD LAW

1961   God, our Creator and Redeemer, chose Israel for   *62*
himself to be his people and revealed his Law to them,
thus preparing for the coming of Christ. The Law of
Moses expresses many truths naturally accessible to reason. These are stated and authenticated within the
covenant of salvation.

1962   The Old Law is the first stage of revealed Law.
Its moral prescriptions are summed up in the Ten Commandments. The precepts of the Decalogue lay the   *2058*
foundations for the vocation of man fashioned in the
image of God; they prohibit what is contrary to the love
of God and neighbor and prescribe what is essential to
it. The Decalogue is a light offered to the conscience of
every man to make God's call and ways known to him
and to protect him against evil:

---

11 St. Augustine, *Conf.* 2, 4, 9: PL 32, 678.   12 Pius XII, *Humani generis*: DS
3876; cf. *Dei Filius* 2: DS 3005.

God wrote on the tables of the Law what men did not read in their hearts.[13]

1963 According to Christian tradition, the Law is holy, spiritual, and good,[14] yet still imperfect. Like a tutor[15] it shows what must be done, but does not of itself give the strength, the grace of the Spirit, to fulfill it. Because of sin, which it cannot remove, it remains a law of bondage. According to St. Paul, its special function is to denounce and *disclose sin,* which constitutes a "law of concupiscence" in the human heart.[16] However, the Law remains the first stage on the way to the kingdom. It prepares and disposes the chosen people and each Christian for conversion and faith in the Savior God. It provides a teaching which endures for ever, like the Word of God.

1610
2542
2515

1964 The Old Law is a *preparation for the Gospel.* "The Law is a pedagogy and a prophecy of things to come."[17] It prophesies and presages the work of liberation from sin which will be fulfilled in Christ: it provides the New Testament with images, "types," and symbols for expressing the life according to the Spirit. Finally, the Law is completed by the teaching of the sapiential books and the prophets which set its course toward the New Covenant and the Kingdom of heaven.

122

There were ... under the regimen of the Old Covenant, people who possessed the charity and grace of the Holy Spirit and longed above all for the spiritual and eternal promises by which they were associated with the New Law. Conversely, there exist carnal men under the New Covenant, still distanced from the perfection of the New Law: the fear of punishment and certain temporal promises have been necessary, even under the New Covenant, to incite them to virtuous works. In any case, even though the Old Law prescribed charity, it did not give the Holy Spirit, through whom "God's charity has been poured into our hearts."[18]

1828

---

13 St. Augustine, *En. in Ps.* 57, 1: PL 36, 673.   14 Cf. *Rom* 7:12, 14, 16.
15 Cf. *Gal* 3:24.   16 Cf. *Rom* 7.   17 St. Irenæus, *Adv. haeres.* 4, 15, 1: PG 7/1, 1012.   18 St. Thomas Aquinas, *STh* I-II, 107, 1 *ad* 2; cf. *Rom* 5:5.

III.   THE NEW LAW OR THE LAW OF THE GOSPEL

1965 The New Law or the Law of the Gospel is the perfection here on earth of the divine law, natural and revealed. It is the work of Christ and is expressed particularly in the Sermon on the Mount. It is also the work of the Holy Spirit and through him it becomes the interior law of charity: "I will establish a New Covenant with the house of Israel. . . . I will put my laws into their minds, and write them on their hearts, and I will be their God, and they shall be my people."[19]   *459   581   715*

1966 The New Law is the *grace of the Holy Spirit* given to the faithful through faith in Christ. It works through charity; it uses the Sermon on the Mount to teach us what must be done and makes use of the sacraments to give us the grace to do it: *1999*

> If anyone should meditate with devotion and perspicacity on the sermon our Lord gave on the mount, as we read in the Gospel of Saint Matthew, he will doubtless find there . . . the perfect way of the Christian life. . . . This sermon contains . . . all the precepts needed to shape one's life.[20]

1967 The Law of the Gospel "fulfills," refines, surpasses, and leads the Old Law to its perfection.[21] In the Beatitudes, the New Law *fulfills the divine promises* by elevating and orienting them toward the "kingdom of heaven." It is addressed to those open to accepting this new hope with faith—the poor, the humble, the afflicted, the pure of heart, those persecuted on account of Christ—and so marks out the surprising ways of the Kingdom.   *577*

1968 The Law of the Gospel *fulfills the commandments* of the Law. The Lord's Sermon on the Mount, far from abolishing or devaluing the moral prescriptions of the Old Law, releases their hidden potential and has new demands arise from them: it reveals their entire divine and human truth. It does not add new external precepts, but proceeds to reform the heart, the root of hu-   *129*

---

19 *Heb* 8:8, 10; cf. *Jer* 31:31–34.   20 St. Augustine, *De serm. Dom.* 1, 1: PL 34, 1229–1230.   21 Cf. *Mt* 5:17–19.

582   man acts, where man chooses between the pure and the impure,[22] where faith, hope, and charity are formed and with them the other virtues. The Gospel thus brings the Law to its fullness through imitation of the perfection of the heavenly Father, through forgiveness of enemies and prayer for persecutors, in emulation of the divine generosity.[23]

1434   **1969**   The New Law *practices the acts of religion:* almsgiving, prayer and fasting, directing them to the "Father who sees in secret," in contrast with the desire to "be seen by men."[24] Its prayer is the Our Father.[25]

1970   The Law of the Gospel requires us to make the decisive choice between "the two ways" and to put into

1696   practice the words of the Lord.[26] It is summed up in the

1789   *Golden Rule,* "Whatever you wish that men would do to you, do so to them; this is the law and the prophets."[27]

1823   The entire Law of the Gospel is contained in the *"new commandment"* of Jesus, to love one another as he has loved us.[28]

1971   To the Lord's Sermon on the Mount it is fitting to add the *moral catechesis of the apostolic teachings,* such as *Romans* 12–15, *1 Corinthians* 12–13, *Colossians* 3–4, *Ephesians* 4–5, etc. This doctrine hands on the Lord's teaching with the authority of the apostles, particularly in the presentation of the virtues that flow from faith in Christ and are animated by charity, the principal gift of the Holy Spirit. "Let charity be genuine. . . . Love one another with brotherly affection. . . . Rejoice in your hope, be patient in tribulation, be constant in prayer. Contribute to the needs of the saints, practice

1789   hospitality."[29] This catechesis also teaches us to deal with cases of conscience in the light of our relationship to Christ and to the Church.[30]

---

22 Cf. *Mt* 15:18–19.   23 Cf. *Mt* 5:44, 48.   24 Cf. *Mt* 6:1–6; 16–18.   25 Cf. *Mt* 6:9–13; *Lk* 11:2–4.   26 Cf. *Mt* 7:13–14, 21–27.   27 *Mt* 7:12; cf. *Lk* 6:31. 28 Cf. *Jn* 15:12; 13:34.   29 *Rom* 12:9–13.   30 Cf. *Rom* 14; *1 Cor* 5–10.

1972 The New Law is called a *law of love* because it 782
makes us act out of the love infused by the Holy Spirit,
rather than from fear; a *law of grace,* because it confers
the strength of grace to act, by means of faith and the
sacraments; a *law of freedom,* because it sets us free
from the ritual and juridical observances of the Old
Law, inclines us to act spontaneously by the prompting
of charity and, finally, lets us pass from the condition of 1828
a servant who "does not know what his master is doing" to that of a friend of Christ—"For all that I have
heard from my Father I have made known to you"—or
even to the status of son and heir.[31]

1973 Besides its precepts, the New Law also includes 2053
the *evangelical counsels.* The traditional distinction between God's commandments and the evangelical counsels is drawn in relation to charity, the perfection of
Christian life. The precepts are intended to remove 915
whatever is incompatible with charity. The aim of the
counsels is to remove whatever might hinder the development of charity, even if it is not contrary to it.[32]

1974 The evangelical counsels manifest the living fullness of charity, which is never satisfied with not giving
more. They attest its vitality and call forth our spiritual
readiness. The perfection of the New Law consists essentially in the precepts of love of God and neighbor. 2013
The counsels point out the more direct ways, the read-
ier means, and are to be practiced in keeping with the
vocation of each:

> [God] does not want each person to keep all the
> counsels, but only those appropriate to the diversity
> of persons, times, opportunities, and strengths, as
> charity requires; for it is charity, as queen of all
> virtues, all commandments, all counsels, and, in
> short, of all laws and all Christian actions, that
> gives to all of them their rank, order, time, and
> value.[33]

---

31 *Jn* 15:15; cf. *Jas* 1:25; 2:12; *Gal* 4:1–7. 21–31; *Rom* 8:15.   32 Cf. St. Thomas
Aquinas, *STh* II-II, 184, 3.   33 St. Francis de Sales, *Love of God* 8, 6.

IN BRIEF

1975 According to Scripture the Law is a fatherly instruction by God which prescribes for man the ways that lead to the promised beatitude, and proscribes the ways of evil.

1976 "Law is an ordinance of reason for the common good, promulgated by the one who is in charge of the community" (St. Thomas Aquinas, *STh* I-II, 90, 4).

1977 Christ is the end of the law (cf. *Rom* 10:4); only he teaches and bestows the justice of God.

1978 The natural law is a participation in God's wisdom and goodness by man formed in the image of his Creator. It expresses the dignity of the human person and forms the basis of his fundamental rights and duties.

1979 The natural law is immutable, permanent throughout history. The rules that express it remain substantially valid. It is a necessary foundation for the erection of moral rules and civil law.

1980 The Old Law is the first stage of revealed law. Its moral prescriptions are summed up in the Ten Commandments.

1981 The Law of Moses contains many truths naturally accessible to reason. God has revealed them because men did not read them in their hearts.

1982 The Old Law is a preparation for the Gospel.

1983 The New Law is the grace of the Holy Spirit received by faith in Christ, operating through charity. It finds expression above all in the Lord's Sermon on the Mount and uses the sacraments to communicate grace to us.

1984 The Law of the Gospel fulfills and surpasses the Old Law and brings it to perfection: its promises, through the Beatitudes of the Kingdom of heaven; its commandments, by reforming the heart, the root of human acts.

1985 The New Law is a law of love, a law of grace, a law of freedom.

1986 Besides its precepts the New Law includes the evangelical counsels. "The Church's holiness is fostered in a special way by the manifold counsels which the Lord proposes to his disciples in the Gospel" (*LG* 42 § 2).

ARTICLE 2
GRACE AND JUSTIFICATION

I.   JUSTIFICATION

1987 The grace of the Holy Spirit has the power to justify us, that is, to cleanse us from our sins and to communicate to us "the righteousness of God through 734 faith in Jesus Christ" and through Baptism:[34]

> But if we have died with Christ, we believe that we shall also live with him. For we know that Christ being raised from the dead will never die again; death no longer has dominion over him. The death he died he died to sin, once for all, but the life he lives he lives to God. So you also must consider yourselves as dead to sin and alive to God in Christ Jesus.[35]

1988 Through the power of the Holy Spirit we take part in Christ's Passion by dying to sin, and in his Resurrection by being born to a new life; we are members 654 of his Body which is the Church, branches grafted onto the vine which is himself:[36]

> [God] gave himself to us through his Spirit. By the participation of the Spirit, we become communi- 460 cants in the divine nature. . . . For this reason, those in whom the Spirit dwells are divinized.[37]

1989 The first work of the grace of the Holy Spirit is *conversion*, effecting justification in accordance with Je-

---

34 *Rom* 3:22; cf. 6:3–4.   35 *Rom* 6:8–11.   36 Cf. *1 Cor* 12; *Jn* 15:1–4.   37 St. Athanasius, *Ep. Serap.* 1, 24: PG 26, 585 and 588.

1427 sus' proclamation at the beginning of the Gospel: "Repent, for the kingdom of heaven is at hand."[38] Moved by grace, man turns toward God and away from sin, thus accepting forgiveness and righteousness from on high. "Justification is not only the remission of sins, but also the sanctification and renewal of the interior man."[39]

1990 Justification *detaches man from sin* which contradicts the love of God, and purifies his heart of sin. Justification follows upon God's merciful initiative of
1446 offering forgiveness. It reconciles man with God. It frees
1733 from the enslavement to sin, and it heals.

1991 Justification is at the same time *the acceptance of God's righteousness* through faith in Jesus Christ. Righteousness (or "justice") here means the rectitude of divine love. With justification, faith, hope, and charity
1812 are poured into our hearts, and obedience to the divine will is granted us.

617 **1992** Justification has been *merited for us by the Passion of Christ* who offered himself on the cross as a living victim, holy and pleasing to God, and whose blood has become the instrument of atonement for the sins of all men. Justification is conferred in Baptism, the sacra-
1266 ment of faith. It conforms us to the righteousness of God, who makes us inwardly just by the power of his
294 mercy. Its purpose is the glory of God and of Christ, and the gift of eternal life:[40]

> But now the righteousness of God has been manifested apart from law, although the law and the prophets bear witness to it, the righteousness of God through faith in Jesus Christ for all who believe. For there is no distinction: since all have sinned and fall short of the glory of God, they are justified by his grace as a gift, through the redemption which is in Christ Jesus, whom God put forward as an expiation by his blood, to be received by faith. This was to show God's righteousness, be-

---

38 *Mt* 4:17.   39 Council of Trent (1547): DS 1528.   40 Cf. Council of Trent (1547): DS 1529.

cause in his divine forbearance he had passed over former sins; it was to prove at the present time that he himself is righteous and that he justifies him who has faith in Jesus.[41]

1993 Justification establishes *cooperation between* 2008 *God's grace and man's freedom.* On man's part it is expressed by the assent of faith to the Word of God, which invites him to conversion, and in the cooperation of charity with the prompting of the Holy Spirit who precedes and preserves his assent:

> When God touches man's heart through the illumi- 2068
> nation of the Holy Spirit, man himself is not inactive while receiving that inspiration, since he could reject it; and yet, without God's grace, he cannot by his own free will move himself toward justice in God's sight.[42]

1994 Justification is the *most excellent work of God's love* made manifest in Christ Jesus and granted by the Holy Spirit. It is the opinion of St. Augustine that "the justification of the wicked is a greater work than the creation of heaven and earth," because "heaven and 312 earth will pass away but the salvation and justification of the elect . . . will not pass away."[43] He holds also that the justification of sinners surpasses the creation of the 412 angels in justice, in that it bears witness to a greater mercy.

1995 The Holy Spirit is the master of the interior life. 741 By giving birth to the "inner man,"[44] justification entails the *sanctification* of his whole being:

> Just as you once yielded your members to impurity and to greater and greater iniquity, so now yield your members to righteousness for sanctification. . . . But now that you have been set free from sin and have become slaves of God, the return you get is sanctification and its end, eternal life.[45]

---

41 *Rom* 3:21–26.   42 Council of Trent (1547): DS 1525.   43 St. Augustine, *In Jo. ev.* 72, 3: PL 35, 1823.   44 Cf. *Rom* 7:22; *Eph* 3:16.   45 *Rom* 6:19, 22.

II.   GRACE

1996   Our justification comes from the grace of God. Grace is *favor,* the *free and undeserved help* that God gives us to respond to his call to become children of *153* God, adoptive sons, partakers of the divine nature and of eternal life.[46]

375 **1997**   Grace is a *participation in the life of God.* It in-
260 troduces us into the intimacy of Trinitarian life: by Baptism the Christian participates in the grace of Christ, the Head of his Body. As an "adopted son" he can henceforth call God "Father," in union with the only Son. He receives the life of the Spirit who breathes charity into him and who forms the Church.

1719 **1998**   This vocation to eternal life is *supernatural.* It depends entirely on God's gratuitous initiative, for he alone can reveal and give himself. It surpasses the power of human intellect and will, as that of every other creature.[47]

1999   The grace of Christ is the gratuitous gift that God makes to us of his own life, infused by the Holy *1966* Spirit into our soul to heal it of sin and to sanctify it. It is the *sanctifying* or *deifying grace* received in Baptism. It is in us the source of the work of sanctification:[48]

> Therefore if any one is in Christ, he is a new creation; the old has passed away, behold, the new has come. All this is from God, who through Christ reconciled us to himself.[49]

2000   Sanctifying grace is an habitual gift, a stable and supernatural disposition that perfects the soul itself to enable it to live with God, to act by his love. *Habitual grace,* the permanent disposition to live and act in keeping with God's call, is distinguished from *actual graces* which refer to God's interventions, whether at the beginning of conversion or in the course of the work of sanctification.

---

46 Cf. *Jn* 1:12–18; 17:3; *Rom* 8:14–17; *2 Pet* 1:3–4.   47 Cf. *1 Cor* 2:7–9.
48 Cf. *Jn* 4:14; 7:38–39.   49 *2 Cor* 5:17–18.

2001 The *preparation of man* for the reception of grace is already a work of grace. This latter is needed to arouse and sustain our collaboration in justification through faith, and in sanctification through charity. God brings to completion in us what he has begun, "since he who completes his work by cooperating with our will began by working so that we might will it:"[50]

> Indeed we also work, but we are only collaborating with God who works, for his mercy has gone before us. It has gone before us so that we may be healed, and follows us so that once healed, we may be given life; it goes before us so that we may be called, and follows us so that we may be glorified; it goes before us so that we may live devoutly, and follows us so that we may always live with God: for without him we can do nothing.[51]

2002 God's free initiative demands *man's free response,* for God has created man in his image by conferring on him, along with freedom, the power to know him and love him. The soul only enters freely into the communion of love. God immediately touches and directly moves the heart of man. He has placed in man a longing for truth and goodness that only he can satisfy. The promises of "eternal life" respond, beyond all hope, to this desire:

> If at the end of your very good works . . . , you rested on the seventh day, it was to foretell by the voice of your book that at the end of our works, which are indeed "very good" since you have given them to us, we shall also rest in you on the sabbath of eternal life.[52]

2003 Grace is first and foremost the gift of the Spirit who justifies and sanctifies us. But grace also includes the gifts that the Spirit grants us to associate us with his work, to enable us to collaborate in the salvation of others and in the growth of the Body of Christ, the Church. There are *sacramental graces,* gifts proper to the different sacraments. There are furthermore *special graces,*

---

50 St. Augustine, *De gratia et libero arbitrio,* 17: PL 44, 901.   51 St. Augustine, *De natura et gratia,* 31: PL 44, 264.   52 St. Augustine, *Conf.* 13, 36, 51: PL 32, 868; cf. *Gen* 1:31.

also called *charisms* after the Greek term used by St. Paul and meaning "favor," "gratuitous gift," "benefit."[53] Whatever their character—sometimes it is extraordinary, such as the gift of miracles or of tongues—charisms are oriented toward sanctifying grace and are intended for the common good of the Church. They are at the service of charity which builds up the Church.[54]

799–801

2004   Among the special graces ought to be mentioned the *graces of state* that accompany the exercise of the responsibilities of the Christian life and of the ministries within the Church:

> Having gifts that differ according to the grace given to us, let us use them: if prophecy, in proportion to our faith; if service, in our serving; he who teaches, in his teaching; he who exhorts, in his exhortation; he who contributes, in liberality; he who gives aid, with zeal; he who does acts of mercy, with cheerfulness.[55]

2005   Since it belongs to the supernatural order, grace *escapes our experience* and cannot be known except by faith. We cannot therefore rely on our feelings or our works to conclude that we are justified and saved.[56] However, according to the Lord's words—"Thus you will know them by their fruits"[57]—reflection on God's blessings in our life and in the lives of the saints offers us a guarantee that grace is at work in us and spurs us on to an ever greater faith and an attitude of trustful poverty.

> A pleasing illustration of this attitude is found in the reply of St. Joan of Arc to a question posed as a trap by her ecclesiastical judges: "Asked if she knew that she was in God's grace, she replied: 'If I am not, may it please God to put me in it; if I am, may it please God to keep me there.'"[58]

---

53 Cf. *LG* 12.   54 Cf. *1 Cor* 12.   55 *Rom* 12:6–8.   56 Cf. Council of Trent (1547): DS 1533–1534.   57 *Mt* 7:20.   58 Acts of the trial of St. Joan of Arc.

III.   MERIT

You are glorified in the assembly of your Holy
Ones, for in crowning their merits you are crowning your own gifts.[59]

2006 The term "merit" refers in general to the *recom-*   *1723*
pense owed by a community or a society for the action
of one of its members, experienced either as beneficial
or harmful, deserving reward or punishment. Merit is
relative to the virtue of justice, in conformity with the   *1807*
principle of equality which governs it.

2007 With regard to God, there is no strict right to
any merit on the part of man. Between God and us there   *42*
is an immeasurable inequality, for we have received
everything from him, our Creator.

2008 The merit of man before God in the Christian
life arises from the fact that *God has freely chosen to as-*
sociate man with the work of his grace. The fatherly ac-   *306*
tion of God is first on his own initiative, and then follows man's free acting through his collaboration, so that   *155*
the merit of good works is to be attributed in the first   *970*
place to the grace of God, then to the faithful. Man's
merit, moreover, itself is due to God, for his good actions proceed in Christ, from the predispositions and assistance given by the Holy Spirit.

2009 Filial adoption, in making us partakers by grace
in the divine nature, can bestow *true merit* on us as a result of God's gratuitous justice. This is our right by
grace, the full right of love, making us "co-heirs" with
Christ and worthy of obtaining "the promised inheritance of eternal life."[60] The merits of our good works
are gifts of the divine goodness.[61] "Grace has gone before us; now we are given what is due. . . . Our merits
are God's gifts."[62]   *604*

2010 Since the initiative belongs to God in the order   *1998*

---

59 *Roman Missal*, Prefatio I de Sanctis; *Qui in Sanctorum concilio celebraris, et
eorum coronando merita tua dona coronas,* citing the "Doctor of grace," St.
Augustine, *En. in Ps.* 102, 7: PL 37, 1321–1322.   60 Council of Trent (1547): DS
1546.   61 Cf. Council of Trent (1547): DS 1548.   62 St. Augustine, *Sermo* 298,
4–5: PL 38, 1367.

of grace, *no one can merit the initial grace* of forgiveness and justification, at the beginning of conversion. Moved by the Holy Spirit and by charity, *we can
then merit* for ourselves and for others the graces
needed for our sanctification, for the increase of grace
and charity, and for the attainment of eternal life.
Even temporal goods like health and friendship can
be merited in accordance with God's wisdom. These
graces and goods are the object of Christian prayer.
Prayer attends to the grace we need for meritorious actions.

492   **2011**   *The charity of Christ is the source in us of all our
merits* before God. Grace, by uniting us to Christ in active love, ensures the supernatural quality of our acts
and consequently their merit before God and before
men. The saints have always had a lively awareness that
their merits were pure grace.

> After earth's exile, I hope to go and enjoy you in the
> fatherland, but I do not want to lay up merits for
> heaven. I want to work for your *love alone.* . . . In
> the evening of this life, I shall appear before you
> with empty hands, for I do not ask you, Lord, to
1460   count my works. All our justice is blemished in
> your eyes. I wish, then, to be clothed in your own
> *justice* and to receive from your *love* the eternal
> possession of *yourself.*[63]

IV.   CHRISTIAN HOLINESS

2012   "We know that in everything God works for
good with those who love him . . . For those whom he
459   foreknew he also predestined to be conformed to the
image of his Son, in order that he might be the first-
born among many brethren. And those whom he predestined he also called; and those whom he called he
also justified; and those whom he justified he also glorified."[64]

2013   "All Christians in any state or walk of life are
915, 2545   called to the fullness of Christian life and to the perfec-

---

63 St. Thérèse of Lisieux, "Act of Offering" in *Story of a Soul,* tr. John Clarke
(Washington DC: ICS, 1981), 277.   64 *Rom* 8:28–30.

tion of charity."[65] All are called to holiness: "Be perfect, as your heavenly Father is perfect."[66]   825

> In order to reach this perfection the faithful should use the strength dealt out to them by Christ's gift, so that . . . doing the will of the Father in everything, they may wholeheartedly devote themselves to the glory of God and to the service of their neighbor. Thus the holiness of the People of God will grow in fruitful abundance, as is clearly shown in the history of the Church through the lives of so many saints.[67]

2014 Spiritual progress tends toward ever more intimate union with Christ. This union is called "mystical" because it participates in the mystery of Christ through the sacraments—"the holy mysteries"—and, in him, in   774
the mystery of the Holy Trinity. God calls us all to this intimate union with him, even if the special graces or extraordinary signs of this mystical life are granted only to some for the sake of manifesting the gratuitous gift given to all.

2015 The way of perfection passes by way of the Cross. There is no holiness without renunciation and spiritual battle.[68] Spiritual progress entails the ascesis   407, 2725
and mortification that gradually lead to living in the   1438
peace and joy of the Beatitudes:

> He who climbs never stops going from beginning to beginning, through beginnings that have no end. He never stops desiring what he already knows.[69]

2016 The children of our holy mother the Church rightly hope for *the grace of final perseverance and the recompense* of God their Father for the good works ac-   162, 1821
complished with his grace in communion with Jesus.[70] Keeping the same rule of life, believers share the "blessed hope" of those whom the divine mercy gathers   1274
into the "holy city, the new Jerusalem, coming down out of heaven from God, prepared as a bride adorned for her husband."[71]

---

65 *LG* 40 § 2.   66 *Mt* 5:48.   67 *LG* 40 § 2.   68 Cf. *2 Tim* 4.   69 St. Gregory of Nyssa, *Hom. in Cant.* 8: PG 44, 941C.   70 Cf. Council of Trent (1547): DS 1576.   71 *Rev* 21:2.

IN BRIEF

2017 The grace of the Holy Spirit confers upon us the righteousness of God. Uniting us by faith and Baptism to the Passion and Resurrection of Christ, the Spirit makes us sharers in his life.

2018 Like conversion, justification has two aspects. Moved by grace, man turns toward God and away from sin, and so accepts forgiveness and righteousness from on high.

2019 Justification includes the remission of sins, sanctification, and the renewal of the inner man.

2020 Justification has been merited for us by the Passion of Christ. It is granted us through Baptism. It conforms us to the righteousness of God, who justifies us. It has for its goal the glory of God and of Christ, and the gift of eternal life. It is the most excellent work of God's mercy.

2021 Grace is the help God gives us to respond to our vocation of becoming his adopted sons. It introduces us into the intimacy of the Trinitarian life.

2022 The divine initiative in the work of grace precedes, prepares, and elicits the free response of man. Grace responds to the deepest yearnings of human freedom, calls freedom to cooperate with it, and perfects freedom.

2023 Sanctifying grace is the gratuitous gift of his life that God makes to us; it is infused by the Holy Spirit into the soul to heal it of sin and to sanctify it.

2024 Sanctifying grace makes us "pleasing to God." Charisms, special graces of the Holy Spirit, are oriented to sanctifying grace and are intended for the common good of the Church. God also acts through many actual graces, to be distinguished from habitual grace which is permanent in us.

2025 We can have merit in God's sight only because of

God's free plan to associate man with the work of his grace. Merit is to be ascribed in the first place to the grace of God, and secondly to man's collaboration. Man's merit is due to God.

2026 The grace of the Holy Spirit can confer true merit on us, by virtue of our adoptive filiation, and in accordance with God's gratuitous justice. Charity is the principal source of merit in us before God.

2027 No one can merit the initial grace which is at the origin of conversion. Moved by the Holy Spirit, we can merit for ourselves and for others all the graces needed to attain eternal life, as well as necessary temporal goods.

2028 "All Christians . . . are called to the fullness of Christian life and to the perfection of charity" (*LG* 40 § 2). "Christian perfection has but one limit, that of having none" (St. Gregory of Nyssa, *De vita Mos.:* PG 44, 300D).

2029 "If any man would come after me, let him deny himself and take up his cross and follow me" (*Mt* 16:24).

ARTICLE 3
THE CHURCH, MOTHER AND TEACHER

2030 It is in the Church, in communion with all the baptized, that the Christian fulfills his vocation. From the Church he receives the Word of God containing the teachings of "the law of Christ."[72] From the Church he receives the grace of the sacraments that sustains him on the "way." From the Church he learns the *example of holiness* and recognizes its model and source in the all-holy Virgin Mary; he discerns it in the authentic witness of those who live it; he discovers it in the spiritual tra-   828

---

72 *Gal* 6:2.

dition and long history of the saints who have gone before him and whom the liturgy celebrates in the rhythms
1172 of the sanctoral cycle.

2031 *The moral life is spiritual worship.* We "present
[our] bodies as a living sacrifice, holy and acceptable to
1368 God,"[73] within the Body of Christ that we form and in
communion with the offering of his Eucharist. In the
liturgy and the celebration of the sacraments, prayer
and teaching are conjoined with the grace of Christ to
enlighten and nourish Christian activity. As does the
whole of the Christian life, the moral life finds its source
and summit in the Eucharistic sacrifice.

85-87 **I.   MORAL LIFE AND THE MAGISTERIUM OF THE**
888-892   **CHURCH**

2032 The Church, the "pillar and bulwark of the
truth," "has received this solemn command of Christ
from the apostles to announce the saving truth."[74] "To
the Church belongs the right always and everywhere to
announce moral principles, including those pertaining
2246 to the social order, and to make judgments on any human affairs to the extent that they are required by the
fundamental rights of the human person or the salva-
2420 tion of souls."[75]

2033 The *Magisterium of the Pastors of the Church* in
moral matters is ordinarily exercised in catechesis and
preaching, with the help of the works of theologians
and spiritual authors. Thus from generation to generation, under the aegis and vigilance of the pastors, the
84 "deposit" of Christian moral teaching has been handed
on, a deposit composed of a characteristic body of rules,
commandments, and virtues proceeding from faith in
Christ and animated by charity. Alongside the Creed
and the Our Father, the basis for this catechesis has traditionally been the Decalogue which sets out the principles of moral life valid for all men.

2034 The Roman Pontiff and the bishops are "au-

---

73 *Rom* 12:1.   74 *1 Tim* 3:15; *LG* 17.   75 CIC, can. 747 § 2.

thentic teachers, that is, teachers endowed with the authority of Christ, who preach the faith to the people entrusted to them, the faith to be believed and put into practice."[76] The *ordinary* and universal *Magisterium* of the Pope and the bishops in communion with him teach the faithful the truth to believe, the charity to practice, the beatitude to hope for.

2035 The supreme degree of participation in the authority of Christ is ensured by the charism of *infallibility*. This infallibility extends as far as does the deposit of divine Revelation; it also extends to all those elements of doctrine, including morals, without which the saving truths of the faith cannot be preserved, explained, or observed.[77]

2036 The authority of the Magisterium extends also to the specific precepts of the *natural law,* because their observance, demanded by the Creator, is necessary for *1960* salvation. In recalling the prescriptions of the natural law, the Magisterium of the Church exercises an essential part of its prophetic office of proclaiming to men what they truly are and reminding them of what they should be before God.[78]

2037 The law of God entrusted to the Church is taught to the faithful as the way of life and truth. The faithful therefore have the *right* to be instructed in the divine saving precepts that purify judgment and, with grace, heal wounded human reason.[79] They have the *duty* of observing the constitutions and decrees conveyed by the legitimate authority of the Church. Even if *2041* they concern disciplinary matters, these determinations call for docility in charity.

2038 In the work of teaching and applying Christian morality, the Church needs the dedication of pastors, the knowledge of theologians, and the contribution of all Christians and men of good will. Faith and the prac- *2442* tice of the Gospel provide each person with an experi-

---

76 *LG* 25.   77 Cf. *LG* 25; CDF, declaration, *Mysterium Ecclesiae* 3.   78 Cf. *DH* 14.   79 Cf. *CIC,* can. 213.

ence of life "in Christ," who enlightens him and makes him able to evaluate the divine and human realities according to the Spirit of God.[80] Thus the Holy Spirit can use the humblest to enlighten the learned and those in the highest positions.

2039   Ministries should be exercised in a spirit of fraternal service and dedication to the Church, in the name of the Lord.[81] At the same time the conscience of each person should avoid confining itself to individualistic considerations in its moral judgments of the person's own acts. As far as possible conscience should take account of the good of all, as expressed in the moral law, natural and revealed, and consequently in the law of the Church and in the authoritative teaching of the Magis-

1783   terium on moral questions. Personal conscience and reason should not be set in opposition to the moral law or the Magisterium of the Church.

2040   Thus a true *filial spirit toward the Church* can develop among Christians. It is the normal flowering of the baptismal grace which has begotten us in the womb of the Church and made us members of the Body of Christ. In her motherly care, the Church grants us the mercy of God which prevails over all our sins and is especially at work in the sacrament of reconciliation.

167   With a mother's foresight, she also lavishes on us day after day in her liturgy the nourishment of the Word and Eucharist of the Lord.

II.   THE PRECEPTS OF THE CHURCH

2041   The precepts of the Church are set in the context of a moral life bound to and nourished by liturgical life. The obligatory character of these positive laws decreed by the pastoral authorities is meant to guarantee to the faithful the indispensable minimum in the spirit of prayer and moral effort, in the growth in love of God and neighbor:

2042   The first precept ("You shall attend Mass on Sun-

1389   days and holy days of obligation.") requires the faithful to

---

80 Cf. *1 Cor* 2:10–15.   81 Cf. *Rom* 12:8, 11.

participate in the Eucharistic celebration when the Christian community gathers together on the day commemorating the Resurrection of the Lord.[82]   *2180*

The second precept ("You shall confess your sins at least once a year.") ensures preparation for the Eucharist by the reception of the sacrament of reconciliation, which continues Baptism's work of conversion and forgiveness.[83]   *1457*

The third precept ("You shall humbly receive your Creator in Holy Communion at least during the Easter season.") guarantees as a minimum the reception of the Lord's Body and Blood in connection with the Paschal feasts, the origin and center of the Christian liturgy.[84]   *1389*

2043 The fourth precept ("You shall keep holy the holy days of obligation.") completes the Sunday observance by participation in the principal liturgical feasts which honor the mysteries of the Lord, the Virgin Mary, and the saints.[85]   *2177*

The fifth precept ("You shall observe the prescribed days of fasting and abstinence.") ensures the times of ascesis and penance which prepare us for the liturgical feasts; they help us acquire mastery over our instincts and freedom of heart.[86]   *1387* *1438*

The faithful also have the duty of providing for the material needs of the Church, each according to his abilities.[87]   *1351*

III.   MORAL LIFE AND MISSIONARY WITNESS

2044 The fidelity of the baptized is a primordial condition for the proclamation of the Gospel and for the *Church's mission in the world.* In order that the message of salvation can show the power of its truth and radiance before men, it must be authenticated by the witness of the life of Christians. "The witness of a Christian life and good works done in a supernatural spirit have great power to draw men to the faith and to God."[88]   *852, 905*

2045 Because they are members of the Body whose Head is Christ,[89] Christians contribute to *building up the Church* by the constancy of their convictions and   *753*

82 Cf. CIC, cann. 1246–1248; CCEO, can. 881 § 1, § 2, § 4.   83 Cf. CIC, can. 989; CCEO, can. 719.   84 Cf. CIC, can. 920; CCEO, cann. 708; 881 § 3. 85 Cf. CIC, can. 1246; CCEO, cann. 881 § 1, § 4; 880 § 3.   86 Cf. CIC, cann. 1249–1251; CCEO, can. 882.   87 Cf. CIC, can. 222.   88 *AA* 6 § 2.   89 Cf. *Eph* 1:22.

828   their moral lives. The Church increases, grows, and develops through the holiness of her faithful, until "we all
attain to the unity of the faith and of the knowledge of
the Son of God, to mature manhood, to the measure of
the stature of the fullness of Christ."[90]

2046   By living with the mind of Christ, Christians
hasten the coming of the Reign of God, "a kingdom of
671, 2819   justice, love, and peace."[91] They do not, for all that,
abandon their earthly tasks; faithful to their master,
they fulfill them with uprightness, patience, and love.

IN BRIEF

2047   The moral life is a spiritual worship. Christian
activity finds its nourishment in the liturgy and
the celebration of the sacraments.

2048   The precepts of the Church concern the moral
and Christian life united with the liturgy and
nourished by it.

2049   The Magisterium of the Pastors of the Church in
moral matters is ordinarily exercised in catechesis and preaching, on the basis of the Decalogue
which states the principles of moral life valid for
every man.

2050   The Roman Pontiff and the bishops, as authentic teachers, preach to the People of God the
faith which is to be believed and applied in
moral life. It is also encumbent on them to pronounce on moral questions that fall within the
natural law and reason.

2051   The infallibility of the Magisterium of the Pastors extends to all the elements of doctrine, including moral doctrine, without which the saving truths of the faith cannot be preserved,
expounded, or observed.

---

90 *Eph* 4:13; cf. *LG* 39.   91 *Roman Missal,* Preface of Christ the King.

THE TEN COMMANDMENTS

Exodus 20:2–17	Deuteronomy 5:6–21	A Traditional Catechetical Formula
I am the LORD your God, who brought you out of the land of Egypt, out of the house of bondage.	I am the LORD your God, who brought you out of the land of Egypt, out of the house of bondage.	1. I am the LORD your God: you shall not have strange Gods before me.
You shall have no other gods before me. You shall not make for yourself a graven image, or any likeness of anything that is in heaven above, or that is in the earth beneath, or that is in the water under the earth; you shall not bow down to them or serve them; for I the LORD your God am a jealous God, visiting the iniquity of the fathers upon the children to the third and the fourth generation of those who hate me, but showing steadfast love to thousands of those who love me and keep my commandments.	You shall have no other gods before me . . .	
You shall not take the name of the LORD your God in vain; for the LORD will not hold him guiltless who takes his name in vain.	You shall not take the name of the LORD your God in vain . . .	2. You shall not take the name of the LORD your God in vain.
Remember the sabbath day, to keep it holy. Six days you shall labor, and do all your work; but the seventh day is a sabbath to the LORD your God; in it you shall not do any work, you, or your son, or your daughter, your manservant, or your maidservant, or your cattle,	Observe the sabbath day, to keep it holy . . .	3. Remember to keep holy the LORD's Day.

THE TEN COMMANDMENTS

Exodus 20:2–17	Deuteronomy 5:6–21	A Traditional Catechetical Formula
or the sojourner who is within your gates; for in six days the LORD made heaven and earth, the sea, and all that is in them, and rested the seventh day; therefore the Lord blessed the sabbath day and hallowed it.		
Honor your father and your mother, that your days may be long in the land which the LORD your God gives you.	Honor your father and your mother . . .	4. Honor your father and your mother.
You shall not kill.	You shall not kill.	5. You shall not kill.
You shall not commit adultery.	Neither shall you commit adultery.	6. You shall not commit adultery.
You shall not steal.	Neither shall you steal.	7. You shall not steal.
You shall not bear false witness against your neighbor.	Neither shall you bear false witness against your neighbor.	8. You shall not bear false witness against your neighbor.
You shall not covet your neighbor's house; you shall not covet your neighbor's wife, or his manservant, or his maidservant, or his ox, or his ass, or anything that is your neighbor's.	Neither shall you covet your neighbor's wife . . . You shall not desire . . . anything that is your neighbor's.	9. You shall not covet your neighbor's wife. 10. You shall not covet your neighbor's goods.

SECTION TWO
THE TEN COMMANDMENTS

"Teacher, what must I do . . . ?"

2052 "Teacher, what good deed must I do, to have eternal life?" To the young man who asked this question, Jesus answers first by invoking the necessity to recognize God as the "One there is who is good," as the supreme Good and the source of all good. Then Jesus tells him: "If you would enter life, keep the commandments." And he cites for his questioner the precepts that concern love of neighbor: "You shall not kill, You shall not commit adultery, You shall not steal, You shall not bear false witness, Honor your father and mother." Finally Jesus sums up these commandments positively: "You shall love your neighbor as yourself."[1]   *1858*

2053 To this first reply Jesus adds a second: "If you would be perfect, go, sell what you possess and give to the poor, and you will have treasure in heaven; and come, follow me."[2] This reply does not do away with the first: following Jesus Christ involves keeping the Commandments. The Law has not been abolished,[3] but rather man is invited to rediscover it in the person of his   *1968* Master who is its perfect fulfillment. In the three synoptic Gospels, Jesus' call to the rich young man to follow him, in the obedience of a disciple and in the observance of the Commandments, is joined to the call to poverty and chastity.[4] The evangelical counsels are inseparable from the Commandments.   *1973*

2054 Jesus acknowledged the Ten Commandments, but he also showed the power of the Spirit at work in their letter. He preached a "righteousness [which] exceeds that of the scribes and Pharisees"[5] as well as that   *581* of the Gentiles.[6] He unfolded all the demands of the Commandments. "You have heard that it was said to the men of old, 'You shall not kill.' . . . But I say to you

---

1 *Mt* 19:16–19. 2 *Mt* 19:21. 3 Cf. *Mt* 5:17. 4 Cf. *Mt* 19:6–12, 21, 23–29.
5 *Mt* 5:20. 6 Cf. *Mt* 5:46–47.

that every one who is angry with his brother shall be liable to judgment."[7]

2055 When someone asks him, "Which commandment in the Law is the greatest?"[8] Jesus replies: "You shall love the Lord your God with all your heart, and

129   with all your soul, and with all your mind. This is the greatest and first commandment. And a second is like it: You shall love your neighbor as yourself. On these two commandments hang all the Law and the prophets."[9] The Decalogue must be interpreted in light of this twofold yet single commandment of love, the fullness of the Law:

> The commandments: "You shall not commit adultery, You shall not kill, You shall not steal, You shall not covet," and any other commandment, are summed up in this sentence: "You shall love your neighbor as yourself." Love does no wrong to a neighbor; therefore love is the fulfilling of the law.[10]

The Decalogue in Sacred Scripture

2056 The word "Decalogue" means literally "ten words."[11] God revealed these "ten words" to his people on the holy mountain. They were written "with the fin-

700   ger of God,"[12] unlike the other commandments written

62   by Moses.[13] They are pre-eminently the words of God. They are handed on to us in the books of *Exodus*[14] and *Deuteronomy*.[15] Beginning with the Old Testament, the sacred books refer to the "ten words,"[16] but it is in the New Covenant in Jesus Christ that their full meaning will be revealed.

2057 The Decalogue must first be understood in the context of the Exodus, God's great liberating event

2084   at the center of the Old Covenant. Whether formulated as negative commandments, prohibitions, or as positive precepts such as: "Honor your father and mother,"

---

7 *Mt* 5:21–22.   8 *Mt* 22:36.   9 *Mt* 22:37–40; cf. *Deut* 6:5; *Lev* 19:18.   10 *Rom* 13:9–10.   11 *Ex* 34:28; *Deut* 4:13; 10:4.   12 *Ex* 31:18; *Deut* 5:22.   13 Cf. *Deut* 31:9–24.   14 Cf. *Ex* 20:1–17.   15 Cf. *Deut* 5:6–22.   16 Cf. for example *Hos* 4:2; *Jer* 7:9; *Ezek* 18:5–9.

the "ten words" point out the conditions of a life freed
from the slavery of sin. The Decalogue is a path of
life:

> If you love the LORD your God, by walking in his
> ways, and by keeping his commandments and his
> statutes and his ordinances, then you shall live and
> multiply.[17]

This liberating power of the Decalogue appears, *2170*
for example, in the commandment about the sabbath
rest, directed also to foreigners and slaves:

> You shall remember that you were a servant in the
> land of Egypt, and the LORD your God brought you
> out thence with a mighty hand and an outstretched
> arm.[18]

2058 The "ten words" sum up and proclaim God's *1962*
law: "These words the LORD spoke to all your assembly
at the mountain out of the midst of the fire, the cloud,
and the thick darkness, with a loud voice; and he added
no more. And he wrote them upon two tables of stone,
and gave them to me."[19] For this reason these two tables
are called "the Testimony." In fact, they contain the
terms of the covenant concluded between God and his
people. These "tables of the Testimony" were to be deposited in "the ark."[20]

2059 The "ten words" are pronounced by God in the *707*
midst of a theophany ("The LORD spoke with you face
to face at the mountain, out of the midst of the fire."[21]).
They belong to God's revelation of himself and his
glory. The gift of the Commandments is the gift of God
himself and his holy will. In making his will known, *2823*
God reveals himself to his people.

2060 The gift of the commandments and of the Law is
part of the covenant God sealed with his own. In *Exodus,* the revelation of the "ten words" is granted between the proposal of the covenant[22] and its conclusion—after the people had committed themselves to

---

17 *Deut* 30:16. 18 *Deut* 5:15. 19 *Deut* 5:22. 20 *Ex* 25:16; 31:18; 32:15;
34:29; 40:1–2. 21 *Deut* 5:4. 22 Cf. *Ex* 19.

"do" all that the Lord had said, and to "obey" it.[23] The
62 Decalogue is never handed on without first recalling the
covenant ("The LORD our God made a covenant with us
in Horeb.").[24]

2061 The Commandments take on their full meaning
within the covenant. According to Scripture, man's
moral life has all its meaning in and through the
covenant. The first of the "ten words" recalls that God
loved his people first:

> Since there was a passing from the paradise of free-
> dom to the slavery of this world, in punishment for
> sin, the first phrase of the Decalogue, the first word
> of God's commandments, bears on freedom: "I am
> the LORD your God, who brought you out of the
2086   land of Egypt, out of the house of slavery."[25]

2062 The Commandments properly so-called come in
the second place: they express the implications of belonging to God through the establishment of the
covenant. Moral existence is a *response* to the Lord's
142 loving initiative. It is the acknowledgement and homage
2002 given to God and a worship of thanksgiving. It is cooperation with the plan God pursues in history.

2063 The covenant and dialogue between God and
man are also attested to by the fact that all the obligations are stated in the first person ("I am the Lord.")
and addressed by God to another personal subject
("you"). In all God's commandments, the *singular* per-
878 sonal pronoun designates the recipient. God makes his
will known to each person in particular, at the same
time as he makes it known to the whole people:

> The Lord prescribed love towards God and taught
> justice towards neighbor, so that man would be nei-
> ther unjust, nor unworthy of God. Thus, through
> the Decalogue, God prepared man to become his
> friend and to live in harmony with his neighbor. . . .
> The words of the Decalogue remain likewise for us
> Christians. Far from being abolished, they have re-

---

23 Cf. *Ex* 24:7. 24 *Deut* 5:2. 25 Origen, *Hom. in Ex.* 8, 1: PG 12, 350; cf. *Ex*
20:2; *Deut* 5:6.

ceived amplification and development from the fact
of the coming of the Lord in the flesh.[26]

The Decalogue in the Church's Tradition

2064 In fidelity to Scripture and in conformity with
the example of Jesus, the tradition of the Church has acknowledged the primordial importance and significance
of the Decalogue.

2065 Ever since St. Augustine, the Ten Commandments
have occupied a predominant place in the catechesis of
baptismal candidates and the faithful. In the fifteenth century, the custom arose of expressing the commandments of
the Decalogue in rhymed formulae, easy to memorize and
in positive form. They are still in use today. The catechisms
of the Church have often expounded Christian morality by
following the order of the Ten Commandments.

2066 The division and numbering of the Commandments
have varied in the course of history. The present catechism
follows the division of the Commandments established by
St. Augustine, which has become traditional in the Catholic
Church. It is also that of the Lutheran confessions. The
Greek Fathers worked out a slightly different division,
which is found in the Orthodox Churches and Reformed
communities.

2067 The Ten Commandments state what is required
in the love of God and love of neighbor. The first three
concern love of God, and the other seven love of neighbor.   *1853*

> As charity comprises the two commandments to
> which the Lord related the whole Law and the
> prophets . . . so the Ten Commandments were
> themselves given on two tablets. Three were written
> on one tablet and seven on the other.[27]

2068 The Council of Trent teaches that the Ten Commandments are obligatory for Christians and that the
justified man is still bound to keep them;[28] the Second   *1993*
Vatican Council confirms: "The bishops, successors of
the apostles, receive from the Lord . . . the mission of
teaching all peoples, and of preaching the Gospel to

---

26 St. Irenaeus, *Adv. haeres.*, 4, 16, 3–4: PG 7/1, 1017–1018.   27 St. Augustine, *Sermo* 33, 2, 2: PL 38, 208.   28 Cf. DS 1569–1570.

888   every creature, so that all men may attain salvation through faith, Baptism and the observance of the Commandments."[29]

The unity of the Decalogue

2069   The Decalogue forms a coherent whole. Each "word" refers to each of the others and to all of them; 2534   they reciprocally condition one another. The two tables shed light on one another; they form an organic unity. To transgress one commandment is to infringe all the others.[30] One cannot honor another person without blessing God his Creator. One cannot adore God without loving all men, his creatures. The Decalogue brings man's religious and social life into unity.

The Decalogue and the natural law

1955   2070   The Ten Commandments belong to God's revelation. At the same time they teach us the true humanity of man. They bring to light the essential duties, and therefore, indirectly, the fundamental rights inherent in the nature of the human person. The Decalogue contains a privileged expression of the natural law:

> From the beginning, God had implanted in the heart of man the precepts of the natural law. Then he was content to remind him of them. This was the Decalogue.[31]

2071   The commandments of the Decalogue, although 1960   accessible to reason alone, have been revealed. To attain a complete and certain understanding of the requirements of the natural law, sinful humanity needed this revelation:

> A full explanation of the commandments of the Decalogue became necessary in the state of sin because the light of reason was obscured and the will had gone astray.[32]

We know God's commandments through the di-
1777   vine revelation proposed to us in the Church, and through the voice of moral conscience.

---

29 LG 24.   30 Cf. *Jas* 2:10–11.   31 St. Irenaeus, *Adv. haeres.* 4, 15, 1: PG 7/1, 1012.   32 St. Bonaventure, *Comm. sent.* 4, 37, 1, 3.

The obligation of the Decalogue

2072   Since they express man's fundamental duties towards God and towards his neighbor, the Ten Commandments reveal, in their primordial content, *grave* obligations. They are fundamentally immutable, and they oblige always and everywhere. No one can dispense from them. The Ten Commandments are engraved by God in the human heart.

1858

1958

2073   Obedience to the Commandments also implies obligations in matter which is, in itself, light. Thus abusive language is forbidden by the fifth commandment, but would be a grave offense only as a result of circumstances or the offender's intention.

"Apart from me you can do nothing"

2074   Jesus says: "I am the vine, you are the branches. He who abides in me, and I in him, he it is that bears much fruit, for apart from me you can do nothing."[33] The fruit referred to in this saying is the holiness of a life made fruitful by union with Christ. When we believe in Jesus Christ, partake of his mysteries, and keep his commandments, the Savior himself comes to love, in us, his Father and his brethren, our Father and our brethren. His person becomes, through the Spirit, the living and interior rule of our activity. "This is my commandment, that you love one another as I have loved you."[34]

2732

521

IN BRIEF

2075   "What good deed must I do, to have eternal life?"—"If you would enter into life, keep the commandments" (*Mt* 19:16–17).

2076   By his life and by his preaching Jesus attested to the permanent validity of the Decalogue.

2077   The gift of the Decalogue is bestowed from within the covenant concluded by God with his people. God's commandments take on their true meaning in and through this covenant.

---

33 *Jn* 15:5.   34 *Jn* 15:12.

2078   In fidelity to Scripture and in conformity with Jesus' example, the tradition of the Church has always acknowledged the primordial importance and significance of the Decalogue.

2079   The Decalogue forms an organic unity in which each "word" or "commandment" refers to all the others taken together. To transgress one commandment is to infringe the whole Law (cf. *Jas* 2:10–11).

2080   The Decalogue contains a privileged expression of the natural law. It is made known to us by divine revelation and by human reason.

2081   The Ten Commandments, in their fundamental content, state grave obligations. However, obedience to these precepts also implies obligations in matter which is, in itself, light.

2082   What God commands he makes possible by his grace.

Chapter One
"You Shall Love the Lord Your God with All Your Heart, and with All Your Soul, and with All Your Mind"

367   2083   Jesus summed up man's duties toward God in this saying: "You shall love the Lord your God with all your heart, and with all your soul, and with all your mind."[1] This immediately echoes the solemn call: "Hear, O Israel: the LORD our God is one LORD."[2]

199   God has loved us first. The love of the One God is recalled in the first of the "ten words." The commandments then make explicit the response of love that man is called to give to his God.

---

1 *Mt* 22:37; cf. *Lk* 10:27:". . . and with all your strength."   2 *Deut* 6:4.

ARTICLE 1
THE FIRST COMMANDMENT

> I am the LORD your God, who brought you out of
> the land of Egypt, out of the house of bondage. You
> shall have no other gods before me. You shall not
> make for yourself a graven image, or any likeness
> of anything that is in heaven above, or that is in the
> earth beneath, or that is in the water under the
> earth; you shall not bow down to them or serve
> them.[3]

It is written: "You shall worship the Lord your
God and him only shall you serve."[4]

I. "YOU SHALL WORSHIP THE LORD YOUR GOD AND HIM ONLY SHALL YOU SERVE"

2084 God makes himself known by recalling his
all-powerful, loving, and liberating action in the history of the one he addresses: "I brought you out of
the land of Egypt, out of the house of bondage." The *2057*
first word contains the first commandment of the Law:
"You shall fear the LORD your God; you shall serve
him. . . . You shall not go after other gods."[5] God's first
call and just demand is that man accept him and worship him. *398*

2085 The one and true God first reveals his glory to
Israel.[6] The revelation of the vocation and truth of man
is linked to the revelation of God. Man's vocation is to *200*
make God manifest by acting in conformity with his
creation "in the image and likeness of God": *1701*

> There will never be another God, Trypho, and there
> has been no other since the world began . . . than
> he who made and ordered the universe. We do not
> think that our God is different from yours. He is
> the same who brought your fathers out of Egypt
> "by his powerful hand and his outstretched arm."
> We do not place our hope in some other god, for
> there is none, but in the same God as you do: the
> God of Abraham, Isaac and Jacob.[7]

---

3 Ex 20:2–5; cf. Deut 5:6–9. 4 Mt 4:10. 5 Deut 6:13–14. 6 Cf. Ex 19:16–25;
24:15–18. 7 St. Justin, *Dial. cum Tryphone Judaeo* 11, 1: PG 6, 497.

2086 "The first commandment embraces faith, hope, and charity. When we say 'God' we confess a constant,
212 unchangeable being, always the same, faithful and just, without any evil. It follows that we must necessarily accept his words and have complete faith in him and acknowledge his authority. He is almighty, merciful, and infinitely beneficent. . . . Who could not place all hope in him? Who could not love him when contemplating the treasures of goodness and love he has poured out on us? Hence the formula God employs in the Scripture at
2061 the beginning and end of his commandments: 'I am the LORD.' "[8]

1814-1816 ## Faith

2087 Our moral life has its source in faith in God who reveals his love to us. St. Paul speaks of the "obedience
143 of faith"[9] as our first obligation. He shows that "ignorance of God" is the principle and explanation of all moral deviations.[10] Our duty toward God is to believe in him and to bear witness to him.

2088 The first commandment requires us to nourish and protect our faith with prudence and vigilance, and to reject everything that is opposed to it. There are various ways of sinning against faith:
157   *Voluntary doubt* about the faith disregards or refuses to hold as true what God has revealed and the Church proposes for belief. *Involuntary doubt* refers to hesitation in believing, difficulty in overcoming objections connected with the faith, or also anxiety aroused by its obscurity. If deliberately cultivated doubt can lead to spiritual blindness.

162 **2089** *Incredulity* is the neglect of revealed truth or
817 the willful refusal to assent to it. "*Heresy* is the obstinate post-baptismal denial of some truth which must be believed with divine and catholic faith, or it is likewise an obstinate doubt concerning the same; *apostasy* is the total repudiation of the Christian faith; *schism* is the refusal of submission to the Roman Pontiff or of com-

---

8 *Roman Catechism* 3, 2,4.   9 *Rom* 1:5; 16:26.   10 Cf. *Rom* 1:18–32.

munion with the members of the Church subject to him."[11]

Hope   1817-1821

2090   When God reveals Himself and calls him, man cannot fully respond to the divine love by his own powers. He must hope that God will give him the capacity to love Him in return and to act in conformity with the 1996 commandments of charity. Hope is the confident expectation of divine blessing and the beatific vision of God; it is also the fear of offending God's love and of incurring punishment.

2091   The first commandment is also concerned with sins against hope, namely, despair and presumption:

By *despair,* man ceases to hope for his personal salvation from God, for help in attaining it or for the forgiveness of his sins. Despair is contrary to God's 1864 goodness, to his justice—for the Lord is faithful to his promises—and to his mercy.

2092   There are two kinds of *presumption.* Either man presumes upon his own capacities, (hoping to be able to save himself without help from on high), or he presumes 2732 upon God's almighty power or his mercy (hoping to obtain his forgiveness without conversion and glory without merit).

Charity   1822-1829

2093   Faith in God's love encompasses the call and the obligation to respond with sincere love to divine charity. The first commandment enjoins us to love God above everything and all creatures for him and because of him.[12]

2094   One can sin against God's love in various ways:

—*indifference* neglects or refuses to reflect on divine charity; it fails to consider its prevenient goodness and denies its power.

11 CIC, can. 751: emphasis added.   12 Cf. *Deut* 6:4–5.

—*ingratitude* fails or refuses to acknowledge divine charity and to return him love for love.

—*lukewarmness* is hesitation or negligence in responding to divine love; it can imply refusal to give oneself over to the prompting of charity.

2733 —*acedia* or spiritual sloth goes so far as to refuse the joy that comes from God and to be repelled by divine goodness.

2303 —*hatred of God* comes from pride. It is contrary to love of God, whose goodness it denies, and whom it presumes to curse as the one who forbids sins and inflicts punishments.

II.   "HIM ONLY SHALL YOU SERVE"

2095   The theological virtues of faith, hope, and charity inform and give life to the moral virtues. Thus char-
1807 ity leads us to render to God what we as creatures owe him in all justice. The *virtue of religion* disposes us to have this attitude.

2628 Adoration

2096   Adoration is the first act of the virtue of religion. To adore God is to acknowledge him as God, as the Creator and Savior, the Lord and Master of everything that exists, as infinite and merciful Love. "You shall worship the Lord your God, and him only shall you serve," says Jesus, citing *Deuteronomy.*[13]

2807 **2097**   To adore God is to acknowledge, in respect and absolute submission, the "nothingness of the creature" who would not exist but for God. To adore God is to praise and exalt him and to humble oneself, as Mary did in the Magnificat, confessing with gratitude that he has done great things and holy is his name.[14] The worship of the one God sets man free from turning in on himself, from the slavery of sin and the idolatry of the world.

---

13 *Lk* 4:8; cf. *Deut* 6:13.   14 Cf. *Lk* 1:46–49.

Prayer   *2558*

2098 The acts of faith, hope, and charity enjoined by the first commandment are accomplished in prayer. Lifting up the mind toward God is an expression of our adoration of God: prayer of praise and thanksgiving, intercession and petition. Prayer is an indispensable condition for being able to obey God's commandments. "[We] ought always to pray and not lose heart."[15]   *2742*

Sacrifice

2099 It is right to offer sacrifice to God as a sign of adoration and gratitude, supplication and communion: "Every action done so as to cling to God in communion of holiness, and thus achieve blessedness, is a true sacrifice."[16]   *613*

2100 Outward sacrifice, to be genuine, must be the expression of spiritual sacrifice: "The sacrifice acceptable to God is a broken spirit. . . ."[17] The prophets of the Old   *2711* Covenant often denounced sacrifices that were not from the heart or not coupled with love of neighbor.[18] Jesus recalls the words of the prophet Hosea: "I desire mercy, and not sacrifice."[19] The only perfect sacrifice is the one that Christ offered on the cross as a total offering to the   *614* Father's love and for our salvation.[20] By uniting ourselves with his sacrifice we can make our lives a sacrifice to God.   *618*

Promises and vows

2101 In many circumstances, the Christian is called to   *1237* make *promises* to God. Baptism and Confirmation, Matrimony and Holy Orders always entail promises. Out of personal devotion, the Christian may also promise to God this action, that prayer, this alms-giving, that pilgrimage, and so forth. Fidelity to promises   *1064* made to God is a sign of the respect owed to the divine majesty and of love for a faithful God.

2102 "A *vow* is a deliberate and free promise made to

---

15 *Lk* 18:1. **16** St. Augustine, *De civ. Dei* 10, 6: PL 41, 283. **17** *Ps* 51:17. **18** Cf. *Am* 5:21–25; *Isa* 1:10–20. **19** *Mt* 9:13; 12:7; cf. *Hos* 6:6. **20** Cf. *Heb* 9:13–14.

God concerning a possible and better good which must be fulfilled by reason of the virtue of religion,"[21] A vow is an act of *devotion* in which the Christian dedicates himself to God or promises him some good work. By fulfilling his vows he renders to God what has been promised and consecrated to Him. The *Acts of the Apostles* shows us St. Paul concerned to fulfill the vows he had made.[22]

1973   **2103** The Church recognizes an exemplary value in the vows to practice the *evangelical counsels:*[23]

914

> Mother Church rejoices that she has within herself many men and women who pursue the Savior's self-emptying more closely and show it forth more clearly, by undertaking poverty with the freedom of the children of God, and renouncing their own will: they submit themselves to man for the sake of God, thus going beyond what is of precept in the matter of perfection, so as to conform themselves more fully to the obedient Christ.[24]

The Church can, in certain cases and for proportionate reasons, dispense from vows and promises.[25]

The social duty of religion and the right to religious freedom

2467   **2104**   "All men are bound to seek the truth, especially in what concerns God and his Church, and to embrace it and hold on to it as they come to know it."[26] This duty derives from "the very dignity of the human person."[27] It does not contradict a "sincere respect" for different religions which frequently "reflect a ray of that truth which enlightens all men,"[28] nor the requirement

851   of charity, which urges Christians "to treat with love, prudence and patience those who are in error or ignorance with regard to the faith."[29]

2105   The duty of offering God genuine worship concerns man both individually and socially. This is "the traditional Catholic teaching on the moral duty of indi-

---

21 CIC, can. 1191 § 1.   22 Cf. *Acts* 18:18; 21:23–24.   23 Cf. CIC, can. 654.
24 *LG* 42 § 2.   25 Cf. CIC, cann. 692; 1196–1197.   26 *DH* 1 § 2.   27 *DH* 2 § 1.   28 *NA* 2 § 2.   29 *DH* 14 § 4.

viduals and societies toward the true religion and the
one Church of Christ."[30] By constantly evangelizing
men, the Church works toward enabling them "to in-   854
fuse the Christian spirit into the mentality and mores,
laws and structures of the communities in which [they]   898
live."[31] The social duty of Christians is to respect and
awaken in each man the love of the true and the good.
It requires them to make known the worship of the one
true religion which subsists in the Catholic and apostolic Church.[32] Christians are called to be the light of the
world. Thus, the Church shows forth the kingship of
Christ over all creation and in particular over human
societies.[33]

2106 "Nobody may be forced to act against his con-   160
victions, nor is anyone to be restrained from acting in   1782
accordance with his conscience in religious matters in   1738
private or in public, alone or in association with others,
within due limits."[34] This right is based on the very nature of the human person, whose dignity enables him
freely to assent to the divine truth which transcends the
temporal order. For this reason it "continues to exist
even in those who do not live up to their obligation of
seeking the truth and adhering to it."[35]

2107 "If because of the circumstances of a particular
people special civil recognition is given to one religious
community in the constitutional organization of a state, the
right of all citizens and religious communities to religious
freedom must be recognized and respected as well."[36]

2108 The right to religious liberty is neither a moral li-   1740
cense to adhere to error, nor a supposed right to error,[37]
but rather a natural right of the human person to civil
liberty, i.e., immunity, within just limits, from external
constraint in religious matters by political authorities.
This natural right ought to be acknowledged in the juridical order of society in such a way that it constitutes
a civil right.[38]

---

30 *DH* 1 § 3.   31 *AA* 13 § 1.   32 Cf. *DH* 1.   33 Cf. *AA* 13; Leo XIII,
Immortale Dei 3, 17; Pius XI, *Quas primas* 8, 20.   34 *DH* 2 § 1.   35 *DH* 2 § 2.
36 *DH* 6 § 3.   37 Cf. Leo XIII, *Libertas praestantissimum* 18; Pius XII, *AAS*
1953, 799.   38 Cf. *DH* 2.

2244   **2109**   The right to religious liberty can of itself be neither
unlimited nor limited only by a "public order" conceived in
a positivist or naturalist manner.[39] The "due limits" which
are inherent in it must be determined for each social situation by political prudence, according to the requirements of
the common good, and ratified by the civil authority in accordance with "legal principles which are in conformity
1906   with the objective moral order."[40]

III.   "YOU SHALL HAVE NO OTHER GODS BEFORE ME"

2110   The first commandment forbids honoring gods
other than the one Lord who has revealed himself to his
people. It proscribes superstition and irreligion. Superstition in some sense represents a perverse excess of religion; irreligion is the vice contrary by defect to the
virtue of religion.

Superstition

2111   Superstition is the deviation of religious feeling and of the practices this feeling imposes. It can even
affect the worship we offer the true God, e.g., when one
attributes an importance in some way magical to certain
practices otherwise lawful or necessary. To attribute
the efficacy of prayers or of sacramental signs to their
mere external performance, apart from the interior
dispositions that they demand, is to fall into superstition.[41]

Idolatry

2112   The first commandment condemns *polytheism*.
It requires man neither to believe in, nor to venerate,
210   other divinities than the one true God. Scripture constantly recalls this rejection of "idols, [of] silver and
gold, the work of men's hands. They have mouths, but
do not speak; eyes, but do not see." These empty idols
make their worshippers empty: "Those who make them
are like them; so are all who trust in them."[42] God, how-

---

39 Cf. Pius VI, *Quod aliquantum* (1791)10; Pius IX, *Quanta cura* 3.   40 *DH* 7 §
3.   41 Cf. *Mt* 23:16–22.   42 *Ps* 115:4–5, 8; cf. *Isa* 44:9–20; *Jer* 10:1–16; *Dan*
14:1–30; *Bar* 6; *Wis* 13:1–15:19.

ever, is the "living God"[43] who gives life and intervenes in history.

2113 Idolatry not only refers to false pagan worship. It remains a constant temptation to faith. Idolatry consists in divinizing what is not God. Man commits idolatry whenever he honors and reveres a creature in place of God, whether this be gods or demons (for example, satanism), power, pleasure, race, ancestors, the state, money, etc. Jesus says, "You cannot serve God and mammon."[44] Many martyrs died for not adoring "the Beast"[45] refusing even to simulate such worship. Idolatry rejects the unique Lordship of God; it is therefore incompatible with communion with God.[46]

398, 2534

2289
2473

2114 Human life finds its unity in the adoration of the one God. The commandment to worship the Lord alone integrates man and saves him from an endless disintegration. Idolatry is a perversion of man's innate religious sense. An idolater is someone who "transfers his indestructible notion of God to anything other than God."[47]

Divination and magic

2115 God can reveal the future to his prophets or to other saints. Still, a sound Christian attitude consists in putting oneself confidently into the hands of Providence for whatever concerns the future, and giving up all unhealthy curiosity about it. Improvidence, however, can constitute a lack of responsibility.

305

2116 All forms of *divination* are to be rejected: recourse to Satan or demons, conjuring up the dead or other practices falsely supposed to "unveil" the future.[48] Consulting horoscopes, astrology, palm reading, interpretation of omens and lots, the phenomena of clairvoyance, and recourse to mediums all conceal a desire for power over time, history, and, in the last analysis, other human beings, as well as a wish to conciliate hid-

---

43 *Josh* 3:10; *Ps* 42:3; etc. **44** *Mt* 6:24. **45** Cf. *Rev* 13–14. **46** Cf. *Gal* 5:20; *Eph* 5:5. **47** Origen, *Contra Celsum* 2, 40: PG 11, 861. **48** Cf. *Deut* 18:10; *Jer* 29:8.

den powers. They contradict the honor, respect, and loving fear that we owe to God alone.

2117   All practices of *magic* or *sorcery,* by which one attempts to tame occult powers, so as to place them at one's service and have a supernatural power over others—even if this were for the sake of restoring their health—are gravely contrary to the virtue of religion. These practices are even more to be condemned when accompanied by the intention of harming someone, or when they have recourse to the intervention of demons. Wearing charms is also reprehensible. *Spiritism* often implies divination or magical practices; the Church for her part warns the faithful against it. Recourse to so-called traditional cures does not justify either the invocation of evil powers or the exploitation of another's credulity.

Irreligion

2118   God's first commandment condemns the main sins of irreligion: tempting God, in words or deeds, sacrilege, and simony.

2119   *Tempting God* consists in putting his goodness
394 and almighty power to the test by word or deed. Thus Satan tried to induce Jesus to throw himself down from the Temple and, by this gesture, force God to act.[49] Jesus opposed Satan with the word of God: "You shall not put the LORD your God to the test."[50] The challenge contained in such tempting of God wounds the respect
2088 and trust we owe our Creator and Lord. It always harbors doubt about his love, his providence, and his power.[51]

2120   *Sacrilege* consists in profaning or treating unworthily the sacraments and other liturgical actions, as well as persons, things, or places consecrated to God. Sacrilege is a grave sin especially when committed against the Eucharist, for in this sacrament the true
1374 Body of Christ is made substantially present for us.[52]

---

49 Cf. *Lk* 4:9.   50 *Deut* 6:16.   51 Cf. *1 Cor* 10:9; *Ex* 17:2–7; *Ps* 95:9.   52 Cf. CIC, cann. 1367; 1376.

2121 *Simony* is defined as the buying or selling of spiritual things.[53] To Simon the magician, who wanted to buy the spiritual power he saw at work in the apostles, St. Peter responded: "Your silver perish with you, because you thought you could obtain God's gift with money!"[54] Peter thus held to the words of Jesus: "You received without pay, give without pay."[55] It is impossible to appropriate to oneself spiritual goods and behave toward them as their owner or master, for they have their source in God. One can receive them only from him, without payment.

1578

2122 "The minister should ask nothing for the administration of the sacraments beyond the offerings defined by the competent authority, always being careful that the needy are not deprived of the help of the sacraments because of their poverty."[56] The competent authority determines these "offerings" in accordance with the principle that the Christian people ought to contribute to the support of the Church's ministers. "The laborer deserves his food."[57]

Atheism

2123 "Many . . . of our contemporaries either do not at all perceive, or explicitly reject, this intimate and vital bond of man to God. Atheism must therefore be regarded as one of the most serious problems of our time."[58]

29

2124 The name "atheism" covers many very different phenomena. One common form is the practical materialism which restricts its needs and aspirations to space and time. Atheistic humanism falsely considers man to be "an end to himself, and the sole maker, with supreme control, of his own history."[59] Another form of contemporary atheism looks for the liberation of man through economic and social liberation. "It holds that religion, of its very nature, thwarts such emancipation by raising man's hopes in a future life, thus both deceiving him and discouraging him from working for a better form of life on earth."[60]

---

53 Cf. *Acts* 8:9–24.   54 *Acts* 8:20.   55 *Mt* 10:8; cf. already *Isa* 55:1.   56 CIC, can. 848.   57 *Mt* 10:10; cf. *Lk* 10:7; *1 Cor* 9:5–18; *1 Tim* 5:17–18.   58 GS 19 § 1.   59 GS 20 § 1.   60 GS 20 § 2.

2125 Since it rejects or denies the existence of God, atheism is a sin against the virtue of religion.[61] The imputability of this offense can be significantly diminished
1735 in virtue of the intentions and the circumstances. "Believers can have more than a little to do with the rise of atheism. To the extent that they are careless about their instruction in the faith, or present its teaching falsely, or even fail in their religious, moral, or social life, they must be said to conceal rather than to reveal the true nature of God and of religion."[62]

2126 Atheism is often based on a false conception of human autonomy, exaggerated to the point of refusing
396 any dependence on God.[63] Yet, "to acknowledge God is
154 in no way to oppose the dignity of man, since such dignity is grounded and brought to perfection in God. . . ."[64] "For the Church knows full well that her message is in harmony with the most secret desires of the human heart."[65]

Agnosticism

2127 Agnosticism assumes a number of forms. In certain cases the agnostic refrains from denying God; instead he postulates the existence of a transcendent being which is incapable of revealing itself, and about which nothing can be said. In other cases, the agnostic makes
36 no judgment about God's existence, declaring it impossible to prove, or even to affirm or deny.

2128 Agnosticism can sometimes include a certain
1036 search for God, but it can equally express indifferentism, a flight from the ultimate question of existence, and a sluggish moral conscience. Agnosticism is all too often equivalent to practical atheism.

---

61 Cf. *Rom* 1:18.   62 *GS* 19 § 3.   63 Cf. *GS* 20 § 1.   64 *GS* 21 § 3.   65 *GS* 21 § 7.

IV.   "YOU SHALL NOT MAKE FOR YOURSELF A   *1159-1162*
GRAVEN IMAGE . . ."

2129   The divine injunction included the prohibition of every representation of God by the hand of man. *Deuteronomy* explains: "Since you saw no form on the day that the LORD spoke to you at Horeb out of the midst of the fire, beware lest you act corruptly by making a graven image for yourselves, in the form of any figure. . . ."[66] It is the absolutely transcendent God who revealed himself to Israel. "He is the all," but at the same time "he is greater than all his works."[67] He is "the   *300* author of beauty."[68]   *2500*

2130   Nevertheless, already in the Old Testament, God ordained or permitted the making of images that pointed symbolically toward salvation by the incarnate Word: so it was with the bronze serpent, the ark of the covenant, and the cherubim.[69]

2131   Basing itself on the mystery of the incarnate Word, the seventh ecumenical council at Nicaea (787) justified against the iconoclasts the veneration of icons—of Christ, but also of the Mother of God, the an-   *476* gels, and all the saints. By becoming incarnate, the Son of God introduced a new "economy" of images.

2132   The Christian veneration of images is not contrary to the first commandment which proscribes idols. Indeed, "the honor rendered to an image passes to its prototype," and "whoever venerates an image venerates the person portrayed in it."[70] The honor paid to sacred images is a "respectful veneration," not the adoration due to God alone:

> Religious worship is not directed to images in themselves, considered as mere things, but under their distinctive aspect as images leading us on to God incarnate. The movement toward the image does not terminate in it as image, but tends toward that whose image it is.[71]

---

66 *Deut* 4:15–16.   67 *Sir* 43:27–28.   68 *Wis* 13:3.   69 Cf. *Num* 21:4–9; *Wis* 16:5–14; *Jn* 3:14–15; *Ex* 25:10–22; *1 Kings* 6:23–28; 7:23–26.   70 St. Basil, *De Spiritu Sancto* 18, 45: PG 32, 149C; Council of Nicaea II: DS 601; cf. Council of Trent: DS 1821–1825; Vatican Council II: *SC* 126; *LG* 67.   71 St. Thomas Aquinas, *STh* II-II, 81, 3 *ad* 3.

IN BRIEF

2133 "You shall love the Lord your God with all your heart, and with all your soul and with all your strength" (*Deut* 6:5).

2134 The first commandment summons man to believe in God, to hope in him, and to love him above all else.

2135 "You shall worship the Lord your God" (*Mt* 4:10). Adoring God, praying to him, offering him the worship that belongs to him, fulfilling the promises and vows made to him are acts of the virtue of religion which fall under obedience to the first commandment.

2136 The duty to offer God authentic worship concerns man both as an individual and as a social being.

2137 "Men of the present day want to profess their religion freely in private and in public" (*DH* 15).

2138 Superstition is a departure from the worship that we give to the true God. It is manifested in idolatry, as well as in various forms of divination and magic.

2139 Tempting God in words or deeds, sacrilege, and simony are sins of irreligion forbidden by the first commandment.

2140 Since it rejects or denies the existence of God, atheism is a sin against the first commandment.

2141 The veneration of sacred images is based on the mystery of the Incarnation of the Word of God. It is not contrary to the first commandment.

ARTICLE 2
THE SECOND COMMANDMENT

> You shall not take the name of the Lord your God in vain.[72]

> You have heard that it was said to the men of old, "You shall not swear falsely ... But I say to you, Do not swear at all."[73]

I.   THE NAME OF THE LORD IS HOLY   2807-2815

2142   The second commandment *prescribes respect for the Lord's name*. Like the first commandment, it belongs to the virtue of religion and more particularly it governs our use of speech in sacred matters.

2143   Among all the words of Revelation, there is one which is unique: the revealed name of God. God confides his name to those who believe in him; he reveals himself to them in his personal mystery. The gift of a name belongs to the order of trust and intimacy. "The Lord's name is holy." For this reason man must not abuse it. He must keep it in mind in silent, loving adoration. He will not introduce it into his own speech except to bless, praise, and glorify it.[74]

203

435

2144   Respect for his name is an expression of the respect owed to the mystery of God himself and to the whole sacred reality it evokes. The *sense of the sacred* is part of the virtue of religion:

> Are these feelings of fear and awe Christian feelings or not? ... I say this, then, which I think no one can reasonably dispute. They are the class of feelings we *should* have—yes, have to an intense degree—if we literally had the sight of Almighty God; therefore they are the class of feelings which we shall have, *if* we realize His presence. In proportion as we believe that He is present, we shall have them; and not to have them, is not to realize, not to believe that He is present.[75]

72 Ex 20:7; Deut 5:11.   73 Mt 5:33-34.   74 Cf. Zech 2:13; Ps 29:2; 96:2; 113:1-2.   75 John Henry Cardinal Newman, *Parochial and Plain Sermons* V, 2 (London: Longmans, Green and Co., 1907) 21-22.

2472   **2145** The faithful should bear witness to the Lord's
427   name by confessing the faith without giving way to
fear.[76] Preaching and catechizing should be permeated
with adoration and respect for the name of our Lord Jesus Christ.

2146 The second commandment *forbids the abuse of
God's name,* i.e., every improper use of the names of
God, Jesus Christ, but also of the Virgin Mary and all
the saints.

2101   **2147** *Promises* made to others in God's name engage
the divine honor, fidelity, truthfulness, and authority.
They must be respected in justice. To be unfaithful to
them is to misuse God's name and in some way to make
God out to be a liar.[77]

2148 *Blasphemy* is directly opposed to the second
commandment. It consists in uttering against God—inwardly or outwardly—words of hatred, reproach, or
defiance; in speaking ill of God; in failing in respect toward him in one's speech; in misusing God's name. St.
James condemns those "who blaspheme that honorable
name [of Jesus] by which you are called."[78] The prohibition of blasphemy extends to language against
Christ's Church, the saints, and sacred things. It is also
blasphemous to make use of God's name to cover up
criminal practices, to reduce peoples to servitude, to torture persons or put them to death. The misuse of God's
name to commit a crime can provoke others to repudiate religion.

1756   Blasphemy is contrary to the respect due God
and his holy name. It is in itself a grave sin.[79]

2149 *Oaths* which misuse God's name, though without the intention of blasphemy, show lack of respect for
the Lord. The second commandment also forbids *magical use* of the divine name.

> [God's] name is great when spoken with respect for
> the greatness of his majesty. God's name is holy

---

76 Cf. *Mt* 10:32; *1 Tim* 6:12.   77 Cf. *1 Jn* 1:10.   78 *Jas* 2:7.   79 Cf. CIC, can.
1369.

when said with veneration and fear of offending him.[80]

II. TAKING THE NAME OF THE LORD IN VAIN

2150 The second commandment *forbids false oaths.* Taking an oath or swearing is to take God as witness to what one affirms. It is to invoke the divine truthfulness as a pledge of one's own truthfulness. An oath engages the Lord's name. "You shall fear the LORD your God; you shall serve him, and swear by his name."[81]

2151 Rejection of false oaths is a duty toward God. As Creator and Lord, God is the norm of all truth. Human speech is either in accord with or in opposition to God *215* who is Truth itself. When it is truthful and legitimate, an oath highlights the relationship of human speech with God's truth. A false oath calls on God to be witness to a lie.

2152 A person commits *perjury* when he makes a *2476* promise under oath with no intention of keeping it, or when after promising on oath he does not keep it. Perjury is a grave lack of respect for the Lord of all speech. *1756* Pledging oneself by oath to commit an evil deed is contrary to the holiness of the divine name.

2153 In the Sermon on the Mount, Jesus explained the second commandment: "You have heard that it was said to the men of old, 'You shall not swear falsely, but shall perform to the Lord what you have sworn.' But I say to you, Do not swear at all. . . . Let what you say be simply 'Yes' or 'No'; anything more than this comes from the evil one."[82] Jesus teaches that every oath involves a reference to God and that God's presence and his truth must be honored in all speech. Discretion in calling upon God is allied with a respectful awareness of his presence, which all our assertions either witness to *2466* or mock.

2154 Following St. Paul,[83] the tradition of the Church has understood Jesus' words as not excluding oaths

---

80 St. Augustine, *De serm. Dom. in monte* 2, 5, 19: PL 34, 1278.   81 *Deut* 6:13.
82 *Mt* 5:33–34, 37; cf. *Jas* 5:12.   83 Cf. *2 Cor* 1:23; *Gal* 1:20.

made for grave and right reasons (for example, in court). "An oath, that is the invocation of the divine name as a witness to truth, cannot be taken unless in truth, in judgment, and in justice."[84]

2155 The holiness of the divine name demands that we neither use it for trivial matters, nor take an oath which on the basis of the circumstances could be interpreted as approval of an authority unjustly requiring it. When an oath is required by illegitimate civil authorities, it may be refused. It must be refused when it is re- 1903 quired for purposes contrary to the dignity of persons or to ecclesial communion.

III.   The Christian Name

232 **2156** The sacrament of Baptism is conferred "in the name of the Father and of the Son and of the Holy Spirit."[85] In Baptism, the Lord's name sanctifies man, 1267 and the Christian receives his name in the Church. This can be the name of a saint, that is, of a disciple who has lived a life of exemplary fidelity to the Lord. The patron saint provides a model of charity; we are assured of his intercession. The "baptismal name" can also express a Christian mystery or Christian virtue. "Parents, sponsors, and the pastor are to see that a name is not given which is foreign to Christian sentiment."[86]

2157 The Christian begins his day, his prayers, and his activities with the Sign of the Cross: "in the name of the 1235 Father and of the Son and of the Holy Spirit. Amen." The baptized person dedicates the day to the glory of God and calls on the Savior's grace which lets him act 1668 in the Spirit as a child of the Father. The sign of the cross strengthens us in temptations and difficulties.

2158 God calls each one by name.[87] Everyone's name is sacred. The name is the icon of the person. It demands respect as a sign of the dignity of the one who bears it.

2159 The name one receives is a name for eternity. In the kingdom, the mysterious and unique character of

---

84 CIC, can. 1199 § 1.   85 *Mt* 28:19.   86 CIC, can. 855.   87 Cf. *Isa* 43:1; *Jn* 10:3.

each person marked with God's name will shine forth in splendor. "To him who conquers ... I will give a white stone, with a new name written on the stone which no one knows except him who receives it."[88] "Then I looked, and Lo, on Mount Zion stood the Lamb, and with him a hundred and forty-four thousand who had his name and his Father's name written on their foreheads."[89]

IN BRIEF

2160   "O Lord, our Lord, how majestic is your name in all the earth" (*Ps* 8:1)!

2161   The second commandment enjoins respect for the Lord's name. The name of the Lord is holy.

2162   The second commandment forbids every improper use of God's name. Blasphemy is the use of the name of God, of Jesus Christ, of the Virgin Mary, and of the saints in an offensive way.

2163   False oaths call on God to be witness to a lie. Perjury is a grave offense against the Lord who is always faithful to his promises.

2164   "Do not swear whether by the Creator, or any creature, except truthfully, of necessity, and with reverence" (St. Ignatius of Loyola, *Spiritual Exercises,* 38).

2165   In Baptism, the Christian receives his name in the Church. Parents, godparents, and the pastor are to see that he be given a Christian name. The patron saint provides a model of charity and the assurance of his prayer.

2166   The Christian begins his prayers and activities with the Sign of the Cross: "in the name of the Father and of the Son and of the Holy Spirit. Amen."

2167   God calls each one by name (cf. *Isa* 43:1).

88 *Rev* 2:17.   89 *Rev* 14:1.

ARTICLE 3
THE THIRD COMMANDMENT

> Remember the sabbath day, to keep it holy. Six days
> you shall labor, and do all your work; but the sev-
> enth day is a sabbath to the Lord your God; in it
> you shall not do any work.[90]

> The sabbath was made for man, not man for the
> sabbath; so the Son of Man is lord even of the sab-
> bath.[91]

346-348 **I.   THE SABBATH DAY**

2168   The third commandment of the Decalogue recalls the holiness of the sabbath: "The seventh day is a
sabbath of solemn rest, holy to the LORD."[92]

2057 **2169**   In speaking of the sabbath Scripture recalls creation: "For in six days the LORD made heaven and
earth, the sea, and all that is in them, and rested the seventh day; therefore the LORD blessed the sabbath day
and hallowed it."[93]

2170   Scripture also reveals in the Lord's day a *memorial of Israel's liberation* from bondage in Egypt: "You
shall remember that you were a servant in the land of
Egypt, and the LORD your God brought you out thence
with mighty hand and outstretched arm; therefore the
LORD your God commanded you to keep the sabbath
day."[94]

2171   God entrusted the sabbath to Israel to keep as a
sign of the irrevocable covenant.[95] The sabbath is for the
Lord, holy and set apart for the praise of God, his work
of creation, and his saving actions on behalf of Israel.

2172   God's action is the model for human action. If
God "rested and was refreshed" on the seventh day,
man too ought to "rest" and should let others, espe-
2184 cially the poor, "be refreshed."[96] The sabbath brings
everyday work to a halt and provides a respite. It is a

---

90 *Ex* 20:8–10; cf. *Deut* 5:12–15.   91 *Mk* 2:27–28.   92 *Ex* 31:15.   93 *Ex*
20:11.   94 *Deut* 5:15.   95 Cf. *Ex* 31:16.   96 *Ex* 31:17; cf. 23:12.

day of protest against the servitude of work and the worship of money.[97]

2173 The Gospel reports many incidents when Jesus was accused of violating the sabbath law. But Jesus never fails to respect the holiness of this day.[98] He gives 582 this law its authentic and authoritative interpretation: "The sabbath was made for man, not man for the sabbath."[99] With compassion, Christ declares the sabbath for doing good rather than harm, for saving life rather than killing.[100] The sabbath is the day of the Lord of mercies and a day to honor God.[101] "The Son of Man is lord even of the sabbath."[102]

II.   THE LORD'S DAY

> This is the day which the LORD has made; let us rejoice and be glad in it.[103]

The day of the Resurrection: the new creation

2174 Jesus rose from the dead "on the first day of the 638 week."[104] Because it is the "first day," the day of Christ's Resurrection recalls the first creation. Because it is the "eighth day" following the sabbath,[105] it symbolizes the 349 new creation ushered in by Christ's Resurrection. For Christians it has become the first of all days, the first of all feasts, the Lord's Day *(he kuriake hemera, dies dominica)*—Sunday:

> We all gather on the day of the sun, for it is the first day [after the Jewish sabbath, but also the first day] when God, separating matter from darkness, made the world; and on this same day Jesus Christ our Savior rose from the dead.[106]

Sunday—fulfillment of the sabbath

2175 Sunday is expressly distinguished from the sabbath which it follows chronologically every week; for Christians its ceremonial observance replaces that of the 1166 sabbath. In Christ's Passover, Sunday fulfills the spiri-

---

97 Cf. *Neh* 13:15–22; 2 *Chr* 36:21.   98 Cf. *Mk* 1:21; *Jn* 9:16.   99 *Mk* 2:27.
100 Cf. *Mk* 3:4.   101 Cf. *Mt* 12:5; *Jn* 7:23.   102 *Mk* 2:28.   103 *Ps* 118:24.
104 Cf. *Mt* 28:1; *Mk* 16:2; *Lk* 24:1; *Jn* 20:1.   105 Cf. *Mk* 16:1; *Mt* 28:1.
106 St. Justin, I *Apol.* 67: PG 6, 429 and 432.

tual truth of the Jewish sabbath and announces man's eternal rest in God. For worship under the Law prepared for the mystery of Christ, and what was done there prefigured some aspects of Christ:[107]

> Those who lived according to the old order of things have come to a new hope, no longer keeping the sabbath, but the Lord's Day, in which our life is blessed by him and by his death.[108]

2176 The celebration of Sunday observes the moral commandment inscribed by nature in the human heart to render to God an outward, visible, public, and regular worship "as a sign of his universal beneficence to all."[109] Sunday worship fulfills the moral command of the Old Covenant, taking up its rhythm and spirit in the weekly celebration of the Creator and Redeemer of his people.

The Sunday Eucharist

1167 **2177** The Sunday celebration of the Lord's Day and his Eucharist is at the heart of the Church's life. "Sunday is the day on which the paschal mystery is celebrated in light of the apostolic tradition and is to be observed as the foremost holy day of obligation in the universal Church."[110]

2043   "Also to be observed are the day of the Nativity of Our Lord Jesus Christ, the Epiphany, the Ascension of Christ, the feast of the Body and Blood of Christi, the feast of Mary the Mother of God, her Immaculate Conception, her Assumption, the feast of Saint Joseph, the feast of the Apostles Saints Peter and Paul, and the feast of All Saints."[111]

1343 **2178** This practice of the Christian assembly dates from the beginnings of the apostolic age.[112] The *Letter to the Hebrews* reminds the faithful "not to neglect to meet together, as is the habit of some, but to encourage one another."[113]

---

107 Cf. *1 Cor* 10:11.   108 St. Ignatius of Antioch, *Ad Magn.* 9, 1: SCh 10, 88.
109 St. Thomas Aquinas, *STh* II-II, 122, 4.   110 CIC, can. 1246 § 1.   111 CIC, can. 1246 § 2: "The conference of bishops can abolish certain holy days of obligation or transfer them to a Sunday with prior approval of the Apostolic See."
112 Cf. *Acts* 2:42–46; *1 Cor* 11:17.   113 *Heb* 10:25.

Tradition preserves the memory of an ever-timely exhortation: Come to Church early, approach the Lord, and confess your sins, repent in prayer. . . . Be present at the sacred and divine liturgy, conclude its prayer and do not leave before the dismissal. . . . We have often said: "This day is given to you for prayer and rest. This is the day that the Lord has made, let us rejoice and be glad in it."[114]

2179 "A *parish* is a definite community of the Chris-   1567
tian faithful established on a stable basis within a particular church; the pastoral care of the parish is entrusted
to a pastor as its own shepherd under the authority of
the diocesan bishop."[115] It is the place where all the   2691
faithful can be gathered together for the Sunday celebration of the Eucharist. The parish initiates the Christian people into the ordinary expression of the liturgical   2226
life: it gathers them together in this celebration; it
teaches Christ's saving doctrine; it practices the charity
of the Lord in good works and brotherly love:

> You cannot pray at home as at church, where there
> is a great multitude, where exclamations are cried
> out to God as from one great heart, and where
> there is something more: the union of minds, the
> accord of souls, the bond of charity, the prayers of
> the priests.[116]

The Sunday obligation
2180 The precept of the Church specifies the law of   2042
the Lord more precisely: "On Sundays and other holy
days of obligation the faithful are bound to participate
in the Mass."[117] "The precept of participating in the
Mass is satisfied by assistance at a Mass which is cele-   1389
brated anywhere in a Catholic rite either on the holy
day or on the evening of the preceding day."[118]

2181 The Sunday Eucharist is the foundation and confirmation of all Christian practice. For this reason the
faithful are obliged to participate in the Eucharist on
days of obligation, unless excused for a serious reason

---

114 *Sermo de die dominica* 2 et 6: PG 86/1, 416C and 421C.   115 CIC, can. 515
§ 1.   116 St. John Chrysostom, *De incomprehensibili* 3, 6: PG 48, 725.
117 CIC, can. 1247.   118 CIC, can. 1248 § 1.

(for example, illness, the care of infants) or dispensed by their own pastor.[119] Those who deliberately fail in this obligation commit a grave sin.

2182   Participation in the communal celebration of the Sunday Eucharist is a testimony of belonging and of be-
815   ing faithful to Christ and to his Church. The faithful give witness by this to their communion in faith and charity. Together they testify to God's holiness and their hope of salvation. They strengthen one another under the guidance of the Holy Spirit.

2183   "If because of lack of a sacred minister or for other grave cause participation in the celebration of the Eucharist is impossible, it is specially recommended that the faithful take part in the Liturgy of the Word if it is celebrated in the parish church or in another sacred place according to the prescriptions of the diocesan bishop, or engage in prayer for an appropriate amount of time personally or in a family or, as occasion offers, in groups of families."[120]

A day of grace and rest from work

2184   Just as God "rested on the seventh day from all his work which he had done,"[121] human life has a
2172   rhythm of work and rest. The institution of the Lord's Day helps everyone enjoy adequate rest and leisure to cultivate their familial, cultural, social, and religious lives.[122]

2185   On Sundays and other holy days of obligation, the faithful are to refrain from engaging in work or ac-
2428   tivities that hinder the worship owed to God, the joy proper to the Lord's Day, the performance of the works of mercy, and the appropriate relaxation of mind and body.[123] Family needs or important social service can legitimately excuse one from the obligation of Sunday rest. The faithful should see to it that legitimate excuses do not lead to habits prejudicial to religion, family life, and health.

---

119 Cf. CIC, can. 1245.   120 CIC, can. 1248 § 2.   121 *Gen* 2:2.   122 Cf. *GS* 67 § 3.   123 Cf. CIC, can. 1247.

The charity of truth seeks holy leisure; the necessity of charity accepts just work.[124]

2186 Those Christians who have leisure should be mindful of their brethren who have the same needs and the same rights, yet cannot rest from work because of poverty and misery. Sunday is traditionally consecrated by Christian piety to good works and humble service of the sick, the infirm, and the elderly. Christians will also *2447* sanctify Sunday by devoting time and care to their families and relatives, often difficult to do on other days of the week. Sunday is a time for reflection, silence, cultivation of the mind, and meditation which furthers the growth of the Christian interior life.

2187 Sanctifying Sundays and holy days requires a common effort. Every Christian should avoid making unnecessary demands on others that would hinder them from observing the Lord's Day. Traditional activities (sport, restaurants, etc.), and social necessities (public services, etc.), require some people to work on Sundays, but every- *2289* one should still take care to set aside sufficient time for leisure. With temperance and charity the faithful will see to it that they avoid the excesses and violence sometimes associated with popular leisure activities. In spite of economic constraints, public authorities should ensure citizens a time intended for rest and divine worship. Employers have a similar obligation toward their employees.

2188 In respecting religious liberty and the common *2105* good of all, Christians should seek recognition of Sundays and the Church's holy days as legal holidays. They have to give everyone a public example of prayer, respect, and joy and defend their traditions as a precious contribution to the spiritual life of society. If a country's legislation or other reasons require work on Sunday, the day should nevertheless be lived as the day of our deliverance which lets us share in this "festal gathering," this "assembly of the first-born who are enrolled in heaven."[125]

---

124 St. Augustine, *De civ. Dei* 19, 19: PL 41, 647.   125 *Heb* 12:22–23.

IN BRIEF

2189   "Observe the sabbath day, to keep it holy" (*Deut* 5:12). "The seventh day is a sabbath of solemn rest, holy to the Lord" (*Ex* 31:15).

2190   The sabbath, which represented the completion of the first creation, has been replaced by Sunday which recalls the new creation inaugurated by the Resurrection of Christ.

2191   The Church celebrates the day of Christ's Resurrection on the "eighth day," Sunday, which is rightly called the Lord's Day (cf. SC 106).

2192   "Sunday ... is to be observed as the foremost holy day of obligation in the universal Church" (CIC, can. 1246 § 1). "On Sundays and other holy days of obligation the faithful are bound to participate in the Mass" (CIC, can. 1247).

2193   "On Sundays and other holy days of obligation the faithful are bound ... to abstain from those labors and business concerns which impede the worship to be rendered to God, the joy which is proper to the Lord's Day, or the proper relaxation of mind and body" (CIC, can. 1247).

2194   The institution of Sunday helps all "to be allowed sufficient rest and leisure to cultivate their familial, cultural, social, and religious lives" (GS 67 § 3).

2195   Every Christian should avoid making unnecessary demands on others that would hinder them from observing the Lord's Day.

CHAPTER TWO
"YOU SHALL LOVE YOUR NEIGHBOR AS YOURSELF"

Jesus said to his disciples: "Love one another even as I have loved you."[1]

2196 In response to the question about the first of the commandments, Jesus says: "The first is, 'Hear, O Israel: The Lord our God, the Lord is one; and you shall love the Lord your God with all your heart, and with all your soul, and with all your mind, and with all your strength.' The second is this, 'You shall love your neighbor as yourself.' There is no other commandment greater than these."[2]

The apostle St. Paul reminds us of this: "He who 2822 loves his neighbor has fulfilled the law. The commandments, *'You shall not commit adultery, You shall not kill, You shall not steal, You shall not covet,'* and any other commandment, are summed up in this sentence, 'You shall love your neighbor as yourself.' Love does no wrong to a neighbor; therefore love is the fulfilling of the law."[3]

ARTICLE 4
THE FOURTH COMMANDMENT

Honor your father and your mother, that your days may be long in the land which the Lord your God gives you.[4]

He was obedient to them.[5]

The Lord Jesus himself recalled the force of this "commandment of God."[6] The Apostle teaches: "Children, obey your parents in the Lord, for this is right. 'Honor your father and mother,' (This is the first commandment with a promise.) 'that it may be well with you and that you may live long on the earth.' "[7]

---

1 *Jn* 13:34.   **2** *Mk* 12:29–31; cf. *Deut* 6:4–5; *Lev* 19:18; *Mt* 22:34–40; *Lk* 10:25–28.   **3** *Rom* 13:8–10.   **4** *Ex* 20:12; *Deut* 5:16.   **5** *Lk* 2:51.   **6** *Mk* 7:8–13.   **7** *Eph* 6:1–3; cf. *Deut* 5:16.

2197 The fourth commandment opens the second table of the Decalogue. It shows us the order of charity. God has willed that, after him, we should honor our parents to whom we owe life and who have handed on to us the knowledge of God. We are obliged to honor and respect all those whom God, for our good, has 1897 vested with his authority.

2198 This commandment is expressed in positive terms of duties to be fulfilled. It introduces the subsequent commandments which are concerned with particular respect for life, marriage, earthly goods, and 2419 speech. It constitutes one of the foundations of the social doctrine of the Church.

2199 The fourth commandment is addressed expressly to children in their relationship to their father and mother, because this relationship is the most universal. It likewise concerns the ties of kinship between members of the extended family. It requires honor, affection, and gratitude toward elders and ancestors. Finally, it extends to the duties of pupils to teachers, employees to employers, subordinates to leaders, citizens to their country, and to those who administer or govern it.

This commandment includes and presupposes the duties of parents, instructors, teachers, leaders, magistrates, those who govern, all who exercise authority over others or over a community of persons.

2200 Observing the fourth commandment brings its reward: "Honor your father and your mother, that your days may be long in the land which the LORD your God gives you."[8] Respecting this commandment provides, along with spiritual fruits, temporal fruits of peace and 2304 prosperity. Conversely, failure to observe it brings great harm to communities and to individuals.

---

8 *Ex* 20:12; *Deut* 5:16.

I.   THE FAMILY IN GOD'S PLAN

The nature of the family

2201   The conjugal community is established upon the consent of the spouses. Marriage and the family are ordered to the good of the spouses and to the procreation and education of children. The love of the spouses and the begetting of children create among members of the same family personal relationships and primordial responsibilities.   *1625*

2202   A man and a woman united in marriage, together with their children, form a family. This institution is prior to any recognition by public authority, which has an obligation to recognize it. It should be considered the normal reference point by which the different forms of family relationship are to be evaluated.   *1882*

2203   In creating man and woman, God instituted the human family and endowed it with its fundamental constitution. Its members are persons equal in dignity. For the common good of its members and of society, the family necessarily has manifold responsibilities, rights, and duties.   *369*

The Christian family   *1655-1658*

2204   "The Christian family constitutes a specific revelation and realization of ecclesial communion, and for this reason it can and should be called a *domestic church*."[9] It is a community of faith, hope, and charity; it assumes singular importance in the Church, as is evident in the New Testament.[10]   *533*

2205   The Christian family is a communion of persons, a sign and image of the communion of the Father and the Son in the Holy Spirit. In the procreation and education of children it reflects the Father's work of creation. It is called to partake of the prayer and sacrifice of Christ. Daily prayer and the reading of the Word of   *1702*

---

9 FC 21; cf. LG 11.   **10** Cf. *Eph* 5:21–6:4; *Col* 3:18–21; *1 Pet* 3:1–7.

God strengthen it in charity. The Christian family has an evangelizing and missionary task.

2206 The relationships within the family bring an affinity of feelings, affections and interests, arising above all from the members' respect for one another. The family is a *privileged community* called to achieve a "sharing of thought and common deliberation by the spouses as well as their eager cooperation as parents in the children's upbringing."[11]

II.   THE FAMILY AND SOCIETY

1880 **2207**   The family is the *original cell of social life*. It is the natural society in which husband and wife are called to give themselves in love and in the gift of life. Authority, stability, and a life of relationships within the 372 family constitute the foundations for freedom, security, 1603 and fraternity within society. The family is the community in which, from childhood, one can learn moral values, begin to honor God, and make good use of freedom. Family life is an initiation into life in society.

2208   The family should live in such a way that its members learn to care and take responsibility for the young, the old, the sick, the handicapped, and the poor. There are many families who are at times incapable of providing this help. It devolves then on other persons, other families, and, in a subsidiary way, society to provide for their needs: "Religion that is pure and undefiled before God and the Father is this: to visit orphans and widows in their affliction and to keep oneself unstained from the world."[12]

2209   The family must be helped and defended by appropriate social measures. Where families cannot fulfill their responsibilities, other social bodies have the duty of helping them and of supporting the institution of the 1883 family. Following the principle of subsidiarity, larger communities should take care not to usurp the family's prerogatives or interfere in its life.

---

11 GS 52 § 1.   **12** Jas 1:27.

2210   The importance of the family for the life and well-being of society[13] entails a particular responsibility for society to support and strengthen marriage and the family. Civil authority should consider it a grave duty "to acknowledge the true nature of marriage and the family, to protect and foster them, to safeguard public morality, and promote domestic prosperity."[14]

2211   The political community has a duty to honor the family, to assist it, and to ensure especially:

—the freedom to establish a family, have children, and bring them up in keeping with the family's own moral and religious convictions;

—the protection of the stability of the marriage bond and the institution of the family;

—the freedom to profess one's faith, to hand it on, and raise one's children in it, with the necessary means and institutions;

—the right to private property, to free enterprise, to obtain work and housing, and the right to emigrate;

—in keeping with the country's institutions, the right to medical care, assistance for the aged, and family benefits;

—the protection of security and health, especially with respect to dangers like drugs, pornography, alcoholism, etc.;

—the freedom to form associations with other families and so to have representation before civil authority.[15]

2212   The fourth commandment *illuminates other relationships in society*. In our brothers and sisters we see the children of our parents; in our cousins, the descendants of our ancestors; in our fellow citizens, the children of our country; in the baptized, the children of our mother the Church; in every human person, a son or daughter of the One who wants to be called "our Father." In this way our relationships with our neighbors are recognized as personal in character. The neighbor is not a "unit" in the human collective; he is "someone" who by his known origins deserves particular attention and respect.

225

1931

---

13 Cf. *GS* 47 § 1.   14 *GS* 52 § 2.   15 Cf. *FC* 46.

2213 Human communities are *made up of persons.* Governing them well is not limited to guaranteeing rights and fulfilling duties such as honoring contracts. Right relations between employers and employees, between those who govern and citizens, presuppose a natural good will in keeping with the dignity of human persons concerned for justice and fraternity.

1939

III.   THE DUTIES OF FAMILY MEMBERS

The duties of children

2214 The divine fatherhood is the source of human fatherhood;[16] this is the foundation of the honor owed to parents. The respect of children, whether minors or adults, for their father and mother[17] is nourished by the natural affection born of the bond uniting them. It is required by God's commandment.[18]

1858

2215 Respect for parents *(filial piety)* derives from *gratitude* toward those who, by the gift of life, their love and their work, have brought their children into the world and enabled them to grow in stature, wisdom, and grace. "With all your heart honor your father, and do not forget the birth pangs of your mother. Remember that through your parents you were born; what can you give back to them that equals their gift to you?"[19]

2216 Filial respect is shown by true docility and *obedience.* "My son, keep your father's commandment, and forsake not your mother's teaching. . . . When you walk, they will lead you; when you lie down, they will watch over you; and when you awake, they will talk with you."[20] "A wise son hears his father's instruction, but a scoffer does not listen to rebuke."[21]

532

2217 As long as a child lives at home with his parents, the child should obey his parents in all that they ask of him when it is for his good or that of the family. "Children, obey your parents in everything, for this pleases the Lord."[22] Children should also obey the reasonable direc-

---

16 Cf. *Eph* 3:14.   17 Cf. *Prov* 1:8; *Tob* 4:3–4.   18 Cf. *Ex* 20:12.   19 *Sir* 7:27–28.   20 *Prov* 6:20–22.   21 *Prov* 13:1.   22 *Col* 3:20; cf. *Eph* 6:1.

tions of their teachers and all to whom their parents have entrusted them. But if a child is convinced in conscience that it would be morally wrong to obey a particular order, he must not do so.

As they grow up, children should continue to respect their parents. They should anticipate their wishes, willingly seek their advice, and accept their just admonitions. Obedience toward parents ceases with the emancipation of the children; not so respect, which is always owed to them. This respect has its roots in the fear of God, one of the gifts of the Holy Spirit.

1831

2218 The fourth commandment reminds grown children of their *responsibilities toward their parents*. As much as they can, they must give them material and moral support in old age and in times of illness, loneliness, or distress. Jesus recalls this duty of gratitude.[23]

> For the Lord honored the father above the children, and he confirmed the right of the mother over her sons. Whoever honors his father atones for sins, and whoever glorifies his mother is like one who lays up treasure. Whoever honors his father will be gladdened by his own children, and when he prays he will be heard. Whoever glorifies his father will have long life, and whoever obeys the Lord will refresh his mother.[24]

> O son, help your father in his old age, and do not grieve him as long as he lives; even if he is lacking in understanding, show forbearance; in all your strength do not despise him. . . . Whoever forsakes his father is like a blasphemer, and whoever angers his mother is cursed by the Lord.[25]

2219 Filial respect promotes harmony in all of family life; it also concerns *relationships between brothers and sisters*. Respect toward parents fills the home with light and warmth. "Grandchildren are the crown of the aged."[26] "With all humility and meekness, with patience, [support] one another in charity."[27]

2220 For Christians a special gratitude is due to those from whom they have received the gift of faith, the

---

23 Cf. Mk 7:10–12. 24 Sir 3:2–6. 25 Sir 3:12–13, 16. 26 Prov 17:6. 27 Eph 4:2.

grace of Baptism, and life in the Church. These may include parents, grandparents, other members of the family, pastors, catechists, and other teachers or friends. "I am reminded of your sincere faith, a faith that dwelt first in your grandmother Lois and your mother Eunice and now, I am sure, dwells in you."[28]

The duties of parents

2221 The fecundity of conjugal love cannot be reduced solely to the procreation of children, but must extend to their moral education and their spiritual formation. "The *role of parents in education* is of such 1653 importance that it is almost impossible to provide an adequate substitute."[29] The right and the duty of parents to educate their children are primordial and inalienable.[30]

2222 Parents must regard their children as *children of God* and respect them as *human persons*. Show- 494 ing themselves obedient to the will of the Father in heaven, they educate their children to fulfill God's law.

2223 Parents have the first responsibility for the education of their children. They bear witness to this responsibility first by *creating a home* where tenderness, forgiveness, respect, fidelity, and disinterested service are the rule. The home is well suited for *education in the virtues*. This requires an apprenticeship in self-denial, 1804 sound judgment, and self-mastery—the preconditions of all true freedom. Parents should teach their children to subordinate the "material and instinctual dimensions to interior and spiritual ones."[31] Parents have a grave responsibility to give good example to their children. By knowing how to acknowledge their own failings to their children, parents will be better able to guide and correct them:

> He who loves his son will not spare the rod. . . . He who disciplines his son will profit by him.[32]

---

28 *2 Tim* 1:5.   29 *GE* 3.   30 Cf. *FC* 36.   31 *CA* 36 § 2.   32 *Sir* 30:1–2.

> Fathers, do not provoke your children to anger, but bring them up in the discipline and instruction of the Lord.[33]

2224 The home is the natural environment for initiat- 1939 ing a human being into solidarity and communal responsibilities. Parents should teach children to avoid the compromising and degrading influences which threaten human societies.

2225 Through the grace of the sacrament of marriage, parents receive the responsibility and privilege of *evangelizing their children*. Parents should initiate their children at an early age into the mysteries of the faith of 1656 which they are the "first heralds" for their children. They should associate them from their tenderest years with the life of the Church.[34] A wholesome family life can foster interior dispositions that are a genuine preparation for a living faith and remain a support for it throughout one's life.

2226 *Education in the faith* by the parents should begin in the child's earliest years. This already happens when family members help one another to grow in faith by the witness of a Christian life in keeping with the Gospel. Family catechisms precedes, accompanies, and enriches other forms of instruction in the faith. Parents have the mission of teaching their children to pray and to discover their vocation as children of God.[35] The 2179 parish is the Eucharistic community and the heart of the liturgical life of Christian families; it is a privileged place for the catechesis of children and parents.

2227 Children in turn contribute to the *growth in ho-* 2013 *liness* of their parents.[36] Each and everyone should be generous and tireless in forgiving one another for offenses, quarrels, injustices, and neglect. Mutual affection suggests this. The charity of Christ demands it.[37]

2228 Parents' respect and affection are expressed by the care and attention they devote to bringing up their

---

33 *Eph* 6:4.   34 *LG* 11 § 2.   35 Cf. *LG* 11.   36 Cf. *GS* 48 § 4.   37 Cf. *Mt* 18:21–22; *Lk* 17:4.

young children and *providing for their physical and spiritual needs.* As the children grow up, the same respect and devotion lead parents to educate them in the right use of their reason and freedom.

2229 As those first responsible for the education of their children, parents have the right to *choose a school for them* which corresponds to their own convictions. This right is fundamental. As far as possible parents have the duty of choosing schools that will best help them in their task as Christian educators.[38] Public authorities have the duty of guaranteeing this parental right and of ensuring the concrete conditions for its exercise.

2230 When they become adults, children have the right and duty to *choose their profession and state of life.* They should assume their new responsibilities within a trusting relationship with their parents, willingly asking and receiving their advice and counsel. Parents should be careful not to exert pressure on their children either in the choice of a profession or in that of a spouse. This necessary restraint does not prevent them—quite the contrary—from giving their children judicious advice, particularly when they are planning to start a family.

2231 Some forgo marriage in order to care for their parents or brothers and sisters, to give themselves more completely to a profession, or to serve other honorable ends. They can contribute greatly to the good of the human family.

IV. The Family and the Kingdom

2232 Family ties are important but not absolute. Just as the child grows to maturity and human and spiritual autonomy, so his unique vocation which comes from God asserts itself more clearly and forcefully. Parents should respect this call and encourage their children to follow it. They must be convinced that the first vocation of the Christian is to *follow Jesus:* "He who loves father

---

38 Cf. GE 6.

or mother more than me is not worthy of me; and he who loves son or daughter more than me is not worthy of me."[39]

2233   Becoming a disciple of Jesus means accepting the invitation to belong to *God's family,* to live in conformity with His way of life: "For whoever does the will of my Father in heaven is my brother, and sister, and mother."[40]   *542*

    Parents should welcome and respect with joy and thanksgiving the Lord's call to one of their children to follow him in virginity for the sake of the Kingdom in the consecrated life or in priestly ministry.

V.   THE AUTHORITIES IN CIVIL SOCIETY

2234   God's fourth commandment also enjoins us to honor all who for our good have received authority in society from God. It clarifies the duties of those who exercise authority as well as those who benefit from it.   *1897*

Duties of civil authorities

2235   Those who exercise authority should do so as a service. "Whoever would be great among you must be your servant."[41] The exercise of authority is measured morally in terms of its divine origin, its reasonable nature and its specific object. No one can command or establish what is contrary to the dignity of persons and the natural law.   *1899*

2236   The exercise of authority is meant to give outward expression to a just hierarchy of values in order to facilitate the exercise of freedom and responsibility by all. Those in authority should practice distributive justice wisely, taking account of the needs and contribution of each, with a view to harmony and peace. They should take care that the regulations and measures they adopt are not a source of temptation by setting personal interest against that of the community.[42]   *2411*

2237   *Political authorities* are obliged to respect the

---

39 *Mt* 10:37; cf. 16:25.   40 *Mt* 12:49.   41 *Mt* 20:26.   42 Cf. *CA* 25.

fundamental rights of the human person. They will dis-
357 pense justice humanely by respecting the rights of everyone, especially of families and the disadvantaged.

The political rights attached to citizenship can
and should be granted according to the requirements
of the common good. They cannot be suspended by
public authorities without legitimate and proportionate
reasons. Political rights are meant to be exercised for
the common good of the nation and the human community.

The duties of citizens

2238   Those subject to authority should regard those
in authority as representatives of God, who has made
them stewards of his gifts:[43] "Be subject for the Lord's
1900 sake to every human institution. . . . Live as free men,
yet without using your freedom as a pretext for evil;
but live as servants of God."[44] Their loyal collaboration includes the right, and at times the duty, to voice
their just criticisms of that which seems harmful to
the dignity of persons and to the good of the community.

1915 **2239**   It is the *duty of citizens* to contribute along with
the civil authorities to the good of society in a spirit of
truth, justice, solidarity, and freedom. The love and service of *one's country* follow from the duty of gratitude
2310 and belong to the order of charity. Submission to legitimate authorities and service of the common good require citizens to fulfill their roles in the life of the political community.

2240   Submission to authority and co-responsibility
for the common good make it morally obligatory to pay
taxes, to exercise the right to vote, and to defend one's
2265 country:

> Pay to all of them their dues, taxes to whom taxes
> are due, revenue to whom revenue is due, respect to
> whom respect is due, honor to whom honor is
> due.[45]

---

43 Cf. *Rom* 13:1–2.   44 *1 Pet* 2:13, 16.   45 *Rom* 13:7.

> [Christians] reside in their own nations, but as resident aliens. They participate in all things as citizens and endure all things as foreigners. . . . They obey the established laws and their way of life surpasses the laws. . . . So noble is the position to which God has assigned them that they are not allowed to desert it.[46]

1900 The Apostle exhorts us to offer prayers and thanksgiving for kings and all who exercise authority, "that we may lead a quiet and peaceable life, godly and respectful in every way."[47]

2241 The more prosperous nations are obliged, to the extent they are able, to welcome the *foreigner* in search of the security and the means of livelihood which he cannot find in his country of origin. Public authorities should see to it that the natural right is respected that places a guest under the protection of those who receive him.

Political authorities, for the sake of the common good for which they are responsible, may make the exercise of the right to immigrate subject to various juridical conditions, especially with regard to the immigrants' duties toward their country of adoption. Immigrants are obliged to respect with gratitude the material and spiritual heritage of the country that receives them, to obey its laws and to assist in carrying civic burdens.

2242 The citizen is obliged in conscience not to follow the directives of civil authorities when they are contrary to the demands of the moral order, to the fundamental rights 1903 of persons or the teachings of the Gospel. *Refusing obedi-* 2313 *ence* to civil authorities, when their demands are contrary to those of an upright conscience, finds its justification in the distinction between serving God and serving the political community. "Render therefore to Caesar the things that 450 are Caesar's, and to God the things that are God's."[48] "We must obey God rather than men":[49]

> When citizens are under the oppression of a public 1901 authority which oversteps its competence, they should still not refuse to give or to do what is objectively demanded of them by the common good; but it is legitimate for them to defend their own

---

46 *Ad Diognetum* 5, 5 and 10; 6, 10: PG 2, 1173 and 1176.   47 *1 Tim* 2:2.
48 *Mt* 22:21.   49 *Acts* 5:29.

rights and those of their fellow citizens against the abuse of this authority within the limits of the natural law and the Law of the Gospel.[50]

2309 **2243** Armed *resistance* to oppression by political authority is not legitimate, unless all the following conditions are met: 1) there is certain, grave, and prolonged violation of fundamental rights; 2) all other means of redress have been exhausted; 3) such resistance will not provoke worse disorders; 4) there is well-founded hope of success; and 5) it is impossible reasonably to foresee any better solution.

The political community and the Church

1910 **2244** Every institution is inspired, at least implicitly, by a vision of man and his destiny, from which it derives the point of reference for its judgment, its hierarchy of values, its line of conduct. Most societies have formed their institutions in the recognition of a certain preeminence of man over things. Only the divinely revealed *1881* religion has clearly recognized man's origin and destiny in God, the Creator and Redeemer. The Church invites *2109* political authorities to measure their judgments and decisions against this inspired truth about God and man:

> Societies not recognizing this vision or rejecting it in the name of their independence from God are brought to seek their criteria and goal in themselves or to borrow them from some ideology. Since they do not admit that one can defend an objective criterion of good and evil, they arrogate to themselves an explicit or implicit totalitarian power over man and his destiny, as history shows.[51]

2245 The Church, because of her commission and competence, is not to be confused in any way with the *912* political community. She is both the sign and the safeguard of the transcendent character of the human person. "The Church respects and encourages the political freedom and responsibility of the citizen."[52]

2246 It is a part of the Church's mission "to pass moral judgments even in matters related to politics,

---

50 GS 74 § 5.   51 Cf. CA 45; 46.   52 GS 76 § 3.

whenever the fundamental rights of man or the salvation of souls requires it. The means, the only means, she may use are those which are in accord with the Gospel and the welfare of all men according to the diversity of times and circumstances."[53]

2032
2420

IN BRIEF

2247 "Honor your father and your mother" (*Deut* 5:16; *Mk* 7:10).

2248 According to the fourth commandment, God has willed that, after him, we should honor our parents and those whom he has vested with authority for our good.

2249 The conjugal community is established upon the covenant and consent of the spouses. Marriage and family are ordered to the good of the spouses, to the procreation and the education of children.

2250 "The well-being of the individual person and of both human and Christian society is closely bound up with the healthy state of conjugal and family life" (*GS* 47 § 1).

2251 Children owe their parents respect, gratitude, just obedience, and assistance. Filial respect fosters harmony in all of family life.

2252 Parents have the first responsibility for the education of their children in the faith, prayer, and all the virtues. They have the duty to provide as far as possible for the physical and spiritual needs of their children.

2253 Parents should respect and encourage their children's vocations. They should remember and teach that the first calling of the Christian is to follow Jesus.

2254 Public authority is obliged to respect the funda-

---

53 *GS* 76 § 5.

mental rights of the human person and the conditions for the exercise of his freedom.

2255 It is the duty of citizens to work with civil authority for building up society in a spirit of truth, justice, solidarity, and freedom.

2256 Citizens are obliged in conscience not to follow the directives of civil authorities when they are contrary to the demands of the moral order. "We must obey God rather than men" (*Acts* 5:29).

2257 Every society's judgments and conduct reflect a vision of man and his destiny. Without the light the Gospel sheds on God and man, societies easily become totalitarian.

ARTICLE 5
THE FIFTH COMMANDMENT

You shall not kill.[54]

You have heard that it was said to the men of old, "You shall not kill: and whoever kills shall be liable to judgment." But I say to you that every one who is angry with his brother shall be liable to judgment.[55]

356 **2258** *"Human life is sacred* because from its beginning it involves the creative action of God and it remains for ever in a special relationship with the Creator, who is its sole end. God alone is the Lord of life from its beginning until its end: no one can under any circumstance claim for himself the right directly to destroy an innocent human being."[56]

I.   RESPECT FOR HUMAN LIFE

The witness of sacred history

401 **2259** In the account of Abel's murder by his brother Cain,[57] Scripture reveals the presence of anger and envy

---

54 *Ex* 20:13; cf. *Deut* 5:17.   55 *Mt* 5:21–22.   56 CDF, instruction, *Donum vitae,* intro. 5.   57 Cf. *Gen* 4:8–12.

in man, consequences of original sin, from the beginning of human history. Man has become the enemy of his fellow man. God declares the wickedness of this fratricide: "What have you done? The voice of your brother's blood is crying to me from the ground. And now you are cursed from the ground, which has opened its mouth to receive your brother's blood from your hand."[58]

2260 The covenant between God and mankind is interwoven with reminders of God's gift of human life and man's murderous violence:

> For your lifeblood I will surely require a reckoning. ... Whoever sheds the blood of man, by man shall his blood be shed; for God made man in his own image.[59]

> The Old Testament always considered blood a sacred sign of life.[60] This teaching remains necessary for all time.

2261 Scripture specifies the prohibition contained in the fifth commandment: "Do not slay the innocent and the righteous."[61] The deliberate murder of an innocent person is gravely contrary to the dignity of the human being, to the golden rule, and to the holiness of the Creator. The law forbidding it is universally valid: it obliges each and everyone, always and everywhere.

1756
1956

2262 In the Sermon on the Mount, the Lord recalls the commandment, "You shall not kill,"[62] and adds to it the proscription of anger, hatred, and vengeance. Going further, Christ asks his disciples to turn the other cheek, to love their enemies.[63] He did not defend himself and told Peter to leave his sword in its sheath.[64]

2844

Legitimate defense

2263 The legitimate defense of persons and societies is not an exception to the prohibition against the murder of the innocent that constitutes intentional killing. "The

---

58 *Gen* 4:10–11.   **59** *Gen* 9:5–6.   **60** Cf. *Lev* 17:14.   **61** *Ex* 23:7.   **62** *Mt* 5:21.
63 Cf. *Mt* 5:22–39; 5:44.   **64** Cf. *Mt* 26:52.

act of self-defense can have a double effect: the preser-
1737 vation of one's own life; and the killing of the aggressor. . . . The one is intended, the other is not."[65]

2196 **2264** Love toward oneself remains a fundamental
principle of morality. Therefore it is legitimate to insist
on respect for one's own right to life. Someone who defends his life is not guilty of murder even if he is forced
to deal his aggressor a lethal blow:

> If a man in self-defense uses more than necessary vi-
> olence, it will be unlawful: whereas if he repels
> force with moderation, his defense will be lawful.
> . . . Nor is it necessary for salvation that a man
> omit the act of moderate self-defense to avoid
> killing the other man, since one is bound to take
> more care of one's own life than of another's.[66]

2265 Legitimate defense can be not only a right but a
2240 grave duty for someone responsible for another's life,
the common good of the family or of the state.

2266 Preserving the common good of society requires
rendering the aggressor unable to inflict harm. For this
reason the traditional teaching of the Church has acknowledged as well-founded the right and duty of legit-
1897-1898 imate public authority to punish malefactors by means
of penalties commensurate with the gravity of the crime,
not excluding, in cases of extreme gravity, the death
penalty. For analogous reasons those holding authority
2308 have the right to repel by armed force aggressors against
the community in their charge.
    The primary effect of *punishment* is to redress
the disorder caused by the offense. When his punish-
1449 ment is voluntarily accepted by the offender, it takes on
the value of expiation. Moreover, punishment has the
effect of preserving public order and the safety of persons. Finally punishment has a medicinal value; as far as
possible it should contribute to the correction of the offender.[67]

---

65 St. Thomas Aquinas, *STh* II-II, 64, 7, *corp. art.*   66 St. Thomas Aquinas, *STh*
II-II, 64, 7, *corp. art.*   67 Cf. *Lk* 23:40–43.

2267 If bloodless means are sufficient to defend human lives against an aggressor and to protect public order and the safety of persons, public authority should limit itself to such means, because they better correspond to the concrete conditions of the common good and are more in conformity to the dignity of the human person.

2306

Intentional homicide

2268 The fifth commandment forbids *direct and intentional killing* as gravely sinful. The murderer and those who cooperate voluntarily in murder commit a sin that cries out to heaven for vengeance.[68]

1867

Infanticide,[69] fratricide, parricide, and the murder of a spouse are especially grave crimes by reason of the natural bonds which they break. Concern for eugenics or public health cannot justify any murder, even if commanded by public authority.

2269 The fifth commandment forbids doing anything with the intention of *indirectly* bringing about a person's death. The moral law prohibits exposing someone to mortal danger without grave reason, as well as refusing assistance to a person in danger.

The acceptance by human society of murderous famines, without efforts to remedy them, is a scandalous injustice and a grave offense. Those whose usurious and avaricious dealings lead to the hunger and death of their brethren in the human family indirectly commit homicide, which is imputable to them.[70]

Unintentional killing is not morally imputable. But one is not exonerated from grave offense if, without proportionate reasons, he has acted in a way that brings about someone's death, even without the intention to do so.

2290

Abortion

2270 Human life must be respected and protected absolutely from the moment of conception. From the first moment of his existence, a human being must be

---

68 Cf. *Gen* 4:10.   69 Cf. *GS* 51 § 3.   70 Cf. *Am* 8:4-10.

1703
357 recognized as having the rights of a person—among which is the inviolable right of every innocent being to life.[71]

> Before I formed you in the womb I knew you, and before you were born I consecrated you.[72]

> My frame was not hidden from you, when I was being made in secret, intricately wrought in the depths of the earth.[73]

2271 Since the first century the Church has affirmed the moral evil of every procured abortion. This teaching has not changed and remains unchangeable. Direct abortion, that is to say, abortion willed either as an end or a means, is gravely contrary to the moral law:

> You shall not kill the embryo by abortion and shall not cause the newborn to perish.[74]

> God, the Lord of life, has entrusted to men the noble mission of safeguarding life, and men must carry it out in a manner worthy of themselves. Life must be protected with the utmost care from the moment of conception: abortion and infanticide are abominable crimes.[75]

2272 Formal cooperation in an abortion constitutes a grave offense. The Church attaches the canonical penalty of excommunication to this crime against human life. "A person who procures a completed abortion incurs excommunication *latae sententiae*,"[76] "by the very commission of the offense,"[77] and subject to the
1463 conditions provided by Canon Law.[78] The Church does not thereby intend to restrict the scope of mercy. Rather, she makes clear the gravity of the crime committed, the irreparable harm done to the innocent who is put to death, as well as to the parents and the whole of society.

1930 **2273** The inalienable right to life of every innocent human individual is a *constitutive element of a civil society and its legislation:*

---

71 Cf. CDF, *Donum vitae* I, 1. **72** Jer 1:5; cf. Job 10:8–12; Ps 22:10–11. **73** Ps 139:15. **74** *Didache* 2, 2: SCh 248, 148; cf. *Ep. Barnabae* 19, 5: PG 2, 777; *Ad Diognetum* 5, 6: PG 2, 1173; Tertullian, *Apol.* 9: PL 1, 319–320. **75** GS 51 § 3 **76** CIC, can. 1398. **77** CIC, can. 1314. **78** Cf. CIC, cann. 1323–1324.

"The inalienable rights of the person must be recognized and respected by civil society and the political authority. These human rights depend neither on single individuals nor on parents; nor do they represent a concession made by society and the state; they belong to human nature and are inherent in the person by virtue of the creative act from which the person took his origin. Among such fundamental rights one should mention in this regard every human being's right to life and physical integrity from the moment of conception until death."[79]

"The moment a positive law deprives a category of human beings of the protection which civil legislation ought to accord them, the state is denying the equality of all before the law. When the state does not place its power at the service of the rights of each citizen, and in particular of the more vulnerable, the very foundations of a state based on law are undermined. . . . As a consequence of the respect and protection which must be ensured for the unborn child from the moment of conception, the law must provide appropriate penal sanctions for every deliberate violation of the child's rights."[80]

2274 Since it must be treated from conception as a person, the embryo must be defended in its integrity, cared for, and healed, as far as possible, like any other human being.

Prenatal diagnosis is morally licit, "if it respects the life and integrity of the embryo and the human fetus and is directed toward its safeguarding or healing as an individual. . . . It is gravely opposed to the moral law when this is done with the thought of possibly inducing an abortion, depending upon the results: a diagnosis must not be the equivalent of a death sentence."[81]

2275 "One must hold as licit procedures carried out on the human embryo which respect the life and integrity of the embryo and do not involve disproportionate risks for it, but are directed toward its healing, the improvement of its condition of health, or its individual survival."[82]

"It is immoral to produce human embryos intended for exploitation as disposable biological material."[83]

"Certain attempts to *influence chromosomic or genetic inheritance* are not therapeutic but are aimed at producing human beings selected according to sex or other

79 CDF, *Donum vitae* III.   80 CDF, *Donum vitae* III.   81 CDF, *Donum vitae* I, 2.   82 CDF, *Donum vitae* I, 3.   83 CDF, *Donum vitae* I, 5.

predetermined qualities. Such manipulations are contrary to the personal dignity of the human being and his integrity and identity"[84] which are unique and unrepeatable.

Euthanasia

1503   **2276**   Those whose lives are diminished or weakened deserve special respect. Sick or handicapped persons should be helped to lead lives as normal as possible.

2277   Whatever its motives and means, direct euthanasia consists in putting an end to the lives of handicapped, sick, or dying persons. It is morally unacceptable.

> Thus an act or omission which, of itself or by intention, causes death in order to eliminate suffering constitutes a murder gravely contrary to the dignity of the human person and to the respect due to the living God, his Creator. The error of judgment into which one can fall in good faith does not change the nature of this murderous act, which must always be forbidden and excluded.

2278   Discontinuing medical procedures that are burdensome, dangerous, extraordinary, or disproportionate to the expected outcome can be legitimate; it is the refusal of "over-zealous" treatment. Here one does not will to cause death; one's inability to impede it is merely accepted. The

1007   decisions should be made by the patient if he is competent and able or, if not, by those legally entitled to act for the patient, whose reasonable will and legitimate interests must always be respected.

2279   Even if death is thought imminent, the ordinary care owed to a sick person cannot be legitimately interrupted. The use of painkillers to alleviate the sufferings of the dying, even at the risk of shortening their days, can be morally in conformity with human dignity if death is not willed as either an end or a means, but only foreseen and tolerated as inevitable. Palliative care is a special form of disinterested charity. As such it should be encouraged.

Suicide

2280   Everyone is responsible for his life before God who has given it to him. It is God who remains the sovereign Master of life. We are obliged to accept life grate-

---

84 CDF, *Donum vitae* I, 6.

fully and preserve it for his honor and the salvation of   *2258*
our souls. We are stewards, not owners, of the life God
has entrusted to us. It is not ours to dispose of.

2281 Suicide contradicts the natural inclination of the
human being to preserve and perpetuate his life. It is
gravely contrary to the just love of self. It likewise offends love of neighbor because it unjustly breaks the ties
of solidarity with family, nation, and other human soci-   *2212*
eties to which we continue to have obligations. Suicide
is contrary to love for the living God.

2282 If suicide is committed with the intention of setting an example, especially to the young, it also takes on
the gravity of scandal. Voluntary co-operation in suicide   *1735*
is contrary to the moral law.

    Grave psychological disturbances, anguish, or
grave fear of hardship, suffering, or torture can diminish the responsibility of the one committing suicide.

2283 We should not despair of the eternal salvation of
persons who have taken their own lives. By ways
known to him alone, God can provide the opportunity
for salutary repentance. The Church prays for persons
who have taken their own lives.   *1037*

II.   Respect for the Dignity of Persons

Respect for the souls of others: scandal

2284 Scandal is an attitude or behavior which leads   *2847*
another to do evil. The person who gives scandal becomes his neighbor's tempter. He damages virtue and integrity; he may even draw his brother into spiritual
death. Scandal is a grave offense if by deed or omission
another is deliberately led into a grave offense.

2285 Scandal takes on a particular gravity by reason   *1903*
of the authority of those who cause it or the weakness
of those who are scandalized. It prompted our Lord to
utter this curse: "Whoever causes one of these little ones
who believe in me to sin, it would be better for him to
have a great millstone fastened round his neck and to be

drowned in the depth of the sea."[85] Scandal is grave when given by those who by nature or office are obliged to teach and educate others. Jesus reproaches the scribes and Pharisees on this account: he likens them to wolves in sheep's clothing.[86]

2286   Scandal can be provoked by laws or institutions, by fashion or opinion.

1887   Therefore, they are guilty of scandal who establish laws or social structures leading to the decline of morals and the corruption of religious practice, or to "social conditions that, intentionally or not, make Christian conduct and obedience to the Commandments difficult and practically impossible."[87] This is also true of business leaders who

2498   make rules encouraging fraud, teachers who provoke their children to anger,[88] or manipulators of public opinion who turn it away from moral values.

2287   Anyone who uses the power at his disposal in such a way that it leads others to do wrong becomes guilty of scandal and responsible for the evil that he has directly or indirectly encouraged. "Temptations to sin are sure to come; but woe to him by whom they come!"[89]

Respect for health

1503 **2288**   Life and physical health are precious gifts entrusted to us by God. We must take reasonable care of them, taking into account the needs of others and the common good.

1509   *Concern for the health* of its citizens requires that society help in the attainment of living-conditions that allow them to grow and reach maturity: food and clothing, housing, health care, basic education, employment, and social assistance.

364 **2289**   If morality requires respect for the life of the body, it does not make it an absolute value. It rejects a neo-pagan notion that tends to promote the *cult of the*

2113 *body,* to sacrifice everything for it's sake, to idolize physical perfection and success at sports. By its selective

---

85 *Mt* 18:6; cf. *1 Cor* 8:10–13.   86 Cf. *Mt* 7:15.   87 Pius XII, Discourse, June 1, 1941.   88 Cf. *Eph* 6:4; *Col* 3:21.   89 *Lk* 17:1.

preference of the strong over the weak, such a conception can lead to the perversion of human relationships.

2290 The virtue of temperance disposes us to *avoid every kind of excess:* the abuse of food, alcohol, tobacco, or medicine. Those incur grave guilt who, by drunkenness or a love of speed, endanger their own and others' safety on the road, at sea, or in the air. *1809*

2291 The *use of drugs* inflicts very grave damage on human health and life. Their use, except on strictly therapeutic grounds, is a grave offense. Clandestine production of and trafficking in drugs are scandalous practices. They constitute direct co-operation in evil, since they encourage people to practices gravely contrary to the moral law.

Respect for the person and scientific research

2292 Scientific, medical, or psychological experiments on human individuals or groups can contribute to healing the sick and the advancement of public health.

2293 Basic scientific research, as well as applied research, *159* is a significant expression of man's dominion over creation. Science and technology are precious resources when placed at the service of man and promote his integral development for the benefit of all. By themselves however they cannot disclose the meaning of existence and of human progress. Science and technology are ordered to man, from whom they take their origin and development; hence they find in the person and in his moral values both evidence of their purpose and awareness of their limits. *1703*

2294 It is an illusion to claim moral neutrality in scientific research and its applications. On the other hand, guiding principles cannot be inferred from simple technical efficiency, or from the usefulness accruing to some at the expense of others or, even worse, from prevailing ideologies. Science and technology by their very nature require unconditional respect for fundamental moral criteria. They *2375* must be at the service of the human person, of his inalienable rights, of his true and integral good, in conformity with the plan and the will of God.

2295 Research or experimentation on the human being cannot legitimate acts that are in themselves con-

1753   trary to the dignity of persons and to the moral law. The subjects' potential consent does not justify such acts. Experimentation on human beings is not morally legitimate if it exposes the subject's life or physical and psychological integrity to disproportionate or avoidable risks. Experimentation on human beings does not conform to the dignity of the person if it takes place without the informed consent of the subject or those who legitimately speak for him.

2296   *Organ transplants* are not morally acceptable if the donor or those who legitimately speak for him have not given their informed consent. Organ transplants conform with the moral law and can be meritorious if the physical and psychological dangers and risks incurred by the donor are proportionate to the good sought for the recipient. It is morally inadmissible directly to bring about the disabling mutilation or death of a human being, even in order to delay the death of other persons.

Respect for bodily integrity

2297   *Kidnapping* and *hostage taking* bring on a reign of terror; by means of threats they subject their victims to intolerable pressures. They are morally wrong. *Terrorism* which threatens, wounds, and kills indiscriminately is gravely against justice and charity. *Torture* which uses physical or moral violence to extract confessions, punish the guilty, frighten opponents, or satisfy hatred is contrary to respect for the person and for human dignity. Except when performed for strictly therapeutic medical reasons, directly intended *amputations, mutilations,* and *sterilizations* performed on innocent persons are against the moral law.[90]

2298   In times past, cruel practices were commonly used by legitimate governments to maintain law and order, often without protest from the Pastors of the Church, who themselves adopted in their own tribunals the prescriptions of Roman law concerning torture. Regrettable as these facts are, the Church always taught the duty of clemency and
2267   mercy. She forbade clerics to shed blood. In recent times it has become evident that these cruel practices were neither

---

90 Cf. DS 3722.

necessary for public order, nor in conformity with the legitimate rights of the human person. On the contrary, these practices led to ones even more degrading. It is necessary to work for their abolition. We must pray for the victims and their tormentors.

Respect for the dead

2299 The dying should be given attention and care to help them live their last moments in dignity and peace. They will be helped by the prayer of their relatives, who must see to it that the sick receive at the proper time the *1525* sacraments that prepare them to meet the living God.

2300 The bodies of the dead must be treated with respect and charity, in faith and hope of the Resurrection. *1681-1690* The burial of the dead is a corporal work of mercy;[91] it honors the children of God, who are temples of the Holy Spirit.

2301 Autopsies can be morally permitted for legal inquests or scientific research. The free gift of organs after death is legitimate and can be meritorious.

    The Church permits cremation, provided that it does not demonstrate a denial of faith in the resurrection of the body.[92]

III. SAFEGUARDING PEACE

Peace

2302 By recalling the commandment, "You shall not kill,"[93] our Lord asked for peace of heart and denounced murderous anger and hatred as immoral. *1765*

    Anger is a desire for revenge. "To desire vengeance in order to do evil to someone who should be punished is illicit," but it is praiseworthy to impose restitution "to correct vices and maintain justice."[94] If anger reaches the point of a deliberate desire to kill or seriously wound a neighbor, it is gravely against charity; it is a mortal sin. The Lord says, "Everyone who is angry with his brother shall be liable to judgment."[95]

---

91 Cf. *Tob* 1:16–18.   92 Cf. CIC, can. 1176 § 3.   93 *Mt* 5:21.   94 St. Thomas Aquinas, *STh* II-II, 158, 1 *ad* 3.   95 *Mt* 5:22.

2094 **2303** Deliberate *hatred* is contrary to charity. Hatred of the neighbor is a sin when one deliberately wishes
1933 him evil. Hatred of the neighbor is a grave sin when one deliberately desires him grave harm. "But I say to you, Love your enemies and pray for those who persecute you, so that you may be sons of your Father who is in heaven."[96]

1909 **2304** Respect for and development of human life require *peace*. Peace is not merely the absence of war, and it is not limited to maintaining a balance of powers between adversaries. Peace cannot be attained on earth without safeguarding the goods of persons, free communication among men, respect for the dignity of persons and peoples, and the assiduous practice of frater-
1807 nity. Peace is "the tranquillity of order."[97] Peace is the work of justice and the effect of charity.[98]

2305 Earthly peace is the image and fruit of the *peace of Christ,* the messianic "Prince of Peace."[99] By the blood of his Cross, "in his own person he killed the hos-
1468 tility,"[100] he reconciled men with God and made his Church the sacrament of the unity of the human race and of its union with God. "He is our peace."[101] He has declared: "Blessed are the peacemakers."[102]

2306 Those who renounce violence and bloodshed and, in order to safeguard human rights, make use of those means of defense available to the weakest, bear
2267 witness to evangelical charity, provided they do so without harming the rights and obligations of other men and societies. They bear legitimate witness to the gravity of the physical and moral risks of recourse to violence, with all its destruction and death.[103]

Avoiding war
2307 The fifth commandment forbids the intentional destruction of human life. Because of the evils and injustices that accompany all war, the Church insistently

---

96 *Mt* 5:44–45.   97 St. Augustine, *De civ. Dei,* 19, 13, 1: PL 41, 640.   98 Cf. *Isa* 32:17; cf. *GS* 78 §§ 1–2.   99 *Isa* 9:5.   100 *Eph* 2:16 J.B.; cf. *Col* 1:20–22.   101 *Eph* 2:14.   102 *Mt* 5:9.   103 Cf. *GS* 78 § 5.

urges everyone to prayer and to action so that the divine Goodness may free us from the ancient bondage of war.[104]

2308 All citizens and all governments are obliged to work for the avoidance of war.

However, "as long as the danger of war persists and there is no international authority with the neces-   *2266* sary competence and power, governments cannot be de- nied the right of lawful self-defense, once all peace ef- forts have failed."[105]

2309 The strict conditions for *legitimate defense by* *2243* *military force* require rigorous consideration. The grav- ity of such a decision makes it subject to rigorous conditions of moral legitimacy. At one and the same time:

—the damage inflicted by the aggressor on the nation or community of nations must be lasting, grave, and cer- tain;

—all other means of putting an end to it must have been shown to be impractical or ineffective;

—there must be serious prospects of success;

—the use of arms must not produce evils and disorders graver than the evil to be eliminated. The power of modern means of destruction weighs very heavily in evaluating this condition.

These are the traditional elements enumerated in what is called the "just war" doctrine.

The evaluation of these conditions for moral le- gitimacy belongs to the prudential judgment of those *1897* who have responsibility for the common good.

2310 Public authorities, in this case, have the right and duty to impose on citizens the *obligations necessary for national defense.*

Those who are sworn to serve their country in *2239* the armed forces are servants of the security and free- *1909*

---

104 Cf. *GS* 81 § 4.   105 *GS* 79 § 4.

dom of nations. If they carry out their duty honorably, they truly contribute to the common good of the nation and the maintenance of peace.[106]

2311 Public authorities should make equitable provision for those who for reasons of conscience refuse to bear arms; these are nonetheless obliged to serve the human community in some other way.[107]

1782, 1790

2312 The Church and human reason both assert the permanent validity of the *moral law during armed conflict.* "The mere fact that war has regrettably broken out does not mean that everything becomes licit between the warring parties."[108]

2313 Non-combatants, wounded soldiers, and prisoners must be respected and treated humanely.

Actions deliberately contrary to the law of nations and to its universal principles are crimes, as are the orders that command such actions. Blind obedience does not suffice to excuse those who carry them out. Thus the extermination of a people, nation, or ethnic minority must be condemned as a mortal sin. One is morally bound to resist orders that command genocide.

2242

2314 "Every act of war directed to the indiscriminate destruction of whole cities or vast areas with their inhabitants is a crime against God and man, which merits firm and unequivocal condemnation."[109] A danger of modern warfare is that it provides the opportunity to those who possess modern scientific weapons—especially atomic, biological, or chemical weapons—to commit such crimes.

2315 The *accumulation of arms* strikes many as a paradoxically suitable way of deterring potential adversaries from war. They see it as the most effective means of ensuring peace among nations. This method of deterrence gives rise to strong moral reservations. The *arms race* does not ensure peace. Far from eliminating the causes of war, it risks aggravating them. Spending enor-

---

106 Cf. *GS* 79 § 5.   107 Cf. *GS* 79 § 3.   108 *GS* 79 § 4.   109 *GS* 80 § 3.

mous sums to produce ever new types of weapons impedes efforts to aid needy populations;[110] it thwarts the development of peoples. *Over-armament* multiplies reasons for conflict and increases the danger of escalation.

2316 *The production and the sale of arms* affect the common good of nations and of the international community. Hence public authorities have the right and duty to regulate them. The short-term pursuit of private or collective interests cannot legitimate undertakings that promote violence and conflict among nations and compromise the international juridical order.   *1906*

2317 Injustice, excessive economic or social inequalities, envy, distrust, and pride raging among men and nations constantly threaten peace and cause wars. Everything done to overcome these disorders contributes to building up peace and avoiding war: *1938*
2538

1941

> Insofar as men are sinners, the threat of war hangs over them and will so continue until Christ comes again; but insofar as they can vanquish sin by coming together in charity, violence itself will be vanquished and these words will be fulfilled: "they shall beat their swords into plowshares, and their spears into pruning hooks; nation shall not lift up sword against nation, neither shall they learn war any more."[111]

IN BRIEF

2318 "In [God's] hand is the life of every living thing and the breath of all mankind" (*Job* 12:10).

2319 Every human life, from the moment of conception until death, is sacred because the human person has been willed for its own sake in the image and likeness of the living and holy God.

2320 The murder of a human being is gravely contrary to the dignity of the person and the holiness of the Creator.

2321 The prohibition of murder does not abrogate the

---

110 Cf. Paul VI, *PP* 53.   111 *GS* 78 § 6; cf. *Isa* 2:4.

right to render an unjust aggressor unable to inflict harm. Legitimate defense is a grave duty for whoever is responsible for the lives of others or the common good.

2322   From its conception, the child has the right to life. Direct abortion, that is, abortion willed as an end or as a means, is a "criminal" practice (*GS* 27 § 3), gravely contrary to the moral law. The Church imposes the canonical penalty of excommunication for this crime against human life.

2323   Because it should be treated as a person from conception, the embryo must be defended in its integrity, cared for, and healed like every other human being.

2324   Intentional euthanasia, whatever its forms or motives, is murder. It is gravely contrary to the dignity of the human person and to the respect due to the living God, his Creator.

2325   Suicide is seriously contrary to justice, hope, and charity. It is forbidden by the fifth commandment.

2326   Scandal is a grave offense when by deed or omission it deliberately leads others to sin.

2327   Because of the evils and injustices that all war brings with it, we must do everything reasonably possible to avoid it. The Church prays: "From famine, pestilence, and war, O Lord, deliver us."

2328   The Church and human reason assert the permanent validity of the moral law during armed conflicts. Practices deliberately contrary to the law of nations and to its universal principles are crimes.

2329   "The arms race is one of the greatest curses on the human race and the harm it inflicts on the poor is more than can be endured" (*GS* 81 § 3).

2330 "Blessed are the peacemakers, for they shall be called sons of God" (*Mt* 5:9).

ARTICLE 6
THE SIXTH COMMANDMENT

You shall not commit adultery.[112]

You have heard that it was said, "You shall not commit adultery." But I say to you that every one who looks at a woman lustfully has already committed adultery with her in his heart.[113]

I. "MALE AND FEMALE HE CREATED THEM . . ."

369-373

2331 "God is love and in himself he lives a mystery of personal loving communion. Creating the human race in his own image . . . , God inscribed in the humanity of man and woman the *vocation,* and thus the capacity and responsibility, *of love* and communion."[114]

1604

"God created man in his own image . . . male and female he created them";[115] He blessed them and said, "Be fruitful and multiply";[116] "When God created man, he made him in the likeness of God. Male and female he created them, and he blessed them and named them Man when they were created."[117]

2332 *Sexuality* affects all aspects of the human person in the unity of his body and soul. It especially concerns affectivity, the capacity to love and to procreate, and in a more general way the aptitude for forming bonds of communion with others.

362

2333 Everyone, man and woman, should acknowledge and accept his sexual *identity.* Physical, moral, and spiritual *difference* and *complementarity* are oriented toward the goods of marriage and the flourishing of family life. The harmony of the couple and of society depends in part on the way in which the complemen-

1603

---

112 *Ex* 20:14; *Deut* 5:18. 113 *Mt* 5:27–28. 114 *FC* 11. 115 *Gen* 1:27.
116 *Gen* 1:28. 117 *Gen* 5:1–2.

tarity, needs, and mutual support between the sexes are lived out.

2334 "In creating men 'male and female,' God gives
357 man and woman an equal personal dignity."[118] "Man is a person, man and woman equally so, since both were created in the image and likeness of the personal God."[119]

2335 Each of the two sexes is an image of the power and tenderness of God, with equal dignity though in a different way. The *union of man and woman* in marriage is a way of imitating in the flesh the Creator's generosity and fecundity: "Therefore a man leaves his fa-
2205 ther and his mother and cleaves to his wife, and they become one flesh."[120] All human generations proceed from this union.[121]

1614 **2336** Jesus came to restore creation to the purity of its origins. In the Sermon on the Mount, he interprets God's plan strictly: "You have heard that it was said, 'You shall not commit adultery.' But I say to you that every one who looks at a woman lustfully has already committed adultery with her in his heart."[122] What God has joined together, let not man put asunder.[123]

　　The tradition of the Church has understood the sixth commandment as encompassing the whole of human sexuality.

II.　THE VOCATION TO CHASTITY

2520 **2337** Chastity means the successful integration of sexuality within the person and thus the inner unity of man in his bodily and spiritual being. Sexuality, in which man's belonging to the bodily and biological world is expressed, becomes personal and truly human when it is integrated into the relationship of one person to another, in the complete and lifelong mutual gift of a man and a woman.

---

118 *FC* 22; cf. *GS* 49 § 2.　119 *MD* 6.　120 *Gen* 2:24.　121 Cf. *Gen* 4:1-2, 25-26; 5:1.　122 *Mt* 5:27-28.　123 Cf. *Mt* 19:6.

The virtue of chastity therefore involves the integrity of the person and the integrality of the gift.

The integrity of the person

2338 The chaste person maintains the integrity of the powers of life and love placed in him. This integrity ensures the unity of the person; it is opposed to any behavior that would impair it. It tolerates neither a double life nor duplicity in speech.[124]

2339 Chastity includes an *apprenticeship in self-mastery* which is a training in human freedom. The alternative is clear: either man governs his passions and finds peace, or he lets himself be dominated by them and becomes unhappy.[125] "Man's dignity therefore requires him to act out of conscious and free choice, as moved and drawn in a personal way from within, and not by blind impulses in himself or by mere external constraint. Man gains such dignity when, ridding himself of all slavery to the passions, he presses forward to his goal by freely choosing what is good and, by his diligence and skill, effectively secures for himself the means suited to this end."[126]

1767

2340 Whoever wants to remain faithful to his baptismal promises and resist temptations will want to adopt the *means* for doing so: self-knowledge, practice of an ascesis adapted to the situations that confront him, obedience to God's commandments, exercise of the moral virtues, and fidelity to prayer. "Indeed it is through chastity that we are gathered together and led back to the unity from which we were fragmented into multiplicity."[127]

2015

2341 The virtue of chastity comes under the cardinal virtue of *temperance,* which seeks to permeate the passions and appetites of the senses with reason.

1809

2342 Self-mastery is a *long and exacting work*. One can never consider it acquired once and for all. It pre-

---

124 Cf. *Mt* 5:37.   125 Cf. *Sir* 1:22.   126 *GS* 17.   127 St. Augustine, *Conf.* 10, 29, 40: PL 32, 796.

409   supposes renewed effort at all stages of life.[128] The effort
required can be more intense in certain periods, such as
when the personality is being formed during childhood
and adolescence.

2343   Chastity has *laws of growth* which progress
through stages marked by imperfection and too often by
sin. "Man . . . day by day builds himself up through his
2223   many free decisions; and so he knows, loves, and accomplishes moral good by stages of growth."[129]

2525   **2344**   Chastity represents an eminently personal task;
it also involves a *cultural effort,* for there is "an interdependence between personal betterment and the improvement of society."[130] Chastity presupposes respect
for the rights of the person, in particular the right to receive information and an education that respect the
moral and spiritual dimensions of human life.

1810   **2345**   Chastity is a moral virtue. It is also a gift from
God, a *grace,* a fruit of spiritual effort.[131] The Holy
Spirit enables one whom the water of Baptism has re-
generated to imitate the purity of Christ.[132]

The integrality of the gift of self

1827   **2346**   Charity is the *form* of all the virtues. Under its
influence, chastity appears as a school of the gift of the
person. Self-mastery is ordered to the gift of self.
Chastity leads him who practices it to become a witness
210   to his neighbor of God's fidelity and loving kindness.

374   **2347**   The virtue of chastity blossoms in *friendship.* It
shows the disciple how to follow and imitate him who
has chosen us as his friends,[133] who has given himself totally to us and allows us to participate in his divine es-
tate. Chastity is a promise of immortality.

Chastity is expressed notably in *friendship with
one's neighbor.* Whether it develops between persons of
the same or opposite sex, friendship represents a great
good for all. It leads to spiritual communion.

---

128 Cf. *Titus* 2:1–6.   129 *FC* 34.   130 *GS* 25 § 1.   131 Cf. *Gal* 5:22.   132 Cf.
1 Jn 3:3.   133 Cf. *Jn* 15:15.

The various forms of chastity

2348 All the baptized are called to chastity. The Christian has "put on Christ,"[134] the model for all chastity. All Christ's faithful are called to lead a chaste life in keeping with their particular states of life. At the moment of his Baptism, the Christian is pledged to lead his affective life in chastity.

2349 "People should cultivate [chastity] in the way *1620* that is suited to their state of life. Some profess virginity or consecrated celibacy which enables them to give themselves to God alone with an undivided heart in a remarkable manner. Others live in the way prescribed for all by the moral law, whether they are married or single."[135] Married people are called to live conjugal chastity; others practice chastity in continence:

> There are three forms of the virtue of chastity: the first is that of spouses, the second that of widows, and the third that of virgins. We do not praise any one of them to the exclusion of the others. . . . This is what makes for the richness of the discipline of the Church.[136]

2350 Those who are *engaged to marry* are called to *1632* live chastity in continence. They should see in this time of testing a discovery of mutual respect, an apprenticeship in fidelity, and the hope of receiving one another from God. They should reserve for marriage the expressions of affection that belong to married love. They will help each other grow in chastity.

Offenses against chastity

2351 *Lust* is disordered desire for or inordinate enjoyment of sexual pleasure. Sexual pleasure is morally disordered when sought for itself, isolated from its procreative and unitive purposes.

2352 By *masturbation* is to be understood the deliberate stimulation of the genital organs in order to derive sexual pleasure. "Both the Magisterium of the Church,

---

134 *Gal* 3:27.   135 CDF, *Persona humana* 11.   136 St. Ambrose, *De viduis* 4, 23: PL 16, 255A.

in the course of a constant tradition, and the moral sense of the faithful have been in no doubt and have firmly maintained that masturbation is an intrinsically and gravely disordered action."[137] "The deliberate use of the sexual faculty, for whatever reason, outside of marriage is essentially contrary to its purpose." For here sexual pleasure is sought outside of "the sexual relationship which is demanded by the moral order and in which the total meaning of mutual self-giving and human procreation in the context of true love is achieved."[138]

To form an equitable judgment about the subjects' moral responsibility and to guide pastoral action, one must take into account the affective immaturity, force of acquired habit, conditions of anxiety, or other psychological or social factors that lessen or even extenuate moral culpability.

1735

2353 *Fornication* is carnal union between an unmarried man and an unmarried woman. It is gravely contrary to the dignity of persons and of human sexuality which is naturally ordered to the good of spouses and the generation and education of children. Moreover, it is a grave scandal when there is corruption of the young.

2523 **2354** *Pornography* consists in removing real or simulated sexual acts from the intimacy of the partners, in order to display them deliberately to third parties. It offends against chastity because it perverts the conjugal act, the intimate giving of spouses to each other. It does grave injury to the dignity of its participants (actors, vendors, the public), since each one becomes an object of base pleasure and illicit profit for others. It immerses all who are involved in the illusion of a fantasy world. It is a grave offense. Civil authorities should prevent the production and distribution of pornographic materials.

2355 *Prostitution* does injury to the dignity of the person who engages in it, reducing the person to an instru-

---

137 CDF, *Persona humana* 9.   138 CDF, *Persona humana* 9.

ment of sexual pleasure. The one who pays sins gravely against himself: he violates the chastity to which his Baptism pledged him and defiles his body, the temple of the Holy Spirit.[139] Prostitution is a social scourge. It usually involves women, but also men, children, and adolescents (The latter two cases involve the added sin of scandal.). While it is always gravely sinful to engage in prostitution, the imputability of the offense can be attenuated by destitution, blackmail, or social pressure.   *1735*

2356   *Rape* is the forcible violation of the sexual intimacy of another person. It does injury to justice and charity. Rape deeply wounds the respect, freedom, and physical and moral integrity to which every person has a right. It causes grave damage that can mark the victim for life. It is always an intrinsically evil act. Graver still   *2297* is the rape of children committed by parents (incest) or   *1756* those responsible for the education of the children entrusted to them.   *2388*

Chastity and homosexuality

2357   Homosexuality refers to relations between men or between women who experience an exclusive or predominant sexual attraction toward persons of the same sex. It has taken a great variety of forms through the centuries and in different cultures. Its psychological genesis remains largely unexplained. Basing itself on Sacred Scripture, which presents homosexual acts as acts of grave depravity,[140] tradition has always declared that "homosexual acts are intrinsically disordered."[141] They are contrary to the natural law. They close the sexual act to the gift of life. They do not proceed from a genuine affective and sexual complementarity. Under no   *2333* circumstances can they be approved.

2358   The number of men and women who have deep-seated homosexual tendencies is not negligible. They do not choose their homosexual condition; for most of them it is a trial. They must be accepted with respect,

---

139 Cf. *1 Cor* 6:15–20.   140 Cf. *Gen* 19:1–29; *Rom* 1:24–27; *1 Cor* 6:10; *1 Tim* 1:10.   141 CDF, *Persona humana* 8.

compassion, and sensitivity. Every sign of unjust discrimination in their regard should be avoided. These persons are called to fulfill God's will in their lives and, if they are Christians, to unite to the sacrifice of the Lord's Cross the difficulties they may encounter from their condition.

2347   **2359** Homosexual persons are called to chastity. By the virtues of self-mastery that teach them inner freedom, at times by the support of disinterested friendship, by prayer and sacramental grace, they can and should gradually and resolutely approach Christian perfection.

III.   THE LOVE OF HUSBAND AND WIFE

2360 Sexuality is ordered to the conjugal love of man and woman. In marriage the physical intimacy of the
1601 spouses becomes a sign and pledge of spiritual communion. Marriage bonds between baptized persons are sanctified by the sacrament.

2361 "Sexuality, by means of which man and woman give themselves to one another through the acts which
1643 are proper and exclusive to spouses, is not something simply biological, but concerns the innermost being of
2332 the human person as such. It is realized in a truly human way only if it is an integral part of the love by which a man and woman commit themselves totally to one another until death."[142]

1611   Tobias got out of bed and said to Sarah, "Sister, get up, and let us pray and implore our Lord that he grant us mercy and safety." So she got up, and they began to pray and implore that they might be kept safe. Tobias began by saying, "Blessed are you, O God of our fathers. . . . You made Adam, and for him you made his wife Eve as a helper and support. From the two of them the race of mankind has sprung. You said, 'It is not good that the man should be alone; let us make a helper for him like himself.' I now am taking this kinswoman of mine, not because of lust, but with sincerity. Grant that she and I may find mercy and that we may grow old

---

142 *FC* 11.

together." And they both said, "Amen, Amen." Then they went to sleep for the night.[143]

2362 "The acts in marriage by which the intimate and chaste union of the spouses takes place are noble and honorable; the truly human performance of these acts fosters the self-giving they signify and enriches the spouses in joy and gratitude."[144] Sexuality is a source of joy and pleasure:

> The Creator himself . . . established that in the [generative] function, spouses should experience pleasure and enjoyment of body and spirit. Therefore, the spouses do nothing evil in seeking this pleasure and enjoyment. They accept what the Creator has intended for them. At the same time, spouses should know how to keep themselves within the limits of just moderation.[145]

2363 The spouses' union achieves the twofold end of marriage: the good of the spouses themselves and the transmission of life. These two meanings or values of marriage cannot be separated without altering the couple's spiritual life and compromising the goods of marriage and the future of the family.

The conjugal love of man and woman thus stands under the twofold obligation of fidelity and fecundity.

Conjugal fidelity

1646-1648

2364 The married couple forms "the intimate partnership of life and love established by the Creator and governed by his laws; it is rooted in the conjugal covenant, that is, in their irrevocable personal consent."[146] Both give themselves definitively and totally to one another. They are no longer two; from now on they form one flesh. The covenant they freely contracted imposes on the spouses the obligation to preserve it as unique and indissoluble.[147] "What therefore God has joined together, let not man put asunder."[148]

1603

1615

---

143 *Tob* 8:4-9.   144 *GS* 49 § 2.   145 Pius XII, Discourse, October 29, 1951.
146 *GS* 48 § 1.   147 Cf. CIC, can. 1056.   148 *Mk* 10:9; cf. *Mt* 19:1-12; 1 *Cor* 7:10-11.

2365 Fidelity expresses constancy in keeping one's given word. God is faithful. The Sacrament of Matrimony enables man and woman to enter into Christ's fidelity for his Church. Through conjugal chastity, they bear witness to this mystery before the world.

1640

> St. John Chrysostom suggests that young husbands should say to their wives: I have taken you in my arms, and I love you, and I prefer you to my life itself. For the present life is nothing, and my most ardent dream is to spend it with you in such a way that we may be assured of not being separated in the life reserved for us. . . . I place your love above all things, and nothing would be more bitter or painful to me than to be of a different mind than you.[149]

1652-1653 ## The fecundity of marriage

2366 Fecundity is a gift, an *end of marriage,* for conjugal love naturally tends to be fruitful. A child does not come from outside as something added on to the mutual love of the spouses, but springs from the very heart of that mutual giving, as its fruit and fulfillment. So the Church, which "is on the side of life"[150] teaches that "each and every marriage act must remain open to the transmission of life."[151] "This particular doctrine, expounded on numerous occasions by the Magisterium, is based on the inseparable connection, established by God, which man on his own initiative may not break, between the unitive significance and the procreative significance which are both inherent to the marriage act."[152]

2205 **2367** Called to give life, spouses share in the creative power and fatherhood of God.[153] "Married couples should regard it as their proper mission to transmit human life and to educate their children; they should realize that they are thereby *cooperating with* the love of *God the Creator* and are, in a certain sense, its interpreters. They will fulfill this duty with a sense of human and Christian responsibility."[154]

---

149 St. John Chrysostom, *Hom. in Eph.* 20, 8: PG 62, 146–147.   150 *FC* 30.
151 *HV* 11.   152 *HV* 12; cf. Pius XI, encyclical, *Casti connubii.*   153 Cf. *Eph*
3:14; *Mt* 23:9.   154 *GS* 50 § 2.

2368 A particular aspect of this responsibility concerns the *regulation of births*. For just reasons, spouses may wish to space the births of their children. It is their duty to make certain that their desire is not motivated by selfishness but is in conformity with the generosity appropriate to responsible parenthood. Moreover, they should conform their behavior to the objective criteria of morality:

> When it is a question of harmonizing married love with the responsible transmission of life, the morality of the behavior does not depend on sincere intention and evaluation of motives alone; but it must be determined by objective criteria, criteria drawn from the nature of the person and his acts, criteria that respect the total meaning of mutual self-giving and human procreation in the context of true love; this is possible only if the virtue of married chastity is practiced with sincerity of heart.[155]

2369 "By safeguarding both these essential aspects, the unitive and the procreative, the conjugal act preserves in its fullness the sense of true mutual love and its orientation toward man's exalted vocation to parenthood."[156]

2370 Periodic continence, that is, the methods of birth regulation based on self-observation and the use of infertile periods, is in conformity with the objective criteria of morality.[157] These methods respect the bodies of the spouses, encourage tenderness between them, and favor the education of an authentic freedom. In contrast, "every action which, whether in anticipation of the conjugal act, or in its accomplishment, or in the development of its natural consequences, proposes, whether as an end or as a means, to render procreation impossible" is intrinsically evil:[158]

> Thus the innate language that expresses the total reciprocal self-giving of husband and wife is overlaid, through contraception, by an objectively contradictory language, namely, that of not giving oneself totally to the other. This leads not only to a

---

155 *GS* 51 § 3.   156 Cf. *HV* 12.   157 *HV* 16.   158 *HV* 14.

> positive refusal to be open to life but also to a fal-
> sification of the inner truth of conjugal love, which
> is called upon to give itself in personal totality. . . .
> The difference, both anthropological and moral,
> between contraception and recourse to the rhythm
> of the cycle . . . involves in the final analysis two ir-
> reconcilable concepts of the human person and of
> human sexuality.[159]

2371 "Let all be convinced that human life and the
duty of transmitting it are not limited by the horizons of
this life only: their true evaluation and full significance
can be understood only in reference to *man's eternal*
1703 *destiny.*"[160]

2372 The state has a responsibility for its citizens' well-
being. In this capacity it is legitimate for it to intervene to
orient the demography of the population. This can be done
by means of objective and respectful information, but certainly not by authoritarian, coercive measures. The state
may not legitimately usurp the initiative of spouses, who
2209 have the primary responsibility for the procreation and education of their children.[161] It is not authorized to promote
demographic regulation by means contrary to the moral
law.

The gift of a child

2373 Sacred Scripture and the Church's traditional
practice see in *large families* a sign of God's blessing and
the parents' generosity.[162]

1654 **2374** Couples who discover that they are sterile suffer
greatly. "What will you give me," asks Abraham of
God, "for I continue childless?"[163] And Rachel cries to
her husband Jacob, "Give me children, or I shall die!"[164]

2293 **2375** Research aimed at reducing human sterility is to
be encouraged, on condition that it is placed "at the service of the human person, of his inalienable rights, and
his true and integral good according to the design and
will of God."[165]

2376 Techniques that entail the dissociation of husband

---

159 *FC* 32.   160 *GS* 51 § 4.   161 Cf. *HV* 23; *PP* 37.   162 Cf. *GS* 50 § 2.
163 *Gen* 15:2.   164 *Gen* 30:1.   165 CDF, *Donum vitae.* intro., 2.

and wife, by the intrusion of a person other than the couple (donation of sperm or ovum, surrogate uterus), are gravely immoral. These techniques (heterologous artificial insemination and fertilization) infringe the child's right to be born of a father and mother known to him and bound to each other by marriage. They betray the spouses' "right to become a father and a mother only through each other."[166]

2377 Techniques involving only the married couple (homologous artificial insemination and fertilization) are perhaps less reprehensible, yet remain morally unacceptable. They dissociate the sexual act from the procreative act. The act which brings the child into existence is no longer an act by which two persons give themselves to one another, but one that "entrusts the life and identity of the embryo into the power of doctors and biologists and establishes the domination of technology over the origin and destiny of the human person. Such a relationship of domination is in itself contrary to the dignity and equality that must be common to parents and children."[167] "Under the moral aspect procreation is deprived of its proper perfection when it is not willed as the fruit of the conjugal act, that is to say, of the specific act of the spouses' union. . . . Only respect for the link between the meanings of the conjugal act and respect for the unity of the human being make possible procreation in conformity with the dignity of the person."[168]

2378 A child is not something *owed* to one, but is a *gift*. The "supreme gift of marriage" is a human person. A child may not be considered a piece of property, an idea to which an alleged "right to a child" would lead. In this area, only the child possesses genuine rights: the right "to be the fruit of the specific act of the conjugal love of his parents," and "the right to be respected as a person from the moment of his conception."[169]

2379 The Gospel shows that physical sterility is not an absolute evil. Spouses who still suffer from infertility after exhausting legitimate medical procedures should unite themselves with the Lord's Cross, the source of all spiritual fecundity. They can give expression to their generosity by adopting abandoned children or performing demanding services for others.

---

166 CDF, *Donum vitae* II, 1.   167 CDF, *Donum vitae* II, 5.   168 CDF, *Donum vitae* II, 4.   169 CDF, *Donum vitae* II, 8.

IV.   Offenses against the Dignity
of Marriage

Adultery

2380 *Adultery* refers to marital infidelity. When two partners, of whom at least one is married to another party, have sexual relations—even transient ones—they commit adultery. Christ condemns even adultery of mere desire.[170] The sixth commandment and the New Testament forbid adultery absolutely.[171] The prophets denounce the gravity of adultery; they see it as an image

1611 of the sin of idolatry.[172]

2381 Adultery is an injustice. He who commits adultery fails in his commitment. He does injury to the sign

1640 of the covenant which the marriage bond is, transgresses the rights of the other spouse, and undermines the institution of marriage by breaking the contract on which it is based. He compromises the good of human generation and the welfare of children who need their parents' stable union.

Divorce

2382 The Lord Jesus insisted on the original intention

1614 of the Creator who willed that marriage be indissoluble.[173] He abrogates the accommodations that had slipped into the old Law.[174]

Between the baptized, "a ratified and consummated marriage cannot be dissolved by any human power or for any reason other than death."[175]

1649 **2383** The *separation* of spouses while maintaining the marriage bond can be legitimate in certain cases provided for by canon law.[176]

If civil divorce remains the only possible way of ensuring certain legal rights, the care of the children, or the protection of inheritance, it can be tolerated and does not constitute a moral offense.

---

170 Cf. *Mt* 5:27–28. **171** Cf. *Mt* 5:32; 19:6; *Mk* 10:11; *1 Cor* 6:9–10. **172** Cf. *Hos* 2:7; *Jer* 5:7; 13:27. **173** Cf. *Mt* 5:31–32; 19:3–9; *Mk* 10:9; *Lk* 16:18; *1 Cor* 7:10–11. **174** Cf. *Mt* 19:7–9. **175** CIC, can. 1141. **176** Cf. CIC, cann. 1151–1155.

2384 *Divorce* is a grave offense against the natural 1650 law. It claims to break the contract, to which the spouses freely consented, to live with each other till death. Divorce does injury to the covenant of salvation, of which sacramental marriage is the sign. Contracting a new union, even if it is recognized by civil law, adds to the gravity of the rupture: the remarried spouse is then in a situation of public and permanent adultery:

> If a husband, separated from his wife, approaches another woman, he is an adulterer because he makes that woman commit adultery; and the woman who lives with him is an adulteress, because she has drawn another's husband to herself.[177]

2385 Divorce is immoral also because it introduces disorder into the family and into society. This disorder brings grave harm to the deserted spouse, to children traumatized by the separation of their parents and often torn between them, and because of its contagious effect which makes it truly a plague on society.

2386 It can happen that one of the spouses is the innocent victim of a divorce decreed by civil law; this spouse therefore has not contravened the moral law. There is a considerable difference between a spouse who has sincerely tried to be faithful to the sacrament of marriage and is unjustly abandoned, and one who through his own grave fault destroys a canonically valid 1640 marriage.[178]

Other offenses against the dignity of marriage
2387 The predicament of a man who, desiring to convert to the Gospel, is obliged to repudiate one or more wives with whom he has shared years of conjugal life, is understandable. However *polygamy* is not in accord 1610 with the moral law. "[Conjugal] communion is radically contradicted by polygamy; this, in fact, directly negates the plan of God which was revealed from the beginning, because it is contrary to the equal personal dignity of men and women who in matrimony give themselves

---

177 St. Basil, *Moralia* 73, 1: PG 31, 849–852.   178 Cf. FC 84.

with a love that is total and therefore unique and exclusive."[179] The Christian who has previously lived in polygamy has a grave duty in justice to honor the obligations contracted in regard to his former wives and his children.

2356 **2388** *Incest* designates intimate relations between relatives or in-laws within a degree that prohibits marriage between them.[180] St. Paul stigmatizes this especially grave offense: "It is actually reported that there is immorality among you . . . for a man is living with his father's wife. . . . In the name of the Lord Jesus . . . you are to deliver this man to Satan for the destruction of the flesh. . . ."[181] Incest corrupts family relationships
2207 and marks a regression toward animality.

2389 Connected to incest is any sexual abuse perpetrated by adults on children or adolescents entrusted to their care. The offense is compounded by the scandalous harm done to the physical and moral integrity
2285 of the young, who will remain scarred by it all their lives; and the violation of responsibility for their upbringing.

2390 In a so-called *free union,* a man and a woman refuse to give juridical and public form to a liaison in-
1631 volving sexual intimacy.

The expression "free union" is fallacious: what can "union" mean when the partners make no commitment to one another, each exhibiting a lack of trust in the other, in himself, or in the future?

The expression covers a number of different situations: concubinage, rejection of marriage as such, or inability to make long-term commitments.[182] All these situations offend against the dignity of marriage; they destroy the very idea of the family; they weaken the
2353 sense of fidelity. They are contrary to the moral law. The sexual act must take place exclusively within marriage. Outside of marriage it always constitutes a grave
1385 sin and excludes one from sacramental communion.

---

179 FC 19; cf. GS 47 § 2.   180 Cf. *Lev* 18:7–20.   181 *1 Cor* 5:1, 4–5.   182 Cf. FC 81.

2391 Some today claim a *"right to a trial marriage"* where there is an intention of getting married later. However firm the purpose of those who engage in premature sexual relations may be, "the fact is that such liaisons can scarcely ensure mutual sincerity and fidelity in a relationship between a man and a woman, nor, especially, can they protect it from inconstancy of desires or whim."[183] Carnal union is morally legitimate only when a definitive community of life between a man and woman has been established. Human love does not tolerate "trial marriages." It demands a total and definitive 2364 gift of persons to one another.[184]

IN BRIEF

2392 "Love is the fundamental and innate vocation of every human being" (*FC* 11).

2393 By creating the human being man and woman, God gives personal dignity equally to the one and the other. Each of them, man and woman, should acknowledge and accept his sexual identity.

2394 Christ is the model of chastity. Every baptized person is called to lead a chaste life, each according to his particular state of life.

2395 Chastity means the integration of sexuality within the person. It includes an apprenticeship in self-mastery.

2396 Among the sins gravely contrary to chastity are masturbation, fornication, pornography, and homosexual practices.

2397 The covenant which spouses have freely entered into entails faithful love. It imposes on them the obligation to keep their marriage indissoluble.

2398 Fecundity is a good, a gift and an end of marriage. By giving life, spouses participate in God's fatherhood.

183 CDF, *Persona humana* 7. 184 Cf. *FC* 80.

2399   The regulation of births represents one of the aspects of responsible fatherhood and motherhood. Legitimate intentions on the part of the spouses do not justify recourse to morally unacceptable means (for example, direct sterilization or contraception).

2400   Adultery, divorce, polygamy, and free union are grave offenses against the dignity of marriage.

ARTICLE 7
THE SEVENTH COMMANDMENT

You shall not steal.[185]

2401   The seventh commandment forbids unjustly taking or keeping the goods of one's neighbor and wronging him in any way with respect to his goods. It commands justice and charity in the care of earthly goods and the fruits of men's labor. For the sake of the common good, it requires respect for the universal destination of goods and respect for the right to private property. Christian life strives to order this world's goods to God and to fraternal charity.

1807

952

I.   THE UNIVERSAL DESTINATION AND THE PRIVATE OWNERSHIP OF GOODS

2402   In the beginning God entrusted the earth and its resources to the common stewardship of mankind to take care of them, master them by labor, and enjoy their fruits.[186] The goods of creation are destined for the whole human race. However, the earth is divided up among men to assure the security of their lives, endangered by poverty and threatened by violence. The appropriation of property is legitimate for guaranteeing the freedom and dignity of persons and for helping each of them to meet his basic needs and the needs of those in his charge. It should allow for a natural solidarity to develop between men.

226

1939

---

185 *Ex* 20:15; *Deut* 5:19; *Mt* 19:18.   186 Cf. *Gen* 1:26–29.

2403 The *right to private property*, acquired by work or received from others by inheritance or gift, does not do away with the original gift of the earth to the whole of mankind. The *universal destination of goods* remains primordial, even if the promotion of the common good requires respect for the right to private property and its exercise.

2404 "In his use of things man should regard the external goods he legitimately owns not merely as exclusive to himself but common to others also, in the sense that they can benefit others as well as himself."[187] The ownership of any property makes its holder a steward of Providence, with the task of making it fruitful and communicating its benefits to others, first of all his family. *307*

2405 Goods of production—material or immaterial—such as land, factories, practical or artistic skills, oblige their possessors to employ them in ways that will benefit the greatest number. Those who hold goods for use and consumption should use them with moderation, reserving the better part for guests, for the sick and the poor.

2406 *Political authority* has the right and duty to regulate the legitimate exercise of the right to ownership for the sake of the common good.[188] *1903*

II. RESPECT FOR PERSONS AND THEIR GOODS

2407 In economic matters, respect for human dignity requires the practice of the virtue of *temperance,* so as to moderate attachment to this world's goods; the practice of the virtue of *justice,* to preserve our neighbor's rights and render him what is his due; and the practice of *solidarity,* in accordance with the golden rule and in keeping with the generosity of the Lord, who "though he was rich, yet for your sake . . . became poor so that by his poverty, you might become rich."[189] *1809* *1807* *1939*

---

187 *GS* 69 § 1.   188 Cf. *GS* 71 § 4; *SRS* 42; *CA* 40; 48.   189 2 *Cor* 8:9.

Respect for the goods of others

2408 The seventh commandment forbids *theft,* that is, usurping another's property against the reasonable will of the owner. There is no theft if consent can be presumed or if refusal is contrary to reason and the universal destination of goods. This is the case in obvious and urgent necessity when the only way to provide for immediate, essential needs (food, shelter, clothing . . .) is to put at one's disposal and use the property of others.[190]

2409 Even if it does not contradict the provisions of civil law, any form of unjustly taking and keeping the property of others is against the seventh commandment: thus, deliberate retention of goods lent or of objects *1867* lost; business fraud; paying unjust wages; forcing up prices by taking advantage of the ignorance or hardship of another.[191]

The following are also morally illicit: speculation in which one contrives to manipulate the price of goods artificially in order to gain an advantage to the detriment of others; corruption in which one influences the judgment of those who must make decisions according to law; appropriation and use for private purposes of the common goods of an enterprise; work poorly done; tax evasion; forgery of checks and invoices; excessive expenses and waste. Willfully damaging private or public property is contrary to the moral law and requires reparation.

2101 **2410** *Promises* must be kept and *contracts* strictly observed to the extent that the commitments made in them are morally just. A significant part of economic and social life depends on the honoring of contracts between physical or moral persons—commercial contracts of purchase or sale, rental or labor contracts. All contracts must be agreed to and executed in good faith.

1807 **2411** Contracts are subject to *commutative justice* which regulates exchanges between persons in accordance with a strict respect for their rights. Commutative justice obliges strictly; it requires safeguarding property rights, paying debts, and fulfilling obligations freely

---

190 Cf. *GS* 69 § 1.   191 Cf. *Deut* 25:13–16; 24:14–15; *Jas* 5:4; *Am* 8:4–6.

contracted. Without commutative justice, no other form of justice is possible.

One distinguishes *commutative* justice from *legal* justice which concerns what the citizen owes in fairness to the community, and from *distributive* justice which regulates what the community owes its citizens in proportion to their contributions and needs.

2412 In virtue of commutative justice, *reparation for injustice* committed requires the restitution of stolen goods to their owner: *1459*

Jesus blesses Zacchaeus for his pledge: "If I have defrauded anyone of anything, I restore it fourfold."[192] Those who, directly or indirectly, have taken possession of the goods of another, are obliged to make restitution of them, or to return the equivalent in kind or in money, if the goods have disappeared, as well as the profit or advantages their owner would have legitimately obtained from them. Likewise, all who in some manner have taken part in a theft or who have knowingly benefited from it—for example, those who ordered it, assisted in it, or received the stolen goods—are obliged to make restitution in proportion to their responsibility and to their share of what was stolen. *2487*

2413 *Games of chance* (card games, etc.) or *wagers* are not in themselves contrary to justice. They become morally unacceptable when they deprive someone of what is necessary to provide for his needs and those of others. The passion for gambling risks becoming an enslavement. Unfair wagers and cheating at games constitute grave matter, unless the damage inflicted is so slight that the one who suffers it cannot reasonably consider it significant.

2414 The seventh commandment forbids acts or enterprises that for any reason—selfish or ideological, commercial, or totalitarian—lead to the *enslavement of human beings,* to their being bought, sold and exchanged like merchandise, in disregard for their personal dignity. It is a sin against the dignity of persons and their fundamental rights to reduce them by violence to their productive value or to a source of profit. St. Paul directed a Christian master to treat his Christian slave "no longer as a slave but more than a slave, as a beloved brother, . . . both in the flesh and in the Lord."[193] *2297*

---

192 *Lk* 19:8.   193 *Philem* 16.

Respect for the integrity of creation

226, 358 **2415** The seventh commandment enjoins respect for the integrity of creation. Animals, like plants and inanimate beings, are by nature destined for the common good of past, present, and future humanity.[194] Use of the mineral, vegetable, and animal resources of the universe cannot be divorced from respect for moral imperatives.
373 Man's dominion over inanimate and other living beings granted by the Creator is not absolute; it is limited by concern for the quality of life of his neighbor, including generations to come; it requires a religious respect for
378 the integrity of creation.[195]

2416 *Animals* are God's creatures. He surrounds them with his providential care. By their mere existence they bless him and give him glory.[196] Thus men owe them kindness. We should recall the gentleness with which
344 saints like St. Francis of Assisi or St. Philip Neri treated animals.

2417 God entrusted animals to the stewardship of those whom he created in his own image.[197] Hence it is legitimate to use animals for food and clothing. They may be domesticated to help man in his work and leisure. Medical and scientific experimentation on animals, if it remains within reasonable limits, is a morally
2234 acceptable practice since it contributes to caring for or saving human lives.

2418 It is contrary to human dignity to cause animals to suffer or die needlessly. It is likewise unworthy to spend money on them that should as a priority go to the
2446 relief of human misery. One can love animals; one should not direct to them the affection due only to persons.

III.   THE SOCIAL DOCTRINE OF THE CHURCH

1960 **2419** "Christian revelation . . . promotes deeper un-
359 derstanding of the laws of social living."[198] The Church receives from the Gospel the full revelation of the truth

---

194 Cf. *Gen* 1:28–31.   195 Cf. *CA* 37–38.   196 Cf. *Mt* 6:26; *Dan* 3:79–81.
197 Cf. *Gen* 2:19–20; 9:1–4.   198 *GS* 23 § 1.

about man. When she fulfills her mission of proclaiming the Gospel, she bears witness to man, in the name of Christ, to his dignity and his vocation to the communion of persons. She teaches him the demands of justice and peace in conformity with divine wisdom.

2420 The Church makes a moral judgment about economic and social matters, "when the fundamental rights of the person or the salvation of souls requires it."[199] In the moral order she bears a mission distinct from that of political authorities: the Church is concerned with the temporal aspects of the common good because they are ordered to the sovereign Good, our ultimate end. She strives to inspire right attitudes with respect to earthly goods and in socio-economic relationships.

2032

2246

2421 The social doctrine of the Church developed in the nineteenth century when the Gospel encountered modern industrial society with its new structures for the production of consumer goods, its new concept of society, the state and authority, and its new forms of labor and ownership. The development of the doctrine of the Church on economic and social matters attests the permanent value of the Church's teaching at the same time as it attests the true meaning of her Tradition, always living and active.[200]

2422 The Church's social teaching comprises a body of doctrine, which is articulated as the Church interprets events in the course of history, with the assistance of the Holy Spirit, in the light of the whole of what has been revealed by Jesus Christ.[201] This teaching can be more easily accepted by men of good will, the more the faithful let themselves be guided by it.

2044

2423 The Church's social teaching proposes principles for reflection; it provides criteria for judgment; it gives guidelines for action:

Any system in which social relationships are determined entirely by economic factors is contrary to the nature of the human person and his acts.[202]

2424 A theory that makes profit the exclusive norm and ultimate end of economic activity is morally unacceptable.

---

199 *GS* 76 § 5.   200 Cf. *CA* 3.   201 Cf. *SRS* 1; 41.   202 Cf. *CA* 24.

2317   The disordered desire for money cannot but produce perverse effects. It is one of the causes of the many conflicts which disturb the social order.[203]

A system that "subordinates the basic rights of individuals and of groups to the collective organization of production" is contrary to human dignity.[204] Every practice that reduces persons to nothing more than a means of profit enslaves man, leads to idolizing money, and contributes to the spread of atheism. "You cannot serve God and mammon."[205]

2425   The Church has rejected the totalitarian and atheistic ideologies associated in modern times with "communism" or "socialism." She has likewise refused to accept, in
676   the practice of "capitalism," individualism and the absolute primacy of the law of the marketplace over human labor.[206] Regulating the economy solely by centralized planning perverts the basis of social bonds; regulating it solely by the law of the marketplace fails social justice, for "there are many human needs which cannot be satisfied by the market."[207] Reasonable regulation of the marketplace and economic initiatives, in keeping with a just hierarchy of val-
1886   ues and a view to the common good, is to be commended.

IV.   ECONOMIC ACTIVITY AND SOCIAL JUSTICE
2426   The development of economic activity and growth in production are meant to provide for the needs of human beings. Economic life is not meant solely to multiply goods produced and increase profit or power; it is ordered first of all to the service of persons, of the whole man, and of the entire human community. Economic activity, conducted according to its own proper methods, is to be exercised within the limits of the moral order, in keeping with social justice so as to
1928   correspond to God's plan for man.[208]

307   **2427**   *Human work* proceeds directly from persons created in the image of God and called to prolong the work of creation by subduing the earth, both with and
378   for one another.[209] Hence work is a duty: "If any one will not work, let him not eat."[210] Work honors the Cre-

---

203 Cf. *GS* 63 § 3; *LE* 7; 20; *CA* 35.   204 *GS* 65 § 2.   205 *Mt* 6:24; *Lk* 16:13.
206 Cf. *CA* 10; 13; 44.   207 *CA* 34.   208 Cf. *GS* 64.   209 Cf. *Gen* 1:28; *GS*
34; *CA* 31.   210 2 *Thess* 3:10; cf. 1 *Thess* 4:11.

ator's gifts and the talents received from him. It can also be redemptive. By enduring the hardship of work[211] in union with Jesus, the carpenter of Nazareth and the one crucified on Calvary, man collaborates in a certain fashion with the Son of God in his redemptive work. He shows himself to be a disciple of Christ by carrying the cross, daily, in the work he is called to accomplish.[212] Work can be a means of sanctification and a way of animating earthly realities with the Spirit of Christ.

531

2428 In work, the person exercises and fulfills in part the potential inscribed in his nature. The primordial value of labor stems from man himself, its author and its beneficiary. Work is for man, not man for work.[213]

2834

2185

Everyone should be able to draw from work the means of providing for his life and that of his family, and of serving the human community.

2429 Everyone has the *right of economic initiative;* everyone should make legitimate use of his talents to contribute to the abundance that will benefit all and to harvest the just fruits of his labor. He should seek to observe regulations issued by legitimate authority for the sake of the common good.[214]

2430 *Economic life* brings into play different interests, often opposed to one another. This explains why the conflicts that characterize it arise.[215] Efforts should be made to reduce these conflicts by negotiation that respects the rights and duties of each social partner: those responsible for business enterprises, representatives of wage-earners (for example, trade unions), and public authorities when appropriate.

2431 The *responsibility of the state.* "Economic activity, especially the activity of a market economy, cannot be conducted in an institutional, juridical, or political vacuum. On the contrary, it presupposes sure guarantees of individual freedom and private property, as well as a stable currency and efficient public services. Hence

---

211 Cf. *Gen* 3:14–19.   212 Cf. *LE* 27.   213 Cf. *LE* 6.   214 Cf. *CA* 32; 34.
215 Cf. *LE* 11.

1908 the principal task of the state is to guarantee this security, so that those who work and produce can enjoy the fruits of their labors and thus feel encouraged to work efficiently and honestly. . . . Another task of the state is that of overseeing and directing the exercise of human rights in the economic sector. However, primary re-
1883 sponsibility in this area belongs not to the state but to individuals and to the various groups and associations which make up society."[216]

2432 Those *responsible for business enterprises* are responsible to society for the economic and ecological ef-
2415 fects of their operations.[217] They have an obligation to consider the good of persons and not only the increase of *profits*. Profits are necessary, however. They make possible the investments that ensure the future of a business and they guarantee employment.

2433 *Access to employment* and to professions must be open to all without unjust discrimination: men and women, healthy and disabled, natives and immigrants.[218] For its part society should, according to circumstances, help citizens find work and employment.[219]

1867 **2434** A *just wage* is the legitimate fruit of work. To refuse or withhold it can be a grave injustice.[220] In determining fair pay both the needs and the contributions of each person must be taken into account. "Remuneration for work should guarantee man the opportunity to provide a dignified livelihood for himself and his family on the material, social, cultural, and spiritual level, taking into account the role and the productivity of each, the state of the business, and the common good."[221] Agreement between the parties is not sufficient to justify morally the amount to be received in wages.

2435 Recourse to a *strike* is morally legitimate when it cannot be avoided, or at least when it is necessary to obtain a proportionate benefit. It becomes morally unacceptable when accompanied by violence, or when ob-

---

216 CA 48.   217 Cf. CA 37.   218 Cf. LE 19; 22–23.   219 Cf. CA 48.   220 Cf. *Lev* 19:13; *Deut* 24:14–15; *Jas* 5:4.   221 GS 67 § 2.

jectives are included that are not directly linked to working conditions or are contrary to the common good.

2436 It is unjust not to pay the social security *contributions* required by legitimate authority.

Unemployment almost always wounds its victim's dignity and threatens the equilibrium of his life. Besides the harm done to him personally, it entails many risks for his family.[222]

V. JUSTICE AND SOLIDARITY AMONG NATIONS

2437 On the international level, inequality of resources and economic capability is such that it creates a real "gap" between nations.[223] On the one side there are those nations possessing and developing the means of growth and, on the other, those accumulating debts.   *1938*

2438 Various causes of a religious, political, economic, and financial nature today give "the social question a worldwide dimension."[224] There must be solidarity among nations which are already politically interdependent. It is even more essential when it is a question of dismantling the "perverse mechanisms" that impede the development of the less advanced countries.[225] In place of abusive if not usurious financial systems, iniquitous commercial relations among nations, and the arms race, there must be substituted a common effort to mobilize resources toward objectives of moral, cultural, and economic development, "redefining the *2315* priorities and hierarchies of values."[226]   *1911*

2439 *Rich nations* have a grave moral responsibility toward those which are unable to ensure the means of their development by themselves or have been prevented from doing so by tragic historical events. It is a duty in solidarity and charity; it is also an obligation in justice if the prosperity of the rich nations has come from resources that have not been paid for fairly.

---

222 Cf. *LE* 18.   223 Cf. *SRS* 14.   224 *SRS* 9.   225 Cf. *SRS* 17; 45.   226 *CA* 28; cf. 35.

2440   *Direct aid* is an appropriate response to immediate, extraordinary needs caused by natural catastrophes, epidemics, and the like. But it does not suffice to repair the grave damage resulting from destitution or to provide a lasting solution to a country's needs. It is also necessary to *reform* international economic and financial *institutions* so that they will better promote equitable relationships with less advanced countries.[227] The efforts of poor countries working for growth and liberation must be supported.[228] This doctrine must be applied especially in the area of agricultural labor. Peasants, especially in the Third World, form the overwhelming majority of the poor.

1908   **2441**   An increased sense of God and increased self-awareness are fundamental to any *full development of human society.* This development multiplies material goods and puts them at the service of the person and his freedom. It reduces dire poverty and economic exploitation. It makes for growth in respect for cultural identities and openness to the transcendent.[229]

2442   It is not the role of the Pastors of the Church to intervene directly in the political structuring and organization of social life. This task is part of the vocation of the *lay faithful,* acting on their own initiative with *899* their fellow citizens. Social action can assume various concrete forms. It should always have the common good in view and be in conformity with the message of the Gospel and the teaching of the Church. It is the role of the laity "to animate temporal realities with Christian commitment, by which they show that they are witnesses and agents of peace and justice."[230]

2544-2547   ## VI.   LOVE FOR THE POOR

2443   God blesses those who come to the aid of the poor and rebukes those who turn away from them: "Give to him who begs from you, do not refuse him who would borrow from you"; "you received without

---

227 Cf. *SRS* 16.   228 Cf. *CA* 26.   229 Cf. *SRS* 32; *CA* 51.   230 *SRS* 47 § 6; cf. 42.

pay, give without pay."[231] It is by what they have done
for the poor that Jesus Christ will recognize his chosen
ones.[232] When "the poor have the good news preached
to them," it is the sign of Christ's presence.[233]

786, 525
544, 853

2444 "The Church's love for the poor . . . is a part of
her constant tradition." This love is inspired by the
Gospel of the Beatitudes, of the poverty of Jesus, and of
his concern for the poor.[234] Love for the poor is even one
of the motives for the duty of working so as to "be able
to give to those in need."[235] It extends not only to material poverty but also to the many forms of cultural and
religious poverty.[236]

1716

2445 Love for the poor is incompatible with immoderate love of riches or their selfish use:

2536

> Come now, you rich, weep and howl for the mis-
> eries that are coming upon you. Your riches have
> rotted and your garments are moth-eaten. Your
> gold and silver have rusted, and their rust will be
> evidence against you and will eat your flesh like
> fire. You have laid up treasure for the last days. Be-
> hold, the wages of the laborers who mowed your
> fields, which you kept back by fraud, cry out; and
> the cries of the harvesters have reached the ears of
> the Lord of hosts. You have lived on the earth in
> luxury and in pleasure; you have fattened your
> hearts in a day of slaughter. You have condemned,
> you have killed the righteous man; he does not re-
> sist you.[237]

2547

2446 St. John Chrysostom vigorously recalls this:
"Not to enable the poor to share in our goods is to steal
from them and deprive them of life. The goods we possess are not ours, but theirs."[238] "The demands of justice
must be satisfied first of all; that which is already due in
justice is not to be offered as a gift of charity":[239]

2402

> When we attend to the needs of those in want, we
> give them what is theirs, not ours. More than per-

231 *Mt* 5:42; 10:8. 232 Cf. *Mt* 25:31–36. 233 *Mt* 11:5; cf. *Lk* 4:18. 234 *CA*
57; cf. *Lk* 6:20–22, *Mt* 8:20; *Mk* 12:41–44. 235 *Eph* 4:28. 236 Cf. *CA* 57.
237 *Jas* 5:1–6. 238 St. John Chrysostom, *Hom. in Lazaro* 2, 5: PG 48, 992.
239 *AA* 8 § 5.

forming works of mercy, we are paying a debt of
justice.[240]

1460 **2447** The *works of mercy* are charitable actions by
which we come to the aid of our neighbor in his spiritual and bodily necessities.[241] Instructing, advising, con-
soling, comforting are spiritual works of mercy, as are
forgiving and bearing wrongs patiently. The corporal
works of mercy consist especially in feeding the hungry,
1038 sheltering the homeless, clothing the naked, visiting the
sick and imprisoned, and burying the dead.[242] Among all
1969 these, giving alms to the poor is one of the chief witnesses to fraternal charity: it is also a work of justice
pleasing to God:[243]

> He who has two coats, let him share with him who
> has none; and he who has food must do likewise.[244]
> But give for alms those things which are within;
> and behold, everything is clean for you.[245] If a
> brother or sister is ill-clad and in lack of daily food,
> and one of you says to them, "Go in peace, be
1004 > warmed and filled," without giving them the things
> needed for the body, what does it profit?[246]

2448 "In its various forms—material deprivation, un-
386 just oppression, physical and psychological illness and
death—*human misery* is the obvious sign of the inherited condition of frailty and need for salvation in which
man finds himself as a consequence of original sin. This
misery elicited the compassion of Christ the Savior, who
willingly took it upon himself and identified himself
with the least of his brethren. Hence, those who are op-
1586 pressed by poverty are the object of *a preferential love*
on the part of the Church which, since her origin and in
spite of the failings of many of her members, has not
ceased to work for their relief, defense, and liberation
through numerous works of charity which remain indispensable always and everywhere."[247]

2449 Beginning with the Old Testament, all kinds of

---

240 St. Gregory the Great, *Regula Pastoralis*. 3, 21: PL 77, 87.   241 Cf. *Isa*
58:6–7; *Heb* 13:3.   242 Cf. *Mt* 25:31–46.   243 Cf. *Tob* 4:5–11; *Sir* 17:22; *Mt*
6:2–4.   244 *Lk* 3:11.   245 *Lk* 11:41.   246 *Jas* 2:15–16; cf. 1 *Jn* 3:17.
247 CDF, instruction, *Libertatis conscientia*, 68.

juridical measures (the jubilee year of forgiveness of debts, prohibition of loans at interest and the keeping of collateral, the obligation to tithe, the daily payment of the day-laborer, the right to glean vines and fields) answer the exhortation of *Deuteronomy*: "For the poor will never cease out of the land; therefore I command you, 'You shall open wide your hand to your brother, to the needy and to the poor in the land.' "[248] Jesus makes these words his own: "The poor you always have with you, but you do not always have me."[249] In so doing he does not soften the vehemence of former oracles against "buying the poor for silver and the needy for a pair of sandals . . . ," but invites us to recognize his own presence in the poor who are his brethren:[250]

1397

> When her mother reproached her for caring for the poor and the sick at home, St. Rose of Lima said to her: "When we serve the poor and the sick, we serve Jesus. We must not fail to help our neighbors, because in them we serve Jesus.[251]

786

IN BRIEF

2450 "You shall not steal" (*Ex* 20:15; *Deut* 5:19). "Neither thieves, nor the greedy . . . , nor robbers will inherit the kingdom of God" (*1 Cor* 6:10).

2451 The seventh commandment enjoins the practice of justice and charity in the administration of earthly goods and the fruits of men's labor.

2452 The goods of creation are destined for the entire human race. The right to private property does not abolish the universal destination of goods.

2453 The seventh commandment forbids theft. Theft is the usurpation of another's goods against the reasonable will of the owner.

2454 Every manner of taking and using another's property unjustly is contrary to the seventh com-

---

248 *Deut* 15:11. 249 *Jn* 12:8. 250 *Am* 8:6; cf. *Mt* 25:40. 251 P. Hansen, *Vita mirabilis* (Louvain, 1668).

mandment. The injustice committed requires reparation. Commutative justice requires the restitution of stolen goods.

2455 The moral law forbids acts which, for commercial or totalitarian purposes, lead to the enslavement of human beings, or to their being bought, sold or exchanged like merchandise.

2456 The dominion granted by the Creator over the mineral, vegetable, and animal resources of the universe cannot be separated from respect for moral obligations, including those toward generations to come.

2457 Animals are entrusted to man's stewardship; he must show them kindness. They may be used to serve the just satisfaction of man's needs.

2458 The Church makes a judgment about economic and social matters when the fundamental rights of the person or the salvation of souls requires it. She is concerned with the temporal common good of men because they are ordered to the sovereign Good, their ultimate end.

2459 Man is himself the author, center, and goal of all economic and social life. The decisive point of the social question is that goods created by God for everyone should in fact reach everyone in accordance with justice and with the help of charity.

2460 The primordial value of labor stems from man himself, its author and beneficiary. By means of his labor man participates in the work of creation. Work united to Christ can be redemptive.

2461 True development concerns the whole man. It is concerned with increasing each person's ability to respond to his vocation and hence to God's call (cf. *CA* 29).

2462 Giving alms to the poor is a witness to fraternal

charity: it is also a work of justice pleasing to God.

2463 How can we not recognize Lazarus, the hungry beggar in the parable (cf. *Lk* 17:19–31), in the multitude of human beings without bread, a roof or a place to stay? How can we fail to hear Jesus: "As you did it not to one of the least of these, you did it not to me" (*Mt* 25:45)?

ARTICLE 8
THE EIGHTH COMMANDMENT

You shall not bear false witness against your neighbor.[252]

It was said to the men of old, "You shall not swear falsely, but shall perform to the Lord what you have sworn."[253]

2464 The eighth commandment forbids misrepresenting the truth in our relations with others. This moral prescription flows from the vocation of the holy people to bear witness to their God who is the truth and wills the truth. Offenses against the truth express by word or deed a refusal to commit oneself to moral uprightness: they are fundamental infidelities to God and, in this sense, they undermine the foundations of the covenant.

I.   LIVING IN THE TRUTH

2465 The Old Testament attests that *God is the source* 215
of all truth. His Word is truth. His Law is truth. His "faithfulness endures to all generations."[254] Since God is "true," the members of his people are called to live in the truth.[255]

2466 In Jesus Christ, the whole of God's truth has been made manifest. "Full of grace and truth," he came as the "light of the world," he *is the Truth.*[256] "Whoever

---

252 *Ex* 20:16; cf. *Deut* 5:20.   253 *Mt* 5:33.   254 *Ps* 119:90; cf. *Prov* 8:7; *2 Sam* 7:28; *Ps* 119:142; *Lk* 1:50.   255 *Rom* 3:4; cf. *Ps* 119:30.   256 *Jn* 1:14; 8:12; cf. 14:6.

believes in me may not remain in darkness."[257] The disciple of Jesus continues in his word so as to know "the truth [that] will make you free" and that sanctifies.[258] To follow Jesus is to live in "the Spirit of truth," whom the Father sends in his name and who leads "into all the truth."[259] To his disciples Jesus teaches the uncondi-
2153 tional love of truth: "Let what you say be simply 'Yes or No.' "[260]

2467 Man tends by nature toward the truth. He is obliged to honor and bear witness to it: "It is in accor-
2104 dance with their dignity that all men, because they are persons . . . are both impelled by their nature and bound by a moral obligation to seek the truth, especially religious truth. They are also bound to adhere to the truth once they come to know it and direct their whole lives in accordance with the demands of truth."[261]

2468 Truth as uprightness in human action and speech is called *truthfulness,* sincerity, or candor. Truth or
1458 truthfulness is the virtue which consists in showing oneself true in deeds and truthful in words, and in guarding against duplicity, dissimulation, and hypocrisy.

2469 "Men could not live with one another if there were not mutual confidence that they were being truth-
1807 ful to one another."[262] The virtue of truth gives another his just due. Truthfulness keeps to the just mean between what ought to be expressed and what ought to be kept secret: it entails honesty and discretion. In justice, "as a matter of honor, one man owes it to another to manifest the truth."[263]

2470 The disciple of Christ consents to "live in the truth," that is, in the simplicity of a life in conformity with the Lord's example, abiding in his truth. "If we say we have fellowship with him while we walk in darkness, we lie and do not live according to the truth."[264]

---

257 *Jn* 12:46.   258 *Jn* 8:32; cf. 17:17.   259 *Jn* 16:13.   260 *Mt* 5:37.   261 *DH* 2 § 2.   262 St. Thomas Aquinas, *STh* II-II, 109, 3 *ad* 1.   263 St. Thomas Aquinas, *STh* II-II, 109, 3, corp. art.   264 *1 Jn* 1:6.

II. TO BEAR WITNESS TO THE TRUTH

2471 Before Pilate, Christ proclaims that he "has come into the world, to bear witness to the truth."[265] The Christian is not to "be ashamed then of testifying to our Lord."[266] In situations that require witness to the faith, the Christian must profess it without equivocation, after the example of St. Paul before his judges. We must keep "a clear conscience toward God and toward men."[267]

1816

2472 The duty of Christians to take part in the life of the Church impels them to act as *witnesses of the Gospel* and of the obligations that flow from it. This witness is a transmission of the faith in words and deeds. Witness is an act of justice that establishes the truth or makes it known.[268]

863, 905

1807

> All Christians by the example of their lives and the witness of their word, wherever they live, have an obligation to manifest the new man which they have put on in Baptism and to reveal the power of the Holy Spirit by whom they were strengthened at Confirmation.[269]

2473 *Martyrdom* is the supreme witness given to the truth of the faith: it means bearing witness even unto death. The martyr bears witness to Christ who died and rose, to whom he is united by charity. He bears witness to the truth of the faith and of Christian doctrine. He endures death through an act of fortitude. "Let me become the food of the beasts, through whom it will be given me to reach God."[270]

852

1808

1258

2474 The Church has painstakingly collected the records of those who persevered to the end in witnessing to their faith. These are the acts of the Martyrs. They form the archives of truth written in letters of blood:

> Neither the pleasures of the world nor the kingdoms of this age will be of any use to me. It is better for me to die [in order to unite myself] to Christ

1011

265 *Jn* 18:37.   266 *2 Tim* 1:8.   267 *Acts* 24:16.   268 Cf. *Mt* 18:16.   269 *AG* 11.   270 St. Ignatius of Antioch, *Ad Rom.* 4, 1: SCh 10, 110.

Jesus than to reign over the ends of the earth. I seek him who died for us; I desire him who rose for us. My birth is approaching. . . .[271]

I bless you for having judged me worthy from this day and this hour to be counted among your martyrs. . . . You have kept your promise, God of faithfulness and truth. For this reason and for everything, I praise you, I bless you, I glorify you through the eternal and heavenly High Priest, Jesus Christ, your beloved Son. Through him, who is with you and the Holy Spirit, may glory be given to you, now and in the ages to come. Amen.[272]

III.   OFFENSES AGAINST TRUTH

2475   Christ's disciples have "put on the new man, created after the likeness of God in true righteousness and holiness."[273] By "putting away falsehood," they are to "put away all malice and all guile and insincerity and envy and all slander."[274]

2152   **2476**   *False witness and perjury.* When it is made publicly, a statement contrary to the truth takes on a particular gravity. In court it becomes false witness.[275] When it is under oath, it is perjury. Acts such as these contribute to condemnation of the innocent, exoneration of the guilty, or the increased punishment of the accused.[276] They gravely compromise the exercise of justice and the fairness of judicial decisions.

2477   *Respect for the reputation* of persons forbids every attitude and word likely to cause them unjust injury.[277] He becomes guilty:

—of *rash judgment* who, even tacitly, assumes as true, without sufficient foundation, the moral fault of a neighbor;

—of *detraction* who, without objectively valid reason, discloses another's faults and failings to persons who did not know them;[278]

---

271 St. Ignatius of Antioch, *Ad Rom.* 6, 1–2: SCh 10, 114.   272 *Martyrium Polycarpi* 14, 2–3: PG 5, 1040; SCh 10, 228.   273 *Eph* 4:24.   274 *Eph* 4:25; *1 Pet* 2:1.   275 Cf. *Prov* 19:9.   276 Cf. *Prov* 18:5.   277 Cf. CIC, can. 220. 278 Cf. *Sir* 21:28.

—of *calumny* who, by remarks contrary to the truth, harms the reputation of others and gives occasion for false judgments concerning them.

2478 To avoid rash judgment, everyone should be careful to interpret insofar as possible his neighbor's thoughts, words, and deeds in a favorable way:

> Every good Christian ought to be more ready to give a favorable interpretation to another's statement than to condemn it. But if he cannot do so, let him ask how the other understands it. And if the latter understands it badly, let the former correct him with love. If that does not suffice, let the Christian try all suitable ways to bring the other to a correct interpretation so that he may be saved.[279]

2479 Detraction and calumny destroy the *reputation and honor of one's neighbor*. Honor is the social witness given to human dignity, and everyone enjoys a natural right to the honor of his name and reputation and to respect. Thus, detraction and calumny offend against the virtues of justice and charity.   *1753*

2480 Every word or attitude is forbidden which by *flattery, adulation, or complaisance* encourages and confirms another in malicious acts and perverse conduct. Adulation is a grave fault if it makes one an accomplice in another's vices or grave sins. Neither the desire to be of service nor friendship justifies duplicitous speech. Adulation is a venial sin when it only seeks to be agreeable, to avoid evil, to meet a need, or to obtain legitimate advantages.

2481 *Boasting* or bragging is an offense against truth. So is *irony* aimed at disparaging someone by maliciously caricaturing some aspect of his behavior.

2482 "*A lie* consists in speaking a falsehood with the intention of deceiving."[280] The Lord denounces lying as the work of the devil: "You are of your father the devil, . . . there is no truth in him. When he lies, he speaks ac-

---

279 St. Ignatius of Loyola, *Spiritual Exercises*, 22.   280 St. Augustine, *De mendacio* 4, 5: PL 40, 491.

cording to his own nature, for he is a liar and the father
392   of lies."[281]

2483   Lying is the most direct offense against the truth. To lie is to speak or act against the truth in order to lead into error someone who has the right to know the truth. By injuring man's relation to truth and to his neighbor, a lie offends against the fundamental relation of man and of his word to the Lord.

2484   The *gravity of a lie* is measured against the nature of the truth it deforms, the circumstances, the intentions of the one who lies, and the harm suffered by
1750   its victims. If a lie in itself only constitutes a venial sin, it becomes mortal when it does grave injury to the virtues of justice and charity.

1756   **2485**   By its very nature, lying is to be condemned. It is a profanation of speech, whereas the purpose of speech is to communicate known truth to others. The deliberate intention of leading a neighbor into error by saying things contrary to the truth constitutes a failure in justice and charity. The culpability is greater when the intention of deceiving entails the risk of deadly consequences for those who are led astray.

2486   Since it violates the virtue of truthfulness, a lie does real violence to another. It affects his ability to know, which is a condition of every judgment and decision. It contains the seed of discord and all consequent
1607   evils. Lying is destructive of society; it undermines trust among men and tears apart the fabric of social relationships.

1459   **2487**   Every offense committed against justice and truth entails the *duty of reparation,* even if its author has been forgiven. When it is impossible publicly to make reparation for a wrong, it must be made secretly. If someone who has suffered harm cannot be directly
2412   compensated, he must be given moral satisfaction in the name of charity. This duty of reparation also concerns

---

281 *Jn* 8:44.

offenses against another's reputation. This reparation, moral and sometimes material, must be evaluated in terms of the extent of the damage inflicted. It obliges in conscience.

IV. RESPECT FOR THE TRUTH

2488 The *right to the communication* of the truth is 1740 not unconditional. Everyone must conform his life to the Gospel precept of fraternal love. This requires us in concrete situations to judge whether or not it is appropriate to reveal the truth to someone who asks for it.

2489 Charity and respect for the truth should dictate the response to every *request for information or communication.* The good and safety of others, respect for privacy, and the common good are sufficient reasons for being silent about what ought not be known or for making use of a discreet language. The duty to avoid scandal often commands strict discretion. No one is 2284 bound to reveal the truth to someone who does not have the right to know it.[282]

2490 The *secret of the sacrament of reconciliation* is 1467 sacred, and cannot be violated under any pretext. "The sacramental seal is inviolable; therefore, it is a crime for a confessor in any way to betray a penitent by word or in any other manner or for any reason."[283]

2491 *Professional secrets*—for example, those of political office holders, soldiers, physicians, and lawyers— or confidential information given under the seal of secrecy must be kept, save in exceptional cases where keeping the secret is bound to cause very grave harm to the one who confided it, to the one who received it or to a third party, and where the very grave harm can be avoided only by divulging the truth. Even if not confided under the seal of secrecy, private information prejudicial to another is not to be divulged without a grave and proportionate reason.

2492 Everyone should observe an appropriate reserve 2522

---

282 Cf. *Sir* 27:16; *Prov* 25:9–10. 283 CIC, can. 983 § 1.

concerning persons' private lives. Those in charge of communications should maintain a fair balance between the requirements of the common good and respect for individual rights. Interference by the media in the private lives of persons engaged in political or public activity is to be condemned to the extent that it infringes upon their privacy and freedom.

V.   THE USE OF THE SOCIAL COMMUNICATIONS MEDIA

2493   Within modern society the communications media play a major role in information, cultural promotion, and formation. This role is increasing, as a result of technological progress, the extent and diversity of the news transmitted, and the influence exercised on public opinion.

1906 **2494**   The information provided by the media is at the service of the common good.[284] Society has a right to information based on truth, freedom, justice, and solidarity:

> The proper exercise of this right demands that the content of the communication be true and—within the limits set by justice and charity—complete. Further, it should be communicated honestly and properly. This means that in the gathering and in the publication of news, the moral law and the legitimate rights and dignity of man should be upheld.[285]

906 **2495**   "It is necessary that all members of society meet the demands of justice and charity in this domain. They should help, through the means of social communication, in the formation and diffusion of sound public opinion."[286] Solidarity is a consequence of genuine and right communication and the free circulation of ideas that further knowledge and respect for others.

2496   The means of social communication (especially the mass media) can give rise to a certain passivity among users, making them less than vigilant consumers of what is *2525* said or shown. Users should practice moderation and discipline in their approach to the mass media. They will want

---

284 Cf. *IM* 11.   285 *IM* 5 § 2.   286 *IM* 8.

to form enlightened and correct consciences the more easily to resist unwholesome influences.

2497 By the very nature of their profession, journalists have an obligation to serve the truth and not offend against charity in disseminating information. They should strive to respect, with equal care, the nature of the facts and the limits of critical judgment concerning individuals. They should not stoop to defamation.

2498 *"Civil authorities* have particular responsibilities in this field because of the common good. . . . It is for the civil authority . . . to defend and safeguard a true and just freedom of information."[287] By promulgating laws and overseeing their application, public authorities should ensure that "public morality and social progress are not gravely endangered" through misuse of the media.[288] Civil authorities should punish any violation of the rights of individuals to their reputation and privacy. They should give timely and reliable reports concerning the general good or respond to the well-founded concerns of the people. Nothing can justify recourse to disinformation for manipulating public opinion through the media. Interventions by public authority should avoid injuring the freedom of individuals or groups. 2237 2286

2499 Moral judgment must condemn the plague of totalitarian states which systematically falsify the truth, exercise political control of opinion through the media, manipulate defendants and witnesses at public trials, and imagine that they secure their tyranny by strangling and repressing everything they consider "thought crimes." 1903

VI. TRUTH, BEAUTY, AND SACRED ART

2500 The practice of goodness is accompanied by spontaneous spiritual joy and moral beauty. Likewise, truth carries with it the joy and splendor of spiritual beauty. Truth is beautiful in itself. Truth in words, the rational expression of the knowledge of created and uncreated reality, is necessary to man, who is endowed with intellect. But truth can also find other complementary forms of human expression, above all when it is a matter of evoking what is beyond words: the depths of the human heart, the exaltations of the soul, the mys- 1804

---

287 *IM* 12.   288 *IM* 12 § 2.

tery of God. Even before revealing himself to man in words of truth, God reveals himself to him through the

341 universal language of creation, the work of his Word, of his wisdom: the order and harmony of the cosmos—which both the child and the scientist discover—"from the greatness and beauty of created things comes a corresponding perception of their Creator," "for the author

2129 of beauty created them."[289]

> [Wisdom] is a breath of the power of God, and a pure emanation of the glory of the Almighty; therefore nothing defiled gains entrance into her. For she is a reflection of eternal light, a spotless mirror of the working of God, and an image of his goodness.[290] For [wisdom] is more beautiful than the sun, and excels every constellation of the stars. Compared with the light she is found to be superior, for it is succeeded by the night, but against wisdom evil does not prevail.[291] I became enamored of her beauty.[292]

2501 Created "in the image of God,"[293] man also expresses the truth of his relationship with God the Creator by the beauty of his artistic works. Indeed, *art* is a distinctively human form of expression; beyond the search for the necessities of life which is common to all living creatures, art is a freely given superabundance of the human being's inner riches. Arising from talent given by the Creator and from man's own effort, art is a form of practical wisdom, uniting knowledge and skill,[294] to give form to the truth of reality in a language accessible to sight or hearing. To the extent that it is inspired by truth and love of beings, art bears a certain

339 likeness to God's activity in what he has created. Like any other human activity, art is not an absolute end in itself, but is ordered to and ennobled by the ultimate end of man.[295]

1156-1162 **2502** *Sacred art* is true and beautiful when its form corresponds to its particular vocation: evoking and glorifying, in faith and adoration, the transcendent mystery

---

289 *Wis* 13:3, 5.   290 *Wis* 7:25–26.   291 *Wis* 7:29–30.   292 *Wis* 8:2.
293 *Gen* 1:26.   294 Cf. *Wis* 7:16–17.   295 Cf. Pius XII, *Musicae sacrae disciplina;* Discourses of September 3 and December 25, 1950.

of God—the surpassing invisible beauty of truth and love visible in Christ, who "reflects the glory of God and bears the very stamp of his nature," in whom "the whole fullness of deity dwells bodily."[296] This spiritual beauty of God is reflected in the most holy Virgin Mother of God, the angels, and saints. Genuine sacred art draws man to adoration, to prayer, and to the love of God, Creator and Savior, the Holy One and Sanctifier.

2503 For this reason bishops, personally or through delegates, should see to the promotion of sacred art, old and new, in all its forms and, with the same religious care, remove from the liturgy and from places of worship everything which is not in conformity with the truth of faith and the authentic beauty of *sacred* art.[297]

IN BRIEF

2504 "You shall not bear false witness against your neighbor" (*Ex* 20:16). Christ's disciples have "put on the new man, created after the likeness of God in true righteousness and holiness" (*Eph* 4:24).

2505 Truth or truthfulness is the virtue which consists in showing oneself true in deeds and truthful in words, and guarding against duplicity, dissimulation, and hypocrisy.

2506 The Christian is not to "be ashamed of testifying to our Lord" (*2 Tim* 1:8) in deed and word. Martyrdom is the supreme witness given to the truth of the faith.

2507 Respect for the reputation and honor of persons forbids all detraction and calumny in word or attitude.

2508 Lying consists in saying what is false with the intention of deceiving the neighbor who has the right to the truth.

---

296 *Heb* 1:3; *Col* 2:9.   297 Cf. SC 122–127.

2509 An offense committed against the truth requires reparation.

2510 The golden rule helps one discern, in concrete situations, whether or not it would be appropriate to reveal the truth to someone who asks for it.

2511 "The sacramental seal is inviolable" (CIC, can. 983 § 1). Professional secrets must be kept. Confidences prejudicial to another are not to be divulged.

2512 Society has a right to information based on truth, freedom, and justice. One should practice moderation and discipline in the use of the social communications media.

2513 The fine arts, but above all sacred art, "of their nature are directed toward expressing in some way the infinite beauty of God in works made by human hands. Their dedication to the increase of God's praise and of his glory is more complete, the more exclusively they are devoted to turning men's minds devoutly toward God" (*SC* 122).

ARTICLE 9
THE NINTH COMMANDMENT

You shall not covet your neighbor's house; you shall not covet your neighbor's wife, or his manservant, or his maidservant, or his ox, or his ass, or anything that is your neighbor's.[298]

Every one who looks at a woman lustfully has already committed adultery with her in his heart.[299]

377, 400 **2514** St. John distinguishes three kinds of covetousness or concupiscence: lust of the flesh, lust of the eyes, and pride of life.[300] In the Catholic catechetical tradition,

---

298 *Ex* 20:17.   299 *Mt* 5:28.   300 Cf. *1 Jn* 2:16.

the ninth commandment forbids carnal concupiscence; the tenth forbids coveting another's goods.

2515 Etymologically, "concupiscence" can refer to 405 any intense form of human desire. Christian theology has given it a particular meaning: the movement of the sensitive appetite contrary to the operation of the human reason. The apostle St. Paul identifies it with the rebellion of the "flesh" against the "spirit."[301] Concupiscence stems from the disobedience of the first sin. It unsettles man's moral faculties and, without being in itself an offense, inclines man to commit sins.[302]

2516 Because man is a *composite being, spirit and* 362 *body,* there already exists a certain tension in him; a certain struggle of tendencies between "spirit" and "flesh" develops. But in fact this struggle belongs to the heritage of sin. It is a consequence of sin and at the same time a confirmation of it. It is part of the daily experience of the spiritual battle: 407

> For the Apostle it is not a matter of despising and condemning the body which with the spiritual soul constitutes man's nature and personal subjectivity. Rather, he is concerned with the morally *good or bad* works, or better, the permanent dispositions— virtues and vices—which are the fruit of *submission* (in the first case) or of *resistance* (in the second case) to *the saving action of the Holy Spirit.* For this reason the Apostle writes: "If we live by the Spirit, let us also walk by the Spirit."[303]

I. PURIFICATION OF THE HEART

2517 The heart is the seat of moral personality: "Out 368 of the heart come evil thoughts, murder, adultery, fornication. . . ."[304] The struggle against carnal covetousness entails purifying the heart and practicing temperance: 1809

> Remain simple and innocent, and you will be like little children who do not know the evil that destroys man's life.[305]

---

301 Cf. *Gal* 5:16, 17, 24; *Eph* 2:3.   302 Cf. *Gen* 3:11; Council of Trent: DS 1515.   303 John Paul II, *DeV* 55; cf. *Gal* 5:25.   304 *Mt* 15:19.   305 *Pastor Hermae,* Mandate 2, 1: PG 2, 916.

2518 The sixth beatitude proclaims, "Blessed are the pure in heart, for they shall see God."[306] "Pure in heart" refers to those who have attuned their intellects and wills to the demands of God's holiness, chiefly in three areas: charity;[307] chastity or sexual rectitude;[308] love of truth and orthodoxy of faith.[309] There is a connection

94 between purity of heart, of body, and of faith:

> The faithful must believe the articles of the Creed "so that by believing they may obey God, by obeying may live well, by living well may purify their hearts, and with pure hearts may understand what
>
158 > they believe."[310]

2548 **2519** The "pure in heart" are promised that they will see God face to face and be like him.[311] Purity of heart is the precondition of the vision of God. Even now it enables us to see *according to* God, to accept others as
2819 "neighbors"; it lets us perceive the human body—ours and our neighbor's—as a temple of the Holy Spirit, a
2501 manifestation of divine beauty.

II.   THE BATTLE FOR PURITY

1264 **2520** Baptism confers on its recipient the grace of purification from all sins. But the baptized must continue to struggle against concupiscence of the flesh and disordered desires. With God's grace he will prevail

2337 —by the *virtue* and *gift of chastity,* for chastity lets us love with upright and undivided heart;

1752 —by *purity of intention* which consists in seeking the true end of man: with simplicity of vision, the baptized person seeks to find and to fulfill God's will in everything;[312]

1762 —by *purity of vision,* external and internal; by discipline of feelings and imagination; by refusing all complicity in impure thoughts that incline us to turn aside

---

306 *Mt* 5:8.   307 Cf. *1 Tim* 4:3–9; *2 Tim* 2:22.   308 Cf. *1 Thess* 4:7; *Col* 3:5; *Eph* 4:19.   309 Cf. *Titus* 1:15; *1 Tim* 1:3–4; *2 Tim* 2:23–26.   310 St. Augustine, *De fide et symbolo* 10, 25: PL 40, 196.   311 Cf. *1 Cor* 13:12; *1 Jn* 3:2.   312 Cf. *Rom* 12:2; *Col* 1:10.

from the path of God's commandments: "Appearance arouses yearning in fools";[313]

—by *prayer:* 2846

> I thought that continence arose from one's own powers, which I did not recognize in myself. I was foolish enough not to know . . . that no one can be continent unless you grant it. For you would surely have granted it if my inner groaning had reached your ears and I with firm faith had cast my cares on you.[314]

2521 Purity requires *modesty*, an integral part of temperance. Modesty protects the intimate center of the person. It means refusing to unveil what should remain hidden. It is ordered to chastity to whose sensitivity it bears witness. It guides how one looks at others and behaves toward them in conformity with the dignity of persons and their solidarity.

2522 Modesty protects the mystery of persons and 2492 their love. It encourages patience and moderation in loving relationships; it requires that the conditions for the definitive giving and commitment of man and woman to one another be fulfilled. Modesty is decency. It inspires one's choice of clothing. It keeps silence or reserve where there is evident risk of unhealthy curiosity. It is discreet.

2523 There is a modesty of the feelings as well as of 2354 the body. It protests, for example, against the voyeuristic explorations of the human body in certain advertisements, or against the solicitations of certain media that go too far in the exhibition of intimate things. Modesty inspires a way of life which makes it possible to resist the allurements of fashion and the pressures of prevailing ideologies.

2524 The forms taken by modesty vary from one culture to another. Everywhere, however, modesty exists as an intuition of the spiritual dignity proper to man. It is born with the awakening consciousness of being a subject. Teaching modesty to children and adolescents means awakening in them respect for the human person.

---

313 *Wis* 15:5.   314 St. Augustine, *Conf.* 6, 11, 20: PL 32, 729–730.

2344 **2525** Christian purity requires a *purification of the social climate*. It requires of the communications media that their presentations show concern for respect and restraint. Purity of heart brings freedom from widespread eroticism and avoids entertainment inclined to voyeurism and illusion.

1740 **2526** So-called *moral permissiveness* rests on an erroneous conception of human freedom; the necessary precondition for the development of true freedom is to let oneself be educated in the moral law. Those in charge of education can reasonably be expected to give young people instruction respectful of the truth, the qualities of the heart, and the moral and spiritual dignity of man.

1204 **2527** "The Good News of Christ continually renews the life and culture of fallen man; it combats and removes the error and evil which flow from the ever-present attraction of sin. It never ceases to purify and elevate the morality of peoples. It takes the spiritual qualities and endowments of every age and nation, and with supernatural riches it causes them to blossom, as it were, from within; it fortifies, completes, and restores them in Christ."[315]

IN BRIEF

2528 "Everyone who looks at a woman lustfully has already committed adultery with her in his heart" (*Mt* 5:28).

2529 The ninth commandment warns against lust or carnal concupiscence.

2530 The struggle against carnal lust involves purifying the heart and practicing temperance.

2531 Purity of heart will enable us to see God: it enables us even now to see things according to God.

---

315 *GS* 58 § 4.

2532 Purification of the heart demands prayer, the practice of chastity, purity of intention and of vision.

2533 Purity of heart requires the modesty which is patience, decency, and discretion. Modesty protects the intimate center of the person.

ARTICLE 10
THE TENTH COMMANDMENT

You shall not covet . . . anything that is your neighbor's. . . . You shall not desire your neighbor's house, his field, or his manservant, or his maidservant, or his ox, or his ass, or anything that is your neighbor's.[316]

For where your treasure is, there will your heart be also.[317]

2534 The tenth commandment unfolds and completes the ninth, which is concerned with concupiscence of the flesh. It forbids coveting the goods of another, as the root of theft, robbery, and fraud, which the seventh commandment forbids. "Lust of the eyes" leads to the violence and injustice forbidden by the fifth commandment.[318] Avarice, like fornication, originates in the idolatry prohibited by the first three prescriptions of the Law.[319] The tenth commandment concerns the intentions of the heart; with the ninth, it summarizes all the precepts of the Law.

2112
2069

I. THE DISORDER OF COVETOUS DESIRES
2535 The sensitive appetite leads us to desire pleasant things we do not have, e.g., the desire to eat when we are hungry or to warm ourselves when we are cold. These desires are good in themselves; but often they exceed the limits of reason and drive us to covet unjustly what is not ours and belongs to another or is owed to him.

1767

---

316 *Ex* 20:17; *Deut* 5:21.   317 *Mt* 6:21.   318 Cf. *1 Jn* 2:16; *Mic* 2:2.   319 Cf. *Wis* 14:12.

2536 The tenth commandment forbids *greed* and the desire to amass earthly goods without limit. It forbids *avarice* arising from a passion for riches and their attendant power. It also forbids the desire to commit injustice by harming our neighbor in his temporal goods:

> When the Law says, "You shall not covet," these words mean that we should banish our desires for whatever does not belong to us. Our thirst for another's goods is immense, infinite, never quenched. Thus it is written: "He who loves money never has money enough."[320]

2537 It is not a violation of this commandment to desire to obtain things that belong to one's neighbor, provided this is done by just means. Traditional catechesis realistically mentions "those who have a harder struggle against their criminal desires" and so who "must be urged the more to keep this commandment":

> ... merchants who desire scarcity and rising prices, who cannot bear not to be the only ones buying and selling so that they themselves can sell more dearly and buy more cheaply; those who hope that their peers will be impoverished, in order to realize a profit either by selling to them or buying from them ... physicians who wish disease to spread; lawyers who are eager for many important cases and trials.[321]

2538 The tenth commandment requires that *envy* be banished from the human heart. When the prophet Nathan wanted to spur King David to repentance, he told him the story about the poor man who had only one ewe lamb that he treated like his own daughter and the rich man who, despite the great number of his flocks, envied the poor man and ended by stealing his lamb.[322] Envy can lead to the worst crimes.[323] "Through the devil's envy death entered the world":[324]

> We fight one another, and envy arms us against one another.... If everyone strives to unsettle the Body of Christ, where shall we end up? We are engaged

---

320 *Roman Catechism,* III, 37; cf. *Sir* 5:8.   321 *Roman Catechism,* III, 37.
322 Cf. *2 Sam* 12:1–4.   323 Cf. *Gen* 4:3–7; *1 Kings* 21:1–29.   324 *Wis* 2:24.

> in making Christ's Body a corpse. . . . We declare ourselves members of one and the same organism, yet we devour one another like beasts.[325]

2539 Envy is a capital sin. It refers to the sadness at the sight of another's goods and the immoderate desire to acquire them for oneself, even unjustly. When it wishes grave harm to a neighbor it is a mortal sin: *1866*

> St. Augustine saw envy as *"the* diabolical sin."[326] "From envy are born hatred, detraction, calumny, joy caused by the misfortune of a neighbor, and displeasure caused by his prosperity."[327]

2540 Envy represents a form of sadness and therefore a refusal of charity; the baptized person should struggle against it by exercising good will. Envy often comes from pride; the baptized person should train himself to live in humility: *1829*

> Would you like to see God glorified by you? Then rejoice in your brother's progress and you will immediately give glory to God. Because his servant could conquer envy by rejoicing in the merits of others, God will be praised.[328]

II.   THE DESIRES OF THE SPIRIT

2541 The economy of law and grace turns men's hearts away from avarice and envy. It initiates them into desire for the Sovereign Good; it instructs them in the desires of the Holy Spirit who satisfies man's heart.   *1718*
    2764

The God of the promises always warned man against seduction by what from the beginning has seemed "good for food . . . a delight to the eyes . . . to be desired to make one wise."[329]   *397*

2542 The Law entrusted to Israel never sufficed to justify those subject to it; it even became the instrument of "lust."[330] The gap between wanting and doing points to the conflict between God's Law which is the "law of my   *1963*

---

325 St. John Chrysostom, *Hom. in 2 Cor.* 27, 3–4: PG 61, 588.   326 Cf. St. Augustine, *De catechizandis rudibus* 4, 8: PL 40, 315–316.   327 St. Gregory the Great, *Moralia in Job* 31, 45: PL 76, 621.   328 St. John Chrysostom, *Hom. in Rom.* 71, 5: PG 60, 448.   329 *Gen* 3:6.   330 Cf. *Rom* 7:7.

mind," and another law "making me captive to the law of sin which dwells in my members."[331]

1992 **2543** "But now the righteousness of God has been manifested apart from law, although the law and the prophets bear witness to it, the righteousness of God through faith in Jesus Christ for all who believe."[332] Henceforth, Christ's faithful "have crucified the flesh with its passions and desires"; they are led by the Spirit and follow the desires of the Spirit.[333]

2443-2449 **III.   POVERTY OF HEART**

2544 Jesus enjoins his disciples to prefer him to everything and everyone, and bids them "renounce all that [they have]" for his sake and that of the Gospel.[334] Shortly before his passion he gave them the example of the poor widow of Jerusalem who, out of her poverty, gave all that she had to live on.[335] The precept of detachment from riches is obligatory for entrance into the
544 Kingdom of heaven.

2545 All Christ's faithful are to "direct their affections rightly, lest they be hindered in their pursuit of perfect charity by the use of worldly things and by an adherence to riches which is contrary to the spirit of evangel-
2013 ical poverty."[336]

2546 "Blessed are the poor in spirit."[337] The Beatitudes reveal an order of happiness and grace, of beauty and
1716 peace. Jesus celebrates the joy of the poor, to whom the Kingdom already belongs:[338]

> The Word speaks of voluntary humility as "poverty in spirit"; the Apostle gives an example of God's poverty when he says: "For your sakes he became poor."[339]

2547 The Lord grieves over the rich, because they find their consolation in the abundance of goods.[340] "Let the proud seek and love earthly kingdoms, but blessed are

---

331 *Rom* 7:23; cf. 7:10.   332 *Rom* 3:21–22.   333 *Gal* 5:24; cf. *Rom* 8:14, 27.
334 *Lk* 14:33; cf. *Mk* 8:35.   335 Cf. *Lk* 21:4.   336 *LG* 42 § 3.   337 *Mt* 5:3.
338 Cf. *Lk* 6:20.   339 St. Gregory of Nyssa, *De beatitudinibus* 1: PG 44, 1200D;
cf. *2 Cor* 8:9.   340 *Lk* 6:24.

the poor in spirit for theirs is the Kingdom of heaven."[341] Abandonment to the providence of the Father in heaven frees us from anxiety about tomorrow.[342] 305 Trust in God is a preparation for the blessedness of the poor. They shall see God.

IV. "I WANT TO SEE GOD"

2548 Desire for true happiness frees man from his immoderate attachment to the goods of this world so that he can find his fulfillment in the vision and beatitude of 2519 God. "The promise [of seeing God] surpasses all beatitude.... In Scripture, to see is to possess.... Whoever sees God has obtained all the goods of which he can conceive."[343]

2549 It remains for the holy people to struggle, with grace from on high, to obtain the good things God promises. In order to possess and contemplate God, Christ's faithful mortify their cravings and, with the 2015 grace of God, prevail over the seductions of pleasure and power.

2550 On this way of perfection, the Spirit and the Bride call whoever hears them[344] to perfect communion with God:

> There will true glory be, where no one will be praised by mistake or flattery; true honor will not be refused to the worthy, nor granted to the unworthy; likewise, no one unworthy will pretend to be worthy, where only those who are worthy will be admitted. There true peace will reign, where no one will experience opposition either from self or others. God himself will be virtue's reward; he gives virtue and has promised to give himself as the best and greatest reward that could exist.... "I shall be their God and they will be my people...." This is also the meaning of the Apostle's words: "So that God may be all in all." God himself will be the goal of our desires; we shall contemplate him without end, love him without surfeit, praise him without

---

341 St. Augustine, *De serm. Dom. in monte* 1, 1, 3: PL 34, 1232.   342 Cf. *Mt* 6:25–34.   343 St. Gregory of Nyssa, *De beatitudinibus* 6: PG 44, 1265A.   344 Cf. *Rev* 22:17.

314   weariness. This gift, this state, this act, like eternal
        life itself, will assuredly be common to all.[345]

IN BRIEF

2551   "Where your treasure is, there will your heart be
       also" (*Mt* 6:21).

2552   The tenth commandment forbids avarice arising
       from a passion for riches and their attendant
       power.

2553   Envy is sadness at the sight of another's goods
       and the immoderate desire to have them for one-
       self. It is a capital sin.

2554   The baptized person combats envy through
       good-will, humility, and abandonment to the
       providence of God.

2555   Christ's faithful "have crucified the flesh with its
       passions and desires" (*Gal* 5:24); they are led by
       the Spirit and follow his desires.

2556   Detachment from riches is necessary for entering
       the Kingdom of heaven. "Blessed are the poor in
       spirit."

2557   "I want to see God" expresses the true desire of
       man. Thirst for God is quenched by the water of
       eternal life (cf. *Jn* 4:14).

---

345 St. Augustine, *De civ. Dei*, 22, 30: PL 41, 801–802; cf. *Lev* 26:12; cf. *1 Cor* 15:28.

PART FOUR
CHRISTIAN PRAYER

SECTION ONE
PRAYER IN THE CHRISTIAN LIFE

2558 "Great is the mystery of the faith!" The Church professes this mystery in the Apostles' Creed *(Part One)* and celebrates it in the sacramental liturgy *(Part Two)*, so that the life of the faithful may be conformed to Christ in the Holy Spirit to the glory of God the Father *(Part Three)*. This mystery, then, requires that the faithful believe in it, that they celebrate it, and that they live from it in a vital and personal relationship with the living and true God. This relationship is prayer.

WHAT IS PRAYER?

For me, prayer is a surge of the heart; it is a simple look turned toward heaven, it is a cry of recognition and of love, embracing both trial and joy.[1]

Prayer as God's gift

2559 "Prayer is the raising of one's mind and heart to God or the requesting of good things from God."[2] But when we pray, do we speak from the height of our pride and will, or "out of the depths" of a humble and contrite heart?[3] He who humbles himself will be exalted;[4] *humility* is the foundation of prayer. Only when we humbly acknowledge that "we do not know how to pray as we ought,"[5] are we ready to receive freely the gift of prayer. "Man is a beggar before God."[6]

2613
2763

2560 "If you knew the gift of God!"[7] The wonder of prayer is revealed beside the well where we come seeking water: there, Christ comes to meet every human being. It is he who first seeks us and asks us for a drink. Jesus thirsts; his asking arises from the depths of God's desire for us. Whether we realize it or not, prayer is the

---

1 St. Thérèse of Lisieux, *Manuscrits autobiographiques,* C 25r. **2** St. John Damascene, *De fide orth.* 3, 24: PG 94, 1089C. **3** *Ps* 130:1. **4** Cf. *Lk* 18:9–14. **5** *Rom* 8:26. **6** St. Augustine, *Sermo* 56, 6, 9: PL 38, 381. **7** *Jn* 4:10.

encounter of God's thirst with ours. God thirsts that we may thirst for him.[8]

2561 "You would have asked him, and he would have given you living water."[9] Paradoxically our prayer of petition is a response to the plea of the living God: "They have forsaken me, the fountain of living waters, and hewn out cisterns for themselves, broken cisterns that can hold no water!"[10] Prayer is the response of faith to the free promise of salvation and also a response of love to the thirst of the only Son of God.[11]

Prayer as covenant

2562 Where does prayer come from? Whether prayer is expressed in words or gestures, it is the whole man who prays. But in naming the source of prayer, Scripture speaks sometimes of the soul or the spirit, but most often of the heart (more than a thousand times). According to Scripture, it is the *heart* that prays. If our heart is far from God, the words of prayer are in vain.

2563 The heart is the dwelling-place where I am, where I live; according to the Semitic or Biblical expression, the heart is the place "to which I withdraw." The heart is our hidden center, beyond the grasp of our reason and of others; only the Spirit of God can fathom the human heart and know it fully. The heart is the place of decision, deeper than our psychic drives. It is the place of truth, where we choose life or death. It is the place of encounter, because as image of God we live in relation: it is the place of covenant.

2564 Christian prayer is a covenant relationship between God and man in Christ. It is the action of God and of man, springing forth from both the Holy Spirit and ourselves, wholly directed to the Father, in union with the human will of the Son of God made man.

2699

1696

---

8 Cf. St. Augustine, *De diversis quaestionibus octoginta tribus* 64, 4: PL 40, 56.
9 *Jn* 4:10.   10 *Jer* 2:13.   11 Cf. *Jn* 7:37–39; 19:28; *Isa* 12:3; 51:1; *Zech* 12:10; 13:1.

Prayer as communion

2565 In the New Covenant, prayer is the living relationship of the children of God with their Father who is good beyond measure, with his Son Jesus Christ and with the Holy Spirit. The grace of the Kingdom is "the union of the entire holy and royal Trinity . . . with the whole human spirit."[12] Thus, the life of prayer is the habit of being in the presence of the thrice-holy God and in communion with him. This communion of life is always possible because, through Baptism, we have already been united with Christ.[13] Prayer is *Christian* insofar as it is communion with Christ and extends throughout the Church, which is his Body. Its dimensions are those of Christ's love.[14]

260

792

CHAPTER ONE

THE REVELATION OF PRAYER

THE UNIVERSAL CALL TO PRAYER

2566 *Man is in search of God.* In the act of creation, God calls every being from nothingness into existence. "Crowned with glory and honor," man is, after the angels, capable of acknowledging "how majestic is the name of the Lord in all the earth."[1] Even after losing through his sin his likeness to God, man remains an image of his Creator, and retains the desire for the one who calls him into existence. All religions bear witness to men's essential search for God.[2]

296

355

28

2567 *God calls man first.* Man may forget his Creator or hide far from his face; he may run after idols or accuse the deity of having abandoned him; yet the living and true God tirelessly calls each person to that mysterious encounter known as prayer. In prayer, the faithful God's initiative of love always comes first; our own first step is always a response. As God gradually reveals himself and reveals man to himself, prayer appears as a reciprocal call, a covenant drama. Through words and ac-

30

142

---

12 St. Gregory of Nazianzus, *Oratio,* 16, 9: PG 35, 945.   **13** Cf. *Rom* 6:5.
14 Cf. *Eph* 3:18–21.   **1** *Ps* 8:5; 8:1.   **2** Cf. *Acts* 17:27.

tions, this drama engages the heart. It unfolds throughout the whole history of salvation.

ARTICLE 1
IN THE OLD TESTAMENT

2568 In the Old Testament, the revelation of prayer comes between the fall and the restoration of man, that is, between God's sorrowful call to his first children: "Where are you? . . . What is this that you have done?"[3] and the response of God's only Son on coming into the world: "Lo, I have come to do your will, O God."[4] Prayer is bound up with human history, for it is the relationship with God in historical events.

410
1736
2738

Creation—source of prayer

288

2569 Prayer is lived in the first place beginning with the realities of *creation*. The first nine chapters of Genesis describe this relationship with God as an offering of the first-born of Abel's flock, as the invocation of the divine name at the time of Enosh, and as "walking with God."[5] Noah's offering is pleasing to God, who blesses him and through him all creation, because his heart was upright and undivided; Noah, like Enoch before him, "walks with God."[6] This kind of prayer is lived by many righteous people in all religions.

58

In his indefectible covenant with every living creature,[7] God has always called people to prayer. But it is above all beginning with our father Abraham that prayer is revealed in the Old Testament.

59

God's promise and the prayer of Faith

2570 When God calls him, Abraham goes forth "as the Lord had told him";[8] Abraham's heart is entirely submissive to the Word and so he obeys. Such attentiveness of the heart, whose decisions are made according to God's will, is essential to prayer, while the words used count only in relation to it. Abraham's prayer is

145

---

3 *Gen* 3:9, 13.   4 *Heb* 10:5–7.   5 Cf. *Gen* 4:4, 26; *Gen* 5:24.   6 *Gen* 6:9; 8:20–9:17.   7 *Gen* 9:8–16.   8 *Gen* 12:4.

expressed first by deeds: a man of silence, he constructs an altar to the Lord at each stage of his journey. Only later does Abraham's first prayer in words appear: a veiled complaint reminding God of his promises which seem unfulfilled.[9] Thus one aspect of the drama of prayer appears from the beginning: the test of faith in the fidelity of God.

2571 Because Abraham believed in God and walked in his presence and in covenant with him,[10] the patriarch is ready to welcome a mysterious Guest into his tent. Abraham's remarkable hospitality at Mamre foreshadows the annunciation of the true Son of the promise.[11] *494* After that, once God had confided his plan, Abraham's heart is attuned to his Lord's compassion for men and he dares to intercede for them with bold confidence.[12] *2635*

2572 As a final stage in the purification of his faith, Abraham, "who had received the promises,"[13] is asked to sacrifice the son God had given him. Abraham's faith does not weaken ("God himself will provide the lamb for a burnt offering."), for he "considered that God was able to raise men even from the dead."[14] And so the father of believers is conformed to the likeness of the Father who will not spare his own Son but will deliver him up for us all.[15] Prayer restores man to God's likeness and *603* enables him to share in the power of God's love that saves the multitude.[16]

2573 God renews his promise to Jacob, the ancestor of the twelve tribes of Israel.[17] Before confronting his elder brother Esau, Jacob wrestles all night with a mysterious figure who refuses to reveal his name, but who blesses him before leaving him at dawn. From this account, the spiritual tradition of the Church has retained the symbol of prayer as a battle of faith and as the triumph of perseverance.[18] *162*

---

9 Cf. *Gen* 15:2 f. 10 Cf. *Gen* 15:6; 17:1 f. 11 Cf. *Gen* 18:1–15; *Lk* 1:26–38.
12 Cf. *Gen* 18:16–33. 13 *Heb* 11:17. 14 *Gen* 22:8; *Heb* 11:19. 15 *Rom* 8:32.
16 Cf. *Rom* 8:16–21. 17 Cf. *Gen* 28:10–22. 18 Cf. *Gen* 32:24–30; *Lk* 18:1–8.

Moses and the prayer of the mediator

62 **2574** Once the promise begins to be fulfilled (Passover, the Exodus, the gift of the Law, and the ratification of the covenant), the prayer of Moses becomes the most striking example of intercessory prayer, which will be fulfilled in "the one mediator between God and men, the man Christ Jesus."[19]

205 **2575** Here again the initiative is God's. From the midst of the burning bush he calls Moses.[20] This event will remain one of the primordial images of prayer in the spiritual tradition of Jews and Christians alike. When "the God of Abraham, of Isaac, and of Jacob" calls Moses to be his servant, it is because he is the living God who wants men to live. God reveals himself in order to save them, though he does not do this alone or despite them: he calls Moses to be his messenger, an associate in his compassion, his work of salvation. There is something of a divine plea in this mission, and only after long debate does Moses attune his own will to that of the Savior God. But in the dialogue in which God confides in him, Moses also learns how to pray: he balks, makes excuses, above all questions: and it is in response to his question that the Lord confides his ineffable name, which will be revealed through his mighty deeds.

555 **2576** "Thus the Lord used to speak to Moses face to face, as a man speaks to his friend."[21] Moses' prayer is characteristic of contemplative prayer by which God's servant remains faithful to his mission. Moses converses with God often and at length, climbing the mountain to hear and entreat him and coming down to the people to repeat the words of his God for their guidance. Moses "is entrusted with all my house. With him I speak face to face, clearly, not in riddles," for "Moses was very humble, more so than anyone else on the face of the earth."[22]

210 **2577** From this intimacy with the faithful God, slow

---

19 *1 Tim* 2:5.   **20** *Ex* 3:1–10.   **21** *Ex* 33:11.   **22** *Num* 12:3, 7–8.

to anger and abounding in steadfast love,[23] Moses drew
strength and determination for his intercession. He does   *210*
not pray for himself but for the people whom God made
his own. Moses already intercedes for them during the
battle with the Amalekites and prays to obtain healing
for Miriam.[24] But it is chiefly after their apostasy that   *2635*
Moses "stands in the breach" before God in order to
save the people.[25] The arguments of his prayer—for intercession is also a mysterious battle—will inspire the
boldness of the great intercessors among the Jewish people and in the Church: God is love; he is therefore righteous and faithful; he cannot contradict himself; he   *214*
must remember his marvellous deeds, since his glory is
at stake, and he cannot forsake this people that bears
his name.

David and the prayer of the king

2578 The prayer of the People of God flourishes in the
shadow of God's dwelling place, first the ark of the
covenant and later the Temple. At first the leaders of the
people—the shepherds and the prophets—teach them to
pray. The infant Samuel must have learned from his
mother Hannah how "to stand before the LORD" and
from the priest Eli how to listen to his word: "Speak,
LORD, for your servant is listening."[26] Later, he will
also know the cost and consequence of intercession:
"Moreover, as for me, far be it from me that I should sin
against the LORD by ceasing to pray for you; and I will
instruct you in the good and the right way."[27]

2579 David is par excellence the king "after God's   *709*
own heart," the shepherd who prays for his people and
prays in their name. His submission to the will of God,
his praise, and his repentance, will be a model for the
prayer of the people. His prayer, the prayer of God's
Anointed, is a faithful adherence to the divine promise
and expresses a loving and joyful trust in God, the only   *436*
King and Lord.[28] In the Psalms David, inspired by the

---

23 Cf. *Ex* 34:6.   24 Cf. *Ex* 17:8–12; *Num* 12:13–14.   25 *Ps* 106:23; cf. *Ex*
32:1–34:9.   26 *1 Sam* 3:9–10; cf. 1:9–18.   27 *1 Sam* 12:23.   28 Cf. *2 Sam*
7:18–29.

Holy Spirit, is the first prophet of Jewish and Christian prayer. The prayer of Christ, the true Messiah and Son of David, will reveal and fulfill the meaning of this prayer.

583   **2580**   The Temple of Jerusalem, the house of prayer that David wanted to build, will be the work of his son, Solomon. The prayer at the dedication of the Temple relies on God's promise and covenant, on the active presence of his name among his People, recalling his mighty deeds at the Exodus.[29] The king lifts his hands toward heaven and begs the Lord, on his own behalf, on behalf of the entire people, and of the generations yet to come, for the forgiveness of their sins and for their daily needs, so that the nations may know that He is the only God and that the heart of his people may belong wholly and entirely to him.

Elijah, the prophets and conversion of heart

2581   For the People of God, the Temple was to be the place of their education in prayer: pilgrimages, feasts and sacrifices, the evening offering, the incense, and the

1150   bread of the Presence ("shewbread")—all these signs of the holiness and glory of God Most High and Most Near were appeals to and ways of prayer. But ritualism often encouraged an excessively external worship. The people needed education in faith and conversion of heart; this was the mission of the prophets, both before and after the Exile.

2582   Elijah is the "father" of the prophets, "the generation of those who seek him, who seek the face of the God of Jacob."[30] Elijah's name, "The Lord is my God," foretells the people's cry in response to his prayer on Mount Carmel.[31] St. James refers to Elijah in order to encourage us to pray: "The prayer of the righteous is powerful and effective."[32]

2583   After Elijah had learned mercy during his retreat at the Wadi Cherith, he teaches the widow of Zarephath

---

29 *1 Kings* 8:10–61.   30 *Ps* 24:6.   31 *1 Kings* 18:39.   32 *Jas* 5:16b–18.

to believe in The Word of God and confirms her faith by his urgent prayer: God brings the widow's child back to life.[33]

The sacrifice on Mount Carmel is a decisive test for the faith of the People of God. In response to Elijah's plea, "Answer me, O LORD, answer me," the Lord's fire consumes the holocaust, at the time of the evening oblation. The Eastern liturgies repeat Elijah's plea in the Eucharistic *epiclesis*.   696

Finally, taking the desert road that leads to the place where the living and true God reveals himself to his people, Elijah, like Moses before him, hides "in a cleft of the rock" until the mysterious presence of God has passed by.[34] But only on the mountain of the Transfiguration will Moses and Elijah behold the unveiled face of him whom they sought; "the light of the knowledge of the glory of God [shines] in the face of Christ," crucified and risen.[35]   555

2584 In their "one to one" encounters with God, the prophets draw light and strength for their mission. Their prayer is not flight from this unfaithful world, but rather attentiveness to The Word of God. At times their prayer is an argument or a complaint, but it is always an intercession that awaits and prepares for the intervention of the Savior God, the Lord of history.[36]   2709

The Psalms, the prayer of the assembly

2585 From the time of David to the coming of the Messiah texts appearing in these sacred books show a deepening in prayer for oneself and in prayer for others.[37] Thus the psalms were gradually collected into the five books of the Psalter (or "Praises"), the masterwork of prayer in the Old Testament.   1093

2586 The Psalms both nourished and expressed the prayer of the People of God gathered during the great

---

33 Cf. *1 Kings* 17:7–24.   34 Cf. *1 Kings* 19:1–14; cf. *Ex* 33:19–23.   35 *2 Cor* 4:6; cf. *Lk* 9:30–35.   36 Cf. *Am* 7:2, 5; *Isa* 6:5, 8, 11; *Jer* 1:6; 15:15–18; 20:7–18.   37 *Ezra* 9:6–15; *Neh* 1:4–11; *Jon* 2:3–10; *Tob* 3:11–16; *Jdt* 9:2–14.

feasts at Jerusalem and each Sabbath in the synagogues. Their prayer is inseparably personal and communal; it concerns both those who are praying and all men. The Psalms arose from the communities of the Holy Land and the Diaspora, but embrace all creation. Their prayer recalls the saving events of the past, yet extends into the future, even to the end of history; it commemorates the promises God has already kept, and awaits the Messiah who will fulfill them definitively. Prayed by Christ and fulfilled in him, the Psalms remain essential to the prayer of the Church.[38]

1177

2587 The Psalter is the book in which The Word of God becomes man's prayer. In other books of the Old Testament, "the words proclaim [God's] works and bring to light the mystery they contain."[39] The words of the Psalmist, sung for God, both express and acclaim the Lord's saving works; the same Spirit inspires both God's work and man's response. Christ will unite the two. In him, the psalms continue to teach us how to pray.

2641

2588 The Psalter's many forms of prayer take shape both in the liturgy of the Temple and in the human heart. Whether hymns or prayers of lamentation or thanksgiving, whether individual or communal, whether royal chants, songs of pilgrimage or wisdom-meditations, the Psalms are a mirror of God's marvelous deeds in the history of his people, as well as reflections of the human experiences of the Psalmist. Though a given psalm may reflect an event of the past, it still possesses such direct simplicity that it can be prayed in truth by men of all times and conditions.

2589 Certain constant characteristics appear throughout the Psalms: simplicity and spontaneity of prayer; the desire for God himself through and with all that is good in his creation; the distraught situation of the believer who, in his preferential love for the Lord, is exposed to a host of enemies and temptations, but who waits upon

---

38 Cf. GILH, nn. 100–109. 39 *DV* 2.

what the faithful God will do, in the certitude of his love
and in submission to his will. The prayer of the psalms *304*
is always sustained by praise; that is why the title of this
collection as handed down to us is so fitting: "The
Praises." Collected for the assembly's worship, the
Psalter both sounds the call to prayer and sings the response to that call: *Hallelu-Yah!* ("Alleluia"), "Praise
the Lord!"

> What is more pleasing than a psalm? David ex-
> presses it well: "Praise the Lord, for a psalm is
> good: let there be praise of our God with gladness
> and grace!" Yes, a psalm is a blessing on the lips
> of the people, praise of God, the assembly's
> homage, a general acclamation, a word that speaks
> for all, the voice of the Church, a confession of
> faith in song.[40]

IN BRIEF

2590   "Prayer is the raising of one's mind and heart to
        God or the requesting of good things from God"
        (St. John Damascene, *De fide orth.* 3, 24: PG 94,
        1089C).

2591   God tirelessly calls each person to this mysteri-
        ous encounter with Himself. Prayer unfolds
        throughout the whole history of salvation as a
        reciprocal call between God and man.

2592   The prayer of Abraham and Jacob is presented
        as a battle of faith marked by trust in God's
        faithfulness and by certitude in the victory
        promised to perseverance.

2593   The prayer of Moses responds to the living
        God's initiative for the salvation of his people. It
        foreshadows the prayer of intercession of the
        unique mediator, Christ Jesus.

2594   The prayer of the People of God flourished
        in the shadow of the dwelling place of God's

---

40 St. Ambrose, *In psalmum 1 enarratio*, 1, 9: PL 14, 924; *LH*, Saturday, wk 10,
OR.

presence on earth, the ark of the covenant and the Temple, under the guidance of their shepherds, especially King David, and of the prophets.

2595 The prophets summoned the people to conversion of heart and, while zealously seeking the face of God, like Elijah, they interceded for the people.

2596 The Psalms constitute the masterwork of prayer in the Old Testament. They present two inseparable qualities: the personal, and the communal. They extend to all dimensions of history, recalling God's promises already fulfilled and looking for the coming of the Messiah.

2597 Prayed and fulfilled in Christ, the Psalms are an essential and permanent element of the prayer of the Church. They are suitable for men of every condition and time.

ARTICLE 2
IN THE FULLNESS OF TIME

2598 The drama of prayer is fully revealed to us in the Word who became flesh and dwells among us. To seek to understand his prayer through what his witnesses proclaim to us in the Gospel is to approach the holy Lord Jesus as Moses approached the burning bush: first to contemplate him in prayer, then to hear how he teaches us to pray, in order to know how he hears our prayer.

Jesus prays
470 2599 The Son of God who became Son of the Virgin learned to pray in his human heart. He learns to pray from his mother, who kept all the great things the Almighty had done and treasured them in her heart.[41]

---

41 Cf. *Lk* 1:49; 2:19; 2:51.

He learns to pray in the words and rhythms of the prayer of his people, in the synagogue at Nazareth and the Temple at Jerusalem. But his prayer springs from an otherwise secret source, as he intimates at the age of twelve: "I must be in my Father's house."[42] Here the newness of prayer in the fullness of time begins to be revealed: his *filial prayer,* which the Father awaits from his children, is finally going to be lived out by the only Son in his humanity, with and for men. *584*

534

2600 The Gospel according to St. Luke emphasizes the action of the Holy Spirit and the meaning of prayer in Christ's ministry. Jesus prays *before* the decisive moments of his mission: before his Father's witness to him during his baptism and Transfiguration, and before his own fulfillment of the Father's plan of love by his Passion.[43] He also prays before the decisive moments involving the mission of his apostles: at his election and call of the Twelve, before Peter's confession of him as "the Christ of God," and again that the faith of the chief of the Apostles may not fail when tempted.[44] Jesus' prayer before the events of salvation that the Father has asked him to fulfill is a humble and trusting commitment of his human will to the loving will of the Father. *535, 554*

612

858, 443

2601 "He was praying in a certain place and when he had ceased, one of his disciples said to him, 'Lord, teach us to pray.' "[45] In seeing the Master at prayer the disciple of Christ also wants to pray. By *contemplating* and hearing the Son, the master of prayer, the children learn to pray to the Father. *2765*

2602 Jesus often draws apart to pray *in solitude,* on a mountain, preferably at night.[46] *He includes all men* in his prayer, for he has taken on humanity in his incarnation, and he offers them to the Father when he offers himself. Jesus, the Word who has become flesh, shares by his human prayer in all that "his brethren" experience; he sympathizes with their weaknesses in order to *616*

---

42 *Lk* 2:49.   43 Cf. *Lk* 3:21; 9:28; 22:41–44.   44 Cf. *Lk* 6:12; 9:18–20; 22:32.
45 *Lk* 11:1.   46 Cf. *Mk* 1:35; 6:46; *Lk* 5:16.

free them.[47] It was for this that the Father sent him. His words and works are the visible manifestation of his prayer in secret.

2603   The evangelists have preserved two more explicit prayers offered by Christ during his public ministry. Each begins with thanksgiving. In the first, Jesus confesses the Father, acknowledges, and blesses him because he has hidden the mysteries of the Kingdom from those who think themselves learned and has revealed them to infants, the poor of the Beatitudes.[48] His exclamation, "Yes, Father!" expresses the depth of his heart, his adherence to the Father's "good pleasure," echoing his mother's *Fiat* at the time of his conception and prefiguring what he will say to the Father in his agony. The whole prayer of Jesus is contained in this loving adherence of his human heart to the mystery of the will of the Father.[49]

2604   The second prayer, before the raising of Lazarus, is recorded by St. John.[50] Thanksgiving precedes the event: "Father, I thank you for having heard me," which implies that the Father always hears his petitions. Jesus immediately adds: "I know that you always hear me," which implies that Jesus, on his part, *constantly made such petitions*. Jesus' prayer, characterized by thanksgiving, reveals to us how to ask: *before* the gift is given, Jesus commits himself to the One who in giving gives himself. The Giver is more precious than the gift; he is the "treasure"; in him abides his Son's heart; the gift is given "as well."[51]

The priestly prayer of Jesus holds a unique place in the economy of salvation.[52] A meditation on it will conclude Section One. It reveals the ever present prayer of our High Priest and, at the same time, contains what he teaches us about our prayer to our Father, which will be developed in Section Two.

2605   When the hour had come for him to fulfill the Father's plan of love, Jesus allows a glimpse of the boundless depth of his filial prayer, not only before he

---

47 Cf. *Heb* 2:12, 15; 4:15.   48 Cf. *Mt* 11:25–27 and *Lk* 10:21–23.   49 Cf. *Eph* 1:9.   50 Cf. *Jn* 11:41–42.   51 *Mt* 6:21, 33.   52 Cf. *Jn* 17.

2673
2546
494
478
2746

freely delivered himself up (*"Abba . . .* not my will, but yours."),[53] but even in *his last words* on the Cross, where prayer and the gift of self are but one: "Father, forgive them, for they know not what they do";[54] 614 "Truly, I say to you, today you will be with me in Paradise";[55] "Woman, behold your son"—"Behold your mother";[56] "I thirst.";[57] "My God, My God, why have you forsaken me?";[58] "It is finished";[59] "Father, into your hands I commit my spirit!"[60] until the "loud cry" as he expires, giving up his spirit.[61]

2606 All the troubles, for all time, of humanity en- 403 slaved by sin and death, all the petitions and intercessions of salvation history are summed up in this cry of the incarnate Word. Here the Father accepts them and, beyond all hope, answers them by raising his Son. Thus 653 is fulfilled and brought to completion the drama of prayer in the economy of creation and salvation. The Psalter gives us the key to prayer in Christ. In the "to- 2587 day" of the Resurrection the Father says: "You are my Son, today I have begotten you. Ask of me, and I will make the nations your heritage, and the ends of the earth your possession."[62]

> *The Letter to the Hebrews* expresses in dramatic terms how the prayer of Jesus accomplished the victory of salvation: "In the days of his flesh, Jesus offered up prayers and supplications, with loud cries and tears, to him who was able to save him from death, and he was heard for his godly fear. Although he was a Son, he learned obedience through what he suffered, and being made perfect, he became the source of eternal salvation to all who obey him."[63]

Jesus teaches us how to pray
2607 When Jesus prays he is already teaching us how 520 to pray. His prayer to his Father is the theologal path (the path of faith, hope, and charity) of our prayer to God. But the Gospel also gives us Jesus' explicit teach-

---

53 *Lk* 22:42.   54 *Lk* 23:34.   55 *Lk* 23:43.   56 *Jn* 19:26–27.   57 *Jn* 19:28.
58 *Mk* 15:34; cf. *Ps* 22:2.   59 *Jn* 19:30.   60 *Lk* 23:46.   61 Cf. *Mk* 15:37; *Jn* 19:30b.   62 *Ps* 2:7–8; cf. *Acts* 13:33.   63 *Heb* 5:7–9.

ing on prayer. Like a wise teacher he takes hold of us where we are and leads us progressively toward the Father. Addressing the crowds following him, Jesus builds on what they already know of prayer from the Old Covenant and opens to them the newness of the coming Kingdom. Then he reveals this newness to them in parables. Finally, he will speak openly of the Father and the Holy Spirit to his disciples who will be the teachers of prayer in his Church.

541
1430
2608 From the *Sermon on the Mount* onwards, Jesus insists on *conversion of heart:* reconciliation with one's brother before presenting an offering on the altar, love of enemies, and prayer for persecutors, prayer to the Father in secret, not heaping up empty phrases, prayerful forgiveness from the depths of the heart, purity of heart, and seeking the Kingdom before all else.[64] This filial conversion is entirely directed to the Father.

153
1814
2609 Once committed to conversion, the heart learns to pray in *faith.* Faith is a filial adherence to God beyond what we feel and understand. It is possible because the beloved Son gives us access to the Father. He can ask us to "seek" and to "knock," since he himself is the door and the way.[65]

2610 Just as Jesus prays to the Father and gives thanks before receiving his gifts, so he teaches us *filial boldness:* "Whatever you ask in prayer, believe that you receive it, and you will."[66] Such is the power of prayer and of faith that does not doubt: "all things are possible to him who believes."[67] Jesus is as saddened by the "lack of faith" of his own neighbors and the "little faith" of his own disciples[68] as he is struck with admiration at the great faith of the Roman centurion and the Canaanite woman.[69]

165

2827
2611 The prayer of faith consists not only in saying "Lord, Lord," but in disposing the heart to do the will of the Father.[70] Jesus calls his disciples to bring into their

---

64 Cf. *Mt* 5:23–24, 44–45; 6:7, 14–15, 21, 25, 33.   65 Cf. *Mt* 7:7–11, 13–14.
66 *Mk* 11:24.   67 *Mk* 9:23; cf. *Mt* 21:22.   68 Cf. *Mk* 6:6; *Mt* 8:26.   69 Cf. *Mt* 8:10; 15:28.   70 Cf. *Mt* 7:21.

prayer this concern for cooperating with the divine plan.[71]

2612 In Jesus "the Kingdom of God is at hand."[72] He calls his hearers to conversion and faith, but also to *watchfulness*. In prayer the disciple keeps watch, attentive to Him Who Is and Him Who Comes, in memory   672 of his first coming in the lowliness of the flesh, and in the hope of his second coming in glory.[73] In communion with their Master, the disciples' prayer is a battle; only   2725 by keeping watch in prayer can one avoid falling into temptation.[74]

2613 Three principal *parables* on prayer are transmitted   546 to us by St. Luke:

—The first, "the importunate friend,"[75] invites us to urgent prayer: "Knock, and it will be opened to you." To the one who prays like this, the heavenly Father will "give whatever he needs," and above all the Holy Spirit who contains all gifts.

—The second, "the importunate widow,"[76] is centered on one of the qualities of prayer: it is necessary to pray always without ceasing and with the *patience* of faith. "And yet, when the Son of Man comes, will he find faith on earth?"

—The third parable, "the Pharisee and the tax collector,"[77]   2559 concerns the *humility* of the heart that prays. "God, be merciful to me a sinner!" The Church continues to make this prayer its own: *Kyrie eleison!*

2614 When Jesus openly entrusts to his disciples the mystery of prayer to the Father, he reveals to them what their prayer and ours must be, once he has returned to the Father in his glorified humanity. What is new is to "ask *in his name*."[78] Faith in the Son introduces the dis-   434 ciples into the knowledge of the Father, because Jesus is "the way, and the truth, and the life."[79] Faith bears its fruit in love: it means keeping the word and the commandments of Jesus, it means abiding with him in the Father who, in him, so loves us that he abides with us.

---

71 Cf. Mt 9:38; Lk 10:2; Jn 4:34.   72 Mk 1:15.   73 Cf. Mk 13; Lk 21:34–36.
74 Cf. Lk 22:40, 46.   75 Cf. Lk 11:5–13.   76 Cf. Lk 18:1–8.   77 Cf. Lk
18:9–14.   78 Jn 14:13.   79 Jn 14:6.

In this new covenant the certitude that our petitions will be heard is founded on the prayer of Jesus.[80]

728   **2615**   Even more, what the Father gives us when our prayer is united with that of Jesus is "another Counselor, to be with you for ever, even the Spirit of truth."[81] This new dimension of prayer and of its circumstances is displayed throughout the farewell discourse.[82] In the Holy Spirit, Christian prayer is a communion of love with the Father, not only through Christ but also *in him*: "Hitherto you have asked nothing in my name; ask, and you will receive, that your joy may be full."[83]

Jesus hears our prayer

2616   Prayer *to Jesus* is answered by him already during his ministry, through signs that anticipate the power

548   of his death and Resurrection: Jesus hears the prayer of faith, expressed in words (the leper, Jairus, the Canaanite woman, the good thief)[84] or in silence (the bearers of the paralytic, the woman with a hemorrhage who touches his clothes, the tears and ointment of the sinful woman).[85] The urgent request of the blind men, "Have mercy on us, Son of David" or "Jesus, Son of David, have mercy on me!" has been renewed in the traditional prayer to Jesus known as the *Jesus Prayer*: "Lord Jesus

2667   Christ, Son of God, have mercy on me, a sinner!"[86] Healing infirmities or forgiving sins, Jesus always responds to a prayer offered in faith: "Your faith has made you well; go in peace."

> St. Augustine wonderfully summarizes the three dimensions of Jesus' prayer: "He prays for us as our priest, prays in us as our Head, and is prayed to by us as our God. Therefore let us acknowledge our voice in him and his in us."[87]

---

80 Cf. *Jn* 14:13–14.   81 *Jn* 14:16–17.   82 Cf. *Jn* 14:23–26; 15:7, 16; 16:13–15; 16:23–27.   83 *Jn* 16:24.   84 Cf. *Mk* 1:40–41; 5:36; 7:29; Cf. *Lk* 23:39–43. 85 Cf. *Mk* 2:5; 5:28; *Lk* 7:37–38.   86 *Mt* 9:27; *Mk* 10:48.   87 St. Augustine, *En. in Ps.* 85, 1: PL 37, 1081; cf. GILH 7.

The prayer of the Virgin Mary

2617   Mary's prayer is revealed to us at the dawning of *148*
the fullness of time. Before the incarnation of the Son of
God, and before the outpouring of the Holy Spirit, her
prayer cooperates in a unique way with the Father's
plan of loving kindness: at the Annunciation, for
Christ's conception; at Pentecost, for the formation of *494*
the Church, his Body.[88] In the faith of his humble handmaid, the Gift of God found the acceptance he had
awaited from the beginning of time. She whom the
Almighty made "full of grace" responds by offering her *490*
whole being: "Behold I am the handmaid of the Lord;
let it be [done] to me according to your word." *"Fiat"*:
this is Christian prayer: to be wholly God's, because he
is wholly ours.

2618   The Gospel reveals to us how Mary prays and *2674*
intercedes in faith. At Cana,[89] the mother of Jesus asks
her son for the needs of a wedding feast; this is the sign
of another feast—that of the wedding of the Lamb
where he gives his body and blood at the request of the
Church, his Bride. It is at the hour of the New
Covenant, at the foot of the cross,[90] that Mary is heard
as the Woman, the new Eve, the true "Mother of all the *726*
living."

2619   That is why the Canticle of Mary,[91] the *Magnificat* (Latin) or *Megalynei* (Byzantine) is the song both of
the Mother of God and of the Church; the song of the
Daughter of Zion and of the new People of God; the
song of thanksgiving for the fullness of graces poured
out in the economy of salvation and the song of the *724*
"poor" whose hope is met by the fulfillment of the
promises made to our ancestors, "to Abraham and to
his posterity for ever."

IN BRIEF

2620   Jesus' filial prayer is the perfect model of prayer
in the New Testament. Often done in solitude

---

88 Cf. *Lk* 1:38; *Acts* 1:14.   89 Cf. *Jn* 2:1-12.   90 Cf. *Jn* 19:25-27.   91 Cf. *Lk* 1:46-55.

and in secret, the prayer of Jesus involves a loving adherence to the will of the Father even to the Cross and an absolute confidence in being heard.

2621 In his teaching, Jesus teaches his disciples to pray with a purified heart, with lively and persevering faith, with filial boldness. He calls them to vigilance and invites them to present their petitions to God in his name. Jesus Christ himself answers prayers addressed to him.

2622 The prayers of the Virgin Mary, in her Fiat and Magnificat, are characterized by the generous offering of her whole being in faith.

ARTICLE 3
IN THE AGE OF THE CHURCH

731 **2623** On the day of Pentecost, the Spirit of the Promise was poured out on the disciples, gathered "together in one place."[92] While awaiting the Spirit, "all these with one accord devoted themselves to prayer."[93] The Spirit who teaches the Church and recalls for her everything that Jesus said[94] was also to form her in the life of prayer.

1342 **2624** In the first community of Jerusalem, believers "devoted themselves to the apostles' teaching and fellowship, to the breaking of bread, and the prayers."[95] This sequence is characteristic of the Church's prayer: founded on the apostolic faith; authenticated by charity; nourished in the Eucharist.

2625 In the first place these are prayers that the faithful hear and read in the Scriptures, but also that they make their own—especially those of the Psalms, in view of their fulfillment in Christ.[96] The Holy Spirit, who *1092* thus keeps the memory of Christ alive in his Church at prayer, also leads her toward the fullness of truth and

---

92 *Acts* 2:1.   93 *Acts* 1:14.   94 Cf. *Jn* 14:26.   95 *Acts* 2:42.   96 Cf. *Lk* 24:27, 44.

inspires new formulations expressing the unfathomable mystery of Christ at work in his Church's life, sacraments, and mission. These formulations are developed in the great liturgical and spiritual traditions. The *forms of prayer* revealed in the apostolic and canonical Scriptures remain normative for Christian prayer.   *1200*

I.   BLESSING AND ADORATION

2626   *Blessing* expresses the basic movement of Christian prayer: it is an encounter between God and man. In blessing, God's gift and man's acceptance of it are united in dialogue with each other. The prayer of blessing is man's response to God's gifts: because God blesses, the human heart can in return bless the One who is the source of every blessing.   *1078*

2627   Two fundamental forms express this movement: our prayer *ascends* in the Holy Spirit through Christ to the Father—we bless him for having blessed us;[97] it implores the grace of the Holy Spirit that *descends* through Christ from the Father—he blesses us.[98]   *1083*

2628   *Adoration* is the first attitude of man acknowledging that he is a creature before his Creator. It exalts the greatness of the Lord who made us[99] and the almighty power of the Savior who sets us free from evil. Adoration is homage of the spirit to the "King of Glory,"[100] respectful silence in the presence of the "ever greater" God.[101] Adoration of the thrice-holy and sovereign God of love blends with humility and gives assurance to our supplications.   *2096-2097*   *2559*

II.   PRAYER OF PETITION

2629   The vocabulary of supplication in the New Testament is rich in shades of meaning: ask, beseech, plead, invoke, entreat, cry out, even "struggle in prayer."[102] Its most usual form, because the most spontaneous, is petition: by prayer of petition we express awareness of our

---

97 Cf. *Eph* 1:3–14; *2 Cor* 1:3–7; *1 Pet* 1:3–9.   98 Cf. *2 Cor* 13:14; *Rom* 15:5–6, 13; *Eph* 6:23–24.   99 Cf. *Ps* 95:1–6.   100 *Ps* 24:9–10.   101 Cf. St. Augustine, *En. in Ps.* 62, 16: PL 36, 757–758.   102 Cf. *Rom* 15:30; *Col* 4:12.

relationship with God. We are creatures who are not
396 our own beginning, not the masters of adversity, not our
own last end. We are sinners who as Christians know
that we have turned away from our Father. Our petition
is already a turning back to him.

2630   The New Testament contains scarcely any prayers
of lamentation, so frequent in the Old Testament. In the
2090 risen Christ the Church's petition is buoyed by hope, even
if we still wait in a state of expectation and must be
converted anew every day. Christian petition, what St.
Paul calls "groaning," arises from another depth, that
of creation "in labor pains" and that of ourselves "as we
wait for the redemption of our bodies. For in this hope
we were saved."[103] In the end, however, "with sighs
too deep for words" the Holy Spirit "helps us in our weakness; for we do not know how to pray as we ought, but the
Spirit himself intercedes for us with sighs too deep for
words."[104]

2838 **2631**   The first movement of the prayer of petition is
asking forgiveness, like the tax collector in the parable:
"God, be merciful to me a sinner!"[105] It is a prerequisite
for righteous and pure prayer. A trusting humility brings
us back into the light of communion between the Father
and his Son Jesus Christ and with one another, so that
"we receive from him whatever we ask."[106] Asking forgiveness is the prerequisite for both the Eucharistic
liturgy and personal prayer.

2816 **2632**   Christian petition is centered on the desire and
search for the Kingdom to come, in keeping with the
teaching of Christ.[107] There is a hierarchy in these petitions: we pray first for the Kingdom, then for what
1942 is necessary to welcome it and cooperate with its coming. This collaboration with the mission of Christ and
the Holy Spirit, which is now that of the Church, is the
object of the prayer of the apostolic community.[108] It is
the prayer of Paul, the apostle par excellence, which
reveals to us how the divine solicitude for all the
2854 churches ought to inspire Christian prayer.[109] By prayer

---

103 *Rom* 8:22–24.   104 *Rom* 8:26.   105 *Lk* 18:13.   106 *1 Jn* 3:22; cf. 1:7–2:2.
107 Cf. *Mt* 6:10, 33; *Lk* 11:2, 13.   108 Cf. *Acts* 6:6; 13:3.   109 Cf. *Rom* 10:1;
Eph 1:16–23; *Phil* 1:9–11; *Col* 1:3–6; 4:3–4, 12.

every baptized person works for the coming of the Kingdom.

2633 When we share in God's saving love, we under- 2830 stand that *every need* can become the object of petition. Christ, who assumed all things in order to redeem all things, is glorified by what we ask the Father in his name.[110] It is with this confidence that St. James and St. Paul exhort us to pray *at all times*.[111]

III. PRAYER OF INTERCESSION

2634 Intercession is a prayer of petition which leads us to pray as Jesus did. He is the one intercessor with the Father on behalf of all men, especially sinners.[112] He is 432 "able for all time to save those who draw near to God through him, since he always lives to make intercession for them."[113] The Holy Spirit "himself intercedes for us . . . and intercedes for the saints according to the will of God."[114]

2635 Since Abraham, intercession—asking on behalf 2571 of another—has been characteristic of a heart attuned to God's mercy. In the age of the Church, Christian intercession participates in Christ's, as an expression of the communion of saints. In intercession, he who prays looks "not only to his own interests, but also to the interests of others," even to the point of praying for those who do him harm.[115]   2577

2636 The first Christian communities lived this form of fellowship intensely.[116] Thus the Apostle Paul gives them a share in his ministry of preaching the Gospel[117] but also intercedes for them.[118] The intercession of Christians recognizes no boundaries: "for all men, for kings and all who are in high positions," for persecu- 1900 tors, for the salvation of those who reject the Gospel.[119] 1037

110 Cf. *Jn* 14:13. 111 Cf. *Jas* 1:5–8; *Eph* 5:20; *Phil* 4:6–7; *Col* 3:16–17; *1 Thess* 5:17–18. 112 Cf. *Rom* 8:34; *1 Jn* 2:1; *1 Tim* 2:5–8. 113 *Heb* 7:25. 114 *Rom* 8:26–27. 115 *Phil* 2:4; cf. *Acts* 7:60; *Lk* 23:28, 34. 116 Cf. *Acts* 12:5; 20:36; 21:5; *2 Cor* 9:14. 117 Cf. *Eph* 6:18–20; *Col* 4:3–4; *1 Thess* 5:25. 118 Cf. *2 Thess* 1:11; *Col* 1:3; *Phil* 1:3–4. 119 *1 Tim* 2:1; cf. *Rom* 12:14; 10:1.

IV.   PRAYER OF THANKSGIVING

224   **2637**   Thanksgiving characterizes the prayer of the Church which, in celebrating the Eucharist, reveals and
1328   becomes more fully what she is. Indeed, in the work of salvation, Christ sets creation free from sin and death to consecrate it anew and make it return to the Father, for his glory. The thanksgiving of the members of the Body
2603   participates in that of their Head.

2638   As in the prayer of petition, every event and need can become an offering of thanksgiving. The letters of St. Paul often begin and end with thanksgiving, and the Lord Jesus is always present in it: "Give thanks in all circumstances; for this is the will of God in Christ Jesus for you"; "Continue steadfastly in prayer, being watchful in it with thanksgiving."[120]

V.   PRAYER OF PRAISE

2639   Praise is the form of prayer which recognizes most immediately that God is God. It lauds God for his own sake and gives him glory, quite beyond what he does, but simply because HE IS. It shares in the blessed
213   happiness of the pure of heart who love God in faith before seeing him in glory. By praise, the Spirit is joined to our spirits to bear witness that we are children of God,[121] testifying to the only Son in whom we are adopted and by whom we glorify the Father. Praise embraces the other forms of prayer and carries them toward him who is its source and goal: the "one God, the Father, from whom are all things and for whom we exist."[122]

2640   St. Luke in his gospel often expresses wonder and praise at the marvels of Christ and in his *Acts of the Apostles* stresses them as actions of the Holy Spirit: the community of Jerusalem, the invalid healed by Peter and John, the crowd that gives glory to God for that, and the pagans of Pisidia who "were glad and glorified the word of God."[123]

2641   "[Address] one another in psalms and hymns and spiritual songs, singing and making melody to the Lord

---

120 *1 Thess* 5:18; *Col* 4:2.   **121** Cf. *Rom* 8:16.   **122** *1 Cor* 8:6.   **123** *Acts* 2:47; 3:9; 4:21; 13:48.

with all your heart."[124] Like the inspired writers of the New Testament, the first Christian communities read the Book of Psalms in a new way, singing in it the mystery of Christ. In the newness of the Spirit, they also composed hymns and canticles in the light of the unheard-of event that God accomplished in his Son: his Incarnation, his death which conquered death, his Resurrection, and Ascension to the right hand of the Father.[125] Doxology, the praise of God, arises from this "marvelous work" of the whole economy of salvation.[126]

2587

2642 The *Revelation* of "what must soon take place," the *Apocalypse,* is borne along by the songs of the heavenly liturgy[127] but also by the intercession of the "witnesses" (martyrs).[128] The prophets and the saints, all those who were slain on earth for their witness to Jesus, the vast throng of those who, having come through the great tribulation, have gone before us into the Kingdom, all sing the praise and glory of him who sits on the throne, and of the Lamb.[129] In communion with them, the Church on earth also sings these songs with faith in the midst of trial. By means of petition and intercession, faith hopes against all hope and gives thanks to the "Father of lights," from whom "every perfect gift" comes down.[130] Thus faith is pure praise.

1137

2643 The Eucharist contains and expresses all forms of prayer: it is "the pure offering" of the whole Body of Christ to the glory of God's name[131] and, according to the traditions of East and West, it is *the* "sacrifice of praise."

1330

IN BRIEF

2644 The Holy Spirit who teaches the Church and recalls to her all that Jesus said also instructs her in the life of prayer, inspiring new expressions of the same basic forms of prayer: blessing, petition, intercession, thanksgiving, and praise.

2645 Because God blesses the human heart, it can in

---

124 *Eph* 5:19; *Col* 3:16. 125 Cf. *Phil* 2:6–11; *Col* 1:15–20; *Eph* 5:14; *1 Tim* 3:16; 6:15–16; *2 Tim* 2:11–13. 126 Cf. *Eph* 1:3–14; *Rom* 16:25–27; *Eph* 3:20–21; *Jude* 24–25. 127 Cf. *Rev* 4:8–11; 5:9–14; 7:10–12. 128 *Rev* 6:10. 129 Cf. *Rev* 18:24; 19:1–8. 130 *Jas* 1:17. 131 Cf. *Mal* 1:11.

return bless him who is the source of every blessing.

2646 Forgiveness, the quest for the Kingdom, and
every true need are objects of the prayer of petition.

2647 Prayer of intercession consists in asking on behalf of another. It knows no boundaries and extends to one's enemies.

2648 Every joy and suffering, every event and need
can become the matter for thanksgiving which,
sharing in that of Christ, should fill one's whole
life: "Give thanks in all circumstances" (*1 Thess*
5:18).

2649 Prayer of praise is entirely disinterested and rises
to God, lauds him, and gives him glory for his
own sake, quite beyond what he has done, but
simply because HE IS.

CHAPTER TWO
THE TRADITION OF PRAYER

2650 Prayer cannot be reduced to the spontaneous
outpouring of interior impulse: in order to pray, one
must have the will to pray. Nor is it enough to know
what the Scriptures reveal about prayer: one must also
learn how to pray. Through a living transmission (Sa-
75 cred Tradition) within "the believing and praying
Church,"[1] the Holy Spirit teaches the children of God
how to pray.

94 2651 The tradition of Christian prayer is one of the
ways in which the tradition of faith takes shape and
grows, especially through the contemplation and study
of believers who treasure in their hearts the events and
words of the economy of salvation, and through their
profound grasp of the spiritual realities they experience.[2]

---

1 *DV* 8.   2 Cf. *DV* 8.

ARTICLE 1
AT THE WELLSPRINGS OF PRAYER

2652   The Holy Spirit is the *living water* "welling up to   *694*
eternal life"[3] in the heart that prays. It is he who teaches
us to accept it at its source: Christ. Indeed in the Christian life there are several wellsprings where Christ
awaits us to enable us to drink of the Holy Spirit.

The Word of God
2653   The Church "forcefully and specially exhorts all   *133*
the Christian faithful . . . to learn 'the surpassing
knowledge of Jesus Christ' (Phil 3:8) by frequent reading of the divine Scriptures. . . . Let them remember,
however, that prayer should accompany the reading of
Sacred Scripture, so that a dialogue takes place between
God and man. For 'we speak to him when we pray; we   *1100*
listen to him when we read the divine oracles.' "[4]

2654   The spiritual writers, paraphrasing *Matthew
7:7*, summarize in this way the dispositions of the heart
nourished by the word of God in prayer: "Seek in reading and you will find in meditating; knock in mental
prayer and it will be opened to you by contemplation."[5]

The Liturgy of the Church
2655   In the sacramental liturgy of the Church, the   *1073*
mission of Christ and of the Holy Spirit proclaims,
makes present, and communicates the mystery of salvation, which is continued in the heart that prays. The
spiritual writers sometimes compare the heart to an al-   *368*
tar. Prayer internalizes and assimilates the liturgy during
and after its celebration. Even when it is lived out "in
secret,"[6] prayer is always prayer *of the Church;* it is a
communion with the Holy Trinity.[7]

---

3 *Jn* 4:14   4 *DV* 25; cf. *Phil* 3:8; St. Ambrose, *De officiis ministrorum* 1, 20, 88:
PL 16, 50.   5 Guigo the Carthusian, *Scala Paradisi*: PL 40, 998.   6 Cf. *Mt* 6:6.
7 GILH 9.

1812-1829 **The theological virtues**

2656 One enters into prayer as one enters into liturgy: by the narrow gate of *faith*. Through the signs of his presence, it is the Face of the Lord that we seek and desire; it is his Word that we want to hear and keep.

2657 The Holy Spirit, who instructs us to celebrate the liturgy in expectation of Christ's return, teaches us to pray in *hope*. Conversely, the prayer of the Church and personal prayer nourish hope in us. The psalms especially, with their concrete and varied language, teach us to fix our hope in God: "I waited patiently for the LORD; he inclined to me and heard my cry."[8] As St. Paul prayed: "May the God of hope fill you with all joy and peace in believing, so that by the power of the Holy Spirit you may abound in hope."[9]

2658 "Hope does not disappoint us, because God's *love* has been poured into our hearts by the Holy Spirit who has been given to us."[10] Prayer, formed by the liturgical life, draws everything into the love by which we are loved in Christ and which enables us to respond to

826 him by loving as he has loved us. Love is the source of prayer; whoever draws from it reaches the summit of prayer. In the words of the Curé of Ars:

> I love you, O my God, and my only desire is to love you until the last breath of my life. I love you, O my infinitely lovable God, and I would rather die loving you, than live without loving you. I love you, Lord, and the only grace I ask is to love you eternally. . . . My God, if my tongue cannot say in every moment that I love you, I want my heart to repeat it to you as often as I draw breath.[11]

"Today"

1165 **2659** We learn to pray at certain moments by hearing the Word of the Lord and sharing in his Paschal mystery, but his Spirit is offered us at all times, in the events

2837 of *each day,* to make prayer spring up from us. Jesus'

---

8 *Ps* 40:2.   9 *Rom* 15:13.   10 *Rom* 5:5.   11 St. John Vianney, *Prayer.*

teaching about praying to our Father is in the same vein as his teaching about providence:[12] time is in the Father's hands; it is in the present that we encounter 305 him, not yesterday nor tomorrow, but today: "O that *today* you would hearken to his voice! Harden not your hearts."[13]

2660   Prayer in the events of each day and each moment is one of the secrets of the kingdom revealed to "little children," to the servants of Christ, to the poor of the Beatitudes. It is right and good to pray so that the 2546 coming of the kingdom of justice and peace may influ- 2632 ence the march of history, but it is just as important to bring the help of prayer into humble, everyday situations; all forms of prayer can be the leaven to which the Lord compares the kingdom.[14]

IN BRIEF

2661   By a living transmission—Tradition—the Holy Spirit in the Church teaches the children of God to pray.

2662   The Word of God, the liturgy of the Church, and the virtues of faith, hope, and charity are sources of prayer.

ARTICLE 2
THE WAY OF PRAYER

2663   In the living tradition of prayer, each Church 1201 proposes to its faithful, according to its historic, social, and cultural context, a language for prayer: words, melodies, gestures, iconography. The Magisterium of the Church[15] has the task of discerning the fidelity of these ways of praying to the tradition of apostolic faith; it is for pastors and catechists to explain their meaning, always in relation to Jesus Christ.

---

12 Cf. *Mt* 6:11, 34.   13 *Ps* 95:7–8.   14 Cf. *Lk* 13:20–21.   15 Cf. *DV* 10.

Prayer to the Father

2664 There is no other way of Christian prayer than Christ. Whether our prayer is communal or personal, vocal or interior, it has access to the Father only if we pray "in the name" of Jesus. The sacred humanity of Jesus is therefore the way by which the Holy Spirit teaches us to pray to God our Father.

Prayer to Jesus

2665 The prayer of the Church, nourished by the Word of God and the celebration of the liturgy, teaches us to pray to the Lord Jesus. Even though her prayer is addressed above all to the Father, it includes in all the liturgical traditions forms of prayer addressed to Christ. Certain psalms, given their use in the Prayer of the Church, and the New Testament place on our lips and engrave in our hearts prayer to Christ in the form of invocations: Son of God, Word of God, Lord, Savior, Lamb of God, King, Beloved Son, Son of the Virgin, Good Shepherd, our Life, our Light, our Hope, our Resurrection, Friend of mankind. . . .

2666 But the one name that contains everything is the one that the Son of God received in his incarnation: JESUS. The divine name may not be spoken by human lips, but by assuming our humanity The Word of God hands it over to us and we can invoke it: "Jesus," "YHWH saves."[16] The name "Jesus" contains all: God and man and the whole economy of creation and salvation. To pray "Jesus" is to invoke him and to call him within us. His name is the only one that contains the presence it signifies. Jesus is the Risen One, and whoever invokes the name of Jesus is welcoming the Son of God who loved him and who gave himself up for him.[17]

2667 This simple invocation of faith developed in the tradition of prayer under many forms in East and West. The most usual formulation, transmitted by the spiritual writers of the Sinai, Syria, and Mt. Athos, is the invocation, "Lord Jesus Christ, Son of God, have mercy on us sinners." It

---

16 Cf. *Ex* 3:14; 33:19–23; *Mt* 1:21.   17 *Rom* 10:13; *Acts* 2:21; 3:15–16; *Gal* 2:20.

combines the Christological hymn of *Philippians* 2:6–11
with the cry of the publican and the blind men begging for
light.[18] By it the heart is opened to human wretchedness
and the Savior's mercy.

2668   The invocation of the holy name of Jesus is the sim-   *435*
plest way of praying always. When the holy name is repeated often by a humbly attentive heart, the prayer is not
lost by heaping up empty phrases,[19] but holds fast to the
word and "brings forth fruit with patience."[20] This prayer
is possible "at all times" because it is not one occupation
among others but the only occupation: that of loving God,
which animates and transfigures every action in Christ Jesus.

2669   The prayer of the Church venerates and honors the   *478*
Heart of Jesus just as it invokes his most holy name. It
adores the incarnate Word and his Heart which, out of love
for men, he allowed to be pierced by our sins. Christian
prayer loves to follow *the way of the cross* in the Savior's
steps. The stations from the Praetorium to Golgotha and
the tomb trace the way of Jesus, who by his holy Cross has   *1674*
redeemed the world.

"Come, Holy Spirit"

2670   "No one can say 'Jesus is Lord' except by the   *683*
Holy Spirit."[21] Every time we begin to pray to Jesus it is
the Holy Spirit who draws us on the way of prayer by
his prevenient grace. Since he teaches us to pray by re-   *2001*
calling Christ, how could we not pray to the Spirit too?
That is why the Church invites us to call upon the Holy
Spirit every day, especially at the beginning and the end
of every important action.   *1310*

> If the Spirit should not be worshiped, how can he
> divinize me through Baptism? If he should be
> worshiped, should he not be the object of adora-
> tion?[22]

2671   The traditional form of petition to the Holy
Spirit is to invoke the Father through Christ our Lord to
give us the Consoler Spirit.[23] Jesus insists on this petition
to be made in his name at the very moment when he

---

18 Cf. *Mk* 10:46–52; *Lk* 18:13.   19 Cf. *Mt* 6:7.   20 Cf. *Lk* 8:15.   21 *1 Cor*
12:3.   22 St. Gregory of Nazianzus, *Oratio*, 31, 28: PG 36, 165.   23 Cf. *Lk*
11:13.

promises the gift of the Spirit of Truth.[24] But the simplest and most direct prayer is also traditional, "Come, Holy Spirit," and every liturgical tradition has developed it in antiphons and hymns.

> Come, Holy Spirit, fill the hearts of your faithful and enkindle in them the fire of your love.[25]

> Heavenly King, Consoler Spirit, Spirit of Truth, present everywhere and filling all things, treasure of all good and source of all life, come dwell in us, cleanse and save us, you who are All-Good.[26]

695   **2672**   The Holy Spirit, whose anointing permeates our whole being, is the interior Master of Christian prayer. He is the artisan of the living tradition of prayer. To be sure, there are as many paths of prayer as there are persons who pray, but it is the same Spirit acting in all and with all. It is in the communion of the Holy Spirit that Christian prayer is prayer in the Church.

In communion with the holy Mother of God

689   **2673**   In prayer the Holy Spirit unites us to the person of the only Son, in his glorified humanity, through which and in which our filial prayer unites us in the Church with the Mother of Jesus.[27]

494   **2674**   Mary gave her consent in faith at the Annunciation and maintained it without hesitation at the foot of the Cross. Ever since, her motherhood has extended to the brothers and sisters of her Son "who still journey on earth surrounded by dangers and difficulties."[28] Jesus, the only mediator, is the way of our prayer; Mary, his mother and ours, is wholly transparent to him: she "shows the way" *(hodigitria),* and is herself "the Sign" of the way, according to the traditional iconography of East and West.

970   **2675**   Beginning with Mary's unique cooperation with the working of the Holy Spirit, the Churches developed

---

24 Cf. *Jn* 14:17; 15:26; 16:13.   25 *Roman Missal,* Pentecost, Sequence.   26 Byzantine Liturgy, Pentecost Vespers, Troparion.   27 Cf. *Acts* 1:14.   28 *LG* 62.

their prayer to the holy Mother of God, centering it on the person of Christ manifested in his mysteries. In *512* countless hymns and antiphons expressing this prayer, two movements usually alternate with one another: the first "magnifies" the Lord for the "great things" he did *2619* for his lowly servant and through her for all human beings;[29] the second entrusts the supplications and praises of the children of God to the Mother of Jesus, because she now knows the humanity which, in her, the Son of God espoused.

2676 This twofold movement of prayer to Mary has found a privileged expression in the *Ave Maria:*

Hail Mary [or Rejoice, Mary]: the greeting of the *722* angel Gabriel opens this prayer. It is God himself who, through his angel as intermediary, greets Mary. Our prayer dares to take up this greeting to Mary with the regard God had for the lowliness of his humble servant and to exult in the joy he finds in her.[30]

Full of grace, the Lord is with thee: These two *490* phrases of the angel's greeting shed light on one another. Mary is full of grace because the Lord is with her. The grace with which she is filled is the presence of him who is the source of all grace. "Rejoice . . . O Daughter of Jerusalem . . . the Lord your God is in your midst."[31] Mary, in whom the Lord himself has just made his dwelling, is the daughter of Zion in person, the ark of the covenant, the place where the glory of the Lord dwells. She is "the dwelling of God . . . with men."[32] Full of grace, Mary is wholly given over to him who has come to dwell in her and whom she is about to give to the world.

Blessed art thou among women and blessed is the *435* *fruit of thy womb, Jesus.* After the angel's greeting, we make Elizabeth's greeting our own. "Filled with the Holy Spirit," Elizabeth is the first in the long succession of generations who have called Mary "blessed."[33] "Blessed is she who believed. . . ."[34] Mary is "blessed among women" because she believed in the fulfillment of the Lord's word. Abraham, because of his faith, became a blessing for all the *146* nations of the earth.[35] Mary, because of her faith, became the mother of believers, through whom all nations of the earth receive him who is God's own blessing: Jesus, the "fruit of thy womb."

---

29 Cf. *Lk* 1:46–55.   30 Cf. *Lk* 1:48; *Zeph* 3:17b.   31 *Zeph* 3:14, 17a.   32 *Rev* 21:3.   33 *Lk* 1:41, 48.   34 *Lk* 1:45.   35 Cf. *Gen* 12:3.

495 **2677** *Holy Mary, Mother of God:* With Elizabeth we
marvel, "And why is this granted me, that the mother of
my Lord should come to me?"[36] Because she gives us Jesus,
her son, Mary is Mother of God and our mother; we can
entrust all our cares and petitions to her: she prays for us
as she prayed for herself: "Let it be to me according to your
word."[37] By entrusting ourselves to her prayer, we abandon
ourselves to the will of God together with her: "Thy will be
done."

    *Pray for us sinners, now and at the hour of our
death:* By asking Mary to pray for us, we acknowledge ourselves to be poor sinners and we address ourselves to the
"Mother of Mercy," the All-Holy One. We give ourselves
over to her now, in the Today of our lives. And our trust
broadens further, already at the present moment, to surrender "the hour of our death" wholly to her care. May she
be there as she was at her son's death on the cross. May she
welcome us as our mother at the hour of our passing[38] to
1020 lead us to her son, Jesus, in paradise.

971, 1674 **2678** Medieval piety in the West developed the prayer of
the rosary as a popular substitute for the Liturgy of the
Hours. In the East, the litany called the *Akathistos* and the
Paraclesis remained closer to the choral office in the Byzantine churches, while the Armenian, Coptic, and Syriac traditions preferred popular hymns and songs to the Mother
of God. But in the *Ave Maria,* the *theotokia,* the hymns of
St. Ephrem or St. Gregory of Narek, the tradition of prayer
is basically the same.

967 **2679** Mary is the perfect *Orans* (pray-er), a figure of
the Church. When we pray to her, we are adhering with
her to the plan of the Father, who sends his Son to save
all men. Like the beloved disciple we welcome Jesus'
mother into our homes,[39] for she has become the mother
of all the living. We can pray with and to her. The
prayer of the Church is sustained by the prayer of Mary
972 and united with it in hope.[40]

---

36 *Lk* 1:43. 37 *Lk* 1:38. 38 Cf. *Jn* 19:27. 39 Cf. *Jn* 19:27. 40 Cf. *LG*
68–69.

IN BRIEF

2680 Prayer is primarily addressed to the Father; it can also be directed toward Jesus, particularly by the invocation of his holy name: "Lord Jesus Christ, Son of God, have mercy on us sinners."

2681 "No one can say 'Jesus is Lord', except by the Holy Spirit" (*1 Cor* 12:3). The Church invites us to invoke the Holy Spirit as the interior Teacher of Christian prayer.

2682 Because of Mary's singular cooperation with the action of the Holy Spirit, the Church loves to pray in communion with the Virgin Mary, to magnify with her the great things the Lord has done for her, and to entrust supplications and praises to her.

ARTICLE 3
GUIDES FOR PRAYER

A cloud of witnesses

2683 The witnesses who have preceded us into the kingdom,[41] especially those whom the Church recognizes as saints, share in the living tradition of prayer by the example of their lives, the transmission of their writings, and their prayer today. They contemplate God, praise him and constantly care for those whom they have left on earth. When they entered into the joy of their Master, they were "put in charge of many things."[42] Their intercession is their most exalted service to God's plan. We can and should ask them to intercede for us and for the whole world. 956

2684 In the communion of saints, many and varied *spiritualities* have been developed throughout the history of the churches. The personal charism of some witnesses to God's love for men has been handed on, like 917

---

41 Cf. *Heb* 12:1.   42 Cf. *Mt* 25:21.

919 "the spirit" of Elijah to Elisha and John the Baptist, so
that their followers may have a share in this spirit.[43] A
distinct spirituality can also arise at the point of con-
vergence of liturgical and theological currents, bearing
witness to the integration of the faith into a particular

1202 human environment and its history. The different
schools of Christian spirituality share in the living tradition of prayer and are essential guides for the faithful.
In their rich diversity they are refractions of the one
pure light of the Holy Spirit.

> The Spirit is truly the dwelling of the saints and the
> saints are for the Spirit a place where he dwells as
> in his own home, since they offer themselves as a
> dwelling place for God and are called his temple.[44]

Servants of prayer

1657 **2685** The *Christian family* is the first place of education in prayer. Based on the sacrament of marriage, the
family is the "domestic Church" where God's children
learn to pray "as the Church" and to persevere in
prayer. For young children in particular, daily family
prayer is the first witness of the Church's living memory
as awakened patiently by the Holy Spirit.

1547 **2686** *Ordained ministers* are also responsible for the
formation in prayer of their brothers and sisters in
Christ. Servants of the Good Shepherd, they are ordained to lead the People of God to the living waters of
prayer: the Word of God, the liturgy, the theologal life
(the life of faith, hope, and charity), and the Today of
God in concrete situations.[45]

916 **2687** Many *religious* have consecrated their whole
lives to prayer. Hermits, monks, and nuns since the time
of the desert fathers have devoted their time to praising
God and interceding for his people. The consecrated life
cannot be sustained or spread without prayer; it is one
of the living sources of contemplation and the spiritual
life of the Church.

---

43 Cf. *2 Kings* 2:9; *Lk* 1:1; PC 2.   **44** St. Basil, *De Spiritu Sancto*, 26, 62: PG 32,
184.   **45** Cf. *PO* 4–6.

2688 The *catechesis* of children, young people, and adults aims at teaching them to meditate on The Word of God in personal prayer, practicing it in liturgical prayer, and internalizing it at all times in order to bear fruit in a new life. Catechesis is also a time for the discernment and education of popular piety.[46] The memorization of basic prayers offers an essential support to the life of prayer, but it is important to help learners savor their meaning.

1674

2689 *Prayer groups*, indeed "schools of prayer," are today one of the signs and one of the driving forces of renewal of prayer in the Church, provided they drink from authentic wellsprings of Christian prayer. Concern for ecclesial communion is a sign of true prayer in the Church.

2690 The Holy Spirit gives to certain of the faithful the gifts of wisdom, faith and discernment for the sake of this common good which is prayer *(spiritual direction)*. Men and women so endowed are true servants of the living tradition of prayer.

> According to St. John of the Cross, the person wishing to advance toward perfection should "take care into whose hands he entrusts himself, for as the master is, so will the disciple be, and as the father is so will be the son." And further: "In addition to being learned and discreet a director should be experienced. . . . If the spiritual director has no experience of the spiritual life, he will be incapable of leading into it the souls whom God is calling to it, and he will not even understand them."[47]

Places favorable for prayer

2691 The church, the house of God, is the proper place for the liturgical prayer of the parish community. It is also the privileged place for adoration of the real presence of Christ in the Blessed Sacrament. The choice

1181
2097
1379

---

46 Cf. *CT* 54.   47 St. John of the Cross, *The Living Flame of Love*, stanza 3, 30, in *The Collected Works of St. John of the Cross*, eds K. Kavanaugh OCD and O. Rodriguez OCD (Washington DC: Institute of Carmelite Studies, 1979), 621.

of a favorable place is not a matter of indifference for true prayer.

—For personal prayer, this can be a "prayer corner" with the Sacred Scriptures and icons, in order to be there, in secret, before our Father.[48] In a Christian family, this kind of little oratory fosters prayer in common.

1175   —In regions where monasteries exist, the vocation of these communities is to further the participation of the faithful in the Liturgy of the Hours and to provide necessary solitude for more intense personal prayer.[49]

1674   —Pilgrimages evoke our earthly journey toward heaven and are traditionally very special occasions for renewal in prayer. For pilgrims seeking living water, shrines are special places for living the forms of Christian prayer "in Church."

IN BRIEF

2692   In prayer, the pilgrim Church is associated with that of the saints, whose intercession she asks.

2693   The different schools of Christian spirituality share in the living tradition of prayer and are precious guides for the spiritual life.

2694   The Christian family is the first place for education in prayer.

2695   Ordained ministers, the consecrated life, catechesis, prayer groups, and "spiritual direction" ensure assistance within the Church in the practice of prayer.

2696   The most appropriate places for prayer are personal or family oratories, monasteries, places of pilgrimage, and above all the church, which is the proper place for liturgical prayer for the parish community and the privileged place for Eucharistic adoration.

---

48 Cf. *Mt* 6:6.   49 Cf. *PC* 7.

CHAPTER THREE
THE LIFE OF PRAYER

2697 Prayer is the life of the new heart. It ought to animate us at every moment. But we tend to forget him who is our life and our all. This is why the Fathers of the spiritual life in the Deuteronomic and prophetic traditions insist that prayer is a remembrance of God often awakened by the memory of the heart: "We must remember God more often than we draw breath."[1] But we cannot pray "at all times" if we do not pray at specific times, consciously willing it. These are the special times of Christian prayer, both in intensity and duration.

1099

2698 The Tradition of the Church proposes to the faithful certain rhythms of praying intended to nourish continual prayer. Some are daily, such as morning and evening prayer, grace before and after meals, the Liturgy of the Hours. Sundays, centered on the Eucharist, are kept holy primarily by prayer. The cycle of the liturgical year and its great feasts are also basic rhythms of the Christian's life of prayer.

1168

1174
2177

2699 The Lord leads all persons by paths and in ways pleasing to him, and each believer responds according to his heart's resolve and the personal expressions of his prayer. However, Christian Tradition has retained three major expressions of prayer: vocal, meditative, and contemplative. They have one basic trait in common: composure of heart. This vigilance in keeping the Word and dwelling in the presence of God makes these three expressions intense times in the life of prayer.

2563

---

1 St. Gregory of Nazianzus, *Orat. theo.*, 27, 1, 4: PG 36, 16.

ARTICLE 1
EXPRESSIONS OF PRAYER

I.   VOCAL PRAYER

1176   **2700** Through his Word, God speaks to man. By words, mental or vocal, our prayer takes flesh. Yet it is most important that the heart should be present to him to whom we are speaking in prayer: "Whether or not our prayer is heard depends not on the number of words, but on the fervor of our souls."[2]

2701 Vocal prayer is an essential element of the Christian life. To his disciples, drawn by their Master's silent prayer, Jesus teaches a vocal prayer, the Our Father. He not only prayed aloud the liturgical prayers of the syn-

2603   agogue but, as the Gospels show, he raised his voice to express his personal prayer, from exultant blessing of

612   the Father to the agony of Gethsemani.[3]

2702 The need to involve the senses in interior prayer corresponds to a requirement of our human nature. We

1146   are body and spirit, and we experience the need to translate our feelings externally. We must pray with our whole being to give all power possible to our supplication.

2703 This need also corresponds to a divine requirement. God seeks worshippers in Spirit and in Truth, and consequently living prayer that rises from the depths of the soul. He also wants the external expression that associates the body with interior prayer, for it renders him

2097   that perfect homage which is his due.

2704 Because it is external and so thoroughly human, vocal prayer is the form of prayer most readily accessible to groups. Even interior prayer, however, cannot neglect vocal prayer. Prayer is internalized to the extent that we become aware of him "to whom we speak."[4]

---

2 St. John Chrysostom, *Ecloga de oratione* 2: PG 63, 585.   **3** Cf. *Mt* 11:25–26; *Mk* 14:36.   **4** St. Teresa of Jesus, *The Way of Perfection* 26, 9 in *The Collected Works of St. Teresa of Avila*, tr. K. Kavanaugh, OCD, and O. Rodriguez, OCD (Washington DC: Institute of Carmelite Studies, 1980), II, 136.

Thus vocal prayer becomes an initial form of contemplative prayer.

II. MEDITATION

2705 Meditation is above all a quest. The mind seeks *158*
to understand the why and how of the Christian life, in
order to adhere and respond to what the Lord is asking.
The required attentiveness is difficult to sustain. We are
usually helped by books, and Christians do not want for
them: the Sacred Scriptures, particularly the Gospels,
holy icons, liturgical texts of the day or season, writings *127*
of the spiritual fathers, works of spirituality, the great
book of creation, and that of history—the page on
which the "today" of God is written.

2706 To meditate on what we read helps us to make it
our own by confronting it with ourselves. Here, another
book is opened: the book of life. We pass from thoughts
to reality. To the extent that we are humble and faithful,
we discover in meditation the movements that stir the
heart and we are able to discern them. It is a question of
acting truthfully in order to come into the light: "Lord,
what do you want me to do?"

2707 There are as many and varied methods of medi- *2690*
tation as there are spiritual masters. Christians owe it to
themselves to develop the desire to meditate regularly,
lest they come to resemble the three first kinds of soil in
the parable of the sower.[5] But a method is only a guide;
the important thing is to advance, with the Holy Spirit, *2664*
along the one way of prayer: Christ Jesus.

2708 Meditation engages thought, imagination, emotion, and desire. This mobilization of faculties is necessary in order to deepen our convictions of faith, prompt
the conversion of our heart, and strengthen our will to
follow Christ. Christian prayer tries above all to meditate on the mysteries of Christ, as in *lectio divina* or the
rosary. This form of prayerful reflection is of great *516*
value, but Christian prayer should go further: to the *2678*

---

5 Cf. *Mk* 4:4–7, 15–19.

knowledge of the love of the Lord Jesus, to union with him.

III.   CONTEMPLATIVE PRAYER

2709 What is contemplative prayer? St. Teresa answers: "Contemplative prayer *[oración mental]* in my opinion is nothing else than a close sharing between 2562-2564 friends; it means taking time frequently to be alone with him who we know loves us."[6]

Contemplative prayer seeks him "whom my soul loves."[7] It is Jesus, and in him, the Father. We seek him, because to desire him is always the beginning of love, and we seek him in that pure faith which causes us to be born of him and to live in him. In this inner prayer we can still meditate, but our attention is fixed on the Lord himself.

2710 The choice of the *time and duration of the prayer* arises from a determined will, revealing the secrets of the heart. One does not undertake contempla- 2726 tive prayer only when one has the time: one makes time for the Lord, with the firm determination not to give up, no matter what trials and dryness one may encounter. One cannot always meditate, but one can always enter into inner prayer, independently of the conditions of health, work, or emotional state. The heart is the place of this quest and encounter, in poverty and in faith.

2711 *Entering into contemplative prayer* is like entering into the Eucharistic liturgy: we "gather up" the heart, recollect our whole being under the prompting of 1348 the Holy Spirit, abide in the dwelling place of the Lord which we are, awaken our faith in order to enter into the presence of him who awaits us. We let our masks fall and turn our hearts back to the Lord who loves us, so as to hand ourselves over to him as an offering to be 2100 purified and transformed.

---

6 St. Teresa of Jesus, *The Book of Her Life*, 8, 5 in *The Collected Works of St. Teresa of Avila*, tr. K. Kavanaugh, OCD, and O. Rodriguez, OCD (Washington DC: Institute of Carmelite Studies, 1976), I, 67.   7 *Song* 1:7; cf. 3:1–4.

2712 Contemplative prayer is the prayer of the child of God, of the forgiven sinner who agrees to welcome the love by which he is loved and who wants to respond to it by loving even more.[8] But he knows that the love he is returning is poured out by the Spirit in his heart, for everything is grace from God. Contemplative prayer is the poor and humble surrender to the loving will of the Father in ever deeper union with his beloved Son.

2822

2713 Contemplative prayer is the simplest expression of the mystery of prayer. It is a *gift*, a grace; it can be accepted only in humility and poverty. Contemplative prayer is a *covenant* relationship established by God within our hearts.[9] Contemplative prayer is a *communion* in which the Holy Trinity conforms man, the image of God, "to his likeness."

2559

2714 Contemplative prayer is also the pre-eminently *intense time* of prayer. In it the Father strengthens our inner being with power through his Spirit "that Christ may dwell in [our] hearts through faith" and we may be "grounded in love."[10]

2715 Contemplation is a *gaze* of faith, fixed on Jesus. "I look at him and he looks at me": this is what a certain peasant of Ars used to say to his holy curé about his prayer before the tabernacle. This focus on Jesus is a renunciation of self. His gaze purifies our heart; the light of the countenance of Jesus illumines the eyes of our heart and teaches us to see everything in the light of his truth and his compassion for all men. Contemplation also turns its gaze on the mysteries of the life of Christ. Thus it learns the "interior knowledge of our Lord," the more to love him and follow him.[11]

521

2716 Contemplative prayer is *hearing* the Word of God. Far from being passive, such attentiveness is the obedience of faith, the unconditional acceptance of a servant, and the loving commitment of a child. It par-

494

---

8 Cf. *Lk* 7:36–50; 19:1–10. 9 Cf. *Jer* 31:33. 10 *Eph* 3:16–17. 11 Cf. St. Ignatius of Loyola, *Spiritual Exercises*, 104.

ticipates in the "Yes" of the Son become servant and the *Fiat* of God's lowly handmaid.

533 2717   Contemplative prayer is *silence,* the "symbol of the world to come"[12] or "silent love."[13] Words in this kind of prayer are not speeches; they are like kindling that feeds the fire of love. In this silence, unbearable to the "outer" man, the Father speaks to us his incarnate Word, who suffered, died, and rose; in this silence the Spirit of adoption enables us to share in the prayer of 498 Jesus.

2718   Contemplative prayer is a union with the prayer of Christ insofar as it makes us participate in his mystery. The mystery of Christ is celebrated by the Church in the Eucharist, and the Holy Spirit makes it come alive in contemplative prayer so that our charity will manifest it in our acts.

2719   Contemplative prayer is a communion of love bearing Life for the multitude, to the extent that it con-
165 sents to abide in the night of faith. The Paschal night of the Resurrection passes through the night of the agony and the tomb—the three intense moments of the Hour of Jesus which his Spirit (and not "the flesh [which] is weak") brings to life in prayer. We must be willing to
2730 "keep watch with [him] one hour."[14]

IN BRIEF

2720   The Church invites the faithful to regular prayer: daily prayers, the Liturgy of the Hours, Sunday Eucharist, the feasts of the liturgical year.

2721   The Christian tradition comprises three major expressions of the life of prayer: vocal prayer, meditation, and contemplative prayer. They have in common the recollection of the heart.

2722   Vocal prayer, founded on the union of body and

---

12 Cf. St. Isaac of Nineveh, *Tract. myst.* 66.   13 St. John of the Cross, *Maxims and Counsels,* 53 in *The Collected Works of St. John of the Cross,* tr. K. Kavanaugh, OCD, and O. Rodriguez, OCD (Washington DC: Institute of Carmelite Studies, 1979), 678.   14 Cf. *Mt* 26:40.

soul in human nature, associates the body with the interior prayer of the heart, following Christ's example of praying to his Father and teaching the Our Father to his disciples.

2723 Meditation is a prayerful quest engaging thought, imagination, emotion, and desire. Its goal is to make our own in faith the subject considered, by confronting it with the reality of our own life.

2724 Contemplative prayer is the simple expression of the mystery of prayer. It is a gaze of faith fixed on Jesus, an attentiveness to the Word of God, a silent love. It achieves real union with the prayer of Christ to the extent that it makes us share in his mystery.

ARTICLE 2
THE BATTLE OF PRAYER

2725 Prayer is both a gift of grace and a determined response on our part. It always presupposes effort. The great figures of prayer of the Old Covenant before Christ, as well as the Mother of God, the saints, and he himself, all teach us this: prayer is a battle. Against whom? Against ourselves and against the wiles of the *2612* tempter who does all he can to turn man away from *409* prayer, away from union with God. We pray as we live, because we live as we pray. If we do not want to act habitually according to the Spirit of Christ, neither can we pray habitually in his name. The "spiritual battle" of the Christian's new life is inseparable from the battle of prayer. *2015*

I. OBJECTIONS TO PRAYER

2726 In the battle of prayer, we must face in ourselves and around us *erroneous notions of prayer.* Some people view prayer as a simple psychological activity, others as an effort of concentration to reach a mental void. Still others reduce prayer to ritual words and postures.

Many Christians unconsciously regard prayer as an occupation that is incompatible with all the other things
2710 they have to do: they "don't have the time." Those who
seek God by prayer are quickly discouraged because
they do not know that prayer comes also from the Holy
Spirit and not from themselves alone.

2727 We must also face the fact that certain attitudes
deriving from the *mentality* of "this present world" can
penetrate our lives if we are not vigilant. For example,
some would have it that only that is true which can be
37 verified by reason and science; yet prayer is a mystery
that overflows both our conscious and unconscious
lives. Others overly prize production and profit; thus
prayer, being unproductive, is useless. Still others exalt
sensuality and comfort as the criteria of the true, the
good, and the beautiful; whereas prayer, the "love of
beauty" *(philokalia),* is caught up in the glory of the liv-
2500 ing and true God. Finally, some see prayer as a flight
from the world in reaction against activism; but in fact,
Christian prayer is neither an escape from reality nor a
divorce from life.

2728 Finally, our battle has to confront what we experience as *failure in prayer:* discouragement during periods of dryness; sadness that, because we have "great
possessions,"[15] we have not given all to the Lord; disap-
pointment over not being heard according to our own
will; wounded pride, stiffened by the indignity that is
ours as sinners; our resistance to the idea that prayer is
a free and unmerited gift; and so forth. The conclusion
is always the same: what good does it do to pray? To
overcome these obstacles, we must battle to gain humility, trust, and perseverance.

---

15 Cf. *Mk* 10:22.

II. HUMBLE VIGILANCE OF HEART

Facing difficulties in prayer

2729 The habitual difficulty in prayer is *distraction*. It can affect words and their meaning in vocal prayer; it can concern, more profoundly, him to whom we are praying, in vocal prayer (liturgical or personal), meditation, and contemplative prayer. To set about hunting down distractions would be to fall into their trap, when all that is necessary is to turn back to our heart: for a distraction reveals to us what we are attached to, and *2711* this humble awareness before the Lord should awaken our preferential love for him and lead us resolutely to offer him our heart to be purified. Therein lies the battle, the choice of which master to serve.[16]

2730 In positive terms, the battle against the possessive and dominating self requires *vigilance*, sobriety of heart. When Jesus insists on vigilance, he always relates it to himself, to his coming on the last day and every day: *today*. The bridegroom comes in the middle of the *2659* night; the light that must not be extinguished is that of faith: " 'Come,' my heart says, 'seek his face!' "[17]

2731 Another difficulty, especially for those who sincerely want to pray, is *dryness*. Dryness belongs to contemplative prayer when the heart is separated from God, with no taste for thoughts, memories, and feelings, even spiritual ones. This is the moment of sheer faith clinging faithfully to Jesus in his agony and in his tomb. "Unless a grain of wheat falls into the earth and dies, it remains alone; but if it dies, it bears much fruit."[18] If dryness is due to the lack of roots, because the word has fallen on rocky soil, the battle requires conver- *1426* sion.[19]

Facing temptations in prayer

2732 The most common yet most hidden temptation *2609* is our *lack of faith*. It expresses itself less by declared incredulity than by our actual preferences. When we be- *2089*

---

16 Cf. *Mt* 6:21, 24. 17 *Ps* 27:8. 18 *Jn* 12:24. 19 Cf. *Lk* 8:6, 13.

gin to pray, a thousand labors or cares thought to be urgent vie for priority; once again, it is the moment of truth for the heart: what is its real love? Sometimes we turn to the Lord as a last resort, but do we really believe he is? Sometimes we enlist the Lord as an ally, but our heart remains presumptuous. In each case, our lack of faith reveals that we do not yet share in the disposition of a humble heart: "Apart from me, you can do *nothing.*"[20]

2092, 2074

2094 **2733** Another temptation, to which presumption opens the gate, is *acedia.* The spiritual writers understand by this a form of depression due to lax ascetical practice, decreasing vigilance, carelessness of heart. "The spirit indeed is willing, but the flesh is weak."[21] The greater the height, the harder the fall. Painful as discouragement is, it is the reverse of presumption. The humble are not surprised by their distress; it leads them to trust more, to hold fast in constancy.

2559

III. FILIAL TRUST

2734 Filial trust is tested—it proves itself—in tribulation.[22] The principal difficulty concerns the *prayer of petition,* for oneself or for others in intercession. Some even stop praying because they think their petition is not heard. Here two questions should be asked: Why do we think our petition has not been heard? How is our prayer heard, how is it "efficacious"?

2629

Why do we complain of not being heard?

2735 In the first place, we ought to be astonished by this fact: when we praise God or give him thanks for his benefits in general, we are not particularly concerned whether or not our prayer is acceptable to him. On the other hand, we demand to see the results of our petitions. What is the image of God that motivates our prayer: an instrument to be used? or the Father of our Lord Jesus Christ?

2779

2559 **2736** Are we convinced that "we do not know how to

---

20 *Jn* 15:5. 21 *Mt* 26:41. 22 Cf. *Rom* 5:3–5.

pray as we ought"?[23] Are we asking God for "what is good for us"? Our Father knows what we need before we ask him,[24] but he awaits our petition because the dignity of his children lies in their freedom. We must pray, *1730* then, with his Spirit of freedom, to be able truly to know what he wants.[25]

2737 "You ask and do not receive, because you ask wrongly, to spend it on your passions."[26] If we ask with a divided heart, we are "adulterers";[27] God cannot answer us, for he desires our well-being, our life. "Or do you suppose that it is in vain that the scripture says, 'He yearns jealously over the spirit which he has made to dwell in us?' "[28] That our God is "jealous" for us is the sign of how true his love is. If we enter into the desire of his Spirit, we shall be heard.

> Do not be troubled if you do not immediately receive from God what you ask him; for he desires to do something even greater for you, while you cling to him in prayer.[29]

> God wills that our desire should be exercised in prayer, that we may be able to receive what he is prepared to give.[30]

How is our prayer efficacious?

2738 The revelation of prayer in the economy of salvation teaches us that faith rests on God's action in history. Our filial trust is enkindled by his supreme act: the Passion and Resurrection of his Son. Christian prayer is *2568* cooperation with his providence, his plan of love for *307* men.

2739 For St. Paul, this trust is bold, founded on the *2778* prayer of the Spirit in us and on the faithful love of the Father who has given us his only Son.[31] Transformation of the praying heart is the first response to our petition.

2740 The prayer of Jesus makes Christian prayer an

---

23 *Rom* 8:26.   24 Cf. *Mt* 6:8.   25 Cf. *Rom* 8:27.   26 *Jas* 4:3; cf. the whole context: *Jas* 4:1–10; 1:5–8; 5:16.   27 *Jas* 4:4.   28 *Jas* 4:5.   29 Evagrius Ponticus, *De oratione* 34: PG 79, 1173.   30 St. Augustine, *Ep.* 130, 8, 17: PL 33, 500. 31 Cf. *Rom* 10:12–13; 8:26–39.

efficacious petition. He is its model, he prays in us and with us. Since the heart of the Son seeks only what pleases the Father, how could the prayer of the children of adoption be centered on the gifts rather than the Giver?

2604

2741   Jesus also prays for us—in our place and on our behalf. All our petitions were gathered up, once for all, in his cry on the Cross and, in his Resurrection, heard by the Father. This is why he never ceases to intercede for us with the Father.[32] If our prayer is resolutely united with that of Jesus, in trust and boldness as children, we obtain all that we ask in his name, even more than any particular thing: the Holy Spirit himself, who contains all gifts.

2606

2614

IV.   PERSEVERING IN LOVE

2098   **2742**   "Pray constantly . . . always and for everything giving thanks in the name of our Lord Jesus Christ to God the Father."[33] St. Paul adds, "Pray at all times in the Spirit, with all prayer and supplication. To that end keep alert with all perseverance making supplication for all the saints."[34] For "we have not been commanded to work, to keep watch and to fast constantly, but it has been laid down that we are to pray without ceasing."[35] This tireless fervor can come only from love. Against our dullness and laziness, the battle of prayer is that of humble, trusting, and persevering *love*. This love opens our hearts to three enlightening and life-giving facts of faith about prayer.

162

2743   *It is always possible to pray:* The time of the Christian is that of the risen Christ who is with us always, no matter what tempests may arise.[36] Our time is in the hands of God:

> It is possible to offer fervent prayer even while walking in public or strolling alone, or seated in your shop, . . . while buying or selling, . . . or even while cooking.[37]

---

32 Cf. *Heb* 5:7; 7:25; 9:24.   33 *1 Thess* 5:17; *Eph* 5:20.   34 *Eph* 6:18.
35 Evagrius Ponticus, *Pract.* 49: PG 40, 1245C.   36 Cf. *Mt* 28:20; *Lk* 8:24.
37 St. John Chrysostom, *Ecloga de oratione* 2: PG 63, 585.

2744 *Prayer is a vital necessity.* Proof from the contrary is no less convincing: if we do not allow the Spirit to lead us, we fall back into the slavery of sin.[38] How can the Holy Spirit be our life if our heart is far from him?

> Nothing is equal to prayer; for what is impossible it makes possible, what is difficult, easy. . . . For it is impossible, utterly impossible, for the man who prays eagerly and invokes God ceaselessly ever to sin.[39]

> Those who pray are certainly saved; those who do not pray are certainly damned.[40]

2745 Prayer and *Christian life* are *inseparable,* for they concern the same love and the same renunciation, proceeding from love; the same filial and loving conformity with the Father's plan of love; the same transforming union in the Holy Spirit who conforms us more and more to Christ Jesus; the same love for all men, the love with which Jesus has loved us. "Whatever you ask the   2660 Father in my name, he [will] give it to you. This I command you, to love one another."[41]

> He "prays without ceasing" who unites prayer to works and good works to prayer. Only in this way can we consider as realizable the principle of praying without ceasing.[42]

ARTICLE 3
THE PRAYER OF THE HOUR OF JESUS

2746 When "his hour" came, Jesus prayed to the Father.[43] His prayer, the longest transmitted by the Gospel, embraces the whole economy of creation and salvation, as well as his death and Resurrection. The prayer of the   1085 Hour of Jesus always remains his own, just as his Passover "once for all" remains ever present in the liturgy of his Church.

---

38 Cf. *Gal* 5:16–25.   39 St. John Chrysostom, *De Anna* 4, 5: PG 54, 666.
40 St. Alphonsus Liguori, *Del gran mezzo della preghiera.*   41 *Jn* 15:16–17.
42 Origen, *De orat.* 12: PG 11, 452C.   43 Cf. *Jn* 17.

2747   Christian Tradition rightly calls this prayer the "priestly" prayer of Jesus. It is the prayer of our high priest, inseparable from his sacrifice, from his passing over (Passover) to the Father to whom he is wholly "consecrated."[44]

518   **2748**   In this Paschal and sacrificial prayer, everything is recapitulated in Christ:[45] God and the world; the Word and the flesh; eternal life and time; the love that hands itself over and the sin that betrays it; the disciples present and those who will believe in him by their word; 820   humiliation and glory. It is the prayer of unity.

2749   Jesus fulfilled the work of the Father completely; his prayer, like his sacrifice, extends until the end of time. The prayer of this hour fills the end-times and carries them toward their consummation. Jesus, the Son to whom the Father has given all things, has given himself wholly back to the Father, yet expresses himself with a sovereign freedom[46] by virtue of the power the Father has given him over all flesh. The Son, who made himself Servant, is Lord, the *Pantocrator*. Our high priest who prays for us is also the one who prays in us and the God 2616   who hears our prayer.

2815   **2750**   By entering into the holy name of the Lord Jesus we can accept, from within, the prayer he teaches us: "Our Father!" His priestly prayer fulfills, from within, the great petitions of the Lord's Prayer: concern for the Father's name;[47] passionate zeal for his kingdom (glory);[48] the accomplishment of the will of the Father, of his plan of salvation;[49] and deliverance from evil.[50]

2751   Finally, in this prayer Jesus reveals and gives to us the "knowledge," inseparably one, of the Father and of the Son,[51] which is the very mystery of the life of 240   prayer.

---

44 Cf. *Jn* 17:11, 13, 19.   **45** Cf. *Eph* 1:10.   **46** Cf. *Jn* 17:11, 13, 19, 24.   **47** Cf. *Jn* 17:6, 11, 12, 26.   **48** Cf. *Jn* 17:1, 5, 10, 22, 23–26.   **49** Cf. *Jn* 17:2, 4, 6, 9, 11, 12, 24.   **50** Cf. *Jn* 17:15.   **51** Cf. *Jn* 17:3, 6–10, 25.

IN BRIEF

2752 Prayer presupposes an effort, a fight against ourselves and the wiles of the Tempter. The battle of
prayer is inseparable from the necessary "spiritual battle" to act habitually according to the
Spirit of Christ: we pray as we live, because we
live as we pray.

2753 In the battle of prayer we must confront erroneous conceptions of prayer, various currents
of thought, and our own experience of failure.
We must respond with humility, trust, and perseverance to these temptations which cast doubt
on the usefulness or even the possibility of
prayer.

2754 The principal difficulties in the practice of prayer
are distraction and dryness. The remedy lies in
faith, conversion, and vigilance of heart.

2755 Two frequent temptations threaten prayer: lack
of faith and acedia—a form of depression stemming from lax ascetical practice that leads to discouragement.

2756 Filial trust is put to the test when we feel that our
prayer is not always heard. The Gospel invites us
to ask ourselves about the conformity of our
prayer to the desire of the Spirit.

2757 "Pray constantly" (*1 Thess* 5:17). It is always
possible to pray. It is even a vital necessity.
Prayer and Christian life are inseparable.

2758 The prayer of the hour of Jesus, rightly called the
"priestly prayer" (cf. *Jn* 17), sums up the whole
economy of creation and salvation. It fulfills the
great petitions of the Our Father.

SECTION TWO
THE LORD'S PRAYER
"OUR FATHER!"

2759 Jesus "was praying at a certain place, and when he ceased, one of his disciples said to him, 'Lord, teach us to pray, as John taught his disciples.' "[1] In response to this request the Lord entrusts to his disciples and to his Church the fundamental Christian prayer. St. Luke presents a brief text of five petitions,[2] while St. Matthew gives a more developed version of seven petitions.[3] The liturgical tradition of the Church has retained St. Matthew's text:

> Our Father who art in heaven,
> hallowed be thy name.
> Thy kingdom come.
> Thy will be done on earth, as it is in heaven.
> Give us this day our daily bread,
> and forgive us our trespasses,
>   as we forgive those who trespass against us,
> and lead us not into temptation,
> but deliver us from evil.

2855 **2760** Very early on, liturgical usage concluded the Lord's Prayer with a doxology. In the *Didache,* we find, "For yours are the power and the glory for ever."[4] The *Apostolic Constitutions* add to the beginning: "the kingdom," and this is the formula retained to our day in ecumenical prayer.[5] The Byzantine tradition adds after "the glory" the words "Father, Son, and Holy Spirit." The *Roman Missal* develops the last petition in the explicit perspective of *2854* "awaiting our blessed hope" and of the Second Coming of our Lord Jesus Christ.[6] Then comes the assembly's acclamation or the repetition of the doxology from the *Apostolic Constitutions.*

---

1 *Lk* 11:1. 2 Cf. *Lk* 11:2–4. 3 Cf. *Mt* 6:9–13. 4 *Didache* 8, 2: SCh 248, 174.
5 *Apostolic Constitutions,* 7, 24, 1: PG 1, 1016. 6 *Titus* 2:13; cf. *Roman Missal* 22, Embolism after the Lord's Prayer.

ARTICLE 1
"THE SUMMARY OF THE WHOLE GOSPEL"

2761 The Lord's Prayer "is truly the summary of the whole gospel."[7] "Since the Lord . . . after handing over the practice of prayer, said elsewhere, 'Ask and you will receive,' and since everyone has petitions which are peculiar to his circumstances, the regular and appropriate prayer [the Lord's Prayer] is said first, as the foundation of further desires."[8]

I.   AT THE CENTER OF THE SCRIPTURES

2762 After showing how the psalms are the principal food of Christian prayer and flow together in the petitions of the Our Father, St. Augustine concludes:

> Run through all the words of the holy prayers [in Scripture], and I do not think that you will find anything in them that is not contained and included in the Lord's Prayer.[9]

2763 All the Scriptures—the Law, the Prophets, and the Psalms—are fulfilled in Christ.[10] The Gospel is this "Good News." Its first proclamation is summarized by St. Matthew in the Sermon on the Mount;[11] the prayer to our Father is at the center of this proclamation. It is in this context that each petition bequeathed to us by the Lord is illuminated: *102*

> The Lord's Prayer is the most perfect of prayers. . . . In it we ask, not only for all the things we can rightly desire, but also in the sequence that they should be desired. This prayer not only teaches us to ask for things, but also in what order we should desire them.[12] *2541*

2764 The Sermon on the Mount is teaching for life, the Our Father is a prayer; but in both the one and the other the Spirit of the Lord gives new form to our desires, those inner movements that animate our lives. Je- *1965*

---

7 Tertullian, *De orat.* 1: PL 1, 1155.   8 Tertullian, *De orat.* 10: PL 1, 1165; cf. *Lk* 11:9.   9 St. Augustine, *Ep.* 130, 12, 22: PL 33, 503.   10 Cf. *Lk* 24:44. 11 Cf. *Mt* 5–7.   12 St. Thomas Aquinas, *STh* II-II, 83, 9.

sus teaches us this new life by his words; he teaches us
1969 to ask for it by our prayer. The rightness of our life in
him will depend on the rightness of our prayer.

II.   "THE LORD'S PRAYER"

2765 The traditional expression "the Lord's Prayer"—
oratio Dominica—means that the prayer to our Father
is taught and given to us by the Lord Jesus. The prayer
that comes to us from Jesus is truly unique: it is "of the
Lord." On the one hand, in the words of this prayer the
2701 only Son gives us the words the Father gave him:[13] he is
the master of our prayer. On the other, as Word incarnate, he knows in his human heart the needs of his human brothers and sisters and reveals them to us: he is
the model of our prayer.

2766 But Jesus does not give us a formula to repeat
mechanically.[14] As in every vocal prayer, it is through the
Word of God that the Holy Spirit teaches the children
of God to pray to their Father. Jesus not only gives us
the words of our filial prayer; at the same time he gives
us the Spirit by whom these words become in us "spirit
and life."[15] Even more, the proof and possibility of our
filial prayer is that the Father "sent the Spirit of his Son
into our hearts, crying, '*Abba!* Father!' "[16] Since our
prayer sets forth our desires before God, it is again the
Father, "he who searches the hearts of men," who
"knows what is the mind of the Spirit, because the Spirit
intercedes for the saints according to the will of God."[17]
690 The prayer to Our Father is inserted into the mysterious
mission of the Son and of the Spirit.

III.   THE PRAYER OF THE CHURCH

2767 This indivisible gift of the Lord's words and of
the Holy Spirit who gives life to them in the hearts of
believers has been received and lived by the Church
from the beginning. The first communities prayed the
Lord's Prayer three times a day,[18] in place of the "Eigh-
teen Benedictions" customary in Jewish piety.

---

13 Cf. *Jn* 17:7.   **14** Cf. *Mt* 6:7; *1 Kings* 18:26–29.   **15** *Jn* 6:63.   **16** *Gal* 4:6.
17 *Rom* 8:27.   **18** Cf. *Didache* 8, 3: SCh 248, 174.

2768 According to the apostolic tradition, the Lord's Prayer is essentially rooted in liturgical prayer:

> [The Lord] teaches us to make prayer in common for all our brethren. For he did not say "my Father" who art in heaven, but "our" Father, offering petitions for the common Body.[19]

In all the liturgical traditions, the Lord's Prayer is an integral part of the major hours of the Divine Office. In the three sacraments of Christian initiation its ecclesial character is especially in evidence:

2769 In *Baptism* and *Confirmation,* the handing on *(traditio)* of the Lord's Prayer signifies new birth into the divine life. Since Christian prayer is our speaking to God with the very word of God, those who are "born anew . . . through the living and abiding word of God"[20] learn to invoke their Father by the one Word he always hears. They can henceforth do so, for the seal of the Holy Spirit's anointing is indelibly placed on their hearts, ears, lips, indeed their whole filial being. This is why most of the patristic commentaries on the Our Father are addressed to catechumens and neophytes. When the Church prays the Lord's Prayer, it is always the people made up of the "new-born" who pray and obtain mercy.[21]   1243

2770 In the *Eucharistic liturgy* the Lord's Prayer appears as the prayer of the whole Church and there reveals its full meaning and efficacy. Placed between the *anaphora* (the Eucharistic prayer) and the communion, the Lord's Prayer sums up on the one hand all the petitions and intercessions expressed in the movement of the *epiclesis* and, on the other, knocks at the door of the Banquet of the kingdom which sacramental communion anticipates.   1350

2771 In the Eucharist, the Lord's Prayer also reveals the *eschatological* character of its petitions. It is the proper prayer of "the end-time," the time of salvation   1403

---

19 St. John Chrysostom, *Hom. in Mt.* 19, 4: PG 57, 278.   20 *1 Pet* 1:23.   21 Cf. *1 Pet* 2:1–10.

that began with the outpouring of the Holy Spirit and will be fulfilled with the Lord's return. The petitions addressed to our Father, as distinct from the prayers of the old covenant, rely on the mystery of salvation already accomplished, once for all, in Christ crucified and risen.

1820   2772 From this unshakeable faith springs forth the hope that sustains each of the seven petitions, which express the groanings of the present age, this time of patience and expectation during which "it does not yet appear what we shall be."[22] The Eucharist and the Lord's Prayer look eagerly for the Lord's return, "until he comes."[23]

IN BRIEF

2773 In response to his disciples' request "Lord, teach us to pray" (*Lk* 11:1), Jesus entrusts them with the fundamental Christian prayer, the Our Father.

2774 "The Lord's Prayer is truly the summary of the whole gospel,"[24] the "most perfect of prayers."[25] It is at the center of the Scriptures.

2775 It is called "the Lord's Prayer" because it comes to us from the Lord Jesus, the master and model of our prayer.

2776 The Lord's Prayer is the quintessential prayer of the Church. It is an integral part of the major hours of the Divine Office and of the sacraments of Christian initiation: Baptism, Confirmation, and Eucharist. Integrated into the Eucharist it reveals the eschatological character of its petitions, hoping for the Lord, "until he comes" (*1 Cor* 11:26).

---

22 *1 Jn* 3:2; cf. *Col* 3:4. 23 *1 Cor* 11:26. 24 Tertullian, *De orat.* 1:PL 1, 1251–1255. 25 St. Thomas Aquinas, *STh* II-II, 83, 9.

ARTICLE 2
"OUR FATHER WHO ART IN HEAVEN"

I. "WE DARE TO SAY"
2777 In the Roman liturgy, the Eucharistic assembly is invited to pray to our heavenly Father with filial boldness; the Eastern liturgies develop and use similar expressions: "dare in all confidence," "make us worthy of. . . ." From the burning bush Moses heard a voice saying to him, "Do not come near; put off your shoes from your feet, for the place on which you are standing is holy ground."[26] Only Jesus could cross that threshold of the divine holiness, for "when he had made purification for sins," he brought us into the Father's presence: "Here am I, and the children God has given me."[27]

> Our awareness of our status as slaves would make us sink into the ground and our earthly condition would dissolve into dust, if the authority of our Father himself and the Spirit of his Son had not impelled us to this cry . . . 'Abba, Father!' . . . When would a mortal dare call God 'Father,' if man's innermost being were not animated by power from on high?"[28]

270

2778 This power of the Spirit who introduces us to the Lord's Prayer is expressed in the liturgies of East and of West by the beautiful, characteristically Christian expression: *parrhesia,* straightforward simplicity, filial trust, joyous assurance, humble boldness, the certainty of being loved.[29]

2828

II. "FATHER!"
2779 Before we make our own this first exclamation of the Lord's Prayer, we must humbly cleanse our hearts of certain false images drawn "from this world." *Humility* makes us recognize that "no one knows the Son except the Father, and no one knows the Father except

---

26 *Ex* 3:5. 27 *Heb* 1:3; 2:13. 28 St. Peter Chrysologus, *Sermo* 71, 3: PL 52, 401CD; cf. *Gal* 4:6. 29 Cf. *Eph* 3:12; *Heb* 3:6; 4:16; 10:19; *1 Jn* 2:28; 3:21; 5:14.

the Son and anyone to whom the Son chooses to reveal him," that is, "to little children."[30] The *purification* of our hearts has to do with paternal or maternal images, stemming from our personal and cultural history, and influencing our relationship with God. God our Father

239 transcends the categories of the created world. To impose our own ideas in this area "upon him" would be to fabricate idols to adore or pull down. To pray to the Father is to enter into his mystery as he is and as the Son has revealed him to us.

> The expression God the Father had never been revealed to anyone. When Moses himself asked God who he was, he heard another name. The Father's name has been revealed to us in the Son, for the name "Son" implies the new name "Father."[31]

240 **2780** We can invoke God as "Father" because *he is revealed to us* by his Son become man and because his Spirit makes him known to us. The personal relation of the Son to the Father is something that man cannot conceive of nor the angelic powers even dimly see: and yet, the Spirit of the Son grants a participation in that very relation to us who believe that Jesus is the Christ and that we are born of God.[32]

2665 **2781** When we pray to the Father, we are *in communion with him* and with his Son, Jesus Christ.[33] Then we know and recognize him with an ever new sense of wonder. The first phrase of the Our Father is a blessing of adoration before it is a supplication. For it is the glory of God that we should recognize him as "Father," the true God. We give him thanks for having revealed his name to us, for the gift of believing in it, and for the indwelling of his Presence in us.

2782 We can adore the Father because he has caused us to be reborn to his life by *adopting* us as his children in his only Son: by Baptism, he incorporates us into the

1267 Body of his Christ; through the anointing of his Spirit

---

30 *Mt* 11:25–27.   31 Tertullian, *De orat.* 3: PL 1, 1155.   32 Cf. *Jn* 1:1; *1 Jn* 5:1.
33 Cf. *1 Jn* 1:3.

who flows from the head to the members, he makes us other "Christs."

> God, indeed, who has predestined us to adoption as his sons, has conformed us to the glorious Body of Christ. So then you who have become sharers in Christ are appropriately called "Christs."[34]

> The new man, reborn and restored to his God by grace, says first of all, "Father!" because he has now begun to be a son.[35]

2783 Thus the Lord's Prayer *reveals us to ourselves* at the same time that it reveals the Father to us.[36] 1701

> O man, you did not dare to raise your face to heaven, you lowered your eyes to the earth, and suddenly you have received the grace of Christ: all your sins have been forgiven. From being a wicked servant you have become a good son. . . . Then raise your eyes to the Father who has begotten you through Baptism, to the Father who has redeemed you through his Son, and say: "Our Father. . . ." But do not claim any privilege. He is the Father in a special way only of Christ, but he is the common Father of us all, because while he has begotten only Christ, he has created us. Then also say by his grace, "Our Father," so that you may merit being his son.[37]

2784 The free gift of adoption requires on our part 1428 continual conversion and *new life.* Praying to our Father should develop in us two fundamental dispositions:

First, *the desire to become like him:* though created in his image, we are restored to his likeness by 1997 grace; and we must respond to this grace.

> We must remember . . . and know that when we call God "our Father" we ought to behave as sons of God.[38]

> You cannot call the God of all kindness your Father if you preserve a cruel and inhuman heart; for in

34 St. Cyril of Jerusalem, *Catech. myst.* 3, 1: PG 33, 1088A. 35 St. Cyprian, *De Dom. orat.* 9: PL 4, 525A. 36 Cf. *GS* 22 § 1. 37 St. Ambrose, *De Sacr.* 5, 4, 19: PL 16:450–451. 38 St. Cyprian, *De Dom. orat.* 11: PL 4:526B.

> this case you no longer have in you the marks of the heavenly Father's kindness.[39]

> We must contemplate the beauty of the Father without ceasing and adorn our own souls accordingly.[40]

2562 **2785** Second, *a humble and trusting heart* that enables us "to turn and become like children":[41] for it is to "little children" that the Father is revealed.[42]

> [The prayer is accomplished] by the contemplation of God alone, and by the warmth of love, through which the soul, molded and directed to love him, speaks very familiarly to God as to its own Father with special devotion.[43]

> Our Father: at this name love is aroused in us ... and the confidence of obtaining what we are about to ask. ... What would he not give to his children who ask, since he has already granted them the gift of being his children?[44]

III.   "OUR" FATHER

443 **2786** "Our" Father refers to God. The adjective, as used by us, does not express possession, but an entirely new relationship with God.

2787 When we say "our" Father, we recognize first that all his promises of love announced by the prophets are fulfilled in the *new and eternal covenant* in his
782 Christ: we have become "his" people and he is henceforth "our" God. This new relationship is the purely gratuitous gift of belonging to each other: we are to respond to "grace and truth" given us in Jesus Christ with love and faithfulness.[45]

2788 Since the Lord's Prayer is that of his people in the "endtime," this "our" also expresses the certitude of our hope in God's ultimate promise: in the new Jerusalem he will say to the victor, "I will be his God and he shall be my son."[46]

---

39 St. John Chrysostom, *De orat Dom.* 3: PG 51, 44.   40 St. Gregory of Nyssa, *De orat. Dom.* 2: PG 44, 1148B.   41 *Mt* 18:3.   42 Cf. *Mt* 11:25.   43 St. John Cassian, *Coll.* 9, 18: PL 49, 788C.   44 St. Augustine, *De serm. Dom. in monte* 2, 4, 16: PL 34, 1276.   45 *Jn* 1:17; cf. *Hos* 2:21–22; 6:1–6.   46 *Rev* 21:7.

2789 When we pray to "our" Father, we personally address the Father of our Lord Jesus Christ. By doing so we do not divide the Godhead, since the Father is its "source and origin," but rather confess that the Son is eternally begotten by him and the Holy Spirit proceeds *245* from him. We are not confusing the persons, for we confess that our communion is with the Father and his Son, Jesus Christ, in their one Holy Spirit. The *Holy Trinity* is consubstantial and indivisible. When we pray *253* to the Father, we adore and glorify him together with the Son and the Holy Spirit.

2790 Grammatically, "our" qualifies a reality common to more than one person. There is only one God, and he is recognized as Father by those who, through faith in his only Son, are reborn of him by water and the Spirit.[47] The *Church* is this new communion of God and *787* men. United with the only Son, who has become "the firstborn among many brethren," she is in communion with one and the same Father in one and the same Holy Spirit.[48] In praying "our" Father, each of the baptized is praying in this communion: "The company of those who believed were of one heart and soul."[49]

2791 For this reason, in spite of the divisions among *821* Christians, this prayer to "our" Father remains our common patrimony and an urgent summons for all the baptized. In communion by faith in Christ and by Baptism, they ought to join in Jesus' prayer for the unity of his disciples.[50]

2792 Finally, if we pray the Our Father sincerely, we leave individualism behind, because the love that we receive frees us from it. The "our" at the beginning of the Lord's Prayer, like the "us" of the last four petitions, excludes no one. If we are to say it truthfully, our divisions and oppositions have to be overcome.[51]

2793 The baptized cannot pray to "our" Father without bringing before him all those for whom he gave his

---

47 Cf. *1 Jn* 5:1; *Jn* 3:5. 48 *Rom* 8:29; cf. *Eph* 4:4–6. 49 *Acts* 4:32. 50 Cf. *UR* 8; 22. 51 Cf. *Mt* 5:23–24; 6:14–15.

604 beloved Son. God's love has no bounds, neither should our prayer.[52] Praying "our" Father opens to us the dimensions of his love revealed in Christ: praying with and for all who do not yet know him, so that Christ may "gather into one the children of God."[53] God's care for all men and for the whole of creation has inspired all the great practitioners of prayer; it should extend our prayer to the full breadth of love whenever we dare to say "our" Father.

IV.   "Who Art in Heaven"

326 **2794** This biblical expression does not mean a place ("space"), but a way of being; it does not mean that God is distant, but majestic. Our Father is not "elsewhere": he transcends everything we can conceive of his holiness. It is precisely because he is thrice-holy that he is so close to the humble and contrite heart.

> "Our Father who art in heaven" is rightly understood to mean that God is in the hearts of the just, as in his holy temple. At the same time, it means that those who pray should desire the one they invoke to dwell in them.[54]

> "Heaven" could also be those who bear the image of the heavenly world, and in whom God dwells and tarries.[55]

2795 The symbol of the heavens refers us back to the mystery of the covenant we are living when we pray to our Father. He is in heaven, his dwelling place; the Father's house is our homeland. Sin has exiled us from the land of the covenant,[56] but conversion of heart en-
1024 ables us to return to the Father, to heaven.[57] In Christ, then, heaven and earth are reconciled,[58] for the Son alone "descended from heaven" and causes us to ascend there with him, by his Cross, Resurrection, and Ascension.[59]

2796 When the Church prays "our Father who art in

---

52 Cf. *NA* 5.   53 *Jn* 11:52.   54 St. Augustine, *De serm. Dom. in monte* 2, 5, 18: PL 34, 1277.   55 St. Cyril of Jerusalem, *Catech. myst.* 5:11: PG 33, 1117.
56 Cf. *Gen* 3.   57 *Jer* 3:19–4:1a; *Lk* 15:18, 21.   58 Cf. *Isa* 45:8; *Ps* 85:12.
59 *Jn* 3:13; 12:32; 14:2–3; 16:28; 20:17; *Eph* 4:9–10; *Heb* 1:3; 2:13.

heaven," she is professing that we are the People of God, already seated "with him in the heavenly places in Christ Jesus" and "hidden with Christ in God;"[60] yet at the same time, "here indeed we groan, and long to put on our heavenly dwelling."[61]

1003

> [Christians] are in the flesh, but do not live according to the flesh. They spend their lives on earth, but are citizens of heaven.[62]

IN BRIEF

2797 Simple and faithful trust, humble and joyous assurance are the proper dispositions for one who prays the Our Father.

2798 We can invoke God as "Father" because the Son of God made man has revealed him to us. In this Son, through Baptism, we are incorporated and adopted as sons of God.

2799 The Lord's Prayer brings us into communion with the Father and with his Son, Jesus Christ. At the same time it reveals us to ourselves (cf. *GS* 22 § 1).

2800 Praying to our Father should develop in us the will to become like him and foster in us a humble and trusting heart.

2801 When we say "Our" Father, we are invoking the new covenant in Jesus Christ, communion with the Holy Trinity, and the divine love which spreads through the Church to encompass the world.

2802 "Who art in heaven" does not refer to a place but to God's majesty and his presence in the hearts of the just. Heaven, the Father's house, is the true homeland toward which we are heading and to which, already, we belong.

---

60 *Eph* 2:6; *Col* 3:3. 61 *2 Cor* 5:2; cf. *Phil* 3:20; *Heb* 13:14. 62 *Ad Diognetum* 5: PG 2, 1173.

ARTICLE 3
THE SEVEN PETITIONS

2803   After we have placed ourselves in the presence of God our Father to adore and to love and to bless him, the Spirit of adoption stirs up in our hearts seven petitions, seven blessings. The first three, more theologal, *2627* draw us toward the glory of the Father; the last four, as ways toward him, commend our wretchedness to his grace. "Deep calls to deep."[63]

2804   The first series of petitions carries us toward him, for his own sake: *thy* name, *thy* kingdom, *thy* will! It is characteristic of love to think first of the one whom we love. In none of the three petitions do we mention ourselves; the burning desire, even anguish, of the beloved Son for his Father's glory seizes us:[64] "hallowed be thy name, thy kingdom come, they will be done. . . ." These three supplications were already answered in the saving sacrifice of Christ, but they are henceforth directed in hope toward their final fulfillment, for God is not yet all in all.[65]

2805   The second series of petitions unfolds with the same movement as certain Eucharistic epicleses: as an *1105* offering up of our expectations, that draws down upon itself the eyes of the Father of mercies. They go up from us and concern us from this very moment, in our present world: "give *us* . . . forgive *us* . . . lead *us* not . . . deliver *us*. . . ." The fourth and fifth petitions concern our life as such—to be fed and to be healed of sin; the last two concern our battle for the victory of life—that battle of prayer.

2656-2658   **2806**   By the three first petitions, we are strengthened in faith, filled with hope, and set aflame by charity. Being creatures and still sinners, we have to petition for us, for that "us" bound by the world and history, which we offer to the boundless love of God. For through the name of his Christ and the reign of his Holy Spirit, our

---

63 *Ps* 42:7.   64 Cf. *Lk* 22:14; 12:50.   65 Cf. *1 Cor* 15:28.

Father accomplishes his plan of salvation, for us and for the whole world.

I. "HALLOWED BE THY NAME" 2142-2159

2807 The term "to hallow" is to be understood here not primarily in its causative sense (only God hallows, makes holy), but above all in an evaluative sense: to recognize as holy, to treat in a holy way. And so, in adoration, this invocation is sometimes understood as praise 2097 and thanksgiving.[66] But this petition is here taught to us by Jesus as an optative: a petition, a desire, and an expectation in which God and man are involved. Beginning with this first petition to our Father, we are immersed in the innermost mystery of his Godhead and the drama of the salvation of our humanity. Asking the Father that his name be made holy draws us into his plan of loving kindness for the fullness of time, "according to his purpose which he set forth in Christ," that we might "be holy and blameless before him in love."[67]

2808 In the decisive moments of his economy God reveals his name, but he does so by accomplishing his work. This work, then, is realized for us and in us only if his name is hallowed by us and in us.

2809 The holiness of God is the inaccessible center of 203, 432 his eternal mystery. What is revealed of it in creation and history, Scripture calls "glory," the radiance of his majesty.[68] In making man in his image and likeness, God 293 "crowned him with glory and honor," but by sinning, man fell "short of the glory of God."[69] From that time on, God was to manifest his holiness by revealing and 705 giving his name, in order to restore man to the image of his Creator.[70]

2810 In the promise to Abraham and the oath that accompanied it,[71] God commits himself but without disclosing his name. He begins to reveal it to Moses and

---

66 Cf. *Ps* 111:9; *Lk* 1:49. 67 *Eph* 1:9, 4. 68 Cf. *Ps* 8; *Isa* 6:3. 69 *Ps* 8:5; *Rom* 3:23; cf. *Gen* 1:26. 70 *Col* 3:10. 71 Cf. *Heb* 6:13.

makes it known clearly before the eyes of the whole people when he saves them from the Egyptians: "he has triumphed gloriously."[72] From the covenant of Sinai onwards, this people is "his own" and it is to be a "holy (or "consecrated": the same word is used for both in Hebrew) nation,"[73] because the name of God dwells in it.

63

2143 **2811** In spite of the holy Law that again and again their Holy God gives them—"You shall be holy, for I the LORD your God am holy"—and although the Lord shows patience for the sake of his name, the people turn away from the Holy One of Israel and profane his name among the nations.[74] For this reason the just ones of the old covenant, the poor survivors returned from exile, and the prophets burned with passion for the name.

434 **2812** Finally, in Jesus the name of the Holy God is revealed and given to us, in the flesh, as Savior, revealed by what he is, by his word, and by his sacrifice.[75] This is the heart of his priestly prayer: "Holy Father ... for their sake I consecrate myself, that they also may be consecrated in truth."[76] Because he "sanctifies" his own name, Jesus reveals to us the name of the Father.[77] At the end of Christ's Passover, the Father gives him the name that is above all names: "Jesus Christ is Lord, to the glory of God the Father."[78]

2013 **2813** In the waters of Baptism, we have been "washed ... sanctified ... justified in the name of the Lord Jesus Christ and in the Spirit of our God."[79] Our Father calls us to holiness in the whole of our life, and since "he is the source of [our] life in Christ Jesus, who became for us wisdom from God, and ... sanctification,"[80] both his glory and our life depend on the hallowing of his name in us and by us. Such is the urgency of our first petition.

---

72 *Ex* 15:1; cf. 3:14.   73 Cf. *Ex* 19:5–6.   74 *Ezek* 20:9; 14, 22, 39; cf. *Lev* 19:2.
75 Cf. *Mt* 1:21; *Lk* 1:31; *Jn* 8:28; 17:8; 17:17–19.   76 *Jn* 17:11, 19.   77 Cf.
Ezek 20:39; 36:20–21; *Jn* 17:6.   78 *Phil* 2:9–11.   79 *1 Cor* 6:11.   80 *1 Cor*
1:30; cf. *1 Thess* 4:7.

By whom is God hallowed, since he is the one who hallows? But since he said, "You shall be holy to me; for I the LORD am holy," we seek and ask that we who were sanctified in Baptism may persevere in what we have begun to be. And we ask this daily, for we need sanctification daily, so that we who fail daily may cleanse away our sins by being sanctified continually. . . . We pray that this sanctification may remain in us.[81]

2814 The sanctification of his name among the nations depends inseparably on our *life* and our *prayer:*   *2045*

We ask God to hallow his name, which by its own holiness saves and makes holy all creation. . . . It is this name that gives salvation to a lost world. But we ask that this name of God should be hallowed in us through our actions. For God's name is blessed when we live well, but is blasphemed when we live wickedly. As the Apostle says: "The name of God is blasphemed among the Gentiles because of you." We ask then that, just as the name of God is holy, so we may obtain his holiness in our souls.[82]

When we say "hallowed be thy name," we ask that it should be hallowed in us, who are in him; but also in others whom God's grace still awaits, that we may obey the precept that obliges us to pray for everyone, even our enemies. That is why we do not say expressly "hallowed be thy name 'in us,' " for we ask that it be so in all men.[83]

2815 This petition embodies all the others. Like the six petitions that follow, it is fulfilled by *the prayer of Christ.* Prayer to our Father is our prayer, if it is prayed *in the name* of Jesus.[84] In his priestly prayer, Jesus asks: *2750* "Holy Father, protect in your name those whom you have given me."[85]

---

81 St. Cyprian, *De Dom. orat.* 12: PL 4, 527A; *Lev* 20:26.   82 St. Peter Chrysologus, *Sermo* 71, 4: PL 52:402A; cf. *Rom* 2:24; *Ezek* 36: 20–22.
83 Tertullian, *De orat.* 3: PL 1:1157A.   84 Cf. *Jn* 14:13; 15:16; 16:24, 26.
85 *Jn* 17:11.

II.   THY KINGDOM COME"

541   **2816**   In the New Testament, the word *basileia* can be
translated by "kingship" (abstract noun), "kingdom"
2632   (concrete noun) or "reign" (action noun). The Kingdom
of God lies ahead of us. It is brought near in the Word
incarnate, it is proclaimed throughout the whole
Gospel, and it has come in Christ's death and Resurrec-
560   tion. The Kingdom of God has been coming since the
1107   Last Supper and, in the Eucharist, it is in our midst. The
kingdom will come in glory when Christ hands it over
to his Father:

> It may even be . . . that the Kingdom of God means
> Christ himself, whom we daily desire to come, and
> whose coming we wish to be manifested quickly to
> us. For as he is our resurrection, since in him we
> rise, so he can also be understood as the Kingdom
> of God, for in him we shall reign.[86]

451, 2632   **2817**   This petition is *"Marana tha,"* the cry of the
671   Spirit and the Bride: "Come, Lord Jesus."

> Even if it had not been prescribed to pray for the
> coming of the kingdom, we would willingly have
> brought forth this speech, eager to embrace our
> hope. In indignation the souls of the martyrs under
> the altar cry out to the Lord: "O Sovereign Lord,
> holy and true, how long before you judge and
> avenge our blood on those who dwell upon the
> earth?" For their retribution is ordained for the end
> of the world. Indeed, as soon as possible, Lord,
> may your kingdom come![87]

769   **2818**   In the Lord's Prayer, "thy kingdom come" refers
primarily to the final coming of the reign of God
through Christ's return.[88] But, far from distracting the
Church from her mission in this present world, this desire commits her to it all the more strongly. Since Pentecost, the coming of that Reign is the work of the Spirit
of the Lord who "complete[s] his work on earth and
brings us the fullness of grace."[89]

---

86 St. Cyprian, *De Dom. orat.* 13: PL 4, 528A.   87 Tertullian, *De orat.* 5: PL 1,
1159A; cf. *Heb* 4:11; *Rev* 6:9; 22:20.   88 Cf. *Titus* 2:13.   89 *Roman Missal*,
Eucharistic Prayer IV, 118.

2819 "The kingdom of God [is] righteousness and 2046 peace and joy in the Holy Spirit."[90] The end-time in which we live is the age of the outpouring of the Spirit. Ever since Pentecost, a decisive battle has been joined 2516 between "the flesh" and the Spirit.[91]

> Only a pure soul can boldly say: "Thy kingdom 2519 come." One who has heard Paul say, "Let not sin therefore reign in your mortal bodies," and has purified himself in action, thought, and word will say to God: "Thy kingdom come!"[92]

2820 By a discernment according to the Spirit, Christians have to distinguish between the growth of the Reign of God and the progress of the culture and society in which they are involved. This distinction is not a 1049 separation. Man's vocation to eternal life does not suppress, but actually reinforces, his duty to put into action in this world the energies and means received from the Creator to serve justice and peace.[93]

2821: This petition is taken up and granted in the 2746 prayer *of* Jesus which is present and effective in the Eucharist; it bears its fruit in new life in keeping with the Beatitudes.[94]

III.   "THY WILL BE DONE ON EARTH AS IT IS IN HEAVEN"

2822 Our Father "desires all men to be saved and to 851 come to the knowledge of the truth."[95] He "is forbearing toward you, not wishing that any should perish."[96] His commandment is "that you love one another; even as I have loved you, that you also love one another."[97] 2196 This commandment summarizes all the others and expresses his entire will.

2823 "He has made known to us the mystery of his 59 will, according to his good pleasure that he set forth in Christ . . . to gather up all things in him, things in

---

90 *Rom* 14:17.   91 Cf. *Gal* 5:16–25.   92 St. Cyril of Jerusalem, *Catech. myst.* 5, 13: PG 33, 1120A; cf. *Rom* 6:12.   93 Cf. *GS* 22; 32; 39; 45; *EN* 31.   94 Cf. *Jn* 17:17–20; *Mt* 5:13–16; 6:24; 7:12–13.   95 *1 Tim* 2:3–4.   96 *2 Pet* 3:9; cf. *Mt* 18:14.   97 *Jn* 13:34; cf. *1 Jn* 3; *Lk* 10:25–37.

heaven and things on earth. In Christ we have also obtained an inheritance, having been destined according to the purpose of him who accomplishes all things according to his counsel and will."[98] We ask insistently for this loving plan to be fully realized on earth as it is already in heaven.

475 **2824** In Christ, and through his human will, the will of the Father has been perfectly fulfilled once for all. Jesus said on entering into this world: "Lo, I have come to do your will, O God."[99] Only Jesus can say: "I always do what is pleasing to him."[100] In the prayer of his agony, he consents totally to this will: "not my will, but

612 yours be done."[101] For this reason Jesus "gave himself for our sins to deliver us from the present evil age, according to the will of our God and Father."[102] "And by that will we have been sanctified through the offering of the body of Jesus Christ once for all."[103]

2825 "Although he was a Son, [Jesus] learned obedience through what he suffered."[104] How much more reason have we sinful creatures to learn obedience—we who in him have become children of adoption. We ask our Father to unite our will to his Son's, in order to

615 fulfill his will, his plan of salvation for the life of the world. We are radically incapable of this, but united with Jesus and with the power of his Holy Spirit, we can surrender our will to him and decide to choose what his Son has always chosen: to do what is pleasing to the Father.[105]

> In committing ourselves to [Christ], we can become one spirit with him, and thereby accomplish his will, in such wise that it will be perfect on earth as it is in heaven.[106]

> Consider how [Jesus Christ] teaches us to be humble, by making us see that our virtue does not depend on our work alone but on grace from on high. He commands each of the faithful who prays to do

---

98 *Eph* 1:9–11.   99 *Heb* 10:7; *Ps* 40:7.   100 *Jn* 8:29.   101 *Lk* 22:42; cf. *Jn* 4:34; 5:30; 6:38.   102 *Gal* 1:4.   103 *Heb* 10:10.   104 *Heb* 5:8   105 Cf. *Jn* 8:29.   106 Origen, *De orat.* 26: PG 11, 501B.

so universally, for the whole world. For he did not say "thy will be done in me or in us," but "on earth," the whole earth, so that error may be banished from it, truth take root in it, all vice be destroyed on it, virtue flourish on it, and earth no longer differ from heaven.[107]

2826 By prayer we can discern "what is the will of God" and obtain the endurance to do it.[108] Jesus teaches us that one enters the kingdom of heaven not by speaking words, but by doing "the will of my Father in heaven."[109]

2827 "If anyone is a worshiper of God and does his will, God listens to him."[110] Such is the power of the Church's prayer in the name of her Lord, above all in the Eucharist. Her prayer is also a communion of intercession with the all-holy Mother of God[111] and all the saints who have been pleasing to the Lord because they willed his will alone:

> It would not be inconsistent with the truth to understand the words, "Thy will be done on earth as it is in heaven," to mean: "in the Church as in our Lord Jesus Christ himself"; or "in the Bride who has been betrothed, just as in the Bridegroom who has accomplished the will of the Father."[112]

IV. "GIVE US THIS DAY OUR DAILY BREAD"

2828 *"Give us":* The trust of children who look to their Father for everything is beautiful. "He makes his sun rise on the evil and on the good, and sends rain on the just and on the unjust."[113] He gives to all the living "their food in due season."[114] Jesus teaches us this petition, because it glorifies our Father by acknowledging how good he is, beyond all goodness.

2829 "Give us" also expresses the covenant. We are his and he is ours, for our sake. But this "us" also recognizes him as the Father of all men and we pray to him

2611

796

2778

1939

---

107 St. John Chrysostom, *Hom. in Mt.* 19, 5: PG 57, 280.   108 *Rom* 12:2; cf. *Eph* 5:17; cf. *Heb* 10:36.   109 *Mt* 7:21.   110 *Jn* 9:31; cf. *1 Jn* 5:14.   111 Cf *Lk* 1:38, 49.   112 St. Augustine, *De serm. Dom.* 2, 6, 24: PL 34, 1279.   113 *Mt* 5:45.   114 *Ps* 104:27.

for them all, in solidarity with their needs and sufferings.

2830 *"Our bread"*: The Father who gives us life cannot but give us the nourishment life requires—all appropriate goods and blessings, both material and spiritual. In the Sermon on the Mount, Jesus insists on the filial trust that cooperates with our Father's providence.[115] He is not inviting us to idleness,[116] but wants to relieve us from nagging worry and preoccupation. Such is the filial surrender of the children of God:

> To those who seek the kingdom of God and his righteousness, he has promised to give all else besides. Since everything indeed belongs to God, he who possesses God wants for nothing, if he himself is not found wanting before God.[117]

2831 But the presence of those who hunger because they lack bread opens up another profound meaning of this petition. The drama of hunger in the world calls Christians who pray sincerely to exercise responsibility toward their brethren, both in their personal behavior and in their solidarity with the human family. This petition of the Lord's Prayer cannot be isolated from the parables of the poor man Lazarus and of the Last Judgment.[118]

2832 As leaven in the dough, the newness of the kingdom should make the earth "rise" by the Spirit of Christ.[119] This must be shown by the establishment of justice in personal and social, economic and international relations, without ever forgetting that there are no just structures without people who want to be just.

2833 "Our" bread is the "one" loaf for the "many." In the Beatitudes "poverty" is the virtue of sharing: it calls us to communicate and share both material and spiritual goods, not by coercion but out of love, so that the abundance of some may remedy the needs of others.[120]

2633

227

1038

1928

2790
2546

---

115 Cf. *Mt* 6:25–34.   116 Cf. *2 Thess* 3:6–13.   117 St. Cyprian, *De Dom. orat.* 21: PL 4, 534A.   118 Cf. *Lk* 16:19–31; *Mt* 25:31–46.   119 Cf. AA 5.   120 Cf. *2 Cor* 8:1–15.

2834 "Pray and work."[121] "Pray as if everything de- 2428
pended on God and work as if everything depended on
you."[122] Even when we have done our work, the food
we receive is still a gift from our Father; it is good to ask
him for it with thanksgiving, as Christian families do
when saying grace at meals.

2835 This petition, with the responsibility it involves,
also applies to another hunger from which men are per-
ishing: "Man does not live by bread alone, but ... by
every word that proceeds from the mouth of God,"[123]
that is, by the Word he speaks and the Spirit he breathes
forth. Christians must make every effort "to proclaim
the good news to the poor." There is a famine on earth, 2443
"not a famine of bread, nor a thirst for water, but of
hearing the words of the LORD."[124] For this reason the
specifically Christian sense of this fourth petition concerns the Bread of Life: The Word of God accepted in
faith, the Body of Christ received in the Eucharist.[125] 1384

2836 *"This day"* is also an expression of trust taught 1165
us by the Lord,[126] which we would never have presumed
to invent. Since it refers above all to his Word and to the
Body of his Son, this "today" is not only that of our
mortal time, but also the "today" of God.

> If you receive the bread each day, each day is today
> for you. If Christ is yours today, he rises for you
> every day. How can this be? "You are my Son, to-
> day I have begotten you." Therefore, "today" is
> when Christ rises.[127]

2837 *"Daily"* (epiousios) occurs nowhere else in the 2659
New Testament. Taken in a temporal sense, this word is
a pedagogical repetition of "this day,"[128] to confirm us
in trust "without reservation." Taken in the qualitative 2633
sense, it signifies what is necessary for life, and more
broadly every good thing sufficient for subsistence.[129]

---

121 Cf. St. Benedict, *Regula*, 20, 48. 122 Attributed to St. Ignatius Loyola, cf.
Joseph de Guibert, SJ, *The Jesuits: Their Spiritual Doctrine and Practice*,
(Chicago: Loyola University Press, 1964), 148, n. 55. 123 *Deut* 8:3; *Mt* 4:4.
124 *Am* 8:11. 125 Cf. *Jn* 6:26–58. 126 Cf. *Mt* 6:34; *Ex* 16:19. 127 St.
Ambrose, *De Sacr.* 5, 4, 26: PL 16, 453A; cf. *Ps* 2:7. 128 Cf. *Ex* 16:19–21.
129 Cf. *1 Tim* 6:8.

Taken literally (*epi-ousios:* "super-essential"), it refers directly to the Bread of Life, the Body of Christ, the 1405 "medicine of immortality," without which we have no life within us.[130] Finally in this connection, its heavenly meaning is evident: "this day" is the Day of the Lord, 1166 the day of the feast of the kingdom, anticipated in the Eucharist that is already the foretaste of the kingdom to come. For this reason it is fitting for the Eucharistic 1389 liturgy to be celebrated each day.

> The Eucharist is our daily bread. The power belonging to this divine food makes it a bond of union. Its effect is then understood as unity, so that, gathered into his Body and made members of him, we may become what we receive. . . . This also is our daily bread: the readings you hear each day in church and the hymns you hear and sing. All these are necessities for our pilgrimage.[131]

> The Father in heaven urges us, as children of heaven, to ask for the bread of heaven. [Christ] himself is the bread who, sown in the Virgin, raised up in the flesh, kneaded in the Passion, baked in the oven of the tomb, reserved in churches, brought to altars, furnishes the faithful each day with food from heaven.[132]

V. "AND FORGIVE US OUR TRESPASSES, AS WE FORGIVE THOSE WHO TRESPASS AGAINST US"

1425 **2838** This petition is astonishing. If it consisted only of the first phrase, "And forgive us our trespasses," it might have been included, implicitly, in the first three petitions of the Lord's Prayer, since Christ's sacrifice is 1933 "that sins may be forgiven." But, according to the second phrase, our petition will not be heard unless we have first met a strict requirement. Our petition looks to 2631 the future, but our response must come first, for the two parts are joined by the single word "as."

---

130 St. Ignatius of Antioch, *Ad Eph.* 20, 2: PG 5, 661; *Jn* 6:53–56.   131 St. Augustine, *Sermo* 57, 7: PL 38, 389.   132 St. Peter Chrysologus, *Sermo* 67: PL 52, 392; cf. *Jn* 6:51.

And forgive us our trespasses . . .

2839 With bold confidence, we began praying to our Father. In begging him that his name be hallowed, we were in fact asking him that we ourselves might be always made more holy. But though we are clothed with the baptismal garment, we do not cease to sin, to turn away from God. Now, in this new petition, we return to him like the prodigal son and, like the tax collector, recognize that we are sinners before him.[133] Our petition begins with a "confession" of our wretchedness and his mercy. Our hope is firm because, in his Son, "we have redemption, the forgiveness of sins."[134] We find the efficacious and undoubted sign of his forgiveness in the sacraments of his Church.[135]

1425
1439

1422

2840 Now—and this is daunting—this outpouring of mercy cannot penetrate our hearts as long as we have not forgiven those who have trespassed against us. Love, like the Body of Christ, is indivisible; we cannot love the God we cannot see if we do not love the brother or sister we do see.[136] In refusing to forgive our brothers and sisters, our hearts are closed and their hardness makes them impervious to the Father's merciful love; but in confessing our sins, our hearts are opened to his grace.

1864

2841 This petition is so important that it is the only one to which the Lord returns and which he develops explicitly in the Sermon on the Mount.[137] This crucial requirement of the covenant mystery is impossible for man. But "with God all things are possible."[138]

. . . as we forgive those who trespass against us

2842 This "as" is not unique in Jesus' teaching: "You, therefore, must be perfect, *as* your heavenly Father is perfect"; "Be merciful, even *as* your Father is merciful"; "A new commandment I give to you, that you love one another, even *as* I have loved you, that you also love one another."[139] It is impossible to keep the Lord's com-

---

133 Cf. *Lk* 15:11–32; 18:13. 134 *Col* 1:14; *Eph* 1:7. 135 Cf. *Mt* 26:28; *Jn* 20:23. 136 Cf. *1 Jn* 4:20. 137 Cf. *Mt* 6:14–15; 5:23–24; *Mk* 11:25. 138 *Mt* 19:26. 139 *Mt* 5:48; *Lk* 6:36; *Jn* 13:34.

mandment by imitating the divine model from outside;
521 there has to be a vital participation, coming from the depths of the heart, in the holiness and the mercy and the love of our God. Only the Spirit by whom we live can make "ours" the same mind that was in Christ Jesus.[140] Then the unity of forgiveness becomes possible and we find ourselves "forgiving one another, *as* God in Christ forgave" us.[141]

2843 Thus the Lord's words on forgiveness, the love that loves to the end,[142] become a living reality. The parable of the merciless servant, which crowns the Lord's teaching on ecclesial communion, ends with these words: "So also my heavenly Father will do to every one of you, if you do not forgive your brother from your heart."[143] It is there, in fact, "in the depths of
368 the *heart,*" that everything is bound and loosed. It is not in our power not to feel or to forget an offense; but the heart that offers itself to the Holy Spirit turns injury into compassion and purifies the memory in transforming the hurt into intercession.

2262 **2844** Christian prayer extends to the *forgiveness of enemies,*[144] transfiguring the disciple by configuring him to his Master. Forgiveness is a high-point of Christian prayer; only hearts attuned to God's compassion can receive the gift of prayer. Forgiveness also bears witness that, in our world, love is stronger than sin. The martyrs of yesterday and today bear this witness to Jesus. Forgiveness is the fundamental condition of the reconciliation of the children of God with their Father and of men with one another.[145]

1441 **2845** There is no limit or measure to this essentially divine forgiveness,[146] whether one speaks of "sins" as in *Luke* (11:4), or "debts" as in *Matthew* (6:12). We are always debtors: "Owe no one anything, except to love one another."[147] The communion of the Holy Trinity is the source and criterion of truth in every relation-

---

140 Cf. *Gal* 5:25; *Phil* 2:1, 5.   141 *Eph* 4:32.   142 Cf. *Jn* 13:1.   143 Cf. *Mt* 18:23–35.   144 Cf. *Mt* 5:43–44.   145 Cf. *2 Cor* 5:18–21; John Paul II, *DM* 14. 146 Cf. *Mt* 18:21–22; *Lk* 17:3–4.   147 *Rom* 13:8.

ship. It is lived out in prayer, above all in the Eucharist.[148]

> God does not accept the sacrifice of a sower of disunion, but commands that he depart from the altar so that he may first be reconciled with his brother. For God can be appeased only by prayers that make peace. To God, the better offering is peace, brotherly concord, and a people made one in the unity of the Father, Son, and Holy Spirit.[149]

VI. "AND LEAD US NOT INTO TEMPTATION"

2846 This petition goes to the root of the preceding one, for our sins result from our consenting to temptation; we therefore ask our Father not to "lead" us *164* into temptation. It is difficult to translate the Greek verb used by a single English word: the Greek means both "do not allow us to enter into temptation" and "do not let us yield to temptation."[150] "God cannot be tempted by evil and he himself tempts no one";[151] on the contrary, he wants to set us free from evil. We ask him not to allow us to take the way that leads to sin. We are engaged in the battle "between flesh and spirit"; *2516* this petition implores the Spirit of discernment and strength.

2847 The Holy Spirit makes us *discern* between trials, which are necessary for the growth of the inner man,[152] and temptation, which leads to sin and death.[153] We must also discern between being tempted and consenting to temptation. Finally, discernment unmasks the lie *2284* of temptation, whose object appears to be good, a "delight to the eyes" and desirable,[154] when in reality its fruit is death.

> God does not want to impose the good, but wants free beings.... There is a certain usefulness to temptation. No one but God knows what our soul has received from him, not even we ourselves. But temptation reveals it in order to teach us to know ourselves, and in this way we discover our evil in-

---

148 Cf. *Mt* 5:23–24; *1 Jn* 3:19–24.   149 St. Cyprian, *De Dom. orat.* 23: PL 4, 535–536; cf. *Mt* 5:24.   150 Cf. *Mt* 26:41.   151 *Jas* 1:13.   152 Cf. *Lk* 8:13–15; *Acts* 14:22; *Rom* 5:3–5; *2 Tim* 3:12.   153 Cf. *Jas* 1:14–15.   154 Cf. *Gen* 3:6.

clinations and are obliged to give thanks for the
goods that temptation has revealed to us.[155]

2848 "Lead us not into temptation" implies a *decision
of the heart:* "For where your treasure is, there will your
heart be also. . . . No one can serve two masters."[156] "If
we live by the Spirit, let us also walk by the Spirit."[157] In
this assent to the Holy Spirit the Father gives us
strength. "No testing has overtaken you that is not
1808 common to man. God is faithful, and he will not let you
be tempted beyond your strength, but with the temptation will also provide the way of escape, so that you
may be able to endure it."[158]

2849 Such a battle and such a victory become possible
only through prayer. It is by his prayer that Jesus van-
quishes the tempter, both at the outset of his public mission and in the ultimate struggle of his agony.[159] In this
petition to our heavenly Father, Christ unites us to his
540, 612 battle and his agony. He urges us to *vigilance* of the
heart in communion with his own. Vigilance is "custody
2612 of the heart," and Jesus prayed for us to the Father:
"Keep them in your name."[160] The Holy Spirit constantly seeks to awaken us to keep watch.[161] Finally, this
petition takes on all its dramatic meaning in relation to
the last temptation of our earthly battle; it asks for *final
perseverance.* "Lo, I am coming like a thief! Blessed is
162 he who is awake."[162]

VII. "BUT DELIVER US FROM EVIL"
2850 The last petition to our Father is also included in
Jesus' prayer: "I am not asking you to take them out of
the world, but I ask you to protect them from the evil
one."[163] It touches each of us personally, but it is always
"we" who pray, in communion with the whole Church,
for the deliverance of the whole human family. The
Lord's Prayer continually opens us to the range of God's
economy of salvation. Our interdependence in the

155 Origen, *De orat.* 29: PG 11, 544CD.   156 *Mt* 6:21, 24.   157 *Gal* 5:25.
158 *1 Cor* 10:13.   159 Cf. *Mt* 4:1–11; 26:36–44.   160 *Jn* 17:11; cf. *Mk* 13:9,
23, 33–37; 14:38; *Lk* 12:35–40.   161 Cf. *1 Cor* 16:13; *Col* 4:2; *1 Thess* 5:6;
1 Pet 5:8.   162 *Rev* 16:15.   163 *Jn* 17:15.

drama of sin and death is turned into solidarity in the Body of Christ, the "communion of saints."[164]   *309*

2851 In this petition, evil is not an abstraction, but refers to a person, Satan, the Evil One, the angel who opposes God. The devil *(dia-bolos)* is the one who "throws himself across" God's plan and his work of sal-   *391* vation accomplished in Christ.

2852 "A murderer from the beginning, . . . a liar and the father of lies," Satan is "the deceiver of the whole world."[165] Through him sin and death entered the world and by his definitive defeat all creation will be "freed from the corruption of sin and death."[166] Now "we know that anyone born of God does not sin, but He who was born of God keeps him, and the evil one does not touch him. We know that we are of God, and the whole world is in the power of the evil one."[167]

> The Lord who has taken away your sin and pardoned your faults also protects you and keeps you from the wiles of your adversary the devil, so that the enemy, who is accustomed to leading into sin, may not surprise you. One who entrusts himself to God does not dread the devil. "If God is for us, who is against us?"[168]

2853 Victory over the "prince of this world"[169] was   *677* won once for all at the Hour when Jesus freely gave himself up to death to give us his life. This is the judgment of this world, and the prince of this world is "cast out."[170] "He pursued the woman"[171] but had no hold on her: the new Eve, "full of grace" of the Holy Spirit, is preserved from sin and the corruption of death (the Im- *490* maculate Conception and the Assumption of the Most *972* Holy Mother of God, Mary, ever virgin). "Then the dragon was angry with the woman, and went off to make war on the rest of her offspring."[172] Therefore the Spirit and the Church pray: "Come, Lord Jesus,"[173] since his coming will deliver us from the Evil One.

---

164 Cf. *RP* 16.   165 *Jn* 8:44; *Rev* 12:9.   166 *Roman Missal,* Eucharistic Prayer IV, 125.   167 *1 Jn* 5:18–19.   168 St. Ambrose, *De Sacr.* 5, 4, 30: PL 16, 454; cf. *Rom* 8:31.   169 *Jn* 14:30.   170 *Jn* 12:31; *Rev* 12:10.   171 *Rev* 12:13–16. 172 *Rev* 12:17.   173 *Rev* 22:17, 20.

2854 When we ask to be delivered from the Evil One, we pray as well to be freed from all evils, present, past, and future, of which he is the author or instigator. In this final petition, the Church brings before the Father all the distress of the world. Along with deliverance from the evils that overwhelm humanity, she implores the precious gift of peace and the grace of perseverance
2632 in expectation of Christ's return. By praying in this way, she anticipates in humility of faith the gathering together of everyone and everything in him who has "the keys of Death and Hades," who "is and who was and who is to come, the Almighty."[174]

> Deliver us, Lord, we beseech you, from every evil and grant us peace in our day, so that aided by your mercy we might be ever free from sin and protected from all anxiety, as we await the blessed hope and
> 1041   the coming of our Savior, Jesus Christ.[175]

ARTICLE 4
THE FINAL DOXOLOGY

2760 **2855** The final doxology, "For the kingdom, the power and the glory are yours, now and forever," takes up again, by inclusion, the first three petitions to our Father: the glorification of his name, the coming of his reign, and the power of his saving will. But these prayers are now proclaimed as adoration and thanksgiving, as in the liturgy of heaven.[176] The ruler of this world has mendaciously attributed to himself the three titles of kingship, power, and glory.[177] Christ, the Lord, restores them to his Father and our Father, until he hands over the kingdom to him when the mystery of salvation will be brought to its completion and God will be all in all.[178]

1061-1065 **2856** "Then, after the prayer is over you say 'Amen,'

---

174 *Rev* 1:8, 18; cf. *Rev* 1:4; *Eph* 1:10.   175 *Roman Missal*, Embolism after the Lord's Prayer, 126: *Libera nos, quæsumus, Domine, ab omnibus malis, da propitius pacem in diebus nostris, ut, ope misericordiæ tuæ adiuti, et a peccato simus semper liberi, et ab omni perturbatione securi: expectantes beatam spem et adventum Salvatoris nostri Iesu Christi.*   176 Cf. *Rev* 1:6; 4:11; 5:13.   177 Cf. *Lk* 4:5–6.   178 1 *Cor* 15:24–28.

which means 'So be it,' thus ratifying with our 'Amen' what is contained in the prayer that God has taught us."[179]

IN BRIEF

2857   In the Our Father, the object of the first three petitions is the glory of the Father: the sanctification of his name, the coming of the kingdom, and the fulfillment of his will. The four others present our wants to him: they ask that our lives be nourished, healed of sin, and made victorious in the struggle of good over evil.

2858   By asking "hallowed be thy name" we enter into God's plan, the sanctification of his name—revealed first to Moses and then in Jesus—by us and in us, in every nation and in each man.

2859   By the second petition, the Church looks first to Christ's return and the final coming of the Reign of God. It also prays for the growth of the Kingdom of God in the "today" of our own lives.

2860   In the third petition, we ask our Father to unite our will to that of his Son, so as to fulfill his plan of salvation in the life of the world.

2861   In the fourth petition, by saying "give us," we express in communion with our brethren our filial trust in our heavenly Father. "Our daily bread" refers to the earthly nourishment necessary to everyone for subsistence, and also to the Bread of Life: the Word of God and the Body of Christ. It is received in God's "today," as the indispensable, (super-) essential nourishment of the feast of the coming Kingdom anticipated in the Eucharist.

2862   The fifth petition begs God's mercy for our offences, mercy which can penetrate our hearts

---

179 St. Cyril of Jerusalem, *Catech. myst.* 5, 18: PG 33, 1124; cf. *Lk* 1:38.

only if we have learned to forgive our enemies, with the example and help of Christ.

2863   When we say "lead us not into temptation" we are asking God not to allow us to take the path that leads to sin. This petition implores the Spirit of discernment and strength; it requests the grace of vigilance and final perseverance.

2864   In the last petition, "but deliver us from evil," Christians pray to God with the Church to show forth the victory, already won by Christ, over the "ruler of this world," Satan, the angel personally opposed to God and to his plan of salvation.

2865   By the final "Amen," we express our "fiat" concerning the seven petitions: "So be it."

SUBJECT INDEX

Prefatory Note to Index
The main entry words are printed in bold type as are references to definitions or exact descriptions (for example, **Angels; demons: 327–330**). References to "In Brief" texts are printed in italics (for example, **Angels; demons:** *350*). The sub-headings that follow main entries provide additional information about the same or closely related topics (for example: **Abraham:** call of Abraham: *59, 72, 762*). Cross references with "see" or "see also" supply information about relevant main entry words. The primary objective in constructing this index was to provide the most comprehensive survey possible of the contents, not the most complete listing of all references to a given subject.

Abortion: 2270–75
condemnation in the early Church: 2271
excommunication as penalty: 2272
inalienable right to life: 2273
protection of human life from the moment of conception: 2270, *2319, 2322–23*
Abraham
call of Abraham: 59, 72, 762
faith of Abraham: 144–46, 165, 1080, 2676
hope of Abraham: 1819
in the Muslim religion: 841
prayer of Abraham: 2570–72, *2592, 2635*
promise to Abraham: 705–6, 762, 1222, 1716, 2810
fulfillment of the promises: 422, *1725,* 2619

Absolution: see Penance, sacrament of: as liturgical celebration
Acedia: (spiritual sloth)
as capital sin: 1866
as sin against love: 2094
as temptation in prayer: 2733
Act; action
beatitude as meaning and end: 1719, 1723
circumstances and consequences: 1754
end does not justify the means: 1753, *1759*
intention and goal: 1752–53
judgment as good or bad: 1749–50, 1755–56, *1757, 1760*
object: 1751, *1758*
Adoration
and blessing: 1078, 2628, 2781
and respect for God's name: 2143, 2145

and sacred art: 2502
of the Blessed Sacrament:
    1178, 1183, 1378–81,
    1418, 2691, *2696*
prayer as expression of:
    2098
sacrifice as sign of: 2099
worship of God by the
    Church: 1083
see also: Worship
Adultery: 2380–81
as grave sin: 1756, 1856,
    1858, *2400*
importance of conjugal
    fidelity: 1646, 2364–65,
    2397
in Jesus' preaching: 2336
Advent: 524, 1095
see also Liturgy: liturgical
    seasons
Agnosticism
as practical atheism: 2128
forms: 2127
Alcohol
abuse: 2290
Almsgiving
as act of religion: 1969
as expression of penance:
    1434, 1438
as form of piety: 575, 2101
as witness to fraternal
    charity: 2447, *2462*
on behalf of the dead:
    1032
**Altar: 1181–82, 1383,
    2570**
Amputation: see Medical
    treatment
Analogy
between Creator and
    creature: 41
of faith: 114
Anamnesis
in the Eucharistic
    celebration: 1354, 1362
in the general liturgical
    celebration: 1103

in the sacramental
    celebration: 1106
**Angels; demons: 327–330,
    *350***
as servants of Christ: 331,
    351, 1034, 1038
"fall" of angels:
    as irrevocable sin:
        392–93, *414*
    by their free decision:
        391–92
    Satan as a "fallen
        angel": 391, *414*
given intelligence and free
    will: 311
guardian angels: 336
heaven as "place" of
    angels: 326, 1023
in salvation history:
    332–33
significance for the
    Church: 334–35, *352*
"son of God" as title for
    angels: 441
Anger; wrath
as passion: 1765
as sin:
    consequence of original
        sin: 2259
    desire for vengeance:
        2302
    forbidden in Sermon on
        the Mount: 2262
    mortal sin: 1866, 2302
Animals
experimentation on: 2417
exploitation forbidden:
    2415, 2418
place in creation: 2415–16
relationship to man:
    2417–18, *2457*
Anointing
Anointing of the Sick:
    1523
as sign of the Holy Spirit:
    695
Baptism: 1237

Confirmation: 1289,
    1293–96
ordination of priests and
    bishops: 1574
Anointing of the Sick
administration by priests
    and bishops: 1516, *1530*
as a sacrament:
    one of the seven
    sacraments: 1113, 1210
    "sacrament of the
    dying": 1523
    since the beginning of
    the Church: 1510
liturgical celebration:
    1517
    elements of the
    celebration: 1518–19,
    1531
main effects: 1520–23,
    1532
    comfort, peace, and
    courage: 1520
    forgiveness of sins: 1520
    preparation for death:
    1523
    sanctification of the
    Church: 1522
    union with the Passion
    of Christ: 1521
purpose: 1499, 1511,
    1526–27
reception:
    Eucharist as "viaticum":
    1517, 1524–25
    preparation: 1516–17
    reception recommended:
    1515, *1528*
    recipient: 1514
    repeated reception:
    1515, *1529*
rite: 1513
tradition of "Extreme
    Unction": 1512
Antichrist: 675
see also: Jesus: Second
    Coming

Anxiety: 2088
Apostasy: 2089, 817
Apostles
apostolic teaching as way
    to heaven: 75–77, 1724
called by Jesus to follow
    him: 1506
Church built on the
    foundation of the
    apostles: 857, 860
commissioned by Jesus: 2,
    858–60
power of the keys: 981
preach the Paschal
    mystery: 571
share in Christ's ministry
    of healing: 1506,
    1510–11
share in Christ's power of
    sanctification: 1087
successors: 3
witnesses of the
    Resurrection: 860
see also: Apostolic
    succession
Apostolate: 863, 864, 900,
    905
Apostolic succession
and the sacrament of Holy
    Orders: 1576
apostles' appointment of
    successors: 77, 860–62
as bond of the Church's
    unity: 815
as sign of the Church's
    catholicity: 830, 833
in the Eastern Churches:
    1399
significance for the liturgy:
    1087
see also: Apostles
Armed forces; soldiers:
    2310
Arms production: 2316
Arms trade: 2316
Art: 2501, *2513*
task of sacred art: 2502–3

truth and beauty: 2500
Artificial insemination: see
  Matrimony: purpose
Ascension: see Jesus Christ
Ascesis
as means to self-mastery:
  1734, 2340
as way to perfection: 2015
Astrology: 2116
Atheism: 2123–26, 2128,
  2140
Authority
and common good: 1906
and duties of citizens:
  2238–43
and family: 2199, 2207
basis for authority:
  God: 1899
  human nature: 1898
  respect for the human
    person: 1930
duty to respect public
  authority: 2234
legitimate exercise of
  authority: 1903, 2236
limitations: 2235
necessary for human
  community: 1898
role of service: 2235
tasks: 1902, 2236
Autopsy: 2301
Avarice: 1866, 2539, *2541,*
  2552
Aversion: see Passions:
  diversity
Baptism
administration and
  reception:
  administration by the
    laity: 903
  cannot be repeated:
    1272
  eligibility: 1246
  in emergency: *1284*
  ordinary ministers:
    1256
as sacrament:

common character of
  Baptism, Confirmation,
  and Holy Orders: 1121
one of the seven
  sacraments: 1113, 1210
sacrament of Christian
  initiation: 1212
sacrament of faith: 1253
sacrament of
  regeneration: 1213
Baptism and sin:
  Baptism erases effects of
    original sin: 405
  first sacrament of
    forgiveness of sins:
    977–78, *985*
  further struggle against
    sin is necessary: 978,
    1264, 2520
  justification granted:
    1266, 1992
  loss of baptismal grace
    through sin: 1446
  makes a "new creation"
    of the neophyte: 1265
  remission of all sins and
    punishment for sins:
    1263, 2520
Baptism and the
  sacrament of Penance:
  1425–26
Baptism in the Church:
  1226–28, *1277*
Baptism of adults:
  1247–49
Baptism of infants:
  and catechetical
    instruction: 1231
  and parental duty: 1251
  as practice from the
    beginning of the Church:
    1252, *1282*
  needed to free from
    original sin: 1250
Baptism of Jesus:
  Baptism of Jesus by
    John: 438

Baptism of the Holy Spirit compared to John's baptism: 720
importance of Jesus' Baptism: 536–37, 1223
baptismal name: 2156, 2165
baptismal promises: 2340
basic contents: 14
called:
  "Baptism": 1214
  "illumination": 1216
  "washing of regeneration and renewal in the Holy Spirit": 1215
effects: 1279:
  ability to celebrate the liturgy: 1119, 1141
  builds up the Body of Christ: 798
  entrance into eternal beatitude: 1257
  gives the gifts of the Holy Spirit: 1266
  gives the moral virtues: 1266
  gives the theological virtues: 1266
  grace of rebirth in God: 683
  grants participation in the common priesthood: 1268
  reception as son of God: 1997
  reception into People of God: 804
  reception into the "Body of Christ": 790, 1267
  reception into the Church of Christ: 1267–70
  rights and duties: 1269–70
  seals with an indelible spiritual mark: 1272–74, 1280

unites with Christ: 790
importance of godparents: 1253–55
interpretation and importance:
  being set apart for God: 931
  connected with faith: 1226
  dying with Christ: 628
  foundation of Christian life: 1213
  foundation of Christian unity: 838, 855, 1271
  in the Apostle Paul: 1227
  "nuptial mystery": 1617
  prefigured in salvation history: 1217–22
  symbol of Christ's death on the Cross: 1220
necessity:
  "Baptism of blood": 1258
  Baptism of desire: 1258, 1260, 1281
  for salvation: 846, 1257
  unbaptized infants: 1261
rite: 1235–45
  anointing with chrism: 1241–42
  blessing: 1245
  blessing of baptismal water: 1238
    water as symbol: 694
  essential rite: 1239, 1278
  exorcism: 1237
  First Holy Communion: 1244
  formula for administering: 189, 232, 1240
  proclamation of the Word of God: 1236

profession of faith: 1237
renunciation of evil:
1427
sign of the Cross: 1235
white garment and
candle: 1243
see also: Catechumenate
Baptism of infants: see
Baptism
Beatific vision
as fulfillment of all man's
longing: 2548
as goal of life: 163
perfect communion with
God: 2550
see also: Beatitude
Beatitude
as God's gift of grace:
1722
as meaning and end of
human acts: 1719, 1723,
2548
Christian path to
beatitude: 1724
in the New Testament:
1720
see also: Beatific vision
Beatitudes
as central proclamation of
Jesus' preaching: 1716
contents and importance:
1717, *1726*
correspond to man's desire
for happiness: 1718
portray Christian hope:
1820
reveal the meaning and
goal of human acts:
1719
shed light on
characteristics of
Christian life: 1717,
1728
Benevolence: 1829
Births, regulation of: see
Matrimony: purpose
Bishop; Episcopate

as degree in the sacrament
of Holy Orders: 1536
as most important office of
service: 1555
as successor of the
apostles: see Apostolic
succession
power and position: 895
preaching and teaching:
888
presider at the Eucharistic
celebration: 1142, 1561
responsible for his
particular Church: 879,
1560
steward of grace: 893
task of governing in the
Church: 873, 894
see also: Orders, sacrament
of Holy
Bishops, college of
as expression of the
universality of the People
of God: 885
bishop, college of bishops,
and the Pope: 877, 879,
881, 883, 886
charism of infallibility: 891
common concern for the
universal Church: 879,
1560
instituted by Christ: 880
Blasphemy: 2148
magical use of God's name
forbidden: 2149
Blessing
and hope: 2090
every baptized person
called to bless: 1669
in God's plan of salvation:
1079–81, *2645*
of God in the liturgy of the
Church: 1082–83
of the Creator: 1078
Boasting: 2481
Body
body and soul: 364–65

Call: see vocation

Calumny (slander): 2475, 2477, 2479, 2507

Capitalism: 2425

Catechesis: 5
and the liturgy: 1074–75
catechesis on creation as decisive: 282
Christ as the heart of catechesis: 426–29, 1698
exercise of catechesis:
   by the laity: 906
   in preaching and teaching: 2033
goal: 4
in the family: 2226
parable of the two ways: 1696
significance for the Church: 6–10
task: 1697, 2688

"Catechism of the Catholic Church"
adaptations and inculturation: 24
addressees: 12
as organic presentation of the faith: 18
development: 10
division and numbering of the Decalogue: 2066
goal: 11
main sources: 11
orientation to the Apostles' Creed: 196
pastoral principle: 25
precursors: 9
presentation of the liturgy: 1075
structure: 13–17

Catechumenate; Catechumens
as members of the Church: 1249
as way of Christian initiation: 1229

Baptism of desire: 1258–60
for adults: 1232
in the first centuries of the Church: 1230
inculturation of the initiation rites: 1232
see also: Baptism

Catechumens, oil of
in the anointing at Baptism: 1237
see also: Baptism

"Catholic": 830

Celibacy
in the Eastern Churches: 1580
in the Roman Catholic Church: 1579
see also: Orders, sacrament of Holy; Virginity; Chastity

Charisms: 799
are to be tested: 801
as gift of grace: 2003
as place of encounter with the Holy Spirit: 688
as means by which the Church is built up: 951, 2003
meaning and purpose: 799–801
special charisms:
   healing: 1508
   infallibility of the Pastors of the Church: 890
   infallibility of the Pope: 2035

Charity: (see also Love)
as theological virtue: 1813, 1822–29, *1844*
and hope: 1818
fruit of the Holy Spirit: 736, 1832
in the Decalogue: *2086*, 2093–94, 2197
interpretation and place and the Law of Christ: 1824

as "soul of the apostolate": 864

as most important social commandment: 1889

as virtue:
love of enemies: 1825
new commandment of love: 1823

bond of the Church's unity: 815

fulfillment of the Law: 2055

sin as offense against charity: 1849, 1855, 2094

Charms (amulets): 2117

Chastity

as fruit of the Holy Spirit: 1832

as evangelical counsel: see Evangelical counsels

see also: Virtues: cardinal virtues; Matrimony

Children; Childrearing: see Parents

Choir

as liturgical ministry: 1143

Chrism: 1241

reservation: 1183

see also: Anointing

"Chrismation"

as name for Confirmation in the Eastern Churches: 1113, 1289

Christ: see Jesus Christ: names and designations: titles; Messiah

Christian

called to sanctity: 825

Christians as "temple of the Holy Spirit": 1695

commission to imitate Christ: 1694

life and activity of the Christian:
according to the evangelical counsels: 915

depicted in the Sermon on the Mount: 1717

for the building up of the Church: 2045

for the coming of the Kingdom of Christ: 2046

fundamental: 1692, 1695

goal is to attain the mind of Christ: 1694

in the mission of the Church: 2044

sustained by the gifts of the Holy Spirit: 1830

relations between Catholics and non-Catholics: 818

Christmas: 525

Church

and non-Christians: 839
Church as assembly of men scattered and led astray by sin: 845
common origin and goal of all men: 842
limitations and errors in men's image of God: 844
necessity of the Church for salvation: 846–48
search for God in non-Christian religions: 843
the Church and the Jews: 839–40
the Church and the Moslems: 841

and revelation:
judgment of the Church about the meaning of Scripture: 119
place of the Gospels: 127
relation with the Old Testament: 128–29
respect of the Church for revelation: 82
revelation about man: 2419
revelation of the Church: 726

revelation of the Holy
Spirit: 688
Sacred Scripture: 104,
113, 119, 127, 131, 572
veneration of Sacred
Scripture: 103
as communion:
as priestly communion:
1119
as sacrament of
communion in the
liturgy: 1108
communion as deepest
vocation of the Church:
959
communion in
charisms: 951
communion of faith:
949
communion in charity:
953
"communion of saints":
946–48, 953, *960*
with Jesus: 787–96
with the dead: *958*
with the saints: 954–57,
961
attributes: 750, 811,
825–26, 865
historical dimension:
770
point to essential
characteristics: 811, *870*
the "apostolic" Church:
857–65, *869*
apostolic character of
the Church: 863
"apostolic" in
threefold sense: 857
apostolicity of
bishops: 862
successors appointed
by apostles: 859, 861
the "catholic" Church:
830–35, 838, *868*
by virtue of Christ:
831

by virtue of her divine
source: 812
call to catholic unity
of the People of God:
836
"catholic": 830
contact with non-
Catholic Churches:
838
full incorporation into
the Church: 837
missionary work as
furthering catholicity:
849
the "holy" Church:
823–29, *867*
and Mary: 829
both holy and sinful:
825, 827
by virtue of Christ:
823
canonization: 828
sanctifying by virtue
of Christ: 824
the "one" Church:
813–22, *866*
by virtue of her source
and "soul": 813
Christ's concern to
maintain unity:
820–22
diversity within this
unity: 814
missionary work
toward unity: 855
non-Catholic Christian
Churches: 818–19
Pope and bishops as
bond of unity: 815–16
renewal to preserve
unity: 821
wounds to Church
unity: 817
built on confession of Jesus
Christ as Messiah: 424
Christ as Head: 669
Church and State

principles of the Church-
State relationship:
2244–46
protection of the
transcendent character of
the human person by the
Church: 2245
Church of Rome presides:
834
goal:
proclaiming the Paschal
mystery: 571
sanctification of men:
824
union of mankind with
God: 772, 773
important aspects:
aid in social
development: 2442
catechesis: 6, 7
Church at the end of
time: 665–67, 675, 686,
1042
"depositum fidei": 84,
97, 175
discrepancy between the
message proclaimed and
the human reality: 672,
853
faith of the Church:
1124
guidance and support by
the Holy Spirit: 737,
768
Mary's place in the
mystery of the Church:
963–75
presence of Christ in the
Church: 1380
interpretation:
Body of Christ: 779,
789, 805:
Christ as Head of the
Body: 792, 807
close union of the
faithful with Christ:
790

individual members
and the Body: 791
instrument of Christ:
775–76
provided with
charisms and
ministries by Christ:
794, 806
Bride of Christ: 796, 808
"goal of all things": 760
historical as well as
spiritual reality: 770–71
mystery and sacrament:
774–76
pilgrim Church on the
way to perfection: 769
sacrament of the life of
God: 932
sacrament of the mission
of Christ and the Holy
Spirit: 738
temple of the Holy
Spirit: 797–98, 809
universal sacrament of
salvation: 849, 780
liturgy:
Church and Eucharist:
Church made by the
Eucharist: 1396
Eucharist as center of
the Church's life:
1343, 2177
Eucharist as mystery
of communion with
God: 1118
examination of forms of
prayer by the
Magisterium: 2663
liturgy as action of the
Church: 1070–72
presence of Christ in the
liturgy: 1088
sacraments:
belonging to the
Church: 1118
Church as dispenser:
1117

communication of
Christ: 947
mission of Christ and the
Holy Spirit accomplished
in the Church: 737,
778
name "Church": 751–52,
777
necessity for salvation:
correct understanding of
concept: 846–48
origin:
from the pierced heart of
Jesus: 766
in the call of the Twelve:
763–65
prepared in the Old
Covenant: 762
revelation of the Church
at Pentecost: 767, 1076
the Father's decision:
759, 761
particular Churches with
their own traditions: 814
structure, states, and
constitution:
apostles as foundation
stones: 642, *935*
catechumens: 1249
Christ as source of
ministry: 874
hierarchical constitution:
771, 874–87, 914
importance of the family
as "domestic church":
1656–58, *1666*
Israel as root: 60
Jesus as Head: 669
laity in the Church:
897–913, *940–43*
ministry: 888–96
ministry of
sanctification: 893
state of consecrated life:
914, *944–45*
approval of new
forms: 919

consecrated virginity:
922–24
eremitical life: 920–21
in the Church from
the beginning: 918
not part of
hierarchical structure:
914
religious life:
all religious as
collaborators of
diocesan bishop:
927
and the spread of
the Gospel: 927
as expression of
God's love: 926
characteristic
features: 925
in institutes
canonically erected
by the Church: 925
profession of the
evangelical counsels:
915
secular institutes:
928–29
significance: 916,
931–33
societies of apostolic
life: 930
various forms: 917
task of governing:
as ministry of service:
876, 894–95
bishops' conferences
and patriarchates: 887
bond between the
Pope and the college
of bishops: 879
collegial character:
877
cooperation of the
laity in governing
Church: 911
personal character:
878

Peter and the apostles: 881, 936
place of an Ecumenical Council: 884
place of individual bishops: 886, 938
place of the college of bishops: 883, 939
place of the Pope: 882, 937
sacramental conferral: 875
symbolism of the college of bishops: 885

teaching ministry: 888–92
  as service to the Word of God: 86
  authority over the natural law: 2036
  bishop commissioned by Christ to preach and teach: 888
  charism of infallibility:
    of an Ecumenical Council: 891
    of the Church: 889
    of the college of bishops: 891
    of the faithful's "supernatural sense of the faith": 889
    of the Pope: 891, 2035
    of the shepherds of the Church: 890, 2051
  exercised through catechesis and preaching: 2033, 2049–50
  laity in the teaching ministry: 906
  meaning: 890

necessity to instruct the faithful: 2037
obedience to: 87, 892, 2037
regular teaching office of the Pope and bishops: 2034
spirit in which exercised: 2039
task: 85, 100, 2032
the three states: 954, 934

symbols: 753
  building: 756
  cultivated field: 755
  "holy remnant": 710
  "Jerusalem above": 757
  Mary as "type" of the Church: 507, 967
  Mother: 169, 757
  olive tree: 755
  sheepfold: 754
  teacher in faith: 169
  temple of God: 756

tasks and opportunities:
  accompanying the dead: 1683
  attestation to the goodness of creation: 299
  concern for the temporal common good: 2420, 2458
  confession:
    of faith: 172–75
    of the Kingship of Christ: 2105
    of the triune God: 152, 258, 738
  conversion as a continuing task: 1428
  example of Christian holiness: 2030
  mission in the world: 2044–45
  moral judgment: 2420
  preservation of the faith: 98, 168, 171, 173

remission of sins:
  commanded by
  Christ: 1442
  granting of
  indulgences: 1478
  power of
  absolution: 827,
  979–83, 1442
speaking about God: 39
transmission and
  interpretation of
  revelation: 82
vocation:
  as missionary Church:
  767
  as People of God from
  the Jews and Gentiles:
  781–86
  as pilgrim Church: 671
  as the "family of God":
  1
  to the service of God:
  783–86
Clairvoyance: 2116
Collectivism: 1885
Commandment: see
  Decalogue; Law
Common good: 1906
acceptance of personal
  responsibility: 1914
and society: 1905
and the State: 1910
concern of the Church with
  temporal aspects: 2420
elements: 1906–9
  peace and security: 1909
  respect for the person:
  1907
  social well-being: 1908
obligation of all to
  promote: 1913
universal common good:
  1911
Communion: see Eucharist;
  Eucharistic celebration
Communion of saints: see
  Church: as communion

Concubinage: 2390
Concupiscence: 1264,
  1426
see also: Desires,
  disordered
Confession: see Penance,
  sacrament of
Confirmation
administration:
  bishop as ordinary
  minister: 1312–13
  by a priest: 1313–14
  given only once: 1304
as one of the seven
  sacraments: 1113,
  1210
as sacrament of Christian
  initiation: 1212, 1285
celebration:
  anointing: 1293–96
  biblical and ancient
  meaning: 1293
  kiss of peace: 1301
  sacramental meaning
  in Confirmation:
  1294–95
consecration of the holy
  chrism: 1297
different traditions in the
  East and in the West:
  1290–92, *1318*
essential rite: 1300, *1320*
invocation for the
  outpouring of the Holy
  Spirit: 1299
renewal of baptismal
  promises: 1298, *1321*
effects:
  confers indelible spiritual
  mark: 1304, *1317*
  deepens baptismal grace:
  1303
  deeper rooting in the
  divine sonship: 1303
  gives special power to
  confess the Christian
  faith: 1303

increases the gifts of the Holy Spirit: 1303
inner union with Christ: 1303
more perfect bond with the Church: 1303
outpouring of the Holy Spirit: 1302
perfects the common priesthood of the faithful: 1305
necessary to complete the grace of Baptism: 1285, 1306, 1314, *1316*
reception:
at the "age of discretion": 1306–8, *1319*
in danger of death: 1307
preparation for reception: 1309–10
roots:
anointing with chrism: 1289
descent of the Holy Spirit on Jesus: 1286
early Christian practice: 1288, *1315*
outpouring of the Holy Spirit on Pentecost: 1287
significance of the name "Confirmation": 1242, 1289
sponsor: 1311
the "Chrismation" of the Eastern Churches: 1242
Conscience, examination of
as preparation to receive the sacrament of Penance: 1454
Conscience: 1778; *1795–96*
decisions in conformity with: 1780, 1786–89, *1799–1800*, 1806
effect: 1776–77, *1797*

erroneous judgment: 1790–94
formation of: 1783–85, *1798*, 1971
need to examine: 1779
permits acceptance of responsibility: 1781
right to act according to: 1782
sin as offense against: 1849
stirring of: 1453
Conscientious objectors: 2311
Consecration
at administration of the sacrament of Holy Orders: 1538
of the Eucharistic species: 1377
Consecration of virgins: see Evangelical counsels
Consummation at the end of time
of heaven and earth: 1042–44
of man: 1045
of the Church: 1042, 1053
of the cosmos: 1046–47
precise time unknown: 1048
Contraception: see Matrimony: purpose
Contracts: 2410–11
Contrition; conversion
as confidence in God's grace: 1431
as first act of the penitent: 1451
as hope for God's mercy: 1431
as the work of God: 1432–33, *1489*
as turning from evil: 1431, *1490*
as turning toward God: 821–22

call to conversion in the proclamation of the Gospel: 1427

conversion:
continuing task for the Christian: 1428
continuing task of the whole Church: 1428

described in the parable of the prodigal son: 1439

expressions:
almsgiving: 1434
fasting: 1434
prayer: 1434

external expression necessary: 1430

"imperfect contrition": 1453

interior contrition important: 1430

"perfect contrition": 1452

Conversion: see Contrition

Correction: 1829

Cosmos
as source of knowledge about God: 1147
see Creation; World

Council
infallibility of a Council: 891
place of Ecumenical Councils: 884
see also: Church

Counsel
as gift of the Holy Spirit: 1831

Creation:
act of creation as beginning of God's work: 198, 280, 338
adoration of God as task of all creation: 347
beauty of creation: 341
conservation of creation: 2415–18, 2456
creatures:

consequences of original sin for creation: 400
goodness of every creature: 339
hierarchy: 342
importance of the order of creation: 346
interdependence of creatures: 340
man as summit of the work of creation: 343, *353, 355*
man created in God's image: *355, 374, 380*
purpose of the creation of man: *356, 381*
solidarity: 344

culmination of creation in the redemption: 349

entrusted to man: 299

God creates "out of nothing": *296, 317–18*

God the Creator:
beauty of the Creator: 341
Christ is Lord of creation: 668
created in freedom: 296
mystery of Christ as illumination of the mystery of creation: 280
revelation of the Creator God:
in Genesis: 289
inseparable from the Covenant: 288
through reason: 286
to the People Israel: 287
sustains creation: 301, *320*
transcends creation: 300

order of creation: *299, 354*

origin in the Trinity: 258, *291–92, 316, 320*

reason for creation:
293–94, *315, 319*
respect for creation: 2415
Sabbath rest: 314, 345,
347
spiritual and corporeal
creation: 327
theology of creation and
natural science: 283, 284
theology of creation and
philosophy: 285
see also: World
"Credo": see Faith,
profession of
Creed
as name of a profession of
faith: 187
important creeds: 193–95
structure: 190–91
see also: Faith, profession
of
Cremation: 2301
**Cross: see Jesus: death of
Jesus**
Cult: see Worship
Damage
of private or public
property: 2409
Deacon; diaconate
as degree of ordination:
1536, 1543, 1569,
1593
grace of office: 1588
"permanent diaconate":
1571
tasks: 1570, 1596, 1630
see also: Orders, sacrament
of Holy
Death
after death:
"beatific vision": 1028
consummation of heaven
and earth: 1042–50
God predestines no one
to damnation: 1037
heaven: 1023–29, *1053*
hell: 1033–37, *1056–58*

inconceivable mystery of
beatific union with God:
1027
Last Judgment: 1038–41,
1051–52, 1059
no "reincarnation":
1013
Purgatory: 1030–32,
1054
as limitation of earthly life:
1021
Christian dealings with
death:
bodies of the deceased:
2300–2301
Christian interpretation
expressed in the liturgy:
1012
good preparation
important: 1014
importance of burial:
2300
reception of the
sacraments for the dying:
2299
reverence and attention
for the dying: 2299
Christian interpretation of
death:
as entrance into eternal
life: 1020
consequence of original
sin: 400–403, *413,* 1008,
1018
contradiction of the
Good News: 164
end of earthly life: 1007
last enemy of man: 1008
participation in the
death of the Lord: 1006
the positive meaning in
the Christian
interpretation: 1010–14
death of Jesus:
human death
transformed by Christ's
obedience: 1009

Jesus as dead: 650
the descent of Jesus to
the dead: 632–35
separation of soul and
body: 1005, *1016*
Death penalty: see
Punishment
Decalogue: 2056
and the evangelical
counsels: 2053
contents:
basic: 2067, *2080–81*
faith, hope, and charity
in the Decalogue: 2086
the most important
commandment: 2055
division and numbering
of the Decalogue:
2066
full meaning revealed in
New Covenant: 2056
in the preaching of Jesus:
2052–55, *2075–76*
made fruitful only in union
with Jesus: 2074
meaning:
as announcement of
God's will: 2063
as expression of man's
fundamental duties:
2072, *2081*
as foundation and light
of the conscience:
1962
as part of God's
revelation: 2059,
2070–71
as path to the Kingdom
of heaven: 1724
basic: 2070
moral life as response to
God's initiative: 2062
obligation of the
Decalogue: 2072
place in the Church's
Tradition: 2064–68,
2078

place in the Old Covenant:
2056–63, *2077*
the unity of the text: 2069,
2079
Decision, arriving at: see
Conscience
Defense
conditions for military
defense: 2309
legitimate defense and
murder: 2263
obligation to legitimate
defense: 2265, *2231*
right to collective and
personal self-defense:
1909
right to defend society:
2266
right to preserve life: 2263
Deism: 285
Demons: see Angels
"depositum fidei": see
Church: important
aspects; Tradition
Desires, disordered: 2515,
2514–17, 2535–37
see also: Concupiscence
Despair: 2091
Detraction: 2477, 2479,
2507
Development aid
direct aid: 2440
fundamental reforms: 2440
goal: 2441
necessity: 2437–38
responsibility of wealthy
nations: 2439
see also: Poverty; Justice
Devil; Satan
as "fallen" angel: 391, *414*
his activity permitted by
divine providence: 395
his rebellion against God:
392
Jesus' exorcisms: 550
power of the devil is
limited: 395

temptation of Jesus by the devil: 538–40

temptation of man by the devil: 397–98

through sin a certain control over man: 394, 407

Diocese: 833

Disciples

achieve miracles in Christ's name: 434

Jesus gathers them around him: 542, 787

Jesus reveals himself to them as the Risen One: 645, 647

receive the Holy Spirit from Jesus: 730

tasks:
preserve and hand on the message of Christ: 425, 1816

take up the cross and follow: 618

will be guided by the Holy Spirit: 243, 725

Dissension: 1852

Divination: 2116

Divine service: see Liturgy

Divorce: 1650–51, 2382, 2384–86

Church annulment: 1629

conjugal separation: 1649, 2383

consequences for the family: 2385

contracting a new civil marriage: 2384, 1665

immorality of divorce: 2384–85

see also: Matrimony; Adultery

Docetism: 465

Dogma: 88

and the spiritual life: 89

"hierarchy of truths": 90, 234

understanding and formulation: 94

Doubt

voluntary and involuntary: 2088

Dove

as symbol for the Holy Spirit: 701

Doxology: 1103, 2639–49, 2760, 2855

see also: Prayer, forms of

Drug traffic; drug consumption: 2291

Drugs: 2291

Dualism: 285

Dying

accompanied by the Church: 1683

significance of dying: end of the sacramental life: 1682

homeward journey to God: 1681

see also: Death

Earth: see Creation; World

Easter

as central Christian feast: 638, 1169

date of Easter: 1170

Easter event: 639, 640

institution of the Eucharist: 1339–40

Paschal feast as memorial of God's act of salvation: 1363–64

twofold Paschal mystery: 654

Ecclesiastical provinces: 887

Economy

different economic interests: 2430

goal and service of economic activity: 2426

responsibility of business managers: 2432

responsibility of the state: 2431

right to economic initiative: 2429

Economy of salvation: 489, 1092, 1095, 1168

Ecumenism: 820–22
see also: Baptism: interpretation and importance

Embryo
a human person from conception on: 2274
duty to protect embryos: 2274
see also: Matrimony

Emmanuel
as name for the Messiah: 712

Emotions: see Passions

Endtime: see Jesus Christ: Second Coming

Enmity: 1852

Environment: see Creation

Envy: 2539
as capital sin and mortal sin: 1866, 2538–39, 2553–54
roots and consequences: 2540

Eparchy: 833

Epiclesis
as prayer for communion with the mystery of Christ: 1109
in the celebration of the liturgy: 1105
in the sacramental celebration: 1106, 1127

Episcopal conferences: 887

Episcopate: see Bishop

Eremitical life: see Evangelical counsels; Church: structure

Eternal life
death as entrance into eternal life: 1020

vision of the divine being: 1023
see also: Resurrection of the dead

Eucharist
as sacrament:
as one of the seven sacraments: 1113, 1210
as the central Christian sacrament: 1211, 1324
of Christian initiation: 1212, 1322
of passage from death to life: 1524
of those in full communion of the Church: 1395
called:
as designation of the Eucharistic form: 1355
"Breaking of the Bread": 1329
"Communion": 1331
"Eucharist": 1328
"Eucharistic assembly": 1329
"Holy and Divine Liturgy": 1330
"Holy Mass": 1332
"Holy Sacrifice" or "Sacrifice of the Mass": 1330
"Lord's Supper": 1329
"Memorial": 1330
"wedding feast": 1617
Christ's presence:
adoration of the Eucharistic species: 1378, *1418*
in the Eucharistic species: 1088, 1373–77, *1413*
presence of the mystery of Christ: 737
significance of Christ's presence in the Church: 1380–81

commits us to the poor: 1397

eschatological interpretation:
  as anticipation of heavenly glory: 1402
  as manifest sign of hope: 1405
  Jesus' interpretation at the Last Supper: 1403
  the Church's continuation of this interpretation: 1404

importance:
  as abridgment and summation of faith: 1327
  as enabling participation in the divine life: 1325
  as enabling the unity of the People of God: 1325
  as foretaste of the resurrection: 1000, 1370
  as memorial of the mystery of salvation: 1099
  as source and summit of Christian life: 1324–27
  as source of strength for the priestly ministry: 1566
  as union with Christ: 790, 1382, 1416
  as union with God: 1118
  in the Church's ministry of sanctification: 893

institution:
  by Jesus Christ: 611, 1323, 1337–40, 1406
  "for the forgiveness of sins": 1846

main effects:
  delivers from sin: 1393–94
  increases the grace of Baptism: 1392
  increases union with Christ: 1391, 1416
  makes the Church: 1396, 1407
  preserves from future mortal sins: 1395
  strengthens the spiritual life: 1394

only validly ordained priests can preside: 1411

reception of Communion: 1415, 1417

sacrificial character:
  as sacrifice of praise: 1359–61, 2643
  Eucharist as sacrifice: 1365–72, 1410, 1414
  full participation of the faithful: 1372
  represents the sacrifice of the Cross: 1366
  sacrifice offered for the faithful departed: 1371
  union of the entire Church in the Eucharistic sacrifice: 1369
  union with the heavenly liturgy: 1326, 1370

sacrilege against the Eucharist especially grave: 2120

signs: 1333–36, 1412
  bread and wine: 1333
  bread and wine in the Old Covenant: 1334
  Eucharist as "stumbling block": 1336
  Jesus' use of bread and wine: 1335

"transubstantiation": 1373–77, 1413

Eucharistic celebration; Communion; celebration of Mass
  commanded by Christ: 1341–44

as center of the Church's
life: 1343
as memorial celebration:
1356–57, *1409*
in the Church from the
beginning: 1342–43,
1345
participation as Church
precept: 2042
Eucharistic communion:
with other Churches:
1398–1401
with the Eastern
Churches: 1399
with the Reformed
Churches: 1400
obligation to participate:
1389, 2180
significance of the Sunday
Eucharistic celebration:
2177–79
structure and movement
as action of the
ministerial priesthood:
1552
basic structure:
most important
elements: 1345–55
two parts: 1346, 1408
corresponds to Paschal
meal of the risen Jesus:
1347
movement:
assembly of the
faithful: 1348
collection: 1351
distribution of
Communion:
in danger of death:
1401
by the laity: 903
significance: 1355
Eucharistic prayer:
1352–54
anamnesis and
epiclesis: 1105–6,
1353–54

as memorial:
1362–66
preface: 1352
Liturgy of the Word:
1349
Lord's Prayer: 1355,
2770
presentation of the
gifts: 1350
reception of
Communion:
admission: 1244
as Church precept:
2042
fruits of
Communion:
1391–96
in every celebration
of the Mass: 1388
insistent invitation
to Communion:
1384
preparation:
1385–87
"under both
species": 1390
presider: 1142
significance of bishop's
Eucharistic celebration:
893
Eucharistic ministers: 1348
Eucharistic prayer: see
Eucharistic celebration
Euthanasia
direct euthanasia: 2277,
2324
discontinuing medical
procedures: 2278
duty to protect those who
are weak or
handicapped: 2276
Evangelical counsels
and the Decalogue: 2053
and the Gospel Law:
1973–74
as vows in following Christ
more closely:

as expression of consecrated life: 914–16, *944–45*
consecrated virgins: 922–24
eremitical life: 920–21
eschatological aspect: 931–33
in diverse forms: 917–19
religious life: 925–27
secular institutes: 928–29
societies of apostolic life: 930
recommended as guiding rules for every Christian: 915
see also: Poverty; Obedience; Chastity; Virginity; Church: structure

Evil
Christ delivered us from evil: 1708
Christian faith as answer to evil: 309
consequences of evil:
deception in religious behavior: 844
evil and the resurrection from the dead: 998
further inclination toward evil: 1707
the Kingdom of God and evil: 671, 677
universality of evil in human history: 401
experience of evil: 385, 1606
God can draw good from every evil: 312
invocation of evil powers: 2117
moral evil: 311–12
judging an action as good or bad: 1755–56
origin of evil:

derived from sin: 403, 1607
human limitations: 844
permitted by God: 412
scandal as inducement to evil: 2284
physical evil: 310
prevention of evil: 1431
question about evil to be answered only in faith: 385

Excommunication
absolution: 1463
as penalty: 1463
Exorcism: 1673
Jesus' exorcisms: 550
at Baptism: 1237
Extravagance; waste: 2409
Extreme Unction: see Anointing of the Sick
Faith: 26, 142, 146, 150, 155, *176*
"analogy of faith": 114
and eternal life: 163–65
and science: 159
and understanding: 156–59
as answer to evil: 309
as assent to revealed truths: 150
as foretaste of eternal life: 163, *184*
as God's grace: 153, *179*, 224
as human act: 154–55, *180*
as source of moral life: 2087
as source of prayer: 2656
as theological virtue: 1813–16
certainty of faith: 157
content:
Christian faith:
in God: *178*, 223
in God the Creator: 14, 229
in Jesus Christ: **14,**

108, 147, 151, 202,
463, 573
in the Holy Spirit: 14,
152, 202
in the one God: 150,
200, 202, 222–27,
228, 233, 2086
in the signs of
revelation: 156
in the Trinity: 234
consequence of faith:
222–27
ecclesial faith:
Church as mediator of
faith: 168–69, *181,*
197
Church as preserver of
faith: 171, *181*
faith only possible in
the community of
believers: 166
fundamentally:
act of faith aims at
reality expressed: 170
meaning of the
formulas of faith: 170
rooted in the Church's
faith: 162, *182*
vivid understanding of
the content of
revelation: 158
cooperation of intellect,
will, and grace: 155
crises of faith:
conflict with reason: 159
doubt regarding faith:
2088
separation from God by
one's own free choice:
1033
support from the
witnesses of faith: 165
trials: 164
duties of faith:
duty to a life of faith: 13
duty to preserve faith:
162

duty to protect and
nourish faith: 2088
man's fundamental duty
of faith: 2087
examples and models:
Abraham: 145, 146
Israel: 147, 212
Mary: 148–49, 487
the Church: 1124
freedom of faith: 160
motives for faith: 156
necessity of faith: 161,
183, 846
obedience of faith:
general obedience of
faith: 143, 144
Mary's obedience of
faith: 494
no coercion in faith:
160
preservation of faith: 162
transmission of faith:
in preaching Christ: 425
places for instruction in
the faith: 2226
within the scope of this
Catechism: 18
unity of faith: 172–74
various "recipients": 150,
177
Faith, profession of
as designation for a
formula of faith: 186–89
content of Christian
profession of faith:
confession of faith in one
God: 199–202
mention of the mysteries
of Christ: 512
profession within the
framework of the
Church: 167, 815
faith itself as the first and
most important
confession: 199
formulas of faith:
Apostles' Creed: 194

articles of faith: 190, 191

baptismal profession: 189

formulas of faith throughout history: 192, 193

Nicene Creed: 195

significance of common statement of faith: 185

witnessing to faith necessary for salvation: 1816

see also: Creed

Faithful, the; believers: 871

called to different missions: 873

common priesthood of Christ: 1141

"effects" of faith: 737

equal dignity of all believers: 872

infallibility of the faithful:
as a whole without error in faith: 92
"supernatural sense of the faith": 889

invited to accept the faith of the Church: 1124

obedience of faith:
obedience to the bishop: 896
obedience to the teaching authority: 87, 91, 93, 892, 2073

right:
to free access to Sacred Scripture: 131
to information about God's commandments: 2037

Faithfulness

as gift of the Holy Spirit: 736, 1832

in marriage: see Matrimony; Divorce

Family: 2204

and the call to follow Christ more closely: 2232–33

and the consequences of a divorce: 2385

duties of the family members:
duties of grown children toward parents: 2217–18
obedience of minor children to their parents: 2216–17
respect of children for parents: 2215

family and society:
as privileged community: 2206
family as natural society: 1882
family as original cell of society: 2207

foundation, nature, and purpose: 2201–3

importance of family prayer: 2685

importance of relationships between brothers and sisters: 2219

significance: 1655–58, 2208

see also: Parents

Famine: 2269

Fasting; Lenten fasting

as Church precept: 2043

as expression of penance: 1434, 1438

Jesus' fast and the Lenten season: 538–40

see also: Liturgy: liturgical seasons

Father: see Parents; Trinity; God

Fathers of the Church

and catechesis: 8

as source of knowledge of the Holy Spirit: 688

Fear: 1765
and imputability for an act: 1735

Fear of the Lord
as gift of the Holy Spirit: 1831

Feast days: see Holy Days of Obligation

Fertility; infertility: see Matrimony: purpose

Fertilization: see Matrimony: purpose

"Filioque": 246
Eastern and Western tradition: 248
in the development of the understanding of the faith: 247
see also: Trinity

Fire
as symbol of the Holy Spirit: 696, 718

Flattery: 2480

Force: see Violence

Forgery: 2409

Fornication: 2353, 1852

Fortitude
as cardinal virtue: 1805, 1808
as gift of the Holy Spirit: 1831

Fortune-telling: 2116

Fraternal harmony
and solidarity: 1939
in society: 2213
significance of fraternal harmony for the Church: 815, 821

Fraud: 2409

Freedom: 1731, 1744
and evil: 1733
and responsibility: 1734, 1746
as man's merit: 2008
and the good: 1733
as gift from God:
and grace: 1742

freedom through Christ: 908, 1741, 1748
man was created free: 1730
as possibility to choose between good and evil: 1732
effects and perfection of freedom: 1731
exercise of freedom:
in the relationship between human beings: 1738
possibility of freedom: 1861
prerequisites for the exercise of this right: 1740
right to the exercise of freedom: 1738, 1747
freedom makes man a moral subject: 1749, 1745
limits of freedom: 1739

Freedom of religion
as right: 2108–9
see also: Society: duties of the state

Friendship
and chastity: 2347
and grace: 2010
and solidarity: 1939
friendship with God: 277, 374, 396, 1468

Funerals
gestures and rites: 1687–90
liturgical celebration, not a sacrament: 1684–85
types of funerals: 1686

Games of chance: 2413

Generosity
as fruit of the Holy Spirit: 1832

Genocide: 2313

Gentleness
as fruit of the Holy Spirit: 736, 1832

Gluttony: 1866
Gnosticism: 285
God
actions with respect to
    man:
    adopts men as children:
        2782–85
    calls man: 30, 2567
    desires all men to be
        saved: 74
    does not abandon man
        after the fall: 410
    God alone can satisfy
        man's desire for
        happiness: 1718
    God's work: 1, 275
    predestines no one to
        damnation: 1037
    reveals himself: 35
    reveals himself in history
        as liberator: 2084
    wants glorification of
        man: 2012
attributes:
    characteristics of a
        father: 370
    characteristics of a
        husband: 370
    characteristics of a
        mother: 370
    goodness: 385
    love: 218–21, 733
    neither man nor woman:
        370
    truth: 214–17, 2465
existence of God: 33, *231*
God the Almighty:
    God can reveal the
        future: 2115
    God's omnipotence:
        268–74, *275–78*
        and evil: 277, 309–12,
            314, 395, 412
        in Holy Scripture: 269
        is not despotism: 271
    God's providence: 302–
        14

the mystery of God's
    apparent powerlessness:
    272–74
God the Creator:
    as "first cause": 300,
        304, 308
    Creator of the world:
        295–300
    dignity of creatures: 308
    God is acting in
        creatures: 308
    God transcends creation:
        300, 303
    sustainer of the world:
        301
God the Creator of man:
    allowed man to
        cooperate in his creation:
        307
    created man as rational,
        free person: 1730
    created man: 1
        out of love: 1604
God the Holy One
    as mystery of his
        divinity: 2807
    God's holiness and glory:
        2809
    in the life and prayer of
        the Christian: 2814
    in the revelation of the
        Old Testament: 2810–11
    in the revelation of Jesus:
        2812
name:
    abuse of God's name
        forbidden: 2146,
        2161–62
    God's name in oaths:
        2150, *2164*
    God wants to be called
        personally: 203
    magical use of God's
        name forbidden: 2149
    names of God:
        "Adonai": 209
        "Kyrios": 209

"YHWH": 206, 210–11, 213–14
significance of the revelation of God's names: 203–14, 2143
sin as offense against God: 1850
speaking about God: 39–43, 48
special salvific actions:
  calls Israel: 62–64, 218–19, 2085
  inspires the authors of Holy Scripture: 105–6
  New Covenant: 64
  reveals himself to Moses: 205
  saves Israel from sin: 431
  sends his Son: 422

Good
in judging an action: 1755–56

Goodness
as fruit of the Holy Spirit: 736, 1832

Good News: see Gospel

Gospel
and the Law of the Old Covenant: 1963
as Good News: 571
as revelation of God's mercy: 1846
command to proclaim: 2
formation: 126
place and significance in the New Testament: 125–27
record of Jesus' life: 514–15, 534, 573
two ways of recording Jesus' message: 76

Grace
as God's gift:
  as charism: 2003
  as gift of the Holy Spirit: 2003
as God's gratuitous help: 1996, 2021
effects:
  as uniting with Christ in active love: 2011
  forges the human character: 1810
  justification: 654, 1987, 1989
  parent-child relationship with God: 1997
  participation in the life of God: 1997
  sanctification: 824, 1999, 2023–24
  vocation to eternal life: 1998
faith as grace: 153–55
graces of state: 2004
habitual and actual grace: 2000
reception:
  and human experience: 2005
  meriting grace: 2010, 2025–27
  readiness to receive: 2001
  requirements: 2002
  unbelief as refusal of grace: 678
  within man's earthly life: 1021
role of grace in the man-God relationship: 35, 2022
sacramental grace: 2003

Greed: see Desires, disordered

Habits
and the imputability of an act: 1735

Hail Mary: 435, 2676–78

Happiness
substance of true happiness: 1723

virtue of hope and desire
for happiness: 1818
Hatred
as grave sin: 2303
as passion: 1765
forbidden in Sermon on the
Mount: 2262
Health
and the virtue of
temperance: 2290
and use of drugs: 2291
and worship of the body:
2289
duty of concern for health:
2288
**Heart of Jesus, adoration
of:** 2669, 1439
Heaven:
as "place of God": 326
as "place of the deceased":
1023–29
"seen and unseen" world:
325
see World; Creation
Hell: 1033
as consequence of mortal
sin: 1861
as location of the damned:
633
God predestines no one to
damnation: 1037
in Jesus' preaching: 1034
in the teaching of the
Church: 1035
teaching about hell as
admonition: 1036
Heresy: 2089, 817
Hierarchy
of truths: see Truth;
Dogma
in the Church: see Church:
structure
Holiness; sanctity; saints
holiness:
all Christians called to
holiness: 2013–14,
2028–29

entails asceticism:
2015
God wants man to be
glorified: 2012
taught by the Church:
2030
saints:
and the Holy Spirit's
activity in the Church:
688
and the Holy Spirit's
activity in men: 686
as companions in prayer:
2683–2684
as example of Christian
holiness: 1717, 2030
as patrons: 2156
communion of saints:
946–59
intercession of saints:
956
significance of
canonization: 828
Holy Days of Obligation:
2042–43, 2177, 2180,
2185, 2187–88, *2192,
2193*
Holy Spirit
acts:
in all mankind:
animates all creation:
703
awakens faith: 684
comes unceasingly into
the world: 732
enables
communication with
Christ: 683
grants gifts to all:
2003
helps man grow in
spiritual freedom:
1742
master and source of
prayer: 741, 2652
"principal author" of
Holy Scripture: 304

restores the divine
likeness: 734
reveals God: 687
reveals the Trinity:
244, 684
source of all holiness:
749
in the Church:
brings about the unity
of the Church: 813
Church as temple of
the Holy Spirit:
797–98
directs and supports
the Church: 768, 747
in the liturgy of the
Church: 1091–1109
living memory of the
Church: 1099
mission in the Church:
737, 739
responsible for the
Church's mission: 852
consubstantial with the
Father and the Son: 685,
689
faith in the Holy Spirit: 14,
152, 202, 742
gifts of the Holy Spirit:
768, 798–801, 1830
at Confirmation: 1303
first gift is love: 733,
735
fruits of the Spirit: 736,
1832
in Baptism: 1266
in the Anointing of the
Sick: 1520
in the charism of
healing: 1508
in the sacrament of Holy
Orders: 1585–89
in the sheltering of
sinners: 827
the seven gifts: 1831,
1845
in God's work of salvation:

in the preaching of Jesus:
714, 728
in the theophanies of the
Old Testament: 707
Jesus gives the Holy
Spirit: 730
John the Baptist and the
preparation of the
people: 718, 720
Mary's conception and
the birth of the Son of
God: 723
outpouring on Pentecost:
731
place in the economy of
salvation: 685–86
preparation for the
Messiah: 702
preparation of Mary:
722, 725, 744
prophetic texts: 715
the promised coming of
the Holy Spirit: 706, 729
joint mission with the Son:
689–90, 727, 743
life "in the Holy Spirit":
740, 1699, 2017
conversion: 1433
forgiveness of sins: 976
sin of "blaspheming
against the Holy Spirit":
1864
manifestation as a divine
Person: 731
names:
"Holy Spirit": 691
in the Acts of the
Apostles and Letters of
the New Testament: 693
"Paraclete": 692
"Spirit of Truth": 692
self-revelation: 687
symbols:
cloud and light: 697
"Finger of God": 700
fire: 696
"Hand of God" 699

in anointing: 695
the dove: 701
the seal: 698
water: 694
Holy Water: 1668
Homily: 2033
Homosexuality: 2357
and chastity: 2359
Honor
right to a good reputation
  and honor: 2479
Hope: 2090
as source of prayer: 2657
as theological virtue: 1813,
  1817–21
Christian hope and that of
  the Jewish People: 1819
in the first commandment
  of the Decalogue: 2086
sins against hope: 2091
Horoscopes: 2116
Hostages, taking of: 2297
Humility
and Baptism: 2540
and prayer: 2559, 2628,
  2631, 2706, 2713
of Jesus: *525, 559*
of Mary: 724
Hypostasis; hypostatic
  union: 252, 464–69
see also: Trinity
Icon: 1159
significance: 1160–61,
  2141
Idolatry: 2113, 1852,
  2112–14
Ignorance
and imputability of an act:
  1735
Impurity: 1852
Inadvertence
and imputability of an act:
  1735
Incarnation
as unique event in God's
  economy of salvation:
  464, 470

see also: Jesus Christ: life
  of Jesus
Incest: 2388–2389
Incredulity: 2089
Inculturation
in the catechumenate:
  1232
in the liturgy: 1205–6
in the mission of the
  Church: 854
Indifference
as a sin against love: 2094
Indulgences: 1471
Church's doctrine on
  indulgences: 1472–79,
  1498
Infertility: see Matrimony:
  purpose
Ingratitude
as sin against love: 2094
Initiation: see Baptism;
  Confirmation; Eucharist;
  Catechumenate
Inspiration
of Sacred Scripture: 106
see also: Scripture, Sacred
"Intercommunion": see
  Eucharistic celebration:
  Eucharistic communion
Irony: 2481
Irreligion: 2110, 2112–14
Islam
Church's relationship with
  Muslims: 841
Muslims profess to hold
  the faith of Abraham:
  841
Israel; Israelites
adoration of the Savior
  God in Israel: 433
announcement of Jesus in
  Israel: 436–40, 522
assembly of the People of
  God as "Church": 751
between the giving of the
  Law and the Exile:
  708–10

call of Israel irrevocable: 839

chosen by God: 62–64, 218, 238, 2085

Church formed in advance in Israel: 759–62

God reveals himself to Israel as Creator: 287–88

God reveals his Law to Israel: 1961

God reveals his name to Israel: 203–4

God's love for Israel: 218–19

Israel as God's "people of the poor": 711, 716

Israel's hope: 674

Israel's reproaches to Jesus: 576, 579

Israel's sin: 401

Jacob as ancestor of the twelve tribes of Israel: 2573

Jesus as fulfillment of Israel's vocation: 539

Sabbath as the heart of Israel's Law: 348

saved from sin by God: 431

"son of God" as title for the Jewish people: 441

see also: Prayer; Liturgy

Jealousy: 1852

Jesus Christ

and the Church:
  communication through the sacraments: 947, 1115
  following of Jesus: 520
  imitation of Jesus: 520
  Jesus acts through the sacraments: 1084
  Jesus as Head of the Church: 669, 792
  liturgy of the Church: 662, 1069, 1084–90

mystery of Christ as something that perdures: 1085

preservation and transmission of Jesus' legacy: 3, 126

as Word of God: 102

Ascension of Jesus: 659–64, 665–67, 670, 673
  as the final apparition of the Risen One to the disciples: 659
  as the beginning of Jesus' lordship over creation: 668
  as the beginning of Jesus' lordship as Messiah: 663–64
  despite the Ascension, Jesus remains present in his Church: 669
  with the Ascension, the final age is with us: 670

Christian confession of Jesus: 202, 422–24

death of Jesus:
  as real death: 619, 627, 629
  burial of Jesus: 624–26, 630
  descent to the underworld: 624, 631–35, 636–37
  God turns murder into salvation: 312, 622
  interpretation of Jesus' death:
    elevation on the Cross and the Ascension: 662
    God "made him to be sin": 602–3
    in the mystery of God's plan: 599, 620
    self-sacrifice of Jesus: 605–18, 621, 623

the death of the
"Servant of God":
601, 713
divine Sonship:
Jesus as Son of God and
of the Virgin: 724
Jesus declares himself to
be the Son of God: 443
significance first realized
in the Paschal mystery:
444–45
the Father gives witness
to it: 444
divinity:
"homoousios" 465
Jesus as true God and
true Man: 464–69,
480–82
the two natures in the
Church's confession:
469
interpretation and
significance:
"Amen" of God's love
for us: 1065
center of angelic world:
331
center of Christian life:
1618
deliverer from Satan and
from sin: 1708
end of the Law: 1953
eschatological judge: 679
heart of catechesis: 426
illuminator of the
mystery of creation: 280
liberator of men for
freedom: 908, 1741
Lord over history: 450,
668
model: 520–21
model of the Beatitudes:
459
new creation: 349
perfect man: 520
physician: 1503–5
priest: 1544–45

restoration of man to the
Father: 518
revelation: 516
Risen One: 625
Servant of God: 555,
580, 601, 608, 615
teacher: 427
"Jesus event," the:
preparation in salvation
history: 522–24
the Gospel account:
514–15
Jewish protest against his
teaching:
attitude toward the Law,
the Temple, and
monotheism: 576
contact with "tax
collectors and sinners":
588
mercy toward and
forgiveness of sinners:
589
relation with the
Sabbath law: 2173
reproach of blasphemy:
591
role in forgiving sins:
587, 594
statements about
himself: 590
life of Jesus:
agony in Gethsemane:
612
as mystery of
Redemption: 517,
561–62
Baptism by John the
Baptist: 535–36, 556,
565, 1223–25
birth of Jesus: 437, 525
call of the apostles: 551,
858
entry into Jerusalem:
559–60, 570
events of childhood:
527–30, 534, 563

exorcisms: 517
healings as sign of his divinity: 517, 1507
hidden life of Jesus:
    daily life: 531, 533
    obedience in life of the family: 517, 532, 564
Incarnation: 461–63, 479, 483
    faith in Incarnation as distinguishing sign of Christian faith: 463
Incarnation in relation to salvation:
    as preparation for the marriage of the Lamb: 1612
    Incarnation and Ascension: 661
    Incarnation and Resurrection: 653–54
    mystery of the Incarnation and the mystery of man: 359
    preparation:
        in God's plan of salvation: 522
        through John the Baptist: 523
    questions with respect to the Incarnation:
        full humanity of Jesus: 470
        Jesus' divine ability to know: 473
        Jesus' human ability to know: 472
        Jesus' human body: 476
        Jesus' human will: 475
        thesis of Apollinaris of Laodicia: 471
Incarnation, reasons for:
    according to the Creed: 456

that men might come to know the love of God: 458
to be our model of holiness: 459
to inaugurate the new creation: 504
to make men partakers of the divine nature: 460
to save and reconcile mankind: 457, 606–7
Last Supper: 610–11
main mysteries of the life of Christ: 429
preaching of Jesus in Galilee: 541
temptation in the desert: 538–40, 566
Transfiguration of Jesus: 554–56, 568
trial against Jesus:
    accusation: 574, 575, 585
    divisions among the Jewish authorities about him: 595–96
    Jesus' suffering: 572
    question of guilt:
        no "collective guilt" of the Jews in Jesus' death: 597
        sinners are guilty of the death of Jesus: 598
way to Jerusalem: 557–58, 569
names and designations:
    significance of the name "Jesus": 430, 432, 434, 435, 452
    titles:
        "Christ": 429, 436, 453
        "Lord": 209, 429, 446–51, 455

"Son of God": 429,
441, *454*
see also: Messiah
designations:
"Lamb of God": 608
"messianic Son of
David": 439, 727
"New Adam": 411,
504
"Rabbi": 581–82
"YHWH": 211
pictorial representation:
477
prayer of Jesus:
as model for the prayer
of disciples: 2601
as prayer of the Son of
the Father: 2599
before important
salvation events: 2600,
2602
high priestly prayer:
2746–51
important prayers of
Jesus: 2603–6
Jesus hears prayers:
2616
Jesus teaches to pray:
2607–15
"Our Father": 2759
Resurrection of Jesus:
apparitions of the Risen
One: 641
as proof of divine
omnipotence: 272
as transcendent event:
647, *656*
interpretation:
as basis for our
resurrection: 655, *658*
as fulfillment of the
promises of the Old
Covenant: 652
as the final
confirmation of Jesus'
authority: 649–51,
653

as work of the Trinity:
648
Jesus' resurrected body:
645–46
meaning and
significance: 651–55
message:
apostles' living
tradition of the
Resurrection: 639
as the central theme of
Christian preaching:
638
significance for the
apostles: 642–44
significance of the empty
grave: 640, *657*
Sunday as the day of the
Resurrection: 2174
Second Coming:
before Christ's return,
the Antichrist will come:
675
Church remains
universal until Christ's
return: 830
could occur at any
moment: 673
Jesus' messianic
kingship: 440, *680, 1060*
Kingdom of God on
earth not yet achieved:
671
Last Judgment: 677–78,
681–82, 1038–41,
1051–52
Christ as Judge: 679,
1040
message of the Last
Judgment:
as call for
conversion: 1041
in Jesus' preaching
from the beginning:
678
resurrection of the dead:
988

significance for the Church:
  liturgy focused on Christ's return: 1107, 1130
  missionary task of the Church until the end of time: 849
the "hardening" of Israel and the endtime: 674
waiting for the definitive reign: 672
sent by the Father: 422
signs and wonders:
  accompany his preaching: 547
  as messianic signs: 549
  bear witness to his mission:
    exorcisms: 550
themes of Jesus' preaching:
  abandonment to God's providence: 305
  Beatitudes as central: 1716
  Decalogue: 2052–55
  Jewish Law: 577–82, 592
  Kingdom of God: 542–46, 567
  Last Judgment: 678
  marriage:
    indissolubility of: 1614–15
    original meaning of conjugal union: 1614
    significance of the wedding at Cana: 1613
    the "marriage of the Lamb": 1612
  message and mission of the Holy Spirit: 728–30
  parables of Jesus: 546
  "peace of Christ": 2305
  prohibition against murder: 2262

resurrection of the dead: 994
Temple of Jerusalem: 583–86, *593*
the poor: 544, 2444
Jesus Prayer: 2616, 2667–68
Jews: see Israel
John the Baptist
Baptism of Jesus: 535–37
Baptism of repentance: 720, 1224
filled with the Holy Spirit in his mother's womb: 717
fire of the Holy Spirit glows in him: 696, 718
role in salvation history: 523, 719
witness given to Jesus: 608
Journalists: 2497
Joy: 301, 523, 1829
as fruit of the Holy Spirit: 736, 1832
see also: Happiness
Judgment, rash: 2477
Justice: 1807
legal commutative and distributive: 2411
as cardinal virtue: 1805
see also: Virtues: cardinal virtues
Justification: 1987, *2018–19*
as most excellent work of God's love: 1994
as receiving of God's justice: 1991
as sanctification of the whole human being: 1995
collaboration between God's grace and man's freedom: 1993
conferred through Baptism: 1266, 1992

grace of conversion
precedes justification:
1989
in the Paschal mystery: 654
made possible by God's
grace: 1987
merited by Christ's
Passion: 1992, *2020*
possibility to rediscover
grace of justification in
Penance: 1446

Kidnapping: 2297

Killing
concern for eugenics never
justifies: 2268
failure to give assistance:
2277
forbidden in Jesus'
preaching: 2262
forbidden in the Old
Testament: 2261
legitimate defense:
2263–67
murder as sin that cries out
to heaven: 2268
stopping or omitting
medical treatment: 2278
suicide: 2280–83, *2325*
unintentional killing: 2269

Kindness
as fruit of the Holy Spirit:
736, 1832
God's kindness: see God:
attributes

Knowledge
as gift of the Holy Spirit:
1831

Knowledge of God
and human soul: 33
God lets himself be known:
31, 34, 54–55
in historical
circumstances: 37
natural knowledge of
God: 32, 47
through grace: 35
through reason: 35, 36

through revelation: 35,
38

Laity: 897
civil duties: 912
importance:
in catechesis: 906
in governing the Church:
911
in secular institutes:
928–29
in the Church's teaching
office: 906
in the mass media: 906
in the preaching of the
Gospel: 900, 905
mission in the Church and
in the world: 873–75
participation in Christ's
kingly office: 908–13
participation in Christ's
priestly office: 901–3
participation in Christ's
prophetic office: 904
right and duty to manifest
opinions: 907
vocation: 898

Last Judgment: see Jesus
Christ: Second Coming

Last Supper: see Jesus
Christ: life of Jesus

**Law; commandment;
Church precept; natural
moral law: 1951,
*1975–76***
as "scandal": 2286
in God's salvation
pedagogy: 707–10,
1980–82
Law of the Gospel:
and the evangelical
counsels: 1973–74,
1986
as fulfillment of the
Mosaic Law: 1968,
1984
as fulfillment of the
divine promises: 1967

as Law of love, grace, and freedom: 1972, *1983, 1985*
Christ as "end of the law": 1953, *1977*
expressed in the Sermon on the Mount: 1965
"golden rule" and "new commandment": 1970
practices the acts of religion: 1969
transmitted through the moral teaching of the apostles: 1971
Law of the Old Covenant:
  as expression of truths accessible to reason: 1961
  as preparation for the Gospel: 1964
  as sign of the Covenant: 709
  Decalogue: 1962
  to be interpreted in the light of the Gospel: 1963–64
love as fulfillment of the law: 2055
natural moral law: 1954, *1978–79*
  and revealed Law: 1960
  and sin: 1949
  application: 1957
  as "work of divine Wisdom": 1950
  as basis for other laws: 1959
  forms of expression: 1952
  function: 1955
  immutable: 1958
  universality: 1956
precepts of the Church:

and the natural law: 1952
celebration of Sunday: 2180
confession: 2042
feast days: 2043
meaning: 2041
participation in the Eucharistic celebration: 2042
reception of Communion: 2042
times of fast and abstinence: 2043
see also: Decalogue
Laws of nature: 341
Laying on of hands
as sign accompanying the administration of a sacrament:
  at Confirmation: 1288
  at ordination: 1538, 1568, 1569, 1573
  at the Anointing of the Sick: 1507
as sign accompanying the administration of sacramentals: 1668
as sign of authorization of the apostles' successors: 1556
Lectern: 1184
Lectio divina: **1177, 2708**
Lectors: see Readers
Lent: see Liturgy: liturgical seasons
Lie: 2482
and culpability: 2485
gravity: 2484
importance: 2483
violation of the virtue of truthfulness: 2486, *2505*
Life
as God's gift: 2260
God as sole Lord over human life: 2258

intentional murder: 2261,
2320
society has the duty to
protect: 2273
threats to freedom from
bodily harm: 2297
to be protected from the
moment of conception:
2270
Light
as symbol of the Holy
Spirit: 697
Liturgy: 1069–70
as constitutive element of
Tradition: 1124
catechesis in the liturgy:
liturgy and catechesis:
1074–75, 1095
use of images: 1159–62,
1192
celebration:
adaptation in different
cultures: 1204–6
basic form: 1101
elements:
music and song:
1156–58, 1191
sign and symbol:
1145–52, 1189
word and action:
1153–55
how one should
celebrate: 1145–62
in community preferred
to private: 1140
Jewish liturgy as aid in
understanding: 1096
ministers: 1142–44
choir: 1143
commentators: 1143
Eucharistic ministers:
1348
readers: 1143
servers: 1143
modifications of the rite:
1125

of Christ's Paschal
mystery: 1067–68
of entire assembly: 1141,
1188
of saints as examples of
Christian holiness: 2030
place: 1179–86, 1197–
99
who celebrates: 1136–44
contents:
Christ's Paschal mystery
made present: 1104
meeting of Christ and
the Church: 1097
unity of Christ's Paschal
mystery in diverse forms:
1200–1201
different traditions:
1202–3, 1208–9
God in the liturgy:
Christ and the liturgy:
1084–90, 1111, 1187,
1188
Holy Spirit and the
liturgy: 1091–1109,
1112
presence of Christ in the
liturgy: 1088
the Father and the
liturgy: 1077–83, 1110
"heavenly liturgy": 1090,
1137–39
interpretations:
act of the whole Christ:
1136, 1187
action of the Church:
1071–72
carried out by the
community: 1140
exercise of Christ's
priestly office: 1070
expression of the
mystery of Christ: 1068
memorial in the mystery
of salvation: 1099
participation in Christ's
prayer: 1073

response of faith: 1083
source of prayer: 2655
work of the Trinity:
1077–1109
liturgical seasons: 1163–78
liturgical year: 1168–73,
1194
    as unfolding of
    Paschal mystery: 1171
    commemoration of
    Mary: 1172
    commemoration of
    saints: 1173, *1195*
    liturgical
    interpretation from
    Easter on: 1168
    liturgical meaning
    shapes the seasons:
    1095
    Liturgy of the Hours:
        and other forms of
        devotion: 1178
        contents: 1176–77
        participants: 1175
        purpose: 1174, *1196*
    Sunday:
        as Day of Lord:
        1166–67, *1193*
        importance of Sunday
        Eucharistic
        celebration: 2177–79
        occasion for the
        celebration of Sunday:
        1166
        purpose of Sunday:
        1167
mystery of the liturgy:
1075
Word of God in the liturgy:
1100–02, *1190*
Liturgy of the Word
and the Sunday obligation:
2183
as part of the Eucharistic
    celebration: 1346, 1349
function: 1103
Lord's Day: see Sunday

Love: 1766 (see also
    Charity)
conjugal love: 1604, 1643
interpretation and place:
    and freedom: 1828
    and the law of Christ:
    1824
    as "soul of
    sanctification": 826
    as "soul of the
    apostolate": 864
    as fundamental passion:
    1765
    as most important social
    commandment: 1889
    as source of prayer:
    2658
    as virtue:
        love of enemies:
        1825
        new commandment of
        love: 1823
love of God and love of
    neighbor:
    Christ's love as source of
    all human merit before
    God: 2011
    commandment to love
    one's neighbor: 2196
consecrated life as
    expression of God's love:
    914–30
    God created man out of
    love: 1604
    relationship of love of
    God to love of men:
    2069
sin as offense against love:
    1849, 1855
Lukewarmness: 2094
Lust: 2351, 1866, 2514,
    2529, 2530, 2542
Magic: 2117, *2138*
Magisterium: see Church
Man
as creature:
    as a good creation: 374

recognition of limitations
   as creature: 396
with body and soul: 327,
   355, 362–65, 382, 1703,
   1711
with reason: 1704
with understanding and
   free will: 311
characteristics and actions:
   action of man: 16,
   2085
   capacity for natural
   knowledge of God: 32,
   46
   desire for happiness:
   1718
   desire to do good:
   1706–07
   endowed with freedom:
   1705
   expresses himself in signs
   and symbols: 1146
   is a religious being: 28,
   44–45
   constant struggle to
   decide in favor of the
   good: 409
   needs social life:
   1879–80
   obligation to follow his
   conscience: 1706, 1713
   striving of man for truth:
   2467
   virtuous man: 1803–4
Christ's right to judge men:
   679
Church proclaims full
   revelation about man:
   2419
consequences of sin:
   according to Sacred
   Scripture: 399–400
   choice between eternal
   life and eternal death:
   1470
   deprived of resemblance
   to God: 705

every man affected from
   birth on: 403
freedom and original sin:
   396–401
harm through the
   activity of the devil: 395
temptation of man: 394
through sin, the devil
   has a certain power over
   man: 407
woundedness of human
   nature: 405
consummation at the end
   of time: 1045
duty to protect and help
   the sick or handicapped:
   2276
end: 16, 356, 260
equality of all men:
   according to nature,
   origin, and goal: 1934
   human dignity as
   fundamental element:
   1935
   unjust inequalities: 1938
   with differences in
   aptitudes: 1936–37
God-man relationship:
   profession of faith: 199
   question of God's
   existence: 33, 41
human dignity, rights, and
   duties:
   basis for and importance
   of human dignity: 1700
   dignity of the creature's
   cooperation with the
   Creator: 306–8
   human dignity: 27
   human dignity
   manifested in moral life:
   1706
   origin of human rights in
   human dignity: 1930
human sexual identity:
   created as "male and
   female": 355, 383

difference and complementarity of the sexes: 369–73, *1605*, 2333
  equal dignity of both sexes: 369, 2334, *2393*
  vocation to love and communion: 2331–32
in creation:
  goal of creation: 358
  hierarchy of creatures: 342
  importance of the order of creation: 346
  interdependence of creatures: 340
  original harmony: 374–79, *384*
  respect for the order of creation: 339
  responsibility for the world: 373
  unique place of man: 343, 355
in humanity:
  brotherhood of all men: 361, *1947–48*
  origin and goal of the whole human race: 842
  unity of mankind: 360
not abandoned by God after the fall: 410
origin:
  created out of love by God: 1, *315*, 1604
promise to restore man's likeness to God: 705
sin and the rejection of God: 29, 398, 1739
sin as offense to human nature: 1849, *1714*
resemblance to God:
  before and after redemption by Christ: 1701
  created in the image of God: 356–61, *380*, 1702

whole of man willed by God: 362
respect for personal dignity: 1738
right to a good reputation: 2479, *2507*
right to act in accord with one's conscience: 1782
right to freedom of religion: 2106
search for God:
  God calls man first: 2567
  knowledge of God:
    God speaks in human words: 101, 109
    through reason: 50
    through revelation: 35, 50, 52, 208
    ways: 31
  man always in search of God: 30, 2566
sexuality:
  importance: 2332, 2362
  importance of conjugal union: 2335
  integration in the human person: 2337
  twofold purpose of Matrimony: 2360–63
  see also: Matrimony
transmission of life: 372
vocation: *1710*, 1878, *2133*
  divinization of man as Jesus' goal: 460
  to communion with God: 27
  to cooperation in God's creation: *307*, 378
  to eternal beatitude: 1703
  to free submission to God: 144, 396
  to friendship with God: 355, 396

to life in the Holy Spirit:
1699
to manifest God: 2085
Manichaeanism: 285
Market economy
within the state's
responsibility: 2431
Marriage: see Matrimony
Martyrdom
as bearing witness to the
truth: 2473, *2506*
importance for the Church:
2474
Mary
and the Church:
in Mary the Church is
all-holy: 829
Marian dimension of the
Church: 773, 973
Mary supports the
beginning of the Church
through her prayer:
965
place of Mary in the
mystery of the Church:
963–72
place of Mary
inseparable from Christ:
964
as example and model:
Christian example of
holiness: 2030
example of faith in
God's omnipotence: 273
Assumption into heaven:
966, *974*
beliefs about Mary based
on beliefs about Christ:
487
conceived and gave birth to
the Son of God: 485,
509, 723
devotion to Mary:
in the liturgy of the
Church: 971
not adoration: 971
in God's plan of salvation:

"full of God's grace":
490
God's choice of Mary:
488–93, *508*
"Immaculate
Conception": 491–92
preparation in the Old
Covenant: 489
interpretation:
dwelling of the Son and
of the Holy Spirit: 721
"Mother of Grace":
968–70
as mediator, not
source, of God's grace:
970
in restoration of
supernatural life to
souls: 968
intercessor before
God: 969, 975
only through the
mediation of Christ:
970
"Mother of the
Church": 963
"Panagia": 493
personification of the
Church: 507
"Theotokos": 495
"Throne of Wisdom":
721
"Type" of the Church:
967
obedience of faith of Mary:
144, 494, *511*
prayer of Mary: 2617–19
prepared by the Holy
Spirit: 722
prophecy of Jesus' birth:
484
sinless during her life: 411
virginity of Mary:
496–507, *510*
as sign of her faith: 506
in God's plan of
salvation: 502–6

in the faith of the
Church: 499
in the Gospels: 497–98,
500
in the Tradition of the
Fathers: 496
Mass: see Eucharistic
celebration
Masturbation: 2352
Materialism: 285
Matrimony, sacrament of;
marriage; wedding: 1601
and consecrated virginity:
1620
and the unmarried: 2230
as instituted by God: 1603
as one of the seven
sacraments: 1113, 1210
as sacrament:
administration: 1623
as sign of Christ's
presence: 1613
bride and bridegroom
receive the Holy Spirit:
1624
celebration of
Matrimony: 1621–24
grace of the sacrament:
1615, 1641–42
main effects: 1638–40
obligatory form in the
Church: 1630–31
of covenant between
Christ and the Church:
1617, *1661*
preparation for: 1622,
1632
special consecration:
1535
characteristics of conjugal
love: 1643
conjugal chastity: 2349
disparity of cult in
Matrimony: 1633, 1637
in Holy Scripture: 1602
in the order of creation:
1603–05, *1660*

in the preaching of Jesus:
1612–17
in the preaching of Paul:
1616, *1659*
indissolubility:
as required by spousal
love: 1644, *1664*
foundation: 1646–47
in Holy Scripture and
Tradition: 1610, 2382
in the preaching of Jesus:
1614–15, 2336
lifelong duration of
marriage: 1648
matrimonial consent: 1625
as the essential element
of marriage: 1626, *1662*
nature of the consent:
1627–28
receipt by the priest or
deacon: 1630, *1663*
significance for the
family: 2201
significance of witnesses:
1630–31, *1663*
mixed marriages: 1633–36
monogamy: 1644–45
offenses against the dignity
of Matrimony: *2400*
"free union" and
concubinage: 2390
incest: 2388
premarital sexual
relations: 2391
"trial marriage": 2391
polygamy: 2387
purpose:
original meaning: 1614
as a state of life in the
Church: 1631
ordered to the
procreation and
education of offspring:
1652, 2249
marriage union of man
and woman: 2335,
2363

fruitfulness: 1653–54,
2366–67, *2398–99*
    and adoption of
        children: 2379
    and regulation of
        births: 2368
    artificial insemination:
        2376
    as human vocation:
        1604, 2371
    infertility and medical
        techniques: 2375–77
    infertility as a great
        suffering: 2374
    periodic continence
        and contraception:
        2370

Media
and civil authorities:
    2498–99
critical use of mass media:
    2496
importance: 2493
in the service of public
    welfare: 2494–95
obligations and limitations:
    2497

Medical treatment
amputations or
    sterilizations as threats
    to bodily integrity: 2297
organ transplants: 2296
scientific experiments as
    contribution to healing:
    2292
scientific experiments on
    human beings not
    permissible: 2295
stopping or omitting
    medical treatment:
    2278–79

Medicine
abuse: 2290

Meditation: 2705–08

Men
man created as "male and
    female": 355, 383

see also: Man: human
    sexual identity

Mercy: 1829, 2447

Merit: 2006
Christ's love as source of all
    merit before God: 2011
merit of grace: 2010,
    2023–25
no merit on man's part in
    God's sight: 2007–08

Messiah
anointing as sign of the
    Messiah: 695
Ascension as beginning of
    Messiah's reign: 664
characteristics: 712–16
expectation of the Messiah
    in Israel: 711–16
first announcement after
    the fall: 410
in Judaism and
    Christianity: 840
Jesus Christ, the Messiah:
    436–40, 528–29, 535,
    540, 590, 674
messianic kingship of
    Jesus: 440
preparation for his arrival
    by the Holy Spirit: 702
suffering of the Messiah
    "according to Scripture":
    572
see also: Jesus Christ

Millenarianism: 676

Misappropriation of funds:
    2409

Missions; missionary
    work
and consecrated life: 931
and unity of the Church:
    855
Christ's missionary
    mandate in the Church:
    849, 858–59
discrepancy between the
    message proclaimed and
    human reality: 853

Holy Spirit as principal
  agent: 852
importance of
  inculturation: 854
love of God as motive:
  851
origin and goal: 850
respectful dialogue with
  other cultures: 856
Modesty
as fruit of the Holy Spirit:
  1832
different forms of
  expressions: 2523–24
purity requires modesty:
  2521
task: 2522
Monophysitism: 467
Moral Law: see Law
Morality
and sin: 407
Mortal sin: see Sin: mortal
  sin
Mother: see Parents;
  Church; Mary
Murder: see Killing
Music
importance of songs and
  music: 1158
liturgical music as Church's
  treasure: 1156
sign function in the liturgy:
  1157
Muslims: see Islam
Mutilation: 2297
Myron: see Chrism
Mystagogy: 1075
Name
baptismal name: 2156,
  2165
name of God: see God
Natural sciences: 284
Neighbor, love of
and truth: 2488
as Christ's commandment:
  2196
in the parish: 2179

love for the poor as special
  form of love of neighbor:
  2443–49
"to make ourselves the
  neighbor of those
  farthest away" 1825
New Covenant
Law of the Gospel:
  1965–74
relationship between the
  people of the New and
  Old Covenants: 839–40
sacrifice of the New
  Covenant: 612–14
New Testament
contents: 124
Gospels as center of the
  New Testament: 125–27
relationship between Old
  and New Testaments:
  128–30
revelation of the Trinity:
  684
Oaths
breaking an oath: 2152
conditions for refusing an
  oath: 2155
false oaths: 2150–51
in the preaching of Jesus:
  2153
in the Tradition of the
  Church: 2154
perjury: 2152
Obedience
civil obedience and
  disobedience: 2242
duty of obedience to
  government authorities:
  1900
Jesus' obedience: 615
obedience in war: 2313
as evangelical counsel: see
  Evangelical counsels
Oikonomia: 236
Oil: see Chrism
Old Covenant

Law of the Old Covenant:
1961–64
the Church and Judaism:
839–40
priesthood of the Old
Covenant: 1539–41
Old Testament
as indispensable: 121
theophany in the Old
Testament: 697, 707
unity of Old and New
Testaments: 128–30
use in the Church's liturgy:
1093, 1156
Orders, sacrament of Holy:
1536
administration: 1575–76
as one of the seven
sacraments: 1113, 1210
as commission to guide the
Church: 1119
celebration:
essential rite of all three
degrees: 1573, *1597*
external signs of
consecration: 1538
place and time of the
consecration: 1572
consecrated state: 897
obligation to celibacy:
1579, *1599*
designations:
"consecratio": 1538
"ordinatio": 1538
"ordo": 1537
effects:
received as unmerited
gift: 1578
effected through the
grace of the Holy Spirit:
1585
confers full power to
forgive sins: 1461
empowers to act as
representative of Christ:
1581

confers indelible spiritual
character: 1582
not impaired by
unworthiness: 1584
grace granted to bishops:
1586, *1594*
grace granted to priests:
1587, *1595*
grace granted to
deacons: 1588, *1596*
priesthood of the Old
Covenant: 1539–41
priesthood of Christ:
1544–45, *1591*
reception:
fundamental: 1577–80
no one has the right to
receive: 1578
only men: 1577, *1598*
practice in the Eastern
Churches: 1580
three degrees: 1536, 1554,
1593
consecration of bishops:
as conferral of the
mission of the
apostles: 1556
as incorporation into
the college of bishops:
1559
confers the fullness of
the sacrament of Holy
Orders: 1557
confers the office of
sanctification,
teaching, and ruling:
1558
requires approval of
Pope: 1559
see also: Bishop
consecration of deacons:
consecrated to "service
of the bishop": 1569
laying on of hands by
the bishop alone: 1569
stamped with indelible
character: 1570

see also: Deacon
consecretion of priests:
  anointing: 1563
  conferral of the
    priestly ministry by
    the bishop: 1562
  importance of the
    promise of obedience
    to the bishop: 1567
  incorporation into the
    priestly state: 1568
  meaning and tasks:
    1564
  presupposes reception
    of sacraments of
    initiation: 1563
  stamped with indelible
    character: 1563
  see also: Priest
Original justice: 379
Original sin: see Sin
Orthodox Churches: 838
Our Father
  eschatological character:
    2771
  importance: 2761–64,
    2774
  in the sacraments of
    initiation: 2769
  in the Eucharistic
    celebration: 2770
  "Lord's Prayer": 2765–66,
    2773, 2775
  prayer of the Church:
    2767–68, 2776
  seven petitions: 2803–54,
    2857–65
Palliative care
  as exemplary form of
    selfless love: 2279
Pantheism: 285
Parables
  in the preaching of Jesus:
    546
Paraclete
  as name for the Holy
    Spirit: 692
  see also: Holy Spirit

**Parents; children;
  childrearing**
childrearing:
  basic right and duty to
    educate children: 2221
  duty to provide for
    physical and spiritual
    needs: 2228
  duty to educate children
    in the faith: 2225–26
  fundamental right to
    choose a school: 2229
  substance of
    childrearing: 2222–24
children as a sign of God's
  blessing: 2373
commandment to honor
  parents:
  addressees and scope:
    2199
  as foundation of the
    Church's social teaching:
    2198
  in the Decalogue: 2197,
    2247–48
  observance of: 2200
duties of parents: 2221–31,
  2253
duties of children:
  2214–20, *2251*
God's fatherhood and
  human fatherhood: 2214
"right to a child": 2378
see also: Matrimony;
  Family
Parish: 2179
Particular Church: 833
as richness of the Church:
  814, 835
presidency of the Church
  of Rome: 834
Passions: 1763–64, *1771*
and the imputability of an
  action: 1735
and sin: 1860
consummation of the
  passions in Christ: 1769

contribution of the
passions to actions: 1762
diversity in: 1765
influence of love on the
other passions: 1766
love as most fundamental
passion: 1765, 1772
moral perfection: 1770,
1775
moral determination of:
1767, 1773, 2552
**Passover of Christ; Paschal
mystery**: 571
as foundation of Christ's
Reign: 671
as center of Christ's Good
News: 571–72
for the salvation of men:
1067
fullness in the outpouring
of the Holy Spirit: 731
Passover of Israel: 1164
Sunday as the fulfillment of
Christ's Passover: 2175
see also: Easter
Patience
as one of the fruits of the
Holy Spirit: 736, 1832
Patriarch: 61, 205, 707
Patriarchate: 887
Peace: 2304
as fruit of the Holy Spirit:
736, 1832
as fruit of love: 1829
disorders threatening
freedom to be
eliminated: 2317
earthly peace as "image of
the peace of Christ":
2305
Penance: see Penance,
sacrament of; Contri-
tion
**Penance, sacrament of;
Confession**
acts of reconciliation in
daily life: 1435

and Baptism: 1425–26,
1427, 1429
and the Eucharist: 1436
as liturgical celebration:
absolution:
does not dispense
from reparation: 1459
formula of absolution:
1449
in danger of death:
1483
of sins: 1424
confession of sins: 1456,
1458
essential parts: 1491
fundamental structure:
1480
historically: 1447–48
penance imposed by the
confessor: 1460, 1494
preparation: 1454
as sacrament of
reconciliation with God
and the Church: 980,
1440, 1486
called:
"sacrament of
confession": 1424
"sacrament of
conversion": 1423
"sacrament of
forgiveness": 1424
"sacrament of Penance":
1423
"sacrament of
reconciliation": 1424
effects:
basic effects: 1422, 1496
reconciliation with God:
980, 1468
reconciliation with the
Church: 980, 1469
eschatological sense: 1470
further means to obtain
forgiveness of sins: 1434
prayer and the reading
of Scripture: 1437

in communal celebration:
1482
instituted by Christ: 1446,
1485
meaning of contrition:
1430–33, 1452–53,
1492
minister:
through the bishop and
priest: 1461, *1495*
necessity for salvation:
as liturgical expression
of conversion and
forgiveness: 1440
for reconciliation with
God and the Church:
1484
for forgiveness of mortal
sin: 1395
for satisfaction: 1459
for preparation to
receive Communion:
1385
to attain the grace of
justification: 1446
obligation to receive: 1457,
1493, 2042
sacramental seal of
confession: 1467, 2490
Penance, works of
conversion as precondition:
1430
meaning: 1460
on behalf of the dead:
1032
Pentateuch: 702
Pentecost
and Confirmation: 1287
beginning of the "age of
the Church": 1076
completion of Christ's
Passover: 731
opening of the Reign of
God: 732
revelation of the Church in
the world: 726, 830,
1076

revelation of the entire
Trinity: 732
Perfection: see Holiness
Perjury: 2476
see also: Oaths
Permissiveness: 2526
Person: see Trinity; Society;
Man
Peter
as foundation of the
Church: 442
as witness to the
Resurrection: 640–42
authority: 552–53, 765,
816, 862
commissioned by Christ:
881
confession of the Messiah:
440, 442–43, 554–56
power to bind and to
loose: 1444
Piety
as gift of the Holy Spirit:
1831
Piety, forms of
as expression of the
Christian life: 1674,
1679
significance of these forms
and manners of
expression: 1674–76
Plants
exploitation forbidden:
2415
Politics: 407
**Polygamy: 1610, 1645,
2387**
see also: Matrimony
Polytheism: 2112
Pope: see Apostolic
succession; Church:
structure: hierarchical
constitution
Pornography: 2354
Poverty; the poor
active love for the poor:
2443–49, 2462–63

moral responsibility of
   wealthy nations:
   2439–40
poverty as evangelical
   counsel: 915, *944*
poverty of heart in
   imitation of Christ:
   2544–47
see also: Development aid;
   Evangelical counsels;
   Justice
Praise: see Doxology;
   Prayer, forms of
Prayer
and ordained ministers:
   2686, *2695*
as always possible: 2743
as vital necessity: 2744
bound up in the history of
   man:
   between the fall and
   restoration of man: 2568
   conversation at the
   burning bush: 2575
   in creation: 2569
   in Judaism: 2577, 2579,
   2586
   in the Old Covenant:
   2568–89, 2592–97
   prayer of Jesus:
   2598–2616, 2620
   prayer of Mary:
   2617–19, 2622
   prayer of the Church:
   2623–25
Christian prayer: 2564–65
   as cooperation with
   God's
   providence: 2738
   as man's answer to
   God's call: 2560–62
   as precondition for
   obeying God's
   commandments: 2098
   different traditions:
   2650–51, 2684
   Lord's Prayer: 17

meaning of the word
   "Amen": 1061–65
prayer and life as
   inseparable: 2725, 2745,
   2752
relationship to God in:
   2592, 2786–88
special place of Jesus in:
   Jesus' name as heart of
   Christian prayer: 435
   possible only in
   Christ's name: 2664
efficacy: 2738–41
family prayer: 2685, *2694*
for the dying: 2299
God's thirst and human
   thirst: 2560
heaven as God's "place":
   2794–96
humility as foundation:
   2559
importance of catechesis:
   2688
in communion with Mary:
   2673–79, 2682
in the community of
   believers: 2790–93
Jesus teaches how to
   pray:
   by means of his own
   prayer: 2607, *2621*
   conversion of heart:
   2608
   in order to do the will of
   the Father: 2611
   in three important
   parables: 2613
   prayer in faith: 2609
   prayer in filial boldness:
   2610
   prayer in the Holy Spirit:
   2615, *2661*
   to ask in his name: 2614
   vigilance in prayer:
   2612, 2730
meaning and importance:
   17, *2590*

necessary for Church unity:
821
objections to: 2726–27
saints as masters of prayer:
2683–84, 2692
sources of: 2662
every day: 2659–60
faith: 2098, 2656
Holy Spirit: 688, 741,
2652
hope: 2098, 2657
liturgy of the Church:
1073, 2655
love: 2098, 2658
Word of God: 2653–54
to Jesus: 451, 2616,
2665–69, 2681
to the Father: 2680,
2779–85, 2788, 2792,
2797–2802
to the Holy Spirit:
2670–72
trust in prayer: 2777–78
"without ceasing": 2742
Prayer, difficulties in: 2728
inner dryness: 2731
distractions: 2729
doubts: 2735–37, 2756
Prayer, forms of
adoration: 2628
blessing: 2626–27
ecclesial forms of prayer:
2625
great range of forms of
Christian prayer: 2644,
2663, 2684, 2693
petition: 2629
for the "coming of the
Kingdom of God":
2646, 2816
in every need and
occasion: 2633
in Holy Scripture: 2630
intercession: 2634–36,
2647
praise of God: 2639–43,
2649

as foundational
movement of Christian
prayer: 2626
the "hallowing" of
God's name: 2807–15
request for daily bread:
2828–37
request for deliverance
from evil: 2850–54
request for forgiveness:
2631, 2838–41
request for love of
neighbor and of enemies:
2842
request for the spirit of
discernment and power:
2846
thanksgiving: 2637–38
see also: Doxology
see also: Prayer, ways of
Prayer, life of: 2697
Prayer, places of: 2691,
2696
Prayer, temptations at
acedia: 2733, 2755
lack of faith: 2732, 2755
Prayer, ways of
contemplative prayer:
2709–19, 2721, 2724
meditation: 2705–08,
2721, 2723
vocal prayer: 2700–2704,
2721–22
Prayer groups: 2689
Precepts of the Church:
2041–43, 2048
Prenatal diagnosis: 2274
Presumption: 2091, 2092
Pride
capital sin: 1866
root of envy: 2540
sin against love: 2094
Priest; priesthood;
presbyterate
Christ's priesthood: 1551
common priesthood of the
baptized: 1546–47, 1591

human weakness: 1550

ministerial priesthood:
acts "in persona Christi": 1548
acts "in the name of the whole Church": 1552–53
as Christ's means for the building up of his Church: 1547
as connection to Christ and the apostles: 1120
as service to the common priesthood: 1120, 1547, *1592*
complete dependence on the priesthood of Christ: 1544–45
connection to the bishops: 1564
for the sake of men and the community of the Church: 1551
presence of Christ: 1088, 1548–49

presbyterate:
as degree of ordination: 1536
collegiality with bishop: 877
importance of the promise of obedience to the bishop: 1567
"presbyterium": 1567
priesthood of the Old Covenant: 1539–41
subordinate to the office of the bishop: 1562
unity of: 1568

prohibition or release from priestly obligations: 1583

tasks of the priest:
administers the Anointing of the Sick: 1516
administers the sacrament of Penance: 1461–67
cooperation of the laity: 900
co-worker of the bishop: 1562
exercise of obligations and functions: 1583
Liturgy of the Hours: 1175
presides at Eucharist: 1142, 1566
receives marital consent: 1630
represents the bishop in local assembly: 1567
see also: Orders, sacrament of Holy

Private revelations: 67

Proclamation of the Gospel
and catechesis: 6
as liturgy: 1070
Church's obligation to evangelize: 848
command to proclaim the Good News: 2, 3, 58, 74
fulfillment at Christ's descent into hell: 634
motive and source: 49, 429
transmission of Christ's legacy: 3

Profession
access to employment: 2433
free choice of profession: 2230
professional secrets: 2491

Promises: 2410
in God's name: 2147
to God: 2101
see also: Vows

Property
administration of goods: 2407, *2451*
appropriation of goods: 2402

right to private property:
2401, 2403
and political authority:
2406
universal destination of
goods: 2402, *2452*
use of goods: 2404–5
Prophet
as authors of Sacred
Scripture: 702
Christ's function as
prophet: 436
John the Baptist as "more
than a prophet": 719
prophecy of the Holy
Spirit: 715
task of the prophets in
Israel: 64, 218
veneration of the prophets:
61
Prostitution: 2355
Providence
and evil: 309–14, *324*
and the cooperation of the
creature: 306–7, *323*
God can reveal the future:
2115
God's dispositions in
creation: 302, *321*
Jesus asks for
abandonment to
providence: 305, *322*
testimony of Sacred
Scripture: 303
Provinces: see Ecclesiastical provinces
Prudence
as a cardinal virtue:
1805–6
Psalms
as prayer of the People of
God: 2586
as school of prayer: 2587
importance for daily
prayer: 2589
in the Church's liturgy:
1093

in the liturgy of the Old
Covenant: 2588
People of God as expressed
in the Psalms: 716
Psalms as book of the Old
Testament: 2585
"Psalms of David": 2579
Punishment
death penalty:
imposition according
to the traditional
teaching of the Church:
2266
nonaggression as mark
of love: 2306
preference for
punishment without
bloodshed: 2267
limitations on punishment:
2267
meaning and effect: 2266
right of society to protect
itself: 2265
see also: Torture
Purgatory: 1030–32
Purity of heart: 2518
demands purification of
the social atmosphere:
2525
goal: 2519, *2531*
in the struggle against
carnal desires: 2517,
2530
means for preserving
purity: 2520, *2532*
requires modesty: 2521,
2533
Rape: 2356
Readers: 1143
Reason
and faith: 156–59, 286
and Law: 1951
as ability of man: 286
sin as offense against: 1849
Redemption
as center of the Christian
message: 571, 601

as source of Christ's
authority over the
Church: 669
continues in the liturgy:
1069
meaning ascertainable only
in faith: 573
requires perseverance in
charity: 837
Religion, virtue of
duty of religious worship:
2105
oaths as lack of respect for
God: 2149
offenses against virtue of
religion: 2118–22:
sacrilege: 2120
simony: 2121
tempting God: 2119
respect for God's name:
2143
use of words with respect
to holy things: 2142
Religious life; religious: see
Church: structure;
Evangelical counsels
Reparation
in the New Testament:
2412, *2424*
for offenses against the
truth: 2487, *2509*
Reproduction: see
Matrimony: purpose
Resistance
against unjust authority:
2242
with force of arms: 2243
Responsibility
and participation in the
common good: 1914
for the sins of others:
1868
imputability: 1735–36
in virtue of man's freedom:
1734
role of conscience: 1781
Resurrection of Christ: see

Jesus Christ:
Resurrection of Jesus
Resurrection of the dead:
988–1004
already risen with Christ in
Baptism: 1002–4
and Jesus: 994–95, *1019*
as work of the Trinity: 989
in Christianity: 991
in the Old Testament:
992–93
on the last day: 1001
"resurrection of the flesh":
686, 990, *1015, 1017*
the transfigured body of
the resurrected:
999–1000
Revelation
can appear obscure: 157
complete with Jesus Christ:
65–66
contents:
revelation of:
Decalogue in the
context of the
Covenant: 2060
definitive truth: 124
future: 2115
God's love: 1701
God's plan of
salvation: 50
law of the Old and
New Covenants: 1952
man: 2419
Mary's virginity: 502
mercy of God with
sinners: 1846
reason for choosing
Israel: 218
resurrection of the
dead: 992
sinfulness of man:
386–90
the Church: 726, 1076
revelation of God:
God as liberator: 2084
in Israel: 2085

of the Decalogue:
2059, 2070–71
of the Father: 238–42
of the Holy Spirit:
243–48, 688
of the name of God:
203–14, 2143
of the Son: 152, 240,
647–48, 651
of the Trinity:
as mystery of faith:
237
on Pentecost: 732
through the Holy
Spirit: 684, 687
faith as response: 142–43,
153–65
God willed to reveal
himself: 35, 50–53,
68–69
in human words: 101
in Sacred Scripture: 80–83,
124
in salvation history:
after the fall: 55
in Abraham: 59, 72
in Israel: 60–64
in Jesus Christ: 65–67,
73
in Noah: 56–58, 71
in our first parents: 54,
70
in Tradition: 80–83
natural knowledge of God
possible: 36
private revelations: 67
transmission of revelation:
through the apostles: 75
through the bishops: 77
through the Church: 74,
79, 82
through the evangelists:
76
through the teaching
office: 78
Revenge: 2262
Rite

different rites within the
universal Church: 1203
modification of rite: 1125
Rosary: 971, 2678, 2708
Sabbath; Sabbath rest
as center of Israel's Law:
348
as end of God's work of
creation: 345, 347
distinguished from the
Christian Sunday: 2175,
2190
holiness of the Sabbath:
2168
Jesus and the Sabbath
commandment: 2173
meaning and importance of
the third commandment:
2168–73, 2189
meaning of the Sabbath:
as sign of God's
irrevocable covenant:
2171
day of rest based on
God's example: 2172
for the praise of God:
2171
memorial of God's act of
creation: 2169
memorial of Israel's
deliverance: 2170
Sacrament: 1084, 1131
as "masterpieces of God":
1116
concept: 774
ecclesial dimension of the
sacraments:
belong to the Church:
1118
communicate growth
and healing: 798
communicate riches of
Christ: 947
form the bond of the
Church's unity: 815
role of the sacraments:
in catechesis: 6

in liturgical catechesis:
1074–75
in the dialogue for
Christian unity: 1126
sacramental mission of
the Church: 738–40,
1132
effects:
acts "ex opere operato":
1128
confers the grace it
signifies: 1127
fruit benefits all
believers: 950
sacramental grace: *1134,*
2003
stamps with an indelible
mark: 698, 1121
foundation in mysteries of
Jesus' life: 1115
importance of sacramental
signs: 1130
in the life of the Christian:
administration of
sacraments in danger of
death: 1401
as preparation for death:
1680
Baptism as the first
sacrament of the
forgiveness of sins:
977–78
conferral of ministry in
the Church: 875
end of sacramental life at
death: 1682
for strength on the way
to Christian holiness,
1133, 2030
importance of the
sacraments of Christian
initiation: 1212, *1275,*
1425, 1533
sacrament of Holy
Orders and Matrimony
as sacraments of

singular mission:
1534–35
sacraments of healing:
1420–21
instituted by Jesus Christ:
1114, 1210
necessity for salvation:
1129
prefigured by signs of the
Old Covenant: 1150
presence of Christ in the
sacraments: 1088
purpose: 1123
"sacramental economy":
1076
seven in number: 1113,
1117, 1210
unique place of the
Eucharist: 1211
"Sacrament, Most Blessed"
as name for the Eucharistic
elements: 1330
Sacramentals
forms:
blessings: 1669, 1671,
1678
consecration of things
and people: 1672
exorcism: 1673
instituted by the Church:
1667
meaning and purpose:
1667–68, 1670, *1677*
Sacrifice
as sign of adoration and
thanksgiving: 2099
inner and outward acts of
sacrifice: 2100
Sacrilege: 2120
Sadness: 1765, *2553*
Saints: see Holiness
Salvation
and faith: 161
comes from God alone:
169
in the New Testament: 124
in the Old Testament: 122

promised by God: 55
see also: Beatitude;
    Economy of salvation
"Sanctus": 559
Satan: see Devil
Scandal
by persons commanding
    respect: 2285
nature and meaning: 2284,
    2326
provoked by laws,
    institutions, or public
    opinion: 2286
responsibility for: 2287
Schism: 2089
as destruction of the unity
    of the Church: 817
Science
values and dangers:
    2293–94
Scripture, Sacred: 81
and Tradition: 78, 80–84,
    95
authorship and inspiration:
    Christ as the only Word
        of the Father: 102, *134*
    God as author: 105,
        136, 304, 688
    men as inspired authors:
        105, 702
    Sacred Scripture as Word
        of God: 103, 104, *135*
meaning and
    interpretation:
    exegesis: 109, 119
    free access necessary:
        131
    fundamental principle of
        the interpretation: 111,
        137
    multiple senses of
        Scripture: 115–19
    study of Sacred
        Scripture: 132, 133
    task of exegetes: 119
    typology: 128–30
Scripture as a whole:

Christian canon of
    Scripture: 120, 138
Christian reading of the
    whole Scripture: 129,
    140
Jewish arrangement of
    Scripture: 702
New Testament: 124–27
    Christ as central
        theme: 124
    significance of the
        Gospels: 125, 127,
        139
Old Testament: 121–23
    indispensability of:
        123
    special place of the
        book of Genesis:
        289
significance:
    as nourishment for
        Christian life: 141
    as source of prayer:
        2653–54
    as source of strength for
        the Church: 104, 131
teaches the truth: 107
see also: New Testament;
    Old Testament
Seal
as symbol of anointing:
    698
of the Holy Spirit at
    Confirmation: 1295–96
of the sacraments: 1121
sacramental seal: see
    Penance, sacrament of
Seat, cathedra
of priest or bishop in the
    liturgy: 1184
Secular institutes: see
    Evangelical counsels;
    Church: structure
Self-control
as fruit of the Holy Spirit:
    736, 1832

Self-knowledge: 2340
Self-mastery
as life-long task: 2342
means for self-mastery:
   2340
see also: Ascesis; Self-
   control
Servant of God
features of Messiah
   revealed in the songs of
   the Servant: 713
Jesus as "Servant of God":
   555, 580, 601, 608,
   615
Servers: 1143
Sexual abuse: 389
see also: Rape
Sexual identity: see Man:
   human sexual identity
Sexuality: see Man: human
   sexual identity;
   Matrimony: purpose
Sickness
charism of healing as gift
   of the Holy Spirit: 1508
Christ's healing mission:
   1503–05
   in the Church: 1509
   in the disciples: 1506–07
interpretation of sickness
   in the Old Testament:
   1502
significance in human life:
   1500–01
Signs
from the world of men:
   1146–48
liturgical signs: 1149
of the Covenant of the
   People of Israel: 1150
sacramental signs of the
   New Covenant: 1145,
   1152
sign function of music in
   the liturgy: 1157
taken up by Christ: 1151
Simony: 2121

Sin; fall; original sin: 387,
   1440, *1871–72*
and involuntary ignorance:
   1860
and lies: 2484
and the Law: 1949
consequences of:
   death: 1008
   harm to the community
      of believers: 953
   injury to the unity of the
      Church: 817
   punishment:
      as purification of the
         bad consequences of
         sin: 1472
      for mortal sins: 1861
      for venial sins: 1863
      in the communion of
         saints: 1474–75
      "temporal" and
         "eternal": 1472
   robs man of resemblance
      to God: 705
   separation of people
      from each other: 845
   sickness: 1505
   vice: 1865
differentiation of:
   according to their object:
      1853, *1873*
   diversity of sins: 1852
   grave sins:
      capital sins: 1866,
         1876
      difference between
         mortal sins and venial
         sins: 1854
      grave matter of a sin:
         1854, 1858
      loss of eternal life:
         1472
      mortal sins: 1855,
         1874
         and forgiveness:
            1856

as radical possibility of human freedom: 1861
conditions: 1857–59
consequences: 1861
"sins that cry to heaven": 1867
individual grave sins:
anger: 2302
blasphemy: 2148
"blasphemy against the Holy Spirit": 1864
envy: 2539
hatred: 2303
malice: 1860
murder: 2268
neglect of Sunday obligation: 2181
sins against faith: 2088–89
sins against hope: 2091
sins against love: 2094
venial sins: 1855, *1875*
consequences: 1863
nature: 1862
explained by revelation: 388
fall of the angels: 392
gathering together of the People of God: 761
in the Church: 827
interpretations:
personal act: 1868
"social sin": 1869
threat to the unity of the Church: 814
"work of the flesh": 1852
Jesus "died for our sins": 601, 654
man and sin:
afflicted by sin from birth: 403
man sins freely: 1739, *1874*

sin as rejection of God: 398, *415*, 1487
mankind not abandoned by God after the fall: 410, 1609, *1870*
nature: 1849–50
necessity of Baptism: 1250
original sin: 390, 397, *416–17*
and the history of mankind: 390
concupiscence as most important consequence: 405
consequences: 55–58, 399–400, 402–09, *418–19*
meaning of the teaching about original sin: 389
seduction by the devil: 391, *414–15*
transmission to all men: 404
permitted by God: 412
reality: 386–87
responsibility for the sins of others: 1868
sinners are to blame for Christ's suffering: 598
Sins, forgiveness of
absolution during confession: 1424
and profession of faith in the Church: 976
and profession of faith in the Holy Spirit: 976
as "treasury of the Church": 1476–77
as reconciliation with the Church: 1443
exercised by the Church at God's command: *986*, 1442
God alone can forgive sins: 1441

God gives the power to forgive sins to men: *984,* 1441

Gospel as revelation of God's mercy with sinners: 1846

importance of the power to bind and loose: 1444–45

in the course of the Anointing of the Sick: 1520

justification through Jesus' death: *421, 615,* 1708

mandate of punishment for sin: 1473

role of confession of sins:
as essential component in sacrament of Penance: 1456
importance: 1455, 1847
of mortal sins: 1456
of venial sins: 1458
supported by grace: 1848

see also: Penance, sacrament of

Slander: see calumny

Slavery
forbidden: 2414

Sloth: see acedia

Social Communications: see Media

Social Doctrine of the Church
concern with temporal aspects of the common good: 2420
contents: 2422–23
critique of capitalist and communist social theories: 2424–25
occasion for development: 2421

Societies of apostolic life:
see Evangelical counsels; Church: structure

Society: State: 1880
authority in society:
function: 1897–98, *1918–21*
obedience toward: 1899, 2238
stipulations for various forms of government: 1901, *1922*
duties of citizens:
armed resistance: 2243
defense of one's country: 2240
duty of obedience: 1900
exercising the right to vote: 2240
limitations on civil obedience: 2242, *2256*
participation in public life: 1915, *2255*
payment of taxes: 2 240
receiving foreigners: 2241
duties of the state:
concern for the health of citizens: 2288
defense: 2310, 2265
promotion of the common good: *1927,* 2237
protection of the life of every innocent person: 2273
provision for conscientious objectors: 2311
provision for religious worship: 2104–8, *2137*
recognition of neighbors: 1931–33
respect for the dignity of the person: 1907, 1930, *1926, 1943,* 2254
responsibility for the economy: 2431

fundamental principles:
  charity as the most
    important social
    commandment: 1889,
    1896
  common good: *1924–25*
  conditions for a society
    of fraternal harmony:
    1931
  just hierarchy of values:
    1886–87, *1895*
  right to information:
    2494, *2512*
  rule of law: 1904
  solidarity: *1948*
  subsidiarity: 1883–85,
    1894
human person as subject
  and end: 1881, *1892*,
  1929, 2459
natural societies: 1882,
  1891
necessity of life in society:
  1879
primary and subsidiary
  societies: 1883–85
relationships within
  society:
  Church and State:
    fundamental
    relationship:
    2244–46
  dangers of socialization:
    1883
  State and family:
    duty to protect the
      family: 2209–11
    family as the original
      cell of society: 2207
    subsidiary support for
      the family: 2208
  State and its impact on
    population growth: 2372
  State and mass media:
    2498–99
  State and social justice:
    1928

State and the common
    good: 1905–12
  State and the renewal of
    society: 1888
social order: 1912
voluntary associations:
    1882, *1893*
Soldiers: see Armed forces;
    soldiers
Solidarity
in brotherhood: 1939
in Church's role: 1942
in the communion of love:
    953
in the distribution of goods
    and work: 1940
in the economy and
    politics: 1941
Son: see Trinity; Jesus
    Christ
Sorcery: 1852, 2117
see also: Magic
Soul: 363
and "heart" of man: 368
and "spirit" of man: 367
created directly by God:
    366
immortal: 366
one nature with the human
    body: 365
Speculation: 2409
Speed: 2290
Spirit: see Holy Spirit
Spiritism
forbidden: 2117
State: see Society
Sterilization
and integrity of the human
    body: 2297, *2398*
see also: Matrimony;
    Medical treatment
Strikes: 2435
Subsidiarity, principle of
and collectivism: 1885
contents: 1883–85
in the relationship between
    society and family: 2209

see also: Social doctrine of
the Church
Substance: 252
see also Trinity;
Transubstantiation
Suffering
as consequence of original
sin: 1521
as participation in Jesus'
work of salvation: 1508,
1521
experience of suffering:
164
Suicide
as contrary to love of self,
neighbor, and God:
2281, 2325
eschatological importance:
2283
factors that can diminish
responsibility: 2282
responsibility for one's
own life: 2280
voluntary cooperation in
suicide: 2282
Sunday; Sunday rest
as "the Lord's Day": 2174,
2191
as the day of Jesus'
Resurrection: 2174,
2190
celebration:
as Church precept: 2043,
2192–93
as fulfillment of the
commandment of the
Old Covenant: 2176
assembly for Eucharistic
celebration: 1343
early Church practice of
assembly: 2178
importance of sharing in
the Sunday Eucharist:
2182
Sunday Eucharist as
center of the Church's
life: 2177

Sunday Eucharist as
foundation of Christian
life: 2181
Sunday obligation:
as precept of the Church:
2180
deliberate failure to
fulfill: 2181
in absence of minister:
2183
obligation for and
dispensation from: 2181
Sunday rest:
as commandment:
2185–86, *2194–95*
protection of Sunday as
day of rest: 2187–88
as opportunity for
family, cultural, and
religious life: 2184
Superstition: 2110–2111,
2138
Surrogate motherhood:
2376
"Symbolon"
as term for a formula of
faith: 188
see also: Creed; Faith,
profession of
Symbols
from the world of men:
1146–49
in the celebration of a
sacrament: 1145
Tabernacle: 1183, 1379
Tax evasion: 2436
Technology: 2293–94
Temperance
as cardinal virtue: 1805
assures the will's mastery
over the instincts:
1809
Terrorism: 2297
Theft: 2408, *2453–54*
in urgent necessity: 2408
obligation for reparation:
2412

Theologal Life: 2607, 2803
see also Virtues, theological
Theology
and the economy of
salvation: 236
importance for the
Magisterium of the
Church: 2033, 2038
Time
and creation: 338
Tobacco
abuse: 2290
Torture
as offense against
mankind: 2297–98
Tradition: 81
and Sacred Scripture: 80,
83, 95, 113, 120
"depositum fidei": 84, 97
liturgy as constitutive
element: 1124
most important content:
638
Transubstantiation:
1373–77, *1413*
see also: Eucharist
Trinity
as central mystery of the
faith: 232, 234, 237,
261, 266
concept of "hypostasis":
252
concept of substance: 252
divine economy as
common work of the
divine Persons: 257–60
divine Persons:
concept of Person: 252
consubstantiality: 242,
253
real distinction between:
254, 267
unity of being: 685, 689
expression of the Trinity:
in Baptism: 233, *265*
in philosophical
concepts: 251

in the early Councils:
250
in the liturgy: 249,
1066
family as image of the
communion of the
Trinity: 2205
"Filioque": 246–48, *264*
indwelling of the triune
God in men: 260
liturgy as work of the
Trinity: 1077–1109
revelation of this mystery:
of God the Father: 238,
240
of God the Holy Spirit:
243–48, *263,* 731
of God the Son: 240,
242, *262,* 663
of the entire Trinity:
684, 732
"Theologia" and
"Oikonomia": 236
the triune God: 202
the unity of the Trinity and
the unity of the Church:
813
unity of God: *228, 255*
and unity of the Church:
813
Truth
and beauty: 2500
giving witness to the truth:
and martyrdom: 2473
duty of Christians:
2472
in the New Testament:
2471
God as source of all truth:
2465
"hierarchy of truths": 90,
234
in communications media:
2492
in following Christ: 2470
in relationships with
others: 2464

in the virtue of
    truthfulness: 2468
man's striving after truth:
    2467
manifestation in Jesus:
    2466
offenses against the truth:
    2464, 2475–87
right to truth not
    unconditional: 2488–92
"Two ways," parable of:
    1696
Understanding
as gift of the Holy Spirit:
    1831
Unity, Christian: see
    Ecumenism
Veneration of images
new "economy" of images
    through Christ's
    Incarnation: 2131
Old Testament prohibition
    of the representation of
    God: 2129
veneration, not adoration:
    2132
Viaticum: see Anointing of
    the Sick: reception
Vice
and capital sins: 1866
and the passions: 1768
see also: Sin
Violence; force
and imputability of an act:
    1735
value of nonaggression:
    2306
Virginity for the Kingdom
    of heaven
and Matrimony: 1620
as unfolding of baptismal
    grace: 1619
in the call by Christ: 1618
see also: Evangelical
    counsels; Virtues
Virtues: 1804, 1833–34

and grace: 1810
and the passions: 1768
cardinal virtues: 1805
    fortitude: 1808, 1837
    justice: 1807, 1836
        as "virtue of religion":
            1807
    prudence: 1806, 1835
    temperance: 1809, 1838
        important for
            reasonable care of
            health: 2290
        in distribution of
            goods: 2407
chastity:
    and homosexuality:
        2359
    as cultural effort: 2344
    as gift of self: 2346
    as grace of God: 2345
    as preservation of the
        integrity of the person:
        2337–38
    as process of personal
        growth: 2343, 2395
    as vocation of all the
        baptized: 2348, 2394
    conjugal chastity: 2349
    engaged couples: 2350
    importance of friendship:
        2347
    lust: 2351
    offenses against chastity:
        2351–56, 2396
    relationship to
        temperance: 2341
    self-mastery: 2339–40
gift at Baptism: 1266
moral virtues: 1839
perfection of through the
    gifts of the Holy Spirit:
    1831
solidarity:
    in the distribution of
        goods: 2407
    virtue of solidarity:
        1942

theological virtues:
and participation in the divine nature: 1812
and the virtue of religion: *1840*, 2095–96
as the foundation of Christian moral activity: 1813, *1840*
faith, hope, and charity as theological virtues: 1813, *1841*
    charity: 1822–29, *1844*
    faith: 1814–16, *1842*
    hope: 1817–21, *1843*
truthfulness: 2468, *2505*
in human relationships: 2469
lies as offense against the virtue of truthfulness: 2486, *2508*

Vocation:
of our first parents: 54
to follow Christ: 1694
to sanctity: 825
to the catholic unity of the People of God: 836
call of all by Jesus: 3, 542–43
call of all by the Creator: 1
see also: Evangelical counsels

Vows: 2102
dispensation from: 2103
of the evangelical counsels: 915, 2103
see also: Evangelical counsels; Promises

Voyeurism: 2523, 2525

Wagers: 2413

Wages
just wage as legitimate fruit of work: 2434
unjust wages: 2409

War
and the moral law: 2312, *2328*

arms race: 2315, 2329
disorders threatening peace: 2317
duty to prevent war: 2307–08, *2327*
"just war": 2309
obedience in war: 2313
production and sale of arms: 2316
treatment of the wounded and civilians: 2313
weapons: 2314

Way of the Cross: 2669

Wedding: see Matrimony

Will
faith and will: 143, 155
strengthening the will's mastery: 1734
see also: Man

Wisdom
as gift of the Holy Spirit: 1831

Witchcraft: see Sorcery

Women
as image of the Church: 2853
in the salvation history of the Old Covenant: 489
man "created as male and female": 355, *383*
ordination of: 1577
see also: Mary; Man: human sexual identity

Work
access to employment: 2433
just wage as legitimate fruit: 2434
meaning and value: 2427–28, *2460*
strikes: 2435
unemployment: 2436

World
created by God: 295
creation of the "visible world": 325, 337

Jesus as Lord of the world:
    450
"sin of the world": 408
subjugation by man: 373
transitoriness: 677
"world of men": 326
world order and natural
    law: 341
see also: Creation

Worship
as the first act of the virtue
    of religion: 2096, *2135*
meaning of worship: 2097
in liturgical celebration:
    1070
see also: Adoration
**YHWH: see God: names of
    God; Jesus Christ**

ABBREVIATIONS

The following are abbreviations cited in the text:

AA	*Apostolicam actuositatem*	COD	*Conciliorum oecumenicorum decreta*
AAS	*Acta Apostolicae Sedis*	CPG	Solemn Profession of Faith: Credo of the People of God
AF	J. B. Lightfoot, ed., *The Apostolic Fathers* (New York: Macmillan, 1889–1890)		
AG	*Ad gentes*	CSEL	Corpus Scriptorum Ecclesiasticorum Latinorum (Vienna, 1866–)
Ben	*de Benedictionibus* (Book of Blessings)		
CA	*Centesimus annus*	CT	*Catechesi tradendae*
Catech. R.	*Catechismus Romanus*	DeV	*Dominum et Vivificantem*
CCEO	Corpus Canonum Ecclesiarum Orientalium	DH	*Dignitatis humanae*
		DM	*Dives in misericordia*
CCL	Corpus Christianorum, Series Latina (Turnhout, 1953–)	DS	Denzinger-Schönmetzer, *Enchiridion Symbolorum, definitionum et declarationum de rebus fidei et morum* (1965)
CD	*Christus Dominus*	DV	*Dei Verbum*
CDF	Congregation for the Doctrine of the Faith	EN	*Evangelii nuntiandi*
		EP	Eucharistic Prayer
CELAM	Consejo Episcopal Latinoamericano	FC	*Familiaris consortio*
CIC	Codex Iuris Canonici	GCD	General Catechetical Directory
CL	*Christifideles laici*	GE	*Gravissimum educationis*

GILH	General Introduction to LH	OCM	*Ordo celebrandi Matrimonium*
GIRM	General Instruction to RomM	OCV	*Ordo consecrationis virginum*
GS	*Gaudium et spes*	OE	*Orientalium ecclesiarum*
HV	*Humanae vitae*	OP	*Ordo paenitentiae*
ICEL	International Commission on English in the Liturgy	OR	Office of Readings
IM	*Inter mirifica*	OT	*Optatam totius*
LE	*Laborem exercens*	PC	*Perfectae caritatis*
LG	*Lumen gentium*	PG	J. P. Migne, ed., Patrologia Graeca (Paris, 1857–1866)
LH	*Liturgy of the Hours*		
LXX	Septuagint	PL	J. P. Migne, ed., Patrologia Latina (Paris: 1841–1855)
MC	*Marialis cultus*		
MD	*Mulieris dignitatem*		
MF	*Mysterium fidei*	PLS	J. P. Migne, ed., Patrologia Latina Supplement
MM	*Mater et magistra*		
NA	*Nostra aetate*	PO	*Presbyterorum ordinis*
NCCB	National Conference of Catholic Bishops (U.S.A.)	PP	*Populorum progressio*
		PT	*Pacem in terris*
ND	Neuner-Dupuis, *The Christian Faith in the Doctrinal Documents of the Catholic Church*	RBC	*Rite of Baptism of Children*
		RCIA	*Rite of Christian initiation of adults*
		RH	*Redemptor hominis*
OBA	*Ordo baptismi adultorum*	RomM	Roman Missal
OC	*Ordo confirmationis*	RMat	*Redemptoris Mater*
OCF	Order of Christian Funerals	RMiss	*Redemptoris Missio*
		RP	*Reconciliatio et paenitentia*

SC	*Sacrosanctum concilium*	*SRS*	*Sollicitudo rei socialis*
SCG	Summa Contra Gentiles	*STh*	Summa Theologiae
SCh	Sources Chrétiennes (Paris: 1942–)	*UR*	*Unitatis redintegratio*

The following abbreviations are used for the books of the Bible cited in the text:

Gen	Genesis	*Am*	Amos
Ex	Exodus	*Jon*	Jonah
Lev	Leviticus	*Mic*	Micah
Num	Numbers	*Zeph*	Zephaniah
Deut	Deuteronomy	*Zech*	Zechariah
Josh	Joshua	*Mal*	Malachi
Judg	Judges	*Mt*	Matthew
1 Sam	1 Samuel	*Mk*	Mark
2 Sam	2 Samuel	*Lk*	Luke
1 Kings	1 Kings	*Jn*	John
2 Kings	2 Kings	*Acts*	Acts of the
1 Chr	1 Chronicles		Apostles
2 Chr	2 Chronicles	*Rom*	Romans
Ezra	Ezra	*1 Cor*	1 Corinthians
Neh	Nehemiah	*2 Cor*	2 Corinthians
Tob	Tobit	*Gal*	Galatians
Jdt	Judith	*Eph*	Ephesians
Esth	Esther	*Phil*	Philippians
2 Macc	2 Maccabees	*Col*	Colossians
Job	Job	*1 Thess*	1 Thessalonians
Ps	Psalms	*2 Thess*	2 Thessalonians
Prov	Proverbs	*1 Tim*	1 Timothy
Eccl	Ecclesiastes	*2 Tim*	2 Timothy
Song	Song of Songs	*Titus*	Titus
Wis	Wisdom	*Philem*	Philemon
Sir	Sirach	*Heb*	Hebrews
Isa	Isaiah	*Jas*	James
Jer	Jeremiah	*1 Pet*	1 Peter
Lam	Lamentations	*2 Pet*	2 Peter
Bar	Baruch	*1 Jn*	1 John
Ezek	Ezekiel	*2 Jn*	2 John
Dan	Daniel	*3 Jn*	3 John
Hos	Hosea	*Jude*	Jude
Joel	Joel	*Rev*	Revelation